PROGRAMMING WITH
ANSI
C++

SECOND EDITION

BHUSHAN TRIVEDI

Director, MCA Programme
GLS Institute of Computer Technology,
Ahmedabad

OXFORD
UNIVERSITY PRESS

Oxford University Press is a department of the University of Oxford.
It furthers the University's objective of excellence in research, scholarship,
and education by publishing worldwide. Oxford is a registered trademark of
Oxford University Press in the UK and in certain other countries.

Published in India by
Oxford University Press
22 Workspace, 2nd Floor, 1/22 Asaf Ali Road, New Delhi 110 002

First Edition published in 2007
Second Edition published in 2012
Eighth impression 2023

ISBN-13: 978-0-19-808396-2
ISBN-10: 0-19-808396-3

Typeset in Times New Roman
by Cameo Corporate Services Limited, Chennai
Printed in India by Gopsons Papers Private Ltd., Sivakasi

For product information and current price, please visit www.india.oup.com

*Dedicated to my
Teachers
who enabled me to learn and write*

Preface to the Second Edition

Even in this age of advanced languages such as Java and DotNet, the age-old C++ is still revered for its versatility. These advanced languages as well as environments such as Windows and Linux would not be around without C++, because they are all written in C++! In fact, the TCP/IP code that a network card runs, the shell that an operating system such as Linux runs, and the graphics library that some of us use are all developed and maintained in C++. It continues to play a major role in coding various embedded systems. It is a vital cog in designing several reliable and high-performance components in various software products. The latest standard of ANSI C++ was released in August 2011; compilers conforming to this standard are expected to be released within a year. This is an important indication that the language is still going strong and in fact *evolving*, nearly four decades after its release!

But why do we need programming languages in the first place? You have probably read about it in the previous semesters—programming languages help us interact with computers. Efficient as they are, computers can simplify tedious tasks and make them look ridiculously easy. They perform computations at a stunning pace and solve complex problems by applying equally complex algorithms. However, we cannot use the word *intelligent* to describe a computer, since every operation requires someone to instruct the computer, in concrete terms, about what it is supposed to do. How does one instruct a computer whose native language (machine codes) is so different from anything we speak? This is where the programs that we create break the language barrier, by providing sets of instructions that the computer can understand.

The next question—why do we have *so many* languages then? This is because, in our attempt to provide instructions in an unambiguous manner and communicate better with the computer, we have gradually developed a range of programming languages.

Where does C++ stand among the group of programming languages? In simple terms, C++ is an object-oriented as well as an object-based language that allows reusability of existing objects. It expresses every programming component as an object in a professionally written program, but it can work without objects as well.

To conclude, C++ is still a professional programmers' favourite when it comes to coding reliable tools. This brings us to the next question—what makes it so versatile? The following are a few reasons from what is almost an endless list:

- C++ codes are compiled directly to a machine's native code. In optimized conditions, it can produce executable codes at a breathtaking speed.
- C++ is an open language and, therefore, it has a range of compilers suitable for different platforms. Its portability allows cross-platform independence. Codes written in one platform can be easily transported to other platforms.
- C++ is reverse compatible with C; in fact, it is almost a superset. It can use existing C libraries with very few or no modifications. It is compatible with C to such an extent that a valid C program (barring very few special cases) is also a valid C++ program.
- C++ lends superior control to the user, unlike most other high-level languages; but it expects the user to know what he/she is typing on the console. Fine control requires more disciplined programming and C++ is no exception. It is a strongly typed language.

NEW TO THE SECOND EDITION

Continuing with the question–answer series, the moot question follows now—why a new edition? In this edition, the attempt has been to make suitable changes based on the useful feedback and comments received from users. Preserving all the basic ingredients that established the first edition, the book now includes the following new features:

- Each chapter contains pedagogical elements such as notes, sidebars, and exhibits spread across the chapters to highlight important statements and concepts.
- Every program is followed by a complete analysis section, 'How the Program Works'. These sections describe the logic behind the programs and the new concepts introduced therein.
- End-chapter exercises now include multiple choice questions in addition to conceptual and practical exercises.

KEY FEATURES

- Contains numerous application-oriented programs, complete with their source codes and test cases
- Includes programs simulating real-life scenarios, to equip the readers to become entry-level professionals
- Discusses advanced topics such as run-time type information (RTTI), casting operators, memberwise initialization list (MIL), reference variables, and templates in detail
- Provides a balance between theory and practice, and covers both elementary as well as advanced topics

EXTENDED CHAPTER MATERIAL

- *Chapter 1* now features the various concepts of object-oriented programming, besides providing an introduction to C++.
- *Chapter 4* provides extended coverage of temporary object creation and destruction. Small code segments have been added to strengthen the discussions on friend functions and how to return a reference.
- *Chapter 5* includes sections on memory leaks and the correct method to copy. Besides, the second edition covers destructors in more detail.
- *Chapter 9* provides a more in-depth analysis of abstract classes.
- *Chapter 10* includes an introduction to virtual destructors and object slicing.
- In *Chapter 11*, the section on polymorphic objects has been strengthened with the help of a code segment and additional descriptions.
- *Chapter 13* contains updated information on operating systems and device drivers. The second edition throws light on file handles and file pointers. A table indicating the differences between binary and ASCII strings has been added.
- *Chapter 14* covers namespaces and dynamism in more depth.
- *Chapter 16* now provides a brief history of Standard Template Library (STL) before moving on to its application areas. The sections on functional and direct addressing models have been significantly improved in the second edition. Additions in this chapter also include a table illustrating different types of iterators.
- The *case study* sports a new look in the second edition. It describes the essential components of the program in an explicit manner. The output is appealing, with direct screenshots

taken at the time of execution. It has a new section 'Possible Extensions', which describes how the same program can be extended further.

CONTENT AND STRUCTURE

Chapter 1 provides an introduction to C++ and explains the philosophical and technical differences between C and C++.

Chapters 2 and 3 present an overview of core C++ and introduce data types, operators, classes, objects, structs, unions, arrays, pointers, and their extensive role in C++.

Chapter 4 discusses the various kinds of functions and their usage.

Chapter 5 deals with constructors and destructors, explaining their need, usage, and execution.

Chapter 6 describes operator overloading along with user-defined conversions. It also discusses the use of either friends or member functions to overload operators, thereby emphasizing the difference between the approaches.

Chapters 7 and 8 discuss the templates and exception handling mechanism in C++ in great detail.

Chapter 9 covers inheritance in detail with all its forms.

Chapter 10 explains the use of virtual functions to implement run-time polymorphism.

Chapter 11 provides an introduction to RTTI, polymorphic objects, different casting operators, limitations of virtual functions, and how RTTI is used to overcome them.

Chapter 12 discusses streams and formatted input/output (I/O), their need and advantages, as also differences between ios functions and manipulators for I/O formatting.

Chapter 13 throws light on text and binary streams, usage of text and binary files, the various operations, as well as error handling in files.

Chapter 14 introduces namespaces, illustrates their need, and explains concepts such as using directive and using declaration, extending namespaces, and namespace aliases.

Chapter 15 discusses ANSI string objects and issues related to normal as well as substring operations.

Chapter 16 provides an introduction to the Standard Template Library in C++.

A comprehensive case study, included at the end of the book as an appendix, demonstrates the application of C++ in maintaining mark sheets of students and displaying them in the requisite format whenever required.

ACKNOWLEDGEMENTS

I gratefully acknowledge the feedback and suggestions given by various faculty members for the improvement of the book.

I am obliged to the editorial team at Oxford University Press, India for bringing out the second edition in quick time and in a very elegant format.

Any suggestions for improving the presentation and contents are welcome. Please send them to the publishers through their website www.oup.com or to the author at bhtrivedi@gmail.com.

Bhushan Trivedi

Preface to the First Edition

C++ is a popular, versatile, and widely used programming language, which supports all features of C language and also provides a number of additional features that make it object-oriented. It includes concepts and features such as classes, objects, dynamic memory management, operator overloading, and many more. Besides learning the syntax, understanding the philosophical background helps the students appreciate the choices made by the creator of the language very easily. It is difficult to answer certain questions such as the following without really knowing the idea behind creating the language: Why is there no standard library for graphics in C++? Why is the base class embedded in the derived class rather than having a pointer to it? Why is there a need for virtual functions? Such questions can only be answered, if one understands the domain of application of C++ and Stroustrup's idea behind creating the language.

ABOUT THE BOOK

Programming with ANSI C++ is designed as a textbook for students of engineering (BE/BTech) and computer applications (BCA/MCA). It discusses the philosophical issues related to the language in order to make the concepts clearer to the users.

The book assumes basic knowledge of the fundamental concepts of C and the art of programming. Those who have already studied C would find this book to be an excellent starter. Wherever possible, comparison with C as well as Java is provided. The book demonstrates and highlights the difference of working in C++, problems with programming in C or Java, and better ways to do the same in C++.

ANSI C and ANSI C++ have been used as the default language throughout the book. The worked examples and codes presented have been specifically designed to demonstrate the concept and syntax as also use in real-life applications. By no means is it claimed that the way to program shown here is the best or most efficient. The variable naming convention is Java-like and care has been taken to use meaningful, though at times very long, variable names.

To make the textbook ideal for classroom learning, several examples and program codes have been included. All of them have been test run with Visual C++.Net (VC++ 7.0) and most of them have also been tested on Linux. 8.0 (gnu C++ 3.2). Numerous review questions, exercises, and project ideas that require knowledge of advanced topics have also been included in every chapter.

ACKNOWLEDGEMENTS

Asheesh Asthana, one of my students sent me a book on C++ in 2002. My real journey of learning C++ actually began then. I have to thank Asheesh for his invaluable gift. While I was writing this book, I kept imagining the kind of queries my readers would pose. Fortunately my students whom I was teaching gave me excellent feedback and suggestions.

I am thankful to all of them. Hardik, Rahul, Hemal, Nimesh, and Shiv are a few names that I can remember at this moment.

My wife Arpita, son Jay, and daughter Sonu all helped me in a way to complete this book. Without their support it would have been impossible. My colleagues, Harshal, Viral, and Hardik, supported me in every way they could.

The editorial team at Oxford University Press has done a great job. The book took a far better shape in the final version than it started with, and I would like to express my sincere thanks to the members of OUP for their interest and support, wealth of good ideas and suggestions, forceful requests and sweet reminders, without which this book would not have happened.

Bhushan Trivedi

Features of the Book

PROGRAM 3.5   Static data members

```
//CStaticVar.cpp
#include <stdio.h>
void Dummy()
{
    static int i = 10;
    int j = 20;
    i+=10;
    j+=5;
    printf("The i value is %d and j value is %d \n",i,j);
}
Output
The i value is 20 and j value is 25
The i value is 30 and j value is 25
```

How the Program Works

In this case, when the first call to Dummy() is made, i is initialized to 10. When the second call is made, it is not initialized even though there is an initialization statement written in the function. Rather, it picks the value of i at the time of its exit from the earlier Dummy(). If it was set to 20 when exiting from the first call to Dummy(), it is retained when the second call is made.

Note   The scope resolution operator is useful in differentiating the functions of different classes with the same name when defined outside the body of a class.

Exhibit 3.2   What separates a static data member from a global data member

1. *Storage:* Both are stored at a global location
2. *Instantiation:* Both are available as a single copy and without any objects being created
3. *Initialization:* Both are initialized to zero at the time of definition
4. *Scope:* The scope of a global variable is the entire program, whereas static variables are restricted to the class in which they are defined.

6.11.4 Wrapper Classes

Some of the built-in types are not objects, for example, int, char, etc. However, for complete object orientation, they should be objects. For instance, if we want to have an integer class, we can specify the functions for reading the integer with proper validation checks. If they are defined as class, we can inherit them to have our own class of, say, positive integers from one to some maximum number. A class that provides a basic data type with such additional facilities is known as a *wrapper class*.

Sometimes, we may need to convert the wrapper class object into built-in type object and vice versa. Converting from built-in type to wrapper is possible using constructors and the inverse is possible using conversion operators. Program 6.13 is an example of the same.

A wrapper class for a built-in data type contains that basic data type and facilities such as error handling, conversion to and fro, initializing to some value (e.g., zero to integer type), and so on.

■ RECAPITULATION ■

- Class is a fundamental requirement for object programming. It represents real-world entities in a program.
- The attributes of entities are represented as data members and function members of a class.
- Class in C++ is similar to struct in C, except that it can have functions as well. The class members can be divided into public and private sections.

- backward compatible with C.
- The function members can also be defined outside the class.
- Static data members are shared between all the objects of the class.
- It is possible to have pointers pointing to class objects and to have pointers to data members of the class, but

Anonymous union   It is a union with no name. It is possible to access members of the union by their name directly, without using the dot (.) notation.

C struct   This refers to the struct data type available in C language.

C++ struct   This refers to the struct data type available in C++ language, which lets us define functions inside the struct. It can have public and private sections. The default section in this case is public unlike the data type

Local class   It is a class defined in a function.

Nested and nesting class   When a class is defined inside another class, it is said to be a nested class. The class inside which the nested class is defined is the nesting class.

Private members   These are members defined inside the private section of the class. Such members are accessible only to other members of the same class and not to the objects of the class.

> Keywords introduced in each chapter are grouped alphabetically, along with their definition.

Multiple Choice Questions

> Objective questions in each chapter provide an easy and quick way to test your understanding of concepts.

1. When overloading unary operators _____.
   (a) no argument is passed explicitly
   (b) one argument is to be passed explicitly
   (c) no argument is passed implicitly
   (d) no argument is passed explicitly only if over-loaded as member functions

2. The advantage of operator overloading is _____.
   (a) better readability
   (b) easy usage
   (c) easy coding

   (b) Always false
   (c) Partially true
   (d) Never true

4. What will the following statement do?
   `Matrix operator *(int multiplier, Matrix tempMatrix);`
   (a) Overload the * (multiplication) operator for Matrix class.
   (b) Compiler will generate an error.
   (c) Overload the * (pointer) operator for Matrix class.

Conceptual Exercises

1. What is the significance of operator overloading?
2. What are the restrictions on operator overloading?
3. List down the operators that cannot be overloaded.
4. List down the operators that cannot be overloaded as a friend.
5. List the differences between an operator overloaded as a member and that overloaded as a friend.
6. Differentiate between overloading of unary and binary operators.
7. Differentiate between overloading postfix and prefix operators.
8. Why are shorthand operators useful when basic

way. (Hint: use friend function to overload).

9. Overload << and >> for the Time class defined in this chapter. When user adds a statement cout << Time or cin >> Time, the overloaded functions should be able to write elements of Time and read from the screen, respectively. The display format for time is HH:MM:SS.

10. For a supermarket, define a bill class. All the bill objects will contain bill number, the name of the clerk preparing the bill, each item with quantity and price, and the total amount to be paid. Total items in the bill are varying. Define dynamic memory allocation constructor for bill class

> Conceptual exercises are designed to test your grasp of the concepts discussed in the chapters.

Practical Exercises

> Practical exercises are designed to put theory into practice and test your programming skills.

1. Write a program to define any class. Define few private and public variables. Try to access them and note down the differences.

2. Define a union with some values inside. Check to see if the address is really shared. Add some functions to it and try to access it like a class member function.

3. Define an inline function inside a program. Call it a few times. Compile and try to look at the size of the compiled code. Again define it as a normal function. Compile again and test the size of the program.

hours the student has already worked for. Check if it exceeds 200 and display message "Welcome <student name>" if it is less than 200. Use pointer to object and pointer to class members for obtaining the value of <student name> by the details.

10. Define a class having one member function in it. Define an object with const declaration. What error does the compiler give when you try to execute the function using that object? Try to define the same function as const and see the difference.

11. Take up any class and define it inside a function, that is, define it as a local class. Test whether the restrictions that we have listed in the text really exist.

Brief Contents

Detailed Contents

Chapter 1

Object-oriented Programming and C++

1.1 NEED FOR C++

Since C is a successful and useful language, a question may arise as to the need for the C++ language. We will first look at the limitations of the C language. Subsequently, we will learn about object orientation and how C++ provides object orientation to solve the problems that cannot be solved using C.

1.1.1 Limitations of C

C is a very powerful language. It has been popular for more than two decades. As compared to other programming languages, programming in C is very efficient and compact. When the C programs are compiled to executable programs, they produce the most compact object code compared to any other high-level language such as Java or Visual Basic (VB). C is frequently used in small- and medium-sized programs. In fact, a large number of programmers are conversant with only the C language. We use so many C programs daily that if everything developed in C is removed from our computer, it will stop functioning. A large portion of operating systems such as Linux and Windows, databases such as Oracle, and network programs such as transmission control protocol/Internet protocol (TCP/IP) are written in C (though a significant part of them is also written in C++). However, C has a few limitations. It lacks a global view and the programming design does not support reusability.

Lack of Global View

Programmers realized the limitations of C only when the C programs were used on a very large scale. It became very difficult for the programmers to remember every part of the program. This is a problem partly with the design and partly due to the inability of the language to express a lengthy program as an abstraction of smaller individual units. Over the years, programmers realized this and found ways to avoid this problem. One such commonly practised method is to make the program *modular*, that is, to divide the program into smaller segments and implement these segments by different functions. To a certain extent, this approach solves the problem. However, when a program grows larger, this solution does not seem

> Lengthy C programs lose a 'global view' and become very difficult to visualize as a single concept.

to work. Although the portions of the program (modules) are separated, these are not totally independent. If a module is to be used at multiple places with a little difference, then it is to be copied and pasted at all such locations and then modified. As a result, the program becomes messy. Another problem with large programs is that they are usually developed by teams and efficient teamwork is not possible without a global view, that is, an abstracted view. For example, while handling a marksheet printing program, a student is an abstraction. We shall assume that all the data that we need for a student is available in the student abstraction (we will soon call this abstraction a *class*) and will not worry about any other details of the student. There may be hundreds of such abstractions available, but we should only be using them and not worry about their internal structure. Thus, we are relieved from the burden of handling a large program to one with only a few abstractions. In addition, we can view the entire program together and can properly reason if a part of it is not working properly and is required to be modified.

Let us try to understand the same concept using an example from our everyday life. Suppose we write something using Microsoft Word. We just use the buttons to save, undo, and so on, without caring about how they work. Let us consider one more example from the programming domain. The application programming for Windows may be done using VB or Visual C++ (VC++), but we can use all facilities such as buttons, text boxes, or tables as controls without worrying about how these controls are implemented or coded. What we get is a control (for example, a text box control) that is programmed for readymade usage. This simplifies our task of programming. This is also true for real-time examples such as driving a car, when we are only worried about the steering wheel, brakes, accelerators, and a few other things and not about how acceleration is actually provided when we press the pedal. Unfortunately, C does not provide any direct mechanism for such abstraction.

Not Designed for Reusability

There is another problem with the style of programming in C. We need many building blocks for a large program. For example, a large payroll program would require all the information about each employee. Management of employee information is one building block for the payroll program. A human resource management program also requires the employee information. Both sets of information may not be exactly the same, though both of them need to be consistent. It would be a better approach to share the information as much as possible between all those who need it, and provide additional information only in special cases. In our case, the employee information is needed by the employee payroll and human resource

> Two serious issues emerge when large programs are to be written in C. The programmer loses a global view of the program and there is no programming construct available for reusing the older code.

departments. In such case, the employee name, address, etc., can be stored at a single location. From this shared pool, both payroll and personnel departments may take the data input. Additional information can be inserted in the individual records of both the departments wherever required. For example, if employee experience is additionally required in the human resource information, then it is stored in its database alone. Here, the idea is to reuse the shared information that is available to all, with little modification at local level. C does not provide any mechanism to reuse the same information with modifications wherever required.

In this chapter, we will see that both these problems encountered in C are very easily and efficiently solved by C++, which follows the paradigm of object orientation. When the new design was termed *object-oriented* or *object-based*, there arose a problem of naming the older method. There are many names given to the old way of coding, the most appropriate one being *procedure-oriented*.

Coding in the C language is commonly based on defining and calling functions for different jobs. To an extent, this helps to distribute the program logic into modules and thus helps to reduce the complexity, but does not completely segregate the components. Object-based programming helps in achieving this. In the following sections, we shall discuss how object-based and object-oriented programming are carried out.

Let us try to understand object-oriented programming in simple terms.

1.1.2 Object-oriented Programming

To overcome the problems listed in Section 1.1.1, the programmers included new features in the C language. The addition of these new features has enabled the advanced language, C++, to suit very large programs.

> **Note** C++ was developed with many additional features to eliminate the problems that C had. The most notable improvements include the support for building reusable components and the ability to provide an abstracted view.

We may even need to change the style of programming and the process of viewing the problem. Programmers have realized this and are researching in this area. There are some interesting outcomes from this research. A new discipline for computer science professionals known as software engineering has emerged. One of the important outcomes of the study of software engineering is a new design for programming. This programming methodology is known as object-based or object-oriented programming. Both are different types of methodologies and the differences between the two will be discussed in detail in Chapter 9.

Programming is a process to provide computer-based solutions to real-world problems. For example, an accounting program solves the accounting-related problems of an organization or a marksheet printing program solves the problem of calculating the marks of an individual student and printing them in the proper format. If one needs to write either a marksheet printing program or an accounting program, he/she first needs to understand the problem itself, that is, the entities involved in the program (marksheet, students, examiners, etc.), their attributes (names, roll numbers, etc.), and the output (examiners provide the marks for the students, students view these marks later in a different format, etc.). This visualization of the system is a design process that must precede the programming phase.

Object-based and object-oriented programming are the methods of visualizing and programming the problem in a global way (by global, we mean that the entire program can be viewed together as a single unit). They provide abstractions for all the entities involved in the process. This abstraction is known as a *class*. Object-based and object-oriented programming help programmers in such a way that the global view is not lost even when the program grows to a large size.

Thus, object-based and object-oriented programming are techniques to envision the problem as a collection of objects that represents real-world entities. Objects are variables of type class. In the C language, we have to define variables of type struct to represent entities such as customer, supplier, or a student (by

> Programming is a process to provide computer-based solutions to real-world problems. Visualizing the real-world problem and finding an appropriate solution in terms of a programming language construct are important prerequisites to develop robust programs.

> An abstraction of a real-world entity is modelled in C++ as a class.

> C++ is almost a super-set of C. Since the syntax of C++ is extended from C, knowledge of C is useful while learning C++.

defining struct Student, struct supplier, or struct customer containing names, addresses, etc.). This mapping is not complete. We can add attributes of an entity student in the struct type variable (e.g., name, address, and marks of respective subjects), but actions related to them (such as enrolment and getting result) cannot be stored within the structure. We usually write functions to perform such activities in C, but these functions are not part of the struct keyword; they are independent.

C++ introduces a new element called class, which is an extension to struct, and provides the facility to store actions in the form of functions within the entities themselves. It is similar to storing the Student object with all the data attributes such as name and address as well as action attributes such as enrolment, reading, and printing details of the concerned Student object. This process of combining data and function attributes of an entity is known as *encapsulation*.

Note A C struct represents only a part of an entity, that is, data. An object represents an entity completely, that is, data as well as methods.

1.1.3 Object-based and Object-oriented Design

C++ is designed for providing both object-based and object-oriented programming. Before we look at the differences between the two, let us assume that the discussion that follows is applicable to both the cases.

It is not easy to provide object orientation in a computer language while maintaining acceptable efficiency levels. A major advantage of the C language is its efficiency. Programs written in C execute faster than if written in any other high-level language. The designers of C++ wanted the same efficiency level in C++ as in C.

> The normal rule of thumb is that the more object-oriented the language, the slower the execution of the program.

In the past, only a few languages such as Smalltalk provided purely object-oriented solutions. These solutions executed far slower than conventional procedural languages such as C. C was also more efficient than such languages. However, C++ provides the extension required for object orientation to C, and at the same time provides almost the same efficiency as C. Therefore, the object-oriented model is not imposed on the developer such as in Java.

> C++ is designed to give freedom to programmers and hence it does not impose the object-oriented model, unlike Java.

We can choose between object-based programming (which is less flexible but more efficient) and object-oriented programming (which is more flexible but less efficient). C++ provides a balance between the efficiency of C and the flexibility of an object-oriented or object-based design. This is why, even after more than a decade of its inception, C++ is still very popular among the developer community.

Differences between Object-based and Object-oriented Programming

> C++ provides a choice to the programmer to decide whether he/she needs an object-based or an object-oriented design.

In this section, we briefly outline the differences between object-based and object-oriented programming.

Object-based programming Object-based programming uses objects and classes but without inheritance. It provides flexibility to the program and is easier to work with. Operator overloading, function overloading, and the use of constructors and destructors are included in object-based programming.

Object-oriented programming Object-oriented programming uses classes and objects with inheritance. It can have classes inherited from other classes and have complex means for calling and using functions of both the classes. Base (or parent) classes (from which we derive or inherit another class) and inherited or derived (from base classes) classes are the two categories of classes. It is possible to inherit a class from multiple classes and it is also possible to inherit multiple classes from a single class. An already inherited class can also be inherited further. Now, once we have such a hierarchy in place, we can decide on the object to process dynamically at run-time. This is an extremely flexible and powerful way of manipulating objects. When we manipulate objects of the hierarchy at run-time, we are providing object-oriented programming.

1.1.4 C++—Not Completely Object-oriented

Pure object-oriented models are never found efficient, but the C++ model is a balanced one chosen to cater to efficiency as the prime requirement. There are other languages such as Java, which offer better object orientation but are less efficient than C++. Hence, C++ does not represent the pure object-oriented model.

The C++ model is very close to the object-oriented philosophy but not completely so. It is also possible to write a C++ program without using the object-oriented methodology. A valid C program without any object orientation feature is usually a valid C++ program as well.

The basic requirements of object orientation and object-based programming include providing classes. Besides, other issues such as encapsulation, inheritance, polymorphism, and reusability of code and objects are required to be implemented. Let us now look at some of the object-oriented concepts that would help us understand the design of the C++ language and the psychology behind its creation.

1.2 CONCEPTS OF OBJECT-ORIENTED PROGRAMMING

Object orientation, as mentioned earlier, is an outcome of the research to find the solution to programming large systems. There are many issues related to object orientation as it has become a discipline of its own today. In this section, we will look at some of the important object-oriented concepts that influenced the C++ design.

Let us begin with an example. Suppose we are given a job to write a program about maintaining the roll call of a college using a C++ program. The roll call is usually done by calling the student's roll number or name one by one and making an entry in the register, by using a special sheet wherein every student present in the class should sign, or through a card-based system, which automatically registers a student when he/she approaches the classroom. This register, sheet, or computer file is then used to provide input to the program. The program should then be able to generate reports such as the individual attendance of a student and the attendance for a particular subject.

To program for the roll call process, we have to decide the entities involved in that process. The first observation yields some entities that are listed here. This list is based on the author's observation. Readers may come up with lists with a few differences. There are no clear-cut guidelines for choosing the entities; it is more a task involving

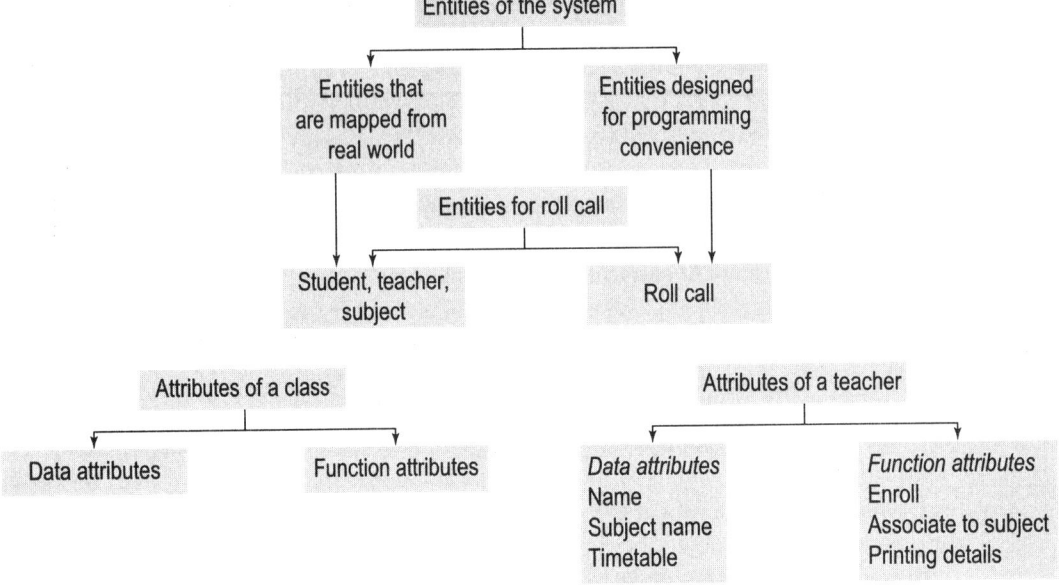

Fig. 1.1   Entities of a system

intuition. The author's list of entities involved in the roll call program, as shown in Fig. 1.1 is as follows:

1. The teacher who is responsible for taking the roll call
2. The subject for which the roll call is taken
3. The roll call itself, where the other details about roll call, for example, the day and time of the roll call, the subject for which it is taken, and so on, are stored. The attendance entries are made for each roll call separately. Individual roll call forms the basis for calculating subject-wise, teacher-wise, or student-wise attendance at later stages.
4. The student who is marked present or absent in a given roll call

As mentioned earlier, this is just a first-hand list; it can and does grow when the actual system is designed. One can easily see that the entities involved in the process are of two different types. The first type has a one-to-one relation with the real-world counterparts. Students, teachers, and subjects happen to exist in the real world. Our entities are computerized counterparts of these entities. The roll call is something that does not exist in the real world, but when we write a program, it is convenient for us to have that entity in our program. So, the first type of entry is directly picked from the real world and the second type is designed by the programmer for programming convenience. Both require some information to be stored in them.

We have already seen the roll call entity and its attributes. Let us take the case of a teacher entity. Some of the details required about this entity are the name of the teacher, the subject he/she teaches, and probably the timetable. We would also like to know how a new teacher is enrolled, how a teacher is associated with a specific subject when he/she is given the assignment of teaching a specific subject or part of it, or how all content related to a teacher can be printed or input. Hence,

One must have a list of entities involved in the program to begin programming. There are two types of such entities. Most of the entities represent real-world counterparts and some of them represent programming constructs that the programmer additionally requires to solve the problem.

there are two different attributes that the teacher entity holds, termed the data and the function attributes. The name, subject name, and timetable information are all data attributes. The rest are all function attributes. The data attributes indicate the status of the teacher object and the function attributes indicate the operations possible. We need to do a similar exercise for the other entities as well. The data and function attributes together describe our understanding of the entity.

> **Note** Entities have two types of attributes, the data and the function attributes. A programmer needs to model both of them in an object.

Once we decide about the data and function attributes of all the entities involved, we may proceed further. It is important to note that the attributes we consider are only those that we may think are important for solving our problem or any extension to the problem that we may foresee. We may not include many other attributes, for example, take the case of the student entity. A real-world entity, student, does have data attributes such as the names of parents, list of friends and hobbies. One can also think of function attributes such as adding a friend, sending a scrap to a specific student, and uploading a photo of a student, as shown in Fig. 1.2. It can easily be seen that such a list is endless. It is an important job of a programmer to weed out those attributes that may not be directly required by the program. This is not all that easy as the choice also depends on the future landscape of the system. If we think that we may need to have a social networking between students additionally in our system later, then some of the attributes weeded out earlier probably should become a part of the system design now. As mentioned earlier, this is a case of an individual expert's judgment based on experience and intuition.

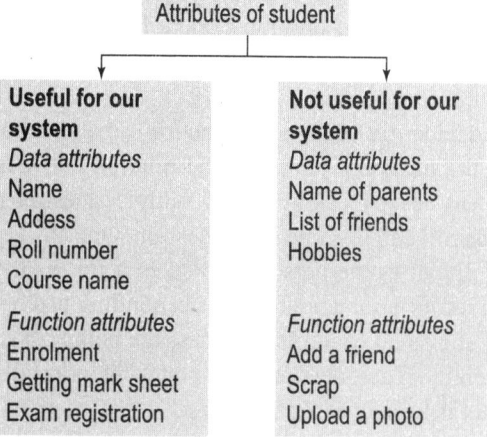

Fig. 1.2 Attributes of a real-world entity

> The real-world entity might have many, potentially infinite, attributes. A programmer decides only those attributes that he/she needs to model in the class to solve the problem at hand.

> A solution involves many entities rather than a single entity to solve a real-world problem.

Usually, a single program such as roll call is not considered while designing classes but a collection of programs that solves the entire college administration process is considered. Here, the roll call management module is just one small fraction of the entire problem. In that case, the list of entities and their attributes are decided looking at the larger scope and not just one program. How to do this is an interesting question that cannot be answered here but students can find it in books on system analysis and design and object-oriented system analysis and design. A better solution still is to just pick some program from this text and extend it further for one's own requirement and understand the first-hand need for the design. If analysis and design is studied after some experimentation, the concepts become much clearer.

For our discussion, it is not necessary to follow the complete system design knowledge. Figure 1.3 represents a small system related to students. Four different programs have been considered as a part of the system here. Usually, we have many programs in the system, but we consider only these four programs for introduction. The first program is the roll call management, the second is

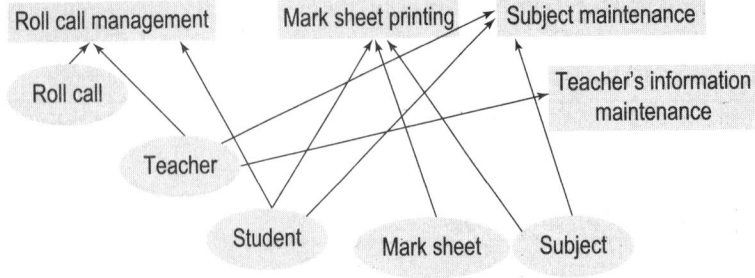

Fig. 1.3 Inter-relationship between programs and entities

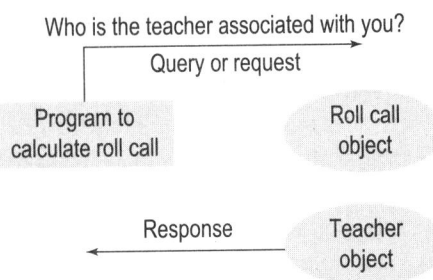

Fig. 1.4 Determining relations among entities

> When a program uses objects to represent real-world entities, its end users ask queries to the objects and seek responses by passing and receiving messages.

marksheet printing, the third is maintaining the subject (i.e., provide adding, deleting, and modifying details of a subject), and the fourth is maintaining the teacher's information (i.e., providing adding, deleting, and modifying details of a teacher). There are five entities considered—roll call, teacher, student, marksheet, and subject. Again, there are possibly many more, but they have not been considered for simplicity. Figure 1.3 shows the association of each entity with each program. The actual system design process might generate a large number of programs and a larger number of entities in more than one way. The following example will illustrate the concept.

Once we decide the data and function attributes of the program, the next step is to find the relation between the different entities by asking a few simple questions. 'How is a teacher associated with the roll call?' is one such question. One answer may associate a teacher with the roll call as the person who takes it for his/her subject. We may need to obtain the information about the corresponding teacher from the roll call entity. Figure 1.4 shows an example of a message being asked and replies being sought from an entity. The question or the query is normally referred to as a *request* and the reply is termed as the *response*.

When we look at our job to be done, we need to have few more such cases of requests and responses, for example, a teacher asking how many students were present on a particular day in the class and the roll call entity answering that question. We may need to find out how many such questions are possible to be asked and how the answers to these questions are sought out. This is the next assignment when we are developing our system. The method to generate the answer of a message must be provided to the receiving entity; otherwise, the receiving entity cannot answer that question. In the case of the question regarding the number of students present, the roll call entity must have a method to calculate the total students present from the data it has. This method is called or invoked by the receiving entity when the other entity asks for that specific information.

1.3 CLASSES AND OBJECTS

A class is an extension to the C struct (the basic C struct is also extended in C++; we will examine the difference later). Let us consider an example of a class Student. The struct Student in C will contain only the attributes of the student such as name and address. On the other hand, in C++, the class Student will have the attributes of the student and it will also store the actions (or functions) related to the student. This means that the student class will contain the student name, address, roll number, subjects, etc., as well as all actions in the form of functions to be performed *on* the variables of that class or *by* the variables of that class (the variables of the class Student are student1, student2, etc., which are actual students and are known as student objects).

The words *on* and *by* used in the previous statement have an important meaning. It is possible to have *any* function inside *any* class, but it is not recommended. Only functions that describe the actions of the entity under consideration should be a part of the entity and others should not be included. We will elaborate this issue further with appropriate examples in Chapter 4.

> **Note** There is no restriction on the type of function a class can have, but a good design requires only related functions to be a part of the class.

There is one design methodology that demands that classes be designed with minimal member functions. It says that when we design classes, we should not keep a function as a member function unless it is necessary. This will make a class 'thin' and easy to modify or extend.

> **Note** The thin class design requires only necessary functions and data attributes to be part of a class, in a way making it easy to administer. When a class has less number of member functions, it is less affected when the class grows or changes.

Thus, the functions for reading and printing information about a student, enrolling of the student in a class, and other functions, which we may consider useful for solving our problem, will also be a part of the Student class. Here, we must understand the difference between the student class and the student object. A class is a data type and an object is a variable of that data type. A Student class is an abstraction describing what a student object should have (name, address, etc.) and should do (printing details, accepting details, checking whether passed or not, etc.), but does not do anything itself. A student object is an instance of that class, which actually has a name, an address, etc. A class is a sketch from where actual objects are derived. If we have a Student class to represent 30 students, we have one student class and 30 objects of it. The action performed by the objects (i.e., the variables of type class) is known as *method* in object-oriented programming, but C++ calls it *function*. So we will use the word 'function' to describe the action that is performed on or by an object of the class.

| Operations are performed by and on objects and not classes. |

The functions that are a part of the class are known as *member functions*. It is also possible to have functions that do not belong to any class; such functions are known as *non-member functions*. In C struct, functions are not a part of the struct; if they need to operate on a structure, it is passed to them. For example, StudentPrintDetails() function is a separate function from struct Student. It cannot become a part of struct Student. A struct variable representing student must be passed to that function for printing the information about the student. If we have defined struct Student Lara, then calling StudentPrintDetails(Lara) requires Lara to be passed to the function. The StudentPrintDetails() function is neither a part of struct Student nor has any compulsion not to be seen by variables other than of type struct. If we define struct Student Mahesh, then we may use StudentPrintDetails(Mahesh) to print details about Mahesh. However, we can also pass something else to the function. If Snoopy is a variable of type struct dog, we can write StudentPrintDetails((Student) Snoopy). This process may print garbage on the screen, but the compiler will not be able to judge

| The functions that are a part of the class are known as member functions. A member function helps programmers to control its access. |

| The objects of the class alone can operate on the functions owned by them. |

that it is an error. Thus, the programmer has no control on how the structure and function interact.

In C++, it is possible to write a member function that is known only to that class, and the rest of the program is not aware of it. There is no direct way to call that member function using objects of other classes. Thus, the objects of class Student can call StudentPrintDetails, but the objects of class dog cannot call this function. This is one of the fundamental differences between C and C++. Thus, we can write Lara.PrintDetails() but we cannot write Snoopy.PrintDetails(). It should be noted that member functions are called using dot notation similar to other data elements. The functions now belong to the class.

The definition of a class is similar to the C struct, as we have mentioned earlier. We can define class Student and can have, say, Student_1 as an object of type Student. If we define class Teacher and then define Bob as a variable of type Teacher, Teacher is a class where Bob is an object.

1.3.1 Object-oriented View of Classes and Objects

We will now take a different look at classes and objects, from the object-oriented point of view. The entities involved in the discussion in the previous sections are implemented in a C++ program as a class. The class is a representation of the real-world entity (e.g., a teacher or a student) or an entity added by a programmer for convenience (e.g., the roll call object) with respective attributes that are required to solve the problem at hand. It can be seen that this description is quite vague. For a given problem, the set of entities that the author has chosen probably is different from that chosen by the readers. The same problem is being solved but handled differently. Moreover, the attributes that the author has chosen probably are very different from that of the readers, even if both are solving the same problem.

All entities that are modelled in the program are implemented as classes. Thus, the classes in one program could be different from that in another when solving the same problem. Such classes (Teacher, Student, or RollCall) do not refer to an individual entity, but we refer to them in general. The entities such as Ganesh as a student, Mathew as a teacher, or roll call 16030903 (roll call created on 16 03 09 and of the third lecture) are instances of the generic entities that we have discussed so far. In object-oriented parlance, they are known as *objects*. Objects are variables of type class and can be defined similar to variables. Assuming that the classes Student, Teacher, and RollCall exist, the following are valid C++ statements, which define the individual entities or objects for respective classes:

```
Student Ganesh;
Teacher Mathew;
RollCall RollCall16030903;
```

In these definitions, the left-hand side (LHS) part is the data type and the right-hand side (RHS) part is the variable. Once the classes have been defined, the class name can indeed be used as a data type. So, in this case, the classes are Student, Teacher, and RollCall. The instances of these classes are Ganesh, Mathew, and RollCall16030903, which are also called the objects of the respective classes. The classes are sometimes referred to as user-defined data types compared to built-in data types, such as int and char. Thus, in our example, Teacher, Student, and RollCall are also called user-defined data types.

Note The analogy of classes and objects with data types and variables does not hold good for the memory allocation in this case. Defining a variable will require a compiler to provide memory. On the contrary, whenever a class definition appears, the memory for the member functions is provided by the compiler. The memory for data members is provided when an object is defined from that class.

It is also important to understand that a single class usually has multiple objects associated with it. For example,

```
Student Mahesh, Jagruti, Rama, Haresh;
```

Here, we have a single `class` `Student` with which we have four objects associated.

The real world also consists of classes and objects. All of us are objects of the class humankind, Delhi is an object of the class city, Amazon is an object of the class river, and so on. Here too, a single class can have multiple objects. Ganges is also an object of the class river and Mumbai is also an example of the class city. The C++ class is derived from this real-world understanding of the class.

What is the difference between city and Bengaluru? We can say that Bengaluru is an instance of city. We have a clear understanding of what a city is. We all know that a city should have a name, have residents living in it, and have houses and shops, streets and roads, water and sewage system, and so on. Every city must share almost all these attributes. Bengaluru, being one such instance, has every attribute that a city should possess. Similarly, Mumbai is also one such instance and has all those attributes as well. Now, can we say something about city and Bengaluru that differentiates a class and an object?

A city is intangible, but Bengaluru is not; a city is conceptual, but Bengaluru is real; a city describes what a city should have and Bengaluru actually has that; a city does not actually have any residents but Bengaluru has; a city can have multiple instances such as Mumbai, Bengaluru, Sydney, and London, which is not true for Bengaluru. Thus, classes and instances are different. Instances are derived from a class, but are tangible and real, whereas the class is an abstract entity. The class city is a concept and contains information about what one would expect in a city. We may include population, dimensions, state or province in which the city lies, and so on as attributes of the city. The city concept itself does not have anybody living in it. Only the instance such as Delhi can have residents. Thus, Delhi requires space to hold them and city does not. Figure 1.5 shows instances of some classes and their objects.

> Class is a data type and object is a variable of that type. A single class may have multiple objects associ-ated with it.

> Classes contain attri-butes that all the objects share.

We have already seen that a class is a sketch containing information about what an object of that class should possess and that the real-world counterparts are also similar.

The identification of the entities of the problem domain results in classes that become part of our program. Finding out the classes that a program will need is the first step in solving any problem in an object-oriented way. The next important thing that we should do is to ask ourselves the question 'What can I do with the objects of this class?' For example, what can I do with an object of the `Student` class? The answer is a set of methods that the object should implement as a response to specific messages. We will look at the methods and messages in Section 1.4.

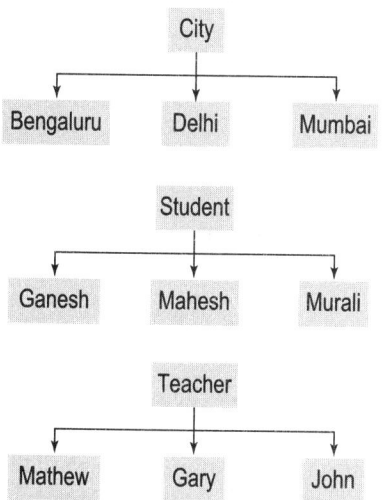

Fig. 1.5 Some classes and their objects.

Let us consider a single example to get some idea about the attributes. City contains population, dimensions, citizens, and so on. Every city object in turn will have all these attributes—Delhi has it, Mumbai has it, Bengaluru has it, and any city that is an object of this class will have it. Thus, these attributes are shared by all objects. Kindly note that only the attributes are shared and their values are different for different cities.

Both Delhi and Bengaluru have population as an attribute but their values are different for both the cities. Two student objects might share an attribute name but its value is different for both the objects. Thus, population, name, and dimensions are attributes associated with the city class and name, roll number, and marks are attributes associated with the student object but each attribute's value can be different. Classes and objects are dealt with in detail in Chapter 3.

1.3.2 Abstract Data Type

When the objects of a class behave like a data type, the class is known as an *abstract data type* (ADT). The string class is an example of ADT. It is possible to define a complex number as a data type using a class. Similarly, we can also define graphic concepts such as point, circle, and rectangle as a class such that the objects behave like a data type. We can write the following statements after properly defining these ADTs.

```
Complex C1(2,3), C2;
Point P(2,3), Q(4,S), R(10,10),S;
Circle C(P,20), Ring;
Rectangle Rect(P,R), PlayGround;
```

These ADTs are defined in two ways, one with initialization and the other without. For example, Point P(2,3) not only defines a point *P* but also defines that the *x* and *y* coordinates of the point *P* are 2 and 3. On the other hand, point *S* is defined without any mention of the coordinates.

Quite a few useful class definitions fall under the category of ADT, including stack, queue, string, vector, and dequeue. We will learn about complex, point, circle, and rectangle while we discuss operator overloading in Chapters 6, 9, and 10. Some of the built-in ADTs are discussed in Chapter 16; the Standard Template Library (STL) and the string ADT are discussed in detail in Chapter 15.

C++ is said to have type extensibility, that is, we can add our own types to the program and use them. STL is a great example of generic data types.

1.4 METHODS AND MESSAGES

Suppose we need to find the teacher who took roll call 16030903 (refer to Fig. 1.1). To accomplish this task, we may write a C++ program with the following statements:

```
Teacher SomeTeacher;
SomeTeacher = RollCall16030903.getTeacher();
```

These statements may not be quite intuitive yet. We will soon learn to write such statements and understand them. For now, they can be understood as follows. The first statement defines an object SomeTeacher of the class Teacher. This definition looks similar to a variable SomeTeacher being defined of the type Teacher. This is indeed so. Here, Teacher is known as a user-defined type and SomeTeacher is a variable of that type, that is, the object of the class

> A member function is invoked similar to a data member with the dot operator after the object name.

`Teacher`. Similar to other variables, this variable can also be used on the LHS of the assignment statement to assign a specific value to it. (This operation is similar to defining `int IntVar` and then writing `IntVar = 20` to assign the value 20 to the integer variable `IntVar`.) Whenever such an object is used as an LHS expression of an assignment statement, the outcome of the RHS expression is assigned to the object. In our case, we get a `Teacher` object by executing the RHS of the assignment statement, which is then assigned to `SomeTeacher`. So, if the outcome of the RHS of the assignment statement is `Mathew`, then `SomeTeacher` now contains `Mathew`.

1.4.1 Message Passing

A more important part is the call to the function, which is defined inside the class `RollCall`. The function can be called by using the object<dot>function name syntax. The function `getTeacher()` is part of the `RollCall` class (if it is not a part of the class, we would not be able to use

> The response in a message passing process is *optional*. Some messages may not return anything.

dot notation to call that function). The statement `RollCall16030903.getTeacher()` calls the function `getTeacher()`, which works on the object `RollCall16030903` and gets the teacher associated with that roll call (object representing Mathew in our case). In the assignment statement `SomeTeacher = RollCall16030903.getTeacher()`, we assign the `Teacher` object (object representing Mathew in our case) returned by that function to `SomeTeacher`. The `getTeacher()` function here must be designed to return the `Teacher` object.

In the entire discussion so far, the `getTeacher()` function is known as a message being passed to an object `RollCall16030903`. The object takes some action (executes the body of the function specified, the `getTeacher()` function in our example) and returns with the response (the `Teacher` object). The code for providing response to the message is known as method (in our case it is the body of the function `getTeacher()`). We can easily see that a specific message invokes a specific method in the object and then the object optionally returns with the response, as shown in Fig. 1.6. It is important to note the word optional. Some messages do not require a response, as can be seen in Fig. 1.7. Assume that `DispInfo()` is a function defined in the `Teacher` class, which displays everything that one would like to know about the teacher, and that we have defined Gary as a teacher. We may type `Gary.`

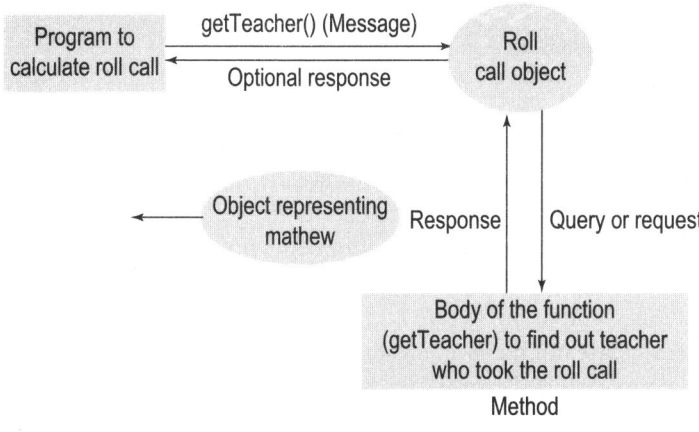

Fig. 1.6 Message, method, and optional response

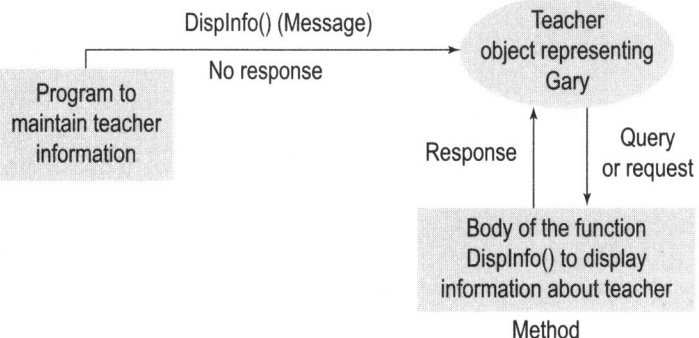

Fig. 1.7 Message, method, and no response

`DispInfo();` and the function will display all information about Gary. Here, the message to display all information is sent to the object of the `Teacher` class (the object named Gary). In response, the object manages to execute the function `DispInfo()` and display the information needed. Here, the object does not need to respond with any information. Thus, the response is optional.

Thus, when we define a function inside the body of a class (i.e., a function that is a member of the class), we can execute that function by using the object<dot>function notation. (We will study about how to define and use functions in Chapter 4.) When we call that function, we are passing a message (which has the same name as the function name) to the object. The object looks at the message and executes the body of the function bearing the same name as the message itself. The body that is executed is called the method in response to the message. Thus, the function name is used as a message and its body is the method that is being executed in response to that message.

> **Note** In C++, the function name is a message and the body is the method that induces optional response and does some job as requested by that message.

Let us look at the process from another angle. We pass the message `getTeacher` to the object, and the object finds out the teacher associated with that roll call and sends it back to us. The message `getTeacher()` is the only thing we are supposed to know. How the object finds the teacher is of no concern to us; we can safely rely on the internal functioning of the `RollCall` object to do that. The object gets us the teacher information by executing some method to find the teacher. Here, the discussion is very much like a real-life scenario, where we are passing some message to an object and getting a response from it. Take the case of riding a motorbike. When we accelerate, we are passing a message to the object (e.g., the bike GJ1-CK-4587). The object responds back with increased speed. How the result is achieved is of no interest to us (unless we are bike mechanics). Probably, moving the accelerator downwards pulls the accelerator wire, which, in turn, opens the petrol valve wider. The widening of the petrol valve results in more petrol being poured into the engine, which results in faster revolution of the engine, which, in turn, speeds the wheels up. As a motorbike rider, how much of this is important to us?

In most real-world activities, we are not really interested in the methods; we are actually interested in the results of our message. When we apply the brakes, we want the vehicle to halt or slow down but how it is done is again of no interest to us. In our case, the bike GJ1-CK-4587 is an example of an object of the class motorbike. The operations such as accelerate and brake are important messages that we would like to pass and get responses to. This is shown in Fig. 1.8. We are not interested in how the responses are achieved, though. Similarly, classes are designed in a manner that the user

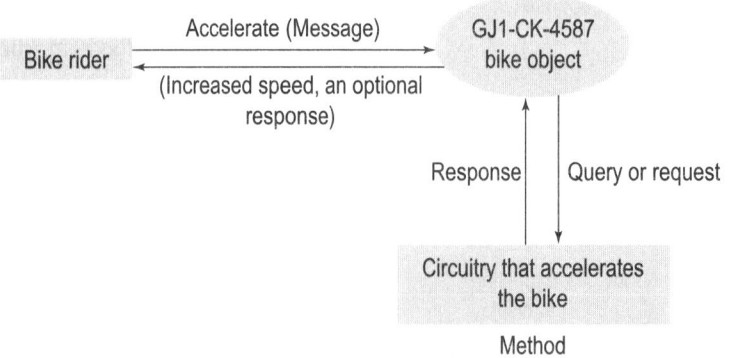

Fig. 1.8 Message, method, and optional response for a motorbike

of the objects of that class can send messages and can get the job done without really being worried about how it is done.

> **Note** Users generally do not bother about how a method is executed, but they are definitely interested in the job being done as per the message.

1.5 ABSTRACTION AND ENCAPSULATION

We have just seen that the caller or user of an object sends the message to the object and is interested in getting the response. We have also seen that the caller usually is not interested in the method used to invoke the response. It is important for the system to keep the method hidden from the user for the sake of simplicity.

Think of the case when one presses the brake pedal and the brakes are applied. All the circuitry that applies the brake is not open to us. What is the advantage of hiding the circuitry? This simplifies our view. We only find the brake pedal to work with. Opening up the circuitry may not make any difference to an experienced bike rider but consider the case of a novice. If everything is open to him/her, it will take quite some time for him/her to figure out how to apply the brakes. The possibility of pressing something other than the brake pedal is also possible. The bottom line is to expose only those entities that the user needs to interact with and hide everything else. This important law is also observed in C++. It is known as the *law of abstraction*, explained in Exhibit 1.1.

> Java has an abstract keyword. When it precedes the definition of the class, the class becomes abstract.

Exhibit 1.1 Law of abstraction

Whenever a programmer designs a class, he/she designs it in a way that only those messages that the user is concerned about can be passed to the object and their responses are sought. How the messages are responded to is not seen. No other messages can be passed to the entity.

For example, we can pass messages such as getTeacher(), getSubject(), and IsStudent Present(Student) to extract data from the RollCall object and get suitable responses. However, we may not be able to send an UpdateRollCallValue() message if such a message is not expected to be received by the RollCall object. We can only send and get responses to valid messages.

Consider a function that searches for a specific entry in the list called Search() defined inside the class. The IsStudentPresent() function may use the Search() function to find out the entry of a specific student to figure out if he/she is present or not. Now, this Search() function may not be available to the user, as he/she does not need that. Moreover, if that function is provided to him/her, he/she would not know what to do with that function and would probably be confused as to whether the IsStudentPresent() function or the Search() function should be used. Ideally, the Search() function should be hidden from the user who is defining a Teacher object and using it, as shown in Fig. 1.9.

> Abstraction hides unnecessary things and reveals only those that the user needs to manipulate.

Defining functions, to some extent, helps us achieve abstraction, even when we are coding with C. We use functions such as printf() and scanf() without really knowing what they contain. Coding these functions can be really complex. One of the important parts of the design of both printf() and scanf() functions

> Proper abstraction can make a complex and large problem a whole lot simpler and manageable.

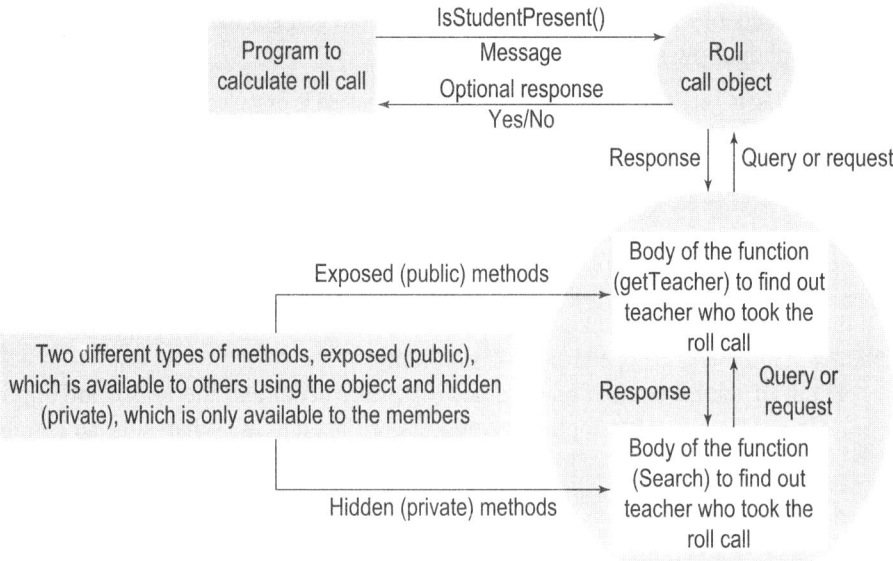

Fig. 1.9 Abstraction implemented as combination of exposed (public) and hidden (private) parts

is that they are able to handle any number of arguments passed to them (printf('Hi'); has one argument, printf('Hi %s', Name); has two arguments, printf('Hi %s your ID is %d', Name, ID); contains three arguments, and so on). Only advanced programmers can manage to write such functions. We use printf() and scanf() functions without really thinking about how that code is implemented. This is the power of abstraction.

The prerequisite of the abstraction process is to have two different types of attributes for a given class, one of which is to be made available to whoever is using the objects of the class and the other is to be hidden. The hidden part is useful to the part that is exposed to the outer world. For example, the Search() function is used to help the IsStudentPresent() function. The exposed attributes are known as public attributes and the hidden attributes are known as private attributes. The decision to make a specific attribute hidden or exposed is based on our plan to make that attribute available to the user for manipulation.

Encapsulation The process of designing a class with some attributes hidden and some exposed is known as *encapsulation*. The entire class is insulated from the outside world. Only the public (or exposed) attributes can be manipulated by the user of that object. Thus, we can have controlled access to the class attributes unlike struct in C. If we define a struct Student with attributes such as name, address, and roll number, then all the attributes are available for manipulation. However, in C++, it is possible to define a class Student where we cannot directly manipulate the name, address, and roll number, but we can only set their values using a function InsertDetails() and print the information using PrintDetails(). Objects have two different types of attributes. The exposed attributes can be manipulated and supplied with inputs, whereas the hidden attributes are meant for internal execution. Such insulation of the class from the rest of the program is called encapsulation. The class attributes are encapsulated within the class and only the public part of it is accessible to the user of the object of that class. The private part is only accessible to those functions that are a part of the capsule, as can be

A friend function can access and manipulate the private entities of a class.

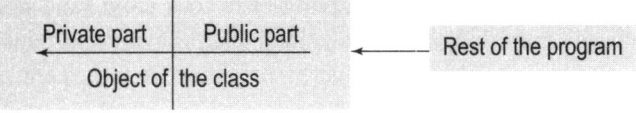

Fig. 1.10 Encapsulation process

seen in Fig. 1.10. The class contains both data and function attributes as part of the capsule. The rest of the program that uses the objects of this class can only access the public part.

Sometimes encapsulation is referred to as combining the data and function together in the class body. The correct way to look at encapsulation is the division of class members in public and private and the idea of hiding the unnecessary and complex part from the user of the object. Encapsulation and abstraction together make the complex system visible as a simpler system. The top view of the system, which was discussed in Section 1.1.1, is possible by abstraction and encapsulation. For extremely large systems, migration from C to C++ is necessary because of these two features of C++. In Chapter 3, we will look at the private and public access specifiers in detail. Section 3.5 explains the need for public and private parts of the class in more detail and also the information hiding principle. Exhibit 1.2 explains the concepts of abstraction and encapsulation.

Exhibit 1.2   Abstraction and encapsulation

Designing a class with public and private attributes carefully makes a complex system easy to work with for the programmer. It helps in hiding the unnecessary things and reveals only those things that are useful for the programmer.

A programmer may define a class as follows, separating the private and public members:

```
class Dummy
{
private:
    ...
public:
    ...
}
```

1.6 INHERITANCE

The idea of extending an already defined class is known as *inheritance*. For example, if we are writing a program to maintain the object MCAStudent and we have a built-in class Student, which has almost all the details needed for our program, except a few, which need to be added manually. The additional information may be anything that an MCA student possesses in addition to the normal student.

Let us now look at inheritance from the point of view of object orientation. The world is full of cases where one class is a specialization of another. Human beings are a specialization of mammals; dogs are a specialization of animals; Indians are a specialization of people. This relationship between two different classes is significant in more than one way. We would be learning about that here and later in Chapter 9.

Inheritance or specialization does not prevent the inherited class to have additional attributes of its own.

There can be quite a large number of relationships possible between any two given entities. Inheritance (or specialization) is one such relationship, where one class inherits all the attributes of some other class. In the examples given, we inherit everything from the mammal class, for example, giving birth to a child (and not laying an egg). Similarly, a dog inherits everything from the animal class (having four legs, very little communicative abilities, and so on) and Indians inherit everything from the people class (Indians have legs, hands, etc.).

The inheritance relationship is sometimes compared with an is-a relationship, which is similar to the mathematical notion of a subset relationship. The word 'is-a' is derived from the fact that we can usually ask the question '*x* is a *y*?' to find if *x* is inherited from *y*. Whenever we have an is-a relationship between two entities, it is inheritance as well. Human being is-a mammal because if *x* is a human, *x* is a mammal; dog is-an animal because if *x* is a dog, *x* is also an animal; and so on. When we have *x* <is-a> *y*, *x* is a subset of *y*. Here, all the attributes of the set are available to the subset as well. Sometimes it is not that obvious.

Take the case of numbers. We know that *N* (the set of natural numbers 1, 2, 3, ... until ∞) is a subset of *R* (the set of real numbers). Is *N* inherited from *R*? It is difficult to understand this. It is better to put forth the question as: 'Is an element of *N* also an element of *R*?' If the answer is yes, *N* is said to have an is-a relationship with *R*. Whenever an entity *x* has an is-a relationship with *y*, *x* is said to be inherited from *y*. Figure 1.11 shows some examples of the is-a relationship.

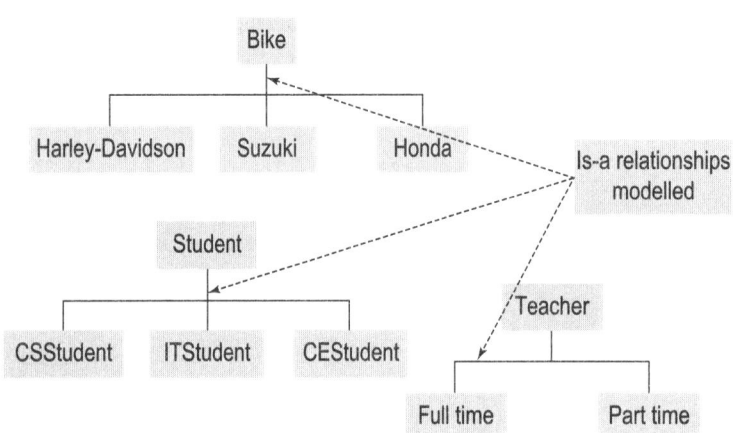

Fig. 1.11   Some classes and inherited subclasses

An is-a relationship exists between two different sets and not between an element and a set. So, dog is-an animal is correct but Snoopy is-a dog is wrong. Sometimes, the instance relationship is modelled as an instance-of relationship and we would write Snoopy instance-of dog and Bengaluru instance-of city. The instance-of relationship, as a diligent reader by now must be able to guess correctly, is the relationship between an object and a class. An object of a class is also an instance of that class (such as Snoopy being an instance of the class dog and Delhi being an instance of the class city).

> **Note**   An is-a relationship is between two objects, and an instance-of relationship is between an element and an object to which the element belongs. The is-a is only one popular type of relation; there are many other relations possible between objects.

1.6.1 Advantages of Deploying Inheritance

Studying inheritance is important for more than one reason. The object-oriented languages including C++ provide means for having inheritance relationship between any two classes. One important reason for such a facility being provided in the language is that inheritance is one intuitive way to model the real-world hierarchy in the program.

Suppose we are programming for graphics shapes and we already have the rectangular shape as a class. Now, we can add square to it using inheritance by providing the specialization

An inherited class is not bound to use the inherited value or function. A class can easily override a function by defining the same function in its own body with a different functionality.

Inheritance is not the only way to provide reusability. C++ provides templates additionally for reusing the same class for different types.

that a square is a rectangle, where the length equals the width. Similarly, ellipse can be inherited into circle, and so on. It is possible to model hierarchy like this in C++.

Reduction in work   One important outcome of modelling this inheritance hierarchy is the reduction in work. We may have defined a function for calculating the area in the `rectangle` class, and when we define a new class `square`, which is inherited from the `rectangle` class, the area function is available to the `square` class automatically. This feature is sometimes referred to as reusability. Reusability is the property of the attributes of the object to be reused in a way such that the maximum utilization of the design is possible. Let us consider one more example. Assume a `Student` class. Now, we inherit that class into a `ComputerScienceStudent` class. We have functions for enrolling new student, reading and printing details about students, etc., defined in the `Student` class. The `ComputerScienceStudent` class will have all these functions when we inherit it from the `Student` class. Interestingly, if we define an `ITStudent` class and inherit that from the same `Student` class, we need not again redefine functions that we already have in the `Student` class. We have written these functions once in the base class and all derived classes use them. This reusability is the second advantage of inheritance.

Myths   There is a point of caution while dealing with inheritance and the issue of reusability. There are two myths associated with reusability, which need to be clarified. These are the following:

Myth 1   For reusability, inheritance is an ideal tool to be used. Whenever one needs to have reusability, he/she should opt for inheritance.

Myth 2   Inheritance is the only way to provide reusability in any object-oriented language.

The first statement is wrong as reusability is an advantage obtained from providing inheritance, but it is not good to opt for inheritance whenever we need to reuse some code. Inheritance should be used only when the class inherited (the derived class) is indeed the specialization of the class inherited from (the base class). Otherwise, unforeseen consequences can occur, and the program design may become rigid and difficult to extend or evolve. Thus, when we want to have some functions in our class, which are available in some other class, we should not inherit from that class unless it has an is-a relationship with that class. Reiterating an important point again, please note that when we use inheritance we get reusability as a side effect and it is a great advantage, but to use inheritance to gain the advantage of reusability is wrong and indicates bad design. A discipline in the programmer community is required to maintain this.

The second statement is also untrue as there are other ways of reusing the same code. C++ provides templates to reuse the code as well as the class definitions. STL, which will be discussed in Chapter 16, is an excellent example of providing reusability without using inheritance. It is also possible to merge the templates and inheritance to provide reusability. We will study about inheritance further in Chapter 9.

1.7 ABSTRACT CLASSES

We have already seen that entities are modelled as classes and their instances are modelled as objects in C++. (This is also true for any another object-based or object-oriented

An abstract class is a class with no objects.

programming language.) We have also stated that there are two different types of entities. One type of entity is directly modelled from the real-world counterpart, that is, a student or a teacher. The other type is what a programmer is required to add to the system to effectively solve the problem. The RollCall class that we have defined earlier is an example of programmer-added entity, which does not have a counterpart in the real world.

There is one more way of looking at the category of classes. The first type of class has a real-world counterpart existing in reality, most of the time having a tangible existence. The other type is the real-world counterpart that exists only in abstract. Take the case of the animal class. An animal is an abstract concept. The animal class does not have any direct object. Every animal is either a dog, a tiger, a lion, or something similar. All these classes are derived from the animal class and due to the transitivity of relationship ($A \rightarrow B$ and $B \rightarrow C$, so $A \rightarrow C$), a dog, a tiger, or a lion is an animal. Snoopy is a dog, so it is an animal as all dogs are animals. Here, Snoopy is not a direct object of the animal class. Plenty of such abstract concepts exist in the real world, and when we need to use them, we should define abstract classes.

It sounds ironic to have abstract classes in the system. We want entities and their instances to be modelled in the program. Now, why would we need entities without any instance? Modelling abstract entities of the real world does not seem to make much sense when we are not going to define and use objects of that class.

Let us try to understand the need for abstract classes from one simple example. It is clear that the abstract class does not represent any real-world tangible entity, which would always have some instances, except when we are dealing with extinct species. Take the case of writing a program for taking the roll call afresh. Assume now that we start with a computer science student and collect his/her attributes. Then, we move on and start working with an IT student, and after finishing that, start with a computer engineering student. We soon realize that there are a few attributes that are common in all these classes, for example, the name and address of a student, and that it is better to keep all these attributes at a single place. Both these attributes appear in all three classes that we have encountered so far. It is better to define aclass Student with all such attributes and let all three classes inherit from it.

Thus, all common attributes are collected and placed in the base class Student. In that case, all three classes will have everything that is defined in the base class and additionally whatever they would like to have individually. This is called bottom-up approach in designing classes and is sometimes very useful. Now, we have a Student class with us from which three classes are derived, namely, CSStudent, ITStudent, and CEStudent. Figure 1.12 shows the steps for designing classes using a bottom-up approach.

One more alternative, but a more practical design, is to learn about the common attributes while working with the first two types of classes and then to program for a CEStudent. Here, the design for CEStudent class becomes easier as it does not need to include anything that is available in the Student class. It is automatically available after inheritance. This is also similar to the real-world case as when we say that man is a mammal, we do not need to ask if man breathes or not. Since all mammals breathe, man having an is-a relationship with the mammal must do so. Unless explicitly stated otherwise, the relationship holds true. Sometimes though, it does not. For

Classes can be designed in the top-down as well as the bottom-up way.

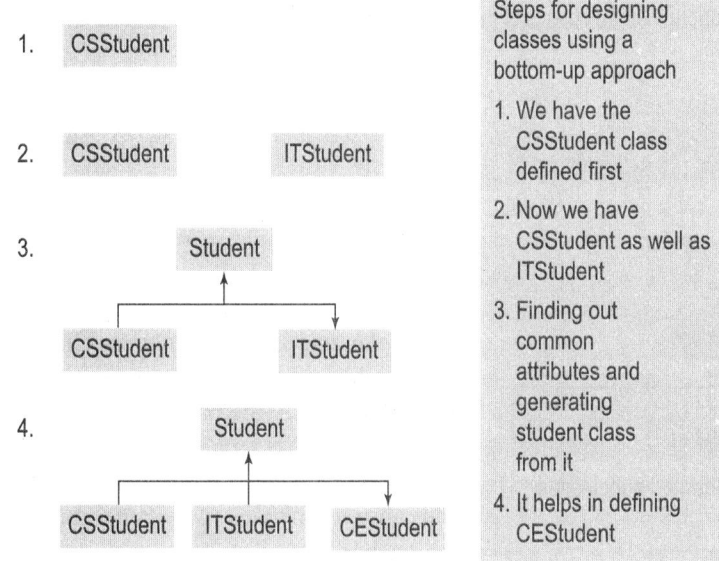

Fig. 1.12 Steps for designing classes using a bottom-up approach

example, all horses have tails but bobtails (a type of horse) do not have any. Similarly, all birds fly but ostriches do not. Such instances are called *exceptions*, which need no further exploration). There are many advantages in the bottom-up design. Some are listed as follows:

1. *There is no redundancy.* The student's name is kept only in the Student class. If we need to change the size or type of the name, we have to change at only one place, the Student class, and nowhere else. As other classes inherit from this class, all of them have the effect of the change automatically.

Hence, there are less chances of ambiguity. Assume that we are not using the base class approach. It is quite possible that the same attribute in two different classes have two different names. Suppose in one class the name of the student is defined as StudName, in the second class the name is defined as Name, and the third class probably calls it StudentName. More than one class representing the same real-world entity or more than one attribute name referring to the same attribute creates a lot of ambiguity in the designer's and developer's mind. This is eliminated here as there is a single class, and the name given to the attribute student name (say StudNm) is the same in all classes because these classes do not define this attribute themselves, but they just inherit them.

> **Note** In C++, we need to recompile the program when the base class changes itself. We need to recompile the program even when the program is not changed a bit. This is not a flaw in the design. Read Section 9.6 in Chapter 9 for finding out the reason.

2. *Adding a new attribute to all the classes is simple.* Suppose we would like to add mobile number as an additional attribute to all three classes, we can do it by placing it in the Student class. We do not need to pick each class one by one and do it individually.

This example, as mentioned earlier, introduces the concept of the bottom-up design. There are sound reasons to follow the bottom-up design approach in many cases.

Let us concentrate now on the class that is generated as a side effect of the design. The class that now contains the shared attributes becomes the base class for all such classes under consideration. This base class, interestingly, is the abstract class. Why? There is nobody who is only student; we may have a CSStudent, a CEStudent, or an ITStudent, but nobody is just a student. Hence, the Student class in this design is an abstract class. We are not going to define any object of the class Student.

Note The abstractness of a class depends on its context. If we do not differentiate students by discipline and store information about them in objects of the Student class, then the Student class is not an abstract class.

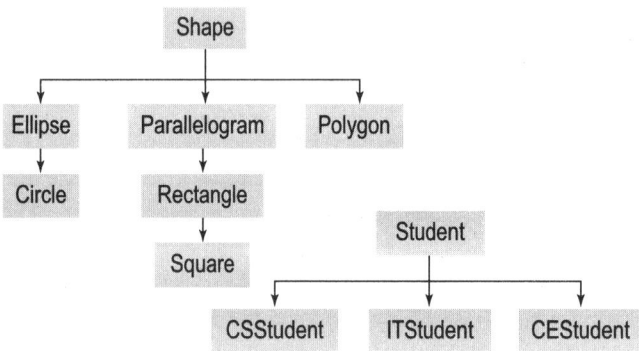

Fig. 1.13   Abstract base classes and inherited subclasses

Let us look at one more example. Suppose we are dealing with graphics objects. If we want to have a single base class for all the graphic shapes, it is bound to be an abstract class. We can name it shape and inherit ellipse, triangle, or rectangle from it. We know that the shape we are planning to draw is either an ellipse, a rectangle, or a triangle, but is definitely not a plain shape (the base class). This is why shape is also an abstract class here. This is shown in Fig. 1.13. It is easy to find abstract classes when the design approach is bottom-up.

Note An abstract class represents an entity with shared attributes of a few related classes. As there is no real counterpart, it does not have any objects associated with it.

This example indicates why the word 'abstract' is chosen. Shape is an abstract concept, which does not have any object associated with it. There are quite a few other abstract concepts such as furniture or electric equipment in the real world, but there are no entities that we can call only furniture or electrical equipment. The entity that is furniture will invariably be a sofa, a chair, or something similar, but not 'furniture' by itself. Similarly, electrical equipment is either a bulb, a holder, or something similar, but not electrical equipment per se.

To model an abstract concept, we need to have an abstract class. In C++, there is no keyword such as 'abstract', which can precede the name of the class to make it abstract. Rather, we need to define a *pure virtual function* in a class to make it abstract. We will study about pure virtual functions in Chapter 10.

The following is an example of inheritance. The class Shape is inherited into Rectangle and Circle. Rectangle is also inherited into Square. It can be seen that Rectangle and Circle are specializations of Shape, and Square is a specialization of Rectangle. The word public means the inheritance is of type public. We will look at different types of inheritance in Chapter 9. The body of the class is irrelevant for the time being, and hence it is not shown.

> If a programmer inadvertently attempts to define an object of an abstract class, the compiler flags an error and does not compile that program.

```
class Shape {…};
class Rectangle: public Shape {…}
class Circle: public Shape {…}
class Square: public Rectangle {…}
```

1.8 POLYMORPHISM

In general, polymorphism is the ability of a single object to appear in many forms. Polymorphism is related to something that behaves differently under different

> Polymorphism allows an object to behave differently under different circumstances, given the same message.

circumstances.One may be a student in a college or an employee in a working place. The same person may be a son or a daughter at home and a friend when sitting with a group of friends. One may respond to 'How are you doing?' differently when playing different roles. The idea is to react differently for the same message in different situations. If one does so, he/she is exhibiting polymorphism.

Many types of polymorphism exist but we will discuss the following three different versions, which have some relation to C++.

1.8.1 Ad-hoc Polymorphism at Compile Time

This type of polymorphism is related to functions that behave differently with different sets of arguments. It is possible to define the same function with different types of arguments or different number of arguments in C++. Let us consider an example to understand this. See Fig. 1.14.

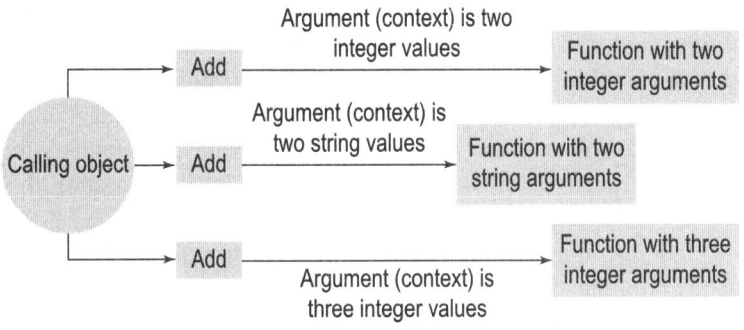

Fig. 1.14 Polymorphism arising from argument set

Here, we have defined three different functions with the same name (Add) but with either *different sets of arguments* or *different number of arguments* or both. All function bodies are different, and thus, we observe a different response when we call the same Add() function with either different sets of arguments or different number of arguments. For example, when we call Add(int, int), we get the addition of two integer values returned from the function, and when we call Add(int, int, int), the function does not return anything but the third argument now contains the summation. Providing different behaviour in different contexts (number or type of arguments) is known as *function overloading* in C++.

The following are the various types of Add () function:

1. Add(int First, int Second)
2. Add(float First, float Second)
3. Add(string First, string Second)
4. Add(int First, int Second, int Third)
5. Add(int First, float Second)
6. Add(int First, float Second, float Third)

> It is possible to define functions with the same name with different sets or types of arguments. This process is known as function overloading.

Function overloading is an example of ad-hoc polymorphism at compile time. We will discuss function overloading in Chapter 4. Function overloading is new for those who have worked with C before. Defining functions in this manner is an error in C as we cannot have two functions with the same name.

We can see that the message is the same for all these Add() functions (remember that the function name is a message, so the message is to add). The message generates different responses depending on the type, number, or ar-

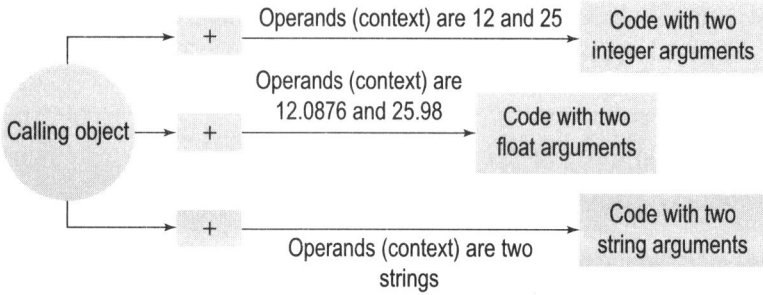

Fig. 1.15 Polymorphism arising from operand types

```
12 + 25                    (Result is 37)
12.0876 + 25.98            (Result is 38.0676)
'Indian' + 'Cricketer'     (Result is 'IndianCricketer')
```

guments as all these different functions have a different body. Hence, this is an example of polymorphism.

One more type of ad-hoc polymorphism is observed when the operators behave differently with different operands. This can be understood better using Fig. 1.15.

The + operator in these three cases behaves differently. In the first case, it adds two integers; in the second case, it adds two double values; and in the third case, it concatenates two different strings into one. The string is available in C++ as a data type. + is overloaded in the string class. So, the given operation makes sense. When the operator behaves differently for different types of operands, it is also a type of ad-hoc polymorphism. In C++ parlance, this is called *operator overloading*. We will discuss operator overloading in Chapter 6.

In C++, both function and operator overloading are resolved at compile time. The compiler, while compiling the program, decides the operation to be performed and generates the object code that describes that operation. In the given example, when 12 + 25 is seen in the source code, the compiler provides the code that adds two integer values and adds that to the object code being generated and when 'Indian' + 'Cricketer' is seen, it adds the string concatenation routine at that place.

Similarly, when the specific Add function is called, for example, Add(20,30), the compiler changes that call to a jump instruction, which jumps to the function body that contains integer addition. Similarly, when Add('Indian','Cricketer') is called, the jump instruction will point to another function that contains the code to concatenate strings. Moreover, when we write Result = Add(FirstVal, SecondVal), the jump instruction points to the function body that adds two integers and returns the answer. When the call is to Add(FirstVal, SecondVal, ThirdVal), the jump instruction points to the function body that does not return anything but where the ThirdVal contains the summation. Thus, the decision about which function to call is done at the compile time. So, ad-hoc polymorphism is also compile time polymorphism in C++.

> When an operator behaves differently for different types of operands, it is known as operator overloading. Java has no such features.

Note It is not necessary that ad-hoc polymorphism must take place at compile time. If the language (Smalltalk is an example) resolves the function call at run-time, then the ad-hoc polymorphism happens at run-time. Such languages are sometimes denoted as late-binding languages.

1.8.2 Dynamic Polymorphism at Run-time

This is a case when the resolution of the function happens at run-time. The restriction here is to choose the function only from the hierarchy of classes and not from elsewhere. Let us consider the example shown in Fig. 1.16 to understand this concept.

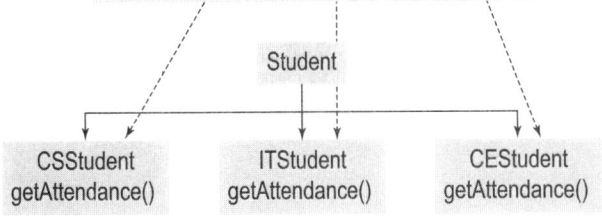

The pointer to student class is named as ptrStudent. When this pointer points to any class derived from student, the statement ptrStudent -> getAttendance() executes the getAttendance() function, which belongs to that class and is a virtual function.

Student

CSStudent
getAttendance()

ITStudent
getAttendance()

CEStudent
getAttendance()

Fig. 1.16 An example of a hierarchy for run-time polymorphism

1. Suppose we define `Student` as a base class.
2. Then, we define three derived classes, `CSStudent`, `ITStudent`, and `CEStudent`, from `Student`.
3. Next, we define function `getAttendance()` in all these classes. (It is important to define this function as virtual to achieve polymorphism. We will study how to define and use virtual functions in Chapter 10.)
4. Now, we define a pointer to the base class `Student`. Let us call it `PtrStudent`. It is important to note that this pointer can point to an object of any class in the hierarchy mentioned.
5. Whenever we type `PtrStudent->getAttendance()` (i.e., execute the function `getAttendance()` of the object `PtrStudent` is pointing to at the moment), the member function of the object being pointed to is executed. So, if our `PtrStudent` is pointing to Ganesh, a CS student, a function `getAttendance()` defined in `CSStudent` class will be executed. When the same pointer points to Mahesh, an IT student, the `getAttendance()` defined inside the `ITStudent` is executed. Both the `getAttendance()`functions could be quite different. For example, in the `CSStudent` case, only the theory class attendance is returned, whereas in the `ITStudent` case both the theory and the practical attendance are returned. The caller does not need to modify his/her call even if the functions behave differently. This is known as *dynamic polymorphism*, as it requires dynamic information about where the pointer is pointing to at run-time. Sometimes, this polymorphism is also referred to as *subtyping* or *inclusion polymorphism*. As mentioned earlier, the function `getAttendance()` mentioned here is to be defined as virtual in C++ to achieve the effect of polymorphism.

The following code snippet shows how polymorphism is provided using virtual functions.

```
/* Assuming class Student is defined with a virtual function
getAttendance() and all the three classes CSStudent, ITStudent, and
CEStudent are inherited from Student */

ITStudent Mahesh;
CSStudent Ganesh;
Student Jayesh CEStudent;
Student *ptrStudent;
...
ptrStudent = *Mahesh;
ptrStudent -> getAttendance()
// it calls the getAttendance() function of ITStudent class
ptrStudent = *Ganesh;
ptrStudent -> getAttendance()
// it calls the getAttendance() function of CSStudent class
```

Dynamic polymorphism can also be achieved by using references.

Polymorphism can be of three types, static or ad-hoc, dynamic, and parametric.

1.8.3 Parametric Polymorphism

The third type of polymorphism seen in C++ is known as parametric polymorphism. Using parametric polymorphism, a function or a data type (user-defined data type, i.e., classes) can be written generically so that it can handle values identically without depending on their type. C++ provides templates as typeless descriptions of classes and functions to provide parametric polymorphism. While programming with parametric polymorphism, we can code functions and classes without specifying their type, and when they are used, the type is passed as an argument. This type-resolution process happens at compile time in C++, so it is a kind of compile type polymorphism. We will study about templates in Chapter 7. An excellent example of type-independent coding is the STL. We will study about STL in Chapter 16.

1.9 OBJECT-ORIENTED DESIGN AND C++

While discussing about object-oriented concepts and C++, it is better to look at a few other issues related to object-oriented design.

The first issue is related to static and dynamic binding. Static binding happens at the compile time, whereas dynamic or late binding happens at run-time. The term binding refers to the function resolution. Suppose our code contains a function f(), and there is more than one f(). If the decision about which f() to call is done at compile time, it is static binding. If the same decision is kept pending until the run-time, it is known as late binding. We will discuss the same issue later in Chapters 9, 10, and 11, wherein we will be discussing about inheritance, virtual functions, and run-time type identification, respectively.

The second issue is related to object-based and object-oriented programming. Although the concepts discussed so far apply to both types of programming in general, inheritance and run-time polymorphism are applicable only to object-oriented programming and not to object-based programming.

A valid C program that does not use classes or any other feature discussed so far is usually a valid C++ program as well.

The third issue relates to how C++ is placed vis-à-vis other object-oriented languages. This comparison can be found at various places in this text .

The last but a very important issue is of flexibility. The designers of C++ designed it for flexibility and a programmer can choose to either use or not use a particular feature of the language. The object orientation feature is also not forced on the programmer in C++.

1.10 PRINCIPLE OF INFORMATION HIDING

Earlier, we found that abstraction is related to the principle of information hiding. Here, we will see what this principle is and the advantages it offers to us. Let us start with an example.

An examination system might have entities such as student, teacher, examiner, question paper, and syllabus. The entities here can have both data members and function members. For example, a question paper object may have the data members such as the subject for which the paper is set, total marks, and marks to pass. The function members may include printing question paper, insert new or modify old contents, etc.

One must also decide what part of the object is to be hidden from the outer world and what is to be shown. Consider an example of a student object, which may allow printing

The functions that are available to all the users are known as public functions. The functions that are not available to outsiders are known as private functions.

its name and address but may not allow doing other actions such as changing the birth date of the student. We may not even be able to change the name and address (though we can see and print them). We may not be able to see and use the function that allocates the roll number uniquely. As a user of an object of a `class` (in our case, `class Student`), we may be able to use the functions provided by that class publicly and nothing else. This is the principle of information hiding. The name is a misnomer. It should be garbage hiding. To understand this, let us assume a `Student` object containing information such as the student name and the roll number. It has functions for reading all the required information from the screen and may be printing on the screen. It also has a function that uniquely allocates a roll number to the `Student` object. If a marksheet printing program is using the `Student` object, the function that gets a unique roll number for the student is useless for that program. The marksheet printing program should deal only with printing the correct roll number with the right set of marks. The roll number creation process is better hidden. Thus, the unique roll number creation function should be defined in a way that it is not accessible to the users of the `Student` object.

Note A class should make the required functions available and hide the other data and functions. This process helps the user to have an uncluttered view and is useful to have objects as an abstraction. This is the principle of information hiding.

An important fact is that the information that is not useful for one may be precious for another. Some of the member functions of the `Student` class may need to use the roll number generating function, such as the one that enrols a new student. The roll number allocation function is definitely not garbage for an enrolment function, so it must be visible to the enrolment function. C does not differentiate between such functions, whereas C++ does. Here, the roll number allocation function is said to be a private function, accessible only to the members of the class (member functions such as enrolment function) but not to users who are using the `Student` object.

1.11 DIFFERENCES BETWEEN C AND C++

In this section, we will discuss the important differences between C and C++.

1.11.1 Philosophical Differences

Every language designer has some vision about the problem to be solved. The language philosophy is the approach the designer deems fit to solve the problem. Different languages are designed by different philosophies for a specific set of problems. In the following paragraphs, the philosophy of C is compared with that of C++.

C++ is Not Just Extended C

Though the syntax of C++ is very similar to that of C, it is much more than extended C. It has a radically different philosophy and needs a different approach to programming.

Going from C-type (procedural) programming to object-based programming itself introduces a lot of designing differences. For object-based or object-oriented programming, one must need to visualize the problem as a collection of interrelated objects, and their attributes and methods.

Implementation of Information Hiding in C++

We have already seen that objects of any class in C++ have two parts—a private part, which is not visible to any element outside the class, and a public part, which is visible to outsiders. Thus, when we want to hide something from others (i.e., other than member functions), we define that in the private part of the class definition, such as the roll number allocation function in the earlier example.

There is an exception to this case as well. In some special cases, a class designer can allow visibility of a private part of an object to some specific outsiders. These special outsiders are known as friend functions.

Let us now concentrate on how information hiding principle is applicable to C++ programs. Two different types of attributes and functions are provided to make this principle possible in C++. Whenever somebody uses an object, anything that is private is simply hidden. Only the data and function members defined as public are accessible. Once we know that we can segregate our class elements into private and public, the next step is to decide what to define as private and public.

Suppose the Student object of our discussion has an attribute named birthdate. This attribute is available to a function that prints the details about a student. It is also available to a function that enrols a new student and similar other functions belonging to the same class. However, it is not required to be available to functions other than class member functions. The function that prints the details about the student is useful to anybody using that Student object. Hence, the first attribute, the birthdate, should be defined in the private part of the class and the PrintDetails() function should be defined in the public part of the class. Here, variables such as birthdate are known as the private members of the class and member functions such as PrintDetails() are known as the public members of the class.

It is possible to classify the functions into two categories. One type consists of functions that are used in the maintenance of the object and need to have access to the private information about the object. The other type consists of functions that need to use the objects of that class only for doing their own job. They use the object only for their purpose and have nothing to do with the maintenance of the object. An analogy from the real world could be a user of a car and a mechanic. A mechanic may need to access the inner engine parts, but a normal user only accesses the interface functions such as the steering wheel, brake, and clutch.

> Objects in C++ can have one more part called protected. The protected portion of the object is public to classes derived from the class under consideration and private to others. So, it is public for some and private for others.

The functions that can have access to the private part of the object are usually made a part of the object itself. Other functions, which do not need to have access to the private part of the object, can reside anywhere (usually) outside the class. In later chapters, we will see more examples to understand the differences between the member and non-member functions in a more precise manner.

> Only those functions that require the private entities of an object are kept as members, the rest can be non-members.

The functions that are a part of the object can also be of two types—one that is not known to outside entities and the other that is known to the outside entities. Here, the functions defined in the private part are known as private functions and the functions defined in the public part are known as public functions. Private functions, similar to private data members, are not known to outside entities, but public functions are known. C does not offer such categorization of functions.

Availability of Off-the-shelf Objects

Another important difference between C and C++ is that C++ offers readymade objects 'off-the-shelf' and a possibility to use them with required changes. This is known as reusability advantage. In C++, it is possible to have built-in objects such as vector and queue, which have requisite functionality for users to use. Such objects can also be tailored for our use, for example, we may define a new `class PriorityQueue` from the built-in `queue` class. This option not only reduces the programming time, but also reduces the chances of errors and enables more modular programming. One such built-in object is the `string`, which we will use in examples throughout this book.

One good example of a collection of readymade objects is the Microsoft Foundation Class (MFC) library. The MFCs have built-in functionality to deal with complicated Windows programming. While using MFC, the job of the programmers is reduced to a large extent. They must have knowledge about the built-in MFC objects and their respective functions. Complicated Windows-based operations such as messaging and event-driven processing are automatically provided when we use objects of appropriate classes.

The reusability advantage is also extended to the users of C++. There are so many classes designed by experts (known as third-party developers) for specific applications such as graphics. As a user of C++, we just have to use them. This kind of software is also available for C but the difference in C++ is that we can actually extend these classes for our own need into newer classes as well (without having the source code). It is done using the concept of inheritance. C++ itself offers one such library that is very powerful and useful. It is known as the STL. Object-based model, on which STL is based, does offer such extension, but is not as extensible as an object-oriented model.

Standard Template Library

An STL is available with all C++ compilers. It has built-in classes that can provide the reusability advantage. It provides means for having different types of collection of objects into container classes. Container classes collect the objects in such a way that efficient operations such as sorting and searching can be done on them. The STL is also equipped with general operations such as find, search, and sort. The beauty of the STL lies in the generality of the object collections (known as containers) and algorithms applicable to them in a generic way. We will study about the STL in Chapter 16.

Similarity of User-defined Types with Built-in Objects

The developers of C++ wanted the user-defined types to behave as similar to the built-in types as possible. This is why some new features such as constructors, destructors, and operator overloading are defined.

Constructors and destructors are provided for initialization and termination effects for objects defined in a C++ program. Initialization effects are applied when the object definition appears in the program and termination effects are applied when the object goes out of scope.

Example of constructors   Take a look at the following code.

```
class Student
{
    int roll no;
    char name[20];

    /* A constructor function, bearing the same name as the class */
```

A constructor is a function that bears the same name as the class. It is automatically called when the object of the class is defined.

```
Student()

{
roll no = 0;
}
};
Student st1;

/* Defining an object of class Student, notice the use of
class name 'Student' instead of 'class Student' as a type */
```

Here st1.roll no is initialized to zero *automatically* when the statement Student st1; gets executed. It is because the function Student() is defined inside the class Student. The function Student() (not the class Student) is called a constructor. The constructor is automatically called when the object is defined. In this case, when we define Student st1; the Student() function is called. The effect of calling that function initializes the roll number to zero. The advantage is that we do not need to explicitly initialize the roll number to zero when we define an object of student. Suppose we define 100 students or an array of students. Each time the constructor function is automatically called, the roll number for all those students is initialized to zero. We will study about constructors and destructors in detail in Chapter 5.

Operator Overloading

Suppose we have defined a class for complex variables. A complex variable has two parts, a real part and an imaginary part. If we have named the class as complex, then it is possible to define

```
complex c1, c2;
```

Here, complex is the class name and c1 and c2 are variables of the complex type, that is, the objects of the class complex. It is possible to write c1 + c2 as an expression where + will add the real and imaginary values, respectively. By default + adds only built-in types such as int, float, and double. C++ provides the facility to assign a new meaning to + such that it can now also add two complex variables. This facility is known as operator overloading. Here, we have to overload the + operator to have the required effect. (Readers interested in knowing how this is done can see Chapter 6 on operator overloading wherein the program for addition of complex objects is provided.)

The ultimate goal for providing all such facilities is to make user-defined objects to behave as naturally as possible. In C++, user-defined objects can actually behave in a natural way. Just by looking at the use of the user-defined objects, it is almost impossible to differentiate them from the built-in objects. In C, user-defined data types always look different from the built-in ones (the word 'struct', for example, struct Student, struct employee, and so on).

1.11.2 Syntactical Differences

There are a number of syntactical differences between C and C++. The major ones derive from the need to provide the class construct and related issues. Almost all C syntax works fine with all C++ compilers. A few syntactical differences are summarized as follows.

Comments

The comments in C++ are of two types. The C-like comments (anything enclosed within /* and */) are acceptable and comments that begin with a // are also allowed. When a //

is provided somewhere in the line, the rest of the line is ignored. Look at the following code:

```
/* This itself is a C-like comment, whereas the
following is a C++-like comment */

if (a > b) // checking for a greater than b
printf ("a is greater!");
```

The following is an example that shows how C++ comments replace C-like comments:

```
/* This is the first line of comment.
This is the second line of it.
And this is the third! */

// This is the first line of comment.
// This is the second line of it.
// And this is the third!
```

In short, // is useful for a single-line comment, but for multiple lines, one may prefer to use /* and */.

Moreover, // is valid until the end of the line, so it cannot replace a C-like comment used within the following statement:

```
if (a > b)              /* checking for a > b!*/
printf("a is greater!");
```

Input/Output Operators

Though printf() is used in the program statements given in Section 1.11.2, it is usually not used in the C++ programs.

```
cout << "a is greater";
```

can do the same job in C++ as printf().

> While coding the C++ programs, one should use cin for reading rather than scanf() and cout for printing rather than printf(). These constructs are simpler and better.

Here, cout is an object of the standard output stream class. It is one of the most useful objects of C++. We have to include <iostream> file for the prototype of iostream (input output stream, to be precise) objects. We can see that iostream is similar to stdio.h used in C. It should be remembered that we still need to use stdio.h for the prototypes of the functions using input and output stream such as printf() and scanf().

> In the case of compilers that can compile both the C and C++ programs, the file name extension determines the type of code. In TurboC or VC++, '.c' is a C program whereas '.cpp' is a C++ program.

If it is possible to use stdout in C++ (i.e., printf(), scanf(), etc.), then why do we need a new way to output? This question is answered in detail in Chapter 12. In summary, the newer approach is better and easier to program. At times, this approach is the only way while providing the input and output of user-defined objects similar to built-in types. For example, it is possible to have a student Lara and then use cout<< Lara to print the details about Lara. We need to overload operator << for the same. This is not possible with printf(). As mentioned earlier, if printf() is used, one needs to include <stdio.h>. The user running the program finds no difference between the output produced by printf() and cout.

While using ANSI C++, one should use <cstdio> and not <stdio.h>. The usage of <cstdio> is similar to the functionality of <stdio.h>, that is, either

<cstdio> or <stdio.h> will provide printf(), scanf(), etc. in exactly the same way. Still, there is a huge difference between them. This difference is explained in Chapter 14. Similarly, there is a difference if we want to use the other C header files (e.g., <math.h> becomes <cmath>).

> The << operator used by cout and >> used by cin are examples of operator overloading.

There is another seemingly minor difference between using the functions such as printf() in C and C++. With most of the C compilers, it is possible to use printf() or scanf() while not including <stdio.h>. Such programs can be compiled and will also work as expected. The inclusion of <stdio.h> does not seem to be necessary (because the stdio.h only contains the prototype of the function). Why is it so? Let us try to understand this.

The compiled code of printf()(and other functions as well) is kept in the library. The library contains the object code for all functions that are a part of the library. The code of printf() and scanf() gets added to the program code after compilation and before the executable code is generated.

Note A C program does not need a prototype to use a function. The C compiler might flag a warning at the most if the prototype of the function is missing. A C++ program, on the contrary, will not compile unless the prototype is available. Prototyping is a must in C++. If we use printf() or scanf() and do not have a header for stdio.h, the program will not compile in C++.

In the case of cout, << is actually an overloaded operator. This means that <<, which is basically a *bitwise left shift operator*, is given a new meaning here. The process of providing a new additional meaning to an existing operator is known as operator overloading. It should be remembered that we can still use << as a bitwise left shift operator. The new meaning given is an extra one (in addition to the original meaning).

Similarly, we can use >> operator (again, overloaded) for reading purpose. We use an object of standard input stream cin for this purpose. A built-in object of iostream class, cin is used to read an element from the console. So, the following statement can be used to read a string variable, where its name is assumed to be StringVariable:

```
cin >> StringVariable
```

We do not need to provide the data type with cin or cout (such as %d or %s), nor do we need to append an & operator in front of the variable while reading a variable value as in scanf. In C++, cout formats the output in a default way, which is suited for most of the cases. We will learn how to format the data different than the default way in Chapter 12.

C++ Headers

We cannot use stdio.h for using cout or cin. We need to write #include <iostream> to use cout and cin in our program. The omission of .h in the name of the header file <iostream> should be noted. This is a new style in ANSI C++. Older C++ programs use a file <iostream.h>. If we write <iostream.h> instead of <iostream>, and it might work with most of the existing C++ compilers. Please understand that it is provided only for backward compatibility. The use of <iostream.h> is no longer recommended in C++.

We will see the difference between using iostream and iostream.h when we learn about namespaces in Chapter 14.

Return Types

The return type in C is by default int, whereas in C++, it is not so and hence we must specify it. For example,

```
my_func(one, two, three)
```

will by default return `int` in C. That is, it is equivalent to writing

```
int my_func(one, two, three)
```

In C++,

```
my_func(one, two, three)
```

is actually treated as

```
void my_func(one, two, three)
```

C does not require `main()` to provide a return type whereas it is mandatory in C++. So, `main()` is not acceptable; either `void main()` or `int main()` has to be written. Moreover, if we have `int main()`, there must be a return statement in `main()` that returns an integer.

Note Linux GNU C++ does not allow `void main()`; hence, `int main()` must be used.

Compiling the C++ Program

In UNIX, the C++ programs have extension C (uppercase c) rather than c (lowercase c) and we may use CC (again, uppercase) to compile rather than cc. In Linux, the C++ programs have extension .cpp and we may use c++ or g++ to compile (GNU C++).

In VC++ and Borland C++ compilers, the program needs to have a .cpp extension to be compiled as a C++ program.

Support for both Object-based and Object-oriented Programming

It is important to know that C++ provides support for both types of programming, object-based and object-oriented. However, we are going to program without using any inheritance in the initial chapters. So, the object-based approach will be followed in the initial chapters. Later on, we will see how object-oriented programming can be done.

When we have more than one approach to solve (object-based and object-oriented, to be precise), how to choose between the two approaches is an important question. That is, if it is possible to solve a problem with and without using inheritance, then which approach should be chosen? The solution without inheritance is preferred in most of the cases for its simplicity and efficiency.

Note There are two different ways to code—object-based and object-oriented. Which approach should be chosen then? The solution without inheritance is preferred in most of the cases for simplicity and efficiency. A normal industry program usually contains both object-based and object-oriented coding in the same program.

1.11.3 Exception-based Design

In the C language, the errors need to be checked explicitly by the programmer and the respective directions are to be provided then and there. C++ has additionally provided a new mechanism to handle errors. It is based on exceptions. When an error occurs, an exception is thrown, which is to be caught by an error-handling routine. The following code shows an example:

```
try
{
```

```
    int i, j;
    <some C++ statements>
    if  <some condition> throw i;
    if  <some other condition> throw j;
}

catch (int)
{
    <error handling routine which works
    for both i and j>
}
```

Thus, error checking and handling are separated. This is a more orderly way of processing errors.

As mentioned earlier, C++ has everything that C has; so, C-style error checking can still be used. C++ exception handling does not replace the error-handling mechanisms that were used in C. Yet, it is an important facility to know and use when required. We will be learning more about exceptions in Chapter 8.

1.11.4 Templates as Generic Programming Elements

Templates are a type-less way of writing codes in C++.

Templates are extensions provided to C++ long after the inception of the language. Templates are produced to support flexible object-based programming. They are far superior to the library of C-like functions. C functions can actually be combined in object-based versions in a library, which can then be used in other programs by referencing that library. We are able to use functions such as sqrt(), sin(), and cos() if we use math.lib (which is present by default in C compilers). The problem in this approach is that the solution is bound to the argument types. If cos() function needs double, we have to pass double argument to it. If we need to have cosine of an integer, we need to cast it into a double value and then pass it to the cos() function. This (casting) does not always work. If a generic function for a quick sort is written, then sorting any data (such as sorting students on their total marks for getting a merit list or on student name for printing sitting arrangement for internal examination) is not possible in a straightforward way. We cannot design a quick sort function to sort integers and then pass names after casting them to integers.

Type is also an argument to be passed to the templates at the time of definition. The code becomes much more flexible and the coding work is reduced if the templates are properly used. Considering the earlier-mentioned case, we can write a generic quick sort, which can take any argument such as student name or student total marks and sort the data.

Note C++ actually uses template libraries rather than normal libraries for its 'off-the-shelf' objects. It is known as the STL. A major portion of the input output libraries is written as templates.

1.12 C++ OBJECT MODEL

When the compiler compiles a C++ program, it needs to pay special attention, which was not needed by the C programs. A C++ program is to be parsed to find details about the classes defined in the program and their usage. The compiling model that is used to compile the C++ programs is known as the C++ object model. As stated earlier, the C++ object model is designed to provide the efficiency of C object code and the flexibility of object orientation.

Though it is not as flexible as the CORBA (common object request broker architecture) or COM (component object model) models (which are also object-oriented models), it is even more efficient because the C++ designers kept the efficiency as the prime concern. We will be referring to the C++ object model throughout this text.

1.13 VARIATIONS OF C++

C++ was originally designed by Bjarne Stroustrup in 1979. It was initially called 'C with classes'. The incremental operator ++ was added in 1983 to C to indicate that C++ is an incremental version of C. Soon, there were quite a few vendors with different brands of C++ compilers. The enthusiasm to provide better features in competing products led to a lot of incompatible versions of C++ compilers. Products from different vendors provided additions to original standard C++, such as protected members, protected inheritance, templates, and the use of multiple-inheritance. (We will learn about them in due course.) In 1997, the American National Standards Institute (ANSI)/International Organization for Standardization (ISO) standardization committee provided an ANSI/ISO C++ standard, taking into consideration all these changes.

1.14 APPLICATIONS OF C++

The applicability of C++ can be seen in operating system development. The majority of the Windows NT and Windows 2000 code is written in C++. Linux and other UNIX variants also use C++ to a great extent. The client–server architecture needs a middle tier in big applications. It is usually developed using C++ (for creating dynamic link libraries (DLLs)). A lot of work is also being done in computer graphics using C++. It is an area where the efficiency of C++ is considered most useful. Network programming relates to programming for routers, firewalls, and similar devices. Multifunction devices that work as routers, firewalls, intrusion detection system (IDS), and antivirus systems traditionally used C. Now, their programming is also done in C++. Voice over IP (VoIP) service, which enables voice communication using computers and Internet, and the search engines used by the web servers for providing fast and efficient text-based content search also use C++ for their coding.

■ RECAPITULATION ■

- C++ is designed with a goal of backward compatibility with C.
- C style of programming is not very useful for complex and large programs.
- C++ provides abstraction and this provides visualization of the entire program as a single unit.
- C++ provides a construct known as `class`, which is the basic building block for abstraction.
- A class is similar to a C `struct` but additionally has function members as well.
- The variables of type class are known as objects.

- C++ enables us to implement the principle of information hiding, which helps in abstraction.
- C++ provides a lot of additions to the C language besides the introduction of classes.
- Syntactical differences between C and C++
  - C++ headers are different from C
  - New comment syntax is available in C++
  - Input–output is done in a very different way
- Philosophical differences between C and C++
  - The provision of object-based and object-oriented programming

- ○ Exception-based error handling
- ○ Use of templates
- Objects get their job done by passing messages to each other.
- Messages are the names of the member functions of the class of the receiving object.
- The receiving object executes the body of the function with the same name as the message and optionally sends the response back.
- The body of the function that is invoked upon call is known as the method.
- The ability to hide how things are done and only allow certain inputs and provide outputs on the basis of the input is useful in providing an abstracted view of the system.
- Abstraction and encapsulation (insulation of the private part of the class from the rest of the system) help in designing complex systems with simpler interfaces.
- Inheritance is an important relationship between classes, which is denoted by a subset or an 'is-a' relationship.
- Inheritance is the ability to extend the class into a specialization such that all the attributes of the class being inherited (formally known as a base class) are available to the new class (formally known as a derived class).
- C++ does not enforce inheritance on the programmer.
- Abstract classes represent abstract concepts and do not have elements.
- Polymorphism is derived from many forms of a single item. Polymorphism in C++ can be achieved in two different ways, compile time and run-time. Operator overloading and function overloading are the two ways to provide compile time polymorphism. They are also known as ad-hoc polymorphism. The other type of polymorphism provided by C++ is by using virtual functions. This is run-time polymorphism or dynamic polymorphism.
- Parametric polymorphism, wherein a function or class can be written with a generic data type, is also possible in C++ by means of templates. Resolution of a function at compile time is known as static binding and resolution at run-time is known as dynamic binding.
- C++ does not enforce any feature on the programmer. We can easily write a program without any of the features mentioned so far, and the C++ compiler will compile it without any errors.

■ KEYWORDS ■

Abstraction   The data and function attributes are stored together in the class to help the user to concentrate only on what the class offers and not on the internal working of the class. This is known as abstraction.

Abstract classes   These are classes with no objects. In C++, any class with at least one virtual function is an abstract class.

Class   C++ enables us to define a class, which is similar to struct of C but with the addition of function members.

Data member   Variables that are defined inside the class are known as the data members of the class.

Dynamic binding   The binding (function resolution) that occurs at run-time is known as dynamic binding.

Encapsulation   Dividing data and function attributes in a way that some of them are private and some of them are public is known as encapsulation. Only the public part of the encapsulated class is available to the users of the object.

Exception handling   Exceptions are similar to errors in C++. An automated error-handling mechanism known as the exception handling mechanism is provided in C++. However, the use of this mechanism is not mandatory. We can use other conventional mechanisms as well.

Function member   Functions that are defined as a part of the class are known as the function members of the class.

Is-a relationship x is said to have an 'is-a' relationship with y if x is a specialization of y.

Inheritance   The ability to generate specialization of a given class is known as inheritance.

Methods   This refers to the code that is executed in response to a message. This code is written as a member function body in C++.

Messages   This is the information or command passed to the object for some action. It is the name of the function in C++.

Object   Objects are the variables of type class.

Object-based programming   Programming wherein the objects are used but without inheritance is known as object-based programming.

Object-oriented programming Programming wherein the real-world entities are defined as class hierarchies and can be manipulated using a pointer to the root or base class of the hierarchy is known as object-oriented programming.

Programmer-designed entities These are the entities that do not occur in our problem domain and are added by programmer for programming convenience.

Real-world entity This refers to the entity that occurs in our problem domain and we would like to model that entity as a class.

Static binding The binding (function resolution) that occurs at compile time is known as static binding.

Templates Templates are typeless programming mechanisms to define classes and functions with generic types. These classes and functions can work with any type.

▪ EXERCISES ▪

Multiple Choice Questions

1. Function prototype is _____.
   (a) compulsory in C and C++
   (b) not compulsory in either of them
   (c) compulsory in C++ but not in C
   (d) none of the above

2. The _____ is automatically called when the class is _____.
   (a) constructor, defined
   (b) object, used
   (c) class, constructed
   (d) destructor, defined

3. cout is _____.
   (a) an object of output stream
   (b) an output operator
   (c) an extraction operator
   (d) a printing operator

4. The idea of extending an already-defined class is known as _____.
   (a) inheritance
   (b) reuse
   (c) extension
   (d) enhancing

5. The functions available to all the users are called _____.
   (a) private functions
   (b) public functions
   (c) protected functions
   (d) global functions

6. Struct of C is extended with _____ as a member to make it a class.
   (a) functions
   (b) variables
   (c) arrays
   (d) linked lists

7. The C++ facility that provides a new meaning to an operator is called _____.

   (a) operator overloading
   (b) operator modifying
   (c) operator enhancing
   (d) operator extension

8. What is the difference between ANSI C++ and old C++?
   (a) iostream is used in ANSI C++ and iostream.h is used in old C++.
   (b) stdio.h is used in ANSI C++ and cstdio is used in old C++.
   (c) iostream.h is used in ANSI C++ and iostream is used in old C++.
   (d) Both of them use both types of headers.

9. We can override the function provided by the original base class by _____.
   (a) defining a new function in our own derived class
   (b) defining a new function outside both classes
   (c) defining a new function in the base class
   (d) it is not possible to do so

10. Lengthy programs in C cannot be easily abstracted as smaller _____, which are totally independent.
    (a) individual units
    (b) combined units
    (c) global units
    (d) dependent units

Conceptual Exercises

1. Discuss the syntactical differences between C and C++ that are not mentioned in this chapter.

2. Find and read the history of C++ evolution. Some of the Stroustrup's papers are available on the Internet. Find and read them.

3. Why does the object-oriented philosophy need functions to be defined inside the classes? What could be the advantage? Provide your own logical answer.

4. Try to get more information about other object-oriented languages such as Smalltalk and Java. Compare their features with C++.

5. Try to find out different C++ compilers available in your institute, for example, GNU C++ with Linux, VC++ with Windows, TC++ and BC++ for DOS-based and Windows-based C++ programming, etc. Try to compare them on the grounds discussed in this chapter.

6. Recall some of the problems that you have faced in programming with C. Try to see if C++ provides an answer to them.

7. What are entities? What are the two different types? Pick some other system of your choice. Write down the entities involved in that system. Now, differentiate them into two types—one that has a real-world counterpart and the other that the programmer needs for programming convenience.

8. What are data and function attributes of the system? Take the same system and design a few data and function attributes of the entities involved.

9. What are programs of the system? Take some other system of your choice and decide at least four programs that you may need to code that system.

10. What are methods? Pick at least three different entities of the system that you have chosen and write a few methods for that object. Show how these methods are used for queries and how these methods respond back.

11. How are classes and objects modelled in C++? Why do we usually have multiple objects associated with a single class? How are real-world classes and objects related with C++ classes and objects?

12. What is the law of abstraction? How does it help the user of the objects? Give an example of your choice to illustrate the need for abstraction.

13. Explain the difference between the public and private attributes of the class. For your own system, decide which attribute will be public and which attribute will remain private. Give your reasons for deciding so.

14. What is encapsulation? How does it help a programmer to design the system better?

15. What is inheritance? Try to enhance the system in a way that at least two classes are inherited further.

16. What is an is-a relationship? How is it connected with inheritance?

17. What are the myths associated with inheritance? What is wrong with those myths?

18. How does inheritance help the programmer? Take your system as an example and explain the answer.

19. What are abstract classes? Give a few examples of abstract classes.

20. What is a bottom-up design? How does bottom-up design result into abstract classes?

21. What are the advantages of bottom-up design? Pick your own system and show with an example.

22. What is polymorphism? What are the different types of polymorphism? Give some examples of the real world where polymorphism is achieved.

23. Differentiate between static and dynamic binding.

Practical Exercise

Pick any C program that you have written earlier. Rename that program as a '.cpp' program. Try to compile and run it. It should compile and run without any trouble. Are there any problems? Take the help of your teacher to sort them out.

Overview of the C++ Language

2.1 IDENTIFIERS AND CONSTANTS (LITERALS)

Every programming language has certain rules for defining the names of variables, functions, classes, etc. Such names are known as *identifiers*. C++ follows almost the same set of rules for defining an identifier as C does. C++ accepts all constants that are acceptable in C, including the backslash constants such as '\0' (null) and '\a' (bell). An important difference is that a C++ identifier has no limit on the length of the name. In C, only the first 32 characters are significant, whereas C++ does not have any such limit. Thus, in C++, an identifier can be arbitrarily long and each character of the name can be still significant.

> **Note** All references to C in this text refer to ANSI C and those to C++ refer to ANSI C++.

C++ supports all literals supported by C, though there are some additional ones as well. In C++, it is possible to define L'A' as a wide character constant. This constant is wide, that is, it is of 16-bit storage rather than the normal 8-bit ASCII (hence L precedes 'A'). Using wide characters, it is possible to accommodate characters in the unicode format. Some languages such as Chinese and Japanese have thousands of characters, which do not conform to the small footprint of ASCII. The unicode format enables C++ to read, print, and store characters of such languages. The constant L'A' is actually of type wchar_t, which is an addition to the C++ standard.

2.2 KEYWORDS

C++ has all the keywords of C and the earlier (older) version of C++. It has some more keywords to provide added functionalities. The complete list of these keywords is given in Table 2.1.

As can be observed from Table 2.1, the C++ standard has added 14 keywords to the original C++ from Stroustrup. C++11 (the latest C++ standard, which was revised in 2011) does have a few more additions but it is not yet stable at the point of this writing and so the keywords included in that standard are not discussed here.

Though the C++ standard does not impose any limit on the length of the identifier name, a compiler may impose one.

Table 2.1   C++ keywords

asm	**do**	**if**	**return**	typedef
auto	**double**	inline	**short**	*typeid*
bool	*dynamic_ cast*	**Int**	**signed**	*typename*
break	else	**long**	**sizeof**	**union**
case	**enum**	*mutable*	static	**unsigned**
catch	*explicit*	*namespace*	*static_cast*	*using*
char	*export*	new	**struct**	virtual
class	**extern**	operator	**switch**	**void**
const	*false*	private	template	**volatile**
const_cast	**float**	protected	this	*wchar_t*
continue	**for**	public	throw	**while**
default	friend	**register**	*true*	
delete	**goto**	*reinterpret_cast*	try	

The **boldface** words are ANSI C keywords. Normal typeface words are original C++ keywords (from Stroustrup), and *italic* words are ANSI C++ additions to earlier C++ keyword set.

2.3 DATA TYPES

The C++ data types in C++ can be divided into three categories. The first category represents the data types borrowed directly from C and forms the largest set. The second category represents the data types that were available in C and are also available in C++, but with extended meanings. The third category represents the new data types that have been introduced in C++ and were not available in C.

2.3.1 Borrowed from C

The data types void, int, char, float, and double and the modifiers to these data types, namely, signed, unsigned, long, and short, operate in the same way as in C. Moreover, pointers, except for void pointers, and arrays, unless containing data of newly added data types, also operate in the same manner as in C.

2.3.2 Borrowed from C with Modifications

Some data types of C included in C++ have been adapted to be compatible with the features and compiler requirements of C++. These data types are structure, union, enumeration, and pointers.

In C++, struct(structure) is extended to be compatible with the data type class. The class data type and the difference between class and struct in C++ are discussed in Chapter 3. The span of union is also extended in C++ and is discussed in detail in Chapter 3.

In C, `enum`(enumeration) literals are globally visible even if they are defined locally; however, in C++ these are visible only to the class (or structure) in which they are defined.

Pointer definitions in C++ operate just like those in C, with the exception of void pointers and two new types of pointers, the *constant pointer* and *pointer to constant*. Pointers in C++ are discussed in detail in Section 2.4.

2.3.3 Newly Added Data Types

Some newly added data types in C++ are described in this section. Classes are the central constructs in C++. A class has the capability to represent an entity of the real world in a true sense. Classes are discussed in detail in Chapter 3.

Strings in C++ are much simpler to use than in C. In C, they are treated as character arrays, but C++ has a special string class for defining strings. Strings are used throughout this book and have been discussed in detail in Chapter 15. Strictly speaking, a string is still an outside entity for a C++ program and the `<string>` file needs to be included to provide operations on strings. There are a few other classes such as `queue` and `vector`, which are part of the Standard Template Library (STL). These are covered in Chapter 16.

Abstract Data Types

One may argue that strings, queues, and stacks are not native or built-in data types but are user-defined. The distinction between a built-in and a user-defined data type, which was clear in C, is quite blurred in C++. Moreover, these data types are given by a standard, and thus, for an end user, they are quite similar to built-in data types. They are sometimes denoted as *abstract data types* and can only be found in object-based languages.

An interesting new data type added in C++ is `bool` (Boolean). It can have only two values, `true` or `false`, both of which are keywords in C++.

Consider the following program. It tests the input and comes out of the program if the input is zero.

```
//TestBool.cpp
#include <iostream>
using namespace std;
void main()
{
   bool flag;
   flag = true;
   int test;
   while(flag)
   {
      cin >> test;
      if(!test)
      flag = false;
   }
}
```

Notice the use of 'flag' as a `bool` variable. A `bool` variable can be used where any relational or logical expression is used. Providing a Boolean operation was the additional job assigned to the integer type variables in C. We can spare integer variables in C++ if our purpose is to test the veracity and nothing else. The use of the `bool` variable makes this testing easier and also makes the program more readable. It can have either true or false value as shown.

2.4 POINTERS

Though pointers are available in C++ also, they have some characteristics that are different from those in C that are discussed in the following sections.

2.4.1 Void Pointer

Void pointer is an important type of pointer borrowed from C. One may question the need for void pointers. As a pointer must point to a variable (i.e., it has an address of some variable), the idea of a void pointer (a pointer pointing to nothing) may sound ironic. However, such pointers are useful in C for returning a pointer value of an unknown type. The `malloc()` function is an example.

> **Note** The `malloc()` function can be used for acquiring memory for any data type. This is why it is designed to return a void pointer which the user cast to whatever required. It is also needed to write a generic algorithm that can accept any pointer type by defining the algorithm to accept a void pointer in the argument.

The essence of the void pointer in C++ is better captured by the term *pointer to void*. A void pointer points to a value that does not have a type (such as `int` and `float`). This means that the value pointed to by the void pointer has an undetermined length and undetermined dereferencing properties. The difference between the definitions of void pointers in C and C++ can be brought out by considering the following code segment:

```
int* FirstPointer;
void* SecondPointer;
```

The statement

```
SecondPointer = FirstPointer;
```

is valid both in C and in C++. However, the reverse, that is,

```
FirstPointer = SecondPointer;
```

does not work in C++ though it works fine in C. This is because C++ is a strictly typed language.

> **Note** C++ is a strictly typed language. When one writes a function as `xyz()`; and assuming that it returns an integer, writes the statement `int i = xyz()`; one relies on `xyz()` returning `int` which is not specified explicitly at the time of definition. Such statements rely on the default behaviour of the compiler to consider `int` even when not specified. When the compiler does not default to `int`, such code results in errors that are hard to debug.

To have the same effect as in C, the second pointer must be explicitly cast in the following manner:

```
FirstPointer = (int*) SecondPointer;
```

The earlier statement produces a compilation error, whereas this one does not.

2.4.2 Constant Pointer

A constant pointer is one that cannot point to anything other than what *it is pointing to at the time of its definition*. It is analogous to the `const int` or `const float` types, where the value assigned at the time of definition cannot be changed throughout the program. The value stored in the `const` pointer is the address of another variable.

When the constant pointer is used, the address itself cannot be changed; however, it must be noted that the content of that address can be changed. So, if we define

```
int * const SecondPointer = &Content1;
```

then the following is allowed:

```
*SecondPointer = AnotherContent;
// Changing the content of the integer pointed to
```

However, the following is not allowed:

```
SecondPointer++;
```

or

```
SecondPointer = &AnotherContent;
// Changing the pointer value itself
```

Consider the following code:

```
void main()
int Content1 = 10;
int Content2 = 20;
int *FirstPointer = &Content1;
// Normal pointer; operation is allowed
int *const SecondPointer = &Content2;
// SecondPointer is a constant pointer
*SecondPointer = 100;
// Operation is allowed; contents can be changed
FirstPointer++;
// Normal pointer, operation is allowed
SecondPointer++;
/* Erroneous statement; not allowed as pointer address itself cannot be changed */
// Error: lvalue specifies const object
// Lvalue is a variable-like construct, which can be assigned a value
```

The expressions `int* const`, `int* const`, and `int *const` are correct and mean the same. Same is the case with expressions such as `int &Name`, `int & Name`, and `int& Name`.

When it is not possible to assign a value to a construct such as a `const` object, it is an error. It is already known from the knowledge of C that a pointer to an integer can be defined as

```
int* FirstPointer = &Content1;
```

C++ allows inserting the keyword `const` between * and the name of the pointer. Such a pointer then becomes a *constant pointer*, that is, the address pointed to by it cannot be manipulated. However, the content of that address can be manipulated. So, the following statement is acceptable:

```
SecondPointer = &Content2;
```

The statement `FirstPointer++;` will increment `FirstPointer` by the size of one integer variable. This is possible for normal pointers such as `FirstPointer`. However, it is not possible to write `SecondPointer++`. The C++ compiler will report an error if such a statement is written. This is because `SecondPointer` is a constant pointer and the value stored in it cannot be altered. Exhibit 2.1 gives an explanation about the constant pointer and other constants.

Exhibit 2.1   Constant pointer and other constants

A constant pointer is similar to a constant of any other data type, except the fact that other constants can store any random value (depending on their data type), whereas a constant pointer stores the address of a particular memory location. This stored address cannot be changed for a constant pointer, but the data stored at that address can be changed. The statement

```
*SecondPointer = 100;
```

is a valid statement in C++ and changes the value of `Content2` to 100. It should be noted that constant pointers must have an assignment at the time of their definition. Therefore, `int  *const SecondPointer  = &Content2;` is acceptable, but `int* const  SecondPointer;` is not acceptable because the constant has not been initialized at the time of definition and it cannot be assigned any value later as it is a constant. It is similar to writing `const  int`(incorrect) instead of `const int i = 5;` (correct).

2.4.3 Pointer to Constant

A *pointer to constant* is a pointer variable that can point to any memory location, but the content of the memory location to which it points cannot be modified. Thus, if one defines

```
int const* SecondPointer = &Content;
```

it is not possible to modify `Content` using `SecondPointer`. Hence, the statement `*SecondPointer = 100;` will now become invalid.

However, the following statement is valid:

```
SecondPointer = &AnotherContent;
```

Consider the following code:

```
void main()
{
    int Content1 = 10;
    int Content2 = 20;
    int* FirstPointer = &Content1;
    // A normal integer pointer
    int const* SecondPointer = &Content2;
    // A pointer to constant
    /* ... Note the difference between this SecondPointer and the SecondPointer in the
    earlier program. Earlier, the word const was placed between * and SecondPointer, but
    now it is between int and *... */
    // The following is an erroneous statement
```

```
    *SecondPointer = 100;
    // Now the contents cannot be changed
    // Error: lvalue specifies const object
    FirstPointer++;
    SecondPointer++;    // is a valid statement
}
```

It is also possible to write

```
const int* SecondPointer = &Content2;
```

instead of

```
int const* SecondPointer = &Content2;
```

The meaning of both these statements is the same.

2.4.4 Use of Constant Pointers and Pointers to Constant

The constant pointers and pointers to constant are two new types of pointers in C++. Functions can receive and return pointer type arguments similar to other data types such as `int` and `float`. Both these pointers are very useful when passed as arguments to functions. Passing a pointer as an argument to a function is always a precarious task in C. For a user, calling a function, for example, `Test_Function(int MyArgument)`, is like a black box. When the function returns, `MyArgument` contains the same value as before, irrespective of what the function does with it.

Sometimes, there is a need to change the value after a function call. A classic example is the `swap` function, which requires the values passed to that function to be interchanged. For example, if one passes `swap(Argument1, Argument2)`, one expects `Argument1` to have the value of `Argument2` and vice versa. It is necessary to use pointers to the specified variables in C.

To return the changed value, a pointer to that value is passed as a parameter to the function. For example, if one passes `MyFunction(&MyVariable)` to `MyFunction(int* PtrToInt)`, then changes made to `*PtrToInt` in the function are reflected in the calling function, that is, in the variable `MyVariable`.

If two integer arguments `Integer1` and `Integer2` need to be swapped, one needs to call `swap(&Integer1, &Integer2)` and hence the pointers to both the integer values. Thus, when a normal value is passed, C does not make any changes to the argument, irrespective of whatever is done with those values in the function. On the contrary, when the pointers to those arguments are passed, the arguments changed in the function remain thus and do not reset to their original values. Unfortunately, there are times when one would like to pass pointers as normal arguments, which is a point of concern. This is the theme of the following discussion.

In C (or C++), the argument passed to a function may change in the function, but the results are not returned to the calling function.

C assumes (incorrectly) that if a pointer is passed to the function, the item to which it is pointing is available for modification. Passing a pointer to the item is the only way to modify it in C, though, at times, the pointer itself is an argument. For example, passing an array to the function requires an array name (pointer to the first element) to be passed. Consider the following code:

```
int Array[10];
int *p = Array;
sort(p);
```

```
for(int i=0; i<10; i++);
   cout << p[i];
```

The function sort, which accepts pointer p, should not change the value of p. If it does so accidently, the program code from then onwards may not be executed as expected.

It is important that the content of the pointer variable is not changed accidentally. Consider a case of passing a C string (char array) to a function that calculates the length of the string. When a C string is passed as an argument to a function, it is the pointer to the first character of the string that is actually passed. It may be necessary to use the pointer (maybe to move over the string to find its length), but it is not necessary to change the content of the string.

There is another situation where passing a pointer instead of values may be useful. Suppose a big struct variable is passed to a function by passing the value, that is, the changes made to the struct variable in the function need not be reflected in the calling function. This program has to follow some serious time constraints. It is always better to pass a *pointer to struct* to a function in such a case. The time taken for stack loading and unloading for a pointer variable is definitely less than that for the big structure. The time for copying the structure to and fro (calling function to called function and vice versa) is also reduced. In this case, a pointer is used to reduce the context-switching time, but the content of the pointer used should not be changed. Therefore, it is better to pass a const pointer than the normal pointer. Consider the following program:

Note All graphics programs working with real-time graphics display have serious time constraints; for example, a cartoon film is not supposed to show jerky pictures. Similarly, many commercial programs require very stringent time-bound operations; for example, a railway reservation system should not wait for five minutes before providing the seat information requested for. In such cases, it is useful to pass a pointer instead of normal data.

```cpp
#include <iostream>
using namespace std;
struct LargeStruct
{
    int ID;
    ...
    public:
      getId()
      {
              cout << "input ID" << endl;
              cin >> ID;
              ...
      }
    ...
}
test1(struct LargeStruct)
{ ... }
test2(struct *LargeStruct)
{ ... }
int main()
{
```

```
    LargeStruct, L1, L2, *ptrLargeStruct;
    ...
    test1(L1);
    ptrLargeStruct = &L2;
    test2(ptrLargeStruct);
}
```

What is the difference between the two functions defined in this code, that is, test1 and test2? The main function contains two calls—the first one is test1 where LargeStruct is passed and the second one contains a pointer to the structure passed to it. Assume LargeStruct contains a video file of size 5 GB. The first case requires that the entire file be passed (copied) to the function and processed. In the second case, the pointer to that structure is passed and the function works on the same structure and does not require a copy. The size of the pointer passed to the function is only 4 bytes. It can be easily understand that the time saved in the second operation is substantial.

In other words, if pointers are passed without the const specifier, the content would be *open* to functions. This means that the contents can be inadvertently modified by the function. In C, it is not possible to prevent the called function from accidentally changing the content. However, this is possible in C++ through the use of constant pointers. Consider Program 2.1:

PROGRAM 2.1   Const pointer

```cpp
#include <iostream>
using namespace std;
struct Employee
{
    char Name[100];
    char Address[200];
    char JobProfile[500];
    char EducationalQualifications[300];
    char OtherDetails[200];
};
void ReadEmployee(Employee* TempEmployee)
{
    cout << "\n Please enter the name:";
    cin >> TempEmployee -> Name;
    cout << "\n Please enter the address:";
    cin >> TempEmployee -> Address;
    cout << "\n Please enter the job profile:";
    cin >> TempEmployee -> JobProfile;
    cout << "\n Please enter educational qualification:";
    cin >> TempEmployee -> EducationalQualifications;
    cout << "\n Please enter other details:";
    cin >> TempEmployee -> OtherDetails;
}

void DangerousDisplay(Employee* TempEmployee)
{
    cout << "\n Name:";
    cout << TempEmployee -> Name;
    cout << "\n Address:";
    cout << TempEmployee -> Address;
```

```
    cout << "\n Job profile:";
    cout << TempEmployee -> JobProfile;
    cout << "\n Educational qualification:";
    cout << TempEmployee -> EducationalQualifications;
    cout << "\n Other details:";
    cout << TempEmployee -> OtherDetails;
/* The following is a dangerous statement as user unknowingly changes the content of the
OtherDetails of TempEmployee and should not be used */
    cin >> TempEmployee -> OtherDetails;
}

void SafeDisplay(Employee const *TempEmployee)
{
    cout << "\n Name:";
    cout << TempEmployee -> Name;
    cout << "\n Address:";
    cout << TempEmployee -> Address;
    cout << "\n Job profile:";
    cout << TempEmployee -> JobProfile;
    cout << "\n Educational qualification:";
    cout << TempEmployee -> EducationalQualifications;
    cout << "\n Other details:";
    cout << TempEmployee -> OtherDetails;
/* The following is a dangerous statement and should not be used */
    cin >> TempEmployee -> OtherDetails;
}

int main()
{
    struct Employee Lara, Beckham;
    ReadEmployee(&Lara);
    ReadEmployee(&Beckham);
    DangerousDisplay(&Lara);
    SafeDisplay(&Beckham);
    SafeDisplay(&Lara);
    DangerousDisplay(&Beckham);
}
```

Output
INPUT SCREEN
Please enter the name: Brian Lara
Please enter the address: West Indies
Please enter the job profile: Cricketer
Please enter educational qualification: ODI and Test passed
Please enter other details: Captain
Please enter the name: David Beckham
Please enter the address: England
Please enter the job profile: Footballer
Please enter educational qualification: Football Test passed
Please enter other details: Captain

OUTPUT SCREEN
Name: Brian Lara
Address: West Indies
Job profile: Cricketer
Educational qualification: ODI and Test passed
Other details: Captain
a /* This is the place where the user unknowingly places 'a' to go */

```
Name: David Beckham
Address: England
Job profile: Footballer
Educational qualification: Football Test passed
Other details: Captain

Name: Brian Lara
Address: West Indies
Job profile: Cricketer
Educational qualification: ODI and Test passed
Other details: a
//OtherDetails information is lost here
```

How the Program Works

This program has one function for reading from and two different functions for writing into struct `Employee`. In all three functions, the address of struct `Employee` is passed. In the `ReadEmployee()` function, it is essential to pass a pointer to struct as the values of struct `Employee` need to be changed. They are initially garbage when defined and new values are to be filled in.

It is not semantically necessary to pass pointers in both display functions—`DangerousDisplay()` and `SafeDisplay()`. Even if one passes struct as it is and modifies the function to manipulate the structure instead of its pointer, the function would work in the same way. It is important to pass the pointer for efficiency reasons. Passing and receiving a big structure consumes more time than passing and receiving a pointer. Passing a structure to and fro needs 1,300 bytes, whereas a pointer needs only 32 bits, that is, 4 bytes, to do the same.

When a pointer is passed instead of the entire structure, another problem is encountered. The pointer content can be modified as it is shown in the case of `DangerousDisplay()` function. If a programmer forgets to remove a `cin` statement while cutting and pasting code from the read routine, it can create a serious problem. Though the function displays the content properly now, it changes after this accidental input. In the output, if the user unknowingly enters 'a' at the end of displaying details about Lara, the `OtherDetails` information is changed. In normal circumstances, errors such as this are very difficult to trace. Fortunately, here Lara's information is displayed again and it is possible to see that the display is improper.

Pointer to Constant

By defining a pointer as a pointer to constant, it is possible to prevent the content from being unknowingly changed. This can be better understood with the help of Program 2.2.

PROGRAM 2.2 Pointer to constant

```cpp
// ConstContent.cpp
#include <iostream>
using namespace std;
#include <string.h>
void main()
{
    void PrintName(char* name, char* AnotherName);
    void PrintConstName(char *const name, char* AnotherName);
    char *MyName = "Lara";
```

```
    char *HisName = "Ravan";
    char *AnotherName = "Beckham";
    PrintName(MyName);
    cout << MyName << "\n";
    PrintConstName(HisName);
    cout << HisName << "\n";
}

void PrintName(char *name, char *AnotherName)
{
    name = AnotherName;
    cout << "Changed name in function is" << name << "\n";
}

void PrintConstName(char *const name, char *AnotherName)
{
    // name = AnotherName;
    /* If this line is not indicated as a comment, the program will not be compiled,
    because for this function, name is a constant pointer and its value may not be
    altered. */
    cout << "Changed name in function is"<< name << "\n";
}
```

How the Program Works

In this program, PrintConstName has been called. In the function, name is declared as a const pointer and the statement name = AnotherName is given as a comment to prevent accidental change to the data. If it is not commented, the C++ compiler will flag an error similar to "lvalue is a constant object" because the program will try to change the value of const pointer and will not compile the program. It should be noted that the function PrintName is the same function without const pointer and so it cannot prevent the assignment. Consider the following example to reiterate the point.

```
#include <iostream>
using namespace std;
int DangerousStringLength(char* String)
{
    int length; (*String) = 'a';
    for(length=0; (*String); length++, String++);
    return length;
}
int ConstStringLength(char *const String)
{
    int length;
    char* Count = String;
    for(length=0; (*Count); length++, Count++);
    return length;
}
int main()
char *Name = "Lara";
char *Address = "West Indies";
```

```
int L1 = DangerousStringLength(Name);
int L2 = ConstStringLength(Address);
cout << L1 << "is the length of the name \n";
cout << L2 << "is the length of the address \n";
cout << "The name and address are \n";
cout << Name << "\n";
cout << Address << "\n";
Output
10 is the length of the name
7 is the length of the address
The name and address are
aara
West Indies
```

It can be observed that here too the DangerousStringLength version of the function changes the first character of name 'Lara' to make it appear as 'aara'. Moreover, it can be observed that the pointer to constant helps in solving the problem.

It is also possible to make both the pointer and the content as constants, as mentioned earlier, for some specific cases. Suppose one passes a string to a function and does not want either the pointer or the content to change, then the argument must be passed as MyFunction(const char *const the_string).

2.5 REFERENCE VARIABLES

Reference variables are introduced in C++ to eliminate some of the problems associated with pointers that were discussed in Programs 2.2–2.5. They provide better readability while the operation is similar to pointer variables. A reference variable is a reference to another variable that is already defined. It provides a kind of a link to the original variable and becomes an *alias* for the original variable. One can even assume it to be a *named pointer*, with two differences:

1. A pointer can be null, that is, not pointing to any valid item, whereas a reference variable should always refer to a valid variable.
2. A pointer can change (except as const) either its address or its content, whereas a reference variable cannot do it. The syntax for defining a reference variable is as follows:

   `<data type> &ReferenceVariable = OriginalVariable;`

Here, OriginalVariable is an already defined variable. The ReferenceVariable is now a reference to OriginalVariable. The & operator used here is *not* the address of the operator. It is used for indicating the reference.

Before defining a reference variable, one should ensure the following:

1. The OriginalVariable must be defined previously.
2. The & operator must precede the ReferenceVariable name.
3. The = sign should be present between the ReferenceVariable name and the OriginalVariable name.

It is not possible to define <data type> &ReferenceVariable; (i.e., without = sign), because in this case, it is not clear as to which variable it refers to. Some languages allow unreferenced reference variables (i.e., `int& RefVariable`), but C++ does not allow a reference variable that does not refer to a valid item.

After defining a reference variable to an original variable, changing *either* of their values results in a change in the value of *both* the variables. This is illustrated by the program given in Section 2.5.1.

2.5.1 Using Standalone Reference Variables

The following program will help us understand how reference variables are used in a program.

> **Note** Before moving on, let us have a brief discussion on 'namespace', which is being repeatedly used in every program. A namespace is a type of enclosure. One can have multiple namespaces in a C++ program to differentiate different sets of classes and functions having the same name. `std` is a standard namespace provided by the C++ system itself.

```
//ReferenceVar.cpp
#include <iostream>
using namespace std;
int main()
{
   int OriginalVariable;
   int& ReferenceVariable = OriginalVariable;
   /* Note the & operator between the data type and the name of the variable */
   OriginalVariable = 100;
   cout << ReferenceVariable << " " << OriginalVariable << "\n";
   ReferenceVariable = 200;
   cout << ReferenceVariable << " " << OriginalVariable << "\n";
   OriginalVariable++;
   cout << ReferenceVariable << " " << OriginalVariable << "\n";
   ReferenceVariable++;
   cout << ReferenceVariable << " " << OriginalVariable << "\n";
}
```

```
Output
100        100
200        200
201        201
202        202
```

The concept of reference variables is very simple to understand. A reference variable is actually an alias of the referred variable, which can be any normal variable defined before the reference variable. Both reference and referred variables now have the same effect if an operation is performed on *either* of them and hence either of them can be used anywhere in the program.

2.5.2 Reference Variables as Dummy Parameters for Functions

Reference variables can be used as dummy parameters, that are parameters defined in the function argument list within the body of the function. At the time of execution, these arguments are replaced by actual parameters passed to the function and hence they are called dummy parameters.

A reference variable as a dummy argument makes the dummy argument an alias of the actual argument. Thus, the manipulations that are done to the dummy argument

A reference variable as a dummy argument makes the dummy argument an alias of the actual argument.

also apply to the actual argument. This can be explained by the well-known swapping variable example of C. It is known that function arguments are by default passed as a value and do not return to the called function. This problem is solved in C using pointers, but C++ has a better solution using reference variables.

There are two functions in Program 2.3: one is written in C++ using a reference variable and the other is written in C using pointers.

PROGRAM 2.3   Swap using reference variable

```
//SwapUsingRef.cpp
#include <iostream>
using namespace std;
main()
{
    int FirstVariable, SecondVariable;
    void SwapInt(int&, int&);        // Function, the C++ reference way
    void SwapPointer(int*, int*);       // Function, the C pointer way
    cin >> FirstVariable;
    cin >> Second Variable;

    SwapInt(FirstVariable, SecondVariable);
    /* variable is passed, not the address */

    cout << FirstVariable;
    cout << SecondVariable;
    SwapPointer(&FirstVariable, &SecondVariable);
    cout << FirstVariable;
    cout << SecondVariable;
}
// The following is a way to swap in C++
/* Look at the reference variable arguments. They are references of the variable arguments
passed; that is, First is the reference to the first argument passed and Second is the
reference to the second argument passed */

void SwapInt(int& First, int& Second)
{
    int temp;
    temp = First;
    First = Second;
    Second = temp;
}

// The following is the old, conventional way used in C to swap
void SwapPointer(int* First, int* Second)
{
    int temp;
    temp = *First;
    *First = *Second;
    *Second = temp;
}
```

How the Program Works

Observe both the versions of Swap. The first one is with reference variables. The second is a conventional C-type solution. Instead of passing variable addresses and receiving them in

One just passes variables as parameters while using reference variables and receives them in reference variables.

Passing a non-pointer argument in C++ does not guarantee passing the value as in C and thus the value returning from the function may be altered. One will have to check the prototype of the function to be sure.

the function as pointers, the code in the first version is far better and easier to understand. This is the advantage of reference variables.

In the function SwapInt(), FirstVariable and SecondVariable are passed to the function and are accepted as int& First and int& Second. Henceforth, First is a reference to FirstVariable and Second is a reference to SecondVariable. As they are reference variables, whatever manipulation is done to First and Second will be reflected in FirstVariable and SecondVariable, respectively, in the main program. Thus, the function using reference variables achieves the same effect as that using pointers, but in a simpler way. This makes the function code more readable.

However, a problem arises while using reference variables as function dummy parameters, as in the example shown. Suppose the Swap() function is a library function; then its definition will not be directly visible. Passing these two variables as value parameters is safe in C. It is known that the function called cannot change the values of the variables inadvertently or maliciously. In order to get the values changed, the addresses of these variables have to be passed. However, in C++, in order to ensure that the values of the variables are not changed, the prototype of the function has to be checked. This is because whether one passes value or reference parameters, the calling function is the same, that is, variables, and not addresses of variables, are being passed in both the cases.

2.5.3 Reference Variables as Return Types

Consider Program 2.4.

PROGRAM 2.4   Return a reference variable

```
//ReturnRef.cpp
#include <iostream>
using namespace std;

void main()

{
    int FirstInt = 10, SecondInt = 20;
    int ThirdInt, FourthInt = 100;
    int& RetRefTest(int, int);
    ThirdInt = RetRefTest(FirstInt, SecondInt);

    // The following is a special use of returning as reference
    RetRefTest(FirstInt, SecondInt) = FourthInt;
    int& RetRefTest(int i, int j)
    {
        return(i>j?i:j);
    }
}
```

How the Program Works

It is very easy to understand this code except the line following the comment. The line preceding the comment is the normal way of calling a function in C, where a variable is passed from a function as a return value. This value is accepted in the left-hand side (LHS) variable. Here, the function is passing a reference instead of the variable itself, but it does not make any difference to the effect. The variable will be assigned the same value as a normal variable.

The second case is different and needs explanation. The function call is on the left side of an assignment. This is not possible in C. It is known that writing A = 2 and 2 = A are different. The first case is acceptable because the LHS is a variable and it can be assigned a value 2. In the second case, the LHS is 2, which is a constant and cannot be assigned any value. Similarly, a function call is like a constant (having the value returned by the function), which cannot be used on the LHS of an assignment statement.

> **Note** If a function that returns a normal variable is used on the LHS, the C++ compiler will flag an error indicating 'lvalue required' (lvalue refers to the LHS value of an assignment). This error indicates that the LHS value of an assignment statement must be a variable to which the value of the RHS expression can be assigned.

Passing a reference changes the scenario in an interesting way. Instead of a variable, a reference is returned, which is a reference (or alias) to an existing variable of the calling function. Now, the function call is not like a constant but is similar to a variable. The variable which is being returned from the *called* function is an alias of some other variable belongs to the *calling* function. It means that a function call that returns a reference can be used as a variable. This is what the line following the comment does. Understandably, the variable with the maximum value will now have the value of FourthInt. So, in this case, the value of SecondInt will become 100.

> **Note** When a function returns a reference, it can be used on the LHS of an assignment statement. The function, in this case, should return only a global variable or a variable local to the calling function and this variable is assigned the RHS value. A function cannot use a variable local to the scope of the function as a returning value.

2.5.4 Chaining Inputs using Reference Variables

There is yet another interesting use of reference variables. Using this option, it is possible to chain inputs to the object. Consider a case of cout.

```
cout << "Hi";
```
or
```
cout << "Hi" << SomeStringVariable << "Your number is" <<
SomeIntegerNumber;
```

The C++ object model implements the references by converting them to pointers internally. Hence, using references or pointers does not make any difference with regard to speed.

Here, the input provided to cout is chained in such a way that once cout << "Hi" is performed, the same output stream is provided to SomeStringVariable, then to "Your number is", and then to SomeIntegerNumber. cout is already programmed to provide this functionality. The programmers can also provide such functionality to their own objects (user-defined objects) while programming. We will see how the use of returning reference helps in chaining the inputs to objects when we discuss operator overloading in Chapter 6.

2.5.5 More on Reference Variables

The & operator is not an address-of operator that is used in C. It actually is read as 'reference to', that is,

```
int& OneVar = AnotherVar
```

C++ allows const
values to be used
in defining array
dimensions unlike C.

is read as OneVar reference to AnotherVar. Though the & operator still holds its meaning in C++, the difference can be easily understood from the context in which the operator is used. The reference operator is always used as `<data type name>& <variable name>` whereas the address-of operator is used as a prefix to a variable name as `&<variable name>`.

For example,

```
char& CharVar = AnotherCharVar
```

is a reference, whereas in

```
MyFunction(float &FloatVar)
```

&FloatVar is again a reference but it is always an address too.

Currently, both the reference and the pointer have similar (address) implementation in the C++ object model. Thus, references are internally converted to pointers during compilation, which means that there will be no difference in efficiency if either of them is used. Thus, both the versions of swapping explained in Program 2.3 will work with similar efficiency.

2.6 ACCESS MODIFIERS

Modifiers in C++ are used to modify the declarations of data types. Access modifiers are used to specify the declared accessibility of data types.

2.6.1 const

const has the same meaning in C++ as in C but with one notable difference, which is explained by the following code snippet:

```
//ConstDifference.cpp
#define SIZE 10
void main()
{
    const int size = 10;
    char name1[size];        // Only C++ accepts this
    char name2[SIZE];        // C and C++ both accept this
}
```

Though SIZE and size seem similar to us, they are actually treated differently by the C compiler, which does not find any SIZE in the program. It is replaced with its value by the preprocessor before the compiler sees it. C, unlike C++, does not accept the const argument in the character array definition. The array argument must either be an integer or a symbolic constant.

2.6.2 volatile

It has the same meaning as in C. There are some specific variables the values of which can be modified by external means. Statements using those variables should not be optimized by the compiler during compilation. The access modifier volatile instructs the compiler not to optimize the expressions that are using such variables.

2.7 STORAGE CLASS SPECIFIERS

There are four storage class specifiers, extern, register, auto, and static. Declarations with the auto or register storage class specifier result in automatic storage and those with the extern or static storage class specifier result in static storage. Out of these, extern, register, and auto have effects similar to that in C, but static is extended in C++ for use in some specific circumstances and is explained in detail in Chapter 3.

2.8 INITIALIZATION

When declaring a regular local variable, its value is, by default, undetermined. For a variable to store a concrete value as it is declared, it needs to be initialized. There are two ways of doing this in C++. These are discussed in Sections 2.8.1 and 2.8.2.

2.8.1 Normal Initialization

To understand the normal initialization method, consider the following code:

```
#include <iostream>
using namespace std;
void main()
{
   int i;
   i = 50;          // Some other code related to i
   int j;           // This will not work in C
   j = 20;
}
```

This method of initialization is the same as that in C. However, C++ has a philosophical diversion from C in this case. It assumes that if a variable is defined near to its usage, it is easier and more readable. So, it allows a variable definition to appear after executable statements. In C++, a variable can be defined anywhere in the program *before its first usage*. The declaration style that suits the programmer can be followed. Whether it is the C style of defining all variables before the actual program or the C++ style of postponing the defining of a variable until its first usage, it does not have any impact on the efficiency of the program.

2.8.2 Variable Initialization

In C++, variables can be initialized at run-time. Let us consider the following program:

```
//VarInitialization.cpp
#include <iostream>
using namespace std;
#include <cmath>                  // This is math.h in C and in older C++
void main()
{
   int FirstVariable;
   FirstVariable = 50;
   // some other code related to FirstVariable
```

```
        int SecondVariable;
        cin >> SecondVariable;
        double ThirdVariable = sqrt(double(SecondVariable));
    }
```

A C++ variable may be initialized at run-time.

The value of sqrt of SecondVariable is not available at the time of compilation. The ThirdVariable is initialized at run-time after the square root of SecondVariable is found. This is not possible with C compilers. Thus, it is more logical to build C++ compilers than C compilers because of the availability of such facilities.

2.9 OPERATORS

The operators in C++ and those in C work in an identical manner. However, some of the operators have new meanings in C++. These new meanings do not have any effect on the old and conventional meanings. The new meaning of the & operator in C++ and the use of << and >> operators with cin and cout have already been discussed. Programmers can, on their own, provide a new meaning to most of the existing operators (see Chapter 6 for more details on overloading).

Some of the new operators introduced in C++ and their meaning are listed in Table 2.2.

Table 2.2   Various operators and their meaning in C++

Operator	Meanings
::	Scope resolution operator: it is used to indicate a member of a specified class
::*	A member-pointer operator
.*	Pointer-to-member-using-object: It is used to indicate a pointer to member of a specified class. Though it is mentioned as a pointer, it is not of type pointer, i.e., it does not contain an address of any variable. It is an offset value to the member from the beginning of the class. The same is also true for the following operator.
->*	Pointer-to-member-using-pointer-to-object operator
delete	Memory release operator
new	Memory allocation operator
reinterpret_cast	Casting operator for C-style casting from any type to any other irrelevant type
const_cast	Removing the const nature of a variable while casting
dynamic_cast	Casting operator that can be used to safeguard against irrelevant casting, used in case of polymorphic classes (classes part of inheritance chain)
typeid	Used to find type of an object at run-time
throw	Useful for throwing an exception at the time of an error

> **Note** An operator used in C can have a new meaning in C++. One can use it in a context different from the one in which they are defined to work.

2.9.1 Scope Resolution Operator

In C, if a variable is defined globally and a local variable *with the same name* is also defined in the same program, then the global variable is not available in the local variable's context. However, in C++, the scope resolution operator helps in the visualization of a global variable in the context of the local variable with the same name. Consider Program 2.5 to understand this better.

PROGRAM 2.5 Scope resolution operator

```cpp
//ScopeRes.cpp
#include <iostream>
using namespace std;

int Variable = 10;   // The global variable
void main()
{
    do
    {
        int Variable;    // The local variable
        // The context of local variable starts from here
        cin >> Variable;
        cout << Variable << '\n';
        cout << "Global variable value is";

        // The following will work only in C++
        cout << ::Variable; // Prints the global variable
        cout << "\n";

        if(Variable == 0)
        break;

        /* The if condition checks for the local variable and the context of local variable
        ends here. If this line is commented, the program will not come out of the loop
        because the following while statement checks for the global variable */

    } while(Variable);
    // Global variable being tested

    cout << "The global value outside the loop is";
    cout << Variable;    // Prints the global variable, i.e., 10
}
```

How the Program Works

It can be observed that there are two variables of the same name Variable in this program. One is global and the other is local, defined in the while block. Consider the following statement:

> The scope resolution operator makes it possible for a programmer to use both global and local variables with the same name.

```cpp
cout << ::Variable
```

This statement prints the global variable's value. This is because if only Variable is written, it is assumed to be a local variable as in C, but if it is preceded by the :: operator, that is, ::Variable, the C++ compiler understands it to be a global variable. Thus, it is possible to access the global variable even when a local variable is in effect. The :: operator, which indicates the global variable, is known as the scope resolution operator. Thus, `TheVariable` will be a local variable, whereas `::TheVariable` will be a global variable. There is no such operator in C, and hence, it is not possible to access any global variable when a local variable *of the same name* is in effect.

> **Note** A local variable is said to be in effect and holds meaning only in the block in which it is defined. The area in which the variable holds its meaning is known as the scope of the local variable.

The next three operators in Table 2.2, the member-pointer, pointer-to-member-using object, and pointer-to-member-using-pointer-to-object operators, need the understanding of the `class` construct and are discussed in Chapter 3.

2.9.2 new and delete Operators

In C, `malloc()` and `free()` are normal functions for allocating and deallocating memory. However, C++ has a better mechanism for this. It uses operators that provide the advantage of better efficiency. The `malloc()` and `free()` function calls involve the context switching operation (placing the context of the calling function on the stack and executing `malloc()` or `free()`). Context switching operation, which is explained in Exhibit 2.2, is costly in terms of time and resources.

Exhibit 2.2 Context switching

Whenever a function is called in either C or C++, the current state of the calling function must be stored and the called function's context must be brought in. As soon as the function call is over, the called function's context must vanish and it must be restored to the original status. This is known as context switching.

For example, when the program control enters the called function, the called function's variables are not accessible. When the control comes back, they are again made available. This operation requires loading the called function's variables and a few other details (such as values of those variables at the time when the function is called and the address where the program control should go after the function call gets over) on a stack, at the time of calling the function, and removing them when control returns to the called function. It involves a lot of work. Such overheads are not present for operators because the code related to operators is built-in, that is, it is inserted by the C++ compiler while compiling. The use of operators does not involve the costly operation of context switching.

Though most C++ compilers implement `new` and `delete` operators in terms of function operators `malloc()` and `free()`, this is not mandatory by the standard. Thus, the advantage of efficiency may not be available for some C++ compilers.

The operator `new` is used for allocation of memory. The syntax of `new` is very simple. To get memory for an integer and assign the address of the allocated memory to pointer `p`, the following is written:

```
int *p = new int
```

Casting or size specification is not necessary here as in `malloc()`. However, a pointer variable should be used only after memory allocation. (This is also true for a pointer getting memory using `malloc()`.) Consider Program 2.6 to see the use of `new` and how the pointer variable can be wrongly manipulated without assigning memory to it.

PROGRAM 2.6 new and delete operators

```cpp
#include <iostream>
using namespace std;

void main()
{
    // Look at the use of new;
    int *PointerToInt = new int;
    *PointerToInt = 10;
    int *DangerousPointerToInt;
    /* DangerousPointerToInt is a variable that is defined as pointer but is not yet initialized
    to anything and contains garbage */

    *DangerousPointerToInt = 10;
    int *PointToArrayOfInt = new int[5];

    /* Defines an array of five integers and allocates memory for the same */

    PointToArrayOfInt[2] = 5;
    // Assigns the third element a value 5

    int *PointToInt3 = new int(3);
    // Initializes the content of PointToInt3 to 3 after allocating memory

    cout <<"Explicitly initialized value "<< PointToArrayOfInt[2];
    cout << "\n implicitly initialized at the time of definition" << *PointToInt3;

    int *PointerToArrayOfInt2 = (int *) new int[4][3];
    int FirstDimension = 4;
    int *PointerToArrayOfInt3 = (int *) new int[FirstDimension][3];

    delete PointerToInt;
    delete[]PointToArrayOfInt;
}
```

How the Program Works

It is necessary to pay attention to some statements of this program. The first one is

```cpp
int *PointerToInt = new int;
```

This statement allocates sufficient memory for holding an integer value and then the address of that memory location is stored in `PointerToInt` variable, which, as the name suggests, is a pointer to integer. Next is the following statement:

```cpp
*PointerToInt = 10;
```

The memory to which `PointerToInt` points to is allocated by a heap manager, which allocates memory from a memory area called heap. Therefore, it is safe to write in that memory area. Now, look at the following statement:

```cpp
*DangerousPointerToInt = 10;
```

This line of code assigns 10 to the content of `DangerousPointerToInt`. The place at which 10 is written depends on the value of the address pointed to by `DangerousPointerToInt`.

At the moment, `DangerousPointerToInt` contains uncertain bits of information, generated from the last usage of the memory area and one cannot be sure of its value. It may be an address of some place in the operating system (OS), a user area, or any place in the memory.

C++ differentiates between a pointer to an array and a pointer to a data type. When a programmer needs to change their usage, casting is required.

If the address belongs to the memory area occupied by the OS, running this program will try to write in a protected area of the OS, which will then crash the program or itself (DOS is known to crash because of such reasons whereas Windows shows a blue screen instead).

If the address belongs to a user area, it leads to two possibilities. It may try to write at a place that is already occupied by something (usually, a variable). The other possibility is that nothing is stored at the place to which the dangerous pointer is currently pointing.

In the first case, when our code inadvertently changes the value of a variable, it generates the wrong output. Though it is a hard error to crack, a clever and experienced developer can debug such an error.

In the second case, when the dangerous pointer points to an area that is empty, nothing wrong happens at the moment, and hence, there is no visual feedback to the programmer that there is something wrong. It is, however, more serious and frustrating because, if something is written later at this area (e.g., when the array size is increased), it may produce strange results. If a compiler initializes the value of such non-initialized pointers to null, there may be a run-time error because the program is trying to write at an undefined or illegal address.

> **Note** When a pointer is not initialized, it may have strange consequences. For example, variables may start changing their values between assignment statements or the program may behave properly at one instance while not in another. Sometimes such errors crash the program and the programmer gets immediate notification, but it does not happen every time.

Now, have a look at following statements:

```
int *PointerToArrayOfInt2 = (int *) new int[4][3];
int *PointerToArrayOfInt3 = (int *) new int[FirstDimension][3];
```

These are examples of multidimensional arrays being constructed using dynamic allocation. Here, the pointer returned by new needs to be typecast because it returns the pointer to an array of two dimensions, which is different from the pointer to integer in C++.

You can notice the simplicity of the new operator compared to malloc(). It is not necessary to provide the explicit size or the number of bytes; new takes care of both. Typecasting is also not needed because new does return the type of pointer one wants unlike the void pointer returned from malloc(). As shown in Program 2.6, new can also be used to get memory for the whole array and to initialize the value of the content.

```
int* PointToArrayOfInt = new int[5];
/* Getting memory for the whole array */

int * PointToInt3 = new int(3);
/* Initializing the content of PointToInt3 to 3 after allocating memory */
```

The syntax uses array notation [ ] for allocating memory for arrays and uses () for initializing the variable immediately after acquiring memory.

Unlike malloc(), new does not return null when allocation cannot be performed.

If an old program is being modified, malloc() cannot be replaced with new. This is because unlike malloc(), new does not return null pointer if the memory is not allocated but throws an exception. If a C program has a malloc() function, the function call will have a subsequent test for checking null value.

If the programmer does not want to replace this code with the exception-based code, then new(nothrow) must be used instead of new. The example will now be

```
include <new>
...
int* PointToArrayOfInt = new(nothrow) int[5];
if(!PointerToArrayOfInt)
cout << "error!";
```

> **Note** The new(nothrow) operator does not throw an exception if memory is not allocated but returns null pointer, similar to malloc(). It is advisable, though, to write a new code using exception handling. Error handling using exception is cleaner and more readable. The header file <new> should be included for using the new operator.

> Allocation using new and deallocation using free() or allocation using malloc() and deallocation using delete can have surprising consequences. It is not recommended to use them this way.

Consider the following statements:

```
int* PointerToArrayOfInt2 = (int*) new int[4][3];
```

and

```
int* PointerToArrayOfInt3 = (int*) new int[FirstDimension][3];
```

Both statements are correct. Here, FirstDimension is a variable and is initialized before a call to new is made. (This is possible because the call to new is made at run-time.) The second argument, however, must be a constant. The statement

```
int SecondDimension = 5;
int* PointerToArrayOfInt4 = (int*) new int[FirstDimension][SecondDimension];
```

is wrong and is not acceptable because subsequent dimensions after the first dimension cannot be variables.

Consider the last two lines of the program. The delete operator is applied to pointer variables. It is analogous to the free() function of C. These variables were earlier initialized using new. The delete operation performs the job of releasing the memory. Thus, the memory allocated using new is deallocated using delete. It should be noted that the array version of delete uses [] *before the variable name.* So delete[]PointToArrayOfInt is valid, but delete PointToArrayOfInt[] is invalid.

If memory is allocated using malloc() and deallocated using delete, or allocated using new and deallocated using free(), then the results can be surprising. The standard says that the result is undefined, which means that a specific compiler may take any action it deems fit. It may even crash the program.

2.9.3 Placement new

Some ways in which the new operator can be used are as follows:

1. `int* p = new int;`
   `// Normal new call`
2. `int* p = new(nothrow) int;`
   `/* Does not throw exception in case memory is not`
   `allocated and returns the pointer value as null */`
3. `int* p = (int*) new int[3][4];`

```
// For allocating memory to arrays
4. int* p = new int(3);
    // For initializing the variable at the time of memory allocation
```

The 'placement new' is a variant of new. It works in the following manner:

```
int* p = new int;        // normal new
int* q = new(p) int;    // placement new
```

Here, no memory is allocated for the variable q; its address is the same as p. It is useful in some special cases. Suppose images from somewhere are being read and displayed one after the other. Assume that the images are stored in an object of class image one after the other and that a pointer is pointing to the area of memory that holds the image, known as position. Now, when the first image is loaded, the following is written:

```
position = new image(FirstImage);
```

This will create a new object, allocate memory for it, and initialize the memory with FirstImage. For all subsequent images, the code will be

```
position = new(FirstImage) SecondImage
. . .
position = new(SecondImage) ThirdImage
. . .
```

thereby storing every image at the same location where the first image had been stored. Readers may question the need for using placement new in this case, instead of writing a simple assignment such as *position = SecondImage.

If both the images, FirstImage and SecondImage, are of the same size, then this statement is acceptable. If they are of different sizes, placement new is the only option available as it calls the destructor of FirstImage first and then it calls the constructor of SecondImage.

> **Note** Placement new is useful when we want another pointer to occupy the memory given to an earlier pointer. Unlike normal copy operation, placement new calls the destructor of the previous object and the constructor of the new object replacing it, thus avoiding any unwanted consequences. For example, suppose the pointer points to images and the second image is smaller than the first one. Merely copying the values will lead to the second image occupying some part and the remaining part containing the older image. It is advisable to use placement new if such effects are to be avoided.

2.9.4 new vs malloc()

Some of the advantages of new over malloc() are as follows:

1. The syntax of new is simpler than that of malloc(). No size, no void pointer, and no casting are required for the new operator.
2. new is an operator, whereas malloc() is a function. Operators execute faster than functions. Context switching can be avoided with operators as they are not functions. Their equivalent assembly code should be directly pasted by the compiler at the time of compilation.
3. new has various forms as discussed in Section 2.9.3. malloc() does not have such facilities.
4. new is class-aware. It is possible to change the meaning of new to suit the need of a user-defined class. This is known as operator overloading.

Notes

1. It is possible to have an operator implemented as a function in C++. In that case, there will be no advantage if the function is not defined `inline`.

2. Unlike `malloc()`, new can be overloaded such that class objects can be given memory as per the need and at the place the user wants it. When `new` is overloaded for any class, calling `new` with the object of that class follows the process defined by the developer of that class and not by the conventional memory management defined by C++.

2.9.5 Significance of `delete` Operator

The `delete` operation does not seem to be important when used in programs. The use of `delete` is not important in places where the machine is shut down at the end of the day, for example, an educational institute. However, there are places where the machine is not shut down daily and the programs continue to run without any halt for a very long period, for example, web servers and related components. In such cases, the memory space occupied by the new variables will continue to increase while the program is running unless they are deleted periodically. At some point of time, the memory will be exhausted and the program will crash. On the other hand, if the machine is shut down, the space occupied is released automatically and there will be no problem of insufficient memory.

Note Web servers run for long periods. In such programs, if the objects introduced by `new` do not have a corresponding `delete` to be used when they go out of scope, the memory occupied by such objects is not regained and the program crashes when the memory is full. C++11, obviously inspired by Java, added garbage collection; it is a process by which the memory wasted by such objects that have gone out of scope can be reclaimed and problems such as mentioned here can be avoided.

2.9.6 New Casting Operators, `typeid`, and `throw`

C++ has new function-like castings as well as old C-style castings. To convert an `int` variable into a `float` in C, `FloatVar = (float) IntVar;` is used. However, in C++, this is written as

```
FloatVar = float(IntVar);
```

which is more readable. The old C-style casting is still available and is very popular among programmers.

Four new casting operators have been recently added by the C++ Standardization Committee for providing better casting operations than that offered by the old C-style casting. These are `dynamic cast`, `reinterpret cast`, `static cast`, and `const cast`. The old C-style cast is still valid in C++, though using new casting operators is recommended. These are discussed in Sections 11.2–11.5 in Chapter 11. `typeid` also is used in the context of RTTI and `throw` is used when exception handling is used to trap errors in C++.

The following code illustrates how `try`, `throw`, and `catch` can be used in a given circumstance. The block covered by `try` is monitored by C++ during the execution of the program. When a `throw` statement is encountered, the control gets permanently transferred to the corresponding `catch` statement. In the following case, if `throw error1` is executed, the control gets transferred to `catch(ErrorType1 er)`, and if `throw error2` is executed, the control gets transferred to `catch(ErrorType2 er)` block.

```
try
{
    ErrorType1 error1;
```

```
        ErrorType2 error2;
        ...;
        throw error1;
        ...;
        throw error2;
        ...;
}

catch(ErrorType1 er)
{ ... }

catch(ErrorType2 er)
{ ... }
```

The following example suggests how typeid can be used. It requires a typeinfo header to be included. The typeid operator helps getting a typeinfo object associated with that object. The typeinfo object contains information about the type including the name of the type. When one writes cout << typeid(SomeObject).name() and if the type of SomeObject is int, it will display "int". If the type of SomeObject is user-defined class employee, it will display "class employee".

```
#include <typeinfo>
...
void main()
{
    ...
    cout << typeid(SomeObject).name();
}
```

2.10 CONDITIONAL STRUCTURES AND LOOPING CONSTRUCTS

if and else provide conditional execution of code in C and are available in the same form in C++. Switch case is also available in C++.

The use of loops can cause a segment of a program to be repeated a given number of times. This repetition continues until the condition is true; else, the loop ends and the control passes to the statements following the loop. Loops in C++ include while, do-while, and for constructs. All these constructs work in the same way as in C.

■ RECAPITULATION ■

- Identifiers in C++ are similar to that in C except that even identifiers larger than 32 characters are significant in C++.
- Keywords and data types available in C++ are supersets of C.
- There are three different categories of data types in C++. The first category consists of functions available in both C and C++. The second category includes those that are available in C, but have an extended meaning in C++. The third category of data types are the ones that are not available in C but are additionally provided in C++.
- const pointers and pointer to const can be useful in programming to avoid errors while the programmer is required to pass pointers to functions.
- References can be used in three different ways, that is, a standalone reference, dummy arguments passing to a function, and return value from the function.

- References are more readable than a pointer while having the same efficiency.
- C++ introduces a `bool` data type, which can be used for conditional testing in a more readable way.
- C++ provides dynamic initializations of variables.
- C++ introduces the scope resolution operator, which can be used for accessing global variables with the same name as a local variable.
- `new` and `delete` are operators for memory allocation and deallocation in C++. They have multiple forms.
- `try`, `catch` and `throw` operators are used for exception handling, and `typeid` is used for accessing the type of the object associated at run-time.

■ KEYWORDS ■

Bool variable It is a variable that can have only two values, `true` and `false`. It is advised to use `bool` variables for checking the truthfulness of an expression in C++.

Constant pointer It is a pointer that cannot change the address it is referring to. The pointer value (address) cannot be changed, but the content can be changed.

Dynamic initialization In C++, initialization to a variable can take place at the run-time. This is known as dynamic initialization.

new and delete operators `new` is an operator to get memory from heap. It is a better mechanism than `malloc()`. `delete` in C++ does a job similar to the `free()` function in C, that is, it releases the memory occupied by the `new` operator.

new[ ] and delete[ ] operators These operators are similar to `new` and `delete` except that they allocate and deallocate memory for an array.

Pointer to constant It is a pointer that can change its address but the content of the address cannot be modified.

Reference Reference is a mechanism to make an alias of a variable. When a referring variable is made to refer to a referred variable, both variables become alias of each other. Changing the value of either of them changes both their values.

typeid and throw `typeid` is used for obtaining the typeinfo object associated with a given class or an object and `throw` is used for handling exceptions.

■ EXERCISES ■

Multiple Choice Questions

1. When a reference is defined, it can refer to _____.
   (a) a `const` pointer
   (b) a pointer to constant
   (c) a valid defined variable
   (d) an operator

2. C++ keywords _____ those in the original C++ from Stroustrup.
   (a) are exactly the same as
   (b) are completely different from
   (c) have additional keywords than
   (d) have less keywords than

3. `int secondVariable; double thirdVariable = sqrt( double( secondVariable ) ) ;`
   This code will _____.
   (a) give syntax error at the declaration of `thirdVariable`

   (b) will give no error and initialize `thirdVariable` at run-time
   (c) result in the program getting compiled but it is not executed properly
   (d) result in the complier not compiling this program

4. A reference variable provides a kind of _____.
   (a) link to the original variable
   (b) pointer to the original variable
   (c) copy of the original variable
   (d) relation to the original variable

5. In C++, a variable can be declared _____.
   (a) anywhere in the `main()` function declaration
   (b) anywhere in the program before its first usage
   (c) anywhere in the program
   (d) only at the beginning of the program

6. Though C++ standard does not impose any limit on the length of an identifier, the _____ may impose one.
   (a) interpreter
   (b) preprocessor
   (c) compiler
   (d) coder

7. Which of the following is not an operator that is available only in C++?
   (a) : : *
   (b) typeid
   (c) throw
   (d) : :

8. Reference variables are introduced in C++ _____.
   (a) in addition to pointers
   (b) to have more flexibility than pointers
   (c) to remove the usage of pointers
   (d) to eliminate some of the problems associated with the usage of pointers in C

9. Void pointers in C++ _____.
   (a) work in the same manner as in C
   (b) are not available
   (c) cannot be automatically typecasted
   (d) can be automatically typecasted

10. When considering the constants, C++ _____ constants that are acceptable in C.
   (a) accepts only a few
   (b) accepts all
   (c) accepts only backlash
   (d) accepts only symbolic

Conceptual Exercises

1. What is the significance of const pointer? Give two examples.
2. What is the significance of pointer to constant? Give two examples.
3. Suggest a case where both a pointer to constant and a const pointer of type <datatype> const * const <pointer> are used in a single expression, for example, int const * const p=q.
4. Define few string objects. Do strings in C++ behave like a normal data type? What happens if a string is assigned to another using '='? Compare two strings using '= ='. What is the result?
5. What is the advantage of returning a reference from

a function? Suggest some applications of returning a reference other than that given in the chapter.

6. What is the importance of a bool variable? Choose any program written in C that uses conditional expressions. Try to incorporate bool variables in the program and then run it as a C++ program.
7. What is dynamic initialization? Where can it be useful?
8. What is the use of the scope resolution operator? Suggest an example of its use in practical circumstances. Does it have any use other than separating out global variables from local variables?
9. What are the advantages of using new and delete operators over malloc() and free() functions?

Practical Exercises

The following exercises require C programming skills and have references to C programs. If you have written some C programs in the past, use them. Otherwise, write a new one and perform the following exercises.

1. Write a C program with a for or while loop. Include some if conditions in this program and compile the program as a C++ program. (Change the extension to cpp in Windows or Novel and compile or change the extension to C in UNIX and compile using CC, or change the extension to cpp and compile using C++ in Linux.) Verify that all the constructs work in the same way as in C++.
2. Read your compiler manual or have an online help of your compiler. (Use MSDN for VC++.) Try to find out rules for defining identifiers. Try to get the list of valid keywords.
3. Normally, C programming books end with the ordered linked list program. You might have seen or written one program yourself. Rewrite the same program using new and delete instead of malloc() and free().
4. Read the compiler manual to get the list of operators. Try to read the descriptions of the operators studied in the chapter.
5. Rewrite, using reference as an argument, any function that you have earlier written in C using a pointer as an argument.
6. Rewrite any C function that returns a pointer such that it now returns a reference.

Chapter 3

Classes and Objects

3.1 INTRODUCTION TO CLASS AND OBJECT

Class is one of the most fundamental needs for an object-based or object-oriented programming language such as C++. For a problem to be solved in C++, the entities of the problem are to be represented as classes. Backward compatibility with C is considered sacred by C++ designers. Thus, it is theoretically possible to write a program without classes, but practically it is very difficult.

Consider a program to be written for printing student marksheets. The entities in this case are the student, examiner, supervisor, moderator, marksheet, and merit list. Entities are represented as classes in a C++ program. The information about these entities that we are interested in storing is known as the *attribute* of the class. Attributes are of two types—data and methods (functions), as shown in Fig. 3.1.

One of the entities of the marksheet program is the examiner. The data attributes of this entity (examiner) may be the examiner's subject, name, address, phone number, and affiliation. The function attributes of the examiner entity may be activities such as reading and printing details about examiners and assigning the bunch of answer sheets.

Let us look at an example of an object of student class. Consider the problem of printing student information, as shown in Program 3.1.

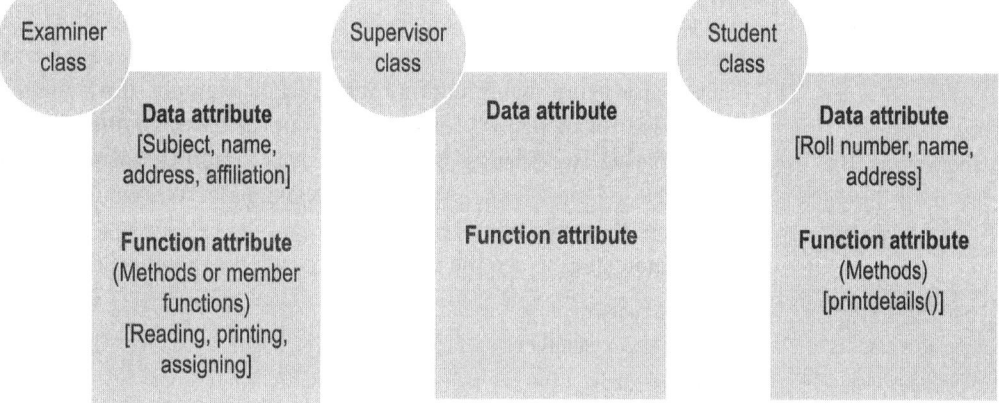

Fig. 3.1   Class and its attributes

PROGRAM 3.1   Example of a class

```cpp
//ClassExample.cpp
#include <iostream>
#include <string>
using namespace std;

class student
{
    public:
        int RollNumber;
        string Name;
        string Address;
        void PrintDetails()
        {
            cout << "Roll number is" << RollNumber << "\n";
            cout << "Name is" << Name << "\n";
            cout << "Address is" << Address << "\n";
        }
};
/* The semicolon is important as it indicates the end of class definition */

void main()
{
    student Student1;
    // The C-like definition will be "class student Student1"
    // The C++ definition is more similar to built-in definitions

    Student1.RollNumber = 1;
    Student1.Name = "Robin Singh";
    Student1.Address = "New Delhi";
    Student1.PrintDetails();
}
```

How the Program Works

In this program, `student` is an example of a class that represents a real-world student (an actual student). The attributes of the `student` class are `RollNumber`, `Name`, `Address`, and `PrintDetails`, where `PrintDetails()` is a function attribute and the rest are data attributes. `Student1` is an object of type `student`. It can be noted from the data types of `Name` and `Address` that string is available as a data type in C++. However, we need to write `#include <string>` for using manipulation routines. For example, this statement needs to be included for using "=" for assigning one string to another or for using "==" for comparing two strings. Technically, it is a built-in class. `Name` and `Address` are objects of the `class string` in this example. We would be using strings throughout the programs in our text.

> String is a built-in class available to C++ programmers. The header file to use this class is `<string>`.

It is interesting to see the way `student` is defined and used.

```cpp
student Student1;
// The C-like definition will be "class student Student1"
// The C++ definition is more like built-in definitions
```

> The second step after defining a class is to define the public and private members of the class.

The definition is more near to the normal data type definitions; it is not necessary to mention `class` before the definition of the object. Look at the

Designing systems
requires looking at
classes and their
attributes before
programming.

familiar dot (.) notation used to access structure elements. It can be used for accessing class elements as well.

The function `PrintDetails()` is defined inside the class. It is known as a *member function* or *function member* of the class. In C, we can have only data members in the structure; the function member is a new type of member available in C++. We will be considering more examples of classes in subsequent sections.

3.2 CLASSES AND THEIR ATTRIBUTES

Finding out entities and their attributes is an important prerequisite for writing a program in C++. Consider, once again, the case of the marksheet problem. A programmer may decide to have entities such as student, examiner, invigilator, question paper, and marksheet.

Consider another class, say `Marksheet` that may have data attributes such as college name, subject, maximum marks, and passing marks. It might have function attributes such as printing the marksheet, reading the marksheet data, providing statistics such as the number of students passed and the number of students with first class, and printing a merit list.

Finding out classes and attributes for a given problem is intuitive for small problems. In most cases, a programmer is able to generate a hierarchy of classes and attributes without any trouble. However, it is very difficult for a large system. A methodical approach is needed to design classes and their attributes. Therefore, we need to study the system in a formal way and have a systematic design for classes and their attributes. Further evolution of the system should also be taken into account. There is a separate discipline dealing with this issue and the scope of this book does not cover the design approach in further detail. However, such a formal design approach is not needed for introduction to C++.

Another important point to be understood is that merely knowing the C++ syntax does not enable one to program in an object-oriented manner and make use of its advantages. One needs to know more for programming in C++. Where to use references, which type of coding to use, whether to use object-based or object-oriented, how to use templates, when to inherit, what to inherit, when to use virtual base classes, when to use virtual function, and so on are some of these aspects. These issues will be discussed as and when needed throughout the text.

The phrase *object-oriented programming* is misleading at times. It means programming by generating a class hierarchy such that we have a pointer to the root class (popularly known as a base class) and then use that pointer to address any object of any class in the entire hierarchy. Programs using C++ can be written in two different and distinct ways—object-based and object-oriented. These details are discussed in depth in Chapter 9.

> **Note** A `class` in C++ is very similar to a `struct` in C. If a `class` contains only data attributes, then it is almost identical to a `struct` of C. The difference is that the `class` defaults to `private` for members, whereas the `struct` defaults to `public`.

3.3 ANATOMY OF CLASS

A class is defined in the following format:

```
class class_name
{
    access_specifier:
        data and functions
```

```
    access_specifier:
        data and functions
    access_specifier:
        data and functions

    ...
} object list;
```

The following is an example of a program with a class definition.

```cpp
//PlayerClassEx.cpp
#include <iostream>
#include <string>
using namespace std;
class player
{
public:
    string PlayerName;
    string PlayerGame;
private:
    int PlayerNo;
    public: void InsertDetails()
    {
        cout << "Insert player number";
        cin >> PlayerNo;
        cout << "Insert player name";
        cin >> PlayerName;
        cout << "Please enter the game he/she plays";
        cin >> PlayerGame;
    }
void DisplayDetails()
{
    cout << "Player number is" << PlayerNo;
    cout << "Player name is" << PlayerName;
    cout << "The game played is" << PlayerGame;
}
};
/* The object list here is usually empty. However, instead of the empty statement, we
can write }VisAnand; and it defines VisAnand as a player object */
void main()
{
    player VisAnand;
    VisAnand.InsertDetails();
    VisAnand.DisplayDetails();
}
```

The definition of a class always starts with the keyword `class` and ends with a semicolon. The object list follows the class definition and contains the objects to be defined for that

A class definition is similar to a struct definition ending with a semicolon. One can define objects immediately after the class definition before the semicolon.

The data defined under public is available to the objects whereas the data defined under private is not available to them.

All member functions can access private as well as public variables of the same class.

class. The object list is optional and is hardly used. (A similar object list is available in struct as well, which again is hardly used.) It should be noted that if the programmer forgets the semicolon at the end of a class definition, the items defined after that are treated as an object list and the C++ compiler gets confused. We have already seen that the variables of type class are known as objects. Private and public are the access specifiers, which specify whether the data defined will be available to the users of the objects of the class.

Look at the modified main() function of this program.

```
void main()
{
    player VisAnand;
    VisAnand.InsertDetails();
    VisAnand.DisplayDetails();

    // The following works because it is a public variable VisAnand
    PlayerName = "Vishwanathan Anand";

    /* The following does not work because it is a private variable and is
    not available to objects */

    // VisAnand.PlayerNo = 5;
    /* Uncomment this statement to see what compilers do when an object tries
    to access a private member */
}
```

VisAnand.PlayerNo is a variable PlayerNo of the object VisAnand of the class player. The PlayerNo variable is defined under the private section, so it cannot be accessed by an object of the class player. If the program contains such a statement, the C++ compiler will flag an error and the program will not be compiled.

Though PlayerNo is not directly available for modification, it is available in an indirect way. When the InsertDetails() function is used for entering information in an object of the type player, the name as well as the player number is entered.

When VisAnand.InsertDetails() is called, the variables of object VisAnand including the private variable PlayerNo are actually manipulated. PlayerNo, earlier having a garbage value, is now modified to have the value specified by the user. The difference between direct access and indirect access must be clearly understood. To reiterate, InsertDetails is a member function of the class player. VisAnand is an object (not a member function) of that class and it cannot have access to PlayerNo directly. If the object wants to access that private variable, it is obtained through InsertDetails().

Note When an object accesses a public member, the access is direct. When an object calls a member function and the member function in turn uses a private variable, it is indirect access. Private members may not be accessed directly; however, indirect access is possible.

The reason behind this is that it provides a way to control the access to the private variables as well as allow only specific types of access. For example, InsertDetails() does not let a user change an old value of PlayerNo or print it; it just takes it as an input.

Unlike PlayerNo, VisAnand.PlayerName is a variable PlayerName of the object VisAnand of the class player. It is defined under the public access specifier unlike the PlayerNo variable.

One can directly access the variable and modify it if it is defined in the public section. Thus, it is possible to write

```
VisAnand.PlayerName = "Vishwanathan Anand";
```

Public data members such as `PlayerName` indicate a bad design. A good design has only member functions in the public section. The reason for this is clearly explained in Section 3.4.

As shown in this example, a programmer is free to decide the order in which public and private derivations appear. However, in this text, the `private` sections are written before the public section, and writing multiple public and private sections has been discouraged, as there is no advantage either way. It is more important to understand the need for access specifiers. This is the point under discussion in Section 3.4.

3.4 ACCESS SPECIFIERS

As mentioned earlier, a problem with large C programs is that a programmer loses its visualization, because a single unit comprises various abstractions. It is difficult for a programmer to look at the entire program and understand what is going on.

A reason for this problem is that the data members and functions are not in the form of comprehensible units of information. Once the function starts, or `struct` is accessed, all the data members defined inside, whether needed or not, are available. This complicates handling the program because one has to deal with unnecessary data members as well.

Ideally, the programmer should refrain from accessing unnecessary items of the class and should have a simplified view of the attributes that need to be used in the program, be it a function or a structure.

For better results, a differentiation is required between the data members that are needed and those that are not accessed by the user. Similar differentiation is also needed between functions necessary for the user and those needed just for maintenance of the object.

> A good class design shields all data members by defining them as private and provides access to them using carefully crafted public functions, thus controlling the way they are manipulated.

This point can be better illustrated using an example of the classic data structure called stack. Stack is a data structure where data is inserted and deleted in a last-in, first-out manner, that is, the value inserted at the end is issued out first. Insertion in a stack is known as *push* and deletion is known as *pop*. Insertion and deletion in the stack are to be done only at the top, and hence, these routines need not provide the location to insert or delete. This location is indicated by a data member called the stack pointer, which can be an index of the array as in Program 3.2 or an actual pointer having the address of an item to push or pop. The use of stack is very common in the system software.

> A C program over-exposes everything it uses, whether it is a function or a structure. C++ helps the programmer by making only the useful parts visible.

Figures 3.2 and 3.3 illustrate the stack operations. A stack can be implemented using arrays or even linked lists as mentioned earlier, though our example of C++ implements a stack as a class using an array.

Let us first define the stack as a structure and identify the problems encountered in doing so. Then, let us see how defining it as a class eliminates these problems.

Hence, first consider the example of the stack being defined as a structure. As far as the member functions are concerned, we have already seen that there are two operations possible on a stack, that is, insertion at the top known as `push()` and deletion from the top known as `pop()`. Though there may be other operations

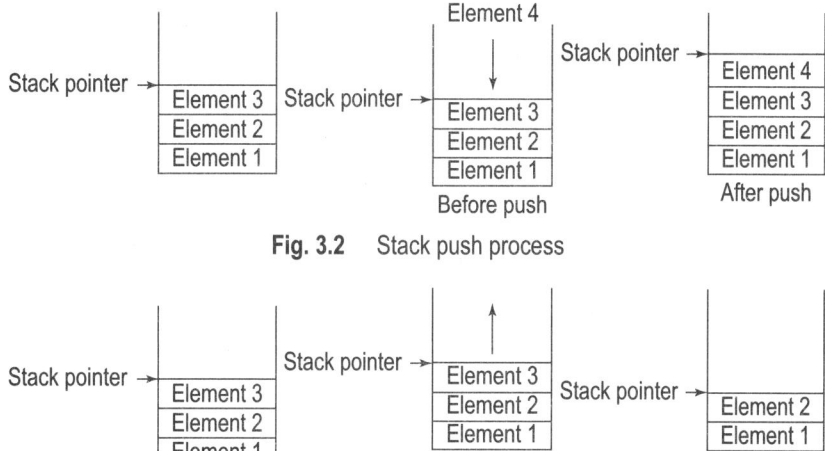

Fig. 3.2 Stack push process

Fig. 3.3 Stack pop process

possible on the stack (such as finding which element is present at the top, without removing it), we will consider only these two functions for our program.

Now, let us consider data members. Again, we will consider only two of them, though there may be more in reality. The first is the array, where the elements will be stored, and the second is the stack pointer, which indicates the place in the array where the addition or removal of elements takes place.

With respect to a class, the stack pointer is manipulated by both the functions present in the stack class. Thus, the push() and pop(), which are the member functions of the stack class, will have access to both the array and the stack pointer, as both are private members.

3.4.1 Expression Parser

Now, think of an external function such as an expression parser. Before we look at how a stack is used by an expression parser, let us understand what it is.

An expression parser is an important component of the compiler. It looks at an expression and separates its basic elements. Then, it converts them into a form understandable by the next routine of the compiler. So, if we provide A + B to an expression parser, it comes out with the answer that there are two variables A and B and they are operated by the operator '+'. Optionally, it can convert the given expression into some other type of expression. An example of an expression parser is one that converts an expression into a postfix expression (i.e., converting A + B into A B+). Similarly, it might convert A + B/C into A BC/ +. This is known as reverse Polish notation and is explained in Exhibit 3.1.

Exhibit 3.1 Reverse Polish notation

Conversion of an expression such as A + B to AB+ is called *infix to postfix conversion* and the notation AB+ is called *reverse Polish notation*. One might wonder why the expression parser does something so weird. The answer is as follows:

An expression might contain variable number of operators and operands. Hence, it is not as straightforward for a complier to look at an expression and decide how to execute it. It needs a simpler (in its view, which is quite contradictory to humans) form to calculate. AB+ is a better way for a compiler to operate than A + B.

Stacks use the popular logic for the expression parser program. The expression parser inserts data members and operators, and takes them out from the stack when needed. In the process, it converts them into the required expressions. The parser needs to call push() and pop() functions to do this process.

We can clearly see that the expression parser program needs help to construct a stack; it pushes a few elements when it deems fit and pops them out when it is appropriate. Does it need to understand the following: How are these operations performed? How is the stack implemented? What is a stack pointer? What is an array? The clear answer is no. The expression parser only requires push() and pop() operations to be available. This is analogous to the example of the car driver discussed in Chapter 1. The car driver only needs to have access to the accelerator, steering wheel, brakes, and clutch, without really worrying about how they work.

It is better if the expression parser is not even aware of the existence of data members, let alone knowing and modifying the stack pointer directly. This helps avoid accidental modification of the stack pointer. Again, this is analogous to the car driver having the access only to the accelerator pedal and not to the petrol valve directly.

This is not possible if we are using C-like structures. Any program that uses a stack has access to the stack pointer data member and can manipulate it. However, a program that uses classes can actually avoid such problems by defining the stack pointer as private.

Program 3.2 demonstrates the stack class and how to manipulate its objects.

 **PROGRAM 3.2**   Private and public members of a class

```cpp
// StackSimple.cpp
#include <iostream>
using namespace std;

class Stack
{
private:
    int StackPointer;
    int StackArray[10];
    /* Data members are hidden from the objects of stack class and hence constructs use those
    objects like an expression parser */
public:
    void InitializeSP()
    {
        StackPointer = 0;
    }

    void push(int value)
    {
        if(StackPointer == 10 )
        /* we have inserted until 9th element */
        cout << "Stack overflow! Cannot insert";
        else
        {
            StackArray[StackPointer] = value;
            StackPointer++;
        }
    }

    int pop()
    {
```

```
            if(StackPointer == 0)
                cout << "Stack underflow! Cannot pop";
            else
            {
                StackPointer--;
                return StackArray[StackPointer];
            }
        }
};

void main()
{
    Stack MyStack;
    MyStack.InitializeSP();
    MyStack.push(1);
    MyStack.push(2);

    cout << MyStack.pop() << "\n"
    /* 2 is the output, inserted later */
    cout << MyStack.pop() << "\n";
    /* The output is now 1, inserted earlier */
}
```

How the Program Works

Using the class objects   This program contains a class stack. It contains two functions, push() (which inserts an integer into the stack) and pop() (which removes one element from the stack). There is an array, StackArray, which can accept ten such pushed elements. There is also a variable, StackPointer, to indicate the index at which elements can be inserted into the stack. StackArray and StackPointer are defined as private.

The program contains an object MyStack of class Stack. Let us see how MyStack works. We need to call MyStack.push(<element>) to push an element into the stack and PopedElement = MyStack.pop() to have the element popped out. MyStack is an object of the class Stack and it cannot access either StackPointer or StackArray directly. Thus, it is good to have MyStack as an object in the expression parser program. The expression parser can create a stack object (using statements such as Stack ExpressionStack;), can push and can pop, but it will not allow expressions such as ExpressionStack.StackPointer = 8 or ExpressionStack. StackArray[8] = 12.

Defining members as public or private   Defining the members as private or public is important from the design point of view. The visibility, service, and the difference in the implementation and interface of a class are maintained by such a selective definition.

When we are using stack, for example, while building an expression parser, we can call push() to insert an element in the stack and pop() to remove an element from the stack, but we need not worry about how the stack is actually implemented. In this example, the stack is implemented using an array, which is not seen by MyStack. Neither the array nor the stack pointer is visible outside the class Stack.

What is to be visualized outside the class is to be defined as public and the rest should be defined as private.

Implementation vs interface problem   Let us visualize this process from the viewpoint of service. The attributes that provide services to outsiders are to be kept public and those that provide services only to member functions are to be defined as private. In our example, push() and pop() provide services to outsiders such as the expression parser, whereas StackPointer and StackArray provide services to their own members such as push() and pop(). This is sometimes referred to as the implementation vs interface problem.

The push() and pop() functions contribute to the interface (to the outside world) and StackPointer and StackArray are a part of implementation. This shows how an interface is actually modelled in the class. An advantage of separating implementation and interface is that we can change the implementation without changing the interface. Thus, if we now decide to implement the push and pop operations using a linked list, both push() and pop() functions need to be rewritten, but the function (e.g., expression parser) that uses them need not change.

Private members, as explained, are hidden from the objects of the class. Though the data members are accessible to member functions, they are hidden from non-member functions. This is an important principle of object-oriented programming; it is known as information hiding and has been discussed earlier. There is an exception to this rule, called *friend functions*, which is described in Chapter 4.

Object initialization   We will now discuss the importance of calling InitializeSP() before doing any push or pop operations on the stack. InitializeSP() initializes the stack pointer to zero. If a member is pushed, it is incremented and makes it possible for the member to be added in the right slot. Without InitializeSP(), the stack pointer will initially contain garbage value. Incrementing and decrementing garbage values also results in garbage. Thus, calls to push() and pop() will result in garbage manipulation. Suppose StackPointer initially has a random value 100. A call to the push() function will result in an element insertion at the array position 100, which is not a place owned by our array. It can result in unforeseen problems.

Need for constructor   As already mentioned, whenever a stack type object is defined, if a programmer fails to call InitializeSP() before any push() operation is performed, it will lead to errors or problems. However, it is possible to automate InitializeSP() in C++ in such a way that when an object is defined, the stack pointer is automatically initialized to zero. This is of great help because a programmer need not worry about mandatory calls to initialize the stack pointer every time a stack is defined, which used to be a common problem. C++ provides a solution to this problem in the form of constructors, which are discussed in detail in Chapter 5.

Other than private and public specifiers, there is one more access specifier called protected. It is useful when inheritance is involved. This specifier is discussed in Chapter 9.

3.5 STORAGE REQUIREMENTS

Classes and variables of classes (objects) in C++ have different memory requirements compared to other data types and variables. Let us try to understand the difference with the help of an example. Consider the following:

```
struct student
{
    int RollNo;
    char Name[30];
    char Address[60];
};
```

This definition in C does not occupy any memory. This is because what is being defined is actually a formation or arrangement for a specific aggregation. We are not defining any variable that needs storage but are only providing an outline of what the student data members should contain. It is analogous to providing a sketch of a machine. The actual machines will be produced later using the same sketch. We need raw materials only when we build the machine and not at the time of drawing the sketch. Similarly, only when we define an object of the class is the memory occupied to hold the data members.

Unlike struct, when we define a class, the memory required for the member functions of the class and the static data members is allocated immediately (static data members are discussed in Section 3.9). On the other hand, when we define objects of the class, only the memory needed for storing non-static data members (normal data members that are not static) is obtained. So far, we have only dealt with non-static members.

Note Memory allocation is done in two phases. In the first phase, the function members and static members are allocated their memory when the class is defined, that is, only once in the lifetime of the program execution. On the other hand, whenever the object is defined, separate memory for that particular object's non-static data members is allocated.

If an object is defined 100 times, memory is accordingly allocated 100 times for those non-static data members. This is due to the fact that, in a C++ object model, the functions and static members are stored only at a single place and are shared, whereas non-static members are not shared and are stored separately with each object. Every object has its own personal copies of non-static members.

Consider the class student defined in Section 3.1. Suppose we add the following code in the main function:

```
student FirstStudent;
student SecondStudent;
```

Then, we have only one PrintDetails() function shared by both the first and the second students. It is defined and memory is allocated immediately when the student class is defined. Details such as roll number, name, and address come into existence and memory is allocated for them when we define the objects of the student class. Having a separate roll number, name, and address for each object is important. If every object does not have a separate set of non-static data attributes, the object will lose its identity and all objects will have the same name, roll number, and address; they will be the same for the user. So, the information displayed by FirstStudent.RollNo is different from that displayed by SecondStudent.RollNo.

This is not the case with the PrintDetails() function. Irrespective of the number of objects defined, there is a single copy of PrintDetails() available to all of them. So, when we call FirstStudent.PrintDetails() or SecondStudent.PrintDetails(), the same function is being called.

How can PrintDetails() print the first student's details in the first case and the second student's details in the second case? We do not seem to pass anything to the function. It is important to note that a pointer to the invoking object (&FirstStudent in the first case and &SecondStudent in the second case) is always passed as an implicit argument to the member function, and this is why it works perfectly in both the cases.

> **Note** `FirstStudent.PrintDetails()` is technically equivalent to `PrintDetails(&FirstStudent)`
> and `SecondStudent.PrintDetails()` to `PrintDetails(&SecondStudent)`. The pointer to
> invoking the object of the class will be passed to the function. The pointer that is passed this way
> (`&FirstStudent` in the first case and `&SecondStudent` in the second case) is called `this` pointer.
> We can actually address the pointer by the keyword `this`.

The passing of a pointer to the invoking object helps in keeping a single copy of the
function for all objects. One needs to understand the importance of sharing the member
function among all the objects. No matter how many objects we create, memory allocation
for a single copy of the member function is enough. Moreover, having separate sets of exactly
the same member functions for each individual object does not make sense.

> **Note** Even if we define l00 student objects, there will be a single copy of the `PrintDetails()` function.
> In the same way, even, if we have 0 student objects, we still have one copy of the `PrintDetails()`
> function. Alternatively, if we have 0 copies of the student object, there are 0 roll numbers. If we have
> l00 copies of the student object, we have l00 roll numbers, one for each object. Therefore, while
> defining a class, the memory for the function is allocated and while defining the objects, the memory
> for the non-static data members is allocated.

3.6 DIFFERENCE BETWEEN STRUCTURE AND CLASS IN C++

The difference between structure and class in C++ is blurred. There is just one (seemingly)
insignificant difference between them. We have seen `public` and `private` access specifiers;
we can omit them in defining a class as shown in Program 3.3.

PROGRAM 3.3   `struct` and `class`

```
// StructClass.cpp
#include <iostream>
#include <string>
using namespace std;
class employee
{
    /* Access specifier is omitted here, so it is private by default */
    int EmpID;
    string Name;
    string Designation;
    string Department;
    int Salary;
public:
    void InsertDetails()
    {
        cout << "Insert employee ID";
        cin >> EmpID;
        cout << "Insert name";
        cin >> Name;
        cout << "Insert designation";
        cin >> Designation;
        cout << "Insert department";
        cin >> Department;
        cout << "Insert salary";
        cin >> Salary;
    }
```

```
        void DisplayDetails()
        {
            cout << EmpID << "\n";
            cout << Name << "\n";
            cout << Designation << "\n";
            cout << Department << "\n";
            cout << Salary << "\n";
        }
};
void main()
{
    employee Robin;
    Robin.InsertDetails();
    Robin.DisplayDetails();
}
```

> **Note** When we define a class and define its data members without writing them under any access specifier, they are treated as `private` by default.

How the Program Works

If this program is slightly modified by replacing the fourth line class `employee` by `struct` `employee`, the program works just the same. However, there is a difference, which is not visible at the moment. Add the following line in both the programs (with `employee` as a class in the first program and as a structure in the second program). The main function is now different as follows:

```
void main()
{
    employee Robin;
    Robin.InsertDetails();
    Robin.DisplayDetails();
    // The following line is added
    Robin.EmpID = 10;
    /* This line will not be compiled in the case of class,
    but it will work fine in a structure */
}
```

The first program is not compiled, but the second one is. The default behaviour in the `struct` definition is different. An attribute without an access specifier name is treated as `public` in *structure* unlike `private` in *class*. Here, `EmpID` in the first program is `private` whereas in the second it is `public`. It can be accessed by the second program's statement but not by that of the first program and hence the second program is compiled. It is not difficult to understand why default is `private` in a class. Unless explicitly specified (i.e., defined under `public`), anything defined should be considered `private` in a class.

It might seem illogical to have the structure which behaves in the same manner as a class, except one seemingly insignificant difference in the default data type. The reason for such behaviour of a structure lies in backward compatibility with C. Consider the following code borrowed from C:

> In the case of a class, the data members and member functions are `private` by default (unless declared otherwise), whereas in the case of a structure, the entities are `public` by default.

```
struct Evaluator
{
```

```
    char Name[30];
    char Address[100];
}
```

If structures are made similar to classes in C++ (i.e., default is `private` when no access specifier is provided), then think what will happen to this code. The program cannot execute statements such as

```
Evaluator MrBaxi;
Strcpy(MrBaxi.Name, "Chandrakant Baxi");
```

The fact that it is able to access `Name` shows that it is a `public` data member. By keeping the default as `public`, the C++ `struct` is still backward compatible with C `struct`. It is a C++ convention to use `class` when we need a class and to use `struct` when we need a C-like structure.

> **Note** If `struct` does not default to `public`, the C code copied to a C++ program will not work. C++ designers needed backward compatibility and wanted a C program to work with minimum modification when compiled by a C++ compiler.

3.7 DIFFERENCE BETWEEN UNIONS AND CLASSES

In C++, unions can have access specifiers and can define both data and functions; similar to structures, their default access specifier is `public`. (The reason is the same as discussed in Section 3.6.) Unions have the important properties of all data elements (but not the member functions) sharing the same memory location. They also have to maintain compatibility with unions in C.

A special type of union defined by C++, which was not available in C, is the *anonymous union*. In this type of union, the name of the union is not provided at the time of definition. An indication that the data elements are sharing the same memory location is provided to the compiler. The members of an anonymous union can be accessed directly, without defining objects of the union type and without using the dot operator. The following is a summary of the points discussed about unions.

1. By and large, unions in C++ remain the same as in C, with the possible addition of member functions.
2. All data members share the same memory as in C.
3. The default access specifier is `public` as in structures.
4. A union without a name, that is, an anonymous union is possible in C++.

Program 3.4 illustrates the types of unions.

PROGRAM 3.4 Unions and classes

```
//UnionExample.cpp
#include <iostream>
using namespace std;

union IntChar

{
    void SetValue()
    // Without access specifier, treated as public
    {
        CharView[0]=0;   // 00000000
```

```
        CharView[1]=1;   // 00000001
        CharView[2]=0;   // 00000000
        CharView[3]=0;   // 00000000
    }
    /* This value is equivalent to 00000000 00000000 00000001 00000000, that is, 2⁸ */

    void GetValue()
    {
        cout << IntView; // displays 256, that is, 2⁸
    }
private:
    unsigned int IntView;
    char CharView[4];
    /* These two data members share the same memory location */
};

void main()
{
    IntChar IC;
    IC.SetValue();
    IC.GetValue();

    // The following is an anonymous union

    union
    {
        int AnoInt;
        char AnoChar[4];
    };
    AnoInt = 65;      // AnoInt is accessed directly
    cout << "\n The AnoChar 1st element is" << AnoChar[0];
    cout << "\n The AnoChar 2nd element is" << AnoChar[1];
    cout << "\n The AnoChar 3rd element is" << AnoChar[2];
    cout << "\n The AnoChar 4th element is" << AnoChar[3] << endl
}
```

Output
```
256
The AnoChar 1st element is A
The AnoChar 2nd element is
The AnoChar 3rd element is
The AnoChar 4th element is
```

How the Program Works

The value of the IntValue data member is printed as 256, that is, 2^8. AnoChar[0] data member prints A (char value of 65) and others print null (char value of zero). The following are some important points to be noted about Program 3.4:

1. The functions SetValue() and GetValue() are not defined under any access specifier and hence are treated as public.
2. AnoChar and AnoInt are accessed without dot notation. It can be seen that the value of AnoChar[0] is "A" when the value of AnoInt is set to 65. This is a simple example to show that AnoChar and AnoInt actually share the same memory location.

> **Note** An anonymous union is defined inside the main union, that is, it is a local union. If we want to define a global anonymous union, we must define it as static in C++. This is not the case with normal unions. In Program 3.4, union IntChar is defined to be global.

There are a number of restrictions when using unions in C++, and hence, it is always better to use classes whenever possible. Unions are to be used only in the context similar to C unions.

Defining data members after function members   We have defined the functions SetValue() and GetValue() before defining the variable values used by them, namely, IntView and CharView. How can the compiler allow usage of something before actual definitions? The reason is interesting. The compiler takes two passes on the class definition. In the first pass, it looks at the function headers, arguments and variable definitions. The function body is taken up in the next pass. When the body is evaluated, the data members, even if defined later, are already known. So, we do not get compiler errors in such cases.

3.8 DEFINING FUNCTION MEMBERS OUTSIDE CLASS

The following example illustrates an important point, that is, it is possible to define the function members outside the class.

```cpp
//FunOutsideClass.cpp
#include <iostream>
#include <string>
using namespace std;
class student
{
public:
    int RollNumber;
    string Name;
    string Address;
    void PrintDetails();
    /* Only the prototype is inside the class definition */
};
void student::PrintDetails()
/* Note that 'student::' is appended at the beginning */
{
    cout << "Roll number is " << RollNumber << "\n";
    cout << "Name is " << Name << "\n";
    cout << "Address is " << Address << "\n";
}
void main()
{
    student Student1;
    Student1.RollNumber = 1;
    Student1.Name = "Robin Singh";
    Student1.Address = "New Delhi";
    Student1.PrintDetails();
}
```

This example shows that it is very simple to define functions outside the class and is recommended if the functions are big. This is dealt with in detail while discussing inline functions in Chapter 4.

Scope Resolution Operator (: :)

When a function does not belong to any class, we call it a non-member function.

Let us now see the use of the scope resolution operator provided before the function definition outside the class, that is, `void student::PrintDetails()` instead of the simple `PrintDetails()`. When the function is defined outside the class, only the prototype remains inside the class. All other details are similar to the definition inside the class. Thus, the statement

```
void PrintDetails();
```

should only be in the body of the class.

The body of a class defines the scope of the member function. When the function is defined inside the body of a class, it is inside the scope of the class, that is, it is implicitly defined to be a member of the same class. There is no need to specify that the function belongs to that class. In Program 3.1, where the `PrintDetails()` function is defined inside the `student` class, we did not mention that `PrintDetails()` belongs to the `student` class.

When the function is defined outside the class, it is defined outside the scope of the class. It is not clear to which class the function belongs or whether the function belongs to any class at all, and hence, the class needs to be explicitly specified with that function. In the previous example, the `PrintDetails()` function is defined outside the class and hence it needs to be specified that it belongs to the `student` class. The definition

```
void student::PrintDetails()
```

states that the `PrintDetails()` function is a member function of the `student` class. The scope resolution operator is named so because it resolves the scope. The scope resolution operator used for a global data member also does the same function of resolving the scope of the data member.

It is also important to note that more than one class can have a function with the same name. In such cases, the scope resolution operator is used to differentiate between them. Consider the class `student` defined in Program 3.1, in which the function `PrintDetails()` is defined inside.

Suppose we have another class `employee` with `PrintDetails()` as one of its functions. If both these functions are defined outside the class, these will be written as follows:

```
student::PrintDetails()
```

and

```
employee::PrintDetails()
```

One can understand at a glance which `PrintDetails()` is being talked about. So, when a compiler encounters `<AnEmployeeObject>.PrintDetails()`, it will be able to call the right function.

Note The scope resolution operator is useful in differentiating the functions of different classes with the same name when defined outside the body of a class.

3.9 STATIC DATA MEMBERS

Static variables in C functions have a specific property that they are initialized only once (when the function is called for the first time) and they retain their values between calls. This is reiterated by Program 3.5.

PROGRAM 3.5   Static data members

```
//CStaticVar.cpp
#include <stdio.h>
void Dummy()
{
    static int i = 10;
    int j = 20;
    i+=10;
    j+=5;
    printf("The i value is %d and j value is %d \n",i,j);
}

void main()
{
    Dummy();
    /* First call to Dummy(). Here, i is initialized to 10. At the end of the call, i
    value changes to 20 */

    Dummy();
    /* Second call to Dummy(). Here, i is not initialized to 10, instead it is 20 as that
    is the value it had while exiting from the first call to Dummy() */
}
```

Output
```
The i value is 20 and j value is 25
The i value is 30 and j value is 25
```

How the Program Works

In this case, when the first call to Dummy() is made, i is initialized to 10. When the second call is made, it is not initialized even though there is an initialization statement written in the function. Rather, it picks the value of i at the time of its exit from the earlier Dummy(). If it was set to 20 when exiting from the first call to Dummy(), it is retained when the second call is made.

The case of variable j is different. It is an automatic (auto) variable, and hence, in both the calls, it is initialized to 20. If it was set to 25 at the end of the first call to Dummy(), it forgets that value immediately after exiting from the function and comes back afresh when the second call is made. This is why it prints the same value 25 in the second call even though the i value is incremented to 30. Another important point needs to be noted here. If i is not initialized in this program, it assumes the value 0. The case with j is different and it contains an arbitrary value left by the previous use of the memory allocated to j.

Note In the context of C++, the meaning of auto is a little extended. If a programmer defines a variable using the statement

```
auto x;
```

the compiler tries to determine the type of x and uses it here. This does not seem to be useful, but when we need to use a large name of a data type, especially when using nested namespaces or using the Standard Template Library (STL), it is quite useful.

Difference between Auto and Static

In C, it is possible to differentiate between auto variables, which lose their values upon exit from the function, and static members, which do not lose them. This is done by storing both

Auto variables lose their values upon exiting from the function whereas static members retain their earlier values.

types of variables at different places. The static members with global variables are stored at a permanent location and the auto variables on the non-permanent stack. (The word 'permanent' here means 'permanent as long as the program execution is on'.) Hence, the auto variables that are stored on the stack upon call to the function are lost when the function exits and their contents are removed from the stack. In short, they are stored at a dynamic place that changes when functions are invoked and exited. On the other hand, the static members are stored in a static place that is retained throughout the execution of the program. Hence, they are called static.

Static members have a similar meaning in C++ as well. Program 3.5 can actually be compiled as a C++ program. All static members are stored with the global variables at a permanent location.

Difference between Static and Global Data Members

A static member defined inside a class is also stored at a permanent location. Static data members of a class are a little different from global data members. Exhibit 3.2 lists out the differences between them.

Exhibit 3.2   What separates a static data member from a global data member

1. *Storage:* Both are stored at a global location
2. *Instantiation:* Both are available as a single copy and without any objects being created
3. *Initialization:* Both are initialized to zero at the time of definition
4. *Scope:* The scope of a global variable is the entire program, whereas static variables are restricted to the class in which they are defined.

As stated earlier, static data members are stored at a location where they are retained throughout the execution of the program and are not stored with class objects. They are stored only as a single copy. This single copy of the static data member is shared between all the objects of the class. Their behaviour is very similar to member functions of the class. Similar to the function `PrintDetails()`, static members exist and are available even if no object of the class is created.

All static data members are initialized to zero at the time of declaration by the C++ compiler. This means that static data members are as good as global data members, with the only difference that they are available only to this class instead of the entire program. Program 3.6 shows how to define and use static members.

PROGRAM 3.6   Static and non-static members

```
//StaticVariable.cpp
#include <iostream>
using namespace std;

class TestStatic
{
private:
    static int StaticVariable;
    /* It does not define the static member; only declaration is provided here */

    int NonStaticVariable;
```

```
public:
    void InitializeVariables(int Stat, int NonStat)
    {
        StaticVariable = Stat;
        NonStaticVariable = NonStat;
    }

    void DisplayVariables()
    {
        cout << "Static member's value is" << StaticVariable << "\n";
        cout << "Non-static member's value is" << NonStaticVariable << "\n";
    }
};

int TestStatic::StaticVariable;
/* Defining the static member */

void main()
{
    TestStatic TS1;
    TestStatic TS2;
    TS1.InitializeVariables(5,5);
    TS1.DisplayVariables();
    TS2.InitializeVariables(10,10);
    TS2.DisplayVariables();
    // Let us again see what are the values for T1
    TS1.DisplayVariables();
}
```

Output
```
Static member's value is 5
Non-static member's value is 5
Static member's value is 10
Non-static member's value is 10
Static member's value is 10
Non-static member's value is 5
```

How the Program Works

This program has a class TestStatic; TS1 is the first object and TS2 is the second object of this class. The class contains two different variables; StaticVariable is defined as static whereas NonStaticVariable is defined as a non-static data member. It should be noted that the static members need two phases of definition. StaticVariable is declared inside the class as

```
static int StaticVariable;
/* this is actually the prototype of the static variable definition */
```

It is defined outside the class as

```
int TestStatic::StaticVariable;
```

> **Note** The keyword static must precede the prototype, but not the definition. Static variables are to be declared inside the class first and then defined outside the class as well.

It should be noted how a static member is declared, defined, and used in this program. Though it is defined as a private variable, it can also be defined as public. Program 3.9 provides an example of a publicly defined static variable.

A static member can be defined as private or public, but usually it is kept public.

In Program 3.6, we assign values to TS1 first and then to TS2. Both NonStaticVariable and StaticVariable are given values. When the static member of TS2 is changed, it can be seen in the output that the static member of TS1 is changed as well. This is because the variables TS1.StaticVariable and TS2.StaticVariable are actually the same. Any number of objects may be defined in the same manner; there will still be only a single copy of StaticVariable.

Static members are needed in a situation when all objects of the class need to share some features. Consider Program 3.7, which deals with another type of student class. It contains two normal variables; SubjectMarks is an array containing the marks of a student object and fail is a Boolean variable indicating whether the student has passed or failed. As discussed in Chapter 1, bool is a new data type added to C++. There are two different member functions: DisplayMarks(), which display the marks of a given student, and SetMarks(), which set the values of marks for a specific object. It should be noted that for the SubjectMark array and fail, the values can be set only by SetMarks() and can only be seen by DisplayMarks(). This is a good example of having a controlled access to an attribute (the marks) of an object.

PROGRAM 3.7   Static members

```cpp
//StaticVar3.cpp
#include <iostream>
using namespace std;

class student
{
public:
    static int PassingMark;
    int SubjectMark[5];
    bool fail;
    void DisplayMarks()
    {
        for(int i=0; i<5; ++i) {
        cout << "Marks of subject no.";
        cout << i << " is " << SubjectMark[i];
    }

    void SetMarks(int Marks[5])
    {
        for(int i=0; i<5; ++i)
        {
            SubjectMark[i] = Marks[i];
        }
    }

    bool CheckPassing()
    {
        fail = false;
        for(int i=0; i<5; ++i)
        {
            if(SubjectMark[i] < PassingMark)
            fail = true;
        }
        if(!fail)
            cout << "Congratulations! You have passed \n";
        else
            cout << "Sorry! You have failed \n";
```

```
            return !fail;
        }
};
int student::PassingMark; // required definition
void main()
{
    student::PassingMark = 35;
    student Robin;
    student Leena;
    student Bob;

    int RobinMarks[] = {75,55,65,56,89};
    int LeenaMarks[] = {15,25,100,98,89};
    int BobMarks[] = {100,70,67,78,98};

    Robin.SetMarks(RobinMarks);
    Bob.SetMarks(BobMarks);
    Leena.SetMarks(LeenaMarks);

    Robin.CheckPassing();
    Leena.CheckPassing();
    Bob.CheckPassing();
}
```

Output
```
Congratulations! You have passed
Sorry! You have failed
Congratulations! You have passed
```

How the Program Works

We will now explain the use of `PassingMark` as a `static` member. Irrespective of the number of students and subjects, we need only one copy of passing marks. Hence, we have defined it to be `static`.

> **Note** When we need to have a single copy of a member irrespective of the number of objects of a class, we need to define it as `static`.

Let us see how `PassingMark` is used. We need to write `student::PassingMark` outside the class to actually define passing marks. The way it is accessed is also interesting. Here, it is accessed as `Student::PassingMark`. A static member can be accessed using either `student::PassingMark`, `Robin.PassingMark` or `Leena.PassingMark`. Thus, there are two ways to access static members:

1. `Class name::Member variable name`
2. `Object name.Member variable name`

The difference must be noted. The scope resolution operator (::) is used along with the class name whereas the dot operator (.) is used with the object name. Though the second form of using the static member is allowed, it is misleading for the reader and is not recommended. We will revisit this while discussing Program 3.8.

Consider the case where we are interested in finding out how many objects of a given class are defined at the moment. Suppose we have a variable called `TotalStudents` for storing information about the total students at present. If this variable is defined as a non-static data member of the class, every object will have its own copy of `TotalStudents` when defined.

For example, we may have `Student1` and `Student2` as two students. `Student1.TotalStudents` and `Student2.TotalStudents` are two different variables. Increasing `TotalStudents` of

Student1 does not increase TotalStudents of Student2. This is similar to changing the roll number of one student, which does not have any effect on that of the other student. Thus, our purpose is not served by using normal variables. The static data member in this case solves the problem. The following program shows how this can be done.

The program contains a student class, containing two functions for setting and printing the details of the students. The student class contains three non-static members, namely, RollNumber, Name, and Address. However, the most important data for us is the static member TotalStudents.

```cpp
// StaticCountVar.cpp
#include <iostream>
#include <string>
using namespace std;
class student
{
public:
    static int TotalStudents;
private:
    int RollNumber;
    string Name;
    string Address;
public:
    void SetDetails(int Roll, string StudentName, string StudentAddress)
    {
        RollNumber = Roll;
        Name = StudentName;
        Address = StudentAddress;
        TotalStudents++;
    }
    void PrintDetails()
    {
        cout << "Roll number is " << RollNumber << "\n";
        cout << "Name is " << Name << "\n";
        cout << "Address is " << Address << "\n";
    }
};
int student::TotalStudents;
/* There is no need to initialize this to zero; the compiler will automatically do it */
void main()
{
    cout << "Total students at the moment " << student::TotalStudents << "\n";
    student Robin;
    Robin.SetDetails(1,"Robin Singh","New Delhi");
    Robin.PrintDetails();
    cout << "Total students at the moment " << student::TotalStudents << "\n";
    student Sonia;
    Sonia.SetDetails(2,"Sonia","Bhopal");
```

```
        Sonia.PrintDetails();
        cout << "Total students at the moment " << student::TotalStudents << "\n";
        if(true)
        {
            student Arti;
            Arti.SetDetails(3,"Arti", "Indore");
            Arti.PrintDetails();
            cout << "Total students at the moment" << student::TotalStudents;
        }
        cout <<"Arti departs! \n";
        /* The following line will not work as expected. Total students are still three */
        cout << "Total students at the moment " << student::TotalStudents <<"\n";
    }
```

Output
```
Total students at the moment 0
Roll number is 1
Name is Robin Singh
Address is New Delhi
Total students at the moment 1
Roll number is 2
Name is Sonia
Address is Bhopal
Total students at the moment 2
Roll number is 3
Name is Arti
Address is Indore
Total students at the moment 3
Arti departs!
Total students at the moment 3
```

As can be seen, this program works successfully and can count the total number of students every time. However, there is a problem. Observe that even after Arti's departure, the number of totals students is displayed as three instead of two. The ways to tackle this problem will be discussed when we study destructors in Chapter 6.

Another interesting factor is to be observed here. TotalStudent has not been initialized to zero. This is because all static and global variables are automatically initialized to zero in C++, as in C.

Let us look at one more example that explains the two ways of calling static functions and also the difference between the two ways. Consider Program 3.8.

PROGRAM 3.8   Two ways of calling static functions

```cpp
//StaticVarDisp.cpp
#include <iostream>
using namespace std;

class TestStatic
{
public:
    static int StaticVariable;
    void DisplayValue()
    {
        cout << "The static member's value is " << StaticVariable << "\n";
    }
};
```

```
int TestStatic::StaticVariable;
void main()
{
    TestStatic::StaticVariable = 100;
    /* Class name to qualify the static member */

    cout << "Static member's value before existence of any object"
    << TestStatic::StaticVariable;

    TestStatic TS1;
    TestStatic TS2;

    TS1.DisplayValue();
    TS2.DisplayValue();
    TS2.StaticVariable = 10;
    // Object name to qualify the same static member
    TS1.DisplayValue();
}
```

How the Program Works

Let us see how the static member is accessed. As mentioned earlier, we can qualify a static member in two different ways.

1. `Object name.Static member name(TS2.StaticVariable = 10;)`
2. `Class name::Static member name(TestStatic::StaticVariable = 100;)`

As can be observed, there is no difference between the results because we are working on the same variable either way. However, the second form is better since it is conceptually clearer. In a true sense, a static member belongs to the class and not the object. The first form is provided just for syntactical convenience and should not be used, because it may confuse the reader and the variable might be taken as a normal variable (normal data member of the class). However, `class name::static member name` clearly states it to be a static member.

> **Note** The other advantage of using the form `class name::static member` is that there is no need to instantiate an object to refer to the static member. Such dummy object instantiation slows down the execution of the program and may lead to unnecessary additions to the program code, which might result in more errors.

We have discussed the unique roll number generator function in Chapter 1. This function can be easily written and used in a program using static members. Consider the following example.

```
//UniqueRollNoGenerator.cpp
#include <iostream>
using namespace std;
class Student
{
private:
    int RollNo;
    static int CurrentRollNo;
    int UniqueRollNoGenerator()
    {
        CurrentRollNo++;
        return CurrentRollNo;
    }
```

```
    public:
      void AssignRollNumber()
      {
         RollNo = UniqueRollNoGenerator();
      }
      void DispRollNo()
      {
         cout << "Roll number of this student is " << RollNo << "\n";
      }
    };
    int Student::CurrentRollNo;
    void main()
    {
      Student Mahesh;
      Mahesh.AssignRollNumber();
      Student Jayesh;
      Jayesh.AssignRollNumber();
      Mahesh.DispRollNo();
      Jayesh.DispRollNo();
    }
```

Output
```
Roll number of this student is 1
Roll number of this student is 2
```

Explanation for this program is not being provided and is left as an exercise for the students. The only important thing to note here is that the `UniqueRollNoGenerator()` function is kept private and is not accessible to any function that uses the student object directly, but it can be accessed by the `AssignRollNumber()` function. The differences between the public and private functions will be discussed in detail in Chapter 4. Functions in C++ can also be static similar to the data members.

3.10 ARRAYS OF OBJECTS

Arrays in C++ can also hold objects. Let us see how an array of objects can be defined and used with the help of an example. Program 3.9, which is an extension to Program 3.1, shows how an array of objects can be manipulated.

> **Note** While coding real-world C++ programs, programmers prefer to use vectors instead of arrays.

PROGRAM 3.9 Defining and using an array of objects

```
//ArrayOfObjects.cpp
#include <iostream>
#include <string>
using namespace std;

class student
{
private:
    int RollNumber;
    string Name;
```

```
        string Address;
public:
        void SetDetails(int Roll, string StudentName, string StudentAddress)
        {
            RollNumber = Roll;
            Name = StudentName;
            Address = StudentAddress;
        }
        void PrintDetails()
        {
            cout << "Roll number is " << RollNumber << "\n";
            cout << "Name is " << Name << "\n";
            cout << "Address is " << Address << "\n";
        }
};

void main()
{
    student ArrayOfStudents[3];

    ArrayOfStudents[0].SetDetails(1,"Robin Singh", "New Delhi");
    ArrayOfStudents[0].PrintDetails();

    ArrayOfStudents[1].SetDetails(2,"Manu", "Bhopal");
    ArrayOfStudents[1].PrintDetails();

    ArrayOfStudents[2].SetDetails(3,"Paras","Indore");
    ArrayOfStudents[2].PrintDetails();
}
```
Output
```
Roll number is 1
Name is Robin Singh
Address is New Delhi
Roll number is 2
Name is Manu
Address is Bhopal
Roll number is 3
Name is Paras
Address is Indore
```

How the Program Works

This is analogous to using an array of structures in C. A subscript notation can be used with the array name to indicate the element of the array. The elements of the array are now objects of type student, which are now indicated by ArrayOfObjects[<subscript variable value>], for example, ArrayOfObjects[2]. A dot (.) notation can be used to access the elements of objects, as is done with structures. The only added feature is function calls. It can be observed that the syntax for accessing function elements is similar to data elements, that is, if PrintDetails() is the function, then ArrayOfObjects[2].PrintDetails() can still be called to print the details of the object stored as the third element of the array.

3.11 POINTER TO OBJECTS AND POINTER TO MEMBERS OF A CLASS

It is almost impossible to write professional programs using C or C++ without pointers. In C++, pointers can also have an address for an object; they are known as *pointers to objects*.

The difference is that pointers themselves are variables that contain addresses. Apart from that, there is no difference.

A pointer to an object contains an address of that object. Pointer increment will increment the address by the size of the object, which is determined by the size of all of its non-static data elements. We have already seen that functions and static data members are not stored with the object and do not count for the size of an object. However, it is a little different in the case of inherited classes, which are complex. Calculating the size of inherited class objects is not straightforward and we defer to discuss that until we study inheritance in Chapter 9. Consider Program 3.10.

PROGRAM 3.10 Object pointer

```cpp
//ObjectPointer.cpp
#include <iostream>
#include <string>
using namespace std;

class student
{
public:
    int RollNumber;
    string Name;
    string Address;

    void PrintDetails()
    {
        cout << "Roll number is " << RollNumber << "\n";
        cout << "Name is " << Name << "\n";
        cout << "Address is " << Address << "\n";
    }
};

void main()
{
    student *StudentPointer;
    StudentPointer = new student;
    /* Instead, these two statements can also be written as a single statement, that is,
    student *StudentPointer = new student; */

    // Section 1
    (*StudentPointer).RollNumber = 1;
    (*StudentPointer).Name = "Robin Singh";
    (*StudentPointer).Address = "New Delhi";
    (*StudentPointer).PrintDetails();

    // Section 2
    StudentPointer->RollNumber = 1;
    StudentPointer->Name = "Robin Singh";
    StudentPointer->Address= "New Delhi";
    StudentPointer->PrintDetails();

    // Section 3
    int student::*RollPoint = &student::RollNumber;
    /* It defines a pointer Rollpoint to point to roll number.
    Note that it is not int *RollPoint = &RollNumber */

    student NewStudent;
    NewStudent.*RollPoint = 2;
    // Same as NewStudent.RollNumber = 2
```

```
    student *NewStudPoint = &NewStudent;
    cout << "\n Now the roll no. is ";
    cout << NewStudPoint->RollNumber; // will display 2
    // Accessing the roll number using pointer to object

    NewStudPoint ->* RollPoint = 3;
    cout << "\n Now the roll no. is ";
    cout << NewStudPoint ->* RollPoint;  // will display 3
    cout << NewStudent.*RollPoint;    // will again display 3
    // Accessing the roll number using object and pointer to member
}
```

Output
```
Roll number is 1
Name is Robin Singh
Address is New Delhi
Roll number is 1
Name is Robin Singh
Address is New Delhi
Now the roll no. is 2
Now the roll no. is 3
Now the roll no. is 3
```

How the Program Works

It is interesting to note that the pointer to an object works in the same way as a pointer to a C structure. We can use either the star–dot combination, which is used in Section 1 of the program, or the popular arrow notation, used in Section 2, to access the elements using object pointers. Pointer to member operators, which are used in Section 3 of the program, are explained in Exhibit 3.3.

Exhibit 3.3   Pointer to member operators

Section 3 of Program 3.10 has two new operators, (.*) and (->*), which are known as *pointer to member operators*. They refer to pointers to members of the class. When we have a pointer to a member and we access the member dereferencing that pointer, we need to use .* operator. The object, (NewStudent in this case), is referred as a normal variable and not by a pointer. It is written as <object name> .* <pointer name>.

The ->* operator is slightly different. It is used when a pointer to a member of a class is used, though, this time, it is accessed using a pointer to the object (NewStudPoint in this case).

Conventional pointers vs pointers to class members   It is important to note that though pointer-to-member-of-the-class is named as pointer, it does not contain any address. It contains only the offset into the class where a member can be found, that is, how far a member is from the beginning of the object. In Program 3.10, RollPoint is actually an offset from the beginning of the class to the variable RollNumber, and is not the address of RollNumber.

This offset is fixed at the time of compilation and works similar to an array index. Students with the knowledge of C may recollect that an array element is accessed by adding the index value to the array name (i.e., address of the beginning byte of the array). By immediately adding the offset to the object address, we can reach the member. This is a very efficient scheme to access an element. There is no need to go and fetch the value from the address; it just gets it from a known location. This has an interesting consequence. Consider the following scenario.

> C++ object model prefers efficiency at the cost of flexibility and thus it sometimes requires that a program be recompiled even when there is no change in the program but there is a change in the library that it uses.

Suppose a library of classes is to be included in a program at the linking time (after compilation and before being executed). Assume that an application has been developed using those classes and the class members are being accessed using pointer to member operators. Later, if there is a new version of the library, in which the format of only one class is different, ideally it should only be linked and not recompiled. This is because the application itself is not changed, but only the library it uses is changed. In our case, however, the application needs to be recompiled, because if the class format is changed, then the offset value will be changed accordingly. The application uses those offsets wherever there are pointers to member expressions.

Though this seems to be a big drawback, the reason why C++ designers have chosen this scheme for the C++ object model is simple. If we have a real pointer, it needs to be checked and traversed every time the member is accessed through it. It will not be much difficult if there is only one class. However, when there is a long inheritance chain where one class in inherited from another, one more from it, and so on, the actual link can be very deep down. Traversing through such a long chain is a very slow process. The C++ object model prefers efficiency to flexibility in this case.

The dynamic linked libraries (DLLs) models of VC++ and CORBA are different than the C++ object one that is being discussed here. Both are more flexible and are obviously less efficient. VC++ has extended the original object model to accommodate DLLs. Here, DLLs are sets of objects added to and removed from the application at run-time. CORBA is a mechanism to access an object from an application without really knowing where the object is (it can be part of a remote machine) and in which language it is implemented. CORBA object model is more advanced in terms of its functionality and provides far more flexibility. However, it does this at the cost of efficiency.

3.12 NESTED CLASSES

It is possible to define a class inside another class as shown in the following example.

```
//NestedClasses.cpp
#include <iostream>
using namespace std;
class Outside
{
private:
    /* The nested class (Inside) is private, hence only the nesting class (Outside) can
    access it, others cannot. */
    class Inside
    {
       int InsideInt;
public:
       void SetInsideInt(int TempInside)
       {
          InsideInt = TempInside;
       }
}; // End of inner class definition
public:
```

```
   int OutsideInt;
   Inside InsideObject;
   void UseInside()
   {
      InsideObject.SetInsideInt(OutsideInt);
      cout << OutsideInt;
   }
}; // End of outer class definition
int main()
{
   Outside OuterClass;
   OuterClass.OutsideInt = 5;
   OuterClass.UseInside();
}
```

There are two classes in this program. `Outside` class is a nesting class and contains the entire body of the `inside` class. The `inside` class, which is defined inside the `outside` class, is also known as the *nested class*. The definition of the class `inside` does not contain anything new and would not be different even if it is defined outside.

It is also interesting to see how the nested class is used. It is defined inside the `outside` class, thus it is referred to as `Outside::Inside`. It can be referred without using the `Outside::`prefix only inside the body of the `outside` class. The importance of defining the nested class as `private` should also be noted. Only the nesting class can refer to it and others cannot. The following program shows how others can make use of a nested class if it is defined as `public`. In this case, it is possible to define an inside class by the user.

```
//PublicInnerClass.cpp
#include <iostream>
using namespace std;
class Outside
{
public:
/* The nested class (Inside) is declared public, which makes it accessible to objects */
   class Inside
   {
      int InsideInt;
      public:
      void SetInsideInt(int TempInside)
      {
            InsideInt = TempInside;
      }
   }; // This class is now accessible to objects
   int OutsideInt;
   Inside InsideObject;
   void UseInside()
   {
      InsideObject.SetInsideInt(OutsideInt);
      cout << OutsideInt;
```

```
    }
}; // End of outer class definition
int main()
{
    Outside OuterClass;
    OuterClass.OutsideInt = 5;
    OuterClass.UseInside();
    Outside::Inside InnerPublicClass;
    InnerPublicClass.SetInsideInt(5);
}
```

If we define a nested class in the public part of the nesting class, it is available to all those who have access to the nesting class. In such a case, it is better that it is defined outside the nesting class as a separate class rather than as the nested class.

It is also possible to define the nested (inner) class outside the nesting (outer) class. The following is an example of the same, where again the nested (inner) class is defined as private.

```
//DefineOutsideNC.cpp
#include <iostream>
using namespace std;
class Outside
{
private:
    class Inside;
public:
    int OutsideInt;
    void UseInside();
}; // End of outer class definition
class Outside::Inside
{
    int InsideInt;
    public:
    void SetInsideInt(int TempInside)
    {
        InsideInt = TempInside;
    }
}; // Inner class is defined outside the class
/* The following function uses the Inside class and so the compiler must allocate
appropriate size for the Inside class for the statement Inside InsideObject; This is why
this function is also defined outside the class after the definition of Inside class */
void Outside::UseInside()
{
    Inside InsideObject;
    InsideObject.SetInsideInt(OutsideInt);
    cout << OutsideInt;
}
int main()
```

```
{
    Outside OuterClass;
    OuterClass.OutsideInt=5;
    OuterClass.UseInside();
}
```

It is important to note that when a nested class is defined outside, the definition cannot be in the scope of the nesting (outer) class. It cannot be defined in the body of the outer class, but must be outside it. Moreover, it can also be observed that the outside class has only the prototype of the class inside its body.

Need for Nested Classes

There are some advantages in defining the inner class outside the inner class and keeping it private. Big projects first need the development of the components. Then, these components are used by other programmers in developing application programs. The team that develops these critical components usually comprises very experienced and talented programmers. The inner or nested class is a component developed and may be maintained by someone from this team, the definition of which is available in the library.

Other teams working in the project are "nearer" to the project and have more insight into the application development. These developers have access to these components and can use them by defining the prototype of that class inside the body of the outer or nesting class. This also makes sure that the developer has the access to the component (the inner class or nested class) but the end user cannot see that class.

If the component is used for performing some really complicated action, it is made sure that even developers do not have access to the code. This is because these components are compiled and available to the developers in the form of object code from the library. It is similar to having string class objects and using them in a program wherein we cannot have access to the code written defining the string class.

3.13 LOCAL CLASSES

For the sake of completeness, C++ allows classes to be defined inside functions as well. These classes are called local classes.

The following example can be used to understand local classes. Consider the class student once again. It is defined inside a function now. TestStudent() is the function that defines the class and uses it within itself. A consequence of defining a class inside a function is quite logical; the class is not visible outside the function. In other words, the scope of the class is confined to the body of the function.

> Local classes are the ones defined inside a function.

Another point to be noted is that the function in which the class is defined is not a member function of the class. It cannot access the private variables of the class.

> **Note** One way to access the private variables of the class is to become a *friend* of it. The friend functions are discussed in Chapter 4.

```
//LocalClasses.cpp
include <iostream>
#include <string>
using namespace std;
void main()
```

```
{
    int RollNo = 3;
    void TestStudent(int);
    /* Prototype of TestStudent function; class student is not known here */
    TestStudent(RollNo);
}
void TestStudent(int Roll)
{
    int TestValue = 100;
    static int StaticTestValue = 200;
    /* This is a local class and is available only inside the TestStudent() function */
    class student
    {
    public:
        int RollNumber;
        string Name;
        string Address;
        void PrintDetails()
        // This function cannot be defined outside the class
        {
                // The following line does not work
                // cout << TestValue;
                /* This class cannot use TestValue because it is a        private variable
                of the class, so it is to be   commented. */
                // The following works
                cout << ::StaticTestValue;
                cout << "Roll number is " << RollNumber << "\n";
                cout << "Name is " << Name << "\n";
                cout << "Address is " << Address << "\n";
        }
    };
    student Student1;
    Student1.RollNumber = Roll;
    Student1.Name = "Robin Singh";
    Student1.Address = "New Delhi";
    Student1.PrintDetails();
}
```

Restrictions of Local Classes

The following are some restrictions on the use of local classes:

1. They cannot use auto local variables of the container function (e.g., TestValue).
2. They can access static local variables or external variables (globally defined) of the container function (e.g., StaticTestValue).
3. They cannot contain static members themselves.
4. They cannot define their functions outside the class boundaries. Here, the PrintDetails() function must be defined inside the class.
5. Their private variables are not available to the container function unless declared as a *friend*.

Note If we define a local class and then define private variables inside it, it hides them within the body of the function. Defining them as public would not let them be known outside the body of the function. We cannot achieve much by defining private variables here, and hence, they are hardly used in local classes.

3.14 ASSIGNING OBJECTS

Objects of similar type can be assigned in a similar manner as other variables. The object assignment is of the form

```
Object1 = Object2
```

It is a simple assignment and is usually not different from a normal variable assignment. However, the object assignment becomes different when the assignment operator for the class for the object is overloaded, which may be needed in some special circumstances. Overloading operators is discussed in detail in Chapter 7.

Assignment is done when a statement of the earlier-mentioned format is executed, whereas initialization is done when the object is defined.

Let us first look at the normal object assignment. The only important point to understand is that *assignment* is different from *initialization*. Assignment is done when a statement of the earlier-mentioned format is executed, whereas initialization is done when the object is defined. This difference is illustrated in Program 3.11.

PROGRAM 3.11 Different forms of assignment and initialization

```cpp
//ObjectAssignment.cpp
#include <iostream>
#include <string>
using namespace std;

class student
{
public:
    int RollNumber;
    string Name;
    string Address;

    void PrintDetails()
    {
        cout << "Roll number is" << RollNumber << "\n";
        cout << "Name is" << Name << "\n";
        cout << "Address is" << Address << "\n";
    }
};
void main()
{
    student Student1;
    Student1.RollNumber = 1;
    Student1.Name = "Robin Singh";
    Student1.Address= "New Delhi";

    Student1.PrintDetails();

    student Student3 = Student1; // Initialization
    student Student2;
    Student2 = Student1; // Assignment
    Student3.PrintDetails();
    Student2.PrintDetails();
}
```

> Assignment observes member-by-member copy while assigning one object to another of the same type.

How the Program Works

Observe the two types of assignments:

```
student Student3 = Student1;        // Initialization
Student2 = Student1;                // Assignment
```

The = operator used in these two cases describe different situations. The assignment operator is applied only in the second case. In the first case, it actually effects initialization and the assignment operator is not applied here. The statement

```
student Student2 = Student1
```

is actually a convenient form allowed for a statement

```
student Student2 (Student1)
```

So, if we overload the assignment operator, the case is applicable to the second example alone. Initialization and the difference between assignment and initialization are dealt with in detail while discussing copy constructors in Chapter 5. Hence, the following discussion is applicable to statements of type Student3 = Student1;

When an assignment is applied to an object, it is copied member by member, that is, the first member of the first object is assigned to the second object and so on (unless, as explained earlier, the assignment operator is overloaded and it provides a different behaviour).

In Program 3.11, the roll number, name and address of Student3 will be assigned the roll number, name and address of Student1. It is obvious that both objects must be of the same type for such an operation, and in most of the cases, as in this example, all members have similar sizes (the roll number of Student3 is of the same size as that of Student1 and so on). So, the compiler takes a shortcut here; it copies all the bits of the entire object to another without looking at member boundaries. This is similar to how one struct is assigned to another in C.

> **Note** For some special cases such as when two objects involved are of *compatible* types but not of the *same* type, it is important to have the assignment operator overloaded to have an exact effect.

3.15 CONSTANT OBJECTS

Constant objects are those that are not modifiable. C++ provides safeguarding against accidental modification by not allowing access of the object to a normal member function. Therefore, a constant object is not allowed to perform operations that modify it and only functions that are defined as const can be accessed by it. Even public variables of the object are not modifiable. Though constant member functions are discussed in detail in Chapter 4, some information is provided here. Constant member functions are those that make sure that an object is not modified. A normal member function cannot be invoked by a const object, which thus maintains its integrity. If there is a need to avoid any accidental change in an object's properties, it should be defined as a const object. Program 3.12 illustrates the use of a const object.

> Constant objects can be accessed only by constant functions.

 **PROGRAM 3.12** Constant objects

```
//ConstObj.cpp
#include <iostream>
#include <string>
using namespace std;
```

```
class student
{
public:
    int RollNumber;
    string Name;
    string Address;
    void PrintDetails() const
    /* This function is now constant; it can now be accessed by the constant object of
    class student */
    {
        cout << "Roll number is " << RollNumber << "\n";
        cout << "Name is " << Name << "\n";
        cout << "Address is " << Address << "\n";
    }
};

void main()
{
    student Student1;
    Student1.RollNumber = 1;
    Student1.Name = "Robin Singh";
    Student1.Address = "New Delhi";

    Student1.PrintDetails();

    student Student2 = Student1;
    student Student3;
    Student3 = Student1;
    Student2.PrintDetails();
    Student3.PrintDetails();

    const student OtherStudent = Student1;

    // The following is erroneous if PrintDetails() is not const
    OtherStudent.PrintDetails();
    /* The following line will not be compiled because it attempts to modify a constant
    object */
    OtherStudent.RollNumber = 5;

    /* The following will work */
    cout << OtherStudent.RollNumber;
}
```

How the Program Works

The following statement defines a constant object:

```
const student OtherStudent = Student1;
```

This definition is analogous to the const definition of other variables. It should be noted that the = operator and another variable to initialize the const object are a *must* here.

A const object definition, similar to other const definitions, must include initialization.

OtherStudent is a constant object, and so, it is not possible for the program to modify it. It should be noted that the PrintDetails() function is defined as const so that the OtherStudent object will be able to access it. Moreover, it is not possible to change RollNumber for OtherStudent because it is a constant object, though printing RollNumber is accepted and executed by a C++ compiler.

■ RECAPITULATION ■

- `Class` is a fundamental requirement for object programming. It represents real-world entities in a program.
- The attributes of entities are represented as data members and function members of a class.
- `Class` in C++ is similar to `struct` in C, except that it can have functions as well. The class members can be divided into `public` and `private` sections.
- The private sections cannot be accessed by non-members, whereas the public sections are accessible to both members and non-members.
- The public member of a class decides the visibility or the service provided to the user. It also forms the interface to the user.
- The private part represents the implementation of the class.
- Memory allocation to objects is not similar to memory allocation to other variables.
- The default type of `struct` of C++ and `union` is `public` unlike `class`. This is done to make them backward compatible with C.
- The function members can also be defined outside the class.
- Static data members are shared between all the objects of the class.
- It is possible to have pointers pointing to class objects and to have pointers to data members of the class, but they are not true pointers.
- When a class is defined inside some other class, it is called a nested class.
- It is also possible to define a class inside a function, which is called a local class.
- When an object is assigned with another object of the same class, each member of the class is copied to another.
- Assignment is different from initialization.
- Objects can also be constant objects, that is, such objects cannot be modified. The constant objects can call only constant member functions.

■ KEYWORDS ■

Anonymous union   It is a union with no name. It is possible to access members of the union by their name directly, without using the dot (.) notation.

C struct   This refers to the `struct` data type available in C language.

C++ struct   This refers to the `struct` data type available in C++ language, which lets us define functions inside the `struct`. It can have public and private sections. The default section in this case is public unlike the data type `class`; otherwise C++ `struct` and `class` are the same.

Class   This is an aggregation of data and function members.

Constant objects   These are objects that cannot be modified. `Const` objects cannot call functions other than `const`.

Data members   These are variables defined in a class. These can either be private or public.

Function members   These are functions defined in a class (may be defined inside or outside the body of the class).

Local class   It is a class defined in a function.

Nested and nesting class   When a class is defined inside another class, it is said to be a nested class. The class inside which the nested class is defined is the nesting class.

Private members   These are members defined inside the `private` section of the class. Such members are accessible only to other members of the same class and not to the objects of the class.

Public members   These are members defined inside the `public` section of the class. Such members are accessible to other members of the class as well as the objects of the class.

Static data members of class   A static data member is defined in the class with the keyword `static` preceding it. It must have a definition outside the body of the class. It is shared between all the objects of the class.

this pointer   It is the pointer used to invoking an object *implicitly* when a member function is called.

▪ EXERCISES ▪

Multiple Choice Questions

1. Which of the following statement is correct?
   - (a) Static functions cannot be declared `volatile`.
   - (b) Static functions cannot access other data members.
   - (c) Static functions cannot be declared `const`.
   - (d) All of the above
2. Which of the following is not the correct syntax of defining a string object?
   - (a) `string myString("Hi");`
   - (b) `string myString(&loqus;H&roqus;);`
   - (c) `string myString(previousStringObject);`
   - (d) All of the above
3. The statement `int *const FirstPointer` _____.
   - (a) is valid
   - (b) needs an assignment
   - (c) needs to remove `const`
   - (d) needs to insert `const` at some other place
4. With exception handling program, both _____ and _____ will sometimes increase substantially.
   - (a) code size, execution time
   - (b) compilation time, linking time
   - (c) linking time, loading time
   - (d) error checking, exception checking
5. It is important to note that it requires programming discipline not to _____ when the relationship is not a subset relationship.
   - (a) inherit
   - (b) overload
   - (c) override
   - (d) discard
6. Plenty of generic algorithms such as find and replace can be applied on strings _____.
   - (a) as they are designed for strings alone
   - (b) as strings can be passed as parameters to these functions
   - (c) as string is a part of STL
   - (d) All of the above
7. The old C++ library used to work in _____ whereas the new C++ library works in _____.
   - (a) global namespace, std namespace
   - (b) std namespace, global namespace
   - (c) global template, std template
   - (d) std template, global template

8. When a function throws a not-allowed exception, it calls unexpected, which in turn calls abort, and abort is not called directly because _____.
   - (a) abort cannot be called directly
   - (b) terminate can only call abort
   - (c) the user can alter the behaviour of unexpected
   - (d) None of the above
9. Dynamic binding enables the function to be linked at _____.
   - (a) compile time
   - (b) load time
   - (c) link time
   - (d) run-time
10. One important difference between virtual and pure virtual functions is that _____.
    - (a) virtual functions with body can be defined inside the class whereas it is not possible with pure virtual
    - (b) virtual functions with body can be defined outside the class whereas it is not possible with pure virtual
    - (c) virtual functions can be called by pointer whereas it is not possible with pure virtual
    - (d) virtual functions can be called by reference whereas it is not possible with pure virtual

Conceptual Exercises

1. What is the difference between `class` and `struct`? Write a program to illustrate the difference.
2. What is the difference between a C union and a C++ union?
3. What is an anonymous union? What is the difference between normal and anonymous unions?
4. Define a class of teacher. What will you define as `private` and `public` in this class? Suppose the class is meant for providing information about teachers to students, what are the function members you would like to have in this class?
5. Take a class of cricketers of Indian cricket team. What would be the data members and function members of this class? Which of them would you like to keep as `private` and `public`? Justify your answer.
6. What is the difference between the storage requirements of a `class` and a C `struct`? What is the reason for the difference?

7. What is this pointer? What is its advantage?

8. Consider a class of film actors. Define a few data members and a function member DisplayFilmNames() to display the names of the films an actor has acted in. Define this function outside the class.

9. How are static members different from normal members of a class? Give an example of the requirement of a static member in the following classes:
   (a) Teacher
   (b) Examiner
   (c) Film actor
   (d) Cricketer
   (e) Politician

10. Take a class of any of the problems defined in the earlier questions or some other class of your choice and show how pointer to members of the class can be used in it.

11. In the case of a pointer to member of a class, why do the pointers contain offsets? Why cannot they contain addresses? Provide a logical reason and justify your answer with an example.

12. Define a nesting class Company. Define a nested class Employee. Show how the Employee class can be used.

13. Define a function ShowFilms() containing a class Film as a local class within. Show how the Film class can be defined and used as a local class using data and function members of your choice.

14. How is one object of the same class assigned to another?

15. What are constant objects and why do we need them?

Practical Exercises

1. Write a program to define any class. Define few private and public variables. Try to access them and note down the differences.

2. Define a union with some values inside. Check to see if the address is really shared. Add some functions to it and try to access it like a class member function.

3. Define an inline function inside a program. Call it a few times. Compile and try to look at the size of the compiled code. Again define it as a normal function. Compile again and test the size of the program.

4. Define any class with a few objects. Use sizeof to check for the size of the objects. Add few functions to the class. Check if the sizeof for the objects shows the same value.

5. In the same class as in Problem 4, add a static member to the class and repeat the experiment. Verify that the static member does not store itself with the objects. Add a normal variable to the class to see the difference in size.

6. Define a class of employees. It should contain employee number, name, address, and the number of dependents for the employee. It should also contain functions to insert and display information about the employees. Define an array of 20 employees. Now write a simple for loop to read information about the employees. Finally, display all employees with more than two dependents.

7. Write a program for the users to log in. Have a class of LoggedInUser. Whenever a user is logged in, a new object of LoggedInUser is to be generated using new. Every time a user logs in, the program should display "You are the nth user" where n − 1 indicates the total number of users logged in before this user.

8. Write a program with more than one class. Try to assign an object of one class to another. What error does the compiler flag? Try to look at its help. Try to assign one object of similar type to another and then display the information of the copied object to verify that the contents are the same as that of the original object.

9. Modify the program of Problem 7 in such a way that the LoggedInUser contains information about the student who is the user of the account. One of the elements of the details is the number of hours the student has already worked for. Check if it exceeds 200 and display message "Welcome <student name>" if it is less than 200. Use pointer to object and pointer to class members for obtaining the value of <student name> by the details.

10. Define a class having one member function in it. Define an object with const declaration. What error does the compiler give when you try to execute the function using that object? Try to define the same function as const and see the difference.

11. Take up any class and define it inside a function, that is, define it as a local class. Test whether the restrictions that we have listed in the text really exist.

Chapter 4

Functions

4.1 INTRODUCTION

Functions in C++ are extended to provide support for object orientation. They have all the properties of C functions and some additional ones. As seen in Chapter 3, a class can have a function as a member. An object can make a function call to a member function using the dot notation (e.g., `Student1.PrintDetails()`). We have already seen examples of this. As in C, the functions that do not belong to any class are acceptable in C++ too; such functions are called as non-member functions and have a call similar to a C-function call, that is, `ShowCustomers()`. The difference between a non-member function and a member function is described in detail in Section 4.10.

4.2 SIMILARITIES WITH C FUNCTIONS

The functions in C++ are very similar to those in C. They are defined in the same manner as in C except the return type `default`, which was discussed in Chapter 1. In this chapter, we shall see in detail how functions are managed in C++.

Consider the following code where `MyFunction()` is called from `main()`:

```
int GlobalVariable
int MyFunction(int FirstArgument, string SecondArgument)
{
    int FunctionVariable;
    // Remaining body of the function
}
int main()
{
    int MainVariable, FirstValue, SecondValue;
    // Other statements
    int Result = MyFunction(FirstValue, SecondValue);
    /* This is the function call */
    cout << Result;
    /* This is the next immediate statement after function call */
    // Other statements
}
```

Writing and executing a program involves three steps, namely, compiling, linking, and loading in memory. When a program is compiled, the

When the program is loaded in the memory, main() is automatically loaded. Other functions (MyFunction() in this case) are not loaded at that point of time.

object codes of all the functions are generated. In this case, main() and MyFunction() are converted to object codes, but separately. When the program is linked, the function object code is attached to the object code of the main() program.

Let us try to understand what happens when a program executes a function call. The process happens in three stages, namely, function call, function execution, and return to calling function.

Stage 1 Let us first see how a function call is made. In our example, main() calls MyFunction(). When this call is made, the object code of the function MyFunction() is loaded in the main memory. The area of the main memory in which functions are loaded is called the *stack*. Once the call is made, the control transfers from the calling function (main() in our case) to the called function (MyFunction()).

Stage 2 The second stage is the execution of the function. Now, the control from main() has been transferred to the function MyFunction(). The local variables of the called function are now available and can be manipulated, that is, it is now possible to assign or print the value of FunctionVariable. However, variables from main() are not available now, that is, it is not possible to assign a value to MainVariable, except those that have been defined as global. In other words, GlobalVariable. FirstArgument, and SecondArgument are dummy arguments of the function MyFunction() and are treated similar to its local variables, with the only difference that they get their values at the time of function call.

It should be noted that FirstValue and SecondValue are needed for calling the function and so have been passed as arguments, and their values are available to FirstArgument and SecondArgument after the call.

Stage 3 The third stage begins when the control returns to the calling function from the called function. When the function execution is over, the control is transferred back to main() at the next statement (cout << Result); after the assignment (int Result = Function call). Now, the local variables of the called function are no longer available, but the local variables of main() are available again. If a function call is made from some function other than main(), the same sequence of operations is applied. Let us suppose that function calls are made from called functions, that is, function1 is calling function2, function2 is calling function3, and so on, until functionN. Then, when functionN is over, the control is transferred to functionN−1; when functionN−1 is over, the control is transferred to functionN−2; and so on until function1.

Context switching It is important here to note that when a function call is made, the context of the *calling* function, that is, the CPU register values and the values of the variables, are to be stored, and when the *called* function is over, they have to be restored. This process is known as *context switching*. This takes some time, which is not significant for a large function whose function execution time will be much more than the context switching time; however, the context switching time does matter for a small function. In the case involving N functions, N context switching operations take place.

Thus, function calling, execution, and return of a C++ function is technically similar to that of a C function.

Difference between C++ and C functions Though C++ functions look similar to C functions, there are two important differences:

1. C++ has inline functions for situations wherein the functions are small and the programmer would like to eliminate the overhead of context switching. Inline functions are discussed in detail in Section 4.4.
2. The *object code* of a C++ function contains some additional information than that of a C function.

4.3 `main()` IN C++

In C, `main()` usually does not need to specify a return type, whereas in C++, either `void` or `int` is a must. If we look at the examples that we have discussed so far, it can be observed that all of them contain `void` as a return type. (If GNU C++ (Linux) is being used, then `int` must be specified as the return type, as `void` is not allowed.) The return type of `main()` can be specified as `int` and an integer value will be returned from `main()`. The operating system (OS) used to invoke the program (UNIX, DOS, or Windows) can get the value passed by `main()` upon the termination of the program. Then, upon looking at the return value, the OS can take appropriate action.

Consider the case of an application running in batch mode. Here, the application contains a series of programs called one after another in a sequence. Assume p1, p2, etc. are called one after another until p*N*. The return status from `main()` is of more importance here. The return value from `main()` of a particular program is considered as an exit status from that program. The convention is to return zero upon normal termination and a non-zero value for abnormal termination. Subsequent programs can be aborted if the program returns something other than zero. For example, if there is an error in p5, the execution of p6–p*N* can be omitted from processing. Thus, it is important to note that it is a good convention to return a value even from `main()`.

4.4 INLINE FUNCTIONS

It has already been mentioned that functions can be defined either inside or outside the class. If they are defined inside the class, they are treated as inline functions.

> **Note** There is an important difference between a function defined inside and that defined outside a class. A function defined inside the class by default becomes inline, while a function defined outside the class by default becomes non-inline. Note that this is a default behaviour, which might not be observed sometimes when the function is not possible to be made inline when it is too complex or recursive.

Inline functions do not behave in the same way as normal functions. Context switching time for a small function is a hindrance to the performance. The body of inline functions replaces the function call statement and thus avoids context switching.

Inline functions eliminate the overhead of context switching.

Another way to avoid context switching is to use macros such as `#define`. (C macros are available in C++ as well, but are not used much because of the availability of the inline facility.) In such a case, the body of the macro with the required parameter substitution replaces the macro call before compilation. The preprocessor does this replacement. Thus, function loading and unloading (i.e., context switching) overhead is removed. Macros, though, have their own problems. Many parentheses are needed and no type checking is possible. Moreover, as they have two phases, namely, pasting and executing, they may evaluate some expressions twice, that is, in both the phases. Functions are very flexible and more readable, but have the drawback of the overhead of context switching time. Hence, inline functions are devised to provide the flexibility of normal functions and the efficiency of macros.

Consider the following code containing a call to `PrintDetails()`, which has been discussed in Section 3.1 of Chapter 3. It should be remembered that a function defined inside a class is treated by the compiler as inline in most cases. Thus, `PrintDetails()` in the following example is an inline function.

```
void main()
{
    student Student1;
    Student1.RollNumber = 1;
    Student1.Name = "Robin Singh";
    Student1.Address = "New Delhi";
    Student1.PrintDetails();
}
```

The compiler generates the code conceptually similar to the following:

```
void main()
{
    student Student1;
    Student1.RollNumber = 1;
    Student1.Name = "Robin Singh";
    Student1.Address = "New Delhi";

    /* The following three statements are replacements for Student1.PrintDetails()
    because PrintDetails() is treated as an inline function */

    cout << "Roll number is " << Student1.RollNumber << "\n";
    cout << "Name is " << Student1.Name << "\n";
    cout << "Address is " << Student1.Address << "\n";
}
```

If `PrintDetails()` is defined outside the class `student`, it is treated as a normal function and the generated code is conceptually similar to the following.

```
void main()
{
    student Student1;
    Student1.RollNumber = 1;
    Student1.Name = "Robin Singh";
    Student1.Address = "New Delhi";
    <Address of PrintDetails() with appropriate arguments>
}
```

When a function defined outside the class, including a non-member function, is preceded by the word `inline`, it is considered to be inline by the compiler.

Let us consider the inline and non-inline cases separately.

Inline function case   The function body replaces the function call statement wherever it appears in the program body. This behaviour is very similar to macros. At the time of execution, the control is transferred to the line after the function is loaded at compile time. It does not require a function call at the execution time. Thus, this solution is more efficient at execution time, as it does not involve context switching, and is important for small functions where context switching time is significant.

Non-inline function case   The address of the function replaces the function call in this case. The non-inline function is better with increase in the size of the compiled program. If a large function is copied at every place it is called, it will increase the code size of the calling function. It is better to have only the address of the function stored at the place of call in such cases. Moreover, for a large function, context switching time is insignificant; they are better as normal functions.

It is also possible to have a function defined outside the class as inline. The only requirement is to precede the function name with the keyword `inline` at the time of definition. This keyword can also precede non-member functions. As mentioned earlier, non-member functions are not associated with any class. We will be looking at an example of a non-member function in Section 4.10.

Note   When a function with no argument is encountered, it should not be assumed that the argument list is null; pointer to Student1 is passed as the only argument in this case. It is an implicit argument called `this` pointer.

Consider Program 4.1 to understand inline functions better.

PROGRAM 4.1   Defining and using inline functions

```cpp
// InlineExample.cpp
#include <iostream>
#include <string>
using namespace std;

class student
{
public:
    int RollNumber;
    string Name;
    string Address;
    void PrintDetails();
};

inline void student::PrintDetails()

/* If we omit the word inline here, the function will be treated as a normal function */

{
    cout << "Roll number is " << RollNumber << "\n";
    cout << "Name is " << Name << "\n";
    cout << "Address is " << Address << "\n";
}
void main()
{
```

```
    student Student1;
    Student1.RollNumber = 1;
    Student1.Name = "Robin Singh";
    Student1.Address = "New Delhi";
    Student1.PrintDetails();
}
```

How the Program Works

Observe how the keyword `inline` is added at the beginning of the function definition to inform the compiler. It is important to note that an inline function must be defined *before* its first use because the code in the function body must be known before making a function call. Only then can it replace the function call statements with the code of the function body. This is different from the other functions, which can be defined after their call. Only the function prototype should precede the call.

> **Note**   A normal function's body may be defined after the call, as only its address is to be replaced with the call. However, an inline function must be defined completely before its call, as the entire body is needed to be replaced with the call.

We have discussed the overhead of context switching for small functions and then having inline functions as a solution. What if the function is large and is defined inside the class? It may add to the program size to a large extent. The best way to solve this problem is to define only small functions inside the class and bigger ones outside. In any case, C++ compilers consider inline as a mere *request*.

There are some obvious cases when it not possible to make functions inline. If the function is found to be too large or too complicated, the inline request is ignored and the function will be treated as a normal function.

Consider a recursive function. A recursive function call cannot be replaced by the function body because the process will never end. Every function body copied will have a call to itself (this is why it is called recursive) where the same body will have to be copied again, which, in turn, will have a call to itself and so on.

Again, consider the case of a function having static variables. The static variables will retain their values between calls. If the compiler pastes copies of the function body where function calls are made, it will be impossible for the function to retain the values of static variables *between the calls*. Suppose we have pasted two copies of the same function at two different places. Assume that in the first copy the variable `StaticVar` is initialized with 10, and it has the value 20 when the copy is executed. How does the second pasted copy of the same function know that the output value of a variable of the earlier copy is 20 and that it should start with 20 rather than 10? This is at the time of compilation. What would happen at execution time? As this is not possible to predict, C++ does not allow inline functions with static variables.

So, it cannot be assumed that the compiler shall necessarily comply with the request for inline when asked for. How then can we know whether the compiler has treated our function as inline or not? A simple way to find that out is to make increasingly more calls to that function in different versions of the same program

Recursive functions and those functions that use static variables are not treated as inline even when they are defined inside the class or preceded by the word `inline`.

If a program's size increases with increasing number of calls to a specific function, it means that the compiler has treated that function as inline.

and look at the increment in the size of the compiled program. If the size grows linearly with the number of function calls made, the compiler has treated it as inline.

4.5 DEFAULT ARGUMENTS

Suppose we want to add a function to our `student` class, which takes the total marks and passing marks and tells us whether a student has passed or not. Let us assume that a student has to score at least 50 marks to pass. Is there a way in C++ to consider the passing marks value as 50 even if it is not provided? In other words, can we tell the C++ compiler to call the function with passing marks (set at 50) as a default argument? It is possible, using the feature known as *default argument*, which is explained in Program 4.2. Let us take a closer look at the function prototype and the way it is invoked in the `main()` function.

> A default argument is considered when the function is called without providing that argument.

PROGRAM 4.2 Default argument example

```cpp
// DefaultArgumentExample.cpp
#include <iostream>
using namespace std;

void add(int NumberOne = 100, int NumberTwo = 200)
{
    cout << "Sum is " << NumberOne + NumberTwo << endl;
}

void main()
{
    int Int1 = 5, Int2 = 7;
    add();
    add(Int1);
    add(Int1, Int2);
    /* If we want to provide only the second argument, it will not work */

    // The following will not work as expected
    add(Int2);
    getchar();
}
```

```
Output
Sum is 300
Sum is 205
Sum is 12
Sum is 207
```

How the Program Works

Program 4.2 shows how default arguments work. Look at the three different calls to the `add()` function. When both the arguments are passed as in the case of the following statement, the output is similar to a function with normal arguments.

```cpp
add(Int1, Int2);
```

It is interesting to observe what happens when the `add()` function is called with no arguments or with one argument as in the following two cases:

```cpp
add();
```

```
add(Int1);
```

In the first case, when we have no argument passed to the function, it is actually called with arguments 100 and 200, respectively, as they are defined as default arguments in the function header. Thus, the number 300 is the output. In the second case, we have provided only one argument. This is considered as the first argument (obviously) and the second argument, which is not explicitly provided by the caller, is taken from default; thus, 5 is added to 200 and we get 205 as the output. Interestingly, if the user's intention is to provide only the second argument and take the first argument as default and if the function is called as follows, it will not give the expected answer.

```
add(Int2);
```

The output is 207, which means that Int2 is considered as the first argument and the second argument was taken by default.

How will the C++ compiler know that Int2 is expected to be the second argument? Is it because it contains 2 in it? What if the arguments are Balance and Interest, which is more likely in a real-world program? There is no way for providing this information to the compiler. So, the first argument is assumed to be the default.

Program 3.9 of Chapter 3 has been modified in Program 4.3. The function CheckPass() is now added to the program. The function is simple enough to understand. It has only one line in the body and returns a bool value, true for passing and false for failing. The value returned depends on the student's marks and the value of the passing marks.

The function PrintDetails() is also changed such that it now also displays whether the student has passed or not, after calling the CheckPass() function. PrintDetails() is called with more than one type of passing marks value to show how a function with default arguments can be called.

PROGRAM 4.3   Default arguments

```cpp
// DefaultArgument.cpp
#include <iostream>
#include <string>
using namespace std;

bool CheckPass(int TotalMarks, int PassingMarks = 50);
// Default value is specified here for an argument

class student
{
public:
    int RollNumber;
    string Name;
    string Address;
    int TotalMarks;

    void SetDetails(int Roll, string StudentName, string StudentAddress, int StudentMarks)
    {
        RollNumber = Roll;
        Name = StudentName;
        Address = StudentAddress;
        TotalMarks = StudentMarks;
    }

    void PrintDetails()
```

```
        {
            cout << "Roll number is " << RollNumber << "\n";
            cout << "Name is " << Name << "\n";
            cout << "Address is " << Address <<  "\n";

            if(CheckPass(TotalMarks))
            // It takes passing marks as 50 here
                cout << "Congratulations! You have passed (passing marks 50)\n";
            if(CheckPass(TotalMarks,40))
                cout << "Congratulations! You have passed (passing marks 40)\n";
            if(CheckPass(TotalMarks, 35))
                cout << "Congratulations! You have passed (passing marks 35)\n";
            else
                cout << "Sorry! Better luck next time\n";
        }
};

bool CheckPass(int TotalMarks, int PassingMarks)
/* Notice the default value for an argument is not repeated here,
it is an error if it is done that way */

{
    return(TotalMarks > PassingMarks);
}

void main()
{
    student ArrayOfStudents[3];
    ArrayOfStudents[0].SetDetails(1, "Umesh Yadav", "New Delhi", 75);
    ArrayOfStudents[0].PrintDetails();
    ArrayOfStudents[1].SetDetails(2, "Varon Aaron", "Jharkhand", 87);
    ArrayOfStudents[1].PrintDetails();
    ArrayOfStudents[2].SetDetails(3, "Vinay Kumar", "Tamil Nadu", 37);
    ArrayOfStudents[2].PrintDetails();
}
```

How the Program Works

Look at the prototype of the CheckPass() function.

```
bool CheckPass(int TotalMarks, int PassingMarks = 50);
```

Here, PassingMarks is a default argument with the default value set as 50. This means that if the function CheckPass() is called with only one argument, the second argument's default value should be taken as 50. The function can be called using CheckPass(72) or CheckPass(30) where the passing marks will be considered to be 50, that is, the second argument is assumed to be 50 *by default*. Thus, the call to CheckPass(72) is equivalent to calling CheckPass(72, 50). It should be noted that the function can also be called using CheckPass(40, 35) where the passing marks are explicitly specified as 35.

In this example, the default arguments are specified in the prototype. If the function is defined before it is used, the prototype can be omitted. In such cases, the function itself will have the default argument specified. If the default arguments are already specified in the prototype, it cannot be redefined in the function header. So, if the function CheckPass() is defined before its call, it will have the following header:

```
bool CheckPass(int TotalMarks, int PassingMarks = 50)
```

instead of

```
bool CheckPass(int TotalMarks, int PassingMarks)
```

and there will be no prototype then.

It is possible to have more than one default argument with more than one normal argument. The rule to pass those arguments is very simple. All the normal arguments must be passed before the default arguments in the argument list.

The CheckPass() function prototype can be rewritten as follows (assuming the code is changed to accommodate usage of other parameters):

```
CheckPass(int Sub1Marks, int Sub2Marks, int PassingMarks = 50)
CheckPass(int Sub1Marks, int Sub2Marks, int PassingMarks1 = 50,
int PassingMarks2 = 35);

CheckPass(int Sub1Marks, int PassingMarks1 = 50, int Sub2Marks,
int PassingMarks2 = 35);

/* This statement is wrong because PassingMarks1 is a default argument written before
Sub2Marks, which is not a default argument. */
```

4.5.1 Using Static Variable as Default Argument to a Function

Functions with default arguments are very handy if, for most of the cases, the value of the argument remains the same. An interesting thing to note here is that a static variable can also be used as a default argument value. So it is possible to write

```
Account(AccountNumber = NextNumber)
```

where NextNumber is a static variable and is incremented every time a new Account object is created. This is an example which shows how an important functionality can be added to a program. As soon as a new account is created, it will get a unique account number automatically. This can be illustrated with a simple example shown in the following program. The getNext() function automatically receives the next immediate number. It can be observed that the static integer value Next is incremented and returned from the function.

This simple solution is possible only in cases where the next number series starts from zero and will not work if the getNext() series is supposed to start from some other number. Such a program will need some changes.

```
#include <iostream>
using namespace std;
static int Next;
int getNext(int NextNumber = Next)
{
    Next++;
    return NextNumber;
}
int main()
{
```

```
   cout << getNext() << endl;
   cout << getNext() << endl;
   cout << getNext() << endl;
   getchar();
}
```

Output

```
0
1
2
```

Readers are encouraged to reason out the following questions:

1. Why should all normal arguments precede all default arguments?
2. How can the compiler determine which argument corresponds to which one?
3. How can a complier know for sure that a particular default argument is passed explicitly?

4.5.2 Functions with Objects as Parameters

Functions in C++ can have any valid data type as an argument or a return type similar to a C function. As an obvious consequence of the availability of objects in C++, functions in C++ can pass as well as return objects. Consider the following program.

Passing an object The function can be passed objects similar to other variables. The following program uses a non-member function PrintValues(), which takes a complex object as an argument and prints it.

```
// ReturnComplexObject.cpp
#include <iostream>

using namespace std;

class Complex
{
public:
   double real;
   double imag;

   void SetValues(int TempReal, int TempImag)
   {
      real = TempReal;
      imag = TempImag;
   }
};

void PrintValues(Complex ComplexNumber)
{
   cout << "(" << ComplexNumber.real << "," << ComplexNumber.imag << ")";
}

int main()
{
```

```
            Complex C1;
            C1.SetValues(10, 30);
            Complex C2;
            C2.SetValues(13, 25);

            PrintValues(C1);
            PrintValues(C2);
            getchar();
            return 0;
        }
```

Output

```
(10, 30)(13, 25)
```

Program 4.4 has a class Time, representing time, which has three fields, namely, Hours, Minutes, and Seconds to represent hour, minute, and second values. The program includes a function called Difference(), which calculates the difference between two times passed to it. Difference() takes two Time objects as input and the difference is returned again in terms of Time object. Here, Difference() is a non-member function.

PROGRAM 4.4   Passing objects to functions

```
// ObjectPassing.cpp
#include <iostream>
using namespace std;

class Time
{
public:
    int Hours;
    int Minutes;
    int Seconds;

    void ShowTime()
    {
        cout << "Time is " << Hours << "hours: " << Minutes << "minutes: and " << seconds <<
        " Seconds \n";
    }

    void SetTime(int TempHours, int TempMinutes, int TempSeconds)
    {
        Hours = TempHours;
        Minutes = TempMinutes;
        Seconds = TempSeconds;
    }
};

void main()
{
    Time Difference(Time, Time);
    // Prototype for our function

    Time Time1, Time2;
    Time1.SetTime(12, 15, 15);
    cout << "The first value \n";
    Time1.ShowTime();
    Time2.SetTime(10, 30, 30);
    cout << "The second value \n";
```

```
    Time2.ShowTime();

    Time Time3;
    Time3 = Difference(Time1, Time2);
    /* Call to the function that accepts and returns the object */

    cout << "And the difference is \n";
    Time3.ShowTime();
}

/* Definition of the function that accepts and returns the object */
Time Difference(Time T1, Time T2)
{
    Time DifferenceTime;
    DifferenceTime.Seconds = T1.Seconds - T2.Seconds;
    if(DifferenceTime.Seconds < 0)
    {
        DifferenceTime.Seconds += 60;
        T1.Minutes--;    // Borrowing from minutes
        if(T1. Minutes < 0)
        {
            T1.Minutes = 59;
            T1.Hours--; // Borrowing from hours
        }
    }

    DifferenceTime.Minutes = T1.Minutes - T2.Minutes;
    if(DifferenceTime.Minutes < 0)
    {
        DifferenceTime.Minutes += 60;
        T1.Hours--; // borrowing from hours
    }

    DifferenceTime.Hours = T1.Hours - T2.Hours;
    if(DifferenceTime.Hours < 0)
    {
        DifferenceTime.Hours = 0;
        DifferenceTime.Minutes = 0;
        DifferenceTime.Seconds = 0;
        // To indicate erroneous input
    }
    return DifferenceTime;
}
```

Output
```
The first value
Time is 12 hours: 15 minutes: and 15 seconds
The second value
Time is 10 hours: 30 minutes: and 30 seconds
And the difference is
Time is 1 hours: 44 minutes: and 45 seconds
```

How the Program Works

See how the function Difference() is used. Two arguments are passed to it, both of type Time. It should be observed that there is no difference in the syntax while passing objects or any other data type to the function. When the function call is made, the actual arguments (objects in this case) are copied to the dummy arguments of the function. By default, an exact copy is made from the actual argument objects to the dummy argument objects in this case. This

Both member and non-member functions can receive as well as return objects. If the values that the function manipulates are defined as `private`, a non-member function will not be able to use them.

means that `Time1` and `Time2` are copied to `T1` and `T2`, respectively. It is possible to change this default element-by-element copy using *copy constructors*, which will be discussed in Chapter 5.

It should be noted that the return type of the `Difference()` function is also of type `Time`. The program has an assumption to simplify the function logic. The first argument must be a time later than the second argument. If not, all zeroes will be returned as the difference. It is possible to write a function that will change the order of the arguments and retry, but it will add to the complexity of the logic, which is not needed now. It is being given as an exercise to the readers.

It should also be noted that the function `Difference()` is not a member function of any class (i.e., it is a non-member function). `Difference()` can use `Hours`, `Minutes` and `Seconds` because they were declared as `public`. If they were declared as `private`, it will not be possible for `Difference()` to access them unless it is defined as a `friend`, which is discussed in Section 4.11.

Observe the statement `Time3 = Difference(Time1, Time2)`. `Difference()` is defined as returning an object of type `Time`. The compiler creates the object, which is returned and assigned to `Time3` when there is a difference. The compiler also destroys it when the assignment statement is over. This creation and deletion of temporary objects is explained in Exhibit 4.1.

Exhibit 4.1 Temporary object creation and destruction

The compiler creates and destroys the objects at run-time. Technically, the compiler creates the code for doing this at compile time. It is similar to defining objects and also defining their constructors and destructors.

In Program 4.4, the temporary object is defined prior to the call to the function and its destructor is called after the assignment statement. So, the compiler is not present at run-time and the code created by the compiler works on its own. Thus, the statements for creating and destroying temporary objects are inserted by the compiler when the program is compiled and they generate and destroy such objects and work as a compiler at run-time.

In C++11, there is no need to destruct the object at run-time. An object that is dangling at run-time can be reclaimed by a garbage collector. Until the release of C++11, garbage collector was available only in Java.

4.5.3 NRV Optimization

Observe the following three code segments. Let us find the minute difference that separates them and makes each one of them unique.

```
Complex Maximum(const Complex c1, const Complex c2)
{
    if(c1.real() > c2.size())
        return c1;
    else
        return c2;
}

Complex Maximum(const Complex &c1, const Complex &c2)
{
```

When a code that returns an object is converted by the C++ compiler to return a reference to that object, thus reducing the overhead of constructing and passing the object itself, it is known as NRV optimization.

```
        if(c1.real() > c2.real())
            return c1;
        else
            return c2;
}

Complex & Maximum(const Complex &c1, const Complex &c2)
{
        if(c1.real() > c2.real())
            return c1;
        else
            return c2;
}
```

The first code uses no references, the second one passes references to objects rather than objects themselves, and the third one returns a reference as well. What is the advantage of the third code when compared with the other two? Passing and returning only references reduces the overhead. When a user writes a code of the second type and it is converted into the third type by the C++ compiler, it is known as name return value (NRV) optimization.

In Program 4.4, the temporary object creation and destruction can be omitted if `Difference()` is passed the reference of `Time3` additionally as third argument and, instead of assigning value to a local variable (i.e., the `DifferenceTime`), the value is directly given to the reference. The compiler can and does convert such codes to have these two optimizations, which is known as NRV optimization. It should be noted that the earlier discussion regarding construction and destruction of temporary objects may not hold true if a compiler applies NRV.

Let us find out what happens when the following statement is executed (assuming no NRV):

```
Time3 = Difference(Time1, Time2);
```

The compiler-generated code does the following operations:

1. Construct temporary variable `Temp` may be by using `Temp = new Time(U);`
2. Assign to `Temp` the value returned by

```
    Difference(Time1, Time2, &Temp);
    // The function code returns the returning value in Temp
```

3. `Time 3 = Temp;`
4. `delete Temp;`

The right-hand side (RHS) of the assignment statement is evaluated first, which in this case requires a function call to be made. A temporary object is created as a side effect of calling and returning the function. The value returned from the function (`Temp` in our example) is passed to the left-hand side (LHS) after the control is returned from the function. Then, `Temp` is assigned to `Time3`. Both the objects (`Temp` and `Time3`) are of the same type, so the assignment will make a member-wise copy. Finally, `Time3` will have the value of `Temp`. At that point of time, the compiler-generated destructor destroys the object returned from the function (i.e., `Temp`). (This is why it is called a temporary object.) Assume that `Difference()` is called without assigning its return value to any object, that is,

```
Difference(Time1, Time2);
```

Then, the object returned from the function is destroyed and is no longer available. It is analogous to calling a C function without using the return type.

Now, consider the following statement:

```
Time3 = Difference(Time1, Time2);
```

The process for this statement can be summarized as follows:

1. The actual arguments are copied to dummy arguments, that is, `Time1` is copied to T1 and `Time2` is copied to `T2`.
2. The function call is made.
3. The function returns the result in a temporary object (`Temp` in our case), defined by compiler at the time of compilation.
4. Temporary object is assigned to `Time3` and is then immediately destroyed by the calling destructor.

It is possible to change the default member-wise copy behaviour while copying from the function to the statement from where the function is called. This can be done using copy constructors, which will be discussed in detail in Chapter 5.

> **Note** Many programmers have a habit of writing functions and ignoring their return values. In C, the `printf()` statement returns the number of characters printed, whereas it is almost always ignored in C++. Statements such as `NoOfCharsWritten = printf("…");` can hardly be found in C++.

Exhibit 4.2 describes a situation where there are arguments with different formats.

Exhibit 4.2   Arguments with different formats

What happens when two arguments passed are of the type `Time` but in different formats? For example, let us suppose that the first time format contains two data fields, hours and minutes, using the 12-hour format and the second time format contains a numeric value indicating seconds elapsed until midnight. What if the result is to be obtained in either first format or second format?

In such a case, both the types will have to be represented by different objects and we need to provide a means of conversion between them.

4.6 CALL BY REFERENCE

The methods to call using a reference variable and to return a reference variable have already been discussed in Chapter 2. We can actually pass as well as return a reference to an object. Program 4.5 illustrates passing object references using the Time class, in which `Time` objects are added now. The importance of returning the reference and the method to do it are described in Program 4.6 in Section 4.7.

PROGRAM 4.5   Passing and returning object references

```
// ObjRefPass2.cpp
#include <iostream>
using namespace std;

class Time
{
```

```
public:
    int Hours;
    int Minutes;
    int Seconds;
    void ShowTime()
    {
        cout << "Time is " << Hours << "hours  : " << Minutes << "minutes : and " << Seconds
        << "seconds \n";
    }

    void SetTime(int TempHours, int TempMinutes, int TempSeconds)
    {
        Hours = TempHours;
        Minutes = TempMinutes;
        Seconds = TempSeconds;
    }
};

void main()
{
    Time AddTimes(Time &, Time &);
    /* Look at this prototype. It has references to two time objects as arguments, though it
    returns a normal object, not a reference */

    Time Time1, Time2;
    Time1.SetTime(12, 15, 15);
    cout << "The first value \n";
    Time1.ShowTime();

    Time2.SetTime(10, 30, 30);
    cout << "The second value \n";
    Time2.ShowTime();

    Time Time3;
    cout << "Now let us add times Time1 and Time2 \n ";

    Time Time4;
    Time3 = AddTimes(Time1, Time2);
    Time3.ShowTime();
    Time4 = AddTimes(Time2, Time3);
    Time4.ShowTime();
    Time4 = AddTimes(Time4, Time1);
    Time4.ShowTime();
    cout << "Now let us add times Time1, Time2, and Time3 as well\n ";
    Time4 = AddTimes(AddTimes(Time2, Time3), Time1);
    Time4.ShowTime();
}

Time AddTimes(Time & Time1, Time & Time2)
{
    Time AddTime;
    AddTime.Seconds = Time1.Seconds + Time2.Seconds;
    AddTime.Minutes = AddTime.Seconds / 60;
    AddTime.Seconds = AddTime.Seconds % 60;
    AddTime.Minutes += Time1.Minutes + Time2.Minutes;
    AddTime.Hours = AddTime.Minutes / 60;
    AddTime.Minutes = AddTime.Minutes % 60;
    AddTime.Hours += Time1.Hours + Time2.Hours;
    return AddTime;
}
```

```
Output
The first value
Time is 12 hours : 15 minutes : and 15 seconds

The second value
Time is 10 hours : 30 minutes : and 30 seconds
Now let us add times Time1 and Time2
Time is 22 hours : 45 minutes : and 45 seconds
Time is 33 hours : 16 minutes : and 15 seconds
Time is 45 hours : 31 minutes : and 30 seconds

Now let us add times Time1, Time2, and Time3 as well
Time is 45 hours : 31 minutes : and 30 seconds
```

How the Program Works

This program has a new `AddTimes()` function for adding two times in the `Time` class. The function definition `Time AddTimes(Time &, Time &);` looks different from the `Difference()` function described earlier. We still have `Time` as a return type. The arguments are changed from `Time` to `Time &`. However, this does not make much difference in the function body. At the time of actual execution, the reference to the argument is passed and not its value. Thus, `AddTimes()` works with `main()` variables and manipulates them directly. One interesting statement is `Time4 = AddTimes(AddTimes(Time2, Time3), Time1)`, which shows how a function call can use itself in the argument.

We have seen that returning a reference enables us to use the function call on the LHS of an assignment statement. If the function call is to be used on the LHS of an assignment statement, a reference needs to be returned. Section 4.7 discusses the situations where the function call needs to be on the LHS, using a classic singly linked list example. The readers are advised to brush up their dynamic memory management and linked list management skills before going through Section 4.7.

4.7 RETURNING A REFERENCE

Program 4.6 shows a function that returns the object. It is used in the LHS of an assignment statement.

PROGRAM 4.6 Function used as LHS

```cpp
// FunctionInLHS.cpp
#include <iostream>
using namespace std;

class Complex
{
public:
    double real;
    double imag;

    void SetValues(int TempReal, int TempImag)
    {
        real = TempReal;
        imag = TempImag;
    }
};
```

```
Complex & Maximum(Complex & Complex1, Complex & Complex2)
{
    if(Complex1.real > Complex2.real)
        return Complex1;
    else
        return Complex2;
}
void PrintValues(Complex ComplexNumber)
{
    cout << "(" << ComplexNumber.real << "," << ComplexNumber.imag <<")";
}

int main()
{
    Complex C1;
    C1.SetValues(10, 30);
    Complex C2;
    C2.SetValues(13, 25);

    PrintValues(C1);
    PrintValues(C2);

    Complex C3 = Maximum(C1, C2);
    PrintValues(C3);

    Maximum(C1, C2) = C3;

    PrintValues(C1);
    PrintValues(C2);

    getchar();
    return 0;
}
```

Output

(10, 30)(13, 25)(13, 25)(10, 30)(13, 25)

How the Program Works

The statement of interest in this program is

```
Maximum(C1, C2) = C3;
```

Here, the maximum of C1 and C2 is assigned the value of C3. It is possible to have such a statement only if the function under consideration returns a reference to a variable of a calling function. Why this happens and where this can be used is explained in Section 4.8 with the help of an example.

Program 4.7 has a linked list of students. A student is represented by an object of class StudentNode. The linked list is represented by an object of class StudentList. Insertion of a new StudentNode is done at the end of the linked list with the help of the function InsertList(). The function InitializeList() is used for making the first pointer to point to null. This is an important function because when a node is inserted in the linked list, a null first pointer indicates empty linked list. Thus, we can make the first pointer to point to that node. In other cases (when the first pointer is not null), the list contains some elements, and hence, we have to traverse the list and reach the end to add that node.

Suppose we want to replace a node of the linked list with an external node of the same type. Here, the node is generated by reading the values from the keyboard but the node may also come from some other program or by some communication channel. It is imperative that the order of the nodes in the list does not change. This operation is analogous to array indexing. Consider the statement

```
a[i] = NewValue;
```

The old value at the ith location in the array changes to NewValue. Though the value changes, the index does not change. A similar process is required in the linked list. The content of the node must be changed but not the position. Therefore, the programmer must ensure that when the node values are copied, the next pointer is found and copied as well. Thus, a statement of the kind

```
"Node at the ith position = NewValue"
```

should change the value of that node to NewValue without changing the position of that node. The way to do this is shown in the following example.

In Program 4.7, class StudentNode uses friend non-member function GenerateStudent Node() and also friend class StudentList. Thus, GenerateStudentNode() and StudentList can access the private members of StudentNode class. Friend functions are discussed in detail in Section 4.11.

PROGRAM 4.7   Returning a reference to an object

```cpp
// ObjRefReturn.cpp
#include <iostream>
#include <string>
using namespace std;

// The following class describes the node in the linked list
class StudentNode
{
    string Name;
    StudentNode *NextStud;
public:
    int RollNo;

    // Inserting roll no., name and setting NextStud value to null
    void SetStud(int TempRollNo, string TempName)
    {
        RollNo = TempRollNo;
        Name = TempName;
        NextStud = '\0';
    }

    void WriteStud()
    {
        cout << "Roll number is " << RollNo << "and the name is " << Name << endl;
    }

    StudentNode * GetNextPtr()
    // Get the next pointer pointing to the next item in the list
    {
        return NextStud;
    }

    void SetNextPtr(StudentNode * TempPointer)
    // Make the next pointer point to the value passed
```

```
        {
            NextStud = TempPointer;
        }

        // Given roll number and name, create an object of student node

        friend StudentNode GenerateStudentNode(int TempRollNo, string TempName);

        /* StudentNode class and all the members of this class are friends of this function.
        Hence, it can access the private members of StudentNode class */

        friend class StudentList;
        /* So all members of StudentList class can refer to our private members */
};
StudentNode GenerateStudentNode(int TempRollNo, string TempName)
{
    StudentNode TempStudNode;
    TempStudNode.RollNo = TempRollNo;
    TempStudNode.Name = TempName;
    return TempStudNode;
};

class StudentList
{
    StudentNode *First;
public:
    void InitializeList()
    {
        First = '\0';
    }

    /* Inserting a student node at the end of a linked list after allocating memory */
    void InsertList(int TempRollNo, string TempName)
    {
        StudentNode *NewStudent = new StudentNode;
        NewStudent -> SetStud(TempRollNo, TempName);
        if(!First)
            First = NewStudent;
            /* If there is no other element, that is, first is null; then, this is the first
            element */
        else
        {
            StudentNode *TempPtr = First;

            while(TempPtr -> NextStud)
                TempPtr = TempPtr->NextStud;
                // Reached the end of the linked list

                TempPtr -> NextStud = NewStudent;
                // Adding an element there
        }
    }

    void DisplayList()
    {
        StudentNode *TempPtr = First;
        while(TempPtr)
        {
            TempPtr -> WriteStud();
```

```
                TempPtr = TempPtr->NextStud;
        }
    }

    /* Finding out the student object containing the required name and return reference to
    that object */
    StudentNode & GetStudent(string TempName)
    {
        StudentNode * TempPtr = First;
        while(TempPtr -> Name != TempName)
        {
            TempPtr = TempPtr -> NextStud;
            if(!TempPtr)
            {
                    cout <<  "Error";
            exit(1);
            }
        }
        return *TempPtr;
    }
};
int main()
{
    StudentList StudList;
    StudList.InsertList(1, "Robin");
    StudList.InsertList(2, "Leena");
    StudList.InsertList(3, "Bob");
    StudList.InsertList(4, "Sam");

    StudList.DisplayList();

    cout << "Insert the name of student you want to change:";
    string OriginalName, NewName;
    cin >> OriginalName;
    cout << "\n Insert new name: ";
    cin >> NewName;
    cout << "\n Insert new roll no.: ";
    int NewRollNo;
    cin >> NewRollNo;

    // Generate a new node with new roll number and new name
    StudentNode NewNode = GenerateStudentNode(NewRollNo, NewName);

    /* Get the next pointer value of the old student node and then set it in the new node */
    NewNode.SetNextPtr(StudList.GetStudent(OriginalName).GetNextPtr());
    /* The following statement is not possible if GetStudent() does not return reference */

    StudList.GetStudent(OriginalName) = NewNode;
    // Replacing the old object with a new one

    StudList.DisplayList();
    return 0;
}
```
Output
```
Roll number is 1 and the name is Robin
Roll number is 2 and the name is Leena
Roll number is 3 and the name is Bob
Roll number is 4 and the name is Sam
Insert the name of student you want to change: Leena
```

```
Insert the new name: Veena

Insert new roll no.: 12
Roll number is 1 and the name is Robin
Roll number is 12 and the name is Veena
Roll number is 3 and the name is Bob
Roll number is 4 and the name is Sam
```

How the Program Works

Let us analyse the program and see what it does.

Classes used in the program   The program contains two classes StudentNode and StudList describing the student and the linked list of students. As mentioned earlier, the addition to the list is made at the end. Look at the definitions of both the classes. StudList has to be made a friend of the StudentNode class because it accesses the private variables of StudentNode class such as the roll number and name. There is an additional friend in this case, that is, the function that generates a node of type StudentNode given the values of roll number and name. Such functions that generate objects are very useful. We will see in Chapter 5 how constructors can do this job instead of a friend.

Functions used   The class StudentNode has four functions. SetStud() fills the value in data members. WriteStud() displays the data members. SetNextPtr() fills the value of the next pointer of the student node and GetNextPtr() gets its value. These functions are useful in preserving the earlier next position and setting it when other values are changed.

Processing   The class StudList is a collection class for StudentNode objects. The InsertList() function adds a student node at the end of the list. DisplayList() displays the contents of the list. InitializeList() is an important function and sets the first pointer to null. As mentioned earlier, the first pointer being null indicates an empty list. The function that is considered to be the most important in this discussion at the moment is GetStudent(), which returns reference to StudentNode object in the list.

Using a function as LHS   When a node needs to be replaced at the same position, it can be done using the following statement:

```
StudList.GetStudent(OriginalName) = NewNode;
```

It replaces the student object reference returned from the GetStudent() function with NewNode. The GetStudent() function returns the reference of the node containing the name as OriginalName; thus, assigning NewNode to it actually replaces that node with NewNode while preserving the position. So, there is no need to set the previous node's next pointer.

Next, the next pointer of the OldNode needs to be preserved. This can be done using GetNextPtr() form the old node and using SetNextPtr() in the NewNode with the same value.

Refer to the earlier statement that assigns a reference of a node to the new node. The reference must be used here because the function call is used in the LHS. Consider the following statement:

```
NewNode = StudList.GetStudent(OriginalName)
```

In this case, the node in the linked list is not updated while the NewNode is updated. In order to prevent this, the function call must be on the LHS and it must return a reference.

Reference to local variable not correct   It should be noted that whenever a reference is being returned, it is not the reference of a local variable. After we exit from the function, all the variables of the function are removed from the stack. If it is a reference (i.e., address; C++ object model implements references as pointers) of a local variable of the function, the address is no longer valid.

In Program 4.5, where a local object was passed, the result was explicitly copied in a main() function object, through the code

```
Time3 = AddTimes(Time1, Time2);
```

That is, the reference was not returned. So, this problem did not arise in that case.

There are two important differences between passing and returning objects and passing and returning references.

1. When the reference is passed to the function instead of an object, only the pointer to the object is passed to the function. It takes far lesser time than passing the whole object. This helps in increasing the efficiency.
2. When the reference is returned, it is possible to use the function as the LHS of an expression, as seen in Program 4.7. We will look at another example when we discuss the overloading operator in Chapter 6.

Function returning a reference used as LHS   What is the difference between returning a reference and returning an object that enables the former to be used on the LHS of an equation? Both cases return a temporary object and the object is destroyed after the assignment is completed. In the first case, where a reference is passed, the temporary object returned is a reference to a known variable, that is, a variable that is either implicitly or explicitly defined in the calling function (main() in our case). The variable here is defined implicitly by one more temporary main() student object generated by the call to GetStudent() function. In that case, assigning a value to the temporary variable actually assigns the value to the known variable to which it is a reference. The temporary object returned is an alias of a node of the linked list, known to us in the StudList class, which is defined in main(). In the case of returning a normal object, such an assignment is meaningless because the object to which the assignment is made is to be destroyed immediately. Hence, it is not allowed by the compiler.

4.8 PROTOTYPING AND OVERLOADING

Whenever a function is to be used, the user should specify how the function should be called. It is important to know the name of the function and the number and type of arguments to be passed in order to call a function. These details are specified by the function prototype. Function prototyping is a mechanism by which a compiler is informed of the number and type of arguments with which the function is likely to be called. Function overloading is a mechanism by which we can define functions with different types or numbers of arguments but retain the same name.

4.8.1 Prototyping

> A function prototype is the function header (excluding the body of a function) with or without the dummy arguments and with the data types of the arguments.

Function prototyping is also a part of ANSI C but is not kept mandatory to support older C programs, which do not require prototyping. In C++, prototyping is made mandatory. (It should be noted that prototyping was first introduced in C++ and then in ANSI C.) A C++ compiler will flag an error when a function call is made but the prototype is not yet defined.

The prototype is not required only in the cases where the function itself is defined before the call. Consider the example given in Section 4.8.2. Observe the prototype for the `Difference()` function. The program will not be compiled if that line is omitted. Such strict measures are required to provide more robust error checking by the compilers. If the prototype is provided, a compiler can easily check for the number of arguments and also their types. For instance, the `Difference()` function should take two `Time` objects. While making a call, if a single `Time` object or three `Time` objects are passed, it will lead to an error at the time of compilation. Moreover, if something other than `Time` object is passed, it will also be detected during compilation. For example, consider the following function prototype:

> A function prototype is useful in checking whether the function is passed the correct set of arguments.

```
MyFunction(int First, char Second)
```

This can also be written as `MyFunction(int, char)`. The important factor is only the datatype; `First` and `Second` are not important for the compiler at the moment.

> When a function is redefined with different sets of arguments, it is known as an overloaded function.

According to this prototype, every call to `MyFunction()` must have two arguments and they can be of types `int` and `char` and nothing else. Compilers can flag a warning if `MyFunction()` is passed one or three arguments or even when two arguments are passed and either the first argument is not `int` or the second is not `char`. This is of immense help when a user unknowingly makes the mistake of sending more number of arguments or a different type of argument.

This is the reason why prototypes were accepted in ANSI C. However, there is another important reason for having function prototypes in C++. They help in function overloading, which is explained in Section 4.8.2.

4.8.2 Function Overloading

In C, it is not possible to redefine a function with the same name. For example, it is not possible to have two `Add()` functions, one with integer arguments and the other with string arguments. However, this is possible in C++ provided both the functions have different sets of arguments. Consider defining a function `Add(int, int)`. If we now redefine `Add(float, float)` then it is known as overloadeded `Add()`. It is also possible to have `Add(int, int, int)` as a separate function. This process is known as function overloading. Let us look at Program 4.8 to understand this concept better.

 **PROGRAM 4.8**   Overloading functions

```
// FunOverLoad1.cpp
#include <iostream>
#include <string>
using namespace std;
```

```
void main()
{
    int Add(int, int);
    double Add(double, double);
    string Add(string, string);

    int IntVar1, IntVar2, IntSum;
    double DoubleVar1, DoubleVar2, DoubleSum;

    IntVar1 = 5;
    IntVar2 = 10;
    DoubleVar1 = 5.25;
    DoubleVar2 = 10.25;

    IntSum = Add(IntVar1, IntVar2);
    cout << IntSum << "\n";
    DoubleSum = Add(DoubleVar1, DoubleVar2);
    cout << DoubleSum << "\n";
    float FloatVar = 1.2;

    /* The following works because the C++ compiler can unambiguously
    convert from float to double */
    cout << Add(DoubleVar1, FloatVar);

    // cout << Add(DoubleVar1, IntVar1);
    /* This statement does not work because it makes the C++ compiler unsure of whether to
    use the int version or the double version of Add */
    string Name = "Robin";
    string Father = "Singh";
    string CompleteName;

    CompleteName = Add(Name,Father);
    cout << endl << CompleteName << endl;
}

int Add(int First, int Second)
{
    return(First + Second);
}
/* The following is an error in C, as we are redefining a function.
It is valid in C++, though */
double Add(double First, double Second)
{
    return(First + Second);
}
string Add(string First, string Second)
{
    return(First + Second);
}
```

How the Program Works

Let us now analyse the program component by component.

Defining overloaded functions   This is a very simple example (there is no class in the program) that shows function overloading. The Add() function is overloaded (defined more than once with int, double, and string arguments) here. The function is not really needed in the program as we could have used + to add two items directly. The purpose of the Add() function is to demonstrate something that is not available in C.

Using overloaded functions   It is possible to not only redefine a function but also call it whenever required, and let C++ pick up the right version for us. When `Add()` is called with two integer arguments, C++ calls `Add()` with integer arguments, and when it is called with two double arguments, C++ automatically calls `Add()` with double arguments. The same happens in the case of strings. It is not necessary to specify *which* `Add()` function to call, because C++ does it automatically by looking at the arguments. The compiler looks at the call, for example, `Add(IntVar1, IntVar2)`, first. It already knows that `IntVar1` and `IntVar2` are integer arguments and is also aware of an overloaded version of `Add()` with two integer arguments. Thus, it is able to judge that the overloaded version of `Add()` with two integer arguments is to be invoked at this place.

Promotions and conversions   C++ applies promotions and conversion similar to C. If a float argument is passed, C++ upgrades it to double and calls the `Add()` function with double arguments. This conversion is helpful because there is no need to define one more function if we need to pass float as an argument now.

Problems with overloading   However, overloading is troublesome at times. Consider the following line, which is commented:

```
// cout << Add(DoubleVar1, IntVar1);
```

This is a call with one double argument and one integer argument; such calls will confuse the C++ compiler, as it cannot decide whether to use the double version or the integer version of `Add()`. This situation is ambiguous. Here, the compiler will flag an error and the program will not be compiled. The solution here is to use casting as follows:

```
Add(DoubleVar1, (double)IntVar1)
```

Methods of Function Overloading
Function overloading is useful when a similar function is required to be called with either variable number of arguments or arguments of different types. It is also possible to use function overloading for both, that is, different types of arguments and different numbers of arguments together. In C, different functions need to be defined with different names, for example, `AddInt()`, `AddDouble()`, etc. In such cases, depending on the arguments, different functions need to be called and generalization is not possible.

Our discussion about difference in two overloaded functions involves only the argument number and type, but does not involve the return type because function calls do not specify the return type. Function calls can be made without using return value, such as `printf()`. A compiler cannot judge from the function call the function to be called if the return type alone is different. Thus, it is not possible to have two `Add()` functions with the same number and type of arguments, but different return types.

Function Overloading and Polymorphism
Polymorphism refers to the ability of the object to react differently to the same command in different contexts. In the context of function overloading, the meaning is one interface for multiple jobs depending on the messages (arguments) passed to the function. Function overloading helps to produce similar behaviour. For example, the same `Add()` function behaves differently when called with strings and with integers (from the user's perspective). In our program, this is implemented using multiple `Add()` functions. For the user, there is only one interface (`Add()` function), which is passed with different messages, that is, either string or integer, and it does different jobs. This type of polymorphism is known as *compile*

time polymorphism. It is also possible to have *run-time* polymorphism, which is achieved using *virtual functions* (discussed in Chapter 10).

Exhibit 4.3 gives a comparison of default argument and function overloading solutions.

Exhibit 4.3 Comparison between default argument and function overloading solutions

At times, a problem can be solved by using either default arguments or function overloading. Consider the following example:

```
bool CheckPassing(int TotalMarks, int PassingMarks = 50)
```

can also be written as two different functions

```
bool CheckPassing(int TotalMarks);
```

and

```
bool CheckPassing(int TotalMarks, int PassingMarks);
```

We can see that the function calls in both the cases (either using a default argument or an overloaded function) do not differ.

The default argument obviously is a simpler way than function overloading. There is no need to write two different versions of the function. However, there is one important difference; in case of default arguments, when the user does not specify the argument, default is *implicitly* passed, whereas in the case of function overloading, only explicitly specified arguments are passed.

4.9 PROGRAM READABILITY AND DEFAULT ARGUMENTS

Program readability can be impacted while using default arguments. When the function CheckPass() is called with one argument, the reader has no clue that there is a second argument automatically being passed. PassingMarks is logically understandable so it is acceptable in this circumstance. If instead of PassingMarks, a student's name is passed to CheckPass() and if CheckPass() sometimes (not always) performs some action on it, it is not apparent to the reader.

Suppose we need to find out a student's parents using his/her name from some database and mail them in case the student has failed. This is not a common case. By looking at the call to CheckPass(), the user will not be able to know what is happening. In such a case, it is better to use an overloaded function that passes the student's name explicitly. For checking whether the student has passed or not, passing marks is an obvious argument and a reasonable candidate for a default argument, whereas student name is not. When in need, the student's name should be passed explicitly using the overloaded version of the program.

> Default arguments are not visible at the function call; this sometimes hinders the readability of the program.

In most cases, such situations arise because of errors in the design. Such functions (reporting failure of students to their parents) should be called explicitly. Passing the name by default to a function that is supposed to check whether the student has passed or not is a wrong design.

4.10 MEMBER AND NON-MEMBER FUNCTIONS

We have already discussed a little about the differences between calling a member function and a non-member function. Let us look at an example to illustrate the difference in detail.

Program 4.9 contains two functions doing the same job of finding out the difference between the Time objects passed to them. One of them MemDiffTime() is a member function, while Difference() is a non-member function.

PROGRAM 4.9   Member and non-member functions

```cpp
// MemNonMem.cpp
#include <iostream>
using namespace std;

class Time
{
public:
    int Hours;
    int Minutes;
    int Seconds;

    void ShowTime()
    {
        cout << "Time is" << Hours << "hours :" << Minutes << "minutes : and" << Seconds <<
        "seconds \n";
    }

    void SetTime(int TempHours, int TempMinutes, int TempSeconds)
    {
        Hours = TempHours;
        Minutes = TempMinutes;
        Seconds = TempSeconds;
    }

    /* The following is a member function doing the same job as a non-member Difference()
    (standalone) function */

    void MemDiffTime(Time Time2)

    /* Only one argument Time2 is passed; this is treated as the second argument. The first
    is an implicit argument, pointer to the calling object (the 'this' pointer), that is,
    pointer to Time4 in our example */

    {
        Seconds = Seconds - Time2.Seconds;

        /* Seconds or hours can now be used without the object.member format, that is, in
        our case, Time4.Seconds */

        if(Seconds < 0)
        {
            Seconds += 60;
            Minutes--;
            if(Minutes < 0)
            {
                Minutes = 59;
                Hours--;
            }
        }

        Minutes = Minutes - Time2.Minutes;
        if(Minutes < 0)
        {
            Minutes += 60;
            Hours--;
        }
```

```
            Hours = Hours - Time2.Hours;
            if(Hours < 0)
            {
                Hours = 0;
                Minutes = 0;
                Seconds = 0;
                // To indicate erroneous input
            }
            /* There is no return statement. The object pointer is implicitly passed. It points
            to the changed object, so we do not need any return statement now */
        }
};
void main()
{
    Time Difference(Time, Time);
    /* Prototype for our non-member function */

    Time Time1, Time2;
    Time1.SetTime(12, 15, 15);
    cout << "The first value \n";
    Time1.ShowTime();
    Time2.SetTime(10, 30, 30);
    cout << "The second value \n";
    Time2.ShowTime();
    Time Time3;
    Time3 = Difference(Time1, Time2);
    cout << "The difference using a non-member function is  \n";
    Time3.ShowTime();
    Time Time4 = Time1;
    Time4.MemDiffTime(Time2);
    cout << "The difference using a member function is  \n";
    Time4.ShowTime();
}

Time Difference(Time T1, Time T2)
{
    Time DifferenceTime;
    DifferenceTime.Seconds = T1.Seconds - T2.Seconds;
    if(DifferenceTime.Seconds < 0)
    {
        DifferenceTime.Seconds += 60;
        T1.Minutes--;
        if(T1.Minutes < 0)
        {
            T1.Minutes = 59;
            T1.Hours--;
        }
    }

    DifferenceTime.Minutes = T1.Minutes - T2.Minutes;
    if(DifferenceTime.Minutes < 0)
    {
        DifferenceTime.Minutes += 60;
        T1.Hours--;
    }

    DifferenceTime.Hours = T1.Hours - T2.Hours;
    if(DifferenceTime.Hours < 0)
    {
```

```
        DifferenceTime.Hours = 0;
        DifferenceTime.Minutes = 0;
        DifferenceTime.Seconds = 0; // To indicate erroneous input
    }
    return DifferenceTime;
}
```

Output
The first value
Time is 12 hours : 15 minutes : and 15 seconds

The second value
Time is 10 hours : 30 minutes : and 30 seconds

The difference using a non-member function is
Time is 1 hours : 44 minutes: and 45 seconds

The difference using a member function is
Time is 1 Hours : 44 minutes: and 45 seconds

How the Program Works

Look at `MemDiffTime()` and `Difference()` functions and observe the difference between the two. Although they are both meant to do the same job, they differ at specific places. Let us look at each one of them in detail.

1. Only one argument needs to be passed in place of two arguments while using a member function. The first argument is implicitly passed. One cannot choose the first argument; it is always the pointer to the object that invoked the function. In the non-member case, `Difference(Time1, Time2)` or `Difference(Time2, Time1)` is possible. It is definitely not possible with `Time4.MemDiffTime(Time2)`, where the pointer to `Time4` will always be the first argument. In `Time2.MemDiffTime(Time4)`, the pointer to `Time2` will always be the first argument. We will revisit this issue again when we discuss operator overloading using friend member functions.

2. We use member variables without specifying their invoking object in the member functions, for example, instead of `T1.Seconds`, we just write `Seconds`. Here again, the invoking object is assumed and writing `Seconds` is similar to writing `this -> Seconds`.

3. Another difference relates to the access specifier of the member variable accessed. `Difference()` works because `Seconds`, `Minutes`, and `Hours` all are public variables. If they are private variables, only `MemDiffTime()` will work and `Difference()` will not work. If the `Difference()` function needs to work even when these variables are defined as private, then it should be made a friend of class `Time`. We will discuss friends in Section 4.11.

4. We do not need an explicit return statement while using a member function. The automatically passed `this` pointer (which points to the invoking object) also takes care of it. The `this` pointer will actually make the function operate on the actual object (because the pointer to it is passed) and we do not need any return. The non-member function works on a temporary copy and needs to return it.

4.10.1 Deciding to Make a Function a Member or a Non-member

This is a design-related issue. Should we define standalone or member functions in cases such as Program 4.9? The thumb rule is to use member functions if it is naturally the member. Why?

From the class design point of view, there are three ways to define a function, namely, non-member non-friend, non-member friend, and member. (It is also possible to define a member function of some other class as friend but it is equivalent to a non-member friend in our case.) For non-member functions, we need to define our data members as public, which otherwise need only private access. Here, the object-oriented (OO) philosophy is not followed and thus non-member functions are least expected to be present in the program. If we use friend functions and keep our variables as private, it is comparatively better, but is still a violation of the OO philosophy (class members are not properly hidden). If we keep the functions as member functions, we are following the OO programming methodology perfectly, which will be a better choice.

> **Note** It requires serious introspection to decide whether the function is to be declared as a member or not. A good design usually requires as few members as possible. The best solution has most of the functions as non-member non-friends and still does the same job. This is called *thin class strategy*. Having thin class reduces class maintenance overhead.

One must test to see whether it is possible to write a non-member non-friend function without needing the conversion of some of the variables to public. This would be the best option. It has two distinct advantages:

1. The class is not cluttered with unnecessary member functions and remains manageable.
2. The function code is not affected if private variables (the implementation of the class) change, as the functions are not using any private variables.

This discussion is for functions that describe the operations of the object. Functions that do not describe the operations of the object and have little relationship with the object in consideration are not supposed to be defined as members. If we can define a function as a non-member non-friend, it should not be defined otherwise.

4.11 FRIEND FUNCTIONS

Look at the following program. A non-member function display() needs access to the data members width and heightof the rectangle class. It is made possible by making the display() function as a friend to rectangle class.

```cpp
// FriendExample.cpp
#include <iostream>
using namespace std;

class Rectangle
{
    int width, height;

public:
    void SetData(int w, int h)
    {
        width = w;
        height = h;
    }
    friend void display(Rectangle &);
};
```

```
void display(Rectangle &r)
{
    cout << "Width is " << r.width << endl << "Height is " << r.height << endl;
}

int main()
{
    Rectangle rect;
    rect.SetData(5, 10);
    display(rect);
    getchar();
    return 0;
}
```

Output

```
Width is 5
Height is 10
```

Friend functions are special. The class grants these functions a special privilege to access its private variables. This privilege must be given by the class itself. It is given by writing the specific function's prototype in the class definition, which should be preceded by the word friend. For example,

```
friend SomeFunction(list of arguments)
```

In Program 4.10, the variables accessed by ListDeptWise() are not public. Here, employee is the class containing the information about an employee of a university. ListDeptWise() is a function that lists the employees for a given department. It should be noted that DeptName is the department name and it is a private variable. If ListDeptWise() needs to access the department name, it must be declared as a friend function.

 **PROGRAM 4.10**   A friend function

```
// FriendSimple.cpp
#include <iostream>
#include <string>
using namespace std;

class employee
{
    int EmpNo;
    string Name;
    string DeptName;
    string Designation;
public:
    void Init(int TempNo, string TempName, string TempDept, string TempDesi)
    {
        EmpNo = TempNo;
        Name = TempName;
        DeptName = TempDept;
        Designation = TempDesi;
    }

    void DisplayDetails()
    {
```

```
            cout << "Details of employee number " << EmpNo << "\n";
            cout << "Name is " << Name << "\n";
            cout << "Department is " << DeptName <<  "\n";
            cout << "Designation is " << Designation <<  "\n\n\n";
        }

        /* The following non-member function is granted access to the private variables of this
        class */

        friend void ListDeptWise(employee[]);
};
void ListDeptWise(employee UniEmp[])
{
    string TempDeptName;
    cout << "Enter the department of the university: ";
    cin >> TempDeptName;
    cout << "\n";

    for(int i = 0; i < 10; ++i)
    {
        if(UniEmp[i].DeptName == TempDeptName)
        /* The access of private variable DeptName is not allowed
        if ListDeptWise() is not friend */
        {
            UniEmp[i].DisplayDetails();
        }
    }
}

void main()
{
    employee UniEmployee[10];
    UniEmployee[1].Init(1, "Robin", "Exam", "Professor");
    UniEmployee[2].Init(2, "Bob", "Marksheet", "Clerk");
    UniEmployee[3].Init(3, "Leena", "Accounts", "HeadClerk");
    UniEmployee[4].Init(4, "Seema", "Exam", "Clerk");
    UniEmployee[5].Init(5, "Rohit", "Accounts", "CAO");
    UniEmployee[6].Init(6, "Vibha", "Exam", "Informer");
    UniEmployee[7].Init(7, "Kesar", "Exam", "Coordinator");
    UniEmployee[8].Init(8, "Michel", "Exam", "Examiner");
    UniEmployee[9].Init(9, "Hari", "Marksheet", "Repeater");
    UniEmployee[0].Init(10, "Meena", "Accounts", "Clerk");

    ListDeptWise(UniEmployee);
}
```

Output
```
Enter the department of the university:  Exam

Details of employee number 1
Name is Robin
Department is Exam
Designation is Professor

Details of employee number 4
Name is Seema
Department is Exam
Designation is Clerk

Details of employee number 6
Name is Vibha
```

```
Department is Exam
Designation is Informer

Details of employee number 7
Name is Kesar
Department is Exam
Designation is Coordinator

Details of employee number 8
Name is Michael
Department is Exam
Designation is Examiner
```

How the Program Works

We have an array of employee objects in this program. The employee object contains employee number, name, department, and designation. It also contains two functions for reading and printing the employee object details. There is a function ListDeptWise(), which takes an array of employee objects as input and produces the list of employees for a given department. This function is defined after the definition of class employee. The ListDeptWise() function has been declared as a friend in the last line of the class definition with the following statement:

```
friend void ListDeptWise(employee[]);
```

This statement indicates that the non-member function ListDeptWise() is granted access to private class variables. The need for a friend function must be noted in this case. ListDeptWise() accesses private variables such as DeptNameof employee class in the following statement:

```
(UniEmp[i].DeptName == TempDeptName);
```

If ListDeptWise() was a non-friend non-member function, it cannot access the private variables of employee such as DeptName and this statement will not be compiled.

4.11.1 Need for Friend Functions

Why do we require friend functions? Why not declare all functions as member functions? Consider making ListDeptWise() a member function. It actually operates on an array of employees and not on a singleton object. If we define ListDeptWise() as a member function, it will be called with a syntax such as UniEmployee[1].ListDeptWise(), which might mislead the reader of the program. ListDeptWise() need not be invoked by UniEmployee[1] alone. If we write UniEmployee[2].ListDeptWise(), the same result is obtained. In fact, even when a dummy employee object such as DummyEmp is defined and DummyEmp.ListDeptWise() is called, the same result will be obtained.

It should be noted that a reader might misinterpret that the object DummyEmp is executing a function and is being manipulated. Such functions should not be defined as members. Why is ListDeptWise() not a member? The reason is that the function under discussion is not the logical part of the object employee. It operates on a bunch of objects. Defining it as a member function will be wrong from the design point of view. Only those functions that describe logical operations from or to the object are to be defined as members (such as reading and printing operations). ListDeptWise() is better defined as a friend in such situations. We need such functions quite frequently,

> Only a function that is a logical part of the object should only be made a member.

especially for sorting objects on some private data, searching objects on some private data, etc.

An even better design would involve adding a public function in the employee class. This public function, known as an access method, returns the value of a private member. In our case, it is DeptName. If the code has a function

> Access methods can be used to convert a friend into non-friend if the friend function is defined to only read a private member's value.

```
getDeptName()
{
    return DeptName;
}
```

then the code

```
(UniEmp[i].DeptName == TempDeptName)
```

could be rewritten as

```
(UniEmp[i].getDeptName() == TempDeptName)
```

This would make it possible to define the ListDeptWise() function as non-member non-friend as it becomes independent of the private variable DeptName of the class.

Situations Where Friend Functions are Preferred

It must be noted that if ListDeptWise() needs to change the value of DeptName, it is not useful as a non-friend. There is one more situation when friend functions are useful. These functions are designed for providing generic utilities and are needed when more than one class would like to share some utility. Consider a case where a function displays the given text in a message box. This is a handy utility for any program that needs to output to a graphic user interface (GUI). (In our program, such a function can be used in place of the respective cout and cin in the InsertDetails() function.) The text and other information that the function uses may be private. The function needs to be defined as a friend to let it access the private variables. As already mentioned, more than one application may be sharing such functions and hence it is not possible to make them a member of a class. So, these types of functions are stored separately and are made friends to the class that uses their functionality.

> Friend functions are useful in two cases; the first one is when we want a utility that works on a bunch of objects and the second one is when a generic class contains functions that other classes need to use for their private members.

Member of Another Class as a Friend

A friend function is sometimes required when a single function needs access to private members of more than one class. Let us assume employee as one class and taxpayer as another class. Now, if we need to write a function that finds out how many employees are taxpayers, it may need to check an employee name with a taxpayer name, both of which are private variables of the respective classes. A function can only be a member of one of these two classes and must be made a friend of another class. Such requirements stem from incorrect design and must be avoided. Hence, this option is used only in cases where the classes might have been designed long back and the code is currently running but needs to be patched for a new requirement of the user. It would be better to opt for rewriting the code and avoid the need for a friend. However, most system administrators dislike the idea of modifying a running code for obvious reasons and friend functions come to their rescue in such cases.

> When a function needs to work with private variables of more than one class, it must be defined as a friend for at least one of the classes.

A friend is usually a non-member but sometimes one needs to have a member function of some class to be a friend of some other class.

Friend Class

It has been shown that it is possible to have a member function of some other class to be a friend of a class. Similarly, it is also possible to have an entire class as a friend, that is, all member functions of that class can access the private variables of the other class. It is important to note that the trust in this case is one directional. Suppose class1 defines class2 to be its friend. Then, class2 member functions can access the private variables of class1 whereas class1 member functions cannot access the private variables of class2. The following program illustrates the use of friend class.

Note Having a friend function in actual terms is a violation of the information hiding principle. If we can have two designs where one is with and the other is without friends, the design without friends is usually better. The thumb rule is that though the facility of friends is available, it should be used sparingly.

The problem of defining functions working on a bunch of objects can be solved by defining a class that is a collection of objects of classes under consideration. For example, define a new class `EmpCollection` that contains an array of employees as the object. All functions that need to operate on the bunch of objects can now be members of such a class. This design is definitely more complicated than one might like it to be. Even in this case, the `employee` class should trust the `EmpCollection` class.

The following program highlights these changes.

```cpp
// FriendClass.cpp
#include <iostream>
#include <string>
using namespace std;

class CollectionEmp; // Forward Definition
class employee
{
    int EmpNo;
    string Name;
    string DeptName;
    string Designation;
public:
    void Init(int TempNo, string TempName, string TempDept, string TempDesi)
    {
        EmpNo = TempNo;
        Name = TempName;
        DeptName = TempDept;
        Designation = TempDesi;
    }
    void DisplayDetails()
    {
        cout << "Details of employee number " << EmpNo << "\n";
        cout << "Name is" << Name << "\n";
        cout << "Department is" << DeptName <<  "\n";
        cout << "Designation is" << Designation <<  "\n";
    }
```

```
/* Member functions of the following class can access the private variables of this
class */
   friend CollectionEmp;
   /* If forward declaration is not provided, this statement would generate an error */
};
class CollectionEmp
{
private:
   employee ColEmp[10];
   /* The collection is in the array form; it can even be a linked list as in Program
   4.9 */

   int Index;
public:
   void InitIndex()
   {
      Index = 0;
   }
   bool AddToCol(employee Emp)
   /* adding an employee to the collection */
   {
      if(Index < 9)
      {
            ColEmp[Index] = Emp;
            Index++;
            return true;
      }
      else
      {
            return false;
      }
   }
   void ListDeptWise()    // Now a member function
   {
      string TempDeptName;
      cout << "Enter the department of the university : ";
      cin >> TempDeptName;
      cout << "\n";
      for(int i = 0; i < 10; ++i)
      {
            if(ColEmp[i].DeptName == TempDeptName)
            {
                  ColEmp[i].DisplayDetails();
            }
      }
   }
}
```

```
};
void main()
{
    CollectionEmp UniEmpCol;
    UniEmpCol.InitIndex();
    employee UniEmployee[10];
    UniEmployee[1].Init(1, "Robin", "Exam", "Professor");
    UniEmployee[2].Init(2, "Bob", "Marksheet", "Clerk");
    UniEmployee[3].Init(3, "Leena", "Accounts", "HeadClerk");
    UniEmployee[4].Init(4, "Seema", "Exam", "Clerk");
    UniEmployee[5].Init(5, "Rohit", "Accounts", "CAO");
    UniEmployee[6].Init(6, "Vibha", "Exam", "Informer");
    UniEmployee[7].Init(7, "Kesar", "Exam", "Coordinator");
    UniEmployee[8].Init(8, "Michel", "Exam", "Examiner");
    UniEmployee[9].Init(9, "Hari", "Marksheet", "Repeater");
    UniEmployee[0].Init(10, "Meena", "Accounts", "Clerk");

    for(int i = 0; i < 10; ++i)
    {
        UniEmpCol.AddToCol(UniEmployee[i]);
        /* Putting the employees in the collection object */
    }
    UniEmpCol.ListDeptWise();
    /* This is a member function now and not a dummy one */
}
```

Execute this program and observe the output. The output is the same as that for Program 4.10. Here, the ListDeptWise() function is a member of a class representing the collection of employees. The collection of employees is implemented using arrays for simplicity. It can even be implemented using linked list as in Program 4.7.

Differentiating Implementation with the Interface

In order to implement the class using linked lists, the AddToCol(),InitIndex(), and ListDeptWise() functions need to be rewritten. For the linked list version, in the InitIndex() function, we will assign null to the first pointer (again similar to the function InitializeList() of Program 4.7) and be ready for input. AddToCol() will add an employee to a linked list (similar to InsertList() of Program 4.7). ListDeptWise() will search in the linked list and produce the required answer. It should be noted that the main()program, which uses these functions as members of UniEmpCol object, will not change. This is an important advantage. The implementation can be changed without changing the interface. Here, implementation is either array based or linked list based; the interface is provided by the three functions mentioned.

> **Note** When a collection of objects is defined as a class, the implementation of operations on that collection such as sorting and searching is hidden from the user. One can replace the default implementation with a more suitable implementation without disturbing the user application.

Thus, there are two ways of implementation, namely, array based and linked list based. It is possible to provide both these methods together by overloading functions. However, in such cases, one must provide different sets of arguments to call a specific function.

This example also illustrates how a class can become a friend of another and how useful it is. Another possibility is that of having a friend class that provides useful though general utilities such as GUI input/output using message boxes as discussed earlier.

4.12 const AND volatile FUNCTIONS

Like C, the `const` and `volatile` variables are available in C++. However, it is also possible to have `const` and `volatile` functions in C++ additionally, unlike in C. A brief introduction is provided in the following sections.

4.12.1 const Functions

Constant objects have already been discussed in Chapter 3 and the definition of a `const` function was shown in Program 3.12. They are defined by placing the keyword `const` between the argument list and the body of the function.

> **Note**   A `const` function can operate on either constant or non-constant objects; however, it cannot modify the objects of the class.

```
<return type><function name>(argument1, argument2, …) const
{
    <The body of the function>
}
```

Program 3.12 in Chapter 3 contains the following function:

```
void PrintDetails()const
/* This function is now constant; it cannot modify
an object of the class student */
{
    cout << "Roll number is " << RollNumber << "\n";
    cout << "Name is " << Name << "\n";
    cout << "Address is " << Address << "\n";
}
```

If this function is modified as follows, we get errors while compiling the program.

```
void PrintDetails()const
{
    cout << "Roll number is" << RollNumber <<   "\n";
    cout << "Name is   " << Name <<   "\n";
    cout << "Address is " << Address << "\n";

    RollNumber = 4;     // This is erroneous
}
```

> **Note**   It is a good programming practice to define member functions as constant when they should not modify the invoking objects. So, later on, if the functions are accidentally modified to change the values of data members, the error can be caught during compilation.

4.12.2 Mutable Data Members

Ordinary data members, as we have seen, cannot be modified by const functions. What if we want a special data member to be modified by a function? If we do not declare the member function as const, it cannot access constant objects. Declaration of a special data member as mutable is the solution here. When a data member is declared mutable, it can be modified even by the const functions.

In the example given, if `RollNumber` definition is changed to

```
mutable int RollNumber;
```

in the `student` class, then the statement

```
void PrintDetails() const
{
    ...
    RollNumber = 4;
}
```

will no longer result in an error. There is no difference between a normal data member and a mutable data member for a normal member function.

4.12.3 volatile Functions

A member function can also be declared as `volatile` if it is invoked by a volatile object. A volatile object's value can be changed by external parameters, which are not under the control of the program. For example, an object taking an input from a network interface card does not take input from our program. As and when the hardware interrupts, the values related to it change without our program's knowledge.

A sample definition of a volatile function and a volatile object are shown in the following code:

```
class NICClass
{
public:
    void CheckValuesForNIC volatile
    // A volatile function definition
    {
        // Function body
    }
    ...
};
volatile NICClass NICObject;
// A volatile object definition
```

4.13 STATIC FUNCTIONS

Some utilities are generic to a set of objects. We have seen the case of dealing with a collection of objects. The utility or the operation does not address a singleton object but works on multiple objects. At times, we need to provide operations that refer to all the objects, such as finding out how many objects are created at the moment. Such cases need static variables, discussed in Chapter 3. We can see that a static variable is an ideal choice for the variable that represents a number of objects alive at the moment. Program 4.11 shows how a static function can be used instead of a member or non-member function.

> **Note** Non-member functions are similar to normal C functions. If we define them as static, they become local to the file in which they are defined. In other words, the scope of that function is the body of the file within which the function is defined.

Program 4.11 is the modified version of the progam in Chapter 3 that counts the number of students defined at the moment. A static function is used here for displaying the total number of students.

PROGRAM 4.11   Static functions for counting the number of students

```cpp
// StaticFunction.cpp
#include <iostream>
#include <string>
using namespace std;

class student
{
public:
    static int TotalStudents;
    static void DispTotal();
    // Declaration of a static member function

private:
    int RollNumber;
    string Name;
    string Address;

public:
    void SetDetails(int Roll, string StudentName, string StudentAddress)
    {
        RollNumber = Roll;
        Name = StudentName;
        Address = StudentAddress;
        TotalStudents++;
    }

    void PrintDetails()
    {
        cout << "Roll number is " << RollNumber << "\n";
        cout << "Name is " << Name << "\n";
        cout << "Address is   " << Address <<   "\n";
    }
};

int student::TotalStudents;
void student::DispTotal()
/* See how the function name is preceded with the class name similar to a member function */
{
    cout << "Total students at the moment" << student::TotalStudents << "\n";
}

void main()
{
    student::DispTotal();
    student Robin;

    Robin.SetDetails(1, "Robin Singh", "New Delhi");
    Robin.PrintDetails();
    student::DispTotal();
```

```
student Sonia;
Sonia.SetDetails(2, "Mathur", "Mumbai");
Sonia.PrintDetails();
student::DispTotal();

if(true)
{
    student Anita;
    Anita.SetDetails(3, "Sharma", "Indore");
    Anita.PrintDetails();
    student::DispTotal();
}
cout << "Anita departs! \n";

/* The following will not work as expected. Total students are still three */
student::DispTotal();
}
```

How the Program Works

DispTotal() is a new function defined as static. A static function is very similar to a non-member function, with the only difference that it is now bound and known only to the class in which it is defined. It should be remembered that non-member functions are known to all the classes of the program. The static functions, similar to member functions, can be invoked only by the objects of the class in which they are declared as static. They can be invoked directly by their name with the class name and scope resolution operator preceding it.

> **Note** In C, if a function is declared as static, it will be treated local to the file in which it is defined. The same concept is applied in the case of a non-member. A static non-member function is local to the file and is not accessible outside that physical file.

The manner in which a static function is defined and used should be noted. Like a non-member function, a static function is defined outside the class. At the same time, it is preceded by the class name and the scope resolution operator, just like a member function defined outside the class.

```
void student::DispTotal()
```

DispTotal() is a static function that is used to display the total number of students and TotalStudents is also a static variable. This did not happen by accident; a static function can act upon only the static variables of the class and cannot have access to other data members of the class. It can also have access to global functions and data.

The most important advantage of static functions is that they increase the readability of the program. Instead of calling Shyam.DispTotal, where Shyam is just a dummy object for counting the total students, we can call student::DispTotal, that is, it should be preceded by the class name, which is far more readable.

4.13.1 Restrictions on Static Function

Static functions have some restrictions as well. Some of the important ones are as follows:

1. They do not have the this pointer because they are not member functions in the true sense. This is why they cannot access the member variables.
2. They cannot access other data members of the class because doing so will implicitly call the this pointer. (Remember: RollNumber is the same as this -> RollNumber.)

3. They cannot be virtual. (We will study virtual functions when we study inheritance in Chapter 10, but again the reason is the same, that is, static functions are not member functions.)

4. They cannot be declared either `const` or `volatile`. (Once again, they are not true members, and hence, there is no point in making them `const` or `volatile`.)

4.14 PRIVATE AND PUBLIC FUNCTIONS

The functions defined in most of our examples are public. They can also be private, that is, they are accessible only to the member functions of the same class. They share the same characteristics of a private data member. Neither are they visible outside the class, nor are they accessible from the object of the same class. The concept of private functions can be understood better using Program 4.12.

Program 4.10 is an example related to a friend function that displays the list of employees for a given department. We will be using the same example with some modifications. We have now added a function `IsPermanent()`, which is a private function that checks whether an employee is permanent or not. In reality, it may look in a database and apply a set of rules to find whether an employee is permanent or not. Here, though, we just check if the employee code is greater than 2000. If so, the employee is permanent; otherwise he/she is temporary.

PROGRAM 4.12   Private and public functions

```cpp
// PrivateFunction.cpp
#include <iostream>
#include <string>
using namespace std;

class employee
{
    int EmpNo;
    string Name;
    string DeptName;
    string Designation;
    bool IsPermanent()
    /* It is a private function. Here, we assume that employee code is less than 2000 for
    temporary employees */
    {
        return(EmpNo > 2000);
    }

public:
    void Init(int TempNo, string TempName, string TempDept, string TempDesi)
    {
        EmpNo = TempNo;
        Name = TempName;
        DeptName = TempDept;
        Designation = TempDesi;
    }

    void DisplayDetails()
    {
        cout << "Details of employee number " << EmpNo << "\n";
        cout << "Name is " << Name << "\n";
        cout << "Department is " << DeptName << "\n";
        cout << "Designation is " << Designation << "\n";
        if(IsPermanent())
```

```
                    cout << "He/She is a permanent employee \n \n";
            else
                    cout << "He/She is a temporary employee \n \n";
    }

    /* The following non-member function can access the private variables of this class */

    friend void ListDeptWise(employee[]);
};
void ListDeptWise(employee UniEmp[])
{
    string TempDeptName;
    cout << "Enter the department of the university:";
    cin >> TempDeptName;
    cout << "\n";

    for(int i = 0; i < 10; ++i)
    {
        if(UniEmp[i].DeptName == TempDeptName)
        {
            UniEmp[i].DisplayDetails();
        }
    }
}

void main()
{
    // employee DummyEmployee = {0, "Dummy", "Dummy", Dummy"};
    employee UniEmployee[10];
    UniEmployee[1].Init(1001, "Robin", "Exam", "Professor");
    UniEmployee[2].Init(1002, "Bob", "Marksheet", "Clerk");
    UniEmployee[3].Init(2003, "Leena", "Accounts", "HeadClerk");
    UniEmployee[4].Init(1004, "Seema", "Exam", "Clerk");
    UniEmployee[5].Init(3005, "Rohit", "Accounts", "CAO");
    UniEmployee[6].Init(2006, "Vibha", "Exam", "Informer");
    UniEmployee[7].Init(1007, "Kesar", "Exam", "Coordinator");
    UniEmployee[8].Init(2008, "Michel", "Exam", "Examiner");
    UniEmployee[9].Init(2009, "Hari", "Marksheet", "Repeater");
    UniEmployee[0].Init(2010, "Meena", "Accounts", "Clerk");

    ListDeptWise(UniEmployee);
}
```

Output
```
Enter the department of the university:  Exam

Details of employee number 1001
Name is Robin
Department is Exam
Designation is Professor
He/She is a temporary employee

Details of employee number 1004
Name is Seema
Department is Exam
Designation is Clerk
He/She is a temporary employee

Details of employee number 2006
Name is Vibha
Department is Exam
```

```
Designation is Informer
He/She is a permanent employee

Details of employee number 1007
Name is Kesar
Department is Exam
Designation is Coordinator
He/She is a temporary employee

Details of employee number 2008
Name is Michel
Department is Exam
Designation is Examiner
He/She is a permanent employee
```

How the Program Works

> Private member functions get the implicit this pointer passed to them by the member function that calls these private functions.

Private functions The function IsPermanent() is an example of a private function. It is not possible to write UniEmployee[1].IsPermanent() because IsPermanent() is a private member of the employee class and UniEmplyee[1] is an object of that class. The object cannot access the private member IsPermanent(). If we define IsPermanent() in the public section instead, the statement is acceptable. However, such access of the IsPermanent() function is not desired here, and hence, it has been defined as a private function.

Calling private functions Another important point to note is that the IsPermanent() function is called without invoking an object. The call is not EmployeeObjectName.IsPermanent(). It is a member function and needs this pointer. To understand how this works, look closely at the call to the function. It is called *within* DisplayDetails(), which is also a member function. When DisplayDetails() is invoked, it is passed the this pointer; for example, UniEmp[i].DisplayDetails() is passed the this pointer of the UniEmp[i]. The pointer is also passed to IsPermanent() by DisplayDetails() at the time of call, that is, the call is equivalent to this -> IsPermanent(). This is true for all private function members. Whenever they are called by other member functions (it should be remembered that they cannot be called by non-member functions as they are private), they are passed this pointer in possession with that member function at the time of call.

4.15 FUNCTIONS THAT RETURN OBJECTS

A function can also return an object. We have earlier seen examples of the Difference() function with Time class. Let us see one more example, which is a modified version of the employee class program. Here, the objective of the problem is to obtain the employee objects related to an employee name, which is given as an input by the user. Thus, our function (GetEmp()) is passed with the employee name and it returns the matching employee objects.

A similar problem is to obtain the manager name of a given employee. Manager is also an object of type employee and has the designation manager and the same department as the employee. Thus, our function (GetManager()) now accepts employee as an input and returns one more employee object representing the manager of the employee object passed.

The following program provides two different functions for these problems, and both of them return objects. One is a member function whereas the other is a non-member function. The program also reinforces the difference between member and non-member functions.

Here, the non-member function (GetEmp()) can also access the private variables of the employee object, and hence, it needs to be defined as a friend of the employee class.

It should be noted that the GetEmp() function is defined as a friend. It cannot be defined as a member function because the argument to that function is only a string (the employee name), and not an object. If it is forcibly converted to a member function, the calling object will be a dummy one.

> **Note** Sometimes, we need to have a function that returns an object from other data. Such functions can be converted to constructors. If such functions are not converted, the objects constructed are called *factory objects* and such functions are known as *factory methods*.

The other function, GetManager(), returns the manager object for a given employee object. One more attribute has been added to the employee object, namely, the variable ManagerName. This function compares the value of ManagerName for the invoking object with the employee whose designation value is Manager. It also checks whether both of them belong to the same department. Thus, it is understandable that GetManager() depends on the employee object invoking it and is a right candidate for being a member function.

```cpp
// ReturnObj.cpp
#include <iostream>
#include <string>
using namespace std;

class employee
{
    int EmpNo;
    string Name;
    string DeptName;
    string Designation;
    string ManagerName;
public:
    void Init(int TempNo, string TempName, string TempDept, string TempDesi, string
    TempManager)
    {
        EmpNo = TempNo;
        Name = TempName;
        DeptName = TempDept;
        Designation = TempDesi;
        ManagerName = TempManager;
    }
    void DisplayDetails()
    {
        cout << "Details of employee number " << EmpNo << "\n";
        cout << "Name is " << Name << "\n";
        cout << "Department is   " << DeptName << "\n";
        cout << "Designation is   " << Designation << "\n";
        cout << "Manager is   " << ManagerName << "\n";
    }
```

```
    employee GetManager(employee EmpArray[])
    {
        for(int i = 0; i < 10; ++i)
        {
            if((ManagerName == EmpArray[i].Name) && (DeptName == EmpArray[i].DeptName))
            return EmpArray[i];
        }
    }
    friend employee GetEmp(string, employee[]);
};
employee GetEmp(string EmpName, employee EmpArray[])
{
    for(int i = 0; i < 10; ++i)
    {
        if(EmpArray[i].Name == EmpName)
                return EmpArray[i];
    }
}
void main()
{
    employee UniEmployee[10];
    UniEmployee[1].Init(1001, "Robin", "Exam", "Manager", "Robin");
    UniEmployee[2].Init(1002, "Bob", "Marksheet", "Manager", "Bob");
    UniEmployee[3].Init(2003, "Leena", "Accounts", "Manager", "Leena");
    UniEmployee[4].Init(1004, "Seema", "Exam", "Clerk", "Robin");
    UniEmployee[5].Init(3005, "Rohit", "Accounts", "CAO", "Leena");
    UniEmployee[6].Init(2006, "Vibha", "Exam", "Informer", "Robin");
    UniEmployee[7].Init(1007, "Kesar", "Exam", "Coordinator", "Robin");
    UniEmployee[8].Init(2008, "Michel", "Exam", "Examiner", "Robin");
    UniEmployee[9].Init(2009, "Hari", "Marksheet", "Repeater", "Bob");
    UniEmployee[0].Init(2010, "Meena", "Accounts", "Clerk", "Leena");
    cout << "Enter name of an employee:";
    string EmpName;
    cin >> EmpName;
    employee Emp = GetEmp(EmpName, UniEmployee);
    Emp.DisplayDetails();
    employee Manager = Emp.GetManager(UniEmployee);
    cout << "\n \n The details of his/her manager are\n";
    Manager.DisplayDetails();
}
```

Output
```
Enter name of an employee: Rohit
Details of employee number 3005
Name is Rohit
Department is Accounts
Designation is CAO
```

Manager is Leena

The details of hisX/her manager are

Details of employee number 2003

Name is Leena

Department is Accounts

Designation is Manager

Manager is Leena

The simplicity with which both functions, GetEmp() and GetManager(), can be called and used is noteworthy.

Using objects while passing an argument or returning is similar to using C structures because they do not store member functions with them. Passing and returning objects actually passes and returns only data members.

4.16 FUNCTION POINTERS

Pointer to function is considered to be a very powerful feature of C programming. When a program contains a large number of functions to choose from, this feature becomes very useful. If the switch-case statement is used instead, it will have a longer code and is less efficient. Such a code needs to check whether each and every function name exists. This is done to find which function is called and then call that function. Instead, if the function pointer is passed, it will automatically call the required function.

Non-member function pointers in C++ behave in the same way as in C. Program 4.13 explains how to use non-member function pointers.

PROGRAM 4.13   *Non-member function pointers*

```cpp
// StandaloneFunctionPointer.cpp
#include <iostream>
#include <string>
using namespace std;

void main()
{
    int PointAccess(int Dummy1, int Dummy2);    // Prototype
    int MainArgl = 10;
    int MainArg2 = 20;

    cout << PointAccess(MainArg1,MainArg2);
    int(*PointFun)(int, int);
    /* Defining pointer to a function that has two arguments, both of which are integers */

    PointFun = PointAccess;
    // Making PointFun point to one such function

    int PointArg1 = 20;
    int PointArg2 = 30;

    cout << (*PointFun)(PointArg1, PointArg2);
    // Same as calling PointAccess

    cout << PointFun(PointArg1, PointArg2);
}

int PointAccess(int Dummy1, int Dummy2)
{
```

```
        cout << "Dummy1 is " << Dummy1 <<"\n";
        cout << "Dummy2 is " << Dummy2 << "\n";
        return Dummy1 + Dummy2;
}
```

Output
```
Dummy1 is 10
Dummy2 is 20 30
Dummy1 is 20
Dummy2 is 30 50
```

How the Program Works
Observe the definition of the pointer to function:

```
int(*PointFun)(int, int);
```

A function is not a variable and thus does not have an address. The function pointer actually contains an address of a d, if will have a long the first exe-cutable statement of the function.

It says that `PointFun` is a pointer to a function. Otherwise, it would not contain function-like braces on the RHS. It also indicates that the function takes two integer arguments. This format is the same as in C. It should be noted that `int * PointFun(int, int)` is a function that returns a pointer to integer and is different from `int(*PointFun)(int, int)`.

The definition of a member function pointer and its use are very simple to understand if we have a clear idea of member pointers. We have discussed in detail pointer to class members in Chapter 3.

Program 4.14 will help to understand the member function pointers.

PROGRAM 4.14   Pointer to member functions

```cpp
// MemberFunctionPointer.cpp
#include <iostream>
#include <string>
using namespace  std;

class PointFunEx
{
    int Arg1;
    int Arg2;
public:
    int PointAccess();
    PointFunEx(int Value1, int Value2)
    {
        Arg1 = Value1;
        Arg2 = Value2;
    }
    /* This function is called a constructor */
};

// The following is the function of our interest
int PointFunEx::PointAccess()
    {
        cout <<  "\n Arg1 is  " << Arg1;
        cout << "\n Arg2 is  " << Arg2 <<  "\n";
        return Arg1 + Arg2;
    }

void main()
```

```
{
    PointFunEx PFE(10, 20);
    /* This initializes the object with values 10 to Arg1 and 20 to Arg2. This calls the
    constructor function here */

    cout << "\n Normal object accessing the function ";
    cout << "   " << PFE.PointAccess();

    /* Instead of int(*PA)(), in the case of a non-member function, the classname is followed
    by a scope resolution operator as shown in the following statements. Moreover, note the
    difference in the arguments. We no longer need to pass both the arguments, as they are
    passed implicitly with the invoking object */

    int(PointFunEx::*PA)();   // Function pointer PA is defined here

    PA = PointFunEx::PointAccess;

    /* Note the difference in this statement */

    /* Instead of assigning PA = PointAccess directly, the name of the function is
    preceded by the class name in which the member function is used and a scope resolution
    operator */

    /* It does not make any difference whether & is present before the function name or not.
    Both the cases will get us the function "address" */

    cout << "\n Normal object accessing the function using a function pointer";
    cout << "   " << (PFE.*PA)();

    /* Again note the difference here: when calling a function with an object, the .*
    notation needs to be used */

    PointFunEx PFE2(20, 30);
    PointFunEx *PointerPFE = &PFE2;

    cout << "\n Pointer to object accessing the function using a function pointer";
    cout << "   " << (PointerPFE->*PA)();

    /* Now we are accessing it using a pointer to an object, so we need a ->* operator */

    int(PointFunEx::*PB)();
    /* A function pointer PB is defined here */

    PB = &PointFunEx::PointAccess;

    /* Note the difference in this statement. Instead of assigning PA = PointAccess directly,
    the name of thefunction is preceded by the class name and a scope resolution operator.
    Moreover, note the use of the optional & operator */

    cout << "\n Normal object accessing the function using a function pointer";
    cout << "   " << (PFE.*PB)();
}
```

Output
```
Normal object accessing the function
Arg1 is 10
Arg2 is 20 30

Normal object accessing the function using a function pointer
Arg1 is 10
Arg2 is 20 30

Pointer to object accessing the function using a function pointer
Arg1 is 20
Arg2 is 30 50
```

```
Normal object accessing the function using a function pointer
Arg1 is 10
Arg2 is 20 30
```

How the Program Works

A few points need to be noted while using a pointer to member functions:

1. We need to use the `<class name>` to precede the function while defining a pointer to the function and making a call.
2. This operator is used for defining pointer to a member function. The syntax for defining such a pointer requires this operator.
3. We need to use the .* operator for accessing a member pointer using an object.
4. We need the ->* operator for accessing a member pointer using a pointer to an object.

The following is an interesting assignment:

```
PA = &PointFunEx::PointAccess; (or PointFunEx::PointAccess without &)
```

If `PointAccess` is a non-member function, it will be `PA = PointAccess`; without braces, as the function name itself is a pointer to the function. Why, then, is & needed here? It is not actually needed. Examine the definition of PB later. We have PA and PB with similar definition except the & operator. Both `<function name>` and `&<function name>` yield the same entry point (address) of the function.

The function is, however, not a variable; it cannot have an address like a variable. When we take the address of a function in either C or C++, it returns the entry point address of the function. It is the memory location from where the execution of the function starts.

4.17 USING POINTER TO MEMBER FUNCTION

The pointer to member syntax is very difficult to remember at first sight. It is also not very intuitive. Let us see how to simplify the syntax and also look at its use. Let us consider an example that is first solved without using the pointer to member function (Program 4.15) and then solved using the function (Program 4.16). The two programs can then be compared to understand how the solution with pointer to member function is better.

Let us again use the `student` class. Now, there are three more requirements to the class. We need to store information about the assignments the students have completed, the projects that he/she has done, and the references that he/she has got. Hence, three more functions are added, namely, `AddAssignment()`, `AddProject()`, and `AddReference()`. There will be three arrays containing details about the assignments, projects, and references.

It is important to note that the number of assignments, projects, or references is different for each student. If we define arrays to store the information, we need to define arrays large enough to accommodate information about a student with the maximum number of assignments, projects, or references. The array size can be kept at 100 for assignments as most students do not have more than five assignments. A better solution is to have a linked list for storing student information. Program 4.15 uses the simpler approach of having arrays large enough for accepting details about students having the maximum number of assignments, projects, or references.

PROGRAM 4.15 Solution without using pointer to member functions

```cpp
// NotUsingPointersToMembers.cpp
#include <iostream>
#include <string>
using namespace std;

enum jobs {ASSIGNMENT, PROJECT, REFERENCE};
class Student
{
private:
    int RollNumber;
    string Name;
    string Address;

    string Assignments[100];
    string Projects[20];
    string References[10];
public:
    static int NextAssignment;
    static int NextProject;
    static int NextReference;
    void GetDetails()
    {
        cout << "\n Enterroll number: ";
        cin >> RollNumber;
        cout << "\n Enter Name: ";
        cin >> Name;
        cout << "\n Enter address: ";
        cin >> Address;
    }
    void AddAssignment()
    {
        string NewAssignment;
        cout << "Enter next assignment \n";
        cin >> NewAssignment;
        Assignments[NextAssignment] = NewAssignment;
        NextAssignment++;
    }
    void AddProject()
    {
        string NewProject;
        cout << "Enter next project \n";
        cin >> NewProject;
        Projects[NextProject] = NewProject;
        NextProject++;
    }

    void AddReference()
    {
        string NewReference;
        cout << "Enter next reference \n";
        cin >> NewReference;
        References[NextReference] = NewReference;
        NextReference++;
    }

    void AddJob(jobs StudentJobs, int NoOfJobs)
    {
```

```cpp
        int i;
        switch(StudentJobs)
        {

        case ASSIGNMENT:
            for(i = 0; i < NoOfJobs; i++)
            {
                AddAssignment();
            }
            break;

        case PROJECT:
            for(i = 0; i < NoOfJobs; i++)
            {
                AddProject();
            }
            break;

        case REFERENCE:
            for(i = 0; i < NoOfJobs; i++)
            {
                AddReference();
            }
            break;

        default:
            break;
        }
    }
    void PrintDetails()
    {
        int i;
        cout << "Roll number is " << RollNumber << "\n";
        cout << "Name is " << Name << "\n";
        cout << "Address is " << Address << "\n";

        cout << "Assignments are \n";
        for(i = 0; i < NextAssignment; i++)
        {
            cout << Assignments[i]<< "\n";
        }
        cout << "Projects are \n";
        for(i = 0; i < NextProject; i++)
        {
            cout << Projects[i]<< "\n";
        }
        cout << "References are \n";
        for(i = 0; i < NextReference; i++)
        {
            cout << References[i]<< "\n";
        }
    }
};
// Mandatory definitions of static variables required at linking time
int Student::NextAssignment;
int Student::NextProject;
int Student::NextReference;

void main()
{
```

```
        Student Lara;
        jobs StudentJobs = ASSIGNMENT;
        Lara.GetDetails();
        Lara.AddJob(StudentJobs,3);
        Lara.PrintDetails();

        // Some other job to be done
        Lara.AddJob(StudentJobs,2);
}
```

Output
```
Enter roll number: 1
Enter name: BrianCharlesLara
Enter address: TheWestIndies

Enter next assignment
Captainship

Enter next assignment
BatsmanShip

Enter next assignment
LeadForTheWorldCup

Roll number is 1
Name is BrianCharlesLara
Address is TheWestIndies

Assignments are
Captainship
BatsmanShip
LeadForTheWorldCup

Projects are
References are

Enter next assignment // Asking for two more assignments
MaintainDisipline
Enter next assignment
CheckPhysicalFitness
```

How the Program Works

Let us now analyse each module of this program.

Definitions Look at the definition of the three arrays for Assignments, Projects, and References.

```
string Assignments[100];
string Projects[20];
string References[10];
```

Detailed informed is not being stored. If we need to do that, then we have to define Assignment as a class and have an array of objects of Assignment class; the same needs to be done for projects and references. We have taken a simpler approach here where we store information in a string alone. This approach will not help if we need to find how many students have done C++ assignments or have executed projects involving OO modelling. As mentioned earlier, such questions can be answered only if assignments, projects, and references are defined as classes in which a function for providing such information is available. However, the objective here is to showcase the need of pointer to member function, for which this solution is good enough.

Using static variables One interesting aspect of this program is that it also shows the usefulness of the static variables.

```
static int NextAssignment;
static int NextProject;
static int NextReference;
```

It is important here to remember that all these variables are initialized to zero by the compiler. It is possible to add assignments (or projects or references) multiple times to a student such as the following:

```
jobs StudentJobs = ASSIGNMENT;
Lara.AddJob(StudentJobs, 3);
// other code
Lara.AddJob(StudentJobs, 2);
(Lara has completed two additional assignments)
```

The second call requires us to find the place where we can add data in the array. We need to remember which assignment we are adding. The static variable NextAssignment provides us that value. It remembers the last assigned value 3, and automatically increments to give us 4. Various AddJob() calls can be made and every time the data is inserted at the right place.

Entering data in the array Let us now see how an assignment is actually added to an array. The index, as mentioned earlier, is the static variable value itself. We just need to increment that variable after the assignment statement.

```
void AddAssignment()
{
    string NewAssignment;
    cout << "Enter next assignment \n";
    cin >> NewAssignment;
    Assignments[NextAssignment] = NewAssignment;
    NextAssignment++;
}
```

The other two functions AddProject() and AddReference() work in a similar way. In fact, the only difference among the three functions is that AddAssignment() adds to the assignment array, AddProject() adds to the project array, and AddReference() adds to the reference array. It is also important to note that all three functions have a similar signature, that is, void <function name>(). The importance of this will be discussed subsequently.

Using global enum Observe the global enum definition.

```
enum jobs {ASSIGNMENT, PROJECT, REFERENCE};
```

We can now use ASSIGNMENT, PROJECT, and REFERENCE as case labels. The most important function in this case is the AddJob() function.

```
void AddJob(jobs StudentJobs, int NoOfJobs)
{
    int i;
    switch(StudentJobs)
    {
```

```
        case ASSIGNMENT:
        for(i = 0; i < NoOfJobs; i++)
        {
            AddAssignment();
        }
        break;

        case PROJECT:

        ...

        }
    }
```

Function to add information, AddJob()   The AddJob() function takes two arguments. The first is the enum value, which refers to what we are interested in inserting. We can pass ASSIGNMENT for adding an assignment to the Assignments array. Similarly, we can pass PROJECT for adding a project and REFERENCE for adding a reference in the corresponding arrays. The second argument is for multiple operations. It is not unusual to add multiple values of projects, assignments, and references together, thus calling the respective function that many times. In this example, we have added three assignments of Lara the first time and then have added two more assignments. Look at the calls made to AddJob() in the program.

```
Lara.AddJob(StudentJobs, 3);
Lara.AddJob(StudentJobs, 2);
```

Here, 3 and 2 are values passed to AddJob(), informing it that the first call needs to add three and second call needs to add two assignments. The StudentJobs value in both the cases is ASSIGNMENT, so in both the cases AddJob() adds to the Assignments array.

Limitation of the solution   Now, the question is, what is the problem with this program? Suppose we need students to have a list of practicals completed. We should have a function such as AddPractical() that adds practicals. The AddJob() function needs to be modified to add one more case and the global enum also needs to be changed. Adding a function AddPractical() cannot be avoided, but is it possible to avoid changing AddJob() and the enum? It is possible if pointer to member functions are used. It solves the problem in such a way that adding one or more functions does not require a change in the AddJob() function and there is no further need for enum.

   Program 4.16 is the same as Program 4.15 but uses a pointer to member function.

PROGRAM 4.16   Solution using pointer to member function

```cpp
// UsingPointerToMember.cpp
#include <iostream>
#include <string>
using namespace std;
// enum jobs {ASSIGNMENT, PROJECT, REFERENCE};

class Student
{
private:
    int RollNumber;
    string Name;
    string Address;
```

```
    string Assignments[100];
    string Projects[20];
    string References[10];
public:
    static int NextAssignment;
    static int NextProject;
    static int NextReference;
    void GetDetails()
    {
        cout << "\n Enter roll number: ";
        cin >> RollNumber;
        cout << "\n Enter name: ";
        cin >> Name;
        cout << "\n Enter address: ";
        cin >> Address;
    }

    void AddAssignment()
    {
        string NewAssignment;
        cout << "Enter next assignment \n";
        cin >> NewAssignment;
        Assignments[NextAssignment] = NewAssignment;
        NextAssignment++;
    }

    void AddProject()
    {
        string NewProject;
        cout << "Enter next project \n";
        cin >> NewProject;
        Projects[NextProject] = NewProject;
        NextProject++;
    }

    void AddReference()
    {
        string NewReference;
        cout << "Enter next reference \n";
        cin >> NewReference;
        References[NextReference] = NewReference;
        NextReference++;
    }

    void AddJob(void(Student::*FPtr)(), int NoOfJobs)
    {
        for(int i = 0; i < NoOfJobs; i++)
        {
            (this ->* FPtr)();
            /* Call the function using this pointer, that is, the invoking object */
        }
    }

    void PrintDetails()
    {
        int i;
        cout << "Roll number is " << RollNumber << "\n";
        cout << "Name is " << Name <<  "\n";
        cout << "Address is " << Address <<  "\n";

        cout << "Assignments are \n";
```

```
            for(i = 0; i < NextAssignment; i++)
            {
                cout << Assignments[i] << "\n";
            }

            cout << "Projects are \n";
            for(i = 0; i < NextProject; i++)
            {
                cout << References[i]<< "\n";
            }
        }
};

int Student::NextAssignment;
int Student::NextProject;
int Student::NextReference;

void main()
{
    void (Student::*JobFunPtr)();  // Defining a function pointer
    Student Lara;
    // jobs StudentJobs = ASSIGNMENT;
    JobFunPtr = Student::AddAssignment;
    // no() after the function name

    Lara.GetDetails();
    // Lara.AddJob(StudentJobs,3);
    Lara.AddJob(JobFunPtr, 3);
    Lara.PrintDetails();
}
```

How the Program Works

The output of the program is the same except that two additional assignments are not given to Lara now. Let us look at the changes made to the earlier program one by one. The first change is that the enum is commented now as it is no longer needed. The second change is that the AddJob() function has now become much shorter. It is defined as

```
void AddJob(void(Student::*FPtr)(), int NoOfJobs)
{
    for(int i = 0; i < NoOfJobs; i++)
    {
        (this ->* FPtr)();
        // Call the function using this pointer, that is, invoking object
    }
}
```

The first argument is important now. It is void(Student::FPtr)(); that is, the pointer to a function is a member of the Student class, which has no arguments, and returns void. Any function that does not have an argument returns void and the member of the student class can be made to point to any member that has the same signature by this pointer. All three of our AddJob() functions have the same signature and the FPtr can point to all of them. Thus, it is possible to pass pointer to AddAssignment(), AddProject(), or AddReference() or any other function with the same signature, such as void AddPractical() or void AddGroupMembers().

Adding a new function without trouble This adds to the flexibility of the function. We only need a function pointer to pass to this function. We need not worry about the *name* of the function as only the *signature* is important. The code does not need to change if any additional function with the same signature is added to the program and called using the `AddJob()` function. Suppose we have defined the following

```
void AddPracticals();
```

in the program. Then, the statement

```
Lara.AddJob(Student::*AddPracticals, 3)
```

adds to practicals. The code of `AddJob()` does not change. Compare this with the earlier example and the amount of code revision required. A lot of work is being done towards making the program design flexible. For example, compilers use this method extensively for system level coding.

Exhibit 4.4 explains why switch-case statement is to be avoided.

Exhibit 4.4 Why switch-case statement should be avoided

The solution using pointer to member function offers an important advantage. It does not employ switch-case statements. In programs with a large number of functions, the switch-case option might consume a substantial amount of time, which is saved here.

In the case of graphics programming or gaming, operations such as moving up, down, right, or left multiple times and, therefore, functions for each operation are needed. Without pointer to member functions, a switch statement with four functions is needed.

Thus, a lot of time will be saved by using pointer to member functions, especially when the operations are carried out multiple times. Even a small amount of time saved in graphics is important.

Using pointer to member function Let us understand the body of the function. It contains a single `for` loop.

```
for(int i = 0; i < NoOfJobs; i++)
{
    (this ->* FPtr)();
    // Call the function using this pointer, that is, the invoking object
}
```

This statement needs explanation. What does the statement `Lara.AddJob(Student::Assignment,3);` do? It calls `Student::AddAssignment()` three times. The `for` loop in the body of the function takes care of calling the respective function three times. Now, `FPtr` is a pointer to the function member of `student` class containing no arguments and returning void. Thus, `(... *FPtr)()` calls the function pointed to by `FPtr`. The only catch is determining what should come in the place of ... (the three dots). Here, the `AddJob()` function for Lara is being called. We need `Lara.AddAssignment()` to be called. This is equivalent to calling `(Lara.*FPtr)()`. Now, `this` pointer value is `&Lara` at the moment as it is invoked by `Lara` object. Thus, `this->` is similar to `Lara::*`. So, we now write `(this ->* FPtr)()` to call the invoking object's respective function.

Calling the function indirectly Finally, the calls made to `AddJob()` are to be explained. Note how the `FunPtr` variable is defined and assigned to `AddAssignment()` function and observe the call as well.

```
void(Student::*JobFunPtr)();
// Defining a function pointer

JobFunPtr = Student::AddAssignment;
// no () after the function name
Lara.AddJob(JobFunPtr, 3)
```

Obviously, `JobFunPtr` can be replaced by `Student::Assignment` and the call works the same. The solution using function pointer is difficult to understand at a glance, but is advantageous as explained.

4.18 LINKAGE SPECIFICATION

We can call functions defined in C in a C++ program. It is not straightforward though. The important questions here are in what way are the functions in C different from those in C++ and why they cannot be called as they are.

C++ compiler processes its functions in a more rigorous manner than C. It *decorates* the compiled function to represent its arguments and their types. This is needed because of function overloading. This decoration is also known as *mangling.* Whenever a function call is made, C++ must pick up the right version. Finding this out at run-time will hamper the performance of the C++ program. Therefore, it is important that the compiler itself adds information to the function definition to differentiate each overloaded function.

Every overloaded function is changed by the C++ compiler in such a way that it is uniquely identified at run-time and there is no overhead to find the correct version at run-time.

A good solution to the problem is that the name of the function changes to a new name known only to the compiler. This new name is different from the new names given to other overloaded functions with the same name. `Add(int, int)` might change to `Add_int_int(int, int)` and `Add(float, float)` might change to `Add_float_float(float, float)`. The function `Add()`, is renamed by the compiler as `Add_int_int` when an integer argument is passed, and renamed as `Add_float_float` when a float argument is passed. Thus, though the user has defined both functions with the same name `Add`, the compiler inherently defines two different functions with different names and uses them accordingly. So, there is no overhead at run-time. Wherever a function call is made as `Add(FloatVar1, FloatVar2)`, the compiler converts the call to `Add_float_float(FloatVar1, FloatVar2)` after deducing the type of both the arguments to be float and unambiguously deciding in favour of calling the float version of the `Add`. Thus, the run-time system does not encounter different versions of `Add` and does not need to deduce the argument types at run-time to find out which function to call.

When a function name is changed by the compiler for unique identification at run-time, the process is known as *name decoration* or *name mangling.*

A function compiled as a C function does not have this feature. Obviously, the *same* function, when compiled as a C++ function, will have a *different* name than when it is compiled as a C function (because of the additional information obtained and added by compiler to the original function name when compiled). If a function is compiled as a C function, we cannot access it in the same manner as a C++ function.

Linking happens after compilation. Inline functions are processed by the compiler, whereas non-inline functions are processed at run-time.

The non-inline function code is not accessed at compile time; it is accessed at linking time. (The function is also accessed at the time of execution, but we will not discuss that at the moment.) Linking is the next phase after compilation where all scattered functions called by the `main()` program are combined together with the `main()` program to build a single executable. At this point of time, the C or C++

Linkage specification
describes how a
function is linked to a
C++ executable.

functions are added to make the exe file. In order to attach a C function, we need to specify that we are attaching a C function at the time of linking. It should be noted that C++ linkage is by default and we need not specify anything if we need to link our function as a C++ function. This specification is known as *linkage specification*.

A function needs to be used as a C function when only the object code of the function is available and the function needs to be called in a C++ program, that is, whenever the library of functions designed by somebody else is being used and the library contains a C function that is needed in a C++ program. In such a case, linkage specification is used. Study the following example.

```
#include <iostream>
using namespace std;
extern "C" void TestCLinkage();

void main()
{
   TestCLinkage();
}

void TestCLinkage()
{
   cout << "Hi, I am linked the C way.\n";
}
```

The statement

```
extern "C" void TestCLinkage();
```

specifies the linkage specification. Note that the word extern is a must before the language name. Moreover, note that the letter 'C' is in uppercase; lowercase 'c' will not work here. If there are multiple functions to link the C way, it can be done as shown in the following program.

> **Note** It is possible to use a compiled C function from some library in a C++ program. We need to have C linkage specification for such functions.

```
#include <iostream>
using namespace  std;
extern "C"
{
   void TestCLinkage();
   void TestCLinkage2();
}
void main()
{
   TestCLinkage();
   TestCLinkage2();
}
void TestCLinkage()
{
   cout << "Hi, I am function no. 1. I am linked the C way.\n";
}
```

```
void TestCLinkage2()
{
    cout << "Hi, I am function No. 2. I am also linked the C way.\n";
}
```

In some specific compilers, linkage specification for other languages is also possible. However, C linkage specification is possible with all C++ compilers.

If a C library is being used, the prototype can be written in the way mentioned and the functions can be accessed the same way as in C. It should be understood that we are dealing with a stage after compilation, and so, we are dealing with the object code. The source code of the function is not needed here. The object code (.obj file) will do. Therefore, in the case of a function library without source code, providing C linkage is the only solution to use those functions. If the source code is available, a better option is to recompile them as C++ and link using C++ linkage. It is always better to recompile the old C library function as a C++ function and use this. When the source code is available, developers use this method. When the function is recompiled, C linkage which is much slower, which is not preferred.

■ RECAPITULATION ■

- C++ functions are similar to C functions. The functions, such as calling, returning, and executing, work in the same manner and the stack is involved in the same way as in C.
- C++ provides an inline function. This function call is expanded like a macro. Inline functions are very efficient and solve the problems associated with the macros of C. However, it is not possible to make all functions inline.
- It is possible for the arguments to have a default value in C++. The default arguments, if any, must be preceded by all the normal arguments in the argument list.
- Functions in C++ can receive as arguments and return objects additionally.
- It is possible to pass a reference and return a reference from a C++ function.
- When a C++ function returns a reference, it can be on the RHS of an assignment statement. Function prototype is compulsory in C++ when the function is used before the definition.
- It is also possible to overload a function with the same name but different numbers of arguments or different types of arguments in C++. This is known as function overloading.
- A C++ function can be defined as a member function of some class or a non-member function.
- It requires critical introspection to decide whether to make a function a member or a non-member.
- It is also possible to declare a function as a friend of some class. In such a case, the function that is not the member of the specific class will be able to access the private members of the class.
- Like const and volatile variables, we can have const and volatile objects in C++. A function can also be a const or a volatile function.
- A const function cannot alter the value of a data member except for the ones defined as mutable.
- Functions can also be defined as static. These functions are not exactly member functions of a class. They can only work with static data members of the class. Usually, these functions are public.
- A pointer to a non-member function is similar to a function pointer in C. It is also possible to define a function pointer to a function member in C++. They are very useful in making the program more flexible.
- It is possible for a C++ program to use a compiled C function from some library. We need to have a C linkage specification for such functions.
- A normal C function in its compiled form is different from a C++ function because the C++ function is name mangled whereas a C function is not. Thus, a function when compiled as a C function generates a different object code than when the same function is compiled as a C++ function.

■ KEYWORDS ■

Call by reference This refers to defining an object as a reference in the function header and passing and accepting it as a reference argument in a function.

Const function This is a function that guarantees not to modify the invoking object. If the body of the const function contains a statement that modifies the invoking object, the program will not be compiled. One exception here is the mutable data member, which can be modified by the const function.

Default arguments The arguments to the function, when not passed, take the default value either specified in the prototype or the header of the function. All default arguments must come after all normal arguments in the function header or prototype.

Friend function A friend is either a non-member function or a member function of some other class, which is given special permission to access private variables of the class. The function is said to be the friend of the class under consideration.

Function overloading C++ allows more than one function with the same name but with different sets of arguments. This process is known as function overloading and each participating function is known as overloaded function.

Function prototyping The header of the function with or without the name of the arguments but with the type of arguments is known as function prototype. When function itself is defined after the call is made, function prototype must precede the call.

Inline function This is a function whose function statement is replaced by the body of the function at the time of compilation.

Linkage specification This is the specification that tells the linker how to link a function. C++ linkage is by default.

Mutable data member This is a special member of the class that can be modified by a const function.

Name mangling The process of generating a unique name for a function when there is a possibility of confusion (when function overloading is possible) is known as name mangling. This is possible in the case when the function is linked as a C++ function (a default case). Thus, the compiler name mangles all C++ functions.

Non-member function This refers to a function that is not defined as a member function of any class or a standalone function.

Name return value (NRV) optimization When a called function defines and returns the local object to be assigned to an object of a calling function, compiler optimizes the code by adding an additional argument to the function, which is the reference of the calling function object. The definition of the local object and the returnstatement is now eliminated. This is known as NRV ptimization.

Polymorphism The ability of the object to react differently to the same command in different contexts is known as polymorphism.

Return by reference This refers to returning a reference of an object from the function. It should rightly be the reference of a calling function object. Returning a reference of a local object might have unforeseen consequences.

Static function The static function is preceded by the keyword static in the definition. It can only access the static members of the class. Though static member functions are defined like member functions, they are not truly members.

■ EXERCISES ■

Multiple Choice Questions

1. At which point of time is the code of a non-inline function not accessible?
   (a) Linking time
   (b) Compile time
   (c) Loading time
   (d) None of the above
2. Polymorphism refers to the ability of the object to _____ to the same command in _____.
   (a) react differently, same contexts
   (b) react same, same contexts
   (c) react same, different contexts
   (d) react differently, different contexts
3. When we take the address of a function, it returns _____.
   (a) the entry point address of the function
   (b) the exit point address of the function
   (c) the call point address of the function
   (d) the definition point address of the functions
4. Private member functions cannot be called by _____.
   (a) public member functions
   (b) friend functions
   (c) non-member functions
   (d) All of the above

5. We can also have _____ as friend functions of some other class.
   (a) non-member functions of a class
   (b) member functions of a class
   (c) global functions
   (d) All of the above
6. The arguments used in the function call are known as _____.
   (a) actual arguments
   (b) dummy arguments
   (c) dummy parameters
   (d) None of the above
7. The functions that are not associated with class are _____.
   (a) inline functions
   (b) member functions
   (c) non-member functions
   (d) const functions
8. How can a data member be modified even by a const function?
   (a) It is never possible.
   (b) It is possible without any specification.
   (c) It is possible when the member is declared mutable.
   (d) It is possible when the member is declared const.
9. We need to use the `<class name>`_____ to precede the function while defining the pointer to function.
   (a) `.*`
   (b) `::*`
   (c) `->*`
   (d) `::`
10. What can be written in the blank with the function definition?

    ```
    <return type><function name>(argument1, ...)
    _____
    {
        <function body>
    }
    ```
    (a) `static`
    (b) `const`
    (c) `volatile`
    (d) `friend`

Conceptual Exercises

1. List out the differences between C functions and C++ functions.
2. Write a simple program with two or more functions. If you are working with either Turbo C or Visual C++, try to trace the function to look at the sequence of function calling.
3. What are the advantages and disadvantages of inline functions? When are inline functions preferred over normal functions?
4. Write a macro for finding the maximum of two numbers. Use it in finding the maximum of five numbers. Rewrite the same program using inline function for finding the maximum of two numbers and discuss the advantages and disadvantages of both the approaches with respect to your program.
5. Show a case where default arguments are important. Why does a single default argument function prevent the overloading of a same function without any argument?
6. How can you check if your compiler applies NRV? It is made mandatory in the standard. Check with your compiler manual how to enable or disable the NRV.
7. What is the advantage of having `this` pointer? Where can it be useful?
8. List the differences between member and non-member functions. Can you add a few other differences yourself?
9. When we return a reference it is better than returning a large object as it requires more context switching. It also has a disadvantage. One can unknowingly use that function in the LHS with unforeseen consequences. What is the solution to this problem?
10. How is polymorphism related to function over-loading?
11. Give an example where it is better to have over-loaded functions than default arguments.
12. Discuss the importance of friend. Give an example where a friend function is a better choice than a non-member function.
13. Discuss the disadvantages of making more member functions than possible in a class. What are the ways one can make member a function a non-member one?
14. What is the difference between a normal function and a const function? Show a case where const function is more useful than normal function.
15. What is the usefulness of static functions? Compare static functions with normal functions.
16. Differentiate between private and public functions. Give one example of a private function that is useful for a class.
17. How can pointer to function be defined for a class member function? List out the differences between pointer to normal functions and pointer to member functions.

18. How can we define pointer to static functions? Test it using a small program of your choice.
19. What is the advantage of function pointers? Give an example other than shown in the book to explain the advantage. Show the usefulness of the :: * operator.
20. What is name mangling? Why is it required?
21. What is linkage specification? Explain the need for linkage specification.

Practical Exercises

1. Write a function for finding the average age of a class `student`. Pass an array of student objects as a parameter to that function. Assume the default class strength to be 50. Provide default strength as a default argument to the function.
2. Define `Time` class with string containing seconds elapsed until midnight (12:00 AM) as a single data member. Write `AddTime()` function, which adds two different `Time` objects and returns a new `Time` object. Write a `DisplayNormal()` function, which converts the time in seconds and displays it in a normal fashion HH:MM:SS.
3. Modify Program 4.6 in such a way that it does not return zeros in the fields when the first `Time` argument is a later time than the second one. It should find the absolute time difference between both the times and return the result.
4. Modify Program 4.6 to use `Time` class with seconds elapsed until midnight as a single data member rather than `Hours`, `Minutes` and `Seconds`.
5. Modify Program 4.7 such that the use of global variable is eliminated.
6. Modify Program 4.7 such that it returns the absolute time difference between both the times the object is passed and does not return zeros when the first `Time` argument is later than the second one.
7. Modify Program 4.6 in such a way that it uses overloaded function instead of default arguments.
8. Modify Program 4.7 in such a way that it uses overloaded function instead of default arguments.
9. Define a class `Car`. Add `Make`, `Colour`, `Size`, and `Cost` as data members. Write member functions for reading and printing the values of the car. Define one more class as `CarCollection`. This class should contain the member functions `Add()`, `Delete()`, `Modify()`, and `Replace()`. `CarCollection` is to be defined as friend of `Car` class.
10. Use the class `Car` of Problem 9. Provide a friend function `Replace()`, which replaces the content of a `Car` object with another `Car` object.
11. Use classes `Employee` and `CollectionEmp` described in the chapter. Write a friend function `Union` of `CollectionEmp()` with two different `CollectionEmp` objects. It should return the result as one more `CollectionEmp` object.
12. Use classes `Car` and `CarCollection` of Problem 9. Write a friend function `Union` of `CarCollection()` with two different `CarCollection` objects. It should return the result as one more `CarCollection` object.
13. Use classes `Employee` and `CollectionEmp` described in the chapter. Write a friend function `Intersection` of `CollectionEmp()` with two different `CollectionEmp` objects. It should return the result as one more `CollectionEmp` object.
14. Use classes `Car` and `CarCollection` of Problem 9. Write a friend function `Intersection` of `CarCollection()` with two different `CarCollection` objects. It should return the result as one more `CarCollection` object.
15. Use the class `Employee` defined in the chapter and write a static function for finding out the total male and female employees. Modify the class if required.
16. Use the class `Car` of Problem 9 and write a static function that displays the total cars with different makes. Modify the class if required.
17. Define a private function `IsOld()` which, given a make, decides if the car is old or not. Assume that for different makes specific lifetime is provided in an array. A car is considered old if the car is older than half its lifetime. Modify the `Car` class to provide for using this function in a member `CarDescription()` function. The `CarDescription()` function describes the car completely and also tells whether the car is old or not.
18. Use `Employee` and `EmpCollection` classes of the chapter and provide `GetSubordinates()` friend function, which returns an object of `EmpCollection` class containing the details of the subordinates of a manager. The employee object describing the manager is to be passed as a parameter.
19. Define a class `Person` containing the name of the person, names of parents of the person, gender, age, and an array containing the list of interests as the data members. Provide functions `FindFather()`, `FindMother()`, `FindUncle()`, and `FindAunty()`, all of which return the objects of the `Person` class. Provide access using function pointers for all these functions.

Chapter 5

Constructors and Destructors

5.1 SIMILAR-TO-BUILT-IN BEHAVIOUR CONCEPT

One of the major thrusts during C++ design was to make the user-created C++ objects behave in a similar way to the built-in objects as much as possible. C++ provides a host of facilities to make this possible such as the automatic initialization (and destruction) of data types. Let us try to understand this with an example. When we write `int i = 25` in a C++ program, it is similar to writing `int i(25)`. Here, i is initialized with the value 25 while being defined.

It is possible to write the following statement to initialize `CaptainStudent` while defining it:

```
student CaptainStudent(1, "Brian Lara", "West Indies");
```

Constructors are special functions that provide this service; they enable us to initialize user-defined objects while defining them, as shown in the examples. Suppose a class for customer has already been defined. It is possible to write

```
customer Javed("Miandad", "Pakistan", "Cricketer", "Cricket bats");
```

which not only defines Javed to be a customer, but also initializes his data such as the surname, address, category, and what items he is interested in. We have used the `Init` function in Chapter 4 in Programs 4.13, 4.14, 4.16 and 4.17 involving the class `employee`. A constructor for providing the same services in an automated way can be written to replace the `Init` function.

Once proper constructors are introduced in the class, the need for object initialization automatically arises.

5.2 NEED FOR OBJECT INITIALIZATION

The need for initialization of objects arises from various reasons, some of which are listed as follows:

1. When an object is declared, it may be needed to initialize the individual data members to some specific default values. Initializing integer variables to zero and pointer variables to null are two very common initializations. For example, when a stack object is defined, the stack pointer may be initialized to null using a constructor. The following is a sample from the program given in Section 5.3:

```
class Stack
{
private:
   int StackPointer;
   int StackArray[10];
public:
   Stack()
   {
      StackPointer = 0;
   }
};
```

2. Dynamic memory allocation may be required when an object is defined. For example, if a program for billing a customer is made, the items purchased by the individual customers may vary a lot. Only when the customer object is initialized will it be possible to know the number of items being purchased by that particular customer. It is always better to provide just enough memory for those items using dynamic memory allocation, when the object is constructed.

The following is a customer constructor allocating enough memory to hold `TotalItems` number of items. The total number of items purchased by the customer is passed to the constructor and an integer pointer `ItemArray` defined inside `customer` class is now to act as a dynamic array. The memory to hold `TotalItems` number of items is to be obtained, which is done using `new Item[TotalItems]`.

```
Customer(int TotalItems)
{
   ItemArray = new Item[TotalItems];
}
```

3. Objects may need to be set to special values. Constructors help in both defining the objects and giving them special values. When a new student is defined, we can provide his name, address, and other attributes along with it. For example, when `TempName` is passed, the customer's name is initialized with it.

```
Customer(string TempName)
{
   CustomerName = TempName;
}
```

4. When inheritance is in effect, if a base class has a constructor, a derived class must also have one to initialize itself. (If the programmer forgets to do it, then the compiler synthesizes one by itself. However, it may not be the same as what the programmer wants it to be.) We will discuss in detail about the base and inherited classes and the effect on constructors by this hierarchy in Chapter 9.

If a class `IndianCustomer` is inherited from class `Customer` as follows

```
class IndianCustomer:public Customer
{...}
```

and if a constructor has not been defined in this class while the base class `Customer` has a constructor, then it will be provided by the compiler.

5.3 INTRODUCTION TO CONSTRUCTORS

A constructor has the following two main functions:

1. It automatically initializes the object (i.e., the constructor function need not be called explicitly; it is automatically called when the object is defined).
2. It usually provides initial values for the data members of the object.

> **Note** A constructor function always has the same name as the class itself. Constructors are almost always invoked automatically, though they can also be called explicitly.

The following program describes how to define and use constructors. This example is related to building a stack object. Earlier, we needed to call an explicit function for initializing the value of an index to zero after creating a stack object, but now it is done automatically using a constructor. Observe the definition of the Stack() function. It should be noted that it bears the same name as the class itself, that is, Stack is a class that has Stack() as a constructor.

A minor modification has been done to Program 3.3 in Chapter 3 where InitializeSP() was used to initialize the value of the stack pointer after defining the object. However, after introducing constructors, this is no longer needed. In the earlier example, after defining a stack object, if one forgets to call InitializeSP(), one would end up with an erroneous result because the stack pointer will be incremented and decremented with a random value. If the value of the stack pointer is not initialized to zero, both push and pop operations would not work as expected. This problem is avoided using a constructor in the following program. Each time an object of the Stack class is defined, the Stack() function would automatically be called, and the respective stack pointer (belonging to that object—it should be remembered that all objects have their unique copies of data members) would initialize to zero.

```cpp
//SimpleConstructor.cpp
#include <iostream>
using namespace std;
class Stack
{
private:
   int StackPointer;
   int StackArray[10];
public:
   Stack()    // This is the constructor
   {
      StackPointer = 0;
   }
   // Pushing the elements into the stack
   void push(int value)
   {
      if(StackPointer == 9)
      {
         cout << "Stack overflow!  Cannot insert";
      }
      else
```

```
                {
                        StackArray[StackPointer] = value; StackPointer++;
                }
        }
        // popping the elements out of the stack
        int pop()
        {
            if(StackPointer == 0)
            cout << "Stack underflow!  Cannot pop";
            else
            {
                    StackPointer--;
                    return StackArray[StackPointer];
            }
        }
};
void main()
{
    Stack MyStack;
    // MyStack.InitializeSP();
    /* automatically done; there is no need to do it explicitly */
    MyStack.push(1);
    MyStack.push(2);
    cout << MyStack.pop()<< "\n";
    cout << MyStack.pop()<< "\n";
}
```

> **Note** The advantage of a constructor is to have automatic initialization, which results in better operation. If a programmer is required to manually initialize the object every time he/she defines it, there is a huge chance of missing it once in a while and errors getting introduced in the code. The best part of having a constructor is that such errors are eliminated by introducing proper constructors.

This example may be difficult to understand for those who do not know what stacks are. The usefulness of a constructor is shown here. The thumb rule is that at certain times one needs to set the members of an object to a default value; only then will the other operations be meaningful. In this example, the push and pop operations can take place only when the stack pointer is initialized to zero. If the program does not have a constructor, the stack pointer should be explicitly set to zero. Such an approach would be both tedious and error-prone. Thus, the advantage of using constructors is that it provides a simpler and better approach.

5.4 RULES FOR DEFINING CONSTRUCTORS

Certain rules need to be followed when constructors are defined and used; some important ones are as follows:

1. A constructor *must* have the same name as the class.

2. A consequence of rule 1 is that there cannot be more than one constructor with different names and same arguments. If there is a need for more than one constructor, one should have a single constructor and overload it with different sets of arguments.

3. A constructor cannot specify a return type. Even writing void is not allowed (though a constructor always returns the object of the class it belongs to *after constructing it*).

> **Note** Although constructors cannot specify a return type, they always return the object of the class they belong to.

4. A constructor should not have a return statement in the body of the constructor.

5. The address of a constructor cannot be obtained. Hence, there cannot be a function pointer pointing to a constructor.

6. A constructor can be defined as private, but then it would not be possible to define objects using those constructors. This is because defining a constructor as private tries to execute a private function by the object at the time of definition, which is not allowed. Therefore, unless normal definition of the object is not restricted, the constructors should be defined as public.

5.5 DEFAULT CONSTRUCTORS

A default constructor is one with no argument or with all default arguments, that is, it is a constructor with an empty argument list or with all arguments having some default value (so that the constructor can be called without any argument). There are two different types of default constructors. When the user does not define any constructor, it is a compiler-provided default constructor, and when the user provides one, it is a user-defined one. The compiler-defined default constructor may not be synthesized by the compiler in all cases and will be synthesized only when the default constructor is necessary. The user can specify the default constructor whenever he/she wishes to do so. Usually, when a user provides a constructor, the compiler does not provide one.

5.5.1 Compiler-defined Default Constructor

Suppose a few objects of a class are defined but no constructors are defined for them. What will happen when that object is defined? For example, when the statement

```
student CaptainStudent;
```

is executed, what actually happens?

In such a case, memory that is sufficient for storing the complete CaptainStudent is set aside and given the name 'CaptainStudent'. If CaptainStudent is addressed later on, the content of this address is fetched.

When the constructors are not provided by the programmers, C++ will provide the same effect by synthesizing the physical constructor code in some of the non-trivial cases. If only memory allocation for the object is to be performed, the effect is provided but the physical constructor code is not synthesized. It would be interesting to know when the physical coding of a constructor is needed, but this is beyond the scope of an introductory book. Readers are encouraged to refer to Stanly Lippman's classic *Inside the C++ Object Model* for the description. For simplicity, we assume that the constructor is provided and we have the effect of construction

> When the user does not define any constructor, the compiler provides a default constructor.

of the object. This C++ constructor enables us to use the object CaptainStudent later in the program by constructing that object. Constructors of this form, which do not take any parameters, are known as default constructors.

> **Note** Physical constructors are not always synthesized by the compiler. However, there are a few non-trivial cases where the operation demands such synthesis.

5.5.2 User-defined Default Constructor

The default constructors synthesized by the compiler cannot do all the initializations that are needed for a class. The synthesized constructor only fulfils the requirements of the compiler. Even when the physical constructor is not synthesized, the compiler provides only those effects that will suit its own requirements and not that of the users. Thus, memory allocation is provided but initialization is not provided by compiler. When we define CaptainStudent, we expect a memory size good enough to hold the object and would like to use it (by storing information about the members of CaptainStudent and manipulate it). The compiler would provide that memory using this constructor. However, the compiler does not need initialization, so it is not provided by the default constructor. Initialization is the programmer's responsibility and should be done explicitly. Consider an example of a node class for a linked list.

```
class node
{
   int Value;
   int *PtrNextValue; // Other items needed for node
}
```

In this case, suppose the node is used as follows:

```
node First;
// checking for empty list
if(First.PtrNextValue)
/* Wrong! The pointer is not initialized to null */
{
     // Necessary action
}
```

Here, consider the statement

```
node First;
```

Depending on the situation, a compiler may define a default constructor for us. However, it only provides memory allocation to store the object of type node in this case (and no physical constructor is constructed). It will certainly not initialize either Value or PtrNextValue for us. It is a programmer's job and if they need to be initialized, the constructor must be written as follows:

> Compilers provide the additions that suit their own require- ments and not that of the users.

```
class node
{
   int Value;
   int *PtrNextValue;
public:
   node()
```

> A constructor is automatically called every time the object definition appears in the program.

```
{
Value = 0;
PtrNextValue = 0;

/* Assigning zero to a pointer is correct in C++; it is the same as
assigning the pointer a null, i.e., "\0" */
}
// Other items needed for node
};
```

So, writing the following statement

```
node First;
```

would automatically do the following:

```
First.Value = 0;
```

and

```
First.PtrNextValue = 0;      (i.e., "\0" or null)
```

Now, `First.PtrNextValue` would be executed properly. It is to be noted that we are not explicitly writing anything for initializing data member values; it is automatically done when the object is defined.

The constructors used in these two examples are also called user-defined default constructors. A constructor without arguments is called a default constructor. It can be seen that it must be defined by the programmer for cases such as mentioned in the examples.

> **Note** There are two types of default constructors, one provided by the compiler and the other user defined. The compiler automatically provides one when the user does not define the constructor explicitly. The compiler may synthesize it physically (actually add that code in the object code created after compilation) or just provide that effect, depending on the situation.

As mentioned earlier, when the compiler provides a constructor, it does the job that just satisfies the compiler's need and not that of the programmer. For specific needs of the programmer, a user-defined constructor needs to be written. Let us look at one more example to understand the usefulness of a user-defined constructor.

Cases Where a Default Constructor is not Needed

It has already been mentioned that the compiler provides automatic constructors when needed. Sometimes, it becomes redundant if the user also provides a default constructor. Therefore, it is always better to leave it to the compiler in case we do not want any different behaviour.

Program 5.1 is an example where the default constructor for `ItemCollection` is redundant.

PROGRAM 5.1 Redundant default constructor

```
//UselessDefaultConstructor.cpp
#include <iostream>
#include <string>
using namespace  std;

class Item
{
```

```cpp
    int ItemNo;
    string ItemName;
public:
    Item()        // Default constructor
    {
        ItemNo = 0;
        ItemName = "";
        /* This is not required as String object is initialized already by the constructor
        provided in string class */
    }

    void SetDetails(int TempItemNo, string TempItemName)
    {
        ItemNo = TempItemNo;
        ItemName = TempItemName;
    }

    void ShowDetails()
    {
        cout << "\n Item number is" << ItemNo;
        cout << "\n Item name is" << ItemName;
    }
};

class ItemCollection
{
    Item ItemArray[20];
    int ItemIndex;
public:
    ItemCollection()      // Default constructor
    /* If we remove this default constructor, it will not affect the program */
    {
        for(int i=0; i<20; i++)
        ItemArray[i].SetDetails(0, "");
        ItemIndex = 0;
    }

    void SetDetails(Item TempItemArray[])
    {
        for(int i=0; i<20; i++)
        ItemArray[i] = TempItemArray[i];
    }

    void PrintDetails()
    {
        for(int i=0; i<20; i++)
        ItemArray[i].ShowDetails();
    }
};

int main()
{
    ItemCollection IC;
    Item TempItemArray[20];
    for(int i=0; i<20; i++)
    {
        TempItemArray[i].SetDetails(i, "Dummy");
    }
    IC.SetDetails(TempItemArray); IC.PrintDetails();
}
```

The readers are encouraged to try the following. Get the output of the program. Remove the default constructor of `ItemCollection` class and get the output again. Observe the difference.

The output does not change. This is because the default constructor is initialized to zero and " " is redundant. It is just a good programming practice to initialize, so that if one forgets to assign values to it later, one would get a value zero and " " and realize the error. When the constructor is not provided, those values are not initialized. As long as reasonable values are provided to both of them, there will not be any trouble and no significant issue is created.

The `ItemCollection` default constructor is anyway redundant, as `Item` constructor is already initializing `Items`.

Cases Where a Default Constructor must be Present

Sometimes, initialization is very important and the counter begins from there. So, if a default constructor is not provided, the counter is not initialized, which will lead to an incorrect execution.

Program 5.2 is an example where the user-defined default constructor must be present.

 PROGRAM 5.2   Useful default constructor

```cpp
//DefaultConstructor.cpp
#include <iostream>
#include <string>
using namespace std;

class Item
{
    int ItemNo;
    string ItemName;
public:
    Item()      // Default constructor
    {
        ItemNo = 0;
        ItemName = "";
        /* This is redundant as the string constructor must have done this already */
    }

    void SetDetails(int TempItemNo, string TempItemName)
    {
        ItemNo = TempItemNo;
        ItemName = TempItemName;
    }

    void ShowDetails()
    {
        cout << "\n Item number is" << ItemNo;
        cout << "\n Item name is" << ItemName;
    }
};

class ItemCollection
{
    Item ItemArray[20];
    int ItemIndex;
public:
    ItemCollection()// Default constructor
    {
```

```
/* The following for loop is not required. This will actually be added by the
compiler when the array is defined by the class in the first line (Item ItemArray[]20;)
by calling the Item() constructor. */

    for(int i=0; i<20; i++)
        ItemArray[i].SetDetails(0, "");

    // The following is important
    ItemIndex = 0;
}

/* This default constructor is needed as ItemIndex is initialized here and
afterwards incremented. Other parts of the constructor are redundant and can be
removed. */

void PrintDetails()
{
    for(int i=0; i<ItemIndex; i++)
    ItemArray[i].ShowDetails();
}

void InsertItem(int TempItemNo, string TempItemName)
{
    ItemArray[ItemIndex].SetDetails(TempItemNo, TempItemName);
    ItemIndex++;
    /* This statement flags an error in the absence of a default constructor */
}
};
int main()
{
    ItemCollection IC;
    IC.InsertItem(105,"Pentium4 processor"); IC.InsertItem(111,"Seagate HDD");
    IC.InsertItem(122,"Samsung monitor"); IC.InsertItem(220,"Creative sound card");
    IC.PrintDetails();
}
```

How the Program Works

Programs 5.1 and 5.2 have two different classes; one is Item and the other is ItemCollection, which contains an array of items. Both of them have default constructors defined. Let us ignore the default constructor for Item and consider only that for ItemCollection in the second case, because it is important here. Program 5.1 contains functions that insert values in the complete set of items in a single shot, using an array. Program 5.2 inserts items one by one. The default constructor in Program 5.1 initializes item numbers as zeros and names as blank strings and also initializes ItemIndex to zero. If this default constructor is removed, it will have no effect on the program, which would be executed as it is.

However, in Program 5.2, initializing ItemIndex to zero is an important step. If the default constructor is removed, the program will not be able to function properly because the functions InsertItem() and PrintDetails() are dependent on that value. Every time InsertItem() is called, ItemIndex is incremented. When the function is called for the first time, it has to increment from zero. If it is not initialized to zero, InsertItem() inserts items at random locations represented by the value of ItemIndex.

It is also possible to define constructors other then default constructors. Let us discuss this in detail.

5.6 CONSTRUCTORS WITH ONE PARAMETER

A constructor with a single argument is a special type of constructor because it actually defines two operations instead of one. Program 5.3 illustrates this concept. The class brother has a single data member, a string indicating the brother name. Here, a single-argument constructor is introduced. When a string containing the name of the brother is passed to this, it constructs an object of type brother.

PROGRAM 5.3 Single-argument constructor

```cpp
//SingleArgCons.cpp
#include <iostream>
#include <string>
using namespace  std;

class brother
{
    string Name;
public:
    brother(string BrotherName)
    {
        Name = BrotherName;
    }
};

void main()
{
    int j(5);    /* int j = 5 is its shorthand notation */
    int i = int(5);
    double f(3.4);   /* Equivalent of double f = 3.4 */
    brother FirstBrother = brother("Steve Waugh");
    brother SecondBrother("Mark Waugh");
    brother ThirdBrother("Gilchrist");
    brother FourthBrother = "Ricky Ponting";
}
```

How the Program Works

This program is very simple to understand. Given a single argument to brother constructor, it constructs an object of type brother.

An interesting point to note is the possible ways to invoke a constructor while defining an object. It should be observed that int i = 5; is understood by the compiler as int i(5); this means that the compiler obtains memory that can hold an int, gives the value 5 to it and then assigns it to I; the statement int i = int(5); is also a case of initialization. The object referred by i is initialized by the temporary object created by the compiler. This temporary object is created earlier with initialization to value 5 from int(5).

It can be observed that the same shorthand notations also work for user-defined objects.

```
brother FirstBrother = brother("Steve Waugh");
(explicit call to brother function; i.e., the constructor)
brother SecondBrother("Mark Waugh");
brother FourthBrother = "Ricky Ponting";
```

Here, the second statement is similar to the third one. In all three cases, the compiler calls the user-defined constructor function (brother function defined in the class here) and constructs

> Whenever a constructor containing a single argument is defined, the compiler automatically defines a conversion operator to convert between the argument type and the user-defined object type.

and initializes the object being defined with it. There is a difference, though. In the first case, the constructor function is called explicitly and in the other two it is called automatically (implicitly). There is a technical difference as well. The first case has an overhead of a temporary object while the other two cases do not have it.

Automatic Generation of Conversion Operator

Now, let us look at another interesting point. The readers might wonder why the last statement of the program, that is,

```
brother FourthBrother = "Ricky Ponting";
```

is compiled without an error. The left-hand side (LHS) is an object of type brother and the right-hand side (RHS) is a C-type string. The program does not have any converter for converting a C-type string to brother class. A brother object is being initialized with a character array (i.e., C-type string). Both the brother object and the C-type string are of different types. How could C++ provide this conversion without our specific instructions? This is because whenever a constructor containing a single argument is defined, the compiler *automatically* defines a conversion operator for converting between the argument type (here, it is a C-type string) and the user-defined object type.

The following program is one more example that shows how a class Number is assigned a built-in item (integer).

In the last statement No2 = 5; we have not specified any conversion operator for converting from an integer to a number, but it is still done automatically.

```cpp
//ImplicitConversion.cpp
#include <iostream>
#include <string>
using namespace std;
class Number
{
   int Value;
public:
   Number()
   {
      Value = 0;
   }
   Number(int TempValue)
   {
      Value = TempValue;
   }
};
void main()
{
   Number No1(5); Number No2;
   No2 = 5;
   /* This is implicit conversion. 5 is converted to Number Object and then assigned
   to No2*/
}
```

We will study about conversion operators in Chapter 6. There are situations wherein we do not want the compiler to do the automatic conversion. The procedure to be followed in such cases is explained in Section 5.7.

5.7 EXPLICIT CONSTRUCTORS

In most cases, automatic conversion adds to readability. It is, therefore, very useful. However, there are times when we can do without such implicit conversion. The creation of the conversion operator can be avoided by using the keyword `explicit` before the class name while defining the object. If we do not want a form of

```
brother FourthBrother = "Ricky Ponting"
```

to work like

```
brother FourthBrother("Ricky Ponting")
```

then we need to precede the constructor name by the keyword `explicit`. Let us discuss this using a modified example given in Program 5.4.

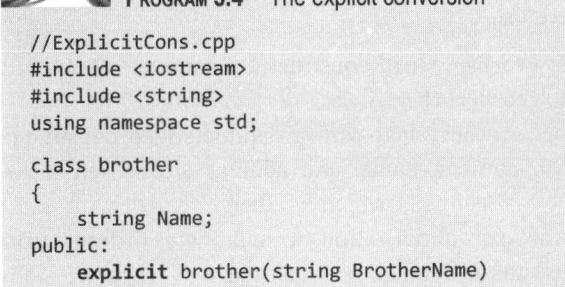

PROGRAM 5.4   The explicit conversion

```
//ExplicitCons.cpp
#include <iostream>
#include <string>
using namespace std;

class brother
{
    string Name;
public:
    explicit brother(string BrotherName)
    /* See the explicit keyword before the constructor */
    {
        Name = BrotherName;
    }
};

void main()
{
    brother FirstBrother = brother("Steve Waugh");
    brother SecondBrother("Mark Waugh");
    brother ThirdBrother("Gilchrist");

    // The following statement is erroneous

    brother FourthBrother = "Ricky Ponting";

    /* A compiler would flag an error such as "initializing":  cannot convert from "char[11]"
    to "brother" */
}
```

How the Program Works

Why is it that the statement

```
brother fourthBrother = "Ricky Ponting"
```

will not work whereas

> It is possible to call a constructor explicitly, which then generates a temporary object of the same class.

```
brother FirstBrother = brother("Steve Waugh")
```

will work? This is because the temporary object in the second case is initialized with Steve Waugh and is then used to initialize FirstBrother. Here, both the objects are of the same type and no conversion is needed. However, in the first case, both the objects of the assignment were of different types.

Note Implicit conversion allows assignments in cases where we have two different objects on both sides.

5.8 PARAMETERIZED CONSTRUCTORS

When the constructor contains a single or multiple arguments, it is known as a parameterized constructor. Thus, the example of a constructor with one argument is also a case of parameterized constructor. This is useful when constructors are needed for creating objects, with required data values initialized.

We need to pass values to parameterized constructors, unlike default constructors. This can be done in two ways. The first way is to pass a setof arguments when the object is defined, as shown in Example 5.6. The other way is to explicitly call the constructor function to (re)initialize an object. For example,

```
brother SecondBrother = brother("Mark Waugh");
```

Here, the explicit call to the constructor brother() will construct a temporary object with Mark Waugh and then is used to initialize SecondBrother.

Program 5.5 extends our definition of student class with a parameterized constructor defined for the student object. The roll number, name, and address are passed to the constructor when the object is defined, which is then created with those parameters. This process is known as initialization. Assignment is different from initialization. We will discuss the difference between the two when we study copy constructors in Section 5.11.

> Initialization is a different process from assignment.

PROGRAM 5.5 *Parameterized constructor*

```cpp
//ParameterizedCon.cpp
#include <iostream>
#include <string>
using namespace std;

class student
{
public:
    int RollNumber; string Name; string Address;

    student(){}
    /* This is an empty default constructor. We need this for object student, which does not
    use a parameterized constructor */

    student(int TempRollNumber, string TempName, string TempAddress)
    // Parameterized constructor
    {
        RollNumber = TempRollNumber;
        Name = TempName;
        Address = TempAddress;
    }

    void PrintDetails()
```

```
    {
        cout << "Roll number is " << RollNumber << "\n";
        cout << "Name is " << Name << "\n";
        cout <<  "Address is   " << Address <<  "\n";
    }
};

void main()
{
    // See the use of constructor to initialize both objects

    student CricketStudent(1, "Brian Lara", "West Indies");
    student FootBallStudent(2, "David Beckham", "England");

    student TennisStudent;
    // The following is an explicit call to a constructor function
    TennisStudent = student(3, "Steffi Graf", "Germany");

    CricketStudent.PrintDetails();
    FootballStudent.PrintDetails();
    TennisStudent.PrintDetails();
}
```

How the Program Works

Empty default constructor The empty default constructor for student should be noted. This is now needed because of the statement

```
    student TennisStudent;
```

If there is no parameterized constructor, this statement will not have any problem, but if a parameterized constructor is present, then this statement will not be compiled.

Parameterized constructor and rerunning objects If a parameterized constructor is provided, then a default constructor (at times an empty one) should also be provided. This is a prerequisite if the objects are to be defined in the normal way.

> **Note** If we do not provide *any* constructor, the C++ compiler provides the effect of a default constructor. If we provide *a* constructor, be it a default or parameterized constructor, then the C++ compiler will not provide one.

Now, look at the explicit call to the constructor.

```
TennisStudent = student(3, "Steffi Graf", "Germany");
```

The constructors are usually not called directly; they are almost always called automatically. Moreover, it has been mentioned that constructors do not have a return statement. Here, student() is called similar to a normal function and it seems to be returning an object of type student class. It might be surprising to observe that a function has been defined without a return type specification, with no return statement, though it returns something.

Let us try to understand this. A constructor always returns the object for which it is written. It returns the object it has constructed, but cannot return anything else. If any return type is specified in the definition of the constructor, it means (to the compiler) that the intention is to send something else back. It means the same even if a return statement is written in the body of the constructor. So, both are prohibited. Though no return type is specified and the constructor contains no return statements inside the function body, it is always implicitly specified to be the native object.

The constructor always returns newly created objects without an explicit return statement.

Hence, in the following statement, when the function `student()` (the student constructor) is called, it creates an object from the data passed and then returns it as a temporary object.

```
TennisStudent = student(3, "Steffi Graf", "Germany");
```

> **Note** When temporary objects are created and destroyed, it puts a lot of overhead. The process of constructing temporary objects, then constructing the LHS objects, and finally copying member by member eats up a lot of time. The latest version of C++ 11 has introduced move semantics, which simplifies this process by just moving the contents of the temporary objects to the LHS objects. This is a great improvement, but we will not explore it further, as its usability can be shown only when we do some advanced programming.

5.9 MULTIPLE CONSTRUCTORS

Consider Program 5.5 once again. The object is used as the RHS of the assignment statement. It is then assigned to the LHS of the assignment, that is, `TennisStudent` object. The temporary object is destroyed as soon as the function exits and the assignment statement is applied. This method of explicitly calling constructors can also be used to dynamically reinitialize objects. We will be discussing this in Section 5.9.3. It is important to note that `TennisStudent` is not constructed by this statement. It has been done before when we have written `student TennisStudent;`. Here, `TennisStudent` is assigned the newly created object using the operation of object assignment. Refer to Chapter 3 for details of object assignment.

As long as their arguments are different, one can have many constructors for a class. A good class design, though, restricts the number of constructors to a few useful ones.

Program 5.5 has two constructors, one is an empty default constructor and the second one is parameterized. It is also possible to have more constructors for a class. One can define as many constructors as required by an application. However, it is always advisable to have as few as possible for efficiency reasons.

The following program uses multiple constructors for the same class. A class is used for storing time in the hours : minutes : seconds format. The time objects are initialized using the constructors. A constructor can be called with arguments of either all three, namely, hours, minutes and seconds, with arguments for hours and minutes, or with arguments for hours alone.

```
//MultipleCons.cpp
#include <iostream>
using namespace std;
class Time
{
public:
    int Hours;
    int Minutes;
    int Seconds;
    void ShowTime()
    {
        cout << " Time is " << Hours << " hours : " << Minutes << " minutes : and" <<
        Seconds << "seconds \n";
    }
    Time(){}
    /* Second constructor */
    Time(int TempHours,  int TempMinutes,  int TempSeconds)
```

```
    {
       Hours = TempHours;
       Minutes = TempMinutes;
       Seconds = TempSeconds;
    }
    /* Third constructor */
    Time(int TempHours, int TempMinutes)
    {
       Hours = TempHours;
       Minutes = TempMinutes;
       Seconds = 0;
    }
    /* Fourth constructor for Time in hours alone */
    Time(int TempHours)
    {
       Hours = TempHours;
       Minutes = 0;
       Seconds = 0;
    }
};
void main()
{
    Time Time1(12,15,15);      // Second constructor is used here
    cout << "Time number 1 \n";
    Time1.ShowTime();
    Time Time2(10,30);         // Third Constructor
    cout << "Time number 2  \n";
    Time2.ShowTime();
    Time Time3;                // First Constructor
    Time3 = Time(12);          // Fourth constructor
    cout << "Time number 3 \n"; Time3.ShowTime();
    Time Time4 = 12;           // Fourth constructor in an implicit way
    cout << "Time number 4 \n"; Time4.ShowTime();
    Time Time5(12);
    /* Using the fourth constructor in an explicit way for Time5 */
    cout << "The Time number 5 \n"; Time5.ShowTime();
}
```

Output
```
Time number 1
Time is 12 hours : 15 minutes : and 15 seconds
Time number 2
Time is 10 hours : 30 minutes : and 0 seconds
Time number 3
Time is 12 hours : 0 minutes : and 0 seconds
Time number 4
Time is 12 hours : 0 minutes : and 0 seconds
Time number 5
Time is 12 hours : 0 minutes : and 0 seconds
```

It should be noted that the constructor for class Time is defined in four different ways. The single-argument constructor can be used in both ways, that is, implicit and explicit. It should also be noted that implicit and explicit calls to an argument constructor leads to the same results.

5.9.1 Constructors with Default Arguments

We have discussed default arguments when we studied functions in Chapter 4. Default arguments are available to constructor functions as well. In the previous program, four constructors have been used, which can be reduced to just two by using default arguments. The following program is a modified version of the previous program, with the constructor now containing default arguments.

```cpp
//DefArgsCons.cpp
#include <iostream>
using namespace  std;
class Time
{
public:
    int Hours;
    int Minutes;
    int Seconds;
    void ShowTime()
    {
        cout << "Time is " << Hours << "hours : " << Minutes << " minutes : and" <<
        Seconds << " seconds \n";
    }
    Time(){}    // We now need a default constructor
    Time(int TempHours, int TempMinutes = 0, int TempSeconds = 0)
    /* See the use of default arguments */
    {
        Hours = TempHours;
        Minutes = TempMinutes;
        Seconds = TempSeconds;
    }
    /* Third and fourth constructors are now not needed */
};
void main()
{
    Time Time1(12,15,15);  /* Second constructor is used here */
    cout << "Time number 1 \n";
    Time1.ShowTime();
    Time Time2(10,30);
    /* Second constructor is used here using the third argument as default */
    cout << "Time number 2  \n"; Time2.ShowTime();
    Time Time3;        /* First constructor is used here */
    Time3 = Time(12);
    /* This is using the second constructor with both second and third arguments as
```

```
defaults in an implicit way */
cout << "Time number 3  \n";
Time3.ShowTime();
Time Time4 = 12;
/* This is again using the second constructor with two default arguments in an
explicit way */
cout << "Time number 4  \n";
Time4.ShowTime();
}
```

Semantic Correctness

> Default arguments must be semantically correct to make them meaningful.

The second constructor can do the job of three separate constructors that were used in the earlier program. Whenever it is *semantically* correct, one must use default arguments with constructors to reduce the number of constructors. It is important to understand the word *semantically*, which means that when the argument is omitted, such as omitting seconds or minutes in the later program, the program must provide default arguments, *which are obvious.*

Let us suppose this program needs to provide default arguments as 30 or 15. This may be needed while preparing a timetable for an institute where a lecture always starts 15 or 30 minutes past any hour. So, when only hours are provided, it is not immediately apparent to the reader that the minute values are non-zero. The minutes in this case are not a proper candidate for a default argument. The discussion about default argument for a function is equally applicable to constructor functions.

In the statement `Time Time4 = 12;` `Time` has more than one argument. Then, how is a conversion operator for converting `12` (integer) to an object `Time` provided? As mentioned earlier, this is specially done just for a single-argument constructor.

A C++ compiler considers a constructor with a single normal argument and the rest default arguments to be equivalent to a single-argument constructor. It can be seen that this is very logical and understandable. It is possible to even omit the default constructor by providing `int hours = 0` as the first argument. Then, when `Time TempTime;` is defined, it will call the same constructor and assign zero to all three data members.

Normal Constructors and Default Argument Constructors

It should be ensured that the compiler is not confused by giving two options, that is, a normal constructor and another constructor with enough default arguments for a given function call. Such programs will not be compiled by the compiler.

Surprisingly, but obviously, constructors with default arguments have an important consequence. If there are constructors for, say, *N* normal arguments and *D* default arguments, it is not possible to have any constructor with any number of arguments between *N* and *N* + *D* with the same type. This means that if there is a Time constructor with one normal argument and two default arguments, it is not possible to overload the Time constructor with a single argument, which is an integer, or with two- or three-integer arguments. If the constructor is modified to have all three as default arguments, it is not possible to even define a default constructor. Let us illustrate this with an example. Assume that we have a constructor

```
Time(int Hours = 0, int Minutes = 0, int Seconds = 0);
```

and that the default constructor is defined here as `Time(){};`

Now, if there is a statement such as `Time TeaTime`, the compiler will be confused as to which constructor to call, that is, the default one or the one with all three arguments as default arguments. Obviously, it will not be able to compile the program.

Likewise, if we have,

```
Time(int Hours, int Minutes, int Seconds = 0)
```

then it is not possible to have

```
Time(int Anything, int AnythingElse)
```

and so on.

5.9.2 Dynamic Initialization and Assignment Operator

In all the examples that we have discussed so far, the object is initialized with constants. The values of constants are available at compile time, that is, the object initialization is done at compile time. This is analogous to initializing the variable with a constant. For example, note the following statement:

```
int i = 5;
```

Here, at the time of compilation, the value of i is known to be 5, so the compiler can insert it there. In the case of `Time Time1(12, 20, 20);` the compiler first allocates the space for all the data members of `Time`. Then, `Time1.Hours` is set to 12, `Time1.Minutes` is set to 20 and `Time1. Seconds` is set to 20 automatically; nothing needs to be done at run-time. It has already been mentioned that it is possible to write statements such as the following:

```
int i;
cin >> i;
int j = i;
```

Here, j is initialized at run-time. Similarly, it is possible to use constructors to initialize objects at run-time. The values to be passed to the constructors are made available at run-time and then the constructor is invoked while defining the object. This is known as dynamic initialization. The same process can even be used to call constructors explicitly and then assigning the returning object to any other object defined earlier. The following program illustrates this point.

```
//DynamicInit.cpp
#include <iostream>
using namespace std;
class Time
{
public:
    int Hours;
    int Minutes;
    int Seconds;
    void ShowTime()
    {
        cout << "Time is " << Hours << "hours : " << Minutes << "minutes : and " <<
        Seconds << "seconds \n";
```

```
    }
    Time(){}    // Empty default constructor
    Time(int TempHours, int TempMinutes = 0, int TempSeconds = 0)
    /* See the use of default arguments in both arguments towards the end */
    {
       Hours = TempHours;
       Minutes = TempMinutes;
       Seconds = TempSeconds;
    }
};
void main()
{
    Time Time1;
    /* The default constructor is applied here at compile time */
    int TempHours, TempMinutes, TempSeconds;
    cout << "\n Please insert hours ";
    cin >> TempHours;
    cout << "\n Please insert minutes ";
    cin >> TempMinutes;
    cout << "\n Please insert seconds ";
    cin >> TempSeconds;
    Time1 = Time(TempHours, TempMinutes, TempSeconds);
    /* Constructor with three arguments is reapplied to temporary object at run-time.
    Then, the temporary object is assigned to our object */
    Time1.ShowTime();
    cout << "\n Please insert hours ";
    cin >> TempHours;
    cout << "\n Please insert minutes ";
    cin >> TempMinutes;
    cout << "\n Please insert seconds ";
    cin >> TempSeconds;
    Time Time2 = Time(TempHours, TempMinutes, TempSeconds);
    /* Similar to the previous case */
    Time2.ShowTime();
    Time Time3(TempHours, TempMinutes, TempSeconds);
    /* The constructor is applied while initializing the object and calling the
    constructor implicitly */
    Time3.ShowTime();
}
```

Output

```
Please insert hours 10
Please insert minutes 10
Please insert seconds 10
Time is 10 hours : 10 minutes : and 10 seconds
Please insert hours 12
```

```
Please insert minutes 12
Please insert seconds 12
Time is 12 hours : 12 minutes : and 12 seconds
Time is 12 hours : 12 minutes : and 12 seconds
```

It can be seen that when `Time Time1;` is written, the empty default constructor is applied and `Time1` is created. Later, it is possible to reinitialize the same object by calling a constructor function explicitly. Although we use words such as reinitialize or initialize, technically this is an assignment and not initialization. This program has a three-argument parameterized constructor. The arguments are taken from the console at run-time using variables and are not constants as in `DefArgsCons.cpp`. Thus, `Time1` is initialized at run-time. With `Time2`, the case is a bit different. C++ defers to initialize the object until the constructor gets the values of the variables at run-time. Only when the values are available, that is, after the user enters the data, the constructor is called and the object is created and initialized.

5.10 CONSTRUCTOR WITH DYNAMIC ALLOCATION

Constructors can use `new` to allocate memory for objects at the time of creation. Such constructors are common when the objects are of varied size and the size is available only at run-time.

Let us consider an example, shown in Program 5.6, which stores the details of the customers. One argument to customer is the number of items he/she is interested in; this list can vary. With each customer, in order to initialize, it is necessary to specify the number of items. Memory for storing those items should then be made available after which those items are stored in that memory.

This type of step was not involved in the earlier constructions. Now, dynamic memory allocation is needed when the object is being initialized. It has already been mentioned that object initialization can be done either at the compile time or at the run-time. It is also possible to reinitialize an object created at compile time or to create an object and initialize it at run-time. Program 5.6 considers both the cases for run-time and uses the modified `Item` and `Customer` classes that were used in Chapter 3.

 **PROGRAM 5.6** Dynamic initialization at the time of construction

```cpp
//DynamicMemAlloc.cpp
#include <iostream>
#include <string>
using namespace std;

class Item
{
    int ItemNo;
    string ItemName;
public:
    Item()
    {
        ItemNo = 0;
        ItemName = "";
    }
```

```
        Item(int TempItemNo, string TempItemName)
        {
            ItemNo = TempItemNo;
            ItemName = TempItemName;
        }

        void ShowDetails()
        {
            cout << "\n Item number is " << ItemNo;
            cout << "\n Item name is " << ItemName;
        }
};
class customer
{
        int CustNo;
        string CustName;
        string CustAddress;
        Item *ItemsInterested;
        /* Pointer to array of items interested */
        int TotalItems;

public:
        customer()
        {
            TotalItems = 0;
            ItemsInterested = 0; // assigning it to null
        }

        customer(int TempCustNo, string TempCustName, string TempCustAddress, Item
        *TempItemsInterested, int TempTotalItems)
        {
            CustNo = TempCustNo;
            CustName = TempCustName;
            CustAddress = TempCustAddress;
            ItemsInterested = new Item[TempTotalItems];

            for(int i=0; i<TempTotalItems; ++i)
            {
                ItemsInterested[i] = TempItemsInterested[i];
            }
            TotalItems = TempTotalItems;
        }
        void ShowDetails()
        {
            cout << "\n Customer number is " << CustNo;
            cout << "\n Customer name is " << CustName;
            cout << "\n Customer address is " << CustAddress;
            cout << "\n" << CustName << " is interested in the following items:" << "\n";

            for(int i=0; i<TotalItems; i++)
            {
                ItemsInterested[i].ShowDetails();
            }
        }
};
void main()
{
        customer Steve;
```

```
    Item  ItemArray[]  =  {Item(3,"Sandwiches"),  Item(4,"PaperBags"),  Item(5,"Napkins"),
    Item(6,"Toys"),Item(10,"Biscuits"),Item(9,"Pen"),Item(1,"Pencil"),Item(2,"Eraser"),};

    Steve = customer(2, "Steve Waugh", "Australia", ItemArray, 5);
    Steve.ShowDetails();
    customer Flintoff(3, "Flintoff the Captain", "England", ItemArray + 2, 6);
    Flintoff.ShowDetails();
}
```

Output
```
Customer number is 2
Customer name is Steve Waugh
Customer address is Australia
Steve Waugh is interested in the following items:
Item number is 3

Customer number is 3
Customer name is Flintoff the Captain
Customer address is England
Flintoff the Captain is interested in the following items:
Item number is 5
Item number is 2
Item name is Eraser
```

How the Program Works

As usual, let us dissect the program and try to understand what it is trying to accomplish. We will look at each section one by one.

Dynamic initialization In this program, the customers have a new data member, that is, a pointer to ItemsInterested. This data member is just a pointer and not an array. When a new customer is defined, an array containing the items that the customer is interested in is passed. The item here is itself an object of the class Item for which the memory is dynamic. Looking at the length of the array passed, the constructor creates a dynamic array in the allocated space, which is then used to store the passed values. At the end, the constructor stores the address of that memory in the pointer variable, so it is now possible to access the customer object with the required set of ItemsInterested. Now, the customer object is initialized with the items that the customer is interested in. The reader might wonder about the need for dynamic initialization and why it will not work if the passed value is just assigned to the pointer. Figures 5.1 and 5.2 show the difference between the cases without and with dynamic initialization.

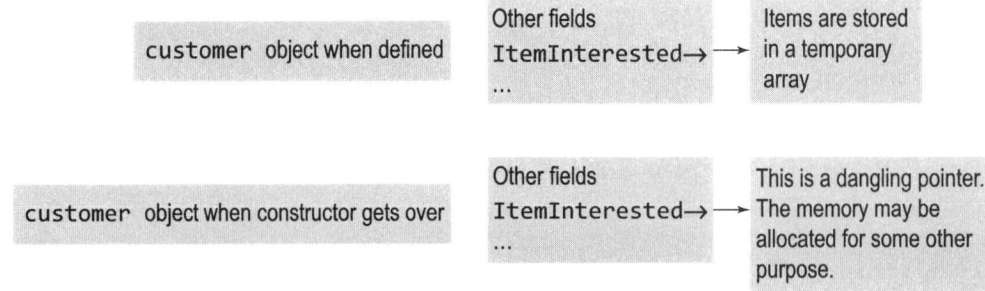

Fig. 5.1 Without dynamic initialization

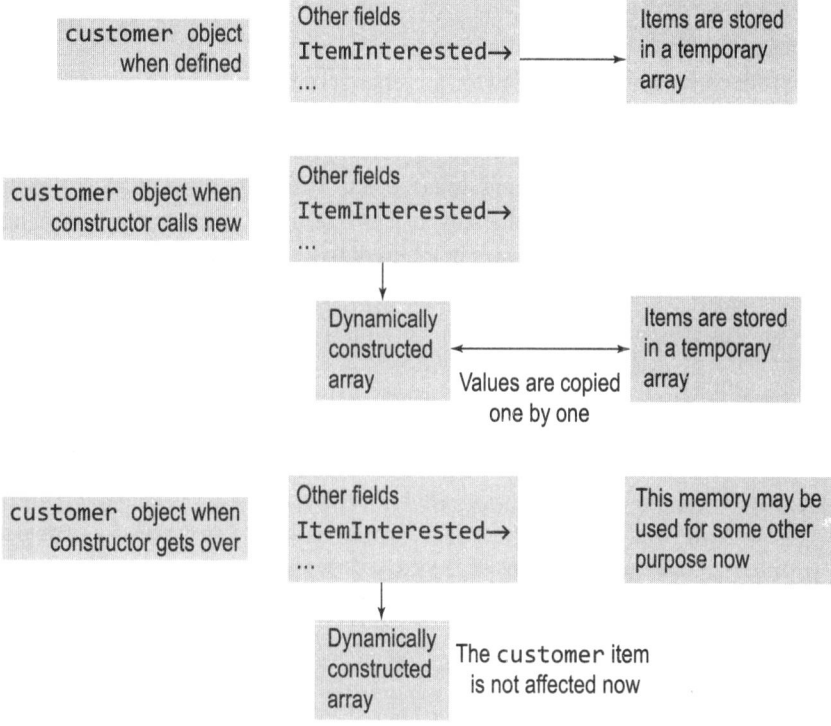

Fig. 5.2 With dynamic initialization

Need for dynamic initialization If the passed array is deleted, the first type of initialization would lead to a dangling pointer whereas in the second case it is not affected. Moreover, if the passed array changes its values in the first case, ItemsInterested would change because we just point to that location, that is, we are sharing the data (the array that is passed) with the calling function. In Program 5.6, if the dynamic allocation part is omitted, the program would look as follows:

```
// Erroneous code
customer(int TempCustNo, string TempCustName, string TempCustAddress, Item
*TempItemsInterested, int TempTotalItems)
{
   CustNo = TempCustNo;
   CustName = TempCustName;
   CustAddress = TempCustAddress;
   ItemsInterested = TempItemInterested; // the erroneous line
   TotalItems = TempTotalItems;
}

// The following is a call to the constructor defined above
Steve = customer(2, "Steve Waugh", "Australia", ItemArray, 5);
```

Now, ItemsInterested will point to ItemArray (the passed array). If the values of ItemArray are changed or deleted, the ItemsInterested pointer would fetch changed values or garbage because it is pointing to the same location to which ItemArray is pointing. It is important to note that the pointer `ItemsInterested` here does not have any memory to store data; it is sharing the memory location with `ItemArray`.

If the values in the constructor are changed, it would inadvertently change the values in the passed array, `ItemArray`. This is similar to passing an array pointer for manipulating it similar to passing an array pointer for sorting functions.

The second case has a separate array into which the passed array has been copied, so, it would not have changed values even if the original passed array is changed. The original array is also immune to changes made to the array items in the constructor function. Exhibit 5.1 shows why copying pointer members is not correct.

Exhibit 5.1 Copying pointer members is not correct

When a constructor uses new to initialize with a dynamic number of values passed to it at run-time, it cannot copy a pointer value. It results in one memory location being shared by multiple objects. Therefore, the changes carried out in the values of one object will reflect as changes in other object values.

Using dynamic memory allocation and giving a new object its own memory helps to avoid this problem by having separate copies of values. Hence, such cases demand dynamic allocation. It is not possible to use static allocation here because the number of items a customer would be interested in is not known in advance.

Objects as members of some other class   Program 5.6 also shows how an object of a class becomes a data member of some other class (`Item` object becoming member of `customer` class). It is important to note that this object is not a normal data member; it is different from normal data members. This difference will be discussed when we learn about inheritance and containership in Chapter 9. When an object is defined as a member of some other class, it is treated differently from other members when the objects of that class are initialized.

Dynamic allocation applied   It should be noted how the customers are initialized using a parameterized constructor. Items such as `CustNo` and `CustName` are initialized in a normal way. `ItemsInterested` is actually a pointer and cannot be initialized in the same way. When the constructor is called, the pointer is passed to an array containing `Item` objects to the constructor.

```
Steve = customer(2, "Steve Waugh", "Australia", ItemArray, 5);
```

Here, `ItemArray` is the name of an array. As in C, it is a static pointer to the array and points to the first item of the array, that is, it contains the address of the first item. As it is static, it cannot be assigned some other value later as done in a normal pointer variable. It is possible to pass any array with any valid length here. This program uses a single array with different starting points and different lengths. It is also possible to pass totally different arrays. In the first example, the array name itself is passed with the total items as five. Array name, as we have discussed earlier, is a pointer to the first item. So, it starts with the first item. In the second example, it starts with `ItemArray + 2`. It should be remembered that this notation is common in C programming and is also used in C++. It is the same as `ItemArray[2]`. It adds two to an item pointer variable and makes it to point to the address of the third item of an array.

Correct way to copy   We need to store an entire array of items and we do not have any space in the data member for it. We must solve this problem by obtaining memory for storing those elements dynamically. It should be remembered that the data member in this program is not an array, but is merely a pointer. The memory needs to be dynamically allocated. It is interesting to see how `ItemsInterested` is initialized dynamically in the following example. `TempTotalItems` is the length of an array. The memory for the length of the array is obtained using the following statement:

```
ItemsInterested = new Item[TempTotalItems];
```

Here, the memory space needed is available. Now, the pointer in the constructor becomes useful. The address of this memory (the dynamically generated array) is stored in the pointer variable, `ItemsInterested`. `new` makes it possible to do both in a single statement.

Then, for all items passed in the array, the `ItemsInterested` array of the object is initialized as follows:

```
for(int i=0; i<TempTotalItems; ++i)
{
    ItemsInterested[i] = TempItemsInterested[i];
}
```

It can be seen that this solves the problem of memory allocation in cases where a priori knowledge of the number of items of `ItemsInterested` array is not available. It is dynamically allocated and the array is available at run-time, which is what was needed.

Though this problem is solved, it is not without cost. Using dynamic allocation will invite more responsibilities. Moreover, copy constructors and overloaded assignment operators as well as destructors are also needed now. The reason for this is given in Exhibit 5.2.

Exhibit 5.2   Memory leaks

Dynamic initialization has a specific problem. When the memory is assigned dynamically for initializing an object, it is essential to deallocate it as well, when the object goes out of scope.

Unlike in the case of other variables, where C++ does the deallocation as soon as the variable goes out of scope, it is not done here until the program execution is over. This problem is known as *memory leak*.

C++ 11 has two important improvements; one is the garbage collector, which takes care of memory leaks, and the second one is that it has better ways of managing temporary objects.

5.11 COPY CONSTRUCTORS

It is possible to pass all types of arguments to a constructor except the object itself. It is obvious why this restriction is provided in C++. If an object is allowed to be passed to the constructor of the same object, for creating a single object, the constructor needs to create one more such object for passing to it while creating that object, and it needs to pass one more such object for creating that object and so on, which is an infinite process. Therefore, C++ would flag an error when a native object is passed to the constructor.

> We can pass all types of arguments to a constructor except the object itself.

However, it is possible to pass the reference of the native object to the constructor, which, in technical sense, is a pointer to the same type of object. This type of constructor is known as copy constructor and it has an important use in C++. Before we study the importance of copy constructor, we must understand the difference between initialization and assignment.

5.11.1 Object Initialization and Object Assignment

We cannot pass the same type of object to a constructor though we may be able to pass a pointer of a reference to that constructor.

We have seen in Chapter 3 that objects can only be assigned to other objects of the same type and that copying is done by copying each member of one class to the other. The compiler takes a shortcut of copying objects bit by bit whenever possible. It is a shortcut as the compiler does not need to remember member boundaries; it can copy one object to another in the same way that the C structure variables are copied.

We have also seen that assignment is different from initialization. Let us review this using the following program.

```cpp
//AssignInit.cpp
#include <iostream>
#include <string>
using namespace  std;
class brother
{
   string Name;
public:
   brother(){};
   brother(string BrotherName)
   {
      Name = BrotherName;
   }
   friend void DisplayBrother(brother);
};
void main()
{
   void DisplayBrother(brother);
   brother AssignBrotherName();
   brother FirstBrother = brother("Steve Waugh");
   /* Initialization using a temporary object */
   brother SecondBrother("Mark Waugh");
   // First case of initialization
   brother ThirdBrother("Gilchrist");
   // First case of initialization
   brother FourthBrother = "Ricky Ponting";
   // This is also first case
   DisplayBrother(FourthBrother);
   // Second case of initialization
   brother FifthBrother = AssignBrotherName();
   /* Third case of initialization; temporary object returned from AssignBrotherName()
   function is used to initialize FifthBrother. */
   DisplayBrother(FifthBrother);
   brother SixthBrother;
   SixthBrother = FirstBrother;
   /* This is assignment, not initialization */
```

```
    DisplayBrother(SixthBrother);
}
void DisplayBrother(brother SomeBrother)
{
    cout << "\n Brother's name is " << SomeBrother.Name << "\n";
}
brother AssignBrotherName()
{
    cout <<  "Give a name for a new brother \n";
    string TempName;
    cin >> TempName;
    cout <<  "New brother is created and sent to main below \n";
    return brother(TempName);
    /* A temporary object is constructed here and passed to Fifth brother; this is the
    third case where initialization is done */
}
```

Note Initialization happens in three cases, when one defines the object with parameters, when an argument containing an object is passed to a function and when a function returns an object.

Three specific cases of initialization are described in the following sections.

Case 1

In the first case, we assign the value using another object of the same type to an object, as and when the object is defined.

```
brother FourthBrother = "Ricky Ponting";      // initialization
brother SecondBrother("Mark Waugh");
brother FirstBrother = brother("Steve Waugh");
/* This is initialization using a temporary object */
```

This definition is an example of the first case. Here, FourthBrother and SecondBrother are initialized at the time of creation to values "Ricky Ponting" and "Mark Waugh". The third example has an additional step of construction of temporary object. This temporary object is constructed from the statement brother("Steve Waugh"); and then assigned to FirstBrother. The third statement is equivalent to writing the following:

```
Brother Temporary("Steve Waugh");
Brother FirstBrother = Temporary;
```

Case 2

The second case is where an object is passed to a function.

```
DisplayBrother(FourthBrother);
```

Again, the temporary object is created and initialized to the object as a parameter and passed to the function. So, the temporary object in this case will be initialized to FourthBrother and then passed. It should be noted that the object used as a parameter (i.e., FourthBrother) itself should not be passed because the original object used in the argument must remain intact after call. Sending another object similar to the object being provided as an argument ensures this. Such seemingly weird behaviour is important for value parameter semantic to be observed. When the original object is kept intact and retains itself when the call is over,

Temporary objects are sometimes denoted as unnamed objects.

whatever changes happened to that object in the function is just ignored. If the function makes any modifications to the passed object, it is done on the copy and not on the original object, so the original object remains unaffected. Hence, the given statement is equivalent to

```
Brother *Temporary = new Brother(FourthBrother);
DisplayBrother(*Temporary);
delete Temporary;
```

Case 3

This case is similar to the case of passing an object back from a function, as seen earlier. Look at the function `AssignBrotherName()` in the following program:

```
brother AssignBrotherName()
{
    // other statements
    return brother(TempName);
    // comments
}
```

and

```
brother FifthBrother = AssignBrotherName();
```

The return statement calls a constructor to construct an object of type `brother` and returns the object. This object is known as *unnamed object*. It is also a temporary object. The lifetime of this temporary object is very small. It is created just on the verge of function exit and is alive until the assignment statement is executed immediately after the function call is over. In the following statement, the function call is made first and then the assignment is done.

```
brother FifthBrother = AssignBrotherName();
```

When the assignment is applied, `FifthBrother` will get that value and the temporary unnamed object is destroyed.

All the three cases described here deal with initialization. In all three cases, when the object is copied, the members are copied one by one. These are not assignments, though they have similar default behaviour. Observe the statement indicating the assignment.

```
SixthBrother = FirstBrother;
```

Here, again memberwise (in our case bitwise) copy is done by default. Then, where and what is the difference between initialization and assignment?

> **Note** Unless a copy constructor or assignment operator is defined for an object, initialization and assignment work the same, that is, they copy everything memberwise (bit by bit whenever possible). Initialization works differently when a copy constructor is defined and assignment works differently when an assignment operator is defined. However, an assignment operator can also be defined for dissimilar types of objects.

5.11.2 Providing Copy Constructors

A copy constructor is one with a single argument as a reference to the very class it belongs to.

When we have a single argument containing an object reference of the same type of object to a constructor, it is known as a copy constructor.

The following program illustrates how a copy constructor is defined and used. This is not an ideal situation to use copy constructors; even if the copy constructor is omitted here, the program would execute the same. The next program is another example, which clearly indicates when one should use them. Note how the copy constructor for Point class is defined and used in this program.

```cpp
//CopyConstructor.cpp
#include <iostream>
using namespace std;
class Point
{
private:
   float x, y;
public:
   Point(Point& OtherPoint)
   // Copy constructor
   {
      x = OtherPoint.x;
      y = OtherPoint.y;
   }
   Point(float TempX = 0, float TempY = 0)
   {
      x = TempX;
      y = TempY;
   }
};
void main()
{
   Point Point1(2,3);        // Calls default constructor
   Point Point2 = Point1;    // Calls copy constructor
   // Point Point2(Point1) is the same as above
   Point1 = Point2;          // Calls assignment operator
}
```

The following is an example of dynamically allocated objects using constructors as discussed earlier, now modified for copy constructors. This is an example of a program where it is necessary to have a copy constructor.

```cpp
//CopyCons.cpp
#include <iostream>
#include <string>
using namespace std;
class customer;
class Item
{
   int ItemNo;
   string ItemName;
public:
   Item()
   {
      ItemNo = 0;
      /* ItemName = ""; */
```

```cpp
      }
      Item(int TempItemNo, string TempItemName)
      {
         ItemNo = TempItemNo;
         ItemName = TempItemName;
      }
      void ShowDetails()
      {
         cout << "\n Item number is " << ItemNo;
         cout << "\n Item name is " << ItemName;
      }
      friend Item ModifyItem(customer & TempCust, int ItemNoToBeReplaced);
};
class customer
{
   int CustNo;
   string CustName;
   string CustAddress;
   Item *ItemsInterested;
   int TotalItems;
public:
   customer()
   {
      TotalItems = 0;
      ItemsInterested = 0;  // assigning it to null
   }
   // The following is a copy constructor
   customer(customer & CustRef)
   {
      CustNo = CustRef.CustNo;
      CustName = CustRef.CustName;
      CustAddress = CustRef.CustAddress;
      ItemsInterested = new Item[CustRef.TotalItems];
      /* New memory for new object. This is the difference.
      Compilers do not do this by default. */
      for(int i=0; i<CustRef.TotalItems; ++i)
      {
              ItemsInterested[i] = CustRef.ItemsInterested[i];
      }
      TotalItems = CustRef.TotalItems;
   }
   customer(int TempCustNo, string TempCustName, string TempCustAddress,
   Item *TempItemsInterested, int TempTotalItems)
   {
      CustNo = TempCustNo;
      CustName = TempCustName;
      CustAddress = TempCustAddress;
      ItemsInterested = new Item[TempTotalItems];
      for(int i=0; i<TempTotalItems; ++i)
      {
```

```
            ItemsInterested[i] = TempItemsInterested[i];
        }
        TotalItems = TempTotalItems;
    }
    void ShowDetails()
    {
        cout << "\n Customer number is " << CustNo;
        cout << "\n Customer name is " << CustName;
        cout << "\n Customer address is " << CustAddress;
        cout << "\n" << CustName << "is interested in following items" << "\n";
        for(int i=0; i<TotalItems; i++)
        {
            ItemsInterested[i].ShowDetails();
        }
    }
    friend Item ModifyItem(customer & TempCust, int ItemNoToBeReplaced);
};
void main()
{
    customer Steve;
    Item ItemArray[]=
    {
        Item(3,"Sandwiches"), Item(4,"Paper Bags"),
        Item(5,"Napkins"), Item(6,"Toys"), Item(10,"Biscuits"),
        Item(9,"Pen"), Item(1,"Pencil"), Item(2,"Eraser"),
    };
    Steve = customer(2, "Steve Waugh", "Australia", ItemArray, 5);
    customer Mark(Steve);
    Steve.ShowDetails();
    Mark.ShowDetails();
    ModifyItem(Mark, 3);
    Mark.ShowDetails();
    Steve.ShowDetails();
    // Without copy constructor, it would show the same result
}
/* The following function is using private variables of both the classes, so it is made
friend of both */
Item ModifyItem(customer & TempCust, int ItemNoToBeReplaced)
{
    for(int i=0; i<TempCust.TotalItems; ++i)
    {
        if(TempCust.ItemsInterested[i].ItemNo) == ItemNoToBeReplaced)
        {
                cout << "Enter new details for item to be replaced \n";
                cout << "Enter item no. \n";
                int TempItemNo;
                cin >> TempItemNo;
                cout << "Enter item name \n";
                string TempItemName;
                cin >> TempItemName;
```

```
                    TempCust.ItemsInterested[i].ItemNo=TempItemNo;
                    TempCust.ItemsInterested[i].ItemName=TempItemName;
            }
        }
    }
```

Changes in this Program

The following modifications were made to Program 5.6:

1. A new function ModifyItem() for modifying the details of items for customers is added. A customer reference is passed, so the changes made to it are reflected back in the customer data.

2. The function ModifyItem() needs to operate on private variables of both the classes, namely, Item and customer. Therefore, it is defined as a friend in both the classes. Such type of "bridge" friend function is sometimes very useful (though a careful designer can and should avoid such functions).

3. We need to know about class customer while discussing class Item and vice versa. (This is because both these classes contain friend definition, which contains both customer and Item.) It is not a problem for the class customer because the class Item is introduced before it and the compiler knows about the class Item while dealing with the class customer. However, this is not the case for the class Item. So, we need a forward reference to class customer. This is done initially when we write

```
    class customer;
```

just before the definition of class Item.

> **Note** When two classes refer to each other, the class defined earlier needs to have a forward reference for the class defined later.

4. We have now introduced a copy constructor. According to the definition, it has the reference to the customer as a single argument.

Case with no copy constructor Let us see what would happen if the copy constructor is not available when ModifyItem(Mark, 3) is called.

To understand this, let us try to recap what happens when we write customer Mark(Steve). The content of Steve is copied into Mark. (Assume that the copy constructor is not available at the moment, so it would follow default behaviour.) The pointer to ItemsInterested is also copied *as it is*. It should be remembered that the contents of ItemsInterested do not have a separate storage in this case. Both Steve and Mark share the same address in ItemsInterested, and hence, the same array items. So, when we modify Mark's details while calling ModifyItem, we are indirectly accessing the same set of items pointed to by the pointer in the Steve object. Thus, our change would change both objects, Mark and Steve. This undesirable behaviour can be eliminated using copy constructors.

A copy constructor, during initialization, overrides the default copy of objects member by member.

Solving the problem using copy constructors Let us look at the copy constructor now. It takes a reference of the class as a single argument. Then, it copies each item, except the pointer, to ItemsInterested. It obtains memory using new. It gets the memory good enough for storing the same number of items as the reference and it stores the items there. It should be noted that the contents of ItemsInterested are not shared in this case. We get a new array. So, if ItemsInterested of Mark is changed later, it would not have any effect on that of Steve.

The copy constructor, as shown here, is a must if an item contains a dynamic constructor, that is, when a constructor is defined using the new operator.

5.12 PRIVATE COPY CONSTRUCTORS

If the copy constructor is defined in a private section, the objects of the class cannot call it. In a way, it stops the operations of the form customer Mark(Steve) or customer Mark = Steve.

If such statements are written when the copy constructor is private, the program will not be compiled. This is very useful when a class is designed and the object code is provided to the user for using it. It should be noted that if the definition of the copy constructor is omitted, C++ would provide a default copy constructor (may not synthesize the physical one) and the user cannot be stopped from writing erroneous statements such as mentioned earlier . In this case, the contents of the copy constructor body are not executed, and hence, the body is usually left empty:

```
customer(customer & dummy){};
// see the empty body
```

5.12.1 Member Initialization List

Memberwise initialization list or member initialization list (MIL) is the method for initialization of the members of a class using the constructor function. It provides an alternative for providing initializations outside the constructor body. Let us consider the following program to understand it.

```
//SimpleMemberInitilizationList.cpp
#include <iostream>
using namespace std;
class Time
{
public:
    int Hours;
    int Minutes;
    int Seconds;
    void ShowTime()
    {
        cout << "Time is " << Hours << " hours : " << Minutes << " minutes : and "
        << Seconds << " seconds \n";
    }
    Time(){}
    /* The following is a constructor using MIL */
    Time(int TempHours, int TempMinutes, int TempSeconds)
    :Hours(TempHours),
    Minutes(TempMinutes),
    Seconds(TempSeconds)
    { } // The empty body
    /* Second constructor */
};
```

```
void main()
{
    Time Time1(12,15,15);
    /* Second constructor with MIL is used here */
    cout << "Time number 1 \n";
    Time1.ShowTime();
}
```

An MIL appears in bet-ween the header and the body, starting with a colon.

The initialization list has been used in the second constructor for the Time class to initialize the Time object. Earlier, the same was done using assignment statements in the constructor body. Let us compare the two methods syntactically. The earlier approach was as follows:

```
Time(int TempHours, int TempMinutes, int TempSeconds)
{
    Hours = TempHours;
    Minutes = TempMinutes;
    Seconds = TempSeconds;
}
```

The MIL approach is as follows:

```
Time(int TempHours, int TempMinutes, int TempSeconds)
:Hours(TempHours),
Minutes(TempMinutes),
Seconds(TempSeconds)
{ }  // the empty body
```

Syntactically, the MIL appears in between the body of the constructor and the header. It starts with a colon (:) and has all the initializations separated by a comma. The initialization has the normal syntax of initialization, that is, Variable(value) for initializing a variable with a value. In the given example, both the approaches yield the same result.

Need for Initialization List

However, it is not true that both these approaches always yield the same result. There are some cases where the use of the second approach is a must (or is better). The difference between assignment and initialization has already been elaborated in Section 5.11.1. The assignment statements in the function body invoke the assignment operator whereas the MIL invokes initialization. The following sub-sections discuss the advantages of using the MIL approach.

Readability

When the MIL is used in a constructor function, it is separated from the rest of the code, and thus, the program becomes more readable. (There is an argument against this. Those who are new to C++ claim that the syntax of the MIL is a bit cryptic and one can easily misunderstand it for a function call.) MIL has not been used in the examples in this book, but its use is advisable while writing commercial programs.

Efficiency

The MIL is more efficient in certain cases. Consider the following program.

```
//MILandAssignment.cpp
#include <iostream>
#include <string>
using namespace std;
class student
{
public:
    int RollNumber; string Name; string Address;
    student(){}
    student(int TempRollNumber, string TempName, string TempAddress)
    :Name(TempName),
    Address(TempAddress)
    {
        RollNumber = TempRollNumber;
    }
    void PrintDetails()
    {
        cout << "Roll number is " << RollNumber << "\n";
        cout << "Name is " << Name << "\n";
        cout <<  "Address is  " << Address <<  "\n";
    }
};
void main()
{
    student CricketStudent(1, "Brian Lara", "West Indies");
    CricketStudent.PrintDetails();
}
```

This program is the modified version of Program 5.5. Observe how student name and address are initialized here.

```
student(int TempRollNumber, string TempName, string TempAddress) :Name(TempName),
Address(TempAddress)
{
    RollNumber = TempRollNumber;
}
```

Earlier, these have been defined as follows:

```
student(int TempRollNumber, string TempName, string TempAddress)
{
    RollNumber = TempRollNumber;
    Name = TempName;
    Address = TempAddress;
}
```

In the second case (earlier approach), TempName and TempAddress are first initialized to an empty string (string is a class and TempName and TempAddresses are its objects; the default constructor for string class is invoked when the arguments are processed). Then, they are

MIL is preferred over assignment whenever possible. It provides a single copy compared to assignment, which might require two copies in many cases.

assigned respective values when the assignment is executed using the statements `Name = TempName` and `Address = TempAddress`. However, in the first case, the arguments are initialized with the respective values directly. This involves only one operation and not two. This is again similar to providing a parameterized constructor at the definition of the object. Thus, the first approach using the MIL is more efficient. It is worth remembering that the MIL uses initialization, whereas using assignment in the body of the constructor uses assignment.

Initializing Constants, References, and Member Objects using MIL

The MIL is the only way to initialize constants, references and objects that are data members of a class for which the constructor is being written. Let us consider the following program.

```cpp
//MILImportance.cpp
#include <iostream>
#include <string>
using namespace  std;
class student
{
public:
   const int SchoolNo;
   int RollNumber;
   string Name;
   string & ShortName;
   string Address;
   student(int TempRollNumber, string TempName, string TempAddress)
   :Name(TempName),
   Address(TempAddress),
   SchoolNo(123),
   // const can only be initialized outside the body
   ShortName(Name)     // so the reference
   {
      RollNumber = TempRollNumber;
   }
   void PrintDetails()
   {
      cout << "School number is " << SchoolNo<< "\n";
      cout << "Roll number is " << RollNumber << "\n";
      cout << "Name is   " << Name << "\n";
      cout << "Short name is " << ShortName << "\n";
      cout << "Address is " << Address << "\n";
   }
};
void main()
{
   student CricketStudent(1, "Brian Lara", "West Indies");
   student FootBallStudent(2, "David Beckham", "England");
   CricketStudent.PrintDetails();
   FootBallStudent.PrintDetails();
}
```

This example contains the school number and short name data members. Both of them must be initialized using MIL. Initializing them in the body of the constructor is not allowed. If they are not initialized at all, it is again an error. MIL is the only solution here. It is also important to note that if the program contains a class in which one of the data members is an object of some other class, MIL is needed to initialize that specific data member.

Some of the researchers on C++ demand to make MIL a mandatory standard for initializing values for object-attributes for the following reasons:

1. It is more type-safe if used with templates; when the types are not known, it is safer to use MIL than assignments in the constructor body, because it will then work for any type. Assignments do not work for all the types. Templates are classes or functions to work for generic types.
2. Objects of some other class, constants, and references can be initialized only using MIL. They are more efficient in some cases.

5.12.2 MIL as Replacement for Constructors

It is possible to use MIL to replace the code of a constructor. In the following program, we will look at `Time` class with two constructors, both of which have a constructor with an empty body. Both the constructors actually look at the values passed to them and solve two distinct problems.

Suppose we have time represented in seconds elapsed until some event format. Such formats are common in operating systems (UNIX is one such example). The first problem we would like to solve is to convert such time into our usual format of hours : minutes : seconds. The second problem relates to the correct values, which are otherwise not acceptable. Suppose the time provided in hours : minutes : seconds format passes seconds or minutes more than 60, then we need to convert them to proper values, that is, 65 seconds means five seconds and one minute, which should be added to minutes now. Let us now look at the program.

```cpp
//MILwithExpr.cpp
#include <iostream>
using namespace std;
class Time
{
public:
    int Seconds;
    int Minutes;
    int Hours;
    void ShowTime()
    {
        cout << "Time is " << Hours << " hours : " << Minutes << " minutes : and " << Seconds
        << " seconds \n";
    }
    Time(){}
    // The following is a constructor using MIL
    Time(int TempHours, int TempMinutes, int TempSeconds)
    :Hours(TempHours + TempMinutes / 60),
    Minutes(TempMinutes % 60 + TempSeconds / 60),
    Seconds(TempSeconds % 60)
    { }        // the empty body
```

```
            Time(int TotalSecondsElapsed)
            :Hours((TotalSecondsElapsed / 60) / 60),
            Minutes((TotalSecondsElapsed / 60) % 60),
            Seconds(TotalSecondsElapsed % 60)
            { }                    // the empty body
        };
        void main()
        {
            Time Time1(18305); // 5 * 60 * 60 + 5 * 60 + 5, i.e., 5 : 5 : 5
            cout << "Time number 1 \n";
            Time1.ShowTime();
            Time Time2(12,65,65);
            cout << "Time number 2\n";
            Time2.ShowTime();
        }
```

Output
```
Time number 1
Time is 5 hours : 5 minutes : and 5 seconds
Time number 2
Time is 13 hours : 6 minutes : and 5 seconds
```

It should be noted that both the constructors now have an empty body.

5.12.3 Order of Initialization

When the MIL is used, the order of initialization is not the same as when they are defined in the list. It is in the order of their *declaration* in the class. In Program 5.7, though SchoolNo(123) is written after Name and Address initializations, it will be initialized before them because it is defined prior to them in the class declarations. This leads to surprising consequences. Look at the following code segment:

PROGRAM 5.7   Order of initialization with MIL

```
//OrderOfInit.cpp
#include <iostream>
using namespace  std;

class TestOrder
{
public:
    int First;
    int Second;
    int Third;
    TestOrder(int Value)
    :Third(Second / 10),
    Second(First / 10),
    First(Value)
    { }
    TestOrder(unsigned Value)
    :Third(Value /= 10),
    Second(Value /= 10),
    First(Value /= 10)
    { }
```

```
    void PrintValues()
    {
        cout << "First is " << First << "\n";
        cout << "Second is " << Second << "\n";
        cout << "Third is " << Third << "\n";
    }
};
void main()
{
    int SignedValue = 1234;
    unsigned UnsignedValue = 1234;
    TestOrder TO(SignedValue);
    cout << "\n" << "The first example " << "\n";
    TO.PrintValues();
    cout << "\n" << "The next example " << "\n";
    TestOrder TO2(UnsignedValue);
    TO2.PrintValues();
}
```

Output
```
The first example
First is 1234
Second is 123
Third is 12
The next example
First is 123
Second is 12
Third is 1
```

How the Program Works

MIL definition   Observe carefully the MIL for `TestOrder` class with the first constructor having int as an argument.

```
TestOrder(int Value)
:Third(Second / 10),  Second(First / 10), First(Value)
```

If the evaluation is done in the same order of defining them in the MIL, the code could return arbitrary values, because `Third` is using `Second`, which is still to be initialized, and similarly `Second` is using `First`, which is not yet initialized. The right answer is obtained only because `First` is initialized before the other two and Second is initialized next.

We can actually check the same using one more constructor. Look at the MIL of the second constructor.

```
TestOrder(unsigned Value)
:Third(Value /= 10),  Second(Value /= 10), First(Value /= 10)
```

Order of evaluation   If the order of MIL is preserved, when we encounter the statement,

```
TestOrder TO2(UnsignedValue);
```

we should get `Third` as 123, `Second` as 12, `First` as 1, but a different answer is obtained. The reason is again the same. The MIL evaluation is done on the basis of the declaration of variables in the class itself and not on the order of appearance in the MIL.

If the programmer mistakenly provides an initialization, which does not preserve the order, it is a difficult error to catch. On the contrary, the statements in the constructor body

MIL initialization depends on the order of definition of the variables rather than their order of appearance in the MIL.

execute in the same order. It is even possible to provide function calls in the MIL, though it is not recommended because function call dependencies are not known precisely and hence may lead to serious errors.

Initialization and assignment   The difference between initialization and assignment discussed in Section 5.12.1 also applies in this case.

Class object members can be initialized only using MIL. This is also true for constants and references. This means that when we use assignment, it is first defined and then assigned a value, which is wrong as these items are constants. Constants can only be given values at the time of initialization.

Assignment always follows initialization   It has already been mentioned that the order of initialization depends on the order of definition of data members in the class, which may be different than the order of appearance and that the constructor body behaves in a different (rather normal) way. Let us see what is done in the following case.

```
TestOrder(unsigned Value)
:Third(Value /= 10),
Second(Value /= 10)
{
    Value /= 10
    First = Value;
}
```

The initialization of First has been moved in the constructor body. Now, Second is assigned first, then Third and finally First, that is, First will be 1, Second will be 123 and Third will be 12. This is because of the simple rule that all initializations should be carried out before the constructor body statements. This means that assignments will be carried out only after initializations take place.

5.13 DESTRUCTORS

When a variable is defined in C++, it continues to be in effect until its scope is over. If a variable is defined as a global variable, it remains in effect throughout the execution of the program. If a variable is defined as a local variable, say, in a function, it remains in effect until the function exits. If a variable is defined as follows:

```
for(int i=0;  i<10; ++i)
{
    // statements
}
```

The allocated memory must be released back after its use. If a constructor uses new, the class also needs a destructor that uses delete.

i is known only in the for loop. As soon as the for loop is over, i will cease to exist.

The compiler achieves this effect by creating a variable when it is defined and destroying it after its scope is over. The memory allocated at the time of creation is regained at the end and may be reused for some other purpose. This memory allocation is done on the stack. Dynamically created objects in C++ are an exception to this rule.

If customer is defined as given in the program, the memory obtained for ItemsInterested using new operator would not be regained after customer goes out of scope. This is because the programmer and not the compiler has obtained that memory, and hence, it is the programmer's job to release it back. In the given example, all objects of customer are a part of the main. The scope of the customer object is the main itself. Even if that memory (i.e., the new memory for ItemsInterested) is not returned, after the program execution is over the memory will be returned anyway. In this case, no harm is done if we do not deallocate the memory ourselves. If some of the customer objects were defined inside some function, the situation would be more serious. After claiming that memory, it will not be possible to return it even after coming back from that function. The memory allocated will be freed only after the execution of the program is over.

What should be done to get the allocated memory back immediately after the function call is over, that is, when the variable goes out of scope? The answer is to define *destructors*. As the name suggests, destructors are opposite to constructors. They come into effect when the object goes out of scope. Like constructors, they are automatically applied and calling them explicitly is also possible.

> **Note** The primary use of destructors is to free the memory dynamically allocated; however, they are also useful for providing terminating effects. If we would like to do something other than releasing memory when the object goes out of scope, such as reducing the value of a variable, say, by one, a destructor can be used.

5.13.1 Use of Destructors

Destructors are special functions that are used to execute automatically when the object of the class goes out of scope. They have the same name as of the class prefixed by "~", for example, ~customer() is a destructor for class customer. The code written in the body of function ~customer() would be executed when the object of type customer goes out of scope. The destructor would also be called when delete is executed as shown in the following example.

```
Customer *pCust = new customer;
delete pCust;  // the destructor is called at this place
```

In the following program, a destructor is defined for the point class. The point class now has a destructor, which displays the point that is going out of scope.

```
//PointDestructor.cpp
#include <iostream>
using namespace std;
class Point
{
private:
   float x, y;
public:
   Point(Point& OtherPoint)
   {
      x = OtherPoint.x;
      y = OtherPoint.y;
   }
   Point(float TempX = 0, float TempY = 0)
```

```
        {
            x = TempX;
            y = TempY;
        }
        ~Point()
        {
            cout << "Point at X = " << x << " Y= " << y << " Destroyed";
        }
    };
    void main()
    {
        Point Point1(2,3);
        Point Point2(4,5);
    } // destructor is called here
    Output
    Point at X = 4 Y = 5 Destroyed
    Point at X = 2 Y = 3 Destroyed
```

An interesting observation is that the destructor for the point defined later is executed before the point defined earlier. This is because when the objects are created, they are pushed on stack, which are destroyed by popping them, obviously in the reverse order.

Let us consider Program 5.8 to understand more about destructors. A destructor is provided for the customer class. It deletes the memory gained by new when the variable goes out of scope or when delete is called for customer object.

PROGRAM 5.8 Using destructors

```cpp
//Destructor1.cpp
#include <iostream>
#include <string>
using namespace std;

class Item
{
    int ItemNo; string ItemName;
public:
    Item()
    {
        ItemNo = 0;
    }
    Item(int TempItemNo, string TempItemName)
    {
        ItemNo = TempItemNo;
        ItemName = TempItemName;
    }
    void ShowDetails()
    {
        cout << "\n Item number is " << ItemNo;
        cout << "\n Item name is " << ItemName;
    }
};
```

```
class customer
{
    int CustNo;
    string CustName;
    string CustAddress;
    Item *ItemsInterested;
    int TotalItems;
public:
    ~customer(); customer()
    {
        TotalItems = 0;
        ItemsInterested = 0; // assigning it to null
        cout << "Constructor is called";
    }

    void operator = (customer & CustRef)
    {
        CustNo = CustRef.CustNo;
        CustName = CustRef.CustName;
        CustAddress = CustRef.CustAddress;
        ItemsInterested = new Item[CustRef.TotalItems];
        // New memory for new object; this is the difference

        for(int i=0; i<CustRef.TotalItems; ++i)
        {
            ItemsInterested[i] = CustRef.ItemsInterested[i];
        }
        TotalItems = CustRef.TotalItems;
    }

    customer(int TempCustNo, string TempCustName, string TempCustAddress, Item
    *TempItemsInterested, int TempTotalItems)
    {
        CustNo = TempCustNo;
        CustName = TempCustName;
        CustAddress = TempCustAddress;
        ItemsInterested = new Item[TempTotalItems];
        for(int i=0; i<TempTotalItems; ++i)
        {
            ItemsInterested[i] = TempItemsInterested[i];
        }
        TotalItems = TempTotalItems;
        cout << "Parameterized constructor is called for " << CustName;
    }

    void ShowDetails()
    {
        cout << "\n Customer number is " << CustNo;
        cout << "\n Customer name is " << CustName;
        cout << "\n Customer address is " << CustAddress;
        cout << "\n" << CustName << " is interested in the following items:" << "\n";
        for(int i=0; i<TotalItems; i++)
        {
            ItemsInterested[i].ShowDetails();
        }
    }
};

// The following is the destructor
```

```
customer::~customer()
{
    cout <<  "Destructor is called for " << CustName;
    delete [] ItemsInterested;
}

void main()
{
    Item ItemArray[]=
    {
        Item(3,"Sandwiches"),    Item(4,"PaperBags"),    Item(5,"Napkins"),    Item(6,"Toys"),
        Item(10,"Biscuits"), Item(9,"Pen"), Item(1,"Pencil"), Item(2,"Eraser"),
    };
    customer SteveWaugh(2, "Steve Waugh", "Australia", ItemArray, 5);
    SteveWaugh.ShowDetails();
    customer Ricky(3, "Susan", "London", ItemArray + 2, 6); Ricky.ShowDetails();
    customer Dummy;
    Dummy = customer(5, "Dummy", "Dummy", ItemArray + 2, 3); Dummy.ShowDetails();
}
```

How the Program Works

The code for ~customer() contains just two lines.

```
cout << "Destructor is called for " << CustName;
delete [] ItemsInterested;
```

Only the second line in this case is significant. It removes the dynamically allocated memory. It is important to note the syntax of delete. **delete [ItemsInterested]** would result in an error. It must be **delete [] ItemsInterested**.

In the following output, note that the destructors are called in the reverse order to that of the constructors. This is because the stack is used to store these (local) objects. So, the object defined last is to be removed first and so destroyed first.

The complete output has not been provided for better readability. The output shown here is a small portion that appears at the end of the actual output.

```
Constructor is called
Parameterized constructor is called for Dummy
Destructor is called for Dummy
Customer number is 5
Customer name is Dummy
Customer address is Dummy
Dummy is interested in the following items:

Item number is 5
Item name is Napkins
Item number is 6
Item name is Toys
Item number is 10
Item name is Biscuits
Destructor is called for Dummy
Destructor is called for Susan
Destructor is called for Steve Waugh
```

Look at the special case of dummy. The normal constructor is called once; then, the parameterized constructor and, immediately after that, the destructor are called. (Look at the bold lines in the output.) To understand the reason behind this, look at the statement again.

```
Dummy = customer(5, "Dummy", "Dummy", ItemArray + 2, 3);
```

The call to customer in this case creates a temporary object of type customer, and at the end of assignment, it is automatically destroyed. The parameterized constructor and the destructor are called for that *temporary object* (which has Dummy stored as its name). One more destructor is called for Dummy at the end, which is for the Dummy object that bears the same structure as the temporary object assigned to it.

Processing Objects at the end of their Lifetime

Destructors are also used for any processing at the end for a specific object. Consider a program that maintains a count of logged-in users. Whenever a user logs in or logs out, the number of users currently logged in is displayed. The following is an example of such a program:

```cpp
//LoggedInUsers.cpp
#include <iostream>
#include <string>
using namespace std;
class LoggedInUser
{
    string Name; int TokenNo;
    static int TotalLoggedIn;
public:
    LoggedInUser()
    {
        TotalLoggedIn++;
        cout << "\n You are user number " << TotalLoggedIn << "\n Welcome! \n";
    }
    ~LoggedInUser()
    {
        TotalLoggedIn--;
        cout << "\n Good bye! \n";
        cout << "Now total no. of users in the system are " <<
        TotalLoggedIn;
    }
};
int LoggedInUser::TotalLoggedIn;
void main()
{
    LoggedInUser *ArrayOfUsers[100];
    int index = 0;
    int Choice;
    while(true)
    {
        cout << "\n 1.  New user \n";
        cout << "2.  Logout \n";
        cout << "3.  Exit from the program \n";
```

```
        cout << "Enter your choice ";
        cin >> Choice;
        if(Choice == 1)
        {
                if(index == 100)
                {
                        cout << "\n Too many users! \n";
                        exit(1);
                }
                ArrayOfUsers[index] = new LoggedInUser; index++;
        }
        else if(Choice == 2)
        {
                if(index == 0)
                {
                        cout << "No users to log out! \n";
                        exit(1);
                }
                delete ArrayOfUsers[index - 1];
                index--;
        }
        else
        exit(0);
    }
}
```

Output
```
1. New user
2. Logout
3. Exit from the program
Enter your choice 1
You are user number 1 Welcome!
1. New user
2. Logout
3. Exit from the program
Enter your choice 1
You are user number 2 Welcome!
1. New user
2. Logout
3. Exit from the program
Enter your choice 2
Good bye!
Now total no. of users in the system are 1
1. New user
2. Logout
3. Exit from the program
Enter your choice 2
Good bye!
Now total no. of users in the system are 0
1. New user
2. Logout
3. Exit from the program
Enter your choice 2
No users to log out!
```

Destructor Code

The destructor here is used to reduce the number of users by one.

```
~LoggedInUser()
{
    TotalLoggedIn--;
    cout << "\n Good bye! \n";
    cout << "Now total no. of users in the system are" << TotalLoggedIn;
}
```

The importance of the static variable `TotalLoggedIn` must also be noted. It is possible to determine the number of users logged in at the moment from the index value of the array. There is no need to write the code in the destructor in that case.

If the array implementation is changed to a linked list, a case of real scenario where users log in and log out randomly, then the code of the destructor is needed to release the memory and also to reduce the number of users. Moreover, it should be noted that the destructor call is made when the delete operation is executed. `Delete` moves the object out of scope, and hence, the destructor is called at that point of time.

5.14 USAGE OF CONSTRUCTORS AND DESTRUCTORS FOR CONSTANT OBJECTS

Only constant functions are allowed to operate on constant objects. Constructors and destructors are an exception to this rule and can be applied on constant objects. This is because only after the constructor is applied, the object comes into existence; so, its *constancy* starts from that point. Similarly, destructors are applied after the object goes out of scope. This means that the *constancy* ends before the destructors are applied.

> **Note** Constructors are applied before the object comes into existence and destructors are applied when the object goes out of scope.

5.15 SYNTHESIS AND EXECUTION OF CONSTRUCTORS AND DESTRUCTORS

Constructors are defined anywhere, but C++ requires the constructors to be synthesized only prior *to the first use of the object.* A compiler can delay the synthesizing constructor until its first use. The constructor call (explicit or implicit) constructs the object and then the object comes into existence. Similarly, destructors are executed upon exit from the block where the object is defined, that is, after the object goes out of scope. It is possible to have a large number of blocks in the program and most of the blocks have variables having destructors. In such a case, every time the program exits the block, the destructor is invoked.

Whenever a compiler needs to create and destroy temporary objects of a specific class, the constructor and destructor are called, if defined in that specific class.

> **Note** The lifetime of a global object is throughout the execution of the program. Otherwise, the object comes into existence when the constructor is over and is alive until it goes out of scope, that is, just before the destructor is applied.

5.16 IMPLEMENTATION OF THE IMPORTANT TRIO

Copy constructor, assignment operator, and destructor are usually implemented together. Let us see why this is so. If we use a copy constructor, we have a dynamic memory allocation in the constructor. In such a case, it becomes imperative for the programmer to deallocate the memory when the object goes out of scope. Hence, the situation demands a destructor. Now, the normal assignment also does not work properly. The assigned object also needs dynamic memory allocation, and therefore, the assignment operator is also overloaded in that case.

■ RECAPITULATION ■

- C++ has user-defined objects similar to the built-in data types.
- Constructor and destructors provide initialization and termination effects to user-defined objects similar to built-in data types.
- User-defined objects may need to initialize themselves when defined.
- Constructors are functions having the same name as class. They can be either default or parameterized.
- Single-argument constructor is a special one. The compiler automatically generates a conversion operator when such a constructor is defined.
- Explicit constructor avoids automatic generation of conversion operator.
- Whenever the user has not defined any constructor, C++ provides the effect of one. It may or may not physically synthesize a constructor depending on the situation.
- The compiler-provided destructor cannot do the job of a programmer. The programmer must initialize members using user-defined constructors in cases where the compiler-provided default constructor is not appropriate.
- It is possible to have multiple constructors for a single class. In this case, all the constructors must have either different numbers of arguments or different types of arguments.
- It is also possible to have default arguments to the constructor similar to a normal function.
- The objects can be dynamically initialized by explicitly calling a constructor function. It is also possible to have a constructor with dynamic allocation.
- A destructor is also to be defined and the assignment operator to be overloaded in most of the cases where a dynamic constructor is used.
- The assignment operator and the copy constructor are different. The copy constructor changes the behaviour of initialization whereas an assignment operator overloading changes the behaviour of the assignment.
- MIL is a better method for some cases and a must for constant, references and object members of the class.
- The order in which MIL is executed depends on the order of declaration of data members and not on the order in which MIL is specified.
- Destructors are needed to provide user-defined termination effects when the object goes out of scope.
- The lifetime of the object is after the construction function is executed and just before the destructor is executed.

■ KEYWORDS ■

Constructor   This is a function with the same name as the class itself and is responsible for constructing and returning the objects of the class.

Copy constructor   An object is copied to another using *initialization* by executing the copy constructor.

Default constructor   This is a constructor without any argument.

Default constructor provided by compiler   This refers to the constructor that is provided by the compiler when the user has not defined any. It may not be physically synthesized by the compiler.

Destructor   This is a function that bears the same name as the class itself and is preceded by ~. The destructor is automatically called when the object goes out of scope.

Dynamic initialization   The initialization that happens at run-time is known as dynamic initialization.

Explicit constructor   This is the single-argument constructor that is defined with the keyword `explicit` before the definition. It prohibits the generation of a conversion operator for a single-argument constructor.

Initialization of the object Giving specific values to the objects at the time they are defined is known as initialization of the object.

Member initialization list (MIL) This is the list that follows the constructor header and ends before the body of the constructor begins. It is preceded by the word ":" and contains initializations of data members separated by "," .

Parameterized constructor A constructor with one or more than one argument is known as a parameterized constructor.

■ EXERCISES ■

Multiple Choice Questions

1. What should be the return type of a constructor?
   (a) `void`
   (b) `int`
   (c) It cannot have any return type
   (d) It can have any return type

2. What type of values do constructors provide to the object?
   (a) New values
   (b) Initial values
   (c) Dynamic values
   (d) Constant values

3. How is the constructor function called?
   (a) It is automatically called when the object is created.
   (b) It is to be called soon after the object is created.
   (c) It can be called anywhere in the program.
   (d) It needs to be explicitly called before object creation.

4. Unless a copy constructor or an assignment operator is defined for an object, _____ and _____ work in a similar way.
   (a) object declaration and creation
   (b) constructor and member function
   (c) initialization and assignment
   (d) ordinary and default parameters

5. Whenever possible, the compiler takes a shortcut of copying the objects _____.
   (a) byte by byte, bit by bit
   (b) char by char
   (c) Member by member
   (d) None

6. Destructors are invoked _____.
   (a) explicitly when needed
   (b) explicitly when object goes out of scope
   (c) automatically when object goes out of scope
   (d) automatically at the end of a program

7. How many constructors are possible to define?
   (a) Only one
   (b) Exactly two
   (c) Any number of constructors
   (d) Any number of constructors, though it is advisable to have as few constructors as possible

8. Which of the following is the correct syntax of a copy constructor?
   (a) `Player (Player) ;`
   (b) `Player (Player &, Player & ) ;`
   (c) `Player (Player *) ;`
   (d) `Player (Player &) ;`

9. The constructor body cannot have _____.
   (a) `malloc` statement
   (b) `new` statement
   (c) `return` statement
   (d) `exit` statement

10. What will happen if we write following two statements in a program for a class named `Time`?
    `Time(int hours=0,int minutes=0,int seconds=0) { }`
    `Time ( ) { }`
    (a) Only second one is permissible
    (b) Only first one is permissible
    (c) Compiler gives an error
    (d) Linker gives an error

Conceptual Exercises

1. Give examples of C++ object definitions and usage that demonstrate the similar-to-built-in behaviour concept.

2. What is the need for initialization of objects using a constructor? What could be the problems if the constructors are not provided in C++?

3. What are the functions of constructors? How are they different from normal functions?

4. What is the difference between a default constructor provided by the compiler and a user-defined default constructor?

5. List the cases where default constructor provided by the user becomes necessary.
6. What is the need for explicit constructor?
7. What is the difference between a parameterized constructor and a default constructor?
8. Give some examples other than those shown in the chapter where we need multiple constructors in the same class.
9. What is the advantage of default arguments in a constructor? Suggest few cases where default arguments are useful.
10. What is meant by dynamically reinitializing an object? What is the difference between normal initialization and dynamic initialization?
11. What is the need for dynamic allocation in a constructor? List some cases where dynamic allocation is required in the constructor.
12. Give an example where if the copy constructor is not provided, the behaviour of the program becomes unacceptable.
13. What are the three cases in which initialization is required?
14. `ModifyItem()` function in the chapter is a friend of two classes. Suggest some other bridge functions for some other cases.
15. What are the advantages and disadvantages of using MIL over assignment?
16. We may need constructor in every class that we define, but we may need destructors only in few classes. Why?
17. When will the destructors be called?
18. What is the lifetime of an object? What is the relation of the lifetime of an object to the constructors and destructors?
19. When we need the copy constructor in the definition of a class, we also need the assignment operator overloaded and the destructor. Elaborate.

Practical Exercises

1. Program 5.8 uses static variables to count the number of objects alive at the moment. We had a problem of decrementing the count when a user departs. Remove that problem writing a destructor for the class.
2. Write an improved version of `LoggedInUsers.cpp` by implementing the same program using a linked list.
3. Write a program using the `Time` class defined in the chapter. Use a single constructor to provide all functionalities.

4. `SimpleConstructor.cpp` contains a `Stack` class with a fixed stack size. Change the program to provide dynamic memory allocation to determine the size of the stack at the time of initialization using constructors and also provide its destructor.
5. Modify the `Stack` class to use a linked list for its implementation.
6. Provide a `Simple Queue` class with a proper set of constructors.
7. Define a `person` class and define few data and function members to illustrate the usefulness of a default constructor in that class.
8. Give an example where explicit constructor is needed.
9. Define a `person` class with more than three constructors. Define data and function members in the class in such a way that all three constructors are meaningful.
10. Define a `supplier` class. Assume that the items supplied by any given supplier are different and varying in number. Use dynamic memory allocation in the constructor function to achieve the solution.
11. Define an `examiner` class. Provide all necessary data and function members to provide the following: The examiner must access answer sheets of at least one subject and may examine answer sheets of multiple subjects; the examiner represents a college and also a university; and most of the examiners are local and represent the local university. The program should have more than one constructor including one with and one without default argument. Provide a meaningful copy constructor.
12. Modify `ParameterizedCon.cpp` in Program 5.5 to use MIL.
13. Modify Program 5.6 to use MIL.
14. Execute Program 5.6 after removing dynamic memory allocation and assigning pointer directly. What have you concluded? Provide changes in `ItemArray` and also in the constructor `ItemsInterested` array. Observe the difference.
15. We have discussed three cases where copy constructors are applied and the importance of the first case with an example. Provide examples for the other two situations (i.e., passing to and returning from the function).
16. Provide destructors in all the examples for which we have provided copy constructors.

Chapter 6

Operator Overloading and User-defined Conversions

Learning Objectives

- Overloading operators
- Unary and binary operators
- friend operators
- Overloading =, [ ], ( ), new, and delete operators
- Function objects
- Cases where user-defined conversion is necessary
- Constructor and operator-based conversions

6.1 INTRODUCTION

Operator overloading enables the use of our own objects using operators which were reserved for built-in types in C. It is very important to have the facility of defining meaningful operators for user-defined objects, which is the subject of discussion in this chapter.

Let us consider a class `Time`, which represents time; `Time1`, `Time2`, and `Time3` are the objects of the class `Time` having some values. If two times are to be added, that is, `Time3 = Time1 + Time2`, it is achieved by overloading the '+' operator for the class `Time`. Unlike int or float, `Time` is not a built-in data type and hence the operator '+' cannot be used without overloading it.

Similarly, it is possible to overload other operators as well though there are some restrictions. It is possible to overload operators in a novel yet legible way.

Let us consider a class that contains a collection of employees, for example, the `Collection` class. Then, the statement

```
UniEmpCol.AddToCol(UniEmployee[i]);
```

can be rewritten as

```
UniEmpCol + UniEmployee[i]
```

However, in order to do that the operator '+' needs to be overloaded to the Collection class.

Operator overloading is performed by adding special member functions to the class; these functions are known as *operator functions* and can help convert one object into another. We will study these under user-defined conversions in Section 6.12.

6.2 RESTRICTIONS UNDER OPERATOR OVERLOADING

Though operator overloading is possible, it has its own set of restrictions, which are listed as follows:

Operator overloading provides additional meaning to an operator.

1. Operators do not lose their original meaning; instead, they have an additional meaning when overloaded. One cannot change the original meaning of an operator.
2. New operators cannot be devised. Only existing operators with given restrictions can be overloaded.
3. Operators will have an additional meaning, but will not have an additional precedence. The precedence remains the same.
4. Operators cannot change the number of arguments that were available in the original form. Hence, '+' in the binary form can only have two arguments. It cannot be overloaded with three arguments.
5. Operators can only be overloaded for user-defined types. All overloaded operators must have at least one argument as a user-defined type.
6. Except (), no other operator can have a default argument.
7. Some operators can never be overloaded.

6.2.1 Operators that Cannot be Overloaded

The following operators cannot be overloaded:

1. Dot operator for member access (.)
2. Dereference member to class operator (.*)
3. Scope resolution operator (::)
4. Size of operator (sizeof)
5. Conditional ternary operator (?:)
6. Casting operators (static_cast< >, dynamic_cast< >, reinterpret_cast< >, and const_cast<>)
7. # and ## tokens for macro preprocessors

Note One may ask why these operators cannot be overloaded. Consider overloading the dot operator. If it is overloaded, a class member operation gets a new meaning, which may lead to serious errors. A compiler developer must deal with the possible complexities that arise out of such errors and help the programmer by providing probable reasons for the error. If C++ allows such code, it can easily confuse the compiler with unforeseen side effects. It is for the same reason that C++ does not allow adding new operators. C++ also does not allow the global definition of certain operators (e.g., = operator). Many languages, including Java, do not provide operator overloading as it is a very difficult problem to manage.

6.2.2 Operators that Cannot be Overloaded as Friends

As pointed out earlier, operators are overloaded as functions. For a function to operate on a class, it should be either a member or a friend. The consequence is that the operators can be overloaded in two distinct ways, that is, as members or as friends. The following operators cannot be overloaded as friends:

1. Assignment operator =
2. Function call operator ()
3. Array subscript operator [ ]
4. Access to class member using pointer to object operator ->

The syntactical rules for the original meaning should be followed by the operators when overloaded. The following are some examples:

1. All arithmetic operators must return a value. However, it can be of a different type than what is returned by the original operator.
2. Unary operators do not have any explicit arguments. If overloaded as a friend, they take one reference argument.
3. Binary operators take one explicit argument if overloaded as a member and two explicit arguments if overloaded as a friend.

6.3 OPERATOR OVERLOADING THROUGH MEMBER FUNCTION

The syntax of the operator function as a member is similar to that of the normal member function with a specific naming convention. Let us look at Program 6.1, which deals with a complex number.

PROGRAM 6.1   Adding two complex numbers using an overloaded operator

```cpp
//OO+.cpp
#include <iostream>
#include <string>
using namespace std;

class Complex
{
    float Real;
    float Imag;
public:
    Complex(float TempReal = 0, float TempImag = 0)
    {
        Real = TempReal;
        Imag = TempImag;
    }

    Complex Add(Complex Comp2)
    {
        float TempReal;
        float TempImag;
        TempReal = Real + Comp2.Real;
        TempImag = Imag + Comp2.Imag;
        return Complex(TempReal, TempImag);
    }

    Complex operator +(Complex Comp2)
    {
        float TempReal;
        float TempImag;
        TempReal = Real + Comp2.Real;
        TempImag = Imag + Comp2.Imag;
        return Complex(TempReal, TempImag);
    }

    void Display()
    {
        cout << Real << "+" << Imag << "i \n";
    }
};
```

```
void main()
{
    Complex Comp1(10, 20);
    Complex Comp2(20, 30);
    Complex CompResult1, CompResult2;
    CompResult1 = Comp1.Add(Comp2);
    CompResult1.Display();
    CompResult2 = Comp1 + Comp2;
    CompResult2.Display();
}
```

How the Program Works

Defining a complex number as a class   In this example, complex numbers are considered to be a class. A complex number is always represented as a collection of two parts. The first part is known as the real value and the second part as the imaginary value. It is represented as <real value> + <imaginary value>i, that is, in a complex number $20 + 30i$, 20 is the real part and 30 is the imaginary part. Here, i is considered to be the square root of -1.

Operator overloading with complex class   Our purpose here is to understand how operator overloading is provided in C++ using this particular class. We hereby represent the complex number as two values, real and imaginary, with a few functions.

The following are the three functions present in the program:

1. The first function is a *constructor*. `Complex Comp1(1, 2)` will create a complex number `Comp1` with real value 1 and imaginary value 2.
2. The second function is the `display.Comp1.Display()`, which should display $1 + 2i$.
3. The third is the `Add()` function. It is a member function of a class and has one complex number as an argument. This means that it already has one implicit argument as `this` pointer to the invoking object. It adds the real and imaginary values of two `Complex` objects passed to it and returns the summation of the two objects as another `Complex` object.

Add Function and Overloaded '+'

Let us consider an interesting example where the body of the function is the same as that of the `Add()` function. It functions in the same way as the `Add()` function, but is called in a different way. The call to an operator function is different from the normal function call. Before looking at the difference, attention should be paid to the naming of the function.

The names of all operator functions begin with the keyword `operator`, which is followed by the *actual operator*. In this case, the + operator has been overload, so the function name is `operator +`. Every time the + operator is overloaded, the function name should be given as `operator +`. When the − operator is overloaded, it would be named as `operator −` and so on.

> The names of all operator functions begin with the keyword operator, which is followed by the actual operator.

The operator function is called when the + operator is used with both operands as *complex* arguments. As discussed earlier, it does not look like a function call. Look at the call

> If an operator is properly overloaded, it improves the readability of the program.

```
CompResult2 = Comp1 + Comp2;
```

It is actually

```
CompResult2 = Comp1.operator + (Comp2)
```

> **Note** Though the operators are defined in the same way as functions, they are not called in the same way.

The function is called this way because we want the addition of the complex numbers to look similar to that of any other numeric variable. One of the advantages of operator overloading is that both the functions (`Add()` and `operator +()`) are doing the same activity. Operator overloading is a very good example of how much C++ designers expect the user-defined objects to work similar to built-in objects. However, looking from the readability point of view, the second function looks far better, that is, `CompResult2 = Comp1 + Comp2` is more readable than `CompResult1 = Comp1.add(Comp2)`.

Choosing Complex Numbers to Overload '+'

The reason for choosing the example of complex numbers to illustrate overloading + is that although + can be overloaded for any other operation, it is important to overload it for an operation that is similar in meaning to the original one. If some other operation is chosen to be symbolized by +, then readability will be a problem. For example, if + is used to get a complex number that is a product of the arguments passed, then it will confuse and mislead the reader.

Similarly, overloading + for items other than numeric also creates ambiguity in the reader's mind. At times, though + indicates addition of some type, one can also use it for other than numerical operands.

> It is important to overload an operator for an operation that is similar or almost similar to the original one.

Overloading '+' for User-defined Class

Consider Program 6.2, which is an example of adding an employee to a collection. This program is the same as FriendClass.cpp discussed in Chapter 4. We have overloaded + to indicate addition to the collection.

PROGRAM 6.2 Adding an employee to an employee collection

```cpp
#include <iostream>
#include <string>
using namespace std;

class CollectionEmp;   // Forward definition
class employee
{
    int EmpNo;
    string Name;
    string DeptName;
    string Designation;
public:
    void Init(int TempNo, string TempName, string TempDept, string TempDesi)
    {
        EmpNo = TempNo;
        Name = TempName;
        DeptName = TempDept;
        Designation = TempDesi;
    }

    void DisplayDetails()
    {
        cout << "Details of employee number" << EmpNo << "\n";
        cout << "Name is" << Name << "\n";
        cout << "Department is " << DeptName << "\n";
```

```
            cout << "Designation is " << Designation << "\n";
    }
    /* Now member functions of the following class can access private variables of this class */

    friend CollectionEmp;
    /* If forward declaration is not provided, this statement will give an error */
};

class CollectionEmp
{
private:
    employee ColEmp[10];
    /* The collection is in the array form; it can even be a linked list */

    int Index;
public:
    void InitIndex()
    {
        Index = 0;
    }

    bool operator +(employee Emp)
    {
        if(Index < 9)
        {
            ColEmp[Index] = Emp;
            Index++;
            return true;
        }
        else
        {
            return false;
        }
    }

    void ListDeptWise()
    {
        string TempDeptName;
        cout << "Enter the department of the university:";
        cin >> TempDeptName;
        cout << "\n";

        for(int i = 0; i < 10; ++i)
        {
            if(ColEmp[i].DeptName == TempDeptName)
            {
                ColEmp[i].DisplayDetails();
            }
        }
    }
};

void main()
{
    CollectionEmp UniEmpCol;
    UniEmpCol.InitIndex();
    employee UniEmployee[10];

    UniEmployee[1].Init(1,"Lara", "Exam", "Professor");
    UniEmployee[2].Init(2, "Ponting", "Marksheet", "Clerk");
    UniEmployee[3].Init(3, "Laxman", "Accounts", "Head Clerk");
```

```
    UniEmployee[4].Init(4, "Flintoff", "Exam", "Clerk");
    UniEmployee[5].Init(5, "Muralidharan", "Accounts", "CAO");
    UniEmployee[6].Init(6, "Sarfaraz", "Exam", "Informer");
    UniEmployee[7].Init(7, "Dean Jones", "Exam", "Invigilator");
    UniEmployee[8].Init(8, "Madugalle", "Exam", "Examiner");
    UniEmployee[9].Init(9, "Ganguly", "Marksheet", "Repeater");
    UniEmployee[0].Init(10, "Nafees", "Accounts", "Clerk");
    for(int i = 0; i < 10; ++i)
    {
        UniEmpCol + UniEmployee[i];
        /* Placing the employees in the collection object */
    }

    UniEmpCol.ListDeptWise();
    /* This is a member function now, not a dummy one though! */
}
```

Output
```
Enter the department of the university: Exam

Details of employee number 1
Name is Lara
Department is Exam
Designation is Professor

Details of employee number 4
Name is Flintoff
Department is Exam
Designation is Clerk

Details of employee number 6
Name is Sarfaraz
Department is Exam
Designation is Informer

Details of employee number 7
Name is Dean Jones
Department is Exam
Designation is Sleeper

Details of employee number 8
Name is Madugalle
Department is Exam
Designation is Examiner
```

How the Program Works

Difference while defining and calling Look at the difference between Program 4.14 in Chapter 4 and this program. There is just a mechanical difference. Surprisingly, only two lines differ in both the programs, which are a line defining the function header and the one calling the function. The following are the changes:

1. `bool AddToCol()` changes to `bool operator +()`.
2. `UniEmpCol.AddToCol(UniEmployee[i])` changes to `UniEmpCol + UniEmployee[i]`.

Steps in operator overloading This shows that operator overloading can be simplified using a simple technique. A function for doing a job is written first and tested to check whether it works fine. Then, only two mechanical changes are needed at a few places in the program.

1. Change the name of the function as operator <operator_symbol> (e.g., operator +) where the function is defined.
2. Use that operator as an implicit function call, wherever the function call is made in the program. Thus, Object1.function (Object2) is changed to Object1 <Operator> Object2.

> **Note** Excessive use of overloading operators may reduce readability, whereas using it judiciously improves readability. Overloading an operator for doing something that is not obvious, such as using '+' for subtracting arguments, is bad programming.

Overloading Operators for a Purpose

Program 6.3 shows how + can be overloaded for a purpose. The same Time class discussed earlier has been used, with an overloaded + to add two times. The only additional feature here is the use of the same operator with more than two arguments. The importance of using a constructor can also be noted here.

PROGRAM 6.3 Operator overloading for a purpose

```cpp
//AddTime.cpp
#include <iostream>
using namespace std;

class Time
{
public:
    int Hours;
    int Minutes;
    int Seconds;

    void ShowTime()
    {
        cout << "Time is" << Hours << " hours : " << Minutes << " minutes : and " << Seconds
        << "seconds \n";
    }

    Time(int TempHours = 0, int TempMinutes = 0, int TempSeconds = 0)
    {
        Hours = TempHours;
        Minutes = TempMinutes;
        Seconds = TempSeconds;
    } // It can serve as default constructor as well

    Time operator +(Time Time2)
    {
        int TempHours, TempMinutes, TempSeconds;
        TempHours = Hours + Time2.Hours;
        TempMinutes = Minutes + Time2.Minutes;
        TempSeconds = Seconds + Time2.Seconds;
        TempMinutes += TempSeconds / 60;
        TempSeconds %= 60;
        TempHours += TempMinutes / 60;
        TempMinutes %= 60;
        return Time(TempHours, TempMinutes, TempSeconds);
    }
};

void main()
{
    Time Time1(12, 15, 15);
```

```
      cout << "The first value \n";
      Time1 ShowTime();
      Time Time2(10, 30, 30);
      cout << "The second value \n";
      Time2.ShowTime();
      Time Time3;
      Time3 = Time1 + Time2;
      cout << "And the result is \n";
      Time3.ShowTime();
      Time Time4 = Time1 + Time2 + Time3; // Adding three times
      Time4.ShowTime();

      /* The following will work and would be the same as Time3.ShowTime(). We are not defining
      a temporary object; the compiler will do that for us here. */

      (Time1 + Time2).ShowTime();
}
```

Output
```
The first value
Time is 12 hours : 15 minutes : and 15 seconds

The second value
Time is 10 hours : 30 minutes : and 30 seconds

And the result is
Time is 22 hours : 45 minutes : and 45 seconds
Time is 45 hours : 31 minutes : and 30 seconds
```

How the Program Works

Look at the statement

```
Time Time4 = Time1 + Time2 + Time3;
```

We are trying to add three times here. It is similar to the statement

```
Time1.operator + (Time2.operator + (Time 3));
```

It should be noted that this is not a case of having more than two arguments in the overloaded '+'. An overloaded '+' always has two arguments irrespective of the class for which it is overloaded.

> **Note** We cannot add three items using overloaded '+'. This is because when we overload an operator, we must honour the original construct for using that operator. '+' is designed to work with two operands (a binary operator) and so it must be honoured.

Another interesting statement is

```
(Time1 + Time2).ShowTime();
```

The compiler generates a temporary object from the expression Time1 + Time2 and the member function ShowTime() is called for that object. This statement is a shorthand notation of the following:

```
Time Temporary = Time1 + Time2; Temporary.ShowTIme();
```

6.4 SITUATIONS WHERE OPERATOR OVERLOADING IS USEFUL

Operator overloading is important in the case when we are developing a class library that will be used by other users. In this case, proper overloading of operators would be more advantageous. There is no need for the users to remember the names of functions and the chance of misspelling is also very less.

When operator overloading is provided for a class that is developed as a part of a team, usage and readability of the class depends heavily on the intuitiveness of the definitions of the operators. Consider the case of a linked list. If overloaded + is provided to add a node object to a linked list object, it does make sense and is very readable and less ambiguous.

```
Like LinkedList L, NewList;
Node N;
L = L + N;    // Adding a node to a list
NewList = L + N;    // New list from old list and adding a node
```

It is also important to know that overloaded + in Program 6.2 does not necessarily return the object of the same type. In its original form, the + operator always returns the same type of object; adding two integers returns an integer, adding two float returns a float, and so on. However, in Program 6.2, it returns a Boolean. In the linked list example, it adds two different types of objects and returns the first operand's type. C++ provides flexibility of this kind, which makes operator overloading extremely useful.

Not all operators enjoy the said flexibility. Operators new, delete and -> have the limitation that they can return only the same type of object as the original operator.

Operators can be classified as unary (which have one argument) and binary (which have two arguments). It should be remembered that it is not possible to overload the single ternary operator available.

6.5 OVERLOADING UNARY OPERATORS

Operators that have a single argument are known as unary operators. When these operators are overloaded as member functions, it is not necessary to pass any argument explicitly. The this pointer pointing to the invoking object is passed as an implicit argument.

```
//UnaryOp.cpp
#include <iostream>
using namespace std;
class Matrix
{
    int Element[3][3];
public:
    Matrix(){};        // Default constructor
    Matrix(int TempMatrix[3][3])
    {
        for(int i = 0; i < 3; i++)
            for(int j = 0; j < 3; j++)
                Element[i][j] = TempMatrix[i][j];
    }
    void Read()
    {
        for(int i = 0; i < 3; i++)
            for(int j = 0; j < 3; j++)
                cin >> Element[i][j];
    }
```

```
    void operator -()
    {
       for(int i = 0; i < 3; i++)
           for(int j = 0; j < 3; j++)
               Element[i][j] = -Element[i][j];
    }
    void Display()
    {
    for(int i = 0; i < 3; i++)
       for(int j = 0; j < 3; j++)
       {
           cout << Element[i][j] << "   ";
       }
       cout << "\n";
    }
};
void main()
{
    int ArrayOfInt[][3]={1,2,3,4,5,6,7,8,9};
    Matrix M1(ArrayOfInt);
    cout << "The first matrix before negation \n";
    M1.Display();
    cout << "First matrix after negation \n";
    -M1;
    M1.Display();
    Matrix M2;
    cout << "Enter values for the second matrix \n";
    M2.Read();
    cout << "The second matrix before negation \n";
    M2.Display();
    -M2;
    cout << "Second matrix after negation \n";
    M2.Display();
}
```

Output

```
The first matrix before negation
1    2    3
4    5    6
7    8    9
First matrix after negation
-1    -2        -3
-4    -5        -6
-7    -8        -9
Enter values for the second matrix
3  4  5  6  6  6  7  78  8
```

```
The second matrix before negation
3   4   5
6   6   6
7   78  8
Second matrix after negation
−3   −4   −5
−6   −6   −6
−7   −78  −8
```

Consider this program, which is an example of a class Matrix representing a matrix of 3×3 integer elements. We use '−' to negate all the values of the matrix.

Look at the definition of a simple function to negate. Naming it as operator − has enabled us to use statements of the type −M1 and −M2, which is more readable than M1.negate().

Similarly, it is possible to overload the operator '~' for inverting a matrix and operator '!' for transpose, if the users are familiar with such notations and if using them makes the program more readable. Given a specific domain, it is interesting to find newer meanings to known symbols and operator overloading is of great help in such cases.

6.5.1 Postfix Versions of ++ and −− Operators

Both increment and decrement operators have two versions in C as well as C++, namely, the *prefix* version and the *postfix* version. Both in C and in C++, they are differentiated by their position, which can be specified by overloading.

Though postfix and prefix are the same, they are differentiated by their respective positions by a C++ compiler. It is not possible to do so while overloading them; operator ++() would be the same for both the versions. To differentiate between the versions, operator ++() is considered to be a prefix operator being overloaded, whereas the statement operator ++(int AnyDummyValue) is considered to be a postfix operator being overloaded.

> We need to pass a dummy argument in the case of *postfix* operators.

In Program 6.4, when ++ is applied in the prefix form to a complex number, it adds to the real value, and when applied in the postfix form, it adds to the imaginary value. This has been done to show how postfix and prefix operators are overloaded to provide different operations.

PROGRAM 6.4   Overloading ++ prefix and postfix versions

```cpp
//OO++--.cpp
#include <iostream>
#include <string>
using namespace std;

class Complex
{
    float Real;
    float Imag;
public:
    Complex(float TempReal = 0, float TempImag = 0)
    {
        Real = TempReal;
        Imag = TempImag;
    }

    Complex Add(Complex Comp2)
```

```
    {
        float TempReal;
        float TempImag;
        TempReal = Real + Comp2.Real;
        TempImag = Imag + Comp2.Imag;
        return Complex(TempReal, TempImag);
    }

    Complex operator +(Complex Comp2)
    {
        float TempReal;
        float TempImag;
        TempReal = Real + Comp2.Real;
        TempImag = Imag + Comp2.Imag;
        return Complex(TempReal, TempImag);
    }

    Complex operator ++()        // This is prefix
    {
        Real++;
        return Complex(Real, Imag);
    }

    Complex operator ++(int dummy)    // This is postfix
    {
        Imag++;
        return Complex(Real, Imag);
    }

    void Display()
    {
    cout << Real << " + " << Imag << "i \n";
    }
};

void main()
{
    Complex Comp1(10, 20);
    Complex Comp2(20, 30);
    Complex CompResult1, CompResult2;

    CompResult1 = Comp1.Add(Comp2);
    CompResult1.Display();
    CompResult2 = Comp1 + Comp2;
    CompResult2.Display();

    Comp1++;   // The postfix version with dummy arguments Comp1.Display();

    ++Comp2;   // The prefix version without any arguments Comp2.Display();
}
```

How the Program Works

It should be noted that the program contains only additional parts of the code for overloading ++ in both versions. Here, we will explore only those two functions. It should also be noted that the argument (`int dummy`) is not used in a program. It is to be written just to differentiate between the prefix and postfix versions. It cannot be actually passed. If the postfix operator used in a program is not defined, the C++ compiler will flag a warning similar to following and then apply the prefix version there.

If we define a postfix version and use the prefix notation, the compiler flags an error.

```
No postfix form of 'operator ++' found for type 'Complex'; using prefix form
```

If different operations for both versions of increment or decrement operator are not needed, a single operator function can be used for prefix. This is useful for most of the practical cases.

6.6 OVERLOADING BINARY OPERATORS

Operators that take two operands are known as binary operators. They will have a single argument when defined as member. The first argument to that operator is always the invoking object. We have already seen an example of overloading the '+' operator for complex numbers.

6.6.1 Overloading Shorthand Operators While Overloading Arithmetic Operators

Shorthand operators include +=, −=, *=, and /=. The programmer may have arithmetic operators overloaded for a class in the program. Once the basic operators are in place and the users are familiar with them, the user might like to try shorthand operators. So, when the statement

```
First Case: −Time3 = Time1 + Time 2;
```

works, the user may try the following statement:

```
Second Case:  −Time3 += Time1;
```

which does not work as expected. This is the reason it is necessary to overload shorthand operators too when the basic arithmetic operators are overloaded. It is very important from the design point of view to include such operators in the class.

> **Note** Shorthand operators such as '+=' should be overloaded while overloading normal operators such as '+'.

6.7 OPERATOR OVERLOADING THROUGH FRIEND FUNCTIONS

As mentioned earlier, it is possible to use friends as operator functions. We have already seen that using friends is a violation of the principle of information hiding and is to be avoided as far as possible. It is true here as well. Let us now see why we need friends.

As discussed earlier, member functions cannot choose the first argument and it is always the invoking object. At times, this is a hindrance. There are two cases where it is really important to use friend functions. The first case involves a non-class first argument, while the second case involves conventional overloading of operators that require objects on the right-hand side (RHS) and not on the left-hand side (LHS). For example, the '<<' operator, while using cout, requires the object being read on the RHS, and not on the LHS. Let us look at the first case now. We will look at the second case Section 6.8.

Overloading Non-class Arguments as First Argument

Suppose we want a multiplication operation in a matrix class. Consider a matrix M1. An operation 5 * M1 is needed indicating the multiplication of a scalar value five and a matrix M1. This operation involves multiplying five with all the elements of M1. However, this is not possible using a member operator because the first argument is not an object, whereas it is possible to provide M1 * 5. It is possible to entertain both the cases by using friends. We need to write two different friend functions for both the operations, as shown in Program 6.5.

| Note | 5 * M and M * 5 must yield the same result. The member function definition of the operator '*' allows only the operation M * 5, and not 5 * M. If we want the operation 5 * M, we will have to overload the '*' operator as a friend. Whether it will yield the same result or not is secondary. We may have it if we wish so. |

PROGRAM 6.5 Operator overloading using a friend

```cpp
//OOUsingFriend.cpp
#include <iostream>
using namespace std;

class Matrix
{
    Int Element[3][3];
public:
    Matrix(){};
    Matrix(int TempMatrix[3][3])
    {
        for(int i = 0; i < 3; i++)
            for(int j = 0; j < 3; j++)
                Element[i][j] = TempMatrix[i][j];
    }

    void Read()
    {
        for(int i = 0; i < 3; i++)
            for(int j = 0; j < 3; j++)
                cin >> Element[i][j];
    }

    void Display()
    {
        for(int i = 0; i < 3; i++)
        {
            for(int j = 0; j < 3; j++)
            {
                cout << Element[i][j] << " ";
            }
            cout <<  "\n";
        }
    }
    friend Matrix operator *(Matrix, int);
    friend Matrix operator *(int, Matrix);
};

Matrix operator *(Matrix TempMatrix, int Multiplier)
{
    for(int i = 0; i < 3; i++)
        for(int j = 0; j < 3; j++)
            TempMatrix.Element[i][j] = Multiplier * TempMatrix.Element[i][j];
    return Matrix(TempMatrix.Element);
}

Matrix operator *(int Multiplier, Matrix TempMatrix)
{
    for(int i = 0; i < 3; i++)
        for(int j = 0; j < 3; j++)
            TempMatrix.Element[i][j] = Multiplier * TempMatrix.Element[i][j];
    return Matrix(TempMatrix.Element);
}
```

```
void main()
{
    Int ArrayOfInt1[][3]={1,2,3,4,5,6,7,8,9};
    int ArrayOfInt2[][3]={4,5,6,7,8,9,1,2,3};
    Matrix M1(ArrayOfInt1);
    Matrix M2(ArrayOfInt2);
    Matrix M3, M4;
    M1.Display();
    M3 = M1 * 5;
    M3.Display();
    M2.Display();
    M4 = 5 * M2;
    M4.Display();
}
```

Output
(After inserting explanatory lines)

Matrix before scalar multiplication

```
1   2   3
4   5   6
7   8   9
```

Matrix after scalar multiplication

```
5    10   15
20   25   30
35   40   45
```

Matrix before scalar multiplication

```
4   5   6
7   8   9
1   2   3
```

Matrix after scalar multiplication

```
20   25   30
35   40   45
5    10   15
```

How the Program Works

Friend function   Notice the flexibility to provide expressions such as M1 * 5 and 5 * M2. Both the expressions actually call two different operator * functions.

```
friend Matrix operator *(Matrix, int);
friend Matrix operator *(int, Matrix);
```

These are two friend definitions for the same operator. The operator function is overloaded in this case for the same set of arguments in *different* order. See that the first version can be rewritten by the member operators, but this is not possible for the second one. That is,

```
Matrix operator *(Matrix TempMatrix, int Multiplier)
```

can be written as Matrix operator *(int) as member. However,

```
Matrix operator *(int Multiplier, Matrix TempMatrix)
```

is not possible.

Note A friend is required in cases where we need to provide both the operations, namely, object <operator> value and value <operator> object. For example, both M * v and v * M are required where only M is a class and v is not.

Different bodies for the functions The bodies of both these functions are identical. Here, when the arguments are specified in either order, the same code is executed. It is important to note that one is free to write entirely different codes in both the functions. However, it should be done only if the problem statement justifies the same.

Take the case of a linked list object and a node object. In the case of Node1 + LinkedList1, the node object adds in the beginning, and in the case of LinkedList1 + Node1, it adds in the end. Hence, we may need to write different codes for operator '+' for reversed arguments. Similar is the case for the dequeue where insertion can be made at both the ends; operator '+' can be used to specify not only the insertion but the position of insertion as well. In such situations, friend functions should only be used.

Let us examine another such case in Section 6.8.

6.8 USING FRIENDS TO OVERLOAD << AND >> OPERATORS

It is simple to use cout and cin for reading and writing built-in type data. They can also be used for user-defined objects. Consider the case of a statement

```
cout << "This is testing"
```

cout is an object representing an output stream. A stream is very analogous to a pipe. cout takes "This is testing" as a sequence of characters and passes it to the other end of the pipe, which is attached to the screen; so, "This is Testing" is printed on the screen. The << is overloaded for this purpose. << here has the first argument as an object of the ostream class (the cout). The second argument here is a string.

The same is the case for cin >> MyVariable. cin is an object of the input stream whose other end is attached to the keyboard. >> is overloaded here. The << operator is known as the *insertion operator* and >> is known as the *extraction operator*. Some authors also refer to them as output and input operators.

cin takes the value from the keyboard because it is at one end of the pipe that is represented by cin. The value is then passed by cin to MyVariable because it is now at the other end of the pipe. Here, >> has its first argument as an object of istream class (the cin) and the second argument is MyVariable. Thus,

```
cout << "This is testing"
```

is similar to

As the syntax of cin and cout expects the object to be on the RHS of the operator << and >>, member functions cannot be used to overload << and >>.

```
operator << (ostream & /* the cout */, string & /* the string "This is
testing" */ )
```

Similarly,

```
cin >> MyVariable;
```

is equivalent to

```
operator >> (istream & /* the cin */, int /* MyVariable */)
```

Exhibit 6.1 explains the reason for choosing >> for cin and << for cout.

Program 6.6 shows how << and >> can be overloaded to read and write a user-defined object student. Here, << is used to print **student** object, while >> is used to read one. Thus, when **cout << Mahesh** is used, where Mahesh is a **student** object, it prints Mahesh object in the way specified while overloading <<. Similarly, **cin >> Mahesh** can also be used, which reads the members of **Mahesh** object in a way specified while overloading the >> operator.

PROGRAM 6.6   Friend operator overloading for reading and writing objects

```
//OOReadWrite.cpp
#include <iostream>
#include <string>
using namespace std;

class student
{
private:
    int RollNumber;
    string Name;
    string Address;
public:
    friend ostream & operator <<(ostream &, student &);
    friend istream & operator >>(istream &, student &);
};

ostream & operator <<(ostream & TempOut, student & TempStudent)
{
    TempOut << "Roll number is " << TempStudent.RollNumber << "\n";
    TempOut << "Name is " << TempStudent.Name << "\n";
    TempOut << "Address is " << TempStudent.Address << "\n";
    return TempOut;
}

istream & operator >>(istream & TempIn, student & TempStudent)
{
    cout << "Enter the roll number ";
    TempIn >> TempStudent.RollNumber;
    cout << "\n";
    cout << "Enter the name ";
    cin >> TempStudent.Name; cout << "\n";
    cout << "Enter the address ";
    cin >> TempStudent.Address;
    cout << "\n";
    return TempIn;
}
```

```
void main()
{
    student CaptainStudent;
    cin >> CaptainStudent;
    cout << endl << "Following is CaptainStudent's data \n" << CaptainStudent << "\n Bye!
    \n";
}
```

Output
```
Enter the roll number    1
Enter the name Lara
Enter the address West Indies

Following is CaptainStudent's data
Roll number is 1
Name is Lara
Address is West Indies
Bye!
```

How the Program Works

Using cin and cout for a user-defined object It is very easy to use `cin` and `cout` objects to read and write user-defined objects once the << and >> operators are overloaded. Overloading these operators reduces the difference between a user-defined and a built-in object to a large extent.

> **Note** The designers of C++ have made many efforts to make user-defined objects to behave in a similar manner to built-in objects; the provision of overloading << and >> operators is one of them. After overloading these operators, a user can provide code for reading and writing objects in the program just by inserting `cout << UserDefinedObject` or `cin >> UserDefinedObject`.

Overloading << and >> also simplifies the main function because it now contains only `cin >> UserDefinedObject` or `cout << UserDefinedObject`.

Inability to use a member function It is important to note that it is not possible to use member functions to overload these two operators. While overloading these operators, it is important to pass the first argument as *stream* (`cin` or `cout`) and the second argument as the user-defined object, whereas the first argument to a member function is always the this pointer. Therefore, if we want << to be a member function of student class, then

```
cout << CaptainStudent
```

must be written as

```
CaptainStudent << cout
```

In this statement, the reference to `CaptainStudent` is the first argument. When we use

```
cout << CaptainStudent
```

the reference to `CaptainStudent` is the second argument and requires the friend function.

Returning a reference Another important point here is that the references are passed and received, so that the user works with the same `istream` and `ostream` objects that are passed (`cin` and `cout`) later in the same expression.

Suppose a reference is not returned and the program contains the statement.

```
cout << CaptainStudent << "\n Bye"
```

it will not work. The reason is that

```
cout << CaptainStudent
```

is executed first. Then, it needs to execute the second argument, that is, "\n Bye". If it does not return as reference, it is not possible to have

```
<Reference to ostream> << "\n Bye"
```

Here, <Reference to ostream> is actually cout, which is returned by the operator function. It is analogous to

```
(cout.operator <<(CaptainStudent)) << "\n Bye"
```

This function call (operator <<) is possible on LHS because it returns a reference.

Overloading operators using a reference as an argument and returning the same reference enable the user to return the same object that is passed and not the one that is newly defined in the function.

Operators such as +, −, ++, −−, <<, and << can also be overloaded when the operation matches the original operation of the operator. We will look at =, [ ], ( ), new, and delete operators in the following sections.

6.8.1 Overloading Assignment Operator (=)

Overloading the assignment operator is useful in various circumstances. The first one is when we have dynamic constructors (which use dynamic allocation) and destructors. Consider the following program.

Note We can overload '=' for a given class; it is called local =. When we use '=' in the main program, it is called global =, which cannot be overloaded.

```cpp
// OO=.cpp
#include <iostream>
#include <string>
using namespace std;
class Item
{
   int ItemNo;
   string ItemName;
public:
   Item()
   {
      ItemNo = 0;
      ItemName = "";
   }
   Item(int TempItemNo, string TempItemName)
   {
      ItemNo = TempItemNo;
      ItemName = TempItemName;
   }
   void ShowDetails()
   {
```

```cpp
           cout << "\n Item number is " << ItemNo;
           cout << "\n Item name is " << ItemName;
    }
};
class customer
{
    int CustNo;
    string CustName;
    string CustAddress;
    Item *ItemsInterested;
    int TotalItems;
public:
    customer()
    {
        CustNo = 0;
        ItemsInterested = 0;
        TotalItems = 0;
    }
    ~customer();
    // It is better to write the non-inline destructor
    void operator = (customer & CustRef)
    {
        CustNo = CustRef.CustNo;
        CustName = CustRef.CustName;
        CustAddress = CustRef.CustAddress;
        ItemsInterested = 0;
        ItemsInterested = new Item[CustRef.TotalItems];
        // New memory for new object; this is the difference
        for(int i = 0; i < CustRef.TotalItems; ++i)
        {
            ItemsInterested[i] = CustRef.ItemsInterested[i];
        }
        TotalItems = CustRef.TotalItems;
    }
    customer(int TempCustNo, string TempCustName, string TempCustAddress, Item
    *TempItemsInterested, int TempTotalItems)
    {
        CustNo = TempCustNo;
        CustName = TempCustName;
        CustAddress = TempCustAddress;
        ItemsInterested = new Item[TempTotalItems];
        for(int i = 0; i < TempTotalItems; ++i)
        {
            ItemsInterested[i] = TempItemsInterested[i];
        }
        TotalItems = TempTotalItems;
```

```
        cout << "Parameterized constructor is called for" << CustName << "\n";
    }
    void ShowDetails()
    {
        cout << "\n Customer number is " << CustNo;
        cout << "\n Customer name is " << CustName;
        cout << "\n Customer address is " << CustAddress;
        cout << "\n" << CustName << " is interested in following items" << "\n";
        for(int i = 0; i < TotalItems; i++)
        {
            ItemsInterested[i].ShowDetails();
        }
    }
};
customer::~customer()
{
    cout << "Destructor is called for " << CustName << "\n";
    delete [] ItemsInterested;
}
void main()
{
    Item ItemArray[]=
    {
        Item(3, "Sandwiches"), Item(4, "Paper Bags"), Item(5, "Napkins"), Item(6, "Toys"),
        Item(10, "Bananas"), Item(9, "Pen"), Item(1, "Pencil"), Item(2, "Eraser"),
    };
    customer Steve (1, "Steve Waugh", "Australia", ItemArray + 2, 6);
    Steve.ShowDetails();
    customer Mark (2, "Mark Waugh", "Australia", ItemArray + 2, 3);
    Mark.ShowDetails();
    customer Beckham;
    /* Overloading the assignment operator is mandatory here */
    Beckham = customer (3, "David Beckham", "England", ItemArray, 5);
    Beckham.ShowDetails();
}
```

Need for Overloading Assignment Operator

The following statement will not work if the assignment operator is not overloaded:

```
Beckham = customer(3, "David Beckham", "England", ItemArray, 5)
```

This is because the compiler creates a new temporary object from the RHS expression to pass it on to the LHS. Immediately after the execution of the assignment statement, the temporary object is destroyed. It destroys the dynamically allocated list of items. Memberwise copy will only copy the pointer value and not the content; it would destroy the items that are pointed to by the pointer of Beckham.ItemsInterested as well. This is similar to the problem that occurred during initialization. Copy constructors have been used to solve this problem.

When we assign an object containing dynamically allocated members, we must overload the assignment operator. It is because member -by-member copy (default) copies only the pointers and thus the contents are not copied and are destroyed once the temporary object is destroyed.

We have seen earlier that initialization and assignment are different. We need to provide a separate solution for assignment if only one for the copy constructor is present. This has been done here.

Precautions while Overloading an Operator

Overloading the assignment operator needs some additional care. Let us try to understand this with a few illustrations.

1. Suppose we have an overloading assignment operator for customer class such as the one in the previous program, and we write a statement such as the following. What will happen?

```
Laxman = Laxman;
```

Here, we are assigning an object to itself. The object Laxman needs a dynamic memory management; we have two different areas of memory where the first one is now not pointed to by any pointer. A solution to this problem is a single line added at the beginning of the operator = function.

```
void operator =(customer & CustRef)
{
    if(*this == CustRef)
        /* Both the objects are the same; they do not do anything and jump to the end */
    else
        ...
}
```

2. The second point about assignment operator is that the object that is assigned already exists. Thus, we need to deallocate the memory before allocating a new one. Thus, the following statement

```
ItemsInterested = new Item[CustRef.TotalItems]
```

must be preceded by

```
delete [] ItemsInterested
```

3. Another point about assignment operator is the return type. We have used void as a return type. This is okay for normal cases, but when we write something similar to the following:

```
Laxman = Ponting = Sachin
```

where the RHS assignment operation (Ponting = Sachin) must return an object for the LHS operation [Laxman = (the result of Ponting = Sachin)] to be carried out, our design does not work. We need to return the object that is being assigned within the RHS assignment statement (i.e., Ponting = Sachin).

So, we need to return 'customer' and the code should also have 'return *this' at the end. The code now becomes

```
customer & operator =(customer & CustRef)
{
    ...
    return *this;
}
```

When one type of object is converted into another, the assignment operator can be overloaded. We have seen that if similar types of objects are assigned to one another, they are copied bit by bit. However, this is not the case for different types of objects. We would look at an example when we study object conversion in Section 6.12.

> **Note**   While overloading an operator, one must check whether the same object is being assigned and skip the rest of the code, return a reference of the object being assigned, and delete the object if it exists before assigning.

6.8.2 Array Subscript Operator ([ ])

The array subscript operator is overloaded usually to provide *safe array* operations. Suppose the user has defined an integer array of five elements as int IntegerArray[5]. It has elements 0 to 4 at its disposal. Suppose somewhere the user writes IntegerArray[5] by mistake, C (or C++) would try to access that place. It calculates the address of the sixth position of the array by having the address of the array and then using an offset of the data type for the required number. The integer data type will have a size of either 16 or 32 bit in most of the cases.

Suppose the array starts at position 100, the expression IntegerArray[5] would try to look at the location 100 + 5*(size of integer) and pick up whatever is stored at that location. C or C++ by default does not check for array boundaries. Why is it so? Let us find the reason.

When we write the code containing arrays, if C (or C++) compiler inserts code for checking array boundaries, it not only bloats the size of the executable code generated but also slows the execution as well. This is because every time the array element is referred to, the compiler checks for array boundaries. Such a check might be useful in one out of (may be) hundred cases. C was designed to be used by top-flight programmers; they are not *expected* to commit such errors. So, C has chosen efficiency over robustness.

> **Note**   C or C++ compilers do not check for array boundary errors for the reason that they want to optimize the executable files for time.

It is not possible to have a check in C if it has not been provided by default. However, C++ provides a facility that is easy to use if we know about operator overloading. It provides the facility to create a safe array, which performs checks for array boundaries as well. This is how it is done. If we write an expression such as <array name>[<sub script>] or IntegerArray[5], it is similar to <array name>[]<sub script> or IntegerArray[] (5). Here, [] is treated as an operator similar to the + operator discussed earlier. We can overload it to provide a check for array boundaries. Consider Program 6.7. SafeIntArray is now a class. Suppose we define an object SafeArray of SafeIntArray type, then we are guaranteed to get run-time errors if we try to access the subscript, which is out of range.

> Unlike C, C++ can help the programmer to check for array boundaries by overloading the array subscript operator ([]).

PROGRAM 6.7   Overloading the Array Subscript Operator

```
//OO[].cpp
#include <iostream>
using namespace std;

class SafeIntArray
{
    int Array[5];
public:
    int & operator[](int Index)
```

```
    {
        if((Index < 0) || (Index > 4))
        {
            cout << "Subscript out of range";
            exit(1);
        }
        else
            return Array[Index];
    }
};
void main()
{
    SafeIntArray SafeArray;
    SafeArray[0] = 5;
    SafeArray[-1] = 10;
    // This will produce a run-time error
    SafeArray[5] = 9;  // This will also generate a run-time error
}
```

How the Program Works

Let us understand how the [] operator is overloaded. It has only one argument, the index.

```
int & operator[](int Index)
```

The call `SafeArray[0]` is similar to `SafeArray.operator[](0)`.

This `IndexValue` (0 in this case) is used to check in the overloaded operator function whether it is going out of boundaries.

We have returned *reference to int* rather than *int* itself in the overloaded []. This is needed for having expressions such as `SafeArray[0] = 5;` because only then can we use the function call (`SafeArray[0]`) on the LHS of an assignment statement. If we define the operator function to return `int` instead of `int &`, it would not be possible to use expressions such as `SafeArray[0] = 5;`

We may think that this safe array program is trivial. It has a fixed size (10) and fixed data type (`int`). This is hardly useful in any application. When we study templates in Chapter 7, we will look at an example to see how the problems of providing safe array of any user-specified type and of size can be solved.

> A reference must be returned in case of [] operator being overloaded. Array expressions such as a[5] = 10 will not work otherwise. This is an example of a function returning reference being used as an LHS.

6.8.3 Function Call Operator

Suppose a class `Point` is defined for representing two-dimensional points. It may have definitions such as `Point P1(2, 3)` where 2 and 3 are the *x* and *y* coordinates, respectively. It is possible to use the constructor for the same. Statements such as `Point P1; P1(2, 3);` may be needed, where the explicit call to the constructor is not made, that is, it is not written as `P1 = Point(2, 3)`. `P1(2, 3)` is far simpler and easier to understand than `P1 = Point(2, 3)`. This can be achieved by overloading the () operator.

The () operator is also known as the *function call operator*. It is overloaded for improving the readability of the code. A better usage is to have a function object. Consider the following program. It shows how program readability is improved by overloading the () operator. We have also overloaded << operator for printing the coordinates of the point.

```
//OO().cpp
#include <iostream>
using namespace std;
class Point
{
    int X;
    int Y;
public:
    void operator ()(int TempX, int TempY)
    {
        X = TempX;
        Y = TempY;
    }
    friend ostream & operator <<(ostream & TempOut, Point & Pt);
};

ostream & operator <<(ostream & TempOut, Point & Pt)
{
    TempOut << "(" << Pt.X << "," << Pt.Y << ")\n";
    return TempOut;
}

void main()
{
    Point P1, P2;
    P1(2, 3);
    P2(4, 5);
    cout << P1;
    cout << P2;
}
```

6.9 FUNCTION OBJECTS

When the () operator is overloaded for a class, the objects of that class can be used similar to a function. Such objects are known as *function objects* as it is possible to call them in the same way as a function. In the previous program, P1(2, 3) looks like a function call.

Using such statements helps the users to call the overloaded () operator function. The advantage of using a function object over normal function is twofold.

> When the function call operator is overloaded for a class, the objects are called in the same manner as functions. Such ob-jects are called function objects and are preferred by expert programmers in many cases.

1. The first advantage is that it is possible to store some information in member variables. The execution of function objects can be controlled by these variables.
2. The second advantage is that the code with a function pointer can sometimes be replaced by template-based function objects. This is advantageous because it is not possible to make function pointers inline whereas a function object call can be inline.

Programs 6.8 and 6.9 solve the same problem in different ways. There are multiple functions to call, namely, Plus, Minus, Divide, and Multiply. The signature remains the same for all the four functions, except the name of the function. Program 6.8 uses (non-member) function pointers, whereas Program 6.9 uses function objects, which is the focus of this chapter.

PROGRAM 6.8   Solution using function pointers

```cpp
//UsingFunctionPointer.cpp
#include <iostream>
using namespace std;

int Plus (int TempX, int TempY)
{
    cout << "Plus() function is called \n";
    return TempX + TempY;
}
int Minus (int TempX, int TempY)
{
    cout << "Minus() function is called \n";
    return TempX - TempY;
}

int FunctionPointer(int(*FunPtr) (int, int), int Arg1, int Arg2)
{
    return FunPtr(Arg1, Arg2);
}

void main()
{
    int Arg1 = 20;
    int Arg2 = 5;

    /* The function itself is passed as an argument in the following statements */
    cout << FunctionPointer(Plus, Arg1, Arg2) << "\n";
    cout << FunctionPointer(Minus, Arg1, Arg2) << "\n";
}
```

Output
```
Plus() function is called
25
Minus() function is called
15
```

How the Program Works

The program is simple enough except for the use of a function pointer in calling the function. Observe the call

```cpp
cout << FunctionPointer(Plus, Arg1, Arg2) << "\n";
```

The first argument is the name of a function. Any function can be called here by name and arguments.

Advantage   The advantage of this mechanism is that we do not need a switch statement and the large number of comparisons in it. The function to be called is the first argument. Such a technique is very handy for those who are writing programs for compilers and have to generate object codes for a number of similar function calls. The header of the function that is called must have the argument consisting the function pointer.

```cpp
int FunctionPointer(int(*FunPtr)(int, int), int Arg1,int Arg2)
{
```

```
    return FunPtr(Arg1,Arg2);
}
```

Function pointer argument The first argument is `int(*FunPtr)(int, int)`. This is a pointer to the function, which returns `int` and has two `int` arguments. It should be noted that both functions come under this category. Moreover, the call `FunPtr(Arg1, Arg2)` is a shorthand notation of `(*FunPtr)(Arg1, Arg2)`. It is also apparent that the function call here is an indirect call, which is difficult to inline. Now, look at Program 6.9, which is the next version of the program that solves the same problem in a different way, that is, using function objects. We have classes now representing the concept of Plus and Minus. The process of adding and subtracting is now represented by the operator () of their respective classes.

Note Function pointers are pointers to functions, whereas function objects are objects with the () operator overloaded. We can see that processes such as add and subtract are implemented as a class with () overloaded. The user would still see it like a function but a programmer gets a far better level of control, as there is a class to handle that function call.

 **PROGRAM 6.9** Function objects

```cpp
//FunctionObject.cpp
#include <iostream>
using namespace std;

class Plus
{
    int X; int Y;
public:
    int operator ()(int TempX, int TempY)
    {
        X = TempX;
        Y = TempY;
        cout << "Plus operator () is called \n";
        return X + Y;
    }
};

class Minus
{
    int X; int Y;
public:
    int operator ()(int TempX, int TempY)
    {
        X = TempX;
        Y = TempY;
        cout << "Minus operator () is called \n";
        return X - Y;
    }
};

// Template definition
template <typename TypeFunObj>
FunObj(TypeFunObj fob, int Arg1, int Arg2)
{
    cout << fob(Arg1,Arg2);
    cout << "\n";
}
```

```
void main()
{
    Plus P;
    Minus M;

    int Arg1 = 20;
    int Arg2 = 5;

    /* The function itself is passed as an argument in all following four arguments: */
    cout << FunObj(P, Arg1, Arg2);
    cout << FunObj(M, Arg1, Arg2);
}
```

How the Program Works

> Unlike a function call using pointers, the function object deploys direct calling, which enables the programmer to make the functions inline.

The program is self-explanatory except for the template definition and its use. We will discuss that part alone here.

Readers may wonder why function templates have been used here. We will be studying function templates in detail in Chapter 7, but, for the time being, keep in mind that we need it while using function objects. Unlike function pointers that deal with pointers, function objects deal with classes and call to such objects require the class object (instead of the function pointer) to be passed.

Calling a function object   The call to the function FunObj, the first argument, is the function object. P and M are function objects representing Plus and Minus. Look at the template definition now. As templates are discussed in detail in Chapter 7, as of now assume TypeFunObj to be a user-defined type of some sort; here, it is the type of the first argument.

When FunObj(P, ...) is called, the first argument is of type Plus. Therefore, the compiler takes the value of TypeFunObj to be Plus. Similarly, when FunObj(M, ...) is called, the TypeFunObj is taken as Minus. The code fob(Arg1, Arg2) is replaced by Plus(Arg1, Arg2) by the compiler at the time of compilation, when TypeFunObj is Plus.

```
template <typename TypeFunObj>
FunObj(TypeFunObj fob, int Arg1, int Arg2)
{
    cout << fob(Arg1, Arg2);
    cout <<  "\n";
}
```

The fob(Arg1, Arg2) will be replaced by their respective objects (P and M, respectively). The call fob(Arg1, Arg2) in FunObj(P, Arg1, Arg2) becomes P(Arg1, Arg2). The operator () is overloaded for P object, and we have here a call to this operator. Thus, it is equivalent to calling a function Plus in this case.

The function call here is not indirect as in Program 6.8; hence, it is possible to have the function inline. This is the advantage of function objects. In fact, all operator () in this code are defined inside the body of the class and are thus inline by default.

6.10 OVERLOADING new AND delete

One of the advantages of using new and delete in place of malloc() and free() is their ability to be overloaded. Section 6.11.1 describes how new and delete can be overloaded.

6.10.1 Overloading `new` and `delete` using `malloc()` and `free()`

Consider Program 6.10 to understand how `new` and `delete` operators can be overloaded.

PROGRAM 6.10 Overloading new and delete

```
//OONewDelete.cpp
#include <cstdlib> #include <iostream>
using namespace std;

class Test
{
    int i;
public:
    Test(): i(0)
    {
        cout << "Constructor is called\n";
    };

    ~Test()
    {
        cout << "Destructor is called\n";
    };
    void *operator new(size_t size);
    void operator delete(void *P);
};

void *Test::operator new(size_t size)
{
    void *p = malloc(size);
    if(!p)
    {
        cout << "memory allocation failure";
        exit(0);
    }
    return p;
}

void Test::operator delete(void *p)
{
    free(p);
}

int main()
{
    Test *TestPtr = new Test;
    delete(TestPtr);
}
```

How the Program Works

Overloaded new does not require deciding the type of the pointer it returns. The programmer just returns a void pointer, which is converted to a valid type by the compiler.

Overloading both operators We have overloaded `new` and `delete` for the class `Test` and these operators are called when `new Test` or `delete TestPtr` is invoked. The overloaded operator `new` calls `malloc()` to allocate memory. The header `cstdlib` is included for calling `malloc()`.

Syntax of new and delete `new` takes a single argument of type `size_t`, which is the size of the class. It is important to note that the overloaded `new` does not return the pointer to the specific object; it returns the *void* pointer. It is surprising to find that there is no need to cast this to the respective pointer. In fact, it is done by the

new can be over-loaded using either `malloc()` or global new (`::new`). `delete` can be overloaded using either `free()` (when allocation is overloaded using `malloc()`) or `::delete` (when allocation is overloaded using `::new`).

compiler. Similarly, `delete` is implemented in terms of `free()`. It is defined to accept a void pointer. Again, when we pass a specific pointer such as `TestPtr`, we need not cast it because the compiler automatically does that for us.

Overloading operators such as `new` and `delete` is required if the memory management is to be done by the programmers. It is possible for them to take a big amount of memory and then allocate and deallocate it themselves. The system-defined `new` is known as global `new`. It is possible to overload `new` only for a given class and not the global `new`. The global `new` is available to all classes but the overloaded `new` is available only to the class in which it is overloaded. This is obvious when we want to write something such as the following:

```
SomeClassPtr = new SomeClass;
```

We would like to control how **SomeClass** is assigned the memory space. It is obvious that we cannot overload **global new** as we should not control how C++ allocates memory to different classes. In Section 6.11.2, we will see a case where we define a **tablespace** and allocate memory from that space.

Databases use a similar concept for allocating memory for the tables that they define inside a given `tablespace`. The advantage of such mechanism is that the programmer can control how and from where the memory is allocated. It is possible to exercise more controls while allocating and deallocating (for example, clearing previous contents before allocating, which would be very useful for a banking server).

Program 6.11 shows how memory can be managed by a programmer by overloading `new` and `delete`. Though we have not provided any additional mechanism to control, one can easily extend this program for this purpose.

6.10.2 Overloading new and delete using ::new

Program 6.10 used `malloc()` for memory allocation in the body of the overloaded `new`. We can also use the system-defined `new` in its place. The system-defined original `new` operator is referred to as the `::new`; or the global `new`.

PROGRAM 6.11   Overloading `new` and `delete` for memory management

```cpp
//OONewDeleteForDatabase.cpp
#include <cstdlib>
#include <iostream>
using namespace std;
#define TABLESPACE_SIZE 32

class Test
{
    int i;
public:
    static char *TableSpace;
    static char *CurrentPtr;
    static char *OldPtr;
    static bool FirstTime;

    Test(): i(0)
    {
        cout << "\n Constructor is called";
    }
```

```
    ~Test()
    {
        cout << "Destructor is called";
    };
    void *operator new(size t size);
    void operator delete(void *P, size_t size);
};
char *Test::CurrentPtr;
char *Test::OldPtr;
char *Test::TableSpace;
bool Test::FirstTime = true;

void *Test::operator new(size_t size)
{
    if(Test::FirstTime)
    {
        /* First time! Allocating memory large enough to hold the entire tablespace */

        Test::TableSpace = (char *)::new char[TABLESPACE_SIZE];
        Test::CurrentPtr = Test::TableSpace;
        printf("\n Test::TableSpace pointer is %u", Test::TableSpace);
        printf("\n Current pointer is %u", Test::CurrentPtr);
        printf("\n Old pointer is %u", Test::OldPtr);
        Test::FirstTime = false;
    }

    /* When we want memory space that goes beyond the tablespace available */

    if((Test::CurrentPtr + size) > (Test::TableSpace + TABLESPACE_SIZE))
    {
        cout << "\n Memory allocation failure";
        getchar();
        exit(0);
    }
    Test::OldPtr = Test::CurrentPtr;
    /* Old pointer to be returned. New pointer would be useful for allocation of new memory
    in the next cycle */

    Test::CurrentPtr = Test::CurrentPtr + size;
    cout << "\n Memory allocated \n";
    printf("Current pointer is %u", Test::CurrentPtr);
    printf("\n Old pointer is %u", Test::OldPtr);
    return Test::OldPtr;
}
void Test::operator delete(void *p, size_t size)
{
    ::delete p;
}
int main()
{
    while(true)
    new Test;   // Continue allocating until it runs out of memory
}
```

Output
```
Test::TableSpace pointer is 48770560
Current pointer is 48770560
Old pointer is 0
Memory allocated
```

```
Current pointer is 48770564
Old pointer is 48770560
Constructor is called
Memory allocated

Current pointer is 48770568
Old pointer is 48770564
Constructor is called
Memory allocated

Current pointer is 48770572
Old pointer is 48770568
Constructor is called
Memory allocated

Current pointer is 48770576
Old pointer is 48770572
Constructor is called
Memory allocated

Current pointer is 48770580
Old pointer is 48770576
Constructor is called
Memory allocated

Current pointer is 48770584
Old pointer is 48770580
Constructor is called
Memory allocated

Current pointer is 48770588
Old pointer is 48770584
Constructor is called
Memory allocated

Current pointer is 48770592
Old pointer is 48770588
Constructor is called
Memory allocation failure
```

How the Program Works

For demonstration purposes, we have defined a small tablespace of 32 bytes and 4 bytes will be allocated from that tablespace for each operation. The program centres around the tablespace design and memory allocation. The tablespace is initialized at the beginning by allocating enough memory to it (32 bytes).

Initializing the tablespace   Let us try to understand the program. Let us begin with the definition of the size of tablespace.

```
#define TABLESPACE_SIZE 32
```

The program contains a small tablespace of 32 bytes. It has a class Test having only one data member int i whose size is four bytes. The objects of class Test are stored in the tablespace of size 32. Thus, it is possible to have a total of eight such objects in the memory of 32 bytes. We have overloaded new, which does two things:

1. It allocates 32 bytes to the static char pointer TableSpace at the beginning. Then, out of these 32 bytes, it allocates four bytes for the first object.

2. From then onwards, it allocates four more bytes for the next object every time until it runs out of memory (32 bytes).

This is illustrated in Figs 6.1, 6.2, and 6.3. Figure 6.1 shows how the memory looks just before the first insertion and after the first insertion. It also throws light on how the variables are set with respective values before and after the operation. Figure 6.2 shows the case where the third insertion is made in the same place. It also indicates how the variable values are changed after that operation. Figure 6.3 indicates the case where the memory is completely occupied.

The first call allocates memory for the entire `Tablespace`, which is of 32 bytes, that is, eight chunks of four bytes each.

It is not possible to allocate memory after this and thus the allocation fails.

Using static members We have defined four static variables in the class `Test`. It is important to learn why static members are used here. We need to keep track of the memory places irrespective of the number of objects. These members, in true sense, belong to the class and not the objects.

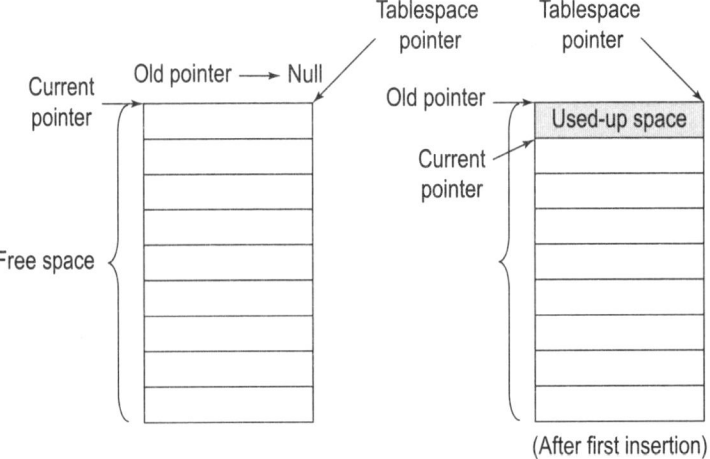

Fig. 6.1 Memory before and after first insertion

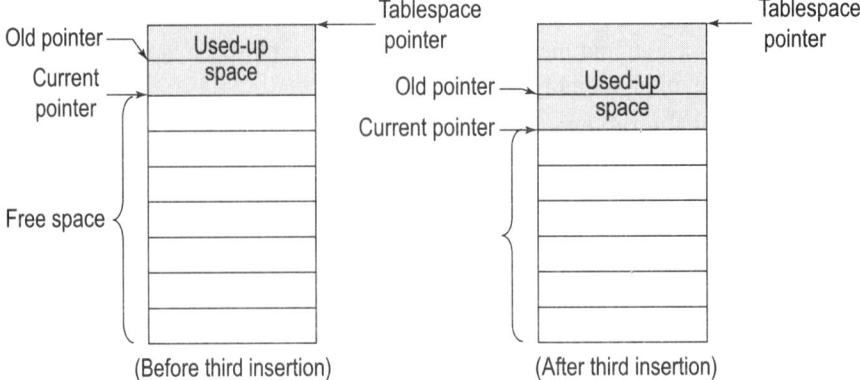

Fig. 6.2 Memory before and after third insertion

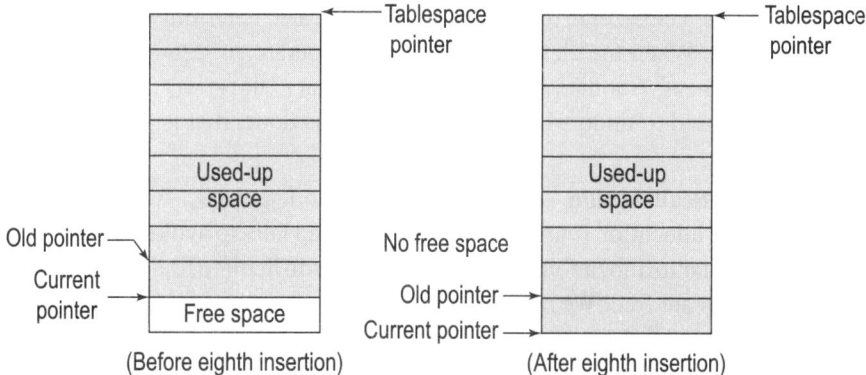

Fig. 6.3   Memory before and after eighth insertion

Let us take a detour to understand this. Suppose we have two statements as follows:

1. Sachin is a man.
2. Men are distributed all over the world.

These statements imply that Sachin is distributed all over the world.

Why is this implication wrong? It is because when the class attribute is inherited into an element, it must be an attribute for the objects and not for the class itself. The example given here is an attribute that is related to the class (the class is distributed all over the world and not the individual objects). Static variables represent class attributes (which are not inherited by the elements of the class, that is, the objects). This is an example where one can see the need for such members and how a programmer can use them.

Memory allocation   The first static variable holds the pointer to the memory that we would like to allocate ourselves. So, when we get memory allocated for the first time, we have to allocate memory (32 bytes in our case) from the heap, and we make the memory pointed to by the pointer as TableSpace. Subsequently, every time allocation is needed, four bytes are taken from that chunk and allocated. Next, the two pointers are for traversing in the memory. The current pointer points to a place where the next memory would be allocated, and the old pointer points to a place where the current memory is allocated. In the first new operation, complete tablespace memory is allocated from the heap; for all subsequent operations, memory is allocated from this tablespace memory and not the heap. The memory has to be allocated differently in the first new call from the other calls. The bool variable FirstTime tells us if new is called for the first time. The process of allocation and movement of the current and old pointers is also shown in Figs 6.1, 6.2, and 6.3.

Constructor calls and ::new   We have defined the constructor and destructor for the Test class as well. It is interesting to see that though we do not call constructor from the overloaded new, it is automatically called. The call to constructor is added by the compiler in the overloaded new function. Moreover, look at the call to ::new in the body of the function operator new(). It will call the global new defined by the system. We use ::new to get the memory required for our tablespace from the heap.

Delete operation   The delete operator is overloaded with two arguments, namely, void pointer and size_t type variable size. The second parameter here is not important. We can call delete with both versions, that is, one argument (void * only) and two arguments (void

* and size_t). The size of the object is automatically determined if the second argument is not provided. When the class in which `delete` operator is defined is inherited, we need the second argument. Another interesting point is that `::delete` is called in the destructor. The `::delete` is used to undo what overloaded `new` has done, that is, deallocate memory pointed to by P.

Stage-wise deallocation Complex deallocation process, which deallocates memory similar to the allocation routine, is not implemented here to avoid complexity. If deallocation routines similar to allocation are written, it will be difficult to find the blocks that are allocated and those that are free. We need an additional array with bool values indicating the slots that are allocated and those that are free. From the list, it will be possible to allocate any slot that is free. Our solution devised for the purpose of showing overloaded `new` and `delete` is not complex. Look at the following condition in the case of the overloaded `new`.

Testing memory allocation failure The following allocation algorithm checks whether the memory we are trying to allocate is within the tablespace limit. If it is beyond the tablespace limit, it displays a failure message and the execution of the program will be terminated.

```
if((Test::CurrentPtr + size) > (Test::TableSpace + TABLESPACE_SIZE))
{
    cout << "\n Memory allocation failure";
    getchar();
    exit(0);
}
```

The output shows how the current and the old pointers are incremented. When the current pointer reaches the end, we get the memory allocation failure message.

6.11 USER-DEFINED CONVERSIONS

Object assignment is straightforward if both the objects involved are of the same type. The assigned object members are copied to the object being assigned. We call it member-by-member copy. However, when they are of different types, say, time in two different formats represented by two different types of objects, then we need user-defined conversion. Why? As the objects are different and the members are not the same, the compiler cannot go for member-by-member copy. Before getting into the details of user-defined conversion, let us see what we mean by implicit conversions, which is automatically provided by the compilers.

> **Note** Normal assignments involve member-by-member copy. However, when both sides of the assignment statement have different types of objects, one must instruct the compiler how to copy. User-defined conversion is a way to solve this problem.

6.11.1 Implicit Conversions

Conversion from one type into another is sometimes needed. C provides a large number of conversions automatically. Moreover, *typecasting* can also be used to provide type conversions. Both these conversions are possible in C++ as well. In addition, it is also possible to provide user-defined conversions (conversion from an object of one class to another, from an object of a class to a built-in type, or from a built-in type to an object of a class).

Implicit conversions are automatically carried out by the compiler as and when encountered in the code. The following is one such example:

```
int I = 0;
float F = 4.5;
I = F + 2;
```

Here, we are assigning 6.5 to the integer variable I. It is implicitly cast to integer to get 6 as an answer in I. Instead, we can write the following expression.

```
I = (int)F + 2
```

This expression is better as we explicitly cast the value; it is more readable as well. Although it is possible to cast one type into another if needed, the C++ compiler provides the automatic casting in a few cases. They are described as follows:

1. When an arithmetic expression contains heterogeneous types: These occur when there is more than one type of operand in an arithmetic type. The compiler picks up the widest type of operand to convert. Look at the following examples. Consider variables defined as

```
int I = 5;
float F = 4.5;
double D = 12.34;
D = I + F
```

   (Here, I and F are both converted to double and then added; this sum is assigned to D. It is analogous to writing

```
D = (double)I + (double)F
```

   If we write

```
float F2 = F + I
```

   then I is cast to float by the compiler similar to the earlier statement.

2. Conversion to bool data type when int is used instead and vice versa: C programmers tend to use integer variable for testing truthfulness. If a similar code is found by a C++ compiler, it will cast that variable into bool data type. Similarly, if the bool variable is used as an RHS in an assignment involving LHS as an integer, the integer variable is assigned the value zero or one depending on the truthfulness of the bool variable. Look at the following examples. Assume int Flag1 and int Flag2 are defined.

   (a) `if(Flag1) cout << "Go Ahead!";` is the same as `if((bool) Flag1) cout ...`
   (b) `if(!Flag2) cout << "Do not move!"` is the same as `if((bool)! Flag2) cout...`
   (c) `I = Flag1` (if Flag1 is true, I is assigned one; otherwise, it is assigned zero after casting the bool value to int) is the same as `I = (int)Flag1`.

3. At the time of initialization, if the value or variable used to initialize is of a different type, then that value or variable is cast to the LHS data type automatically. Following are the examples:

   (a) `int J = 4.5` will assign 4 to J by casting 4.5 to int
   (b) `int J = F` will assign 4 to J by casting F to int

(c) `int *p = 0` (We can assign zero value to a pointer variable). In this case, zero is cast from int to pointer to int; thus, p is made to point to null. Zero is the only value possible to be used here. It is indicative of null value. In the given expression, p now points to null.

> **Note**   It is normal practice by programmers to assign 0 (zero) to a pointer in C++. It means null and the pointer is given a null value. In C++ 11, we have an explicit null pointer.

4. When signed and unsigned values are used together in an expression or short and long are used, then the compiler picks up wider values, which can preserve the meaning of the variable.

> **Note**   If long and short are used in the same expression, short is converted to long. Moreover, if both signed and unsigned are used in the same expression, the signed value is converted to unsigned. If the signed value is negative, an incorrect value is assigned to the unsigned variable but no error is flagged. More importantly, when conversions between other combinations are used, the conversion is compiler dependent.

5. Any pointer can be converted to void * (but not vice versa; a void pointer needs a cast to be converted to any other type unlike C). For example,

```
int *q = &I;
void *p = q;
```

(Here, q is an integer pointer and p is assigned q after implicitly casting it into void pointer by the compiler.)

6. Array name (which is a static pointer pointing to the first element of an array) can be cast to normal pointer when used in assignment. For example,

```
int a[10]; int *p = a;
```

(Static pointer a is cast to normal pointer and assigned to p)

Now, p is pointing to the first element of the array.

7. Enumeration type is converted to `int`: For example,

```
enum employee{DailyWages = 1, Temporary, OnProbation, Permanent};
```

This assigns the values of 2, 3, and 4 to `Temporary`, `OnProbation`, and `Permanent` values, respectively. Now, we can write something like this:

```
int Salary = OnProbation * DaysAttended
```

which is equivalent to multiplying `DaysAttended` and 3.

8. Non-constant is converted to constant: Whenever a const is initialized or assigned with a value or variable that is not constant, the value or variable is cast to constant before assignment.

```
const CI = I
```

This converts the I value to const integer before assignment.

> **Note**   Default member-wise copy does not work if both operands are of dissimilar types. Neither does C++ provide a default behaviour when the objects involved on both the sides of the assignment are different. When such an assignment is provided, it confuses the compiler and the program does not compile.

The bottom line is that when we need to assign different types of objects, we need to write our own conversion routine to guide the compiler what to do when such assignments are provided. User-defined conversions are needed in four different cases as mentioned in the following sections.

6.11.2 Built-in Data Type to Object

One specific method to solve the problem of dissimilar objects assignment is to use constructors. For example, Complex C1 (2, 3) takes two arguments of built-in data type and converts to a Complex object. Wherever we use constructors, we convert the argument types to the native object type of the constructor. Let us see an example of this case. Suppose we define a class Length and would like to have a constructor as follows:

```
class Length
{
   int L
   ...
public:
   Length(int TempLength = 0)
   {
      L = TempLength;
   }
};
```

Now, if we define an object using a statement such as Length DoorLength(8), basically we construct the object from 8, an integer value. In a way, we are converting an integer value into an object.

6.11.3 Object to Built-in Data Type

Suppose we have a LoggedInUser class with contents such as Name, Token (which indicates access rights for the user), and few other information that are important for a program. We may need to print error messages for a given LoggedInUser along with the user's name. In that case, we write cout << LIU1.Name where LIU1 is an object of LoggedInUser class. This has a problem. If Name is declared as private, this statement will not work. We have to either make Name public and face the consequences or write a member function to access the name. The biggest consequence of making Name public is that it defeats the purpose of defining a member as private and keeping the interface to the class uncluttered. It also allows the user to modify the value in any manner that he deems fit, unlike the case where we provide public functions to access that private variable which enables us to have controlled access to that member. When we write a function such as PrintName(), we may need to write LIU1.PrintName(). It is better to write just LoggedInUser to get the user id instead of cout << LIU1. This can easily be done using a conversion function.

Program 6.12 shows how we can convert an object to a built-in data type. In addition, the program also shows the usage of an array of pointers and how it leads to efficient memory management. When a new user is encountered, we allocate memory for the user and then make the pointer point to that location. Thus, we only allocate memory for the users encountered and not for the entire array.

Note   Converting objects of built-in types is a common operation in Java. For example, the `toString` method converts the class object to string. Though string is also an object in Java, it is still useful to have such a feature.

PROGRAM 6.12   Object to built-in data type

```
//ObjectToBuiltIn.cpp
#include <iostream>
#include <string>
using namespace std;
class LoggedInUser
{
    string Name;
    int TokenNo;
    static int TotalLoggedIn;
public:
    LoggedInUser()
    {
        TotalLoggedIn++;
        cout << "\n You are user number " << TotalLoggedIn   << "\n Welcome! \n";
    }
    void InsertName()
    {
        cout << "Insert name of the new user ";
        cin >> Name;
    }
    /* The following is the function of our interest; it converts the object to string
    operator */
    string()
    {
        return Name;
    }
};
int LoggedInUser::TotalLoggedIn;
void main()
{
    LoggedInUser *ArrayOfUsers[100];
    int index = 0;
    int Choice;

    while(true)
    {
        cout << "\n1. New user \n";
        cout << "2. List all users \n";
        cout << "3. Exit from the program \n";
        cout << "Enter your choice ";
        cin >> Choice;

        if(Choice == 1)
        {
            if(index == 100)
            {
                cout << "\n Too many users! \n";
                exit(1);
            }
            ArrayOfUsers[index] = new LoggedInUser; ArrayOfUsers[index]->InsertName();
```

```
        index++;
    }
    else if(Choice == 2)
    {
        for(int i = 0; i < index; ++i)
        {
            /* The conversion takes place here */
            string NameOfUser = *ArrayOfUsers[i];

            /* One of the following could also be used instead */
            cout << (string) *ArrayOfUsers[i] << "\n";
            cout << string (*ArrayOfUsers[i]) << "\n";

            /* In both the cases, the conversion is done with the help of typecasting.
            The first case is C-style casting whereas the next one is a newer cast
            available in C++ */

            cout << NameOfUser;
        }
    }
    else
        exit(0);
    }
}
```

How the Program Works

We will only look at the code that converts the object into a built-in type value. String is considered to be a built-in type in the following. In a strict sense, it is not built in but is a part of Standard Template Library (STL).

Conversion of user object into string   In the following statement

```
string NameOfUser = *ArrayOfUsers[i];
```

we have assigned the object to a string. It is acceptable to the compiler because we have written a conversion function. The conversion function itself is very simple. Let us look at it again.

```
operator string()
{
    return Name;
}
```

The other two statements that perform a similar conversion are as follows:

```
cout << (string) *ArrayOfUsers[i] << "\n";
cout << string (*ArrayOfUsers[i]) << "\n";
```

This function converts the object of type `LoggedInUser` to a string. It tells the compiler to convert `LoggedInUser` to a string, and then copy the `Name` value of `LoggedInUser` to the string.

Operator function   Though we have not specified, we are returning an object of type string in the operator function. We cannot specify a return type in the header of an operator function. The syntax of a header is as follows:

```
operator <built-in type name>()
```

```
{
    body of the function
}
```

The function that provides guidance of conversion from one type into another is called the *operator function*. It contains with the word 'operator', the type to convert to, and the body of function indicating how it will be done.

Here, the return type and the argument are not specified. The return type is actually the built-in-type-name that we have specified after the keyword operator. The argument list must be empty. Here, <built-in-type> (string in the given example) is treated as an operator.

Thus, operator string returns string, operator int returns int, operator float returns float, and so on.

We cannot define an operator function returning a type as a friend. It has to be a member function.

6.11.4 Wrapper Classes

Some of the built-in types are not objects, for example, int, char, etc. However, for complete object orientation, they should be objects. For instance, if we want to have an integer class, we can specify the functions for reading the integer with proper validation checks. If they are defined as class, we can inherit them to have our own class of, say, positive integers from one to some maximum number. A class that provides a basic data type with such additional facilities is known as a *wrapper class*.

> A wrapper class for a built-in data type contains that basic data type and facilities such as error handling, conversion to built in type to and fro, initializing to some value (e.g., zero to integer type), and so on.

Sometimes, we may need to convert the wrapper class object into built-in type object and vice versa. Converting from built-in type to wrapper is possible using constructors and the inverse is possible using conversion operators. Program 6.13 is an example of the same.

 **PROGRAM 6.13** A wrapper class for integer

```cpp
//Wrapper.cpp
#include <iostream>
#include <string>
using namespace std;

class Integer
{
private:
    int Value;
public:
    friend ostream & operator <<(ostream &, Integer &);
    friend istream & operator >>(istream &, Integer &);

    /* Conversion using constructor*/
    Integer(int TempVal = 0)
    {
        Value = TempVal;
    }

    /* Conversion using operator */
```

```
        operator int()
        {
            return Value;
        }
};

ostream & operator <<(ostream & TempOut, Integer & TempInteger)
{
    TempOut << TempInteger.Value;
    return TempOut;
}

istream & operator >>(istream & TempIn, Integer & TempInteger)
{
    TempIn >> TempInteger.Value; return TempIn;
}

void main()
{
    Integer Int1 = 5;
    // The constructor is applied

    Integer Int2;
    int int1;
    int int2 = 7;
    int2 = int2;      // The constructor is applied
    int1 = Int1;      // The operator is applied here

    cout << "Integer value is" << Int1 << "int value is" << int1 <<"\n";
    cout << "Integer value is" << Int2 <<"int value is" << int2 <<"\n";
}
```

How the Program Works

We will only look at the important statements of this program in this section.

Using `Integer` and `int` interchangeably   We have used `Integer` and `int` interchangeably in this example without hinting that `Integer` is actually a class. The advantage of using wrapper class objects compared to the raw data types is that validations of our choice can be provided. When not initialized explicitly, an `Integer` object would be initialized with the value zero.

Inheritance advantage   It is also possible to inherit such classes into classes of our choice. For example, a class of positive integers can be inherited from the `Integer` class. Moreover, the use of the overloaded << and >> should be noted. This makes the wrapper class identical to a built-in data type.

Operator function and constructor   Our concern here is the *operator* int. This function provides the facility of converting the `Integer` type to `int`. Thus, a user-defined object can be converted to that of a built-in type. A conversion from built-in type to a user-defined object is also possible using constructors.

6.11.5 Conversion of Object Type using Constructors

It is possible to convert from one type of object into another using either constructors or conversion functions. There are two different cases in such conversions. They are conversion from a foreign object into a native one and vice versa. The conversion from a foreign object

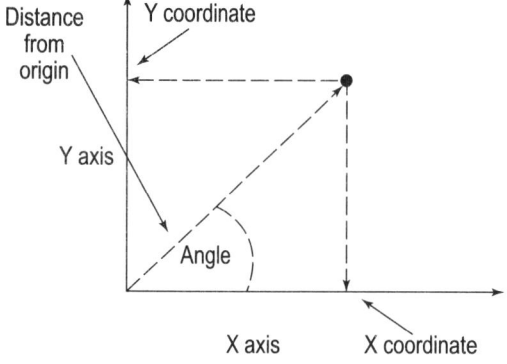

Fig. 6.4   Cartesian and polar coordinates

into native one is done using constructors. We will study how to use constructors to convert one object into another in this section.

Consider a class `Point`, which can be represented in the format in which a point is described by an x and a y coordinate. This format is known as rectangular coordinates or Cartesian coordinates system. `Point` can also be defined using the angle made with the x-axis and the radius as a distance from the origin. This is known as polar coordinates system (refer Fig. 6.4). A system may have both the representations and need a method for conversion between them.

The mathematical formulae for conversion between the two are as follows:

1. Conversion from polar to Cartesian coordinates

```
X = Radius * cos(angle)
Y = Radius * sin(angle)
```

2. Conversion from Cartesian to polar coordinates

```
Angle = atan(X/Y)
Radius = sqrt(X * X + Y * Y)
```

In Program 6.14, conversion is shown using a constructor function.

 **PROGRAM 6.14**   Polar to Cartesian object conversion using constructors

```cpp
//PolarToCartesian1.cpp
#include <iostream>
#include <string>
#include <cmath>
using namespace std;

class Polar
{
    double Radius;
    double Angle;
public:
    Polar(double TempRadius = 0, double TempAngle = 0)
    {
        Radius = TempRadius;
        Angle = TempAngle;
    }

    double GetRadius()
    {
        return Radius;
    }

    double GetAngle()
    {
        return Angle;
    }
};
```

```
class Cartesian
{
    double X;
    double Y;
public:
    Cartesian(double TempX = 0, double TempY = 0)
    {
        X = TempX;
        Y = TempY;
    }

    Cartesian(Polar PolarPoint)
    {
        double TempRadius = PolarPoint.GetRadius();
        double TempAngle = PolarPoint.GetAngle();
        X = TempRadius * cos(TempAngle);
        Y = TempRadius * sin(TempAngle);
    }

    void Show()
    {
        cout << "(" << X << "," << Y << ") \n";
    }
};
void main()
{
    Cartesian CPoint1(10, 10);
    Polar PPoint2(10, 45);
    Polar PPoint1;
    Cartesian CPoint2;
    CPoint2 = PPoint2;

// The following will not work
// PPoint1 = CPoint1;
CPoint2.Show();
}
```

How the Program Works

The statement `Cpoint2 = Ppoint2` is important. It is a shorthand notation of `Cpoint2 = Cartesian (Ppoint2)`, thus casting `Ppoint2` to Cartesian. The C++ compiler will not flag an error here if the conversion is defined. In this case, the conversion is defined using a constructor.

```
Cartesian(Polar PolarPoint)
{
    float TempRadius = PolarPoint.GetRadius();
    float TempAngle = PolarPoint.GetAngle();
    X = TempRadius * cos(TempAngle);
    Y = TempRadius * sin(TempAngle);
}
```

The `Cartesian` constructor has an argument of type `Polar`. It provides a method for converting a polar point to a Cartesian point. The statements in the body of the function are the implementation of the formulae that have been mentioned earlier. However, it is not possible to write PPoint1 = CPoint1 because we do not have any constructor in the Polar class for the Cartesian class. If both the conversions are needed, one way is to use operators as described in Section 6.12.6.

6.11.6 Conversion of Object Type using Conversion Functions

When a native object needs to be converted into a foreign object, operator functions (conversion functions) are used. They can be used in the same manner as used while converting to a basic type from an object. Program 6.15 shows the use of operator functions.

 **PROGRAM 6.15**   Cartesian to polar object conversion using operator function

```cpp
//CartesianToPolar1.cpp
#include <iostream>
#include <string>
#include <cmath>
using namespace std;

class Cartesian;
class Polar
{
    double Radius;
    double Angle;
public:
    Polar(double TempRadius = 0, double TempAngle = 0)
    {
        Radius = TempRadius;
        Angle = TempAngle;
    }

    double GetRadius()
    {
        Return Radius;
    }

    double GetAngle()
    {
        return Angle;
    }
    void Show()
    {
        cout << "(" << Radius <<", "<< Angle <<")\n";
    }
};
class Cartesian
{
    double X;
    double Y;

public:

    Cartesian(double TempX = 0, double TempY = 0)
    {
        X = TempX;
        Y = TempY;
    }

    Cartesian(Polar PolarPoint)
    {
```

```
        double TempRadius = PolarPoint.GetRadius();
        double TempAngle = PolarPoint.GetAngle();
        X = TempRadius * cos(TempAngle);
        Y = TempRadius * sin(TempAngle);
    }

    operator Polar()
    {
        double TempAngle = atan(X/Y);
        double TempRadius = sqrt(X * X + Y * Y);
        return Polar(TempRadius, TempAngle);
    }

    void Show()
    {
        cout << "(" << X << ", " << Y << ") \n";
    }
};

void main()
{
    Cartesian CPoint1(10, 10);
    Polar PPoint2(10, (double)0.5);
    Polar PPoint1;
    Cartesian CPoint2;
    CPoint2 = PPoint2;
    // The following will work
    PPoint1 = CPoint1;
    CPoint2.Show();
    PPoint1.Show();
}
```

How the Program Works

This program contains an operator function that converts from a Cartesian coordinate to a polar coordinate. Look at the function:

```
operator Polar()
{
    double TempAngle = atan(X/Y);
    double TempRadius = sqrt(X * X + Y * Y);
    return Polar(TempRadius, TempAngle);
}
```

This code will generate a polar object from a rectangle object. The syntax of the header of the operator function is as follows:

```
operator <ObjectFromWhichConversionTobeMade>()
```

It should be noted that this function does not have either return type or arguments.

6.11.7 Constructor vs Operator Functions for Conversion

A *constructor* converts a *foreign* object to a *native* one, whereas an operator converts a *native* object to a *foreign* one. Thus, the code for conversion using a constructor needs to be written in the destination class, whereas that using an operator needs to be written in the source class.

> **Note** If we want to convert some other object to a native object, we would write a constructor, whereas if we want a native object to be converted to some other object, we would use operators.

In the constructor method, we need to use functions that return the value of private variables. Programs 6.14 and 6.15 had `GetRadius()` and `GetAngle()` functions for this purpose. These functions are known as *access methods*. They are important because the private variables of the class need to be accessed for conversion.

In the operator method, we need to use a constructor for the foreign object. If it has not been defined, this method cannot be used. In case, a constructor is not available, we need to change the program as follows.

We have to define an object such as `Polar TempPolar`, since we would need `TempPolar.Radius` and `TempPolar.Angle` to be calculated given the values of X and Y. In other words, the following code

```
operator Polar()
{
    float TempAngle = atan(X/Y);
    float TempRadius = sqrt(X * X + Y * Y);
    return Polar(TempRadius, TempAngle);
}
```

will be converted to the following code. This constructor is not provided in the `Polar` class.

```
operator Polar()
{
    Polar TempPolar;
    TempPolar.Angle = atan(X/Y);
    TempPolar.Radius = sqrt(X * X + Y * Y);
    return TempPolar;
}
```

`Radius` and `Angle` are private variables here and are not accessible to non-member functions. Even if access methods such as the first case are defined, the problem is not solved. The access methods provide values of the private variables, but do not permit changing the value of variables. Providing public functions that let the value of a private member change is not a good way to program because then the members do not remain private. If we have a constructor, we can construct the object as we have done in Program 6.14 without any need to access the private variables, which shows the usefulness of the constructor while writing the operator function that converts one user-defined object into another.

6.11.8 Choosing an Appropriate Conversion Method

The differences between the constructor and operator functions are shown in Table 6.1

Choosing an appropriate method of conversion depends on the situation. Suppose we have a built-in object of some kind but do not have an access to the source code of that class. If we want to provide *conversion from* a new class that we are coding, we have to write an *operator* in our class. On the other hand, if we want *conversion to* the new class, we have to write a *constructor.*

Table 6.1 Constructor vs operator functions

Criteria	Constructor	Operator
Place	Source class	Destination class
Convert from	Foreign to native	Native to foreign
Compulsory	Access methods	Constructor of foreign object
Preferred when	Source class code unavailable	Destination class code unavailable

Note Though both constructor and operator functions can convert one object into another, one must carefully decide the method to be used for a given case.

If both the classes are at our disposal, then we have to look at the order of definition of both the classes to find an answer. The conversion routine can only be written for the class defined later. If conversion is needed from the second to the first class, operators are to be used. If it is needed from the first to the second class, a constructor is required.

It should be remembered that access methods are needed to covert an object into another if we opt for a constructor function. However, using access methods only for this purpose is not a good practice as it may inadvertently expose the private variables. So, when both the classes are available, then the operator method is preferred, as it does not require us to add the access methods.

If the access methods are anyway available, we may go for constructors. Otherwise, there is almost no difference in using either of the methods. If both the conversion methods are defined, that is, constructor is defined in the destination object and the operator in the source object, then C++ takes the expression for conversion and examines it. If it is a constructor call, it calls the constructor, whereas if it is a casting, it calls the operator function; otherwise, if the expression is confusing, it flags an error.

■ RECAPITULATION ■

- Operator overloading is an important step to make user-defined object to behave in a similar manner to the built-in types.
- Operator overloading enables us to give an additional meaning to an existing operator for the objects of our own class.
- We can only overload a subset of existing operators. New operators can neither be devised nor be overloaded.
- We can overload operators in two different ways. The first method is to use the operator function as a member function and second one is to use it as a non-member friend function.
- Some of the operators can only be overloaded as a member.
- Operators are overloaded using the operator function.

- Friend functions, being non-member, do not have `this` pointer as the first argument as in member functions and are more flexible.
- Using operators judiciously improves the readability of the program and reduces the chances of spelling mistakes while coding.
- The operators can be categorized as unary and binary operators. The single ternary operator is not possible to be overloaded.
- For implementing the two different versions of operators ++ and −− (postfix and prefix), a special dummy argument is allowed to be specified for the prefix version of the operator function.
- It is wiser for a programmer to overload the shorthand operators such as += when overloading binary operators.

- Friends are useful for cases such as overloading insertion and extraction (>> and <<) operators and also when we want the first argument to the operators to be a built-in type.
- The case where we need dynamic memory allocation in constructor also needs assignment operator.
- The [] operator can be overloaded to provide array boundary checking and the () operator can be overloaded to make objects behave in the same way as functions.

- Function objects improve the readability of the code and make it possible to be inline.
- When we need to allocate and deallocate memory in a non-conventional way, we can overload new and delete.
- It is possible and sometimes useful to convert one type of object into another. It is also possible to convert a built-in type to object and vice versa. Constructors and operator functions help us in these conversions.

▪ KEYWORDS ▪

Built-in type to user-defined This refers to the conversion from built-in type to an object.

Extraction operator The >> operator, which is used to read from the keyboard, is known as the extraction operator. It is also known as the input operator.

Function objects Objects of the classes where the () operator is overloaded can be written with a () and can be treated similar to functions. Such objects that can be called like a function are known as function objects.

Insertion operator The << operator, which is used to write to the console, is known as the insertion operator. It is also known as the output operator.

Forward definition It is a prototype of the class that permits definition of the class name only at the beginning.

Object to built-in type conversion This refers to the conversion from an object to a built-in type.

Operator function Functions beginning with the keyword operator and having an operator specified as the next word in the function name are called operator functions. These functions replace the specified operator when the expression containing that operator is invoked.

Operator overloading This is the process of giving an existing operator an additional meaning.

User-defined conversion When we need to convert between different types, we can guide the compiler how to convert from one type to another by writing operator functions or constructors. These constructors and operator functions are known as user-defined conversions.

Wrapper class This is a class that makes a C-like structure or a built-in type data represented as a class. For example, an Integer wrapper class represents a data type int as a class.

▪ EXERCISES ▪

Multiple Choice Questions

1. When overloading unary operators _____.
   (a) no argument is passed explicitly
   (b) one argument is to be passed explicitly
   (c) no argument is passed implicitly
   (d) no argument is passed explicitly only if overloaded as member functions

2. The advantage of operator overloading is _____.
   (a) better readability
   (b) easy usage
   (c) easy coding
   (d) Both (a) and (b)

3. The operators created using friend function can also be created by member functions.
   (a) Always true

   (b) Always false
   (c) Partially true
   (d) Never true

4. What will the following statement do?
   ```
   Matrix operator *(int multiplier, Matrix tempMatrix);
   ```
   (a) Overload the * (multiplication) operator for Matrix class.
   (b) Compiler will generate an error.
   (c) Overload the * (pointer) operator for Matrix class.
   (d) Linker will generate an error .

5. All operators can be overloaded for _____.
   (a) predefined types
   (b) user-defined types

(c) extended types

(d) All of the above

6. Using operator overloading, one can _____.

   (a) design new operators

   (b) not design new operators

   (c) only overload available operators

   (d) give a meaning to all the available operators

7. If conversion is needed from second class to the first class, _____ is required.

   (a) operator

   (b) conversion function

   (c) constructor

   (d) Any of the above

8. Which of the following is the correct syntax of overloading the `new` operator for a class named `Test`?

   (a) `void Test operator new( int size );`

   (b) `void * Test operator new( int size );`

   (c) `void * Test operator new( size_t size );`

   (d) `Test * Test operator new( size_t size );`

9. When operators are overloaded _____.

   (a) there is a change in their precedence

   (b) there is no change in their precedence

   (c) they get an additional precedence

   (d) None of the above

10. C++ examines the expression for conversion and calls the operator if it is _____.

    (a) a constructor call

    (b) a operator function call

    (c) casting

    (d) All the above

Conceptual Exercises

1. What is the significance of operator overloading?

2. What are the restrictions on operator overloading?

3. List down the operators that cannot be overloaded.

4. List down the operators that cannot be overloaded as a friend.

5. List the differences between an operator overloaded as a member and that overloaded as a friend.

6. Differentiate between overloading of unary and binary operators.

7. Differentiate between overloading postfix and prefix operators.

8. Why are shorthand operators useful when basic operators are already overloaded?

9. Why do we need to pass and return a reference of the stream object when we overload << and >> operators?

10. What are function objects? Why are they useful?

11. Overloading `new` and `delete` may help us in managing memory ourselves. Explain.

12. What are the different types of conversion? Compare them.

Practical Exercises

1. Section 6.3 describes overloading + for a complex class. Overload − , ++, and −− for the same class.

2. For `CollectionEmp` class, add a member operator function −− to remove an employee object from a `CollectionEmp` object.

3. Overload −− for the `Time` class.

4. The * is overloaded for multiplying a scalar value to a matrix. Overload the same operator for multiplying two matrices.

5. Overload + and − for a stack class such that + provides push and − provides pop operations.

6. Overload −− and ++ for the `Integer` class defined in Program 6.13.

7. Overload ++ and −− in prefix and postfix version for the complex class. Prefix ++ adds to the real part and postfix adds to the imaginary part. Similarly, prefix −− subtracts from the real part and postfix subtracts from the imaginary part. For example, if the complex number `ComplexNo` has values $2 + 3i$, then `ComplexNo++` will make it $2 + 4i$, `++ComplexNo` makes it $3 + 3i$, `ComplexNo--` will produce $2 + 2i$ while `--ComplexNo` produces $1 + 3i$.

8. For Program 6.13, overload * and / such that division from and to normal integer work the same way. (Hint: use friend function to overload).

9. Overload << and >> for the `Time` class defined in this chapter. When user adds a statement `cout << Time` or `cin >> Time`, the overloaded functions should be able to write elements of `Time` and read from the screen, respectively. The display format for time is HH:MM:SS.

10. For a supermarket, define a `bill` class. All the `bill` objects will contain bill number, the name of the clerk preparing the bill, each item with quantity and price, and the total amount to be paid. Total items in the bill are varying. Define dynamic memory allocation constructor for `bill` class such that any number of items from 1 to 50 can be accommodated in a single bill. There is an array that describes each item with a price. The price is to be picked up from that array. Now overload

= operator and provide reasons for the need of such operator.

11. Design a safe array for complex numbers. The `complex` class that we have discussed in this chapter should be used as an array element. The program must flag an error when the user tries to refer to an array element outside the boundary.

12. Add two variables `UpperBound` and `LowerBound` to the `Integer` class defined in Program 6.13. Also, add a function `Validate()` to the same class such that when that function is called, it checks to see if the value is between the upper and lower bounds. Overload () operator for the `Integer` class such that the code

```
Integer Int1;

int int1;

Integer (int1).Validate()
```

works properly, that is, it casts `int` to `Integer` object.

13. Define a class `Real` such that the object of that class works as a float or double number and can be interchanged with the float or double. Can we use casting operator here? What is the problem?

14. There are two classes `Emp` and `Employee`. `Emp` is defined in the payroll department containing details of employee id and his/her payment. `Employee` is a Human resource department class containing only basic salary details and full personal details such as the name of the spouse, number of children, and the previous experience of the employee. Add code in the `Emp` class such that conversion from one type of employee object into another is possible. While converting, items that are not available in the source class (such as the number of children when the source class is `Employee`) should take a default value. What could be the problems with such conversions?

15. For Problem 14, modify `Employee` class for its conversion from and to `Emp` class. Again, non-applicable items should take default values.

16. Define a wrapper class `CString` for C-type strings and overload < and == operators such that if we define `CString MyName = "ABC"` and `CString YourName = "DEF"` then statements such as `if(MyName < YourName)`, `if(MyName == "ABC")`, and `if(MyName == YourName)` work properly.

17. In Program 6.11, we have seen a program where `new` is overloaded and memory is allocated in four-byte chunks. We did not have overloaded `delete` to deallocate chunkwise. Now, try to overload `new` and `delete` such that they work in tandem.

Templates

7.1 INTRODUCTION

Software reusability is one of the most-cited advantages of object program-ming. In most cases, it is associated with inheritance and object-oriented programming. However, software reusability can also be provided in other ways. One such method is *templates*. The model used by templates is known as the object-based model of reusability. In other words, it allows reusability without inheritance. Let us try to understand the concept of templates in this chapter.

Two Approaches to Reuse Code

The bubble sort algorithm is used to sort data of any given type. However, there may be a need to use it for multiple data types, say, for float as well as integer data in the same program. There are two very different approaches to solve this problem.

Typecasting approach   One solution is to write a single bubble sort function for float variables and use it for float as well as integer arguments. The integer arguments will be converted to float when the function is called and will then be compared as floats for all the passes.

Overloading approach   It is also possible that the bubble sort with integer values is called most of the times in the program. In such cases, it is better to overload the bubble sort function with integer as well as float arguments. Two different bubble sort functions can be written, one for integers and the other for float values (by overloading the integer bubble sort with float bubble sort). Now, whenever bubble sort is called with integer arguments, the function with integer arguments will be called, and only when the function with float arguments is called will the float bubble sort be called. Thus, it is possible to achieve both generality and high performance at the same time.

The second approach is definitely better than the first one, but it also has an overhead. Even though the sort process itself is independent of data type, the *same* bubble sort function needs to be written twice, with *identical body and different data types.* Thus, the overloading approach is more laborious and prone to errors when more data types are to be added. It is also problematic when the body itself requires some change later because the same change is to be provided at all the places in all the bubble sort functions.

Generic (Template) Functions

Can a single bubble sort function be written, which is independent of data type? Can the data type be specified while using the bubble sort function?

> Templates allow reusability without inheritance.

> Function templates in C++ provide generic functions independent of data type.

Or, even better, can the compiler understand from the call that the argument to bubble sort is an integer or a float, and accordingly call the function for that data type? In other words, can the data type be passed with other arguments when the function for bubble sort is called? The answer is *yes*. This is possible using *function templates*.

Generic (Template) Classes

Similar to functions templates, C++ also has generic classes, which are independent of the data type. Let us discuss how and where they can be utilized. When one thinks of some real-world entities one is interested in programming for, one may need to think of their varieties as well. Consider a queue of programs, a queue of user IDs, or a queue of passengers. All these queues are actually the same except for the data they are dealing with.

Suppose we have a class `Program` and another class called `Passenger`. We are interested in having a queue that can insert at one end and delete from the other end. It is obvious that the queue for the `Passenger` object and that for the `Program` object are the same, except for the type of content they hold. The routines for insertion and deletion work in the same way in both the cases. We can also have a new queue of user IDs, which again works the same way except that its data type is different. Here, what we are interested in is defining a queue class without specifying the type of the content. If it is possible to do that, the same queue will work for all the data types that we have defined earlier and can also be used for other additional data types. When we use that queue class for a specific object type (e.g., `Passenger`), we will have a specific queue class for `Passenger` automatically generated and overloaded. This is possible in C++ using *class templates*, which define such generic types of classes.

> **Note** A generic class is independent of data types. It can generate classes related to specific data types automatically without the programmer having to code them explicitly. In other words, it can provide a solution even without specifying the data type.

The advantage of a class template is that it is possible to define a generic class that works for any data type that is passed to it as a parameter. In this chapter, we will learn about function templates and class templates and see how they help us in generic programming.

7.2 FUNCTION TEMPLATES

Function templates are generic functions that work for any data type that is passed to them. The data type is not specified while writing the function. While using that function, the data type is passed and the required functionality is obtained. It is also possible that the user may not specify the data type at all and it is deduced by the compiler.

> When a function template is written, the argument types are either passed while calling the function or the compiler deduces it from the expression.

7.2.1 Drawbacks of using Macros

A C programmer's solution to this problem is to use macros. Macros are very useful for working on problems without having to depend on types. For instance, suppose it is required to calculate the maximum of two items irrespective of their type, the following can be safely written in a C program.

```
#define MAX(a, b) (a) > (b) ? (a) : (b)
```

If we define the following

```
int i, j;
float f1, f2;
```

it is possible to call MAX as MAX(i, j); and MAX(f1, f2);

A similar functionality can also be achieved in C++ by using macros instead of function templates. However, their use in such cases has the following drawbacks:

1. Macros are not visible to the compiler. A macro is substituted by its body by a *preprocessor* (which processes the program before the compilation starts). If there is some error in the body of the macro, the error is represented in a non-user friendly form. This is more annoying for a user who uses the macros from a library and is not aware of the variables used in the body.
2. The type-related information is lost in macros. Moreover, it is not possible to have any type-related validations in the macros.
3. Macros are evaluated twice, first when they are copied and the next time when they are executed. So, MAX(i++, j) is converted to

   (i++) > j ? (i++) : j

   Do you notice the problem here? Here, i++ is performed twice, incrementing i twice rather than once. Function templates provide a type-independent solution without these problems and are hence preferred.

7.2.2 Single-argument Function Templates

Function templates are very simple to implement. Only a few mechanical changes are needed to make a normal function a function template. To understand the process of writing function templates, we start by writing a bubble sort function for integer elements and also a function template with generic elements as shown in Program 7.1.

 **PROGRAM 7.1** Bubble sort using function templates

```cpp
//TemplateGenericro.cpp
#include <iostream>
#include <string>
using namespace std;

void BubbleSort(int TempIntArray[])
{
    for(int i = 0; i < 9; i++)
    {
        for(int j = i + 1;  j < 10; j++)
        {
            if(TempIntArray[i] < TempIntArray[j])
            {
                int TempInt = TempIntArray[i];
                TempIntArray[i] = TempIntArray[j];
                TempIntArray[j] = TempInt;
            }
        }
    }
}

template <typename Type>
```

```
void GenericBubbleSort(Type TempGenericArray[])
{
    for(int i = 0; i < 9; i++)
    {
        for(int j = i + 1;  j < 10; j++)
        {
            if(TempGenericArray[i] < TempGenericArray[j])
            {
                int TempGeneric = TempGenericArray[i];
                TempGenericArray[i] = TempGenericArray[j];
                TempGenericArray[j] = TempGeneric;
            }
        }
    }
}

void main()
{
    int Array[] = {3,2,6,1,8,9,5,4,12,11};
    int Array2[] = {11,45,23,8 9,65,34,12,44,65,22};
    char Array3[] = "irngiremxc";
    float Array4[] = {1.2,2.3,3.4,2.1,4.4,3.2,2.1};
    cout << "First integer array" << endl;

    /* Calling bubble sort for first array and the compiler deducing it */

    BubbleSort(Array);
    for(int i = 0; i < 10; i++)
    {
        cout << " " << Array[i] << ",";
    }
    cout << "\n";

    /* Calling bubble sort for second array */
    cout << "Second integer array" << endl;
    GenericBubbleSort <int> (Array2);
    for(int i = 0; i < 10; i++)
    {
        cout << "  " << Array2[i] << ",";
    }
    cout <<"\n";
    cout << "Character array" << endl;

    /* Another explicit specification */
    GenericBubbleSort <char> (Array3);
    for(int i = 0; i < 10; i++)
    {
        cout << " " << Array3[i] << ",";
    }
    cout << "\n";
    cout << "Double array" << endl;
    /* Another deduction by compiler */
    GenericBubbleSort(Array4);
    /* Here, the arguments are deduced by the compiler */
    for(int i = 0; i < 10; i++)
    {
        cout << " " << Array4[i] << ",";
    }
    cout <<"\n";
}
```

```
Output
First integer array
12, 11, 9, 8, 6, 5, 4, 3, 2, 1,

Second integer array
89, 65, 65, 45, 44, 34, 23, 22, 12, 11,

Character array
x, r, r, n, m, i, i, g, e, c,

Double array
4.4, 3.2, 3, 2.1, 2, 2, 1, 1.93171e-039, 1.4013e-044, 1.4013e-044,
```

How the Program Works

Let us dissect the program element by element.

Functions   This program contains two different functions. The first one is a simple bubble sort, which sorts the integer array of size 10. The second one is a function template or a generic function. The definitions of both the functions are identical, except the header and the data type.

Defining function template   In the following headers, we can see that the function template differs from the function definition only in terms of its header.

```
void BubbleSort(int TempIntArray[])
```

and

```
template <typename Type>
void GenericBubbleSort(Type TempIntArray[])
```

The definition of a function template always starts with the keyword `template`. It then contains the type declaration section, which defines the types used in the function. In the section that is enclosed within < and >, the generic type names are introduced. Although this program has only one type name, it can contain more definitions as well. The syntax for defining type names is as follows:

```
<typename GenericType1, typename GenericType2, ...>
```

Typename keyword   Here, `typename` is a keyword. It is also possible to use the keyword `class` to have the same effect but it is preferable to use `typename` because it is more readable and is not ambiguous. Most of the older C++ books use the keyword `class` here. These two keywords are interchangeable while defining types with the template.

> **Note**   The keyword `typename` may not work with some older compilers. In such cases, `typename` is changed to `class` and the program is recompiled.

Template vs normal function   Naming a generic function is similar to any other function in C++. However, there is an important difference in the function argument list. It now contains the generic type name that we have introduced with the `template` keyword.

Thus, in Program 7.1, `GenericBubbleSort()` is a function template, with one generic type `Type`, and it takes a pointer to that generic type as a single parameter.

We can use `Type` throughout the function similar to any other data type. For example,

```
Type TempIntArray
```

A template function is a generic function that contains at least one parameter, which is replaced by the actual type when the function is called.

Type replacement   The variable Type is replaced by some valid type when the function call is compiled. If the compiler finds a statement GenericBubbleSort <int> (Array2), it generates a function by converting Type to int in the definition of GenericBubbleSort. It is also possible that GenericBubbleSort(Array2) is called directly without specifying <int>. In this case, the compiler tries to deduce the data type of Array2. If it can deduce it unambiguously, it invokes that function with the deduced type.

> **Note**   typename defines the dummy placeholder for an unspecified type at the time of template specification. Older versions used the keyword class for the same effect.

Type is only a dummy type name. It is a placeholder, a template, and hence the name. The function is also a dummy one. The actual function, as said earlier, is created by the compiler at the time of definition. This is why the definition is known as a *function template*. Template names can be used in the definition as well as declarations. The following three declarations are of the *same* template:

```
template <typename Ty>
void GenericBubbleSort(Ty TempIntArray[]);

template <typename T>
void GenericBubbleSort(T TempIntArray[]);

template <typename TT>
void GenericBubbleSort(TT TempIntArray[]);
```

The definition for these functions may be as follows:

```
template <typename Type>
void GenericBubbleSort(Type TempIntArray[])
{
   Body of the function
}
```

The body of the function GenericBubbleSort() is the same as the BubbleSort() function, except that the temporary variable is also of the generic type. Now, let us look at the function call.

Calling the generated function   The function call for a generic function again has one more section between the function name and the argument list. It is enclosed between < and > and contains all the types that are needed to be passed to a generic function. We may pass the actual data type that is going to call the overloaded function with the specified Type when the function is called.

We have two different calls to GenericBubbleSort(). The first one is with GenericBubbleSort <int> and the second one is with GenericBubbleSort <char>. The first call makes the call to GenericBubbleSort() overloaded with int as an argument.

> **Note**   GenericBubbleSort() is a template, while GenericBubbleSort <int> is an overloaded and actually created function with Type replaced by int. Therefore, in this case, two functions are created from the template GenericBubbleSort(), namely, GenericBubbleSort <int> and GenericBubbleSort <char>.

Deducing arguments   It is also important to note that the middle section enclosed in < > can be omitted if the compiler can deduce the argument by itself. For example, the program contains a statement

```
GenericBubbleSort(Array4);

/* Here, the arguments are deduced by the compiler */
```

When a compiler can unambiguously deduce the argument, a user may leave the < > section while calling a template function.

In this statement, the middle section is missing. Here, the compiler can unambiguously deduce the arguments to be float and can generate and call a float version of the function.

Thus, although the program has only a single `GenericBubbleSort()` function, yet three calls have been made with different types. This is the advantage of using function templates.

7.2.3 Instantiation

When a real function for a specific type is generated from the generic function definition, it is called instantiation of that generic function.

Let us now discuss how `GenericBubbleSort()` works with all the three data types. The template that is defined is not actually a function. The definition of the `GenericBubbleSort()` given earlier does not define any function in the true sense.

The function definition is generated when statements such as the following are encountered.

```
// Create char instance
GenericBubbleSort <char> (Array3);

// Create int instance
GenericBubbleSort <int> (Array2);

// Deduce float and generate float instance
GenericBubbleSort(Array4);
```

This is different from a normal function such as the `BubbleSort()`. When a normal function definition is encountered in the program, the function is generated even if it is not called in the program. However, the template functions are not defined when the template is defined. When a template function such as `GenericBubbleSort <int>` is called for the *first* time, the following happens:

1. The function is generated, that is, *instantiated* from the template definition for the respective type, that is, `int`.
2. The call statement is compiled.

What happens when the following statements are encountered in a program?

```
GenericBubbleSort <char> (Array3);

GenericBubbleSort <char> (Array5);
```

The first call (`Array3`) compilation process generates the function from the template. Then, it compiles the call statement. The second call does not require the generation of function as it is already instantiated. It would only compile the call statement.

> **Note** The difference between a normal function and an instantiated function is that the normal function is generated when the class *definition* is compiled, whereas the instantiated function comes into existence when the first function *call* is compiled.

It is also possible that multiple copies of the same function are instantiated if they are called in different files. We will look at this issue when we discuss compilation models in Section 7.4.

7.2.4 Generic Sorting and Need for Operator Overloading

For any class to work with our generic search, object assignment (=) and less than (<) operators must be overloaded.

Can the generic bubble sort be used for sorting any other data types? Suppose the user wishes to sort an array of strings. If the elements of the array are used as a string object, as we have used so far in this book, the program will be executed as it is. However, if we use *C-type character arrays* to represent strings, the program will not work for the simple reason that the operation `TempGenericArray[i] < TempGenericArray[j]` is undefined for such a data type (`strcmp()` needs to be used here). Even the expressions such as `TempIntArray[i] = TempIntArray[j]` are not defined (this requires `strcpy()`).

The built-in string type has both the < and = operators overloaded. It is possible to compare two string objects using < or >, and also assign one string object to another using =. Hence, the generic sort is able to sort the data of type string. This is the advantage of the string being a class. Moreover, the << operator also needs to be overloaded for using it with `cout`. This, again, is available with the built-in string object. String objects are described in detail in Chapter 15.

Therefore, if we need bubble sort to work with other data types, operations such as =, <, and > must be implemented in the class. Thus, operator overloading allows general algorithms to work without really needing the type of data. The only constraint is that the operations required by the algorithms should be implemented in the class itself. This concept is also fundamental to Standard Template Library (STL), which is discussed in Chapter 16.

> **Note** For generic algorithms (function templates) to work with any class, the class must have some operators (e.g., =, <, >, etc.) overloaded, which is expected by that generic algorithm. It is important to learn about such relations before designing a generic algorithm and classes. A designer must have previously worked with such important relations and built those into the design.

7.2.5 Sorting Employee Objects using Generic Bubble Sort

If the employee objects need to be sorted by employee numbers, it is important to overload < and << operators. There is no problem with the = operator as the assignment is available by default.

Let us write a program for sorting the employee array. The expression `EmpObject1< EmpObject2` requires some form of comparison to be made between two employee objects. In Program 7.2, it is assumed to be based on the employee number. It can be the employee name as well; in that case, only the operator < () function needs to be changed.

PROGRAM 7.2   Generic bubble sort

```
//GenericSortEmployee.cpp
#include <iostream>
#include <string>
using namespace std;

class employee
{
    int EmpNo;
    string Name;
```

```
    string DeptName;
    string Designation;
public:
    employee(int TempNo = 0, string TempName = 0, string TempDept = 0, string TempDesi = 0)
    {
        EmpNo = TempNo;
        Name = TempName;
        DeptName = TempDept;
        Designation = TempDesi;
    }
    bool operator <(employee & OtherEmployee)
    {
        if(EmpNo > OtherEmployee.EmpNo)
            return false;
        else
            return true;
    }
    friend ostream & operator <<(ostream & TempOut, employee & TempEmployee);
};

ostream & operator <<(ostream & TempOut, employee & TempEmployee)
{
    TempOut << "Details of employee number" << TempEmployee.EmpNo <<  "\n";
    TempOut << "Name is" << TempEmployee.Name << "\n";
    TempOut << "Department is" << TempEmployee.DeptName << "\n";
    TempOut << "Designation is" << TempEmployee.Designation << "\n";
    return TempOut;
}

template <typename Type>
void GenericBubbleSort(Type TempGenericArray[])
{
    for(int i = 0; i < 9; i++)
    {
        for(int j = i + 1; j < 10; j++)
        {
            if(TempGenericArray[i] < TempGenericArray[j])
            {
                Type TempGeneric = TempGenericArray[i];
                TempGenericArray[i] = TempGenericArray[j];
                TempGenericArray[j] = TempGeneric;
            }
        }
    }
}

void main()
{
    employee UniEmployee[10] =
    {
        employee(1, "Lara", "Exam", "Professor"),
        employee(2, "Ponting", "Marksheet", "Clerk"),
        employee(3, "Laxman", "Accounts", "Head Clerk"),
        employee(4, "Flintoff", "Exam", "Clerk"),
        employee(5, "Murlidharan", "Accounts", "CAO"),
        employee(6, "Sarfaraz", "Exam", "Informer"),
        employee(7, "Dean Jones", "Exam", "Invigilator"),
        employee(8, "Madugalle", "Exam", "Examiner"),
        employee(9, "Ganguly", "Marksheet", "Repeater"),
```

```
        employee(10, "Nafees", "Accounts", "Clerk")
    };

    GenericBubbleSort <employee> (UniEmployee);
    for(int i = 0; i < 10; i++)
    {
        cout << " " << UniEmployee[i] <<   ",";
    }
}
```

How the Program Works

We will explore only one important point in this section. The `GenericBubbleSort()` does not change at all. Why? Let us see.

The advantage of the generic sort is that it does not depend on the type of data sent to it. If proper operator overloading is provided, `GenericBubbleSort()` can work for any data type, even for user-defined objects. Such algorithms can prove to be very useful when one needs to work with multiple data types. STL contains many such algorithms.

It is important to note that the meaning of < for the `BubbleSort` must be preserved. Semantics (i.e., the meaning) of < here is that the left-hand side (LHS) of the '<' operator must be logically less than the right-hand side (RHS). This is done by defining the employee with the smaller ID value to be logically less than one with the greater ID value. This may be acceptable in some cases, but does not always hold good.

Dealing with built-in types   Sometimes, operator overloading is not possible. For example, when dealing with a built-in data type where overloading an operator is out of question or with a class designed by others where one may not have an access to that class. Program 7.3 is an example that illustrates the problem with built-in C-type string.

In this program, a `Max` function has been defined to find the maximum of the two values passed to it. Three different instantiations are generated from the template. Observe what happens when the `Max` function is called.

 **PROGRAM 7.3**   Finding the maximum of two generic arguments

```
//SemanticInOO.cpp
#include <iostream>
#include <string>
using namespace  std;

template <typename T>
bool Max(T First, T Second)
{
    return(First > Second);
}

int main()
{
    string sAddress = "West Indies";
    string sName = "Brian Charles Lara";

    int i1 = 5;
    int i2 = 7;

    char cAddress[] = "West Indies";
```

```
char cName[] = "Brian Charles Lara";

// Instance 1
if(Max(i1, i2))
    cout << "i1 is bigger\n";
else
    cout << "i2 is bigger\n";

// Instance 2
if(Max(sName, sAddress))
    cout << "sName is bigger\n";
else
    cout << "sAddress is bigger\n";

// Instance 3
if(Max(cName, cAddress))
    cout << "cName is bigger\n";
else
    cout << "cAddress is bigger\n";
}

Output
i2 is bigger
sAddress is bigger
cName is bigger
```

Note Strings are compared in a lexicographical manner. Thus, West Indies is bigger than Brian Charles Lara, as 'B' appears before 'W' in the dictionary. This holds true even when the number of characters in the second string is more than that of the first one.

How the Program Works

The output is *surprising*. The comparison of the two strings yields the correct output but the comparison of two character arrays does not. Why? `cName` and `cAddress` are the names of the character arrays and are pointers to the first elements of the respective array. When they both are compared, the pointer value, that is, the address is compared; so, the item defined next becomes larger. Hence, `cName`, which is defined after `cAddress`, gets a larger address value. On the contrary, the < operator is overloaded in string class, and hence the behaviour there is more meaningful. The < operator yields true if the string on the LHS is lexically smaller than that on the RHS; otherwise, it returns false.

How can this problem be solved? If there is a class, it can be solved by providing an appropriate operator overloading to eliminate this. Unfortunately, that is not possible if the type is built-in (such as C-type arrays) or if the class is defined by others (where the source code is not available to modify the class). The answer to this problem is to overload the template itself for that particular type. We will see an improved version of this program using this solution in Program 7.8.

7.2.6 Function Templates with Multiple Arguments

It is possible to have templates with more than one argument. Other arguments can be generic or normal. Program 7.4 is a simple search program for searching an element in the array. Here, we need to pass two arguments, the array and the element to be searched, both of which are bound to be of generic type.

PROGRAM 7.4   Generic search with two generic arguments

```cpp
//GenericSearch.cpp
#include <iostream>
#include <string>
using namespace std;

class employee
{
    int EmpNo;
    string Name;
    string DeptName;
    string Designation;
public:
    employee(int TempNo = 0, string TempName = 0, string TempDept = 0, string TempDesi = 0)
    {
        EmpNo = TempNo;
        Name = TempName;
        DeptName = TempDept;
        Designation = TempDesi;
    }

    bool operator ==(employee TempEmp)
    {
        return(EmpNo == TempEmp.EmpNo);
    }

    friend ostream & operator <<(ostream & TempOut, employee & TempEmployee);
};

ostream & operator <<(ostream & TempOut, employee & TempEmployee)
{
    TempOut <<   "Details of employee number" << TempEmployee.EmpNo << "\n";
    TempOut <<   "Name is" << TempEmployee.Name << "\n";
    TempOut <<   "Department is" << TempEmployee.DeptName << "\n";
    TempOut << "Designation is" << TempEmployee.Designation << "\n";
    return TempOut;
}

template <typename Type>
int GenericSearch(Type TempGenericArray[], Type EleToBeSearched)
{
    for(int i = 0; i < 10; i++)
    {
        if(EleToBeSearched == TempGenericArray[i])
        return i;
    }
    return −1;
}

void main()
{
    int Array1[] = {11,45,23,8 9,65,34,12,44,65,22};
    char Array2[] = "irngiremxc";
    employee UniEmployee[] =
    {
        employee(1, "Lara", "Exam", "Professor"),
        employee(2, "Ponting", "Marksheet", "Clerk"),
        employee(3, "Laxman", "Accounts", "Head Clerk"),
        employee(4, "Flintoff", "Exam", "Clerk"),
```

```
            employee(5, "Murlidharan" "Accounts", "CAO"),
            employee(6, "Sarfaraz", "Exam", "Informer"),
            employee(7, "Dean Jones", "Exam", "Invigilator"),
            employee(8, "Madugalle", "Exam", "Examiner"),
            employee(9, "Ganguly", "Marksheet", "Repeater"),
            employee(10, "Nafees", "Accounts", "Clerk")
    };

    cout << "\n The integer element 12 is at position" << GenericSearch(Array1,12);
    cout << "\n The char element is at position" << GenericSearch(Array2, 'a');
    cout << "\n";
    int SearchIndex = GenericSearch(UniEmployee, employee (3, " ", " ", " "));
    cout << UniEmployee[SearchIndex];
}

Output
The integer element is at position 6
The char element is at position -1
Details of employee number 3
Name is Laxman
Department is Accounts
Designation is Head Clerk
```

How the Program Works

Note how the two arguments are passed to the function `GenericSearch()`. It looks at the elements to be searched one by one and checks whether it matches with the required element in the `TempGenericArray`. In both the cases, the compiler deduces the right set of arguments. Thus, any number of arguments can be passed to a function template.

7.2.7 Function Templates with Two Generic Arguments

The following example shows how two generic arguments can be passed to a function template. The function `BiggerSize()` determines the size of both the items passed to it and then displays which one of them is bigger.

```cpp
//TwoGenericArguments.cpp
#include <iostream>
#include <string>
using namespace std;

template <typename Type1, typename Type2>
void BiggerSize(Type1 FirstVal, Type2 SecondVal)
{
    if(sizeof(FirstVal) > sizeof(SecondVal))
    {
        cout << "First item's type is bigger\n";
    }
    else
    {
        cout << "Second item's type is bigger\n";
    }
}
```

```
void main()
{
    int i = 10;
    char c = 'A';
    BiggerSize <int, char> (i, c);
    string Name = "Robin Singh";
    char STRING[] = "Robin Singh";
    BiggerSize <string, char *> (Name, STRING);
}
```
Output
```
First item's type is bigger
First item's type is bigger
```

It also reveals an interesting fact that for the same data "Robin Singh" stored in a C-type string and a string object of C++, ANSI C++ string declaration takes more memory space (five bytes more in this case).

7.2.8 Non-generic Parameters in Template Functions

Non-generic arguments can also be passed to a template function. The earlier examples of array definition (Programs 7.2 and 7.4) have the array size fixed to 10. However, it is possible to pass the array size as well to the generic function as shown in Program 7.5. Non-generic type is also known as non-type arguments in short.

 PROGRAM 7.5 Passing non-generic argument to a function template

```
//GenericNonGenericArgs.cpp
#include <iostream>
#include <string>
using namespace std;

template <typename Type>
void GenericBubbleSort(Type TempGenericArray[], int Size)
// Passing a non-generic parameter
{
    for(int i = 0; i < Size - 1; i++)
    {
        for(int j = i + 1;  j < Size; j++)
        {
            if(TempGenericArray[i] < TempGenericArray[j])
            {
                Type TempGeneric = TempGenericArray[i];
                TempGenericArray[i] = TempGenericArray[j];
                TempGenericArray[j] = TempGeneric;
            }
        }
    }
}

void main()
{
    int Array2[] = {1,8,9,5,4,12,11,45,23,89,65,34,12,44,65,22};
    char Array3[] = "irngiremxc";

    GenericBubbleSort(Array2, 16);
```

```
    for(int i = 0; i < 16; i++)
    {
        cout << " " << Array2[i] << ",";
    }
    cout <<"\n";

    GenericBubbleSort(Array3, 10);
    for(int i = 0; i < 10; i++)
    {
        cout << " " << Array3[i] << ",";
    }
}
```

```
Output
89, 65, 65, 45, 44, 34, 23, 22, 12, 12, 11, 9, 8, 5, 4, 1,
x, r, r, n, m, i, i, g, e, c,
```

How the Program Works

Generic arguments are not the only option possible to be provided to templates. One can pass non-generic type arguments as well.

This program is similar to Programs 7.2 and 7.4 except for the size parameter. Those programs assumed that the size of the array is always 10. However, Program 7.5 is better as it can have any number of elements in the array and will still be able to generate a BubbleSort function that sorts the elements. The call to GenericBubbleSort() now requires us to pass the size as the second argument to the function. It is also possible to pass two different data types and use them as two arguments of the function. As mentioned earlier, there is no restriction on the number of arguments as well as the number of types passed to the template function.

Alternative Solution to Avoid Passing 'Size'

Program 7.6 demonstrates how passing the size can also be avoided.

PROGRAM 7.6   A compulsory non-type argument

```
//NonTypeArgument.cpp
#include <iostream>
#include <string>
using namespace std;

template <typename Type, int Size>
void GenericBubbleSort(Type(&TempGenericArray)[Size])
{
    for(int i = 0; i < Size - 1; i++)
    {
        for(int j = i + 1; j < Size; j++)
        {
            if(TempGenericArray[i] < TempGenericArray[j])
            {
                Type TempGeneric = TempGenericArray[i];
                TempGenericArray[i] = TempGenericArray[j];
                TempGenericArray[j] = TempGeneric;
            }
        }
    }
}

void main()
{
```

```
    int Array2[] = {1,8,9,5,4,12,11,45,23,89,65,34,12,44,65,22};
    char Array3[] = "irngiremxc";

    GenericBubbleSort(Array2);
    for(int i = 0; i < 16; i++)
    {
        cout << " " << Array2[i] << ",";
    }
    cout <<"\n";

    GenericBubbleSort(Array3);
    for (int i = 0; i < 10; i++)
    {
        cout << "   " << Array3[i] << ",";
    }
}
```

How the Program Works

Instead of receiving the array as a pointer, the array is now received as a reference with the specification of size. Observe the function header

```
template <typename Type, int Size>
void GenericBubbleSort(Type(&TempGenericArray)[Size])
```

The type of argument now is a reference to an array of size `Size` with elements of type `Type`. The braces surrounding `&TempGenericArray` are important as the precedence of [] is higher than &.

Exhibit 7.1 shows the difference between non-type arguments in the template and in the argument list.

Exhibit 7.1   Non-type argument as function argument and template argument

The first version has the following construct:

```
template <typename Type>
void GenericBubbleSort(Type TempGenericArray[], int Size)
```

   The second version has the following construct:

```
template <typename Type, int Size>
void GenericBubbleSort(Type(&TempGenericArray)[Size])
```

   The first version does not have a non-type argument in the template <> section, while the second one needs it. The `GenericBubbleSort()` function has a non-type argument in the argument list in the first version, while the second one does not have it. Thus, it is imperative that we define it in the template<> section.

7.2.9 Types of Non-generic Arguments

In Program 7.6, we have defined the size as `int`.

```
template <typename Type, int Size>
```

It is not a variable of type `int` because at the time of compilation the value of `Size` is passed to generate the following function:

```
GenericBubbleSort(Array2);
```

The generated function, GenericBubbleSort(), does not contain the size variable but a value 16 (deduced by the compiler) as the size parameter, which is the size of the array passed to the function.

Thus, we can generalize that a value known at the time of compilation is allowed as a non-type argument.

> **Note** In C++, three data types, that is, int constant such as given in the example, pointer or reference to a global function, and pointer or reference to a non-local (i.e., either static or global) object, are allowed as non-type arguments. This is because the address of the global functions and global objects is known at the time of compilation, and hence, pointers to them are allowed. On the contrary, local objects get their addresses when loaded onto a stack at run-time, and so, pointers to them are not allowed.

7.2.10 Template Argument Deduction

It has already been mentioned that the compiler can deduce the type of arguments when they are not specified. Template argument deduction has the following advantages:

1. The user can use the template function as a normal function. In the example, the call to GenericBubbleSort(Array4) function is similar to a normal function call. Thus, if such functions are provided in the library, the user can use them without really knowing that the function is not a normal function but a function template.
2. The data type deduction is done automatically every time the program is executed. If ever the program is modified to accept and process other data types than those provided earlier, for example, if Array4 changes to operate on type double now, the function call need not be changed. Whenever the program runs next time, the compiler deduces the data type to be double and accordingly instantiates the right version of the function.

> **Note** It is always better to leave it to the compiler to deduce the types of arguments, if possible. Only in case of ambiguity should the user supply explicit arguments.

Process of Deduction

The compiler deduces the type of generic parameter from the type and the values of the arguments passed to the function in the function call. The argument deduction process is much more stringent than the normal function call. If the types are not matching, the arguments are not promoted as in normal functions. Thus, the call SumIt(12, 12U) will not work if SumIt() has been defined as follows:

```
template <typename Type>
SumIt(Type, Type);
```

This is because both the arguments passed to SumIt() are not of the same type; one is int and the other is unsigned. However, the definition of template says that SumIt() has to have two exactly same types of arguments, since the Type placeholder cannot have two values at the same point of time. The compiler cannot instantiate a function with a unique Type value in this case.

> When the generic type is to be matched, the compiler does not opt for promotions or standard conversions.

Interestingly, if we define SumIt(unsigned, unsigned) (without using templates), then SumIt(12, 12U) would work, because the integer (12) is promoted to unsigned by the compiler and then the unsigned version of it is called, which is not an error.

There are some cases where deduction is not possible at compile time. In those cases, it is better to use explicit specification of arguments.

1. One such example is the `SumIt()` function given earlier. As already seen, `SumIt(12, 12U)` will not work; instead, one can specify `SumIt <unsigned int> (12, 12U)`. Here, the `Type` is assumed to be `unsigned int` and the value 12 would be converted to unsigned `int` and the process is carried out further.

2. Extending the same function to return `long`, if we write `SumIt <unsigned int>`, it will assume the type of the arguments to be unsigned `int` but not the return type as `long` type. We, therefore, need to specify the return type as `SumIt <long, unsigned int> (12, 12U)`. In such a case, the definition of `SumIt()` would change to

```
template <typename ReturnType, typename Type>

ReturnType SumIt(Type, Type)
```

7.2.11 Template Function and Specialization

It is possible to define a single template function and use it for generating multiple functions with different data types. For example, we have defined `GenericBubbleSort()` with generic type `Type` and used the same function with `int`, `char`, and `employee` types of data. In this section, we will learn how C++ achieves this functionality.

When a template function is defined (e.g., the `GenericBubbleSort()` function in the given example), the compiler automatically generates the correct code for the function actually used. Here, the compiler creates three different versions of `GenericBubbleSort()`, one each for `int`, `char`, and `employee` types. In a way, the compiler automatically overloads `GenericBubbleSort()`. An important fact here is that the *compiler overloads a function only for those types that are used in the program* from potentially a large number of possible functions.

> **Note** A generic function starting with the keyword `template` is known as a template function. The automatically overloaded functions are known as *specializations* or instantiations of the template function. The process of generating specializations is known as *instantiation*.

The compiler generates specializations automatically. Section 7.2.12 explains what happens if we want the compiler to generate specializations for all cases but one.

7.2.12 Overloading a Template

The compiler overloads a function only for those types that are used in the program from potentially a large number of possible functions.

As seen in Section 7.2.11, the template function is automatically overloaded by the compiler itself when needed. It is also possible to provide specific overloading to a template function. Consider the case of employees. We are now interested in sorting them on the basis of department numbers and then on their employee numbers. Obviously, the same algorithm will not work. We need a special algorithm for our employee class. This is shown in Program 7.7.

 **PROGRAM 7.7** Overloading a template

```
//OverloadingTemplates.cpp
#include <iostream>
#include <string>
using namespace  std;

template <typename Type>
void GenericBubbleSort(Type TempGenericArray[], int Size);
```

```cpp
class employee
{
    int EmpNo;
    string Name;
    string DeptName;
    string Designation;
public:
    employee(int TempNo = 0, string TempName = 0, string TempDept = 0, string TempDesi = 0)
    {
        EmpNo = TempNo;
        Name = TempName;
        DeptName = TempDept;
        Designation = TempDesi;
    }

    bool operator <(employee & OtherEmployee)
    {
        if(EmpNo > OtherEmployee.EmpNo)
            return false;
        else
            return true;
    }

    friend ostream & operator <<(ostream & TempOut, employee & TempEmployee);
    template <>
    friend void GenericBubbleSort(employee TempEmployee[], int Size);
};

ostream & operator <<(ostream & TempOut, employee & TempEmployee)
{
    TempOut << "Details of employee number" << TempEmployee.EmpNo << "\n";
    TempOut << "Name is" << TempEmployee.Name << "\n";
    TempOut << "Department is" << TempEmployee.DeptName << "\n";
    TempOut << "Designation is" << TempEmployee.Designation << "\n";
    return TempOut;
}

template <typename Type>
void GenericBubbleSort(Type TempGenericArray[], int Size)
{
    for(int i = 0; i < Size - 1; i++)
    {
        for(int j = i + 1;  j < Size; j++)
        {
            if(TempGenericArray[i]  < TempGenericArray[j])
            {
                Type TempGeneric = TempGenericArray[i];
                TempGenericArray[i] = TempGenericArray[j];
                TempGenericArray[j] = TempGeneric;
            }
        }
    }
}

template<>
void GenericBubbleSort(employee TempEmployee[], int Size)
{
    for(int i = 0; i < Size - 1; i++)
    {
        for(int j = i + 1; j < Size; j++)
```

```
        {
            if(TempEmployee[i].DeptName < TempEmployee[j].DeptName)
            {
                employee TempEmp = TempEmployee[i];
                TempEmployee[i] = TempEmployee[j];
                TempEmployee[j] = TempEmp;
            }
            else
            if(TempEmployee[i].DeptName == TempEmployee[j].DeptName)
            {
                if(TempEmployee[i].EmpNo < TempEmployee[j].EmpNo)
                {
                    employee TempEmp = TempEmployee[i];
                    TempEmployee[i] = TempEmployee[j];
                    TempEmployee[j] = TempEmp;
                }
            }
        }
    }
}

int main()
{
    employee UniEmployee[10] =
    {
        employee(1, "Lara", "Exam", "Professor"),
        employee(2, "Ponting", "Marksheet", "Clerk"),
        employee(3, "Laxman", "Accounts", "Head Clerk"),
        employee(4, "Flintoff", "Exam", "Clerk"),
        employee(5, "Murlidharan", "Accounts", "CAO"),
        employee(6, "Sarfaraz", "Exam", "Informer"),
        employee(7, "Dean Jones", "Exam", "Invigilator"),
        employee(8, "Madugalle", "Exam", "Examiner"),
        employee(9, "Ganguly", "Marksheet", "Repeater"),
        employee(10, "Nafees", "Accounts", "Clerk")
    };

    int Array2[] = {1,8,9,5,4,12,11,45,23,89,65,34,12,44,65,22};
    char Array3[] = "irngiremxc";

    GenericBubbleSort(Array2,16);
    for(int i = 0; i < 16; i++)
    {
        cout << "  " << Array2[i] << ",";
    }
    cout <<"\n";

    GenericBubbleSort (Array3,10);
    for(int i = 0; i < 10; i++)
    {
        cout << " " << Array3[i] << ",";
    }

    GenericBubbleSort(UniEmployee, 10);
    for(int i = 0; i < 10; i++)
    {
        cout <<  "  " << UniEmployee[i]   << ",";
    }
```

```
     return 0;
}
```

Output (*Condensed*)
89, 65, 65, 45, 44, 34, 23, 22, 12, 12, 11, 9, 8, 5, 4, 1,
x, r, r, n, m, i, i, g, e, c,

Details of employee number 9
Name is Ganguly
Department is Marksheet
Designation is Repeater

Details of employee number 3
Name is Laxman
Department is Accounts
Designation is Head Clerk

How the Program Works

The GenericBubbleSort() is now written in two forms, that is, the generic form, which we have seen earlier, and a special form that we have added for the employee class. Examine the declaration of GenericBubbleSort() for the employee objects.

```
template <>
friend void GenericBubbleSort(employee TempEmployee[], int Size);
```

Moreover, note the forward declaration of the template GenericBubbleSort() before the definition of the class Employee.

```
template <typename Type>
void GenericBubbleSort(Type TempGenericArray[], int Size);
```

It is important to have the forward declaration in such a case. The explicit template definition cannot come before the original template definition. The class employee contains the declaration for the explicit template as a friend. If the forward declaration does not precede the *explicit specialization*, the program will not be compiled. Moreover, look at the call

```
GenericBubbleSort(UniEmployee, 10);
```

There is no difference in the function call. Note the following function definition:

```
template<>
void GenericBubbleSort(employee TempEmployee[], int Size)
{
    Body of the function
}
```

Need for Overloading Templates

If an explicit overloaded function (or explicit specialization) is provided, it will override the compiler's version.

The function definition given is actually an overloaded function, which has been written explicitly. It has already been mentioned that the compiler automatically generates a required function if needed. An explicit overloaded function (or *explicit specialization*), if provided, will override the compiler's version. Thus, when the function call is compiled, the compiler does not generate an automatic overloaded version of GenericBubbleSort(); it picks the one that is explicitly defined.

However, why do we need to overload a template in this case? We need to sort the employees first by department and then by employee number. The output shows the required effect. The same effect can also be achieved by modifying the overloaded < for the employee class. It can be done if the employee class source code is accessible. However, sometimes the programmer will not have the source code of that class or the authority to modify a class that is a part of a live application. In such cases, the class designer can be asked to make the required function a friend.

Another example can be the Max function that was discussed in Program 7.3. It was seen that the function does not work properly for C-type strings. Overloading the Max function for handling C strings solves the purpose. Program 7.8 shows how this is done using an explicitly specialized Max function.

 **PROGRAM 7.8** Solving incorrect execution by overloading the template

```cpp
//OverloadingMax.cpp
#include <iostream>
#include <string>
using namespace std;

template <typename T>

bool Max(T First, T Second)
{
    return(First > Second);
}

template <>
bool Max(char *First,  char *Second)
{
    return(strcmp(First, Second) > 0);
}

int main()
{
    string sAddress = "West Indies";
    string sName = "Brian Charles Lara";

    int i1 = 5;
    int i2 = 7;

    char cAddress[] = "West Indies";
    char cName[] = "Brian Charles Lara";
    if(Max(i1, i2))
        cout << "i1 is bigger\n";
    else
        cout << "i2 is bigger\n";

    if(Max(sName, sAddress))
        cout << "sName is bigger\n";
    else
        cout << "sAddress is bigger\n";

    if(Max(cName, cAddress))
        cout << "cName is bigger\n";
    else
        cout << "cAddress is bigger\n";
}
```

How the Program Works

It can be seen that the output is correct now. It should be noted that the definition of the original template is similar to the earlier definition.

```
template <typename T>
bool Max(T First, T Second)
{
    return(First > Second);
}
```

Now, look at the *specialization*.

```
template <>
bool Max(char *First, char *Second)
{
    return(strcmp(First, Second) > 0);
}
```

This is a special version for C-type strings as the arguments to the functions are char * rather than Type. The body now contains the strcmp() function, which can handle C-type strings. The template <> preceding the function header signifies that the definition following it is not a normal function but a specialization.

Template Specialization vs Non-Generic Function

It is also possible to overload template definition with normal non-generic functions. The functions with headers can also be written as

```
void GenericBubbleSort(employee TempEmployee[], int Size)
```

or

```
bool Max(char *First, char *Second)
```

that is, by removing template <> from the definition of template specialization. Here, the original template is being overloaded with a non-generic function. Then, what is the difference between a template specialization and a non-generic (normal) function? The difference is that a generic function argument (the one that is overloaded) matching would be much more stringent than the normal function version.

Assume the SumIt() function is overloaded using a non-generic function for Employee objects. If the program has one more class Person, it is possible to write a conversion operator that converts a Person object to an Employee object in the Person class. We can, therefore, call now GenericBubbleSort() with Person array.

The templatized function would not work as it expects only an Employee object. The templatized version will not be called, as it requires converting the Person object to the Employee object. This, in turn, requires standard conversion, which is not possible with either automatically generated template functions or explicitly specified template functions.

An important step in program design is deciding which version (explicitly specified template instantiation or a non-generic normal function) is to be used when. In the given example, converting a `Person` object to an `Employee` object may be disastrous as the `Person` object may not have `EmpNo` or `Dept`. Thus, a non-generic function should not be used in this case. However, if we expect the Person object to work in the same way with `GenericBubbleSort()` function, we may have a non-generic function instead. Note that in either of the cases, the user may call the function in the same way without really knowing if the overloaded function is a template specification or a non-generic function. Exhibit 7.2 explains the difference between overloading a template with a template specialization and a non-generic function.

Exhibit 7.2   Overloading a template with a template specialization or a non-generic function

When a template is overloaded by a generic function, the argument match is stringent and no conversions or promotions are applied to the arguments. In contrast, when it is overloaded by a non-generic function, such promotions and conversions for arguments are allowed. Look at following definition of an array and the templatized function call.

```
Person Indians[100];
GenericBubbleSort(Indians);
// This is not acceptable for
// template<> GenericBubbleSort(employee *)
// but is acceptable for GenericBubbleSort(employee *)
```

Suppose we have `GenericBubbleSort()` function as a non-generic specialization for the `Employee` class and call it with a `Person` object. The non-generic function would convert the `Person` object into an `Employee` object using the conversion operator and therefore it works.

7.2.13 Overloading One Generic Function with Another

In Section 7.2.12, a template has been overloaded with explicit specialization. It is also possible to overload one template with another.

To overload a generic function with another generic function, the number of arguments must differ (this is because type cannot be differentiated).

The generic sort algorithm is as follows:

```
template <typename Type>
void GenericBubbleSort(Type TempGenericArray[], int Size)
```

If we want that the original array to remain intact and the result to be reflected in another array, we may have one more function as follows:

```
template <typename Type>
        void GenericBubbleSort(Type TempGenericArray[], int Size, Type
TempResultArray[])
```

One can overload a template function with another template function. The number of arguments must differ in such a case.

Now, if the function is called with two arguments as usual, the first function would be called, and if the function is called with three arguments, the second function would be called. So, `GenericBubbleSort()` is a generic function with two arguments, which is overloaded as a generic function with three arguments.

> Templates do not introduce any run-time overhead.

Hence, if we call

```
GenericBubbleSort(Array2, 16, ResultArray);
```

then the `ResultArray` will have the sorted elements.

7.2.14 Manually Overloaded Functions vs Template Instantiations

A template function definition forces the compiler to overload the function as many times as it is used with different types in the program. What is the difference between manually overloaded functions that we have studied earlier and automatically overloaded functions of this kind?

An important difference is that the automatically overloaded functions have different types of arguments but the *same body*. Manually overloaded functions can and usually have different codes. It is possible to have a template function for some cases and manually overloaded functions for some special cases.

> **Note** If we need to introduce more number of specializations in our program, it usually means that the design is faulty and the case should be solved by overloaded functions and not by using template functions.

The other difference is the match of arguments. The template function requires an exact match of arguments. Normal function arguments may not have the exact match but can use integral promotions or standard conversions to match. Hence, manually overloaded function arguments can be promoted or standard converted.

There is an interesting consequence to this. Suppose the following are the function calls in a program using `SumIt()`.

```
template <typename Type>
Type SumIt(Type, Type)

int main()
{
    int i1, i2;
    char ch1, ch2;
    unsigned u1, u2;

    SumIt(i1, i2);  // int version instantiated
    SumIt(ch1, ch2);   // char version instantiated
    SumIt(u1, u2);   // unsigned version instantiated
}
```

> **Note** A generic function overloads a new function for the types that are handled by type promotions in case of a normal non-generic function.

Here, we have three different overloaded functions. As an alternative, we can have only one function for unsigned *without using templates*, which can handle all the three calls. Thus, if the templatized definition of `SumIt()` is replaced by `unsigned SumIt(unsigned, unsigned)`, then it will work for all the cases.

7.2.15 Default Arguments to Function Templates

We have seen that function templates can take generic arguments as well as normal (non-type) arguments. Therefore, can we provide default arguments to the template arguments? The answer is no. It is not possible to write statements such as

```
template <typename Type = int> // This is incorrect
```

Surprisingly, this is allowed in class templates. This is because the default argument to template functions was proposed too late to the standardization committee to accept.

Efficiency

We have seen the usefulness of templates. One of the aims of the designers of template is efficiency. Let us see how efficient it is to use templates. The first problem with template is that it may bloat the code in an unexpected way.

Suppose we have the generic bubble sort as discussed earlier. If we have the following three arrays:

```
int IntArray[10]
short ShortArray[10]
char CharArray[10]
```

and the calls GenericBubbleSort(IntArray), GenericBubbleSort(ShortArray), GenericBubble Sort(CharArray), then three distinct functions are generated. A single function with int as an argument can actually serve the purpose. If we have to solve a problem with such data types, it is not advisable to use template functions.

Another point to be noted is that every manipulation related to templates is done at compile time. Hence, there is almost no run-time overhead when templates are used.

Flexibility

Flexibility is an important advantage of using function templates, which can be used for built-in as well as user-defined types. It has already been mentioned that the algorithms may need the operators to be overloaded if they are to be used with objects as parameters. Algorithms can be flexible only if proper operators are overloaded meaningfully for a given object. For example, Bubblesort(EmpArray, size) is useful and correct only if < and = are defined.

7.3 CLASS TEMPLATES

We have seen generic functions and their uses so far. Similarly, generic classes, which take data type as parameters, are also possible in C++. It is possible to define a stack class, which has all possible functionality of a stack. The objects of the stack class can be defined as follows:

```
stack <int> MyIntStack;
```

Here, the content of the stack class is of type integer. It is also possible to have stack <char>, stack <employee>, etc. How can such a functionality be built? Program 7.9 uses the same stack used in Program 3.2 in Chapter 3, but now with generic type elements.

 **PROGRAM 7.9**   Generic stack class

```
//GenericStackClass.cpp
#include <iostream>
using namespace std;

template <typename ElementType>
```

```
class Stack
{
private:
    int StackPointer;
    ElementType StackArray[10];
public:
    Stack()
    {
        StackPointer = 0;
    }

    void push(ElementType value)
    {
        if(StackPointer == 9)
        {
            cout << "Stack overflow! Cannot insert";
        }
        else
        {
            StackArray[StackPointer] = value; StackPointer++;
        }
    }

    ElementType pop()
    {
        if(StackPointer == 0)
            cout << "Stack underflow! Cannot pop";
        else
        {
            StackPointer--;
            return StackArray[StackPointer];
        }
    }
};

void main()
{
    // Integer stack
    Stack <int> MyStack;
    MyStack.push(1); MyStack.push(2);
    cout << MyStack.pop() << "\n";
    cout << MyStack.pop() << "\n";

    // Character stack
    Stack <char> YourStack;
    YourStack.push('n'); YourStack.push('O');
    cout << YourStack.pop() << "\n";
    cout << YourStack.pop() << "\n";
}
```

How the Program Works

Compare both stack classes (the normal stack class in Program 3.2 and the templatized version in Program 7.9). There are three differences:

1. The class header class Stack changes to

```
template <typename ElementType>
class Stack
```

> Deducing a type is not possible for class templates. We must have the type explicitly specified while defining a class.

`template <typename ElementType>` precedes the class definition for the class to use `ElementType` as a generic type in its body.

2. The definition `Stack MyStack` changes to `Stack <int> MyStack`
3. The `int element type` argument to push and the return type of pop have been replaced here by `ElementType`.

It is also possible to have `char Stack` and `employee Stack` similar to the `int` stack. It can be observed that the program will not have any change in the `Stack` class definition.

It is to be noted that it is not possible to have automatic argument deduction in class templates because the compiler cannot deduce a type from the object declaration such as `Stack MyStack`. It is not similar to a function call where there are arguments and deductions that may tell a compiler the data type for the `Type`.

7.3.1 Defining Functions of Class Templates outside the Class

If the functions `push()` and `pop()` are defined outside the class, `class Stack` will have to be defined in the following way:

```
template <typename ElementType>
class Stack
{
private:
    int StackPointer;
    ElementType StackArray[10];
public:
    Stack()
    {
        StackPointer = 0;
    }
    void push(ElementType);
    ElementType pop();
};

template <typename ElementType>
void Stack <ElementType>::push(ElementType value)
{
    if(StackPointer == 9)
    {
        cout << "Stack overflow! Cannot insert";
    }
    else
    {
        StackArray[StackPointer] = value; StackPointer++;
    }
}

template <typename ElementType>
ElementType Stack <ElementType>::pop()
{
```

```
      if(StackPointer == 0)
         cout << "Stack underflow! Cannot pop";
      else
      {
         StackPointer--;
         return StackArray[StackPointer];
      }
   }
```

The syntax for the function header seems cryptic at first sight. The function header is preceded by template <...>, which is the same as the template specification that preceded the class definition earlier. The class name (e.g., Stack) should also indicate the type variables used in the class (e.g., int) using the same <> pair to indicate names, that is, Stack <int>. Note that the template specification contains typename (it has been mentioned already that it can even be the keyword class instead of typename) followed by the type variable name (e.g., typename ElementType). The class section will only have the type (e.g., ElementType in Program 7.9).

In Program 7.10, the function has been moved outside the template class and the Employee stack has been introduced.

PROGRAM 7.10   Employee stack

```cpp
//EmpStack.cpp
#include <iostream>
#include <string>
using namespace std;

class employee
{
    int EmpNo;
    string Name;
    string DeptName;
    string Designation;
public:
    employee(){};
    employee(int TempNo, string TempName, string TempDept, string TempDesi)
    {
        EmpNo = TempNo;
        Name = TempName;
        DeptName = TempDept;
        Designation = TempDesi;
    }

    friend ostream & operator <<(ostream & TempOut, employee & TempEmployee);
};
ostream & operator <<(ostream & TempOut, employee  & TempEmployee)
{
    TempOut << "Details of employee number" << TempEmployee.EmpNo << "\n";
    TempOut << "Name is" << TempEmployee.Name << "\n";
    TempOut << "Department is" << TempEmployee.DeptName << "\n";
    TempOut << "Designation is" << TempEmployee.Designation << "\n";
    return TempOut;
}
template <typename ElementType>
```

```cpp
class Stack
{
private:
    int StackPointer;
    ElementType StackArray[10];
public:
    Stack()
    {
        StackPointer = 0;
    }
    void push(ElementType); ElementType pop();
};
template <typename ElementType>
void Stack <ElementType>::push(ElementType value)
{
    if(StackPointer > 9)
    {
        cout << "Stack overflow! Cannot insert";
    }
    else
    {
        StackArray[StackPointer] = value; StackPointer++;
    }
}
template <typename ElementType>
ElementType Stack <ElementType>::pop()
{
    if(StackPointer == 0)
        cout << "Stack underflow! Cannot pop";
    else
    {
        StackPointer--;
        return StackArray[StackPointer];
    }
}
void main()
{
    Stack <int> MyStack;
    MyStack.push(1);
    MyStack.push(2);

    cout << MyStack.pop() << "\n";
    cout << MyStack.pop() << "\n";

    Stack <char> YourStack;
    YourStack.push('n');
    YourStack.push('O');

    cout << YourStack.pop() << "\n";
    cout << YourStack.pop() << "\n";

    Stack <employee> EmpStack;
    employee UniEmployee[10] =
    {
        employee(1, "Lara", "Exam", "Professor"),
        employee(2, "Ponting", "Marksheet", "Clerk"),
        employee(3, "Laxman", "Accounts", "Head Clerk"),
        employee(4, "Flintoff", "Exam", "Clerk") ,
```

```
            employee(5, "Murlidharan", "Accounts", "CAO"),
            employee(6, "Sarfaraz", "Exam", "Informer"),
            employee(7, "Dean Jones", "Exam", "Invigilator"),
            employee(8, "Madugalle", "Exam", "Examiner"),
            employee(9, "Ganguly", "Marksheet", "Repeater"),
            employee(10, "Nafees", "Accounts", "Clerk")
    };

    for(int i = 0;  i < 10; i++)
    {
        EmpStack.push(UniEmployee[i]);
    }

    for(int i = 0; i < 10; i++)
    {
        cout << EmpStack.pop();
    }
}
```

How the Program Works

We will see how the real class is generated from a generic class and is used in the program.

Constructing a class   Let us see how `class stack` is used as an `int stack` as well as a `char stack`. Similar to function templates, when a class template is defined, that is, when `template <Type ElementType>` is defined, it informs the compiler that the following class definition contains a generic data type called `ElementType`. This does not define the class, as no functions are generated and no elements are created. This also indicates that when the class is actually defined in the main program, the type of `ElementType` will be known.

The definition of stack in the program, `Stack <int> MyStack`, indicates that `int` is passed as a type to the template class. The compiler creates the class only when such an object is defined. It creates the integer version of `Stack` class template (known as `Stack <int>`) *at that moment*. It also creates an object of that class (`MyStack`). Thus, both the class and the object are created together.

Generating the second class   When the compiler encounters `Stack <char> YourStack`, it creates *another class*, which is a `char` version of `Stack` and an object of that class (`YourStack`). This process (generating normal class from the template class) is known as *instantiation*. Here, it is known as class instantiation from a class template. Both `Stack <int>` and `Stack <char>` are known as *specializations* (instantiations). Now, if we have one more definition `Stack <char> YourStack2`, the compiler will not generate a new class, that is, it would not generate new specialization from `Stack` *template* as it has already instantiated `Stack <char>`. It would only create an object (`YourStack2`) of class `Stack <char>`.

> Generating a normal class for a specific data type from a generic class is known as instantiation and the generated class is known as specialization.

Explicit specialization   If `Stack <employee>` *class* is to behave differently from the `Stack` *template*, it can be defined as an explicit specialization as has been done with template functions.

Program 7.11 is an example of an explicit class specialization. Instead of inserting the complete employee object in the stack, the employee number of the employee object is inserted. When the element is popped, the array needs to be searched to get the employee object with the same employee number. This solution is storage efficient but will take more time to execute because of the search operation involved.

 **PROGRAM 7.11** Explicit class specialization

```cpp
//SpecializationClassTempalte.cpp
#include <iostream>
#include <string>
using namespace std;

class employee
{
    string Name;
    string DeptName;
    string Designation;
public:
    int EmpNo;
    employee(){};
    employee(int TempNo, string TempName, string TempDept, string TempDesi)
    {
        EmpNo = TempNo;
        Name = TempName;
        DeptName = TempDept;
        Designation = TempDesi;
    }

    bool operator ==(employee TempEmp)
    {
        return(EmpNo == TempEmp.EmpNo);
    }

    bool operator <(employee & OtherEmployee)
    {
        return(EmpNo < OtherEmployee.EmpNo);
    }

    friend ostream & operator <<(ostream & TempOut, employee & TempEmployee);
};

ostream & operator <<(ostream & TempOut, employee & TempEmployee)
{
    TempOut << "Details of employee number" << TempEmployee.EmpNo << "\n";
    TempOut << "Name is" << TempEmployee.Name << "\n";
    TempOut << "Department is" << TempEmployee.DeptName << "\n";
    TempOut << "Designation is" << TempEmployee.Designation << "\n";
    return TempOut;
}

employee UniEmployee[10] =
{
    employee(1, "Lara", "Exam", "Professor"),
    employee(2, "Ponting", "Marksheet", "Clerk"),
    employee(3, "Laxman", "Accounts", "Head Clerk"),
    employee(4, "Flintoff", "Exam", "Clerk"),
    employee(5, "Murlidharan", "Accounts", "CAO"),
    employee(6, "Sarfaraz", "Exam", "Informer"),
    employee(7, "Dean Jones", "Exam", "Invigilator"),
    employee(8, "Madugalle", "Exam", "Examiner"),
    employee(9, "Ganguly", "Marksheet", "Repeater"),
    employee(10, "Nafees", "Accounts", "Clerk")
};

template <typename Type>
```

```cpp
int GenericSearch(Type TempGenericArray[], Type EleToBeSearched)
{
    for(int i = 0; i < 10; i++)
    {
        if(EleToBeSearched == TempGenericArray[i])
        return i;
    }
    return -1;
}

template <typename ElementType>
class Stack
{
private:
    int StackPointer;
    ElementType StackArray[10];
public:
    Stack()
    {
        StackPointer = 0;
    }

    void push(ElementType);
    ElementType pop();
};

template <typename ElementType>
void Stack <ElementType>::push(ElementType value)
{
    if(StackPointer > 9)
        cout << "Stack overflow! Cannot insert!";
    else
        StackArray[StackPointer] = value;
        StackPointer++;
}

template <typename ElementType>
ElementType Stack <ElementType>::pop()
{
    if(StackPointer == 0)
        cout << "Stack underflow! Cannot pop";
    else
    {
        StackPointer--;
        return StackArray[StackPointer];
    }
}

template <>
class Stack <employee>
{
private:
    int StackPointer;
    int EmpNoArray[10];
public:
    Stack()
    {
        StackPointer = 0;
    }

    void push(employee);
```

```
        employee pop();
};
template <>
void Stack <employee>::push(employee TempEmp)
{
    if(StackPointer > 9)
        cout << "Stack overflow! Cannot insert";
    else
    {
        EmpNoArray[StackPointer] = TempEmp.EmpNo;
        StackPointer++;
    }
}

template <>
employee Stack <employee>::pop()
{
    if(StackPointer == 0)
        cout << "Stack underflow! Cannot pop";
    else
    {
        StackPointer--;
        int TempEmpNo = EmpNoArray[StackPointer];
        int SearchIndex = GenericSearch(UniEmployee, employee TempEmpNo" "," "));
        return UniEmployee [SearchIndex];
    }
}

void main()
{
    Stack <int> MyStack;
    MyStack.push(1);
    MyStack.push(2);
    cout << MyStack.pop() << "\n";
    cout << MyStack.pop() << "\n";

    Stack <char> YourStack;
    YourStack.push('n');
    YourStack.push ('O');
    cout << YourStack.pop() << "\n";
    cout << YourStack.pop() << "\n";

    Stack <employee> EmpStack;
    for(int i = 0; i < 10; i++)
    {
        EmpStack.push(UniEmployee[i]);
    }

    for(int i = 0; i < 10; i++)
    {
        cout << EmpStack.pop();
    }
}
```

How the Program Works

Generic search routine   We have added a generic search routine, which can sort any array. The employee number (EmpNo) needs to be defined as public and the employee array as global, so that the search routine can operate on it. While programming for a real-world problem, these solutions are not acceptable. It is better to have a linked list of employee numbers, and the function accessing should be defined as a friend rather than defining the employee number as public. However, since the focus here is to learn specialization, we have presented the program in this manner.

Generating `Stack <employee>`   When `Stack <employee>` gets compiled, the compiler will not automatically generate the class from the `Stack` template, but will take the definition that has been provided explicitly and generate that class.

Using a separate class   Another way to accomplish the same task is to define a special class `StackEmp`, which contains the same definition. Then, it is possible to write

```
StackEmp EmpStack;
```

instead of

```
Stack <employee> EmpStack.
```

The difference does not lie in the definition or use, but in the way the compiler treats it. In the case of `StackEmp`, the compiler generates the class when the definition of `StackEmp` is compiled and generates push and pop for it. In the earlier case, only if an object of `Stack <employee>` is defined does the class get instantiated, and the functions come into existence only if they are called, and not otherwise.

If the stack of employees is defined as a template specialization, the user need not be aware of the implementation of employee stack as a special one and can treat the stack object of employees similar to other objects. This adds to the simplicity of the operation for users who use the program's library (where the stack class is defined).

Thus, if the user needs to generate an integer stack, the following could be written:

```
Stack <int>
```

Moreover, if an employee stack is needed, the user would simply write

```
Stack <employee>
```

without having to learn anything else. Instead, if we have a `StackEmp` class, the user has to remember the name `StackEmp` to instantiate the object.

7.3.2 Classes with Multiple Generic Data Types

Classes, similar to function templates, can have more than one generic type. The following program supports this fact.

```
//TwoGenericTypes.cpp
#include <iostream>
#include <string>
using namespace std;

template <typename Type1, typename Type2>
class ClassWithTwoTypes
{
    Type1 FirstValue;
    Type2 SecondValue;

public:
    ClassWithTwoTypes(Type1 TempVal1, Type2 TempVal2)
    {
```

```
        FirstValue = TempVal1; SecondValue = TempVal2;
    }
    void Display()
    {
    cout << FirstValue << " " << SecondValue;
    }
};
void main()
{
    ClassWithTwoTypes <int, char> ObjectIC(12, 'b');
    ClassWithTwoTypes <char, string> ObjectIS('b', "Batsman");
    ObjectIC.Display();
    cout << "\n"; ObjectIS.Display( );
}
```

This example shows two different types, namely, `Type1` and `Type2`, as generic types used in a generic class `ClassWithTwoTypes`. `ObjectIC` is an object of a class instantiated from it. In `objectIC`, the first type is integer and the second one is character. Thus, the object is that of the class instantiated with a character and a string as its two members. Thus, our class is capable of holding any pair of variables of different types.

7.3.3 Using Non-type Arguments

Similar to function templates, class templates can also have non-type arguments in the argument list. Take the case of an array that takes generic data type as elements.

The array is defined with [] overloaded to have a range-safe operation. Here, the size of the array needs to be passed as an argument. The argument cannot be a variable because the size of the array must be known at compile time for the compiler to allocate memory for the specialization of the class it is generating from the template definition. Since the argument is a constant, it cannot be modified even by the class functions. These types of arguments are known as non-type (which do not indicate data type) arguments. As discussed earlier, their values must be available at compile time. The non-type arguments can also be constants of int type or a pointer (or reference) of global data because all three are available at compile time.

Non-type arguments can also be used in class templates.

The following is an extended example of Program 6.7 in Chapter 6. The array is now capable of having any type of elements.

```
//GenericArray.cpp
#include <iostream>
using namespace std;

template <typename Type, int Size>
class SafeGenericArray
{
    Type Array[Size];
public:
    Type & operator [](int Index)
    {
        if((Index < 0) || (Index > Size - 1))
```

```
        {
                cout << "Subscript out of range!";
                exit(1);
        }
        else
                return Array[Index];
    }
};
void main()
{
    SafeGenericArray <int, 5> SafeIntArray;
    SafeGenericArray <char, 3> SafeCharArray;
    int i = 5;
    // SafeGenericArray <char, i> NotAcceptable;
    SafeIntArray[0] = 5;
    // SafeArray[-3] = 7;
    SafeCharArray[5] = 'j';
}
```

> The values of non-type arguments are replaced at compile time.

The use of non-type argument must now be clear. The values five and three in the first two statements of main() will replace Size of the generic array at compile time. The fourth line will not be compiled because the value of i is not available during compilation. If we look at the definition of the template class, Size seems to be a variable of type int. However, it is a constant value that must be known at compile time. This is true for all non-type arguments.

7.3.4 Using Default Arguments

Default arguments can be used with template classes. The previous example can be rewritten as follows with default arguments.

```
//DefArgsGenFunc.cpp
#include <iostream>
using namespace std;
template <typename Type = int, int Size = 10>
// Note the use of default argument

class SafeGenericArray
{
    Type Array[Size];
public:
    Type & operator [](int Index)
    {
        if((Index < 0) || (Index > Size - 1))
        {
                cout << "Subscript out of range!";
                exit(1);
        }
    }
```

```
        else
                return Array[Index];
    }
};
void main()
{
    SafeGenericArray <int, 5> SafeIntArray1;
    SafeGenericArray <char> SafeCharArray1; // Size = 10
    SafeGenericArray <> SafeIntArray2;  // Type = int and Size = 10
    SafeGenericArray <char, 5> SafeCharArray2;
    SafeIntArray1[0] = 5;
    SafeCharArray1[7] = 'j';
    SafeIntArray2[9] = 15;
    SafeCharArray2[2] = 'j';
}
```

> **Note** Unlike template functions, template classes, both generic and non-generic types, can have default arguments. It is important to provide empty angular braces (<>) when the user expects to use default arguments (unlike template function calls).

Both the arguments have been defined in the program as default. It is possible to omit one or both. The class can even be defined with both the arguments. The compiler automatically supplies the missing arguments by taking the default arguments.

7.3.5 Static Data Members

The template class can also have static data members. The static variable will have one instance for one initialization of the template class. Thus, there will be two different static members for Stack <int> and for Stack <char>.

For all the objects of a single class (e.g., Stack <int>), there is only one instance of static member. The way a static member is defined is analogous to the way member functions are defined outside the template class. The TotalStacks variable in the following program defines the total number of stacks of a specified type. Note how the static variable is defined here.

> A template class can have static members. There will be one static member instance for one instance of the template class. When the class is instantiated, static members are instantiated along with it.

```
template <typename ElementType>
int Stack <ElementType>::TotalStacks;
```

The part preceding int Stack contains the same template specification as has been added earlier in the definition of the Stack class, which is provided with <ElementType> to indicate a specific type of stack.

In the following example, the static variable TotalStacks is used to find the total number of stacks for two different types, int and char. The program can easily be extended to provide any other type of stacks, for example, employee stack.

```
//StaticDataMembers.cpp
#include <iostream>
#include <string>
using namespace std;
template <typename ElementType>
```

```
class Stack
{
private:
    int StackPointer;
    ElementType StackArray[10];
public:
    static int TotalStacks;
    Stack()
    {
        StackPointer = 0;
        TotalStacks++;
    }
    void push(ElementType);
    ElementType pop();
};
template <typename ElementType>
int Stack <ElementType>::TotalStacks;

template <typename ElementType>
void Stack <ElementType>::push(ElementType value)
{
    if(StackPointer > 9)
    {
        cout << "Stack overflow! Cannot insert";
    }
    else
    {
        StackArray[StackPointer] = value;
        StackPointer++;
    }
}
template <typename ElementType>
ElementType Stack <ElementType>::pop()
{
    if(StackPointer == 0)
        cout << "Stack underflow! Cannot pop";
    else
    {
        StackPointer--;
        return StackArray[StackPointer];
    }
}
void main()
{
    Stack <int> MyStack1;
    cout << "Integer stack total elements = " << Stack  <int>::TotalStacks << "\t";
```

```
    cout << "Character stack total elements = " << Stack <char>::TotalStacks << "\n";
    Stack <char> YourStack1;
    cout << "Integer stack total elements = " << Stack  <int>::TotalStacks << "\t";
    cout << "Character stack total elements = " << Stack  <char>::TotalStacks << "\n";
    Stack <int> MyStack2;
    cout << "Integer stack total elements = " << Stack  <int>::TotalStacks << "\t";
    cout << "Character stack total elements = "<< Stack <char>::TotalStacks << "\n";
    Stack <char> YourStack2;
    cout << "Integer stack total elements = " << Stack <int>::TotalStacks << "\t";
    cout << "Character stack total elements = " << Stack <char>::TotalStacks << "\n";
    getchar();
}
```

Output

```
Integer stack total elements = 1 Character stack total elements = 0
Integer stack total elements = 1 Character stack total elements = 1
Integer stack total elements = 2 Character stack total elements = 1
Integer stack total elements = 2 Character stack total elements = 2
```

Thus, we have two different `TotalStack` variables, `Stack  <int>::TotalStack` and `Stack <char>::TotalStack`. We can see that multiple instances of classes have separate copies of the static members. The output shows that both the stacks have increasing number of members.

7.3.6 Friends of Class Template

A friend of a class template can be one of the following:

1. Class template
2. Function template
3. Ordinary (non-template) function
4. Ordinary (non-template) class
5. A specialization of class template
6. A specialization of function template

The following code illustrates how it is possible to have many types of friends for a class template.

```
class ClassNo1;  // Forward definition

template <typename Type1>
class TemplateClassNo1
{
    Body of the class
}

template <typename Type2>
class TemplateClassNo2
{
    Body of the class
}

template <typename Type3>
class TemplateClassNo3
{
private:
```

<table>
<tr><td>

When we need to
have a different be-
haviour for a different
set of arguments,
which is a subset of
the original set of
arguments, we need
partial specialization.

</td><td>

```
    ...
public:

    ...
    friend ClassNo1;
    friend SomeNonTemplateFunction();
    friend TemplateClassN01;
    friend TemplateClassNo2 <int>;
    friend SomeTemplateFunction();
    friend SomeTemplateFunction <int>()
    // A specialization of template function
}
```

</td></tr>
</table>

7.3.7 Primary and Partial Specialization

Suppose we want a specialization of the stack class that has been defined to work for pointer-to-any-variable in a different way (say, instead of storing pointers, we may need to store their contents). The specialization here should work for all types of pointers.

For example, if the employee objects are to be inserted in the stack, they are inserted without any change. In contrast, if the pointers to employee are inserted, then we insert their contents (i.e., employee objects pointed to by them). Similarly, if we need to push pointers to the passenger object in the stack, we again insert the contents pointed to by the pointer.

This process is distinctly different from normal overloading, which provides special treatment for only a single-type situation. However, here we are dealing with a set of types (all of type pointers in our case) for which we need a different behaviour. The specialization can be written as follows:

```
template <typename ElementType>
class Stack <ElementType*>
{ . . . }
```

Note the `<ElementType *>` appearing immediately after the class name. This indicates *partial specialization*. The code we have written would work for all pointer types. This is known as partial specialization.

> **Note** A partial specialization is a template definition that begins with a '< >' pair after the class name. It always follows the primary specialization. A primary specialization is the one that is defined before and of which the partial specialization is a subset.

A partial specialization should always *follow* the primary specialization, that is, a template definition without <> pair after the class name. In the given example, it relates to the following definition:

```
template <typename ElementType>
class Stack
{ . . . }
```

This is also applicable to the `SafeArray`. A special case is encountered when C-type strings are passed to the `SafeArray`. We need partial specialization because when we sort the array using techniques such as bubble sort, we need to compare strings and even assign one string to another.

Consider the following case as a definition of a generic safe array.

```
template <typename Type>
class SafeGenericArray
```

Suppose the following are the elements of the array:

```
template <typename Type>
class SafeGenericArray <Type *>
```

Though the content of first C-type string is the same as that of second C-type string, they are not similar because the addresses are not the same. We need to define another algorithm for manipulation in this case. Essentially, this is needed for any array containing pointers. Partial specialization can be used here. We have to define our specialization in the following template class:

```
template <typename Type>
class SafeGenericArray <Type *>
```

Now, it can work for any array as an element. Consider the following example that explains partial specialization.

The partial specialization solution is not ideal. See that the [] operator does not return a reference. This cannot be used in the LHS of the expression. Anyway, it serves the purpose of introducing partial specialization.

```cpp
//PartSpec.cpp
#include <iostream>
using namespace std;
#define Size 10
#include <string.h>
template <typename Type>

class SafeGenericArray
{
    Type Array[Size];
public:
    Type & operator [](int Index)
    {
        if((Index < 0) || (Index > Size - 1))
        {
            cout << "Subscript out of range!";
            exit (1);
        }
        else
            return Array[Index];
    }
};

// The following is partial specialization
template <typename Type>
class SafeGenericArray <Type *>
{
    Type *Array[Size];
```

```
    public:
       Type *operator[](int Index)
       {
          if((Index < 0) || (Index > Size - 1))
          {
                  cout << "Subscript out of range!";
                  exit(1);
          }
          else
          {
                  cout << "Element no. " << Index << "is accessed \n";
          return Array[Index];
       }
    }
};
int main()
{
    SafeGenericArray <int> SafeIntArray1;
    SafeGenericArray <char> SafeCharArray1;

    SafeGenericArray <char *> SafeStringArray;
    char *String = "Lara";
    strcpy(SafeStringArray[1], String);
    SafeIntArray1[0] = 5;
    return 0;
}
```

Output
```
Element no. 1 is accessed
```

We can also have multiple partial specializations for a single primary specialization, that is, we can have class `SafeGenericArray <type &>`, etc.

7.4 COMPILATION MODELS FOR TEMPLATES

When templates are included in the programs, there are two different ways to compile them. One is similar to inline functions where the template body is included when the templates are called; the other is similar to normal functions where the function call is replaced by some sort of jump instruction that calls the template function for a specified type and the control gets transferred to that place. Here we discuss both the types of compilation models.

7.4.1 Inline vs Non-inline Function Calls in Multiple Files

A very important difference between inline functions and normal functions is the way they are defined in a multifile program. It is possible to have a program that contains multiple files. Assume that `Prog1.cpp`, `Prog2.cpp`, and `Prog3.cpp` are three different files containing three different parts of the same program. To execute the program, the individual files are compiled one after another and then all the files are linked together to build a single executable file.

Suppose there is an inline function call in `Prog1.cpp` and `Prog3.cpp`. A copy of the function is needed in both the files. This is because inline functions are pasted at the time of compilation. If the individual file does not contain the body of the inline function, they cannot replace the call with the body.

It is an error to define multiple copies of a non-inline function in multiple files.

This is not the case with non-inline functions, which are defined only at a single place. Suppose, in the given example, a non-inline function `xyz()` is called from all the three `.cpp` files. If the function definition appears in `Prog1.cpp`; then only its declaration or prototype should appear in the other two files (as extern). The function body is not copied to the program at compile time. When all three files are linked together, they all have the call address of the same function.

It is actually an error if multiple copies of the same non-inline function are defined in multiple files. The compiler, at the time of compilation, cannot check this point; however, at the time of linking, when the linker gets multiple copies of the non-inline function, it would be unable to link the program.

Note In multiple source files, inline functions need to have a source copy in all the files. In contrast, non-inline functions need to have only the extern definitions in all the files excluding the one where it is defined.

7.4.2 Template Instantiations in Multiple Files

In this section, we will learn if we need to define templates in every file where a template is to be instantiated, similar to inline functions. We will also learn whether it is possible to have the complete definition in one file and use it elsewhere with just the declaration. In other words, we will know whether template functions should be used like inline functions or non-inline functions.

In fact, both the models are applicable in the case of function templates. The templates can be defined in all the files that are being used. At the time of compilation, the compiler compiles the function as if it is the only definition. At the end of compilation, in a pre-link phase, when multiple copies of the same template instantiation are found, a single copy is taken and the others are ignored. There are a few problems with this approach, which are listed as follows:

1. It may not be possible to copy the template definitions in all the files as the template designer may not want the definition to be seen by others.

One simple way to include templates in a multiple source file case is to copy all of them to all source files. It is called inclusion compilation model.

2. It may not be feasible to copy large template files to every file as it increases the compile time.

3. The template definition is an implementation and the template call is an interface. The interface should be separated from implementation for the following reasons:

(a) Implementation should be independently modifiable without changing the interface. Assume that `template xyz` is defined inside a file `Prog1.cpp` and is used in `Prog2.cpp` and `Prog3.cpp`. These two files should not be recompiled or recoded if the definition of `xyz` (implementation) changes.

When all template definitions are kept at a single place and linked with all other source files at linking time, it is known as separate compilation model.

(b) Implementation, at times, represents the high-quality work from a top-flight programmer. It is better that this is not distributed and is kept at a single place.

(c) Maintenance of the template becomes easy if the definition exists at a single place. If multiple copies of templates exist at multiple places, maintaining them can be problematic.

Thus, a solution similar to the non-inline functions for the templates is needed. It is possible using another model that uses the keyword export (discussed in the following section), where it is possible to define a template function at a single place and use declarations at other places.

export *Keyword*

The keyword export is useful when a template function is defined at a single place and the declarations are used at other places. This is useful in instances where the templates defined while developing one application are found to be useful for other applications or when the templates designed by somebody else are to be used.

Suppose we define BubbleSort.cpp to contain the definition of the generic bubble sort. Then, it is possible to modify the definition as follows:

```
export template <typename Type>
void GenericBubbleSort(Type TempIntArray[])
{
    Body of the function
}
```

Note In separate compilation model, the definition of the template definition is preceded by the keyword export in the file in which the templates are defined. In all other files, only the prototype of the template is specified.

If we want to use the same GenericBubbleSort() in UseIt.cpp, then the code in UseIt.cpp contains only the following:

```
{
    template <typename Type>
    void GenericBubbleSort(Type TempIntArray[]);
    /* Note the semicolon; it indicates the end */
    // No definition of the template
    // Other code
}
```

However, while linking UseIt.cpp, we just need to provide the .obj file of the BubbleSort program.

Note that in the earlier case the entire body of GenericBubbleSort() should be copied to UseIt.cpp.

The first model where template definitions are copied to all the files is called *inclusion compilation model* and the second one is known as *separate compilation model* as implementation is separated from the interface here.

7.5 USE OF typename

The keyword typename indicates that the expression following the keyword is the name of a type. We have used typename in the <> section in the template. It can also be used within the body of the template function (or template class function).

If we write a typename identifier, then that identifier is treated as a type in that function template as shown in Program 7.12.

PROGRAM 7.12   Using typename for unambiguously specifying a type

```cpp
//Typename.cpp
#include <iostream>
using namespace std;

int ptr;
template <class Type>

void Min()
{
    typename Type::Test * ptr;
    // Type::Test *ptr;
    // Other code, which does not concern us here
}

class TestTypeName1
{
public:
    typedef int Test;
};

class TestTypeName2
{
public:
    typedef char Test;
};

void main()
{
    Min <TestTypeName1>();
    Min <TestTypeName2>();
}
```

How the Program Works

Here, we have two classes, TestTypeName1 and TestTypeName2, both of which define a type Test. Min() is a function template with a single Type argument. We have called this function twice, first with the argument TestTypeName1 and the second time with TestTypeName2. When Type is instantiated by TestTypeName1, Type::Test is an integer and when Type is instantiated by TestTypeName2, it is a char. The user here wants to define a variable of type Test. This means that if TestTypeName1 is the argument, then the variable is int, and if TestTypeName2 is the argument, then the variable is char. To define that we cannot write the statement,

```cpp
Test Variable;
```

as it would confuse the compiler that there are two different options

We need to write the following statement as it would not create any ambiguity:

```cpp
Type::Test Variable;
```

We have to refer to it as TestTypeName1::Test if we want to have the Test data type of the first class (which is actually an int). Likewise, we have to write TestTypeName2::Test, which is actually a char, when we are referring to the type of the second class TestTypeName2. The Type contains that type, so the ambiguity no longer exists.

Note that the scope resolution operator is used here to avoid confusion about the Test we are referring to, because we have two different data types having the same name. The name we have used with the class name and the scope resolution operator is known as the *qualified name*.

Now, suppose we need to define a pointer to this type `Test`. Our definition now changes to

```
Type::Test * ptr;
```

which is a source of ambiguity. Why?

A statement such as `Type::Test * ptr;` is valid and acceptable, but the problem is that the use of '*' is *ambiguous*. It can be interpreted in two different ways; the first one is what we intend here, that is, defining a pointer pointing to the type `Type::Test`; it can also be assumed to be a multiplication operation where the result is ignored (i.e., multiplying `Test` with `ptr` and ignoring the outcome). The compiler may take that meaning by default. If we want to treat `Type::Test` as type, we have to tell the compiler explicitly, which we have done in this program by writing `typename` before the definition.

```
typename Type::Test * ptr;
```

It is also possible that the compiler may take the intended meaning by default, but by writing `typename` before the definition, we make the program more portable. It makes a program independent of the defaults of a given compiler by compiling the program using any another compiler.

■ RECAPITULATION ■

- Templates are very helpful in achieving software reusability.
- Templates are type-independent outlines of definitions of classes and functions.
- It is possible to later on instantiate real classes and functions with specific type using these templates.
- Function templates are outlines of generic functions and class templates are outlines of generic classes.
- When a specific class or function is instantiated with some specific type, the body of the instantiation will replace the generic type with the specific type.
- Argument deduction is possible for function templates.
- A function template can have multiple arguments similar to the normal function.
- A non-type parameter can also be passed to a template function.
- We can have specializations that are different from what the compiler otherwise provides. This means that we can always override a specific specialization by providing our own explicit version.
- One template can be overloaded with another by providing different numbers of arguments, as different types cannot be specified.
- Though it is allowed to provide default arguments to a class template, it is not allowed for the function template.
- Static data members of the class templates are instantiated once for one instantiation of the class.
- It is possible to overload the class template with another class template having type specification as a subset of the original type specification. This overloading of class template is known as partial specialization.
- When we are dealing with multiple source files, it is possible to copy the template definitions to all the files, compile each file separately, and then create an executable file.
- It is also possible to define member functions and template functions of template classes at a single place, and use them in other files with just declarations. In this case, the definitions are to be preceded by the keyword `export`.
- `typename` is the keyword that allows the users to specify an expression as a data type, overriding any default meaning that the expression may stand for.

■ KEYWORDS ■

Class template This is a generic class outlined by the specification of a generic type using the keyword `template`. The actual class is defined later using this template.

Explicit specialization When either a function or a class is defined explicitly for a specific type, then that special definition is known as explicit specialization.

The explicit specialization overrides the normal specialization.

export `export` is a keyword required for implementing the separate compilation model. When the template definition is preceded by `export`, the compiler can manage to compile other files without needing the body of the template functions or member functions of the template class.

Inclusion compilation model It is possible to compile the templates spread across multiple files by having the copy of the template text in all the files. This model is known as the inclusion compilation model.

Instantiation Generation of either function or class for a specific type using the class of function template is known as instantiation of the class or function.

Non-type parameters Parameters to either template function or template class that do not specify any specific type but the constant value are known as non-type parameters.

Partial specialization When we define a template class, we can overload that class with other specific set of types, which is a subset of the original set of types. This overloading of the template class is known as partial specialization.

Separate compilation model It is possible to compile templates separately and then use them by providing their prototypes in other files. This model is known as the separate compilation model.

Specialization The function or class generated from the process of instantiation is known as a specialization of the template.

Template argument deduction The compiler, while encountering a call to a function template, tries to find out the actual type for the generic type specified in the definition of the function template. This process is known as template argument deduction. It is only possible in the case of function templates but not in class templates.

Template function or function template The generic function outlined by specification of a generic type using the keyword `template`. The actual function is defined later using this template.

typename or class keyword The `typename` or `class` keyword is used to define the generic name for the type in the function or class templates.

▣ EXERCISES ▣

Multiple Choice Questions

1. `typename` can be used for _____.
   - (a) defining generic data type
   - (b) indicating a data type
   - (c) Both (a) and (b)
   - (d) None of the above
2. The model where template definitions are copied to all the files is called _____.
   - (a) compilation model
   - (b) primary model
   - (c) inclusion compilation model
   - (d) exclusion compilation model
3. What type of pointers or references are allowed as non-type arguments to template functions?
   - (a) Pointers to global function
   - (b) Pointers to non-local objects
   - (c) Both (a) and (b)
   - (d) Pointers are not allowed
4. A friend of a class template can be one of the following:
   - (a) Class template
   - (b) Function template
   - (c) Ordinary non-template class
   - (d) All of the above

5. Is it possible to have templates with two or more generic arguments?
   - (a) Yes
   - (b) No
   - (c) Yes, but only for function templates
   - (d) Yes, but only for class templates
6. When is the template function compiled?
   - (a) When the compiler encounters the declaration of the template function
   - (b) After the template function is instantiated
   - (c) When the compiler encounters the definition of the template function
   - (d) Before other normal functions are compiled
7. What is `typename`?
   - (a) Identifier
   - (b) Preprocessor directive
   - (c) Keyword
   - (d) Conditional construct
8. Which of the following is the correct syntax for declaring function templates?
   - (a) `template <typename T>; void fun(T var1);`
   - (b) `template <T>; void fun(T var1);`
   - (c) `template <type T>; void fun(T var1);`

(d) `template <tname T>; void fun(T var1);`

9. Is there any restriction on the number of arguments as well as the number of types passed to template functions?

(a) Yes

(b) No

(c) Only when the template function is defined outside the class

(d) Only when the template function defined inside the class

10. What are the classes `Stack <int>` and `Stack <char>` known as?

(a) Normal classes

(b) Template classes

(c) Specializations

(d) Special classes

Conceptual Exercises

1. What is the need for template functions in C++? What are their advantages?

2. What are the problems with using macros? Explain using an example other than the one given in the book.

3. Give a few examples of multi-argument templates.

4. What is the difference between `typename` and `class`?

5. What is instantiation? Explain.

6. What is the need for operator overloading when we are using template functions to work with user-defined types? Clarify with an example.

7. What is the difference between generic and non-generic (type and non-type) arguments to function templates?

8. What is the difference between a template function and template class?

9. What are the advantages of template arguments deduction? When is it not possible for the compiler to deduce the argument types?

10. Give a few examples where explicit specialization of template function and template class is required.

11. Why do we need to overload a normal function instead of template specialization in some cases? Give an example to explain the need.

12. Give an example explaining the need for overloading a template with another template.

13. Discuss the efficiency and flexibility issues with templates.

14. What is the difference between manually over loaded functions and template instantiations?

15. Give an example where using the default arguments are useful in class template.

16. How does the behaviour of the static data members of a class template differ from that of static data members of a normal class?

17. What is the need for partial specialization? Differentiate between explicit specialization and partial specialization.

18. Explain the two models for template compilation? Compare.

19. Explain how `typename` can be used to indicate the type giving an example.

Practical Exercises

1. Implement selection sort as a generic function.

2. Implement quick sort as a generic function.

3. Write a program for binary search as a generic function. The function should take arguments as array name, the size, and the element to be searched.

4. Implement selection sort with a non-type size.

5. Implement quick sort with a non-type size.

6. Write a program for generic queue class with two member functions, insert and delete. Use the array to implement the queue.

7. Use the queue class in the previous problem and provide specialization for strings.

Exception Handling

8.1 INTRODUCTION

Exception handling is a mechanism to handle exceptions that are error-like situations. It is difficult to decide when an error becomes an exception. For the purpose of discussion, we will assume exceptions as errors.

C++ provides mechanisms for generating and handling exceptions. When exception handling is in place, instead of providing normal means of execution when an exception occurs, an alternative path of execution needs to be provided. In cases where the exception is not acceptable (most of the cases are such), the program should be terminated. It is a far better and orderly way to handle errors than the traditional C way to handle them. Let us compare both the approaches and see why the C++ error handling mechanism is more effective.

8.2 TRADITIONAL ERROR HANDLING

Traditionally, error handling is done in three different ways, namely, returning error number, global flag manipulation, and abnormal termination. None of these are completely suitable for solving problems. In this section, we will discuss in brief all these mechanisms and their shortcomings.

8.2.1 Returning Error Number

When a function is encountered in a program, arguments are accepted and the processing starts. If the arguments are incorrect or if something goes wrong while processing, the function returns an error code. This mechanism is quite common in C programs where returning zero is considered a successful function call, while a non-zero value indicates an error indicated by the value returned. There is no universal standard for such error codes. Returning error code 1 may indicate a wrong argument type (e.g., int instead of double) in one case, whereas in another case, it may signify that a pointer argument passed contains an invalid address.

8.2.2 Global Flag Manipulation

There are *error variables* that are globally available to all C library functions. They can set the value of errno to indicate errors. After calling the library function, the value of errno can be checked to find the actual error. The function perror() can also be used to get the same effect.

The disadvantage of this method is the reliance on the user to comply and test the value of the global flag every time the function is called. If the

> Exceptions are error-like situations. Exception handling is a mechanism to generate and handle exceptions.

> Returning zero for successful termination and non-zero otherwise is common practice in C programs.

The global variable errno and functions such as perror() to display error are also common methods of handling errors in C.

user does not check the value of errno and continues to work, there is a danger of getting unexpected results.

8.2.3 Abnormal Termination of Program

This is the most common exception handling procedure. Whenever something goes out of bound, exit() or abort() is called. It is a little better to use assert(), which displays a message before terminating. However, if this procedure is used, then an error would eventually crash the program. This is a very rough way to handle the situation and not recommended at all, though it is the only way to end in quite a few cases.

The most common way of handling errors in conventional coding is to call exit() or abort() and leave the user to decide what to do next.

While dealing with objects, crashing a program without properly closing the files and resources held by the object can leave the system in an inconsistent state. It is very difficult and, at times, impossible to recover from such states.

8.3 NEED FOR EXCEPTION HANDLING

Exception handling mechanism is needed in C++ because of the inappropriateness of all the traditional solutions while working with objects and in a distributed environment. The following section explains the need for exception handling.

8.3.1 Dividing Error Handling

While building a library, one may check for errors but may not be able to determine what to do with those errors. This is because one cannot predetermine the way the library is going to be used since it is built to be used in more than one situation. The *library user* on the other hand knows exactly what to do when an error occurs, that is, what files to close, whom to inform, etc. The exception handling mechanism enables the *library designer* to throw exceptions and the library users to accept and handle those exceptions. The error handling, thus, is divided. The library designer reports the errors and the user acts upon it.

Let us consider an example to understand the problem of library builder and library user.

Libraries are designed much before they are actually used in programs. Hence, the library designer must pave way for the users of the library to manage errors in their own way.

Suppose a library is being developed for a multimedia project. It has an argument "dimension" for the figure object. An error is to be reported from the library when the dimensions are not proper (going out of screen at the time of display or not within appropriate scaling with other figures on the screen). The designer can only display "Improper dimensions". However, the user of the class figure knows that the object being dealt with is a space shuttle; hence, when the dimensions of the left wing of that figure is under consideration, the user would display "The left wing does not fit on the screen", which is more understandable. If the same class is used elsewhere to draw a football ground in a multimedia game, the same error may be displayed by the user as "The opposite party's goalpost is drawn out of screen".

8.3.2 Unconditional Termination

In case of an abnormal termination (when abort() or exit() is called in the library), the programmer does not have any control over the program termination process. In such cases, exception handling mechanism helps a great deal by passing the control back to the programmer. Now, the programmer can control the termination process, that is, can close the files and release buffers and other resources before terminating.

> **Note** When users opt for unconditional termination, the objects that are instantiated will be abnormally terminated and their destructors are not executed. Other objects such as file and network connections also run into trouble due to abnormal termination. Exception handling provides a way for programmer-controlled termination.

8.3.3 Separating Error Reporting and Error Handling

> Conventionally, there is no structure for dividing error reporting and handling. Exception handling provides a standard and clear cut method for dividing them and handles the exceptions.

We have already seen the importance of separating error reporting and error handling. The two conventional ways to do it are using error codes and global error numbers. Both the methods generally use integers and are not standardized. In the exception handling mechanism, it is possible to have objects passed to the user, which can throw some more light on the situation related to the error. For example, if a file is not available while the user is making an attempt to read it, then the exception handler can provide functions that ask the user to select some other file instead (if the user has mistyped the name) or create a new file.

8.3.4 Problem of Destroying Objects

> When the program terminates abnormally, the objects created must be destroyed in the reverse order. This is known as stack unwinding problem. Exception handling provides a systematic method for termination with stack unwinding.

When an object is defined for a class with a dynamic constructor (a constructor with dynamic memory allocation), a destructor is needed. When an object contains resources (buffers in RAM, file handles, open connections to other parties in the network, etc.), a destructor is needed to smoothly return the resources and close the connections. The exit() or abort() function does not call the destructor of an object. Hence, if these functions are called, the objects are not destroyed properly, which can create inconsistency. If exception handling is used instead, the object destructors are automatically called and the problem is solved.

8.4 COMPONENTS OF EXCEPTION HANDLING MECHANISM

The exception handling mechanism has three building blocks, namely, try for indicating the program area where the exception can be thrown, throw for throwing an exception, and catch for taking an action for the specific exception. Figure 8.1 shows graphically how the three entities communicate with each other.

Try block	Throw expression	Catch block
Indicates the area where an exception can be thrown	Statement or function with throw	Take action for the specific exception

Fig. 8.1   Three building blocks of exception handling

8.4.1 try Block

> A try block decides the body that is monitored by the system to look for exceptions.

The try block is the one that can throw an exception. The code that is to be monitored for exceptions is placed within this block. Thus, the try block is the scope of exception generation. Whenever a specific code segment is expected to throw an exception, such segment is placed within the try block. Thus, this

| A catch block contains the code that the user has written to handle a particular exception. | block contains either a `throw` statement or a function containing either a `throw` statement or a similar function inside the body. |

8.4.2 catch Block

This is the section where the exception is handled. There are two ways to throw an exception: first, by using an explicit `throw` statement or second, by calling a function which in turn contains a `throw` statement or a similar function call in its body. The exception is handled by the `catch` block, which should immediately follow the `try` block.

8.4.3 throw Expression

This is a mechanism to generate the exception. It is usually a single statement starting with the keyword `throw` or a function call that contains `throw` inside its body. After the execution of this statement, the control is transferred to the corresponding `catch` block written immediately after the `try` block, if the exception is thrown.

The identifier following the `throw` is the name of the variable being thrown. The control now is permanently transferred to the `catch` block and the statements after the `throw` statement are not executed.

Let us examine Program 8.1 to understand these constructs.

PROGRAM 8.1   Exception example

```
//EHExample.cpp
#include <iostream>
#include <string>
using namespace std;

class MyException
{
public:
    int ExNumber;
    string ExMessage;
};

void main()
{
    try
    {
        cout << "Inside try block\n";
        cout << "Assuming error and throwing exception now\n";
        MyException Error1;
        Error1.ExNumber = 20;
        Error1.ExMessage = "Error testing";

        // Assume that the error has occurred
        throw Error1;
        cout << "This statement will not be executed";
    }
    catch (MyException Except)
    {
        cout << "\n Inside catch";
        cout << Except.ExNumber;
        cout << "\n" << Except.ExMessage;
    }
}
```

How the Program Works

Once the control is outside the `try` block, it must get a matching `catch` statement for the exception thrown.

A `throw` statement transfers the control outside the `try` block permanently.

This program does not have any error generating environment. Instead, it is just assumed that an error has occurred. With this simple program, it is very easy to understand all the three entities involved in the exception handling process.

The `try` block contains all the statements that are to be observed for exception generation. A `throw` statement transfers the control outside the `try` block permanently. The statements after the `throw` statement will not be executed in case of an error. In this case, an object of the class `MyException` is thrown. For simplicity, this program contains only two data attributes, namely, error number and error message, in it. Once the control is outside the `try` block, it must get a matching `catch` statement for the exception thrown. It must be noted that the `catch` block immediately follows the `try` block. In this case, the `catch` block (fortunately) contains the type that has been thrown, and hence, the control will pass to that block. Now, the statements inside the `catch` block are executed and then the program is terminated.

It is important to have a matching `catch` block for a thrown exception. If the match is not found, the `catch` block calls a built-in function `terminate()`, which terminates the program by calling `abort()`. We look at both of them in Section 8.12. The matching of `catch` is more restrictive than a normal match. For example, `catch(unsigned)` will not catch `int` or `char`.

Note that this is a two-step process and that it is not possible to have a direct call to `abort()`. First, `terminate()` has to be called, which in turn calls `abort()`. The flexibility of indirect access of this kind is important. The built-in `terminate()` can be replaced with the programmer's own function, which might close the files and connections before calling `abort()`. It is not possible to call `abort()` in certain circumstances. This is what is meant by programmer-controlled termination.

> **Note** An exception thrown that does not receive a proper match calls `terminate()`, which, by default, calls `abort()`. A user can write his/her own `terminate()` function, which can provide the last rituals to the object. In general, the user's own `terminate()` also calls `abort()` to ensure that all possible measures are taken before the termination.

The control transfer from the `try` block to the `catch` block is permanent. This is unlike a function call where, when the function exits, the control would transfer back to the next statement of the calling function. In try-to-catch block transfer, the transfer of control will not come back to the `try` block when the `catch` block execution is over. Even when no matching `catch` block is found, the control would not come back to the `try` block.

8.5 CHALLENGES IN THE NEW APPROACH

The new approach using exception handling is not without its own set of problems. As programmers, it is necessary for the readers to understand the challenges involved in this approach. The behaviour of the program changes substantially under this model. Care needs to be taken while using third-party libraries that throw exceptions. At the time of throwing an exception, the user also needs to take care of all its subsequent effects.

8.5.1 Finding Proper Handlers

It is to be known well in advance how many types of expressions can be thrown from the `try` block, and `catch` blocks must be provided for all such cases. It is very easy to check for

A library user must be aware of the type and nature of exceptions thrown by the functions he/she uses. If the user fails to take account of an exception, the program may terminate abnormally.

A polymorphic object, when thrown, can be caught by its own catch statement or the base class from which it is derived.

When we have two exceptions thrown at the same point of time, the program terminates abnormally.

programs such as Program 8.1. However, it becomes complicated if a function called from the try block throws an exception in the body of the function itself and does not have an appropriate catch block in its body. The programmer needs to provide an error handler in this case. One may assume that such cases are rare but it is not so. Most of the exceptions are thrown by the functions and are not caught by them. The onus is on the calling function to decide what to do when a specific exception is thrown.

Take the case of the new operator. The library implementation of new does not have a catch for a case when memory is not allocated. The operator new just throws an exception of type bad_alloc. It is up to the programmer to provide a catch block for it. If third-party functions are called in a program, a user needs to be aware of the exceptions that might be thrown from those functions and must provide appropriate error handlers for them. Failing to provide a proper exception handler leads to sudden crashes of programs much to the dislike of the users. Thus, it is imperative appropriate handlers are written when exceptions are expected.

In the real sense, the exception handling mechanism is an error-reporting mechanism from the library creator to the user, as mentioned earlier. Both the designers and the programmers are unaware of each other. Exception handling is a standardized mechanism to help them communicate about anomalies. It is imperative that the user of library functions be able to know the type and nature of the exceptions thrown from those functions.

8.5.2 Finding Proper Handlers for Polymorphic Objects

It will be seen in Chapter 9 that it is possible to inherit a class into another class. It is possible to access a derived class object by a base class pointer. The object pointed to by such a pointer is known as a *polymorphic object*. Whenever a polymorphic object of a derived class is thrown, it can be caught either by the base class or by the derived class. This is a challenging task. We defer this discussion until we study inheritance in Chapter 9.

8.5.3 Backtracking until Beginning of try Block

It is important to understand that when an exception is thrown, the control, before being passed to the catch block, travels backwards in the try block, and destroys all the objects generated in due course. This helps in restoring consistency, which was discussed earlier. A programmer must take care while writing *destructors* for objects (if a destructor is required for properly destroying the object) and place them in the try block to ensure consistency. It is also important to note that these destructors should not throw exceptions themselves in such cases. If one exception is not handled and another exception is thrown, the system has no other option but to terminate the program abnormally, as it is not capable of handling more than one exception at the same point of time.

8.6 THROWING WITHIN AND OUTSIDE FUNCTIONS

We have seen that we can throw an exception in the function that is caught outside the *function under consideration* but handled in the calling function. If this exception is not caught by the calling function, it may be caught by a function that has called this calling function. This is true for any level of hierarchy.

Suppose a function `Fun1` calls `Fun2`, which in turn calls `Fun3` and so on until `FunN`. If `FunN` throws an exception that is not caught in `FunN` itself, the control would transfer back to `FunN-1` and would look for the matching `catch` section there. If `FunN-1` does not have the `catch` for the case, it then may be caught by `FunN-2` if it has a matching case and so on.

It should be understood that this is not a normal function return. The control does not come back to the next statement after the function call, but just looks for a matching `catch`. The process would continue until it either gets the matching `catch` or exits `Fun1`. If a matching `catch` is available, the exception is said to be handled by that particular function having the `catch` block, and the function returns from there as a normal return.

As soon as a match is found in a specific function, even when the exception has passed up in the hierarchy, *that* function returns normally. All other functions through which the exception passes do not execute their code.

In the example discussed, if the matching `catch` is found at `Fun5`, it executes the code in the `catch` block in `Fun5` and returns normally to `Fun4` and executes the remaining statements of `Fun4`. There is no function return so far from `FunN` to `Fun5`, and hence, no remaining statements from those functions would be executed there. However, all the objects defined in those functions are systematically destroyed.

When an exception is thrown and not caught in the same function where it is thrown, it passes up in the hierarchy where the calling function has a chance to catch it.

In case the matching `catch` is not found until exiting `Fun1` and still the exception has not been handled (i.e., no exception handler has been found so far), the `terminate()` function would be called as usual. Program 8.2 is an example of a program in which an exception is called from a function. For simplicity, we look at a single layer of hierarchy, that is, `main()` is calling the function `ExGen()`, which is going to throw an exception. Here, the exception will be caught by the `main()` function.

PROGRAM 8.2 Throw using a function

```cpp
//FunctionThrow.cpp
#include <iostream>
#include <string>
using namespace std;

class MyException
{
private:
    int ExNumber;
    string ExMessage;
public:
    MyException(int ErrNo, string Description)
    {
        ExNumber = ErrNo;
        ExMessage = Description;
    }

    void ShowEx()
    {
        cout << "Error number is" << ExNumber << "\n";
        cout << ExMessage << "\n";
    }
};

// Function responsible for exception generation and throw
```

```
void ExGen()
{
    cout << "Inside the function \n";
    cout << "Inside try block\n";
    cout << "Assuming error and throwing exception now\n";
    MyException Error1(20, "Error testing");

    throw Error1;
    cout << "This  statement will not be executed";
}
void main()
{
    try
    {
        cout << "Inside main\n";
        ExGen();     // This would generate exception
        cout << "This will not be executed";
    }
    catch (MyException Except)
    {
        cout << "Inside main catch \n";
        Except.ShowEx();
    }
}
```

How the Program Works

There is very little difference between Program 8.1 and this one. Earlier, the exception generation and throw happened in main, whereas now they are a part of the ExGen() function. There is a matching catch in main rather than the function itself. When ExGen() throws an exception using

throw Error1;

it is not caught at ExGen(). It goes one level up to main to find the matching catch there. Fortunately, it gets one matching catch and executes it. The remaining statements of main will not be executed. Immediately after executing the catch block, main exits.

Catching an Exception by a Caller Function

This program can be modified a bit as shown in Program 8.3 to see how finding a match elsewhere changes the scenario.

PROGRAM 8.3 Catching up in the hierarchy

```
//CatchInHierarchy.cpp
#include <iostream>
#include <string>
using namespace std;

class MyException
{
private:
    int ExNumber;
    string ExMessage;
public:
    MyException(int ErrNo, string Description)
```

```
        {
            ExNumber = ErrNo;
            ExMessage = Description;
        }

        void ShowEx()
        {
            cout << "Error number is" << ExNumber << "\n";
            cout << ExMessage << "\n";
        }
};
/* Function generating exception as well as catching */
void ExGen()
{
    cout << "Inside the function \n";
    cout << "Inside try block\n";
    cout << "Assuming error and throwing exception now\n";

    MyException Error1(20, "Error testing");
    throw Error1;
    cout << "This  statement will not be executed";
}

// Exception is caught in this block
void TestGen()
{
    try
    {
        cout << "Inside TestGen\n";
        ExGen();     // This would generate exception
        cout << "This will not be printed";
    }

    /* When an exception is thrown, the remaining statements of that function will not be
    executed, as the control gets permanently transferred to the catch block */

    catch (MyException Except)
    {
        cout << "Inside main catch \n";
        Except.ShowEx();
    }
}

int main()
{
    TestGen();
    cout << "This statement would be printed\n";
    return 0;
}
```

Output
```
Inside main
Inside the function
Inside try block
Assuming error and throwing exception now
Inside main catch
Error number is 20
Error testing
This statement would be printed
```

> **Note**   It is by design that when an exception is thrown, the control gets permanently transferred to the `catch` block. Such behaviour looks very logical once we learn how real-world problems are solved. Take a case where a library designer develops a graphics library that is used by another user. Suppose the user sends a dimension to the graphics library and the dimensions are incorrect, then there is no point in executing the remaining statements and drawing that object further.

How the Program Works

Exceptions thrown   It should be noted that now the `TestGen()` function calls the `ExGen()` function. The exception thrown from `ExGen()` is caught in `TestGen()`, so it returns normally to `main`. Hence, the remaining single statement of `main` executes after the function call to `TestGen()` is over. It should also be noted that the remaining statements in `TestGen()` do not get executed.

Separation of reporting from handling   Though Programs 8.2 and 8.3 looks similar to Program 8.1, there is a small change. Instead of throwing and catching the exception in the same function, they are done separately. Although it seems to be a simple change, it is big considering the separation of the *error reporting* and *handling* parts. Throwing now happens in `ExGen()` and catching happens in `main` and `TestGen()` in Programs 8.2 and 8.3, respectively.

Inability of designer to provide appropriate messages   `ExGen()` can be used in various cases where exceptions are thrown. It is possible to write an appropriate error message in the `catch` statement for each such case in the program. Here, `ExGen()` is a very simple function and does almost nothing, but in real-life cases, it might do many actions to revert back to a stable state when a specific error occurs.

For example, assume that a globally available big array is present and that `ExGen()` is designed to allocate some memory in the array when the user asks for it. That portion of array may be used to store the information in the calling program. Understand that `ExGen()` is a common function for many objects and is used at different places by different objects for storing different types of objects. One may use `ExGen()` for storing `Employee` objects, another may use it to store the marks of students, and so on. Although the size of `ExGen()` array is big, it is not infinite and hence may run out of memory at some time. At that point, instead of providing space in the array, `ExGen()` throws an exception `NotEnoughMemory`.

Suppose `ExGen()` is used to allocate memory for the `employee` object in `main` where the exception `NotEnoughMemory` is caught, it is possible to display a message "Too many employee objects are created, cannot create any more", which is easily understandable. Suppose an error message is provided in the `ExGen()` itself, then it would be similar to "No space left in the array". `ExGen()` does not have any idea about the `employee` object, so it cannot be as precise as the `main()` function.

> **Note**   There are two reasons for `ExGen()` to have no knowledge about the `employee` array. The library designer has no idea about how that array will be used and which user will store what information in the array. Second, even when the user has an idea about the usage of the library, there is no method that can print a selective message for a specific usage. Take the case of using an aerospace design program and an architect using this library. When the out-of-dimension message is to be printed, what will the library designer prefer to print? In the given example, a user definitely prefers to have "Too many employee objects" rather than "No space left in the array".

Solution   Passing an exception is better in this case. The `ExGen()` function, instead of printing a message, passes the exception to the caller, which decides what to do with that exception, as it is definitely in a better position to print a more user-friendly message. In a way, the library designer passes that message to the user and the user prints an appropriate message. If the same ExGen() is used later for acquiring memory for the students enrolled in a course, an appropriate message may be displayed at the time of exception. So, this approach is more flexible as well.

Exception handling is a more structured mechanism than error handling. If the ExGen() function is provided with an error code, the description may not be obtained right from the function; it may need to be obtained from elsewhere. Moreover, it is known that the error codes are not standardized. It would be impossible for somebody else to use the ExGen() function without knowing the error code values and the meaning of each error code.

In both cases, exception handling is a more orderly and an acceptable form. However, it might bring down the efficiency and performance levels by a few notches. Refer to Section 8.15 to know how the performance of a program gets affected when exception handling is included.

8.6.1 Handling Exceptions

When a catch matches with what is thrown, it can match with any of the following:

1. An exact type
2. A type that is derived from the type used by the catch statement, so that if catch (base) is provided and throw derived is performed, it is caught.
3. A void pointer, which matches with any pointer. Thus, catch (void *) matches with any pointer thrown by the throw statement.

It is possible to write one try block inside another. The thrown exception, if not caught inside the try block, is passed to the outer try block. Suppose we have the following code

```
try
{
   try
   {
      MyException Something;
      throw Something;
   }
   catch (AnotherException AE)
   {
      Body of the catch block
   }
}
catch (MyException ME)
{
   // This is where Something is handled
}
```

Here, Something is not handled in the same try block; rather, it is handled in the outer try block. If it is not handled in the outer try block, it is processed similar to any other exception. It is passed to the calling function and to the calling function of the calling function and so on until it is either caught or reached out of the main when terminate() is called.

8.7 THROWING VARIABLES OTHER THAN OBJECTS

It is also possible to throw other variables such as integers, chars, and strings. They can also be caught in the same way as objects. However, it is advisable to use objects to help users with more elaborate and acceptable handling of errors. At times, the object should also have member functions to solve the problem and recover from the error if possible. Suppose our function needs a file to get some input from that file. If the file is not found, the function can throw an exception as an object. The object may have a member function, which tells the user that the file it needs is not available and asks for an alternate file if available, or if file is not available, it asks the user for permission to use old data available from older fetches. It is important to note that using those member functions the user may provide generic error handling logic irrespective of the situation in which the error has occurred.

Throwing variables instead of objects is similar to the C-type error handling mechanism where we return error codes. It is similar to providing the conventional solution at a higher cost.

In Section 8.8, we will look at a few examples that show how to throw variables other than objects and catch them.

8.8 USING MULTIPLE catch

It is possible to use more than one catch section for a single try block. First, matching the catch block will get executed when an expression is thrown. If no matching catch block is found, the exception is passed one layer up in the block hierarchy. This has already been explained using Program 8.3.

The following program demonstrates the following:

1. There are multiple try blocks, one in the function and one in main as shown.
2. Options are provided for throwing three items, two of them being built-in data types, int and char, and the third an object of type MyException.
3. Two type of exceptions are caught in the function, in which case, the function call terminates in the usual way and the execution resumes in the main with a statement appearing immediately after the function call. Once an exception is caught, it would not be caught at the higher layers; the catch sections of main for char and int are, thus, not executed in this case.
4. The third type of exception, MyException, cannot be caught by the catch statements of the function (which can only handle int and char). Therefore, it goes up in the hierarchy and is caught by a catch statement in the main. In this case, the function call does not terminate properly and the statement after the function call is not executed. The control directly passes to the catch section of main.
5. The fourth type of exception is a string, for which there is no corresponding catch statement either in the function or the main. In such a case, a built-in function terminate() is called. It terminates the program with an indication of abnormal termination.
6. There is one throw statement in the main, which would be caught by the catch of the main(). If catch (int) in the main is removed, it will result in the same error that was obtained while sending a string exception. When an exception is thrown, if the corresponding catch is not found in the current context, it would go up in the hierarchy, and not down. So, in this case, it does not execute the catch of ExGen() if not found in the main.

7. There are two types of `catch` statements, namely, `catch (data type)` and `catch (data type value)`, that is, `catch (int)` in `main` and `catch (int IntEx)` in the function. When one is interested only in identifying the type of exception, one can use the `catch (data type)` syntax; if the actual exception value is need, the `catch (data type value)` format must be used. The `IntEx` value is used for printing in the function, while such printing is not required in the `main`.

```cpp
//MultipleCatch.cpp
#include <iostream>
#include <string>
using namespace std;

class MyException
{
private:
   int ExNumber;
   string ExMessage;
public:
   MyException(int ErrNo, string Description)
   {
      ExNumber = ErrNo;
      ExMessage = Description;
   }
   void ShowEx()
   {
      cout << "Error number is" << ExNumber << "\n";
      cout << ExMessage << "\n";
   }
};

void ExGen()
{
   cout << "Inside the function \n";
   try
   {
      cout << "Inside try block\n";
      MyException Error1(20, "Error testing");
      cout << "Press 1 for int, 2 for char, 3 for MyException, and 4 for string";
      int reply;
      cin >> reply;
      cout << "Assuming error and throwing exception now\n";
      switch(reply)
      {
         case 1:
           throw 10;
         case 2:
           throw 'a';
         case 3:
```

```
                    throw Error1;
                case 4:
                    throw "There is nobody to catch this";
            }
            cout << "This statement will not be executed";
        }
    catch (int IntEx)
    {
        cout << "Integer exception" << IntEx
        << "is caught in the function \n";
    }
    catch (char CharEx)
    {
        cout << "Character exception" << CharEx
        << "is caught in the function \n";
    }
}
void main()
{
    try
    {
        cout << "Inside main\n";
        ExGen();          // It generates exception
        cout << "This will not be executed if the exception is
        not caught in the function\n";
        throw 10;
    }
    catch (int)
    {
        cout << "An integer is caught in main";
    }
    catch (char)
    {
        cout << "A char is caught in main";
    }
    catch (MyException Except)
    {
        cout << "Inside main catch \n";
        Except.ShowEx();
    }
}
```

Output (Edited)
(Two different cases with integer and MyException objects show how the program executes
when an exception is handled inside and outside the function)
Inside main

```
Inside the function
Inside try block
Press 1 for int, 2 for char, 3 for MyException, and 4 for string
1
Assuming error and throwing exception now
Integer exception10 is caught in the function
This will not be executed if the exception is not caught in the function
An integer is caught in main
Inside main
Inside the function
Inside try block
Press 1 for int 2 for char, 3 for MyException, and 4 for string
3
Assuming error and throwing exception now
Inside main catch
Error number is 20
Error testing
```

8.9 CATCH ALL

> catch (...) is used to catch any exception. Here, the three dots play the role of a wild card.

It is possible to catch all types of exceptions in a single catch section by using catch (...) (three dots as an argument).

Consider Program 8.4 which is reworked from the previous one. It has catch (...) (which is commonly known as the *catch all* statement) in the function. Now, whatever is thrown would be caught by that single statement and would not be passed up the hierarchy.

PROGRAM 8.4   Catching all exceptions in a single catch

```cpp
//CatchAll.cpp
#include <iostream>
#include <string>
using namespace std;
class MyException
{
private:
    int ExNumber;
    string ExMessage;
public:
    MyException(int ErrNo, string Description)
    {
        ExNumber = ErrNo;
        ExMessage = Description;
    }

    void ShowEx()
    {
        cout << "Error number is" << ExNumber << "\n";
        cout << ExMessage << "\n";
    }
};
```

```
void ExGen()
{
    cout << "Inside the function \n";
    try
    {
        cout << "Inside try block\n";
        MyException Error1(20, "Error testing");
        cout << "Press 1 for int, 2 for char, 3 for MyException, and 4 for string";

        int reply;
        cin >> reply;
        cout << "Assuming error and throwing exception now\n";
        switch(reply)
        {
            case 1:
                throw 10;
            case 2:
                throw 'a';
            case 3:
                throw Error1;
            case 4:
                throw "Now there is catch all to catch this";
        }

        cout << "This statement will not be executed";
    }

    // Catch-all block
    catch (...)
    {
        cout << "Anything thrown is caught here in the function \n";
    }
}

void main()
{
    try
    {
        cout << "Inside main\n";
        ExGen();
        /* Generates exception and catches itself */
        cout << "This will always be executed now because the exception is always caught in
        the function \n";
    }

    catch (MyException Except)
    {
        cout << "Inside main catch \n";
        Except.ShowEx();
    }
}
```

How the Program Works

Instead of writing just one `catch`, it is possible to provide all the `catch` statements one is interested in and then provide a catch all at the end similar to the following:

```
catch (int IntEx)
{
    cout << "Integer exception" << IntEx << "is caught \n";
```

```
}
catch (char CharEx)
{
    cout << "Character exception" << CharEx << "is caught \n";
}
catch (...)
{
    cout << "Anything thrown is caught here \n";
}
```

This is a better design because in this case it is possible to take care of exceptions of one's interest in the usual manner. If anything other than what is expected is thrown, it can be taken care of as well by the catch all block. The catch all section is very useful in debugging and is as useful as a default statement in switch.

8.10 RESTRICTING EXCEPTIONS FROM FUNCTIONS: EXCEPTION SPECIFICATION

It is possible to specify what kind of exceptions can be thrown from the functions using a specific syntax. The function definition header can be appended with the keyword throw and the possible types of expressions to be thrown in the parenthesis. It is known as *exception specification*. In the following example, the function ExGen() is allowed to throw only int and char exceptions.

```
void ExGen() throw(int, char)
```

When ExGen() tries to throw some exception other than that allowed in exception specification, that is, other than int and char (or a function called by ExGen() throws such an exception and not catching it thereby passing it up to ExGen()), then a built-in function named as unexpected() is called, which in turn terminates the program.

One may wonder what the need for exception specification is. When a third-party function is used, the source code may not be available but the prototype may be available. The programmer can decide to write corresponding catch statements depending on those types that are possible to be thrown from that function. In a way, exception specification works similar to the possible errors that can occur during the use of that specific function and gives one a chance to decide what action one would like to provide in response to such errors.

Look at the following function. It would generate an error if the user selects either 3 or 4.

```
void ExGen() throw(int, char)
{
                cout << "Inside the function \n";
                cout << "Inside try block\n";
                MyException Error1(20, "Error testing");
                cout << "Press 1 for int, 2 for char, 3 for MyException, and 4 for
         string";
            int reply;
            cin >> reply;
            cout << "Assuming error and throwing exception now \n";
            switch(reply)
```

Exception specification specifies what a function can throw. Looking at exception specification, a user decides to provide corresponding catch statements.

When a function tries to throw an exception that is not allowed by the exception specification, a function named unexpected() is called, which in turn calls abort(). The users can change thebehaviour by specifying their own functions instead of unexpected().

```
{
    case 1:
        throw 10;
    case 2:
        throw 'a';
    case 3:
        throw Error1;      // This should not work
    case 4:
        throw "There is nobody to catch this";
        // This too should not work
    }
    cout << "This  statement will not be executed";
}
```

The statement `void ExGen() throw(int, char)` states that out of all the exceptions thrown from the function, only `char` and `int` are allowed to pass through. Here, the list `throw(int, char)` is known as *exception specification*.

> **Note** It is an important job of a library writer to make sure that no exceptions other than what is mentioned in the exception specification is thrown from a function. If such an exception is thrown, the program terminates. One must also ensure before using any library that proper exception specifications are provided.

Other exceptions are not allowed to be thrown outside the function. If they are thrown, they are not acceptable. In case the user selects the choice as 3 or 4, the exception thrown is either of type `MyException` or `string`, neither of which is specified in the exception specification. The built-in function `unexpected()` is called, which in turn calls `terminate()` to abort the program. It should be noted that the following syntax

```
<return type> <function name>(<argument List>)
throw(<only exceptions allowed to be thrown>)
```

will prevent exceptions to be thrown out of the function. It does not provide any restriction on throwing and catching an exception inside the function. Look at the following code. Here, `MyException` is caught inside the function itself, so it will not create any problem. However, the string or user-defined exception will still create a problem.

```
void ExGen() throw(int, char)
{
    cout << "Inside the function \n";
    cout << "Inside try block\n";
    MyException Error1(20, "Error testing");
    cout << "Press 1 for int, 2 for char, 3 for MyException, and 4 for string";
    int reply;
    cin >> reply;
    cout << "Assuming error and throwing exception now\n";
    switch(reply)
    {
        case 1:
                throw 10;
```

```
        case 2:
                throw 'a';
        case 3:
                throw Error1; // This will work
        case 4:
                throw "There is nobody to catch this";
                /* However, this still will not work */
    }
    cout << "This  statement will not be executed";
}
catch(MyException)
{
    // Body of catch block
}
```

Consider the following program, which uses exception specification.

```cpp
//ExSpec.cpp
#include <iostream>
#include <string>
using namespace std;
class MyException
{
private:
    int ExNumber;
    string ExMessage;
public:
    MyException(int ErrNo, string Description)
    {
        ExNumber = ErrNo;
        ExMessage = Description;
    }
    void ShowEx()
    {
        cout << "Error number is" << ExNumber << "\n";
        cout << ExMessage << "\n";
    }
};
void ExGen() throw(int, char)
{
    cout << "Inside the function \n";
    try
    {
        cout << "Inside try block\n";
        MyException Error1(20, "Error testing");
        cout << "Press 1 for int, 2 for char, 3 for MyException, and 4 for string \n";
```

```
        int reply;
        cin >> reply;
        cout << "Assuming error and throwing exception now\n";
        switch(reply)
        {
                case 1:
                        throw 10;
                case 2:
                        throw 'a';
                case 3:
                        throw Error1;
                case 4:
                        throw "There is nobody to catch this \n";
        }
        cout << "This statement will not be executed \n";
    }
    catch (int IntEx)
    {
        cout << "Integer exception" << IntEx << "is caught in the function \n";
    }
    catch (char CharEx)
    {
        cout << "Character exception" << CharEx << "is caught in the function \n";
    }
}
int main()
{
    try
    {
        cout << "Inside main\n";
        ExGen();          // Generates exception
        cout << "This will not be executed if exception is not caught in the function \n";
        throw 20;
    }
    catch (int)
    {
        cout << "An integer is caught in main \n";
    }
    catch (char)
    {
        cout << "A char is caught in main \n";
    }
    catch (MyException Except)
    {
        cout << "Inside main catch \n";
```

```
        Except.ShowEx();
    }
    return 0;
}
```

Output (Edited)
```
Inside main
Inside the function
Inside try block
Press 1 for int, 2 for char, 3 for MyException, and 4 for string
3  // Input is 3
Assuming error and throwing exception now
Inside main catch
Error number is 20
Error testing

Inside main
Inside the function
Inside try block

Press 1 for int, 2 for char, 3 for MyException, and 4 for string
1  // Input is 1

Assuming error and throwing exception now
Integer exception10 is caught in the function
This will not be executed if exception is not caught in the function
An integer is caught in main
```

throw() as Exception Specification

It is also possible to write throw() as an exception specification. This will not let any exception to be thrown from that function. If the function throws an exception, the program would be aborted. Thus, if void ExGen() throw() is written, that is, empty braces to follow the throw, then the function is not allowed to throw any exception. Consider the following program.

```
//ExceptionSpecification.cpp
#include <exception>
#include <iostream>
using namespace std;
#include <string>
class MyException
{
private:
    int ExNumber;
    string ExMessage;
public:
    MyException(int ErrNo, string Description)
    {
        ExNumber = ErrNo;
        ExMessage = Description;
    }
```

```
      void ShowEx()
      {
         cout << "Error number is" << ExNumber << "\n";
         cout << ExMessage << "\n";
      }
};
void ExGen() throw()
{
   cout << "Inside the function \n";
   try
   {
      cout << "Inside try block\n";
      MyException Error1(20, "Error testing");
       throw Error1;
   }
   catch (int)
   {
      cout << "This  statement will not be executed";
   }
}
int main()
{
   try
   {
     cout << "Inside main\n";
     ExGen();         // This would generate exception
     cout << "This will not be executed if exception is not caught in the function \n";
     throw 10;
   }
   catch (int)
   {
     cout << "An integer is caught in main \n";
   }
   catch (char)
   {
     cout <<  "A char is caught in main \n";
   }
   catch(...)
   {
     if(uncaught exception())
     {
             cout << "There is an uncaught exception \n";
     }
     cout << "Come back to main \n";
     }
   return 0;
```

```
}
Output
Inside main
Inside the function
Inside try block
Aborted
```

As the function is specified not to throw any exception, when it tries to throw one, the program is aborted.

It should be noted that the exception specification is used for throwing *outside the function*. It does not have any effect on exceptions thrown inside the function or thrown from any other function called from the current function and caught in the current function.

8.11 RETHROWING EXCEPTIONS

Exceptions can be caught in the same function where the try block has been defined or in the calling function up in the hierarchy. This is actually true with even higher layers. Suppose an exception is thrown from a function N, which is called from the function N-1, which is in turn called from the function N-2, and so on until the function 1. The exception can be caught by function N; if it is not caught there, it can be caught in function N-1; if not, then in function N-2; and so on until function 1.

If we want to catch the exception in function N and also want to pass it on to higher layers, it is achieved by rethrowing an exception *after catching it.*

The use of such rethrowing facility can be explained with an example. Suppose we are in the middle of a function. The function has two arguments and one of the arguments that we are going to use in the denominator of an expression is found to be zero. Then, we may need to suspend the execution, return all the resources allocated, close the files, and do all other types of winding up before passing it to the calling function. We also need to indicate to the calling function that the operation intended is not completed properly.

> When a function wants to take some action when the error occurs and also inform the calling function about the errors, rethrowing is useful.

In such cases, we have to catch the exception in the same function to do the winding up. We also need to make the calling function aware of the mishaps. If we just catch the exception in the function itself, the calling function will get the normal return. It will not know whether the function had performed the task assigned or not. If we do not catch the exception here in the function, it would ultimately be passed to the calling function and the function will then realize that something wrong has happened. In that case, the winding-up process will not be possible. However, we cannot eliminate the winding-up process. To solve this problem, we need to *rethrow* the exception. Let us see how to do it using an example. The syntax for rethrowing is very simple. We need to write a simple throw after the last line of the catch block. Consider the following program.

> A catch block can include throw statements. In that case, the caught expression is again thrown to the upper layer in the hierarchy of calls.

```
//ReThrow.cpp
#include <iostream>
#include <string>
using namespace std;

class MyException
```

```
{
private:
    int ExNumber;
    string ExMessage;
public:
    MyException(int ErrNo, string Description)
    {
        ExNumber = ErrNo;
        ExMessage = Description;
    }
    void ShowEx()
    {
        cout << "Error number is" << ExNumber << "\n";
        cout << ExMessage << "\n";
    }
};
void ExGen()
{
    cout << "Inside the function \n";
    try
    {
        cout << "Inside try block\n";
        MyException Error1(20, "Error testing");
        cout << "Press 1 for int, 2 for char, 3 for MyException, and 4 for string \n";
            int reply;
            cin >> reply;
            cout << "Assuming error and throwing exception now \n";

            switch(reply)
            {
                case 1:
                    throw 10;
                case 2:
                    throw 'a';
                case 3:
                    throw Error1;
                case 4:
                    throw "There is nobody to catch this  \n";
                }
                cout << "This  statement will not be executed \n";
    }
    catch (int IntEx)
    {
        cout << "Integer exception" << IntEx << "is caught in the function \n";
        throw;   // Rethrowing
```

```
    }
    catch (char CharEx)
    {
       cout << "Character exception" << CharEx << "is caught in the function \n";
       throw;    // Rethrowing
    }
}
void main()
{
    try
    {
       cout << "Inside main \n";
       ExGen();          // This would generate exception
       cout << "This will not be executed if exception is not caught in the function \n";
       throw 10;
    }
    catch (int)
    {
       cout << "An integer is caught in main \n";
    }
    catch (char)
    {
       cout << "A char is caught in main \n";
    }
    catch (MyException Except)
    {
       cout << "Inside main catch \n";
       Except.ShowEx();
    }
}
Output
Inside main
Inside the function
Inside try block
Press 1 for int, 2 for char, 3 for MyException, and 4 for string
2
Assuming error and throwing exception now
Character exception a is caught in the function
A char is caught in main
```

Note that the character expression is caught in the function and then rethrown using throw in the catch block. The same exception then is caught again in the main, so it displays message related to it there. In such a case, if the exception is not caught up in the hierarchy, a built-in function terminate() is called, which terminates the program with an indication for abnormal termination.

8.12 `terminate()` AND `unexpected()` FUNCTIONS

As mentioned earlier, `terminate()` is the function that calls `abort()` to exit the program in the event of run-time error related to exceptions. The indirection through `terminate()` function is provided because the user can define his/her own `terminate()` function instead of the built-in `terminate()`, which just calls `abort()` and does nothing else. This way the user may be able to close all open files and deallocate resources before quitting the program. Let us see how this is done using the following program.

```cpp
//SetTerminate.cpp
#include <exception>
#include <iostream>
#include <string>
using namespace std;
class MyException
{
private:
    int ExNumber;
    string ExMessage;
public:
    MyException(int ErrNo, string Description)
    {
        ExNumber = ErrNo;
        ExMessage = Description;
    }
    void ShowEx()
    {
        cout << "Error number is" << ExNumber << "\n";
        cout << ExMessage << "\n";
    }
};
void ExGen()
{
    cout << "Inside the function \n";
    cout << "Inside try block \n";
    cout << "Assuming error and throwing exception now.\n";
    MyException Error1(20, "Error testing");
    throw Error1;
    cout << "This  statement will not be executed";
}
void MyTerminate()
{
    cout << "This is my terminate function";
    /* The cleanup code comes here;, it closes all open files,
    closes open connections, and runs destructors if need be */
    exit(-1);
```

```
   }
void main()
{
   void MyTerminate();
   set_terminate(MyTerminate);
   /* Instead of system's terminate, MyTerminate is called */
   cout << "Inside main\n";
   ExGen();
   // This would generate an exception for which no catch is available
   cout << "This will not be executed";
}
```

We now have our own terminate() function instead of the default terminate() in this case. We can do all the cleaning up here. We can close files, deallocate dynamic memory, close connections if working in the client-server environment so that the connected party becomes aware of our departure, etc.

> **Note** We can have our own terminate() function instead of the default terminate(), which just calls abort(). The set_terminate() function tells the system that there is a new terminate() function specified by the user.

Similarly, for functions with exception specifications, if a function throws an exception that is not allowed, a function unexpected() is called, which in turn calls abort(). It is possible to use set_unexpected() in a similar manner to terminate() to provide our own function in such a case. Consider the following program. The set_unexpected() function is used to tell the system that there is a new unexpected() function specified by the user.

```
//SetUnexpected.cpp
#include <exception>
#include <iostream>
#include <string>
using namespace std;
class MyException
{
private:
   int ExNumber;
   string ExMessage;
public:
   MyException(int ErrNo, string Description)
   {
      ExNumber = ErrNo;
      ExMessage = Description;
   }
   void ShowEx()
   {
      cout << "Error number is" << ExNumber << "\n";
      cout << ExMessage << "\n";
```

```
    }
};
void ExGen() throw()
{
    cout << "Inside the function \n";
    cout << "Inside try block \n";
    cout << "Assuming error and throwing exception now \n";
    MyException Error1(20, "Error testing");
    throw Error1;
    cout << "This statement will not be executed";
}
void MyUnExpected()
{
    cout <<  "This is my unexpected function \n";
    /* The cleanup code comes here; it closes all open files, closes open connections,
    and runs destructors if needed */
    exit(-1);
}
int main()
{
    try
    {
        void MyUnExpected();
        set_unexpected(MyUnExpected);
        cout << "Inside main\n";
        ExGen();
        // This would generate an exception for which no catch is available
        cout << "This will not be executed \n";
    }
    catch(...)
    {
        cout << "Caught it!";
    }
    return 0;
}
```

Output

```
Inside main
Inside the function
Inside try block
Assuming error and throwing exception now
This is my unexpected function
```

The function `ExGen()` has exception specification as `throw()`. If `ExGen()` throws some exception, the `unexpected()` function would be called and the output of this function is "`This is my unexpected function`". In the given example, we have written our own function for unexpected circumstances. We have specified to use that function instead of the built-in unexpected() using the statement

```
set_unexpected(MyUnExpected);
```

As a result, the user-defined MyUnExpected() function is called.

8.13 uncaught_exception() FUNCTION

When an exception is thrown, it automatically invokes stack unwinding process. In this process, all the objects prior to the throw statement to the beginning of the try block are destroyed in the reverse order of their creation. It is possible that some of the objects that are being destroyed have destructors and that the destructor function might also throw an exception.

If at least one of the objects contains such a destructor, we have a situation where the first exception is not completely handled, and the second one is being thrown. It is not possible in C++ to handle two exceptions simultaneously. The normal outcome of such a situation is a call to abort(), which terminates the program. In such situations, a function from built-in exception class, uncaught_exception(), comes handy. It returns true when an exception is thrown. If the destructor checks and finds that an exception has already been thrown when the destructor is called, it will not throw a new one. The algorithm of the function would be as follows:

```
if(uncaught_exception())
{
    Do not call the function that might throw an exception
}
else
{
    Follow the natural sequence of the destructor algorithm
}
```

Uncaught_exception is a handy way of finding out unhandled exceptions.

Program 8.5 demonstrates the use of the uncaught_exception() function. When an exception is thrown, the destructors of all the objects defined in the try block are called one by one. Then, the exception is handled and now it is said to be caught. If we check for the uncaught exception now, it is found to be caught.

PROGRAM 8.5 Using uncaught_exception to find out unhandled exceptions

```cpp
//UncaughtException.cpp
#include <exception>
#include <iostream>
using namespace  std;

class TestClass
{
    char *ptrMessage;
public:
    TestClass(char Message[], int LengthOfMessage)
    {
        ptrMessage = new char [LengthOfMessage + 1];
        for(int i = 0; i < LengthOfMessage; i++)
        {
            ptrMessage[i] = Message[i];
        }
        ptrMessage[LengthOfMessage] = 0;  // Null
```

```
    }
    friend ostream & operator <<(ostream & TempOut, TestClass & TempData);

    // To destroy the objects defined in the try block

    ~TestClass()
    {
        if(uncaught_exception() == true)
        {
            cout << "There is an uncaught exception in process when";
            cout << *this;
            delete [] ptrMessage;
        }
        else
        {
            cout << "There is no uncaught exception in process when";
            cout << *this;
        }
    }
};
ostream & operator <<(ostream & TempOut, TestClass & TempData)
{
    TempOut << TempData.ptrMessage;
    return TempOut;
}

void ExGen()
{
    char FirstMessage[] = "message is not a part of the try block \n";
    char SecondMessage[] = "message is within the try block \n";
    TestClass TestObject1(FirstMessage, strlen(FirstMessage));
    /* This object is created outside the try block */

    try
    {
        /* The following object is created within the try block*/
        TestClass TestObject2(SecondMessage, strlen(SecondMessage));
        cout << "Inside the function \n";
        cout << "Inside try block\n";
        int dummy = 10;

        /* When the following exception is thrown, the destructor for
        TestObject would be called, which finds that the exception is not yet caught */

        throw dummy;
    }

    catch (int)
    {
        cout << "Caught dummy\n";
    }
}

/* Now the destructor for TestObject1 would be called, which finds that the exception has
already been caught */

int main()
{
    ExGen();
    return 0;
}
```

```
Output
Inside the function
Inside try block
There is an uncaught exception in process when message is within the try block
Caught dummy
There is no uncaught exception in process when message is not a part of the try block
```

How the Program Works

This program contains two different objects of TestClass. One object is initialized before the try block starts and the other is initialized within the try block. When the exception is thrown by the statement

```
throw dummy;
```

the objects defined within the try block have to be destroyed (the stack rewinding process), and so, their destructors are called in the reverse order of their initialization. We have only one object TestObject2 defined within the try block, so its destructor is called. At this point, the exception handling is in process, so the uncaught_exception() function returns true. When the exception is handled by the catch block, it would display "Caught dummy" and then the ExGen() function is over. The destructor for TestObject1 is called next, which now goes out of scope. In this case, the uncaught_exception() would yield false, because now the exception has been handled and no more exception is in process.

Note that *this is used as a string to be printed in the destructor. It is a handy way of finding out which object is going out of scope. The TestClass can be easily converted to a string class with more member functions. We have also seen how destructors are used in such classes. A destructor is needed here because we use dynamic constructor to get the memory, and it is our job then to return that memory when the object goes out of scope.

8.14 EXCEPTION HANDLERS AND DEBUGGERS

Some systems such as VC++ have a debugger in place. Sometimes the roles of a debugger and the exception handling system clash and overlap. When an error occurs, the debugger needs all the objects to indicate the user about the problem and the *status of all those objects at that point of time.*

On the other hand, the exception handling system has to delete those objects because of the compulsion to call the destructors. This system need not be aware of the place where the error has occurred and when the exception was thrown. However, the debugger must be aware of such details and help the user out in such circumstances.

Due to mutually conflicting requirements, the C++ compilers that provide debuggers may not provide all the facilities of exception handling. One must refer to the documentation available with the respective compiler for such details.

8.15 DRAWBACKS OF EXCEPTION HANDLING

Uncertain termination is a major drawback of the exception handling mechanism. When library functions are used and the user is unaware of some specific exception, the program would crash if that exception is thrown. Whenever third-party libraries are being used, there is the danger of a program crash. If it cannot be afforded, one cannot use those libraries.

Another disadvantage of exception handling is the overhead. With exception handling, both the executable program code size and the execution time would increase substantially. Simpler

C-type mechanisms would be better in cases where such performance overhead outweighs the advantage gained or when performance is the first priority. Consider writing a compiler, a database management system, or a network controlling program. Here, the task must be finished as quickly as possible. Exception handling is not advised in such cases. Similarly, mobile device programmers do not use exception handling while coding their programs.

Programmers, at times, tend to use exception handler for other purposes where other looping structures can also be used. This is not a good use of this heavy tool. Use of exception handler for other purposes must be avoided.

> **Note** Exception handling is a heavy duty job and is not always an ideal replacement of the simpler conventional methods for handling errors. Exception handling must be confined to standardized message passing between a library designer and user, especially in large projects where it makes sense.

Exception handler is a tool for communicating about anomalies between two different components of the program developed by two different individuals. This is not needed for normal error checking in a program. Hence, normal error checking methods should not be replaced if the user does not gain anything by providing exception handling. When a library is being developed for a large project, one may need to use it. It is important to understand that the library functions that throw exceptions must be standardized. All the users must be aware of the exceptions thrown by the functions used by them. If this is not possible, the exception handling approach will increase and not decrease the problems.

8.16 EXCEPTION CLASS

There are some system-defined exceptions. We already have seen that the operator `new` throws the `bad_alloc` exception when memory cannot be allocated. Other such exceptions are `bad_cast` for `dynamic_cast` when the casting is not acceptable and `bad_typeid` for `typeid` that is not acceptable. We will be learning about using `dynamic_cast` and `typeid` when we study Run-Time Type Information (RTTI) in Chapter 11. All such exceptions are objects derived from the built-in `class exception`.

■ RECAPITULATION ■

- The exception handling mechanism is meant for handling error-like situations.
- The traditional error handling techniques are not sufficient to handle cases in a standard, well-defined way.
- Exception handling is an attempt to manage anomalies between library writers and users.
- The exception handling techniques are able to handle the problem of destroying objects.
- The exception handling mechanism has three keywords.
- The area of the program where an exception is possible to be thrown is written in the `try` block. The `catch` block contains the code to handle the exception.
- We can have multiple `catch` blocks for a single `try` block.
- The exception is thrown using a `throw` statement, which can throw an object or a built-in type.
- The exception handling approach handles exceptions at run-time and is not efficient. It is time consuming to find a proper handler for a given throw. It might require recursive moves from a block inside to a block outside until a proper handler is found.
- If the proper handler is found, the exception handling mechanism will automatically undo whatever is done before, that is, it will call destructors for all the objects defined earlier until the beginning of the `try` block.
- If the proper handler is not found, the exception handling mechanism calls `terminate()`, which in turn calls `abort()`.

- It is possible to have our own `terminate()` function using `set_terminate()`.
- Exception specifications indicate to the user the function that is allowed to throw outside.
- If the function violates the exception specification, the `unexpected()` function is called, which in turn calls the `abort()`.
- We can also have our own `unexpected()` functions.
- If we want the exception to be handled in the local block and also want the same exception to pass up in the hierarchy, we can rethrow that exception.

- It is possible to check if the exception is already thrown when we are about to throw using `uncaught_exception()` function.
- Exception handling adds to run-time overhead and demands a different style of programming than conventional programming.
- It is not the tool to replace normal error handling. If we can use normal error handling to solve our problem satisfactorily, we should not go for exception handling.

■ KEYWORDS ■

Catch all   The expression `catch (...)` is known as catch all.

Exception   This is an error-like situation and is actually a subset of error. It is difficult to decide when an error becomes an exception.

Exception handler   The `catch` block that is executed when a specific exception is thrown is known as the exception handler.

Exception handling   This refers to the mechanism provided by C++ to handle an exception when it occurs.

Exception specification   This is a list contained within the () braces after the function header and the keyword `throw`. The contents of the list are the only valid type of exceptions that can be thrown from that function.

Polymorphic object   This is the object of a class that is inherited and accessed by the pointer to the base class from which it is inherited.

Rethrowing   The exception, once handled by a handler, can be rethrown to a higher block. This process is known as rethrowing.

terminate()   This is the function to call when the exception handling mechanism does not get any proper handler for a thrown exception.

uncaught_exception()   This is the function to call when we want to check before throwing any exception if some other exception is already on.

unexpected()   This is the function to call when the exception handling mechanism encounters an exception not allowed from exception specification.

■ EXERCISES ■

Multiple Choice Questions

1. The statement to generate an exception is _____.
   - (a) `try`
   - (b) `catch`
   - (c) `throw`
   - (d) None of the above
2. For throwing an exception, _____ statement is used.
   - (a) `try`
   - (b) `throw`
   - (c) `catch`
   - (d) `throwing`
3. It is possible to throw _____.
   - (a) built-in types
   - (b) user-defined types
   - (c) Both
   - (d) None

4. Even when no matching of the `catch` block is found, control would _____.
   - (a) come back to the try block
   - (b) not come back to the try block
   - (c) come back to the throw block
   - (d) come back to the catch block
5. When we are interested in finding the type of exception thrown, we use _____.
   - (a) `catch (...)`
   - (b) `catch (<data type> variable name)`
   - (c) `catch (<data type>)`
   - (d) None
6. Which of the following is the correct syntax to throw an exception?
   - (a) `throw error1;`
   - (b) `error1 throw;`

(c) `throw int error1;`

(d) `int error1 throw;`

7. The section where the exception is handled is called _____.

(a) `try`

(b) `throw`

(c) `catch`

(d) `throws`

8. Which function can be used to have our own unexpected() function instead of the built-in unexpected() function?

(a) `set_unexpected`

(b) `user_unexpected`

(c) `new_unexpected`

(d) It is not possible to do so

9. The code that we want to monitor for exceptions is kept in the _____ block.

(a) `try`

(b) `throw`

(c) `catch`

(d) `throws`

10. Which of the following is the correct syntax for a catch block?

(a) `catch (int);`

(b) `catch (int intEx);`

(c) Both

(d) None

Conceptual Exercises

1. What are the different mechanisms of traditional error handling? What is the problem with them?

2. What is the need for a communication mechanism between the library designer and the library user? How does exception handling mechanism help?

3. What is the problem of destroying objects? How can exception handling help here?

4. What is the role of each of the components of the exception handling mechanism?

5. What is the role of the `terminate()` function in exception handling? Why does the exception handling mechanism not call `abort()` directly?

6. What is the difference between throwing exceptions inside and outside the function?

7. What is the importance of throwing objects rather than built-in type values?

8. When do we need multiple `catch` blocks for a single `try` block? Give an example.

9. What is the importance of catch all (`catch (...)`)?

10. What are exception specifications? In which cases are they needed?

11. What is rethrow? What is its use?

12. What is the `set_terminate()` function? Why is it needed?

13. What is the `unexpected()` function? Give an example to explain the need of it.

14. What is `uncaught_exception()` function and why do we need it?

15. What are the disadvantages of the exception handling mechanism?

Practical Exercises

1. Define the `Time` class described in Chapter 7. Provide checking for time and throw exception when an invalid time is input, either from the constructor or the user.

2. Define a `stack` class. The class should throw an exception when the stack underflow and overflow take place.

3. Use the `Time` class to provide an overloaded '–'. Here the time query is also to be recorded in a file. Use C text file to store the query. If a calling function provides expression `Time1 - Time2`, then operator `-()` function should throw an exception if `Time2` is a later time than `Time1`. Before throwing the exception, though, the operator '–' function should close the file.

4. Define a class `TheException`, which contains member functions for displaying messages regarding stack underflow and overflow. When overflow occurs, it asks for increasing the stack size. If the user says yes, it should respond by increasing the stack size. Use dynamically allocated array to implement stack.

5. Using `Time` class, throw an exception when invalid time is input. Write `set_terminate()` to provide your own terminate function, which takes care of this problem.

6. Use the `stack` class of Problem 2. Provide exception specification as `throw()` to push function and throw an exception when stack is overflow. Use `set_unexpected()` to set your own unexpected function to take care of this situation.

7. Write a normal `stack` class and also a `stack` class with exception handling and use them in two different programs. Use the classes a number of times in the respective programs. (You may write a loop, which creates and destroys the class). Compare the efficiency of both the programs when

(a) exceptions are thrown

(b) exceptions are not thrown

In addition check the run-time as well as the resultant code size.

Chapter 9

Inheritance

Learning Objectives

- Introduction to inheritance
- Implementation of inheritance in C++ object model
- Access specifiers and their use in inheritance
- Access declaration
- Multiple inheritance and their limitations
- Virtual base class
- Abstract classes
- Role of constructors and destructors in inheritance
- Advantages of memberwise initialization list (MIL)
- Exception handling during inheritance
- Composite and inherited objects

Many real-world cases fall under the category of multiple inheritance. Modelling such hierarchy becomes simple in C++ because the feature comes inbuilt with the program.

Object-based approach is more efficient than object-oriented approach. Hence, C++ applications generally choose the object-based approach when the stress is more on efficiency.

9.1 INTRODUCTION

Inheritance is an important feature of object-oriented programming. It is a mechanism to create a new class from an already defined class. The new class contains all the attributes of the old class in addition to some of its own attributes. In addition, it can also override some of the features of the old class.

Inheritance allows us to draw the functionalities of an already existing class and modify it to suit our requirement. There is no need to start from scratch. Another advantage is that a class once defined can be used multiple times by other applications after being inherited into a class that suits that application. In simple terms, inheritance allows *reusability*.

Proper use of inheritance helps in getting better and robust solutions quickly. For example, if one designs a class that helps to create and process windows on the screen, then the properties of the designed class can be extended to other applications that provide windows-based user interface. All such applications can inherit the designed class into a new class. The generic class may contain the caption of the window, specific borders, corners, size, look, and feel, and maybe minimize, maximize, and close buttons as well. The application may or may not need all these functionalities, or it may need some additional functionalities than what is provided in the generic class. The inheritance approach is better in this case because one has to concentrate only on the additional part and there is no need to start from scratch. It is more robust because the class one inherits from has already been used by others before, and bugs, if any, have higher probability of being found out and removed.

Inheritance is a mechanism to obtain a *derived* class from a *base* class. Such inheritance relationships are very common in the real-world scenario. For example, mammal is a class derived from living things, people is a class derived from mammal, man and woman are classes derived from people, and Indian people is also derived from people. In all these cases, the properties of the base class are automatically available in the derived class. People give birth to child. This attribute is derived from mammals. Indian people have two hands, two legs, etc., and this attribute is derived from people. Similar hierarchy is possible in C++ classes as well. Inheritance is the natural solution when such real-world hierarchy is to be modelled in a C++ program.

Java has a similar root class called object. C++ has no such notion. It is possible to program without such a hierarchy, as we have done so far, and this is known as object-based programming. Programming using inheritance is known as object-oriented programming. Sometimes both are applicable for providing a solution. In general, the approach using object-based method is more acceptable if the performance issues are taken into consideration.

9.2 ADVANTAGES OF USING INHERITANCE

There are some obvious cases where inheritance is needed. Consider the following cases:

1. There is a need for extending the functionality of an existing class.
2. There are multiple classes with some attributes common to them and problems of inconsistencies need to be avoided between the common attributes.
3. The programmer would like to model a real-world hierarchy in the program in a natural way.

In all the three cases mentioned here, it is better to have inheritance in the program.

9.2.1 Avoiding Creation of Objects from Scratch

Suppose an object of type Employee needs to be defined for a payroll program and a payroll Employee class is needed to know the basic pay of an employee and calculate his/her salary. Assume that there already exists a similar class (called EmployeeBase) with the human resource department, which keeps track of all the employee details.

In this case, if the attributes of EmployeeBase are inherited, then there is no needed to collect the employee details all over again. All that one needs to do is to add to the Employee class a few additional details that are not available in the EmployeeBase class. Hence, there is no need to create the Employee class from scratch.

> **Note** The Microsoft Foundation Class (MFC) provides a number of classes that we can inherit and use in our own way. For example, there is a class named CDialog that contains basic mechanisms for dialog boxes. If we need to use a specialized dialog box in our program, we can derive a new class from CDialog and use it. Hence, we need not define the functionalities such as the header, the border, and the buttons. We can define our own MyDialog class by inheriting it from CDialog and use it inside the employee class.

9.2.2 Avoiding Redundancy and Maintaining Consistency

It is not unusual to find redundant data in classes. The problem with this redundancy is that the same data needs to be stored at multiple places. Consider a case of designing classes that store data related to the students of arts, commerce, and science. If a field is added for entering the phone number of a student, it must be done in all the three classes. If one of the classes is not updated, one may end up having inconsistent data. Hence, it is not a good design.

A better design option is to collect all the common attributes in a separate class called Student, and then store only the additional features in the respective classes (i.e., ArtsStudent, CommerceStudent, ScienceStudent, etc.) while providing inheritance from the Student class. This is a common practice in object-oriented design.

Finding common attributes of real classes and creating an abstract class of such common attributes is called the *bottom-up design approach*. This approach reduces the possibility of redundant data. In the given example, if there are 10 types of Student objects and the Student base class is not used, then the data (phone number) is to be kept at 10 places (10 classes), whereas in the second case, only the Student class contains it.

> Finding common attributes of real classes and creating an abstract class of such common attributes is called the bottom-up design approach.

Redundancy reduction also reduces the code size and the chances of errors. It also adds to flexibility. Later on, if a BCAStudent class needs to be added, the normal attributes are in place. One just needs to inherit the BCAStudent class from the Student class and then add to the inherited class only the new items needed.

9.2.3 Mapping a Real-world Hierarchy

We have natural inheritance in a real-world situation. Objects such as rectangle and ellipse are shapes that are derived from the shape concept. Square is a concept derived from rectangle, whereas circle is a concept derived from ellipse. C++ provides the inheritance mechanisms to map these hierarchies *as it is* in its programs. This facility of C++ makes the programs more intuitive and readable.

9.3 IS-A AND PART OF RELATIONSHIPS

When it is possible to inherit and reuse a class, one may be tempted to do so arbitrarily. It is important to have some form of subset relationship between a derived class and the base class. All the examples mentioned earlier have subset relationships. A subset relationship is also known as an *is-a relationship*. At times, one may be confused between an is-a and a *part of* relationship.

In the CDialog example described earlier, MyDialog is a subset of CDialog whereas it is a part of the Employee class. We will be looking at the differences in details in Section 9.15.

It is important to note that it requires programming discipline not to inherit when the relationship is not a subset of or is-a. If one needs to use functions that are defined in that class, it is better to rewrite them in the new class or design in such a way that such inheritance does not take place.

> **Note** Though it is said time and again that inheritance provides reusability, it does not mean that it should be deployed whenever one needs to reuse. Inheritance must be used in a disciplined way only in places where the is-a relationship holds true.

Meaning of Inheritance in C++

When a class is declared as derived from some other class, the data members of the class are made available to the derived class without redefining. The type of inheritance used determines which data members are available and in which form. This is also determined by the original access specifiers (private, public, or protected) associated with the base class members. We will be studying three different types of inheritance in this chapter and will be exploring the forms of inheritance in the following sections.

9.4 DEFINING DERIVED CLASSES

Let us have a look at an example of inheritance to understand the concept. We start with the simplest type of inheritance. Assume that there is a single base class from which a new class is derived. The syntax of the derivation is very simple. If one has to derive a `DerivedClass` from a `BaseClass`, it needs to be specified while defining the `DerivedClass`. The syntax for defining the `DerivedClass` is as follows:

```
class DerivedClass : <access modifier> BaseClass;
```

Here, the access modifier can be either public, private, or protected. Some authors also use the word *visibility mode* to represent the types of these access modifiers. We have already studied public and private access modifiers. We will be learning about protected access specifier in Section 9.4.3.

9.4.1 Derivation using Public Access Modifier

If the program has the following statements

```
class Base
{
    // Body of the base
}

class Derived : public Base
{
    // Body of the derived
}
```

then the derivation is known as *public derivation*. The members of the base class are now treated as follows:

1. The public members of the base class are treated as the public members of the derived class.
2. The private members are not inherited.
3. If some members have been defined as protected in the base class, they are available as protected in the derived class.

This can be understood better with the help of Program 9.1.

PROGRAM 9.1   Inheriting publicly

```
//PublicInheritance.cpp
class Base
{
    int PrivateBaseInt;
public:
    int PublicBaseInt;
    void SetPrivateBaseInt(int Value)
    {
        PrivateBaseInt = Value;
    }
};

// Public derivation
class DerivedPublic : public Base
{
    int PrivateDerivedInt;
public:
    int PublicDerivedInt;
```

```
    void SetPrivateDerivedInt(int Value)
    {
        PrivateBaseInt = Value;
    }
};

void main()
{
    DerivedPublic DerivedObject;

    // DerivedObject.PrivateBaseInt = 10;
    // DerivedObject.PrivateDerivedInt = 10;
    DerivedObject.PublicBaseInt = 10;
    DerivedObject.PublicDerivedInt = 10;
    DerivedObject.SetPrivateBaseInt(20);
    DerivedObject.SetPrivateDerivedInt(30);
}
```

How the Program Works

Why are the following lines commented in the program?

```
// DerivedObject.PrivateBaseInt = 10;
// DerivedObject.PrivateDerivedInt = 10;
```

In the first line, `PrivateBaseInt` is a private variable of `Base`; so, it is not available to the `DerivedPublic` class. However, `PublicBaseInt` is a public variable, and so, it is available to the `DerivedPublic` class *as public* because of public derivation. Similarly, `SetPrivateBaseInt()` is also available *as public* in `DerivedPublic` because it is public in Base.

The second line `// DerivedObject.PrivateDerivedInt` accesses a private member of the same class, which is not allowed. Similarly, private members of the base class are not inherited, and so, are not available here as well.

Look at the statements using `Set` functions.

```
DerivedObject.SetPrivateBaseInt(20);
DerivedObject.SetPrivateDerivedInt(30);
```

These functions are able to manipulate the private data members because they are member functions. As these functions themselves are public, it is possible to access them.

The private members of the base class are not available directly to a derived class; however, they are available indirectly. The call to `SetPrivateDerivedInt()` actually manipulates that variable.

> **Note** Though private members of the base class are not available to the derived class, they are still accessible using public function members of the base class. In that sense, the private members are still available to the derived class indirectly.

9.4.2 Derivation using Private Access Modifier

If the program contains the following statements,

```
class Base
{
    // Body of the base
```

```
        }
        class Derived : private Base
        {
            // Body of the derived
        }
```

then the derivation is known as *private derivation*. The members of the base class are treated as follows:

1. The public members of the base class are treated as the private members of the derived class.
2. Similar to public derivation, the private members of the base class are not inherited and, thus, are not available to the derived class.
3. If some members have been defined as protected in the base class, they are available as private in the derived class. Protected members are discussed in detail later.

This can be understood better with the help of Program 9.2.

PROGRAM 9.2   Inheriting privately

```cpp
//PrivateInheritance.cpp
class Base
{
    int PrivateBaseInt;
public:
    int PublicBaseInt;
    void SetPrivateBaseInt(int Value)
    {
        PrivateBaseInt = Value;
    }
};
class DerivedPrivate : private Base
{
    int PrivateDerivedInt;
public:
    int PublicDerivedInt;
    void SetPrivateDerivedInt(int Value)
    {
        PrivateDerivedInt = Value;
    }
    void SetPublicPrivateBaseInt(int Value)
    {
        PublicBaseInt = Value;
        SetPrivateBaseInt(Value);
    }
};
void main()
{
    DerivedPrivate DerivedObject;
    // DerivedObject.PrivateBaseInt = 10;
    // DerivedObject.PrivateDerivedInt = 10;
    // DerivedObject.PublicBaseInt = 10;
    DerivedObject.PublicDerivedInt = 10;
```

```
// DerivedObject.SetPrivateBaseInt(20);
DerivedObject.SetPrivateDerivedInt(30);
DerivedObject.SetPublicPrivateBaseInt(10);
}
```

How the Program Works

When a derived class member function calls a base class member, which is available to a derived class after inheritance, the **this** pointer to the derived class object passes from the derived class to the base class function member.

Observe the definition of `DerivedPrivate` class. `PublicBaseInt` and `SetPrivateBaseInt` functions are now not accessible to the object of `DerivedPrivate` class, though a call to a member function `SetPublicPrivateBaseInt()` can still manipulate both of them. The reason is simple. The public members of the base class are now the private members of the derived class. Hence, they cannot be accessed by an object of the derived class but are accessible to a member function of the derived class.

Interestingly, the call to function `SetPrivateBaseInt(Value);` is made without using an invoking object, though the function itself is a member function. How is such a statement acceptable to the C++ compiler?

It should be remembered that whenever a member function is called, the object implicitly pass `this` pointer to the member function. An invoking object is needed for the same. `SetPrivateBaseInt()` is called in the body of `SetPublicPrivateBaseInt()` function. When a call is made to `SetPublicPrivateBaseInt()` function, the pointer to the invoking object `DerivedObject` is passed as an argument to the function. The same pointer is passed to the `SetPrivateBaseInt()` function. Looking from another angle, in this case, a derived class object invokes a derived class public member (the function `SetPublicPrivateBaseInt()`), which in turn accesses a (now changed to) derived class private member (the function `SetPrivateBaseInt()`). This is acceptable because `SetPrivateBaseInt()` function is a member, and can accept `this` pointer of the same class. This is similar to the private function members being used by the public function members.

9.4.3 Protected Access Specifier

The protected access specifier is similar to the private access specifier for a class that is not inherited further. The members defined as protected are accessible to the member functions and friend functions and are not available to objects.

Unlike private data members, when a class containing protected data members is inherited, the protected members are available to the derived class member functions as well, but are not available to the objects of derived class. This can be understood better with Program 9.3.

PROGRAM 9.3   Inheriting in protected manner

```
//ProtectedInheritance.cpp
class Base
{
protected:
    int ProtectedBaseInt;
public:
```

```
    int PublicBaseInt;
    void SetProtectedBaseInt(int Value)
    {
        ProtectedBaseInt = Value;
    }
};
class DerivedProtected : public Base
{
    int PrivateDerivedInt;
public:
    int PublicDerivedInt;
    void SetPrivateDerivedInt(int Value)
    {
        PrivateDerivedInt = Value;
    }

    void SetPublicProtectedBaseInt(int Value)
    {
        PublicBaseInt = Value;
        ProtectedBaseInt = Value;
    }
};

void main()
{
    DerivedProtected DerivedObject;
    // DerivedObject.ProtectedBaseInt = 10;
    // DerivedObject.PrivateDerivedInt = 10;
    // DerivedObject.ProtectedBaseInt = 10; DerivedObject.PublicDerivedInt = 10;
    // DerivedObject.SetPrivateBaseInt(20); DerivedObject.SetPrivateDerivedInt(30);
    DerivedObject.SetPublicProtectedBaseInt(10);
}
```

How the Program Works

Note the difference between Programs 9.2 and 9.3. In Program 9.3, the private member of the base class is removed, and instead, a protected member is added. We have seen that it is as good as private for the base class but acts differently when inherited. The DerivedProtected class is derived in a protected way, which means now it is possible to access ProtectedBaseInt in the member functions of the DerivedProtected class. If ProtectedBaseInt had been a private member, it may not be able to access it directly in the member function of the derived class. One cannot, though, access the ProtectedBaseInt by an object of the derived class. So, the following line is still commented:

```
// DerivedObject.ProtectedBaseInt = 10;
```

The difference between private and protected derivation is that protected derivation can be further derived.

Public derivation has been used in this example. What happens if private derivation is used instead? It does not have any effect on the result of the program. The protected members, when inherited as private, become private members of the derived class. The program behaviour is similar. What is the difference between protected and private members then? The difference is seen when the derived class is further inherited. As we know, private data is not inherited, but protected data can be inherited.

9.4.4 Derivation using Protected Access Modifier

If the program contains the following statements,

```
class Base
{
   // Body of the base
}

class Derived : protected Base
{
   // Body of the derived
}
```

then the derivation is known as *protected derivation*. The base class elements are treated as follows:

1. The public members of the base class are treated as the protected members of the derived class.
2. Private members are not inherited.
3. If some members have been defined as protected in the base class, they are available as protected in the derived class.

> **Note**   The main advantage of protected members over private members is that they are available to the derived class but still remain available to only the member functions and not the objects.

Another advantage is that protected derivation for protected and public members permits further derivation in a protected form. Suppose **Derived1** is derived from **Base** class using protected access modifier and then **Derived2** is derived from **Derived1** using any access specifier, then the protected members of the **Base** class are available to **Derived2**. If **Derived1** is derived as private instead of protected, they are not available. Table 9.1 shows the effective access specifier of the base class member in a derived class.

Table 9.1   Effective access specifier of the base class member in a derived class

Member type in base class	Type of derivation	Member type in derived class
Private	Private	Not available
	Protected	Not available
	Public	Not available
Protected	Private	Private
	Protected	Protected
	Public	Protected
Public	Private	Private
	Protected	Protected
	Public	Public

It is also important to understand the effect of access specifiers used on further derivations.

1. If the access specifier is public, the effective specifier in the derived class is the same as the base class (i.e., public remains public and protected remains protected). If it is further inherited as public, they are again going to retain the same access specifier. So, public in base class is also public in derived class.
2. If the access specifier is protected, the access specifier in the derived class is protected for both the protected and public members of the base class. Further inheriting this even as public does not make the public member of the base class to the further derived class as public; it can only be accessed as protected.
3. The most important difference is observed between a member of the class derived as protected and that derived as private. Once privately derived, the data member is not available for further inheritance, whereas in the case of protected, it is available for further inheritance. This is one of the major differences between private and protected inheritances.
4. When a member is protected, it is not different from private unless the class is inherited.

Figure 9.1 explains this concept.

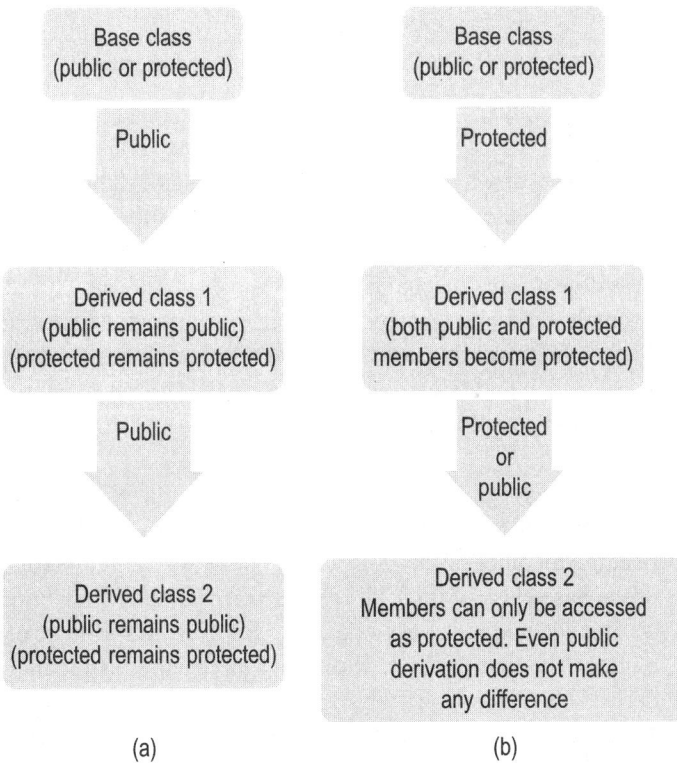

(a)   (b)

Fig. 9.1   Derivations based on access modifiers   (a) Public derivation
(b) Protected derivation

(Contd)

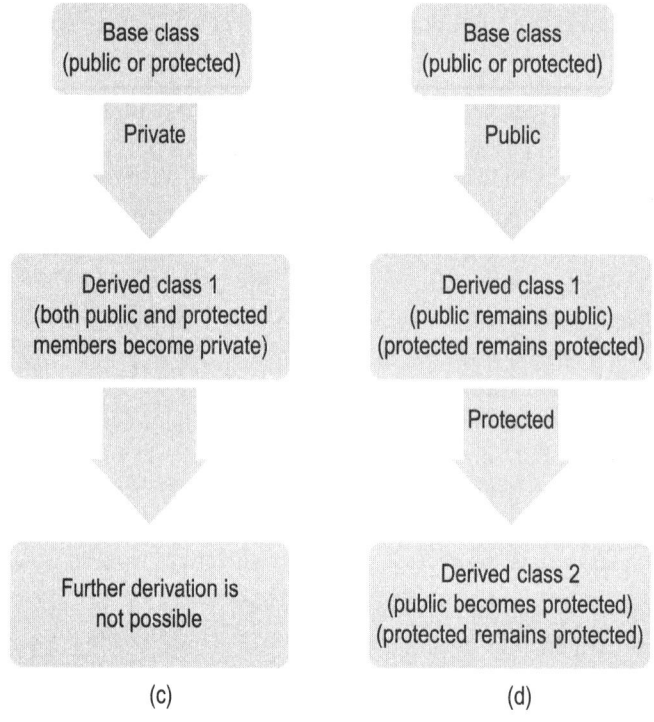

Fig. 9.1 (*Contd*) (c) Private derivation (d) Public and protected derivation

9.5 INHERITANCE IN C++ OBJECT MODEL

There can be a number of ways to implement the points described in Section 9.4. The C++ object model has chosen the simplest one. The compiler embeds the base class completely in a derived class at the time of derivation. Instead, the compiler could have provided a pointer to the base class object. This mechanism would save space.

There is a simple reason as to why a pointer is not provided here. It is possible to have a long inheritance chain where `class1` derives `class2`, which in turn derives `class3`, and so on. In such a case, when one refers to `classN`, one needs to traverse through `N` pointers to the base class to have the complete information about `classN`. This is not efficient in terms of time.

Performance of accessing a base class element is similar to that of referring to a derived class element in terms of time. This provides uniform access to all the members of the class, be it the member of the same class, one of its base class, or one of the base class of the base class of this class, and so on.

As the C++ object model is designed considering efficiency as the prime criteria, it has chosen to copy the base class into the derived class object when the derivation takes place.

This technique is very efficient. However, this kind of efficiency comes with a price. The first problem with using this method is the increase in class size. A derived class is as big as the size of the base class plus its own element's total size. The second problem with this technique is that it leads to strange consequences at times. Consider the case of a library class from which a class has been derived and is being used in a few applications. If the original base class changes, one needs to recompile all the applications that use the derived class. This is because though the original base class has changed, the copy that was made when the derived class was compiled remains unchanged. If it had a pointer to the base class, there is no need to recompile the application because the pointer would automatically point to the new base class.

Program 9.4 verifies the fact that the C++ object model embeds the base classes into the derived ones.

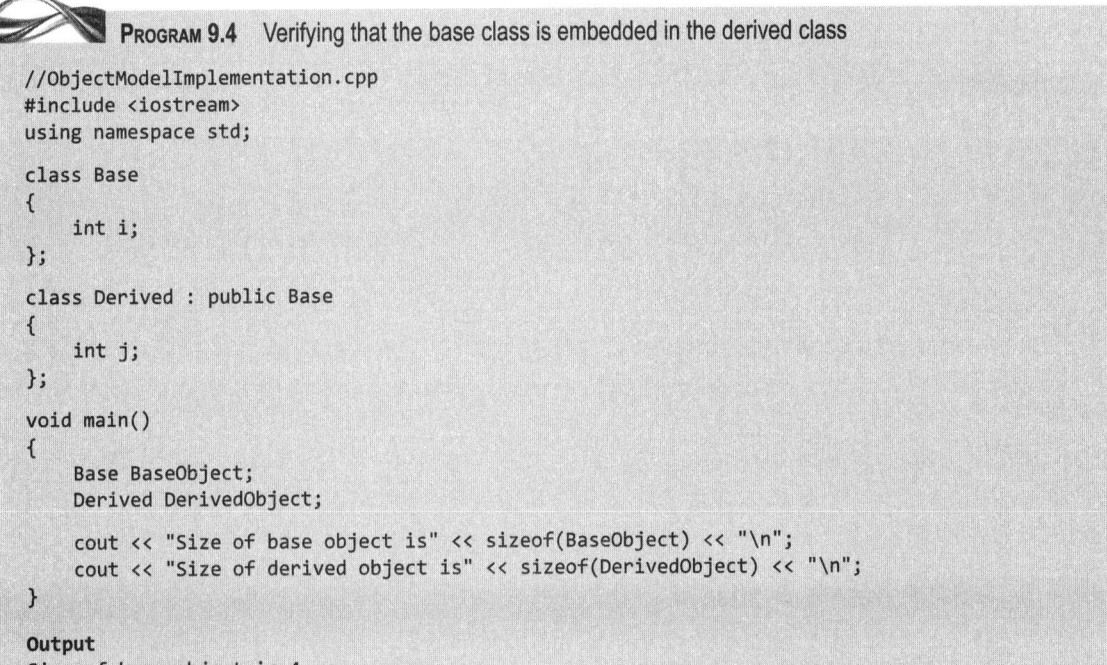

PROGRAM 9.4 Verifying that the base class is embedded in the derived class

```
//ObjectModelImplementation.cpp
#include <iostream>
using namespace std;

class Base
{
    int i;
};

class Derived : public Base
{
    int j;
};

void main()
{
    Base BaseObject;
    Derived DerivedObject;

    cout << "Size of base object is" << sizeof(BaseObject) << "\n";
    cout << "Size of derived object is" << sizeof(DerivedObject) << "\n";
}
```

Output
```
Size of base object is 4
Size of derived object is 8
```

How the Program Works

We will only discuss the architecture of the program and how it serves the purpose. The base class does not have any data as public. The private integer variable is not inherited; so, the size of the derived object must be equal to the size of the base class object (because both of them have a single integer as a member), *but it is not true*. The base class object is embedded within the derived class object, which, therefore, has a size equal to its own size (size of int j) and that of the base class (equal to the size of int i). The example indicates the first disadvantage of the scheme for embedding a base class into a derived class, that is, possible code bloat.

The C++ object model exhibits a different behaviour when virtual base classes are used. We will be learning about virtual base classes in Section 9.12.

Considering the peculiarity of the object model, there are various combinations of access specifiers for the data members and different types of derivations are possible. The following sections deal with the combinations of different access specifiers and different derivations.

9.6 DIFFERENT WAYS TO DERIVE CLASSES

There are three different ways to derive a class from another—public, protected, and private inheritances. All of them result in different types of access restrictions on the members. We will describe each one of them and their respective differences in the following subsections.

9.6.1 Public Derivation

Figure 9.2 shows the first case where a class is derived from the base class using the public access specifier. The private member of the base class is copied to the derived class but is not visible. The public members of the base class are copied as public in the derived class.

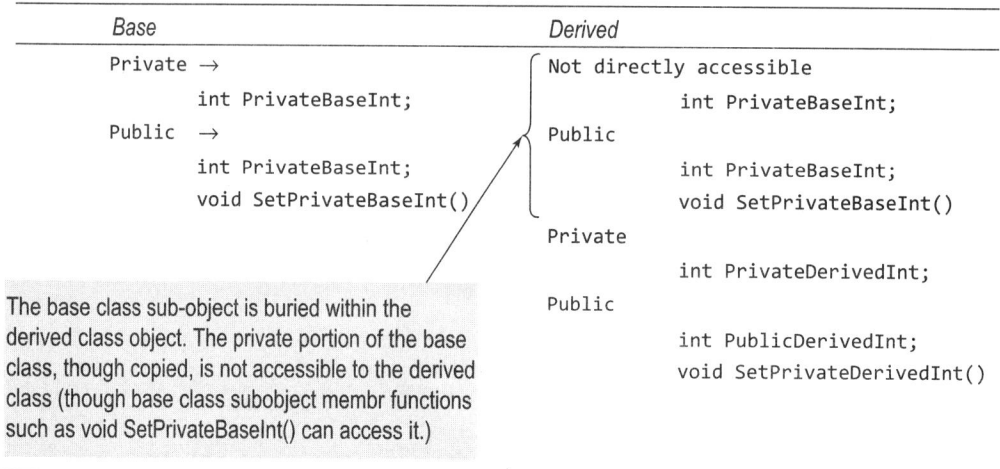

Base	Derived
Private →	Not directly accessible
int PrivateBaseInt;	int PrivateBaseInt;
Public →	Public
int PrivateBaseInt;	int PrivateBaseInt;
void SetPrivateBaseInt()	void SetPrivateBaseInt()
	Private
	int PrivateDerivedInt;
	Public
	int PublicDerivedInt;
	void SetPrivateDerivedInt()

The base class sub-object is buried within the derived class object. The private portion of the base class, though copied, is not accessible to the derived class (though base class subobject membr functions such as void SetPrivateBaseInt() can access it.)

Fig. 9.2 Public derivation

9.6.2 Private Derivation

In this case, the public members of the base class become the private members of the derived class. Again, private members are not inherited. Though the private members of the base class are copied to the derived class, they are not visible. This is shown in Fig. 9.3.

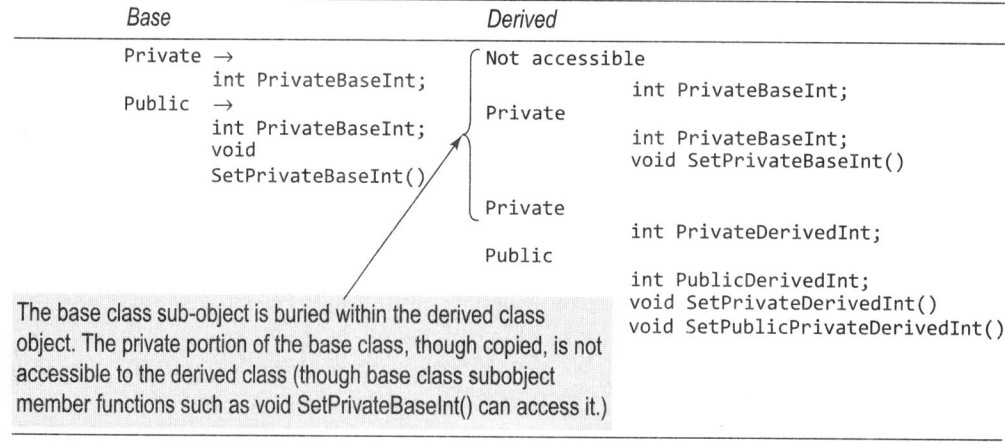

Base	Derived
Private →	Not accessible
int PrivateBaseInt;	int PrivateBaseInt;
Public →	Private
int PrivateBaseInt;	int PrivateBaseInt;
void	void SetPrivateBaseInt()
SetPrivateBaseInt()	
	Private
	int PrivateDerivedInt;
	Public
	int PublicDerivedInt;
	void SetPrivateDerivedInt()
	void SetPublicPrivateDerivedInt()

The base class sub-object is buried within the derived class object. The private portion of the base class, though copied, is not accessible to the derived class (though base class subobject member functions such as void SetPrivateBaseInt() can access it.)

Fig. 9.3 Private derivation

9.6.3 Protected Derivation

In the case of protected derivation, the protected members as well as the public members of the base class become the protected members of the derived class, as shown in Fig. 9.4.

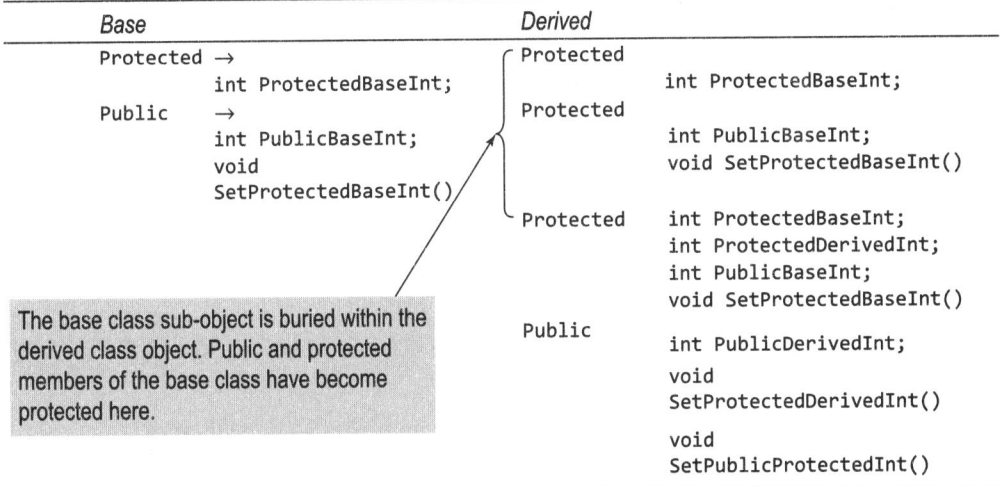

Base		Derived	
Protected →		Protected	
	int ProtectedBaseInt;		int ProtectedBaseInt;
Public →		Protected	
	int PublicBaseInt;		int PublicBaseInt;
	void		void SetProtectedBaseInt()
	SetProtectedBaseInt()		
		Protected	int ProtectedBaseInt;
			int ProtectedDerivedInt;
			int PublicBaseInt;
			void SetProtectedBaseInt()
		Public	int PublicDerivedInt;
			void SetProtectedDerivedInt()
			void SetPublicProtectedInt()

The base class sub-object is buried within the derived class object. Public and protected members of the base class have become protected here.

Fig. 9.4 Protected derivation

9.6.4 Public and Private Derivation of Protected Access Specifier

If the protected members of a class are inherited as public, they remain protected, whereas if inherited as private, they become private. An important impact of this is on further inheritance. If derived public (or protected), the protected members will be available for further inheritance in a public (or protected) derivation (i.e., one can derive one more class from the derived class and the members are still available to the member functions of the same class). Suppose we have following:

```
Class GrandpaBase
{
private:
   int PrivateGB; protected:
   int ProtectedGB;
}
class Base1 : public GrandpaBase
{
private:
   int PrivateB; protected:
   int ProtectedB;
}
class Base2 : private GrandpaBase
{
private:
   int PrivateB; protected:
   int ProtectedB;
}
class Derived1 : public Base1
{ };
```

```
class Derived2 : public Base2
{ };
```

In this case, **ProtectedGB** will be available to **Derived1** (as protected) but not to **Derived2**; this is because **Base2** is privately derived from **GrandpaBase**.

9.7 ACCESS CONTROL

The member functions of the class and of the derived class, friends, and objects can access the different parts of the class. The access for public, private, and protected members is different for all these entities. Access control describes who can access what and in which form. Figure 9.5 shows the access control.

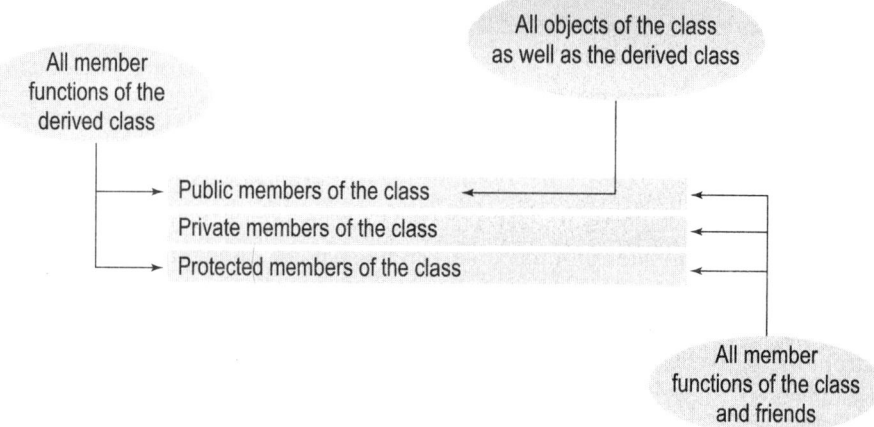

Fig. 9.5   Access control

Available or accessible entities can be determined by the access control. The three entities available for access are as follows:

1. Public
2. Private
3. Protected members

The three types of entities that access them are as follows:

1. The member functions of the class and the friends of the class
2. The member functions of the derived class
3. The objects of the class as well as the derived class

9.8 ACCESS DECLARATION

As mentioned earlier, if a class is derived in a private way, then it is not possible to access the data members of the base class using the derived class objects. In contrast, if the class is derived in a public way, then all the members can be accessed as public. If one wants to derive a class and wants only a few and not all the public members to be available to the objects of the derived class, then one has to provide access declaration. Using access declaration, it is possible to provide public access to some of the base class members even after deriving them as private. Consider Program 9.5 to understand the concept better.

PROGRAM 9.5 Access declaration to use a specific inherited member for a different purpose

```cpp
//AccessDeclaration.cpp
#include <iostream>
using namespace std;

class Base
{
protected:
    int SpecialProtectedInt;
public:
    int SpecialInt;
    int NormalInt;
};

class Derived : private Base
{
protected:
    Base::SpecialProtectedInt;
    /* Making this protected integer specially available to the object of the derived class */

public:
    Base::SpecialInt;
    /* Making this integer specially available to the object of the derived class */

    // Using Base::SpecialInt;
    /* Newer way of writing the same */

    void SetSpecialProtectedIntofBase()
    {
        SpecialProtectedInt = 10;
    }
};

void main()
{
    Derived DerivedObject;
    // DerivedObject.NormalInt = 10;
    /* This statement, if not commented, would not be compiled */

    DerivedObject.SpecialInt = 20;
    DerivedObject.SetSpecialProtectedIntofBase();
}
```

How the Program Works

The statement `Base::SpecialInt;` redefines the `SpecialInt` in the public access specifier header of the derived class, thus making it *specially* public. All other data will remain private. Thus, the `NormalInt` will still be private. Note that `SpecialProtectedInt` has also been redefined to remain protected in the derived class. Access declaration is a great facility; however, it has the following restrictions:

1. The access specifier cannot be modified to raise the status of the original access specifier. It means that if there is a private or protected member in the base, it cannot be redefined in the derived class as public.
2. The consequence of the previous statement is that a member with public access specification can be redefined with public or protected access, whereas the protected member can only be redefined as protected.

The use of access declaration in the form shown Program 9.5 is deprecated, that is, it is not recommended for use in new programs; the same effect of access declaration can also be achieved with the keyword `using`. For writing new programs, one must use this keyword. `using Base::SpecialProtectedInt;` and `using Base::SpecialInt;` are ways to replace older definitions (i.e., just precede older definitions with the keyword `using`). We will be discussing how to use this keyword while studying namespaces in Chapter 14.

9.9 DERIVING MULTIPLE CLASSES FROM A SINGLE CLASS

It is possible to derive multiple classes from a single class. Suppose there are some `Student` classes, say, `SchoolStudent`, `UndergraduateStudent`, and `PostgraduateStudent`. From the design point of view, one must look at all such possible classes and find the common elements in them. Then, the `Student` class (the base class for all of them) is to be created with those elements. Thus, the base class contents are decided *after* the derived class contents are determined. In Program 9.6, we have arts, commerce, and science students inherited from the student class. Suppose the following information needs to be stored for the arts students:

1. Name
2. Address
3. Marks obtained in social science subjects in Class XII
4. Rank obtained in Class XII
5. Name of school in Class XII

Moreover, information for creative art work such as poems or stories written may need to be added.

> **Note** Some books call it *hierarchical inheritance*, which is non-standard; so, we prefer not to use that phrase to describe the situation when multiple classes are derived from a single class.

For the science students, the marks of science subjects and practical subjects, except the language subjects, in Class XII are to be considered. Not only lecture schedules but also practical schedules are considered. For simplicity, both the schedules are assumed to be a string; in real-life scenario, they may be a table to be read from a file.

For commerce students, commerce subject details are to be considered. There may be a need to add details about internship to some private companies. This information is also considered to be contained by a string.

It can be observed that some parts of the details are specific to the type of subject, whereas other details are common. A student class should be created with the common details and then these three classes should be inherited. Consider Program 9.6.

PROGRAM 9.6   Inheriting multiple classes from a single class

```
//StudentInherited.cpp
#include <iostream>
#include <string>
using namespace std;
const int Languages = 2;
const int Science = 3;
const int Commerce = 2;
```

```
class student
{
protected:
    string Name;
    string Address;
    char Grade;
    string NameofSchool;
public:
    student(string TempName, string TempAddress, char TempGrade, string TempNameofSchool)
    {
        Name = TempName;
        Address = TempAddress;
        Grade = TempGrade;
        NameofSchool = TempNameofSchool;
    }
};

// Derived class ArtsStudent
class ArtsStudent : public student
{
    int marks[Languages];
    string LanguageName;
public:
    /* Note how the members are initialized using a member initialization list */
    ArtsStudent(string TempName, string TempAddress,
    char TempGrade, string TempNameofSchool,
    int TempMarks[], string TempLanguageName) : student(TempName, TempAddress, TempGrade,
    TempNameofSchool)
    {
        for(int i = 0; i < Languages; ++i)
        marks[i] = TempMarks[i];
        LanguageName = TempLanguageName;
    }
};

// Derived class ScienceStudent
class ScienceStudent : public student
{
    int marks[Science];
    string ScienceName;
    string PractSchedule;
public:
    ScienceStudent(string TempName, string TempAddress, char TempGrade, string
    TempNameofSchool, int TempMarks[], string TempScienceName, string TempPractSchedule) :
    student(TempName, TempAddress, TempGrade, TempNameofSchool)
    {
        for(int i = 0; i < Science; i++)
        marks[i] = TempMarks[i];
        ScienceName = TempScienceName;
        PractSchedule = TempPractSchedule;
    }
};

// Derived class CommerceStudent
class CommerceStudent : public student
{
    int marks[Commerce];
    string CompanyName;
```

```
    public:
        CommerceStudent(string TempName, string TempAddress, char TempGrade, string
        TempNameofSchool, int TempMarks[], string TempCompanyName) : student(TempName,
        TempAddress, TempGrade, TempNameofSchool)
        {
            for(int i = 0; i < Commerce; i++)
            marks[i] = TempMarks[i];
            CompanyName = TempCompanyName;
        }
};

void main()
{
    int ArtsMarks[] = {55,75};
    int ScienceMarks[] = {89,78,97};
    int CommerceMarks[] = {54,78};

    CommerceStudent Lara("Lara", "West Indies", 'A', "Trinidad beach", CommerceMarks,
    "Under the sun");

    ScienceStudent Beckham("David Beckham", "Karnataka", 'A', "Bangalore school",
    ScienceMarks, "Physics", "12to2daily");

    ArtsStudent Steffi("Steffi", "C/o Agassi's address", 'A', "Germany school", ArtsMarks,
    "Silence");
}
```

How the Program Works

The program contains a `student` class, and there are three classes inherited from it, namely, `ArtsStudent`, `CommerceStudent`, and `ScienceStudent`. The `student` class contains all the data common to the derived classes, that is, name, address, etc. Constructors are provided for all these classes, which are defined and used while defining `student`.

It is a very simplified example, though it has gone a little on the heavy side, particularly the constructor call for the base class in the derived class. It is important to note that the base class constructor is called using the memberwise initialization list (MIL), which has been dealt with while learning constructors in Chapter 5. It has been mentioned that members can be initialized using MIL. When the member is a class (here, the derived class has the base class as a member), it is initialized using MIL. It is also important to note that the base class objects can be initialized only using MIL and not in the body of the constructor of the derived class object. It is also important to note that the derived class constructor must have enough number of arguments for both the base class object, which is a part of the derived class, and the constructor for the other members of the derived class.

> **Note** Base class objects can be initialized only using MIL. The derived class constructor must have enough number of arguments to construct the base class subobject embedded in the derived class object as well as the other members of the derived class.

> One important advantage of inheritance is the facility to store common attributes at a single place in the base class.

This program stresses the advantages of base classes when it is inherited multiple times. A single base class is shared with all the classes that are inherited from it. If the university wants to add the e-mail addresses of all the students of all the disciplines in the `student` data, the information needs to be added at only one place, the `student` class. This is the prime advantage of inheritance. Suppose if at a further period, there is a need to deal with engineering students as well, it is possible to inherit a new class from student class again. Then, there is no need to add those details (name, address, etc.) to the Engineering class, which should only contain information specific to it. This is another advantage of inheritance. If the proper base classes are in place, further programming is easier and faster. It leads to modular and quick programming. It is also robust if the base class is debugged and tested properly.

9.10 MULTIPLE INHERITANCE

It is also possible to derive a single class from more than one class. When a single class is inherited from multiple base classes, it is known as *multiple inheritance*. Many examples of multiple inheritance can be seen in the real world.

For example, Indian people are Indians as well as people at the same point of time; similarly, a personal computer is both personal and computer at the same point of time. When such a concept is implemented as a class, multiple inheritance occurs. If ever a class IndianPeople is derived, it would be multiple inherited from the classes Indian as well as People. Similarly, the class PersonalComputer will be inherited from the classes Personal as well as Computer. The multiple-inherited derived class inherits attributes from all the classes it is derived from. Let us take one specific example to learn how multiple inheritance found in real world can be mapped to a C++ program. Though we would like to come as close to a real-world example as possible, we will fall short of an actual real-world C++ program, because the complexity of such a program would be out of bounds for a text book such as this.

Multiple inheritance is a great idea. There are so many such hierarchies in the real world. An Indian cricket player can be a player from the south, north, east, or west zone. At the same time, he is also either a bowler, a batsman, a wicket keeper, or an all-rounder. One class can be described as a combination of a bowler and a south zone player. The class under consideration inherits from both the south zone player class and the bowler class.

Another example is that of an auto-rickshaw, which is a member of three-wheeler vehicle class and, at the same time, is also a member of the class of vehicles available on rent. Program 9.6 shows Beckham to be an object of the class ScienceStudent; he can as well be an object of the class FootballStudent. In such a case, there is a need to have one more class FootballScienceStudent of which Beckham is a member. Multiple inheritance relates to an entity that inherits attributes from more than one distinct entities. Such natural inheritance becomes easy and intuitive to a program with the facility of multiple inheritance provided by the language.

Implementing Multiple Inheritance in C++

Let us see how one can implement multiple inheritance in a C++ program. Program 9.7 contains a class called SportsStudent, which is inherited from the student class and the SportsPerson class.

The object of SportsStudent class contains properties such as name and address derived from the student class and the details such as the name of the sport one is playing, the national and international sports events taken part in, and medals won so far, which are derived from the SportsPerson class. Moreover, note that there are some other attributes such as sports subjects taken and sports points obtained (from practicals and participation in various events), which are specific to the SportsStudent class. Program 9.7 reinforces what is stated here.

> When a single class is inherited from multiple base classes, it is known as multiple inheritance.

PROGRAM 9.7 Multiple inheritance

```cpp
//MultipleInheritance.cpp
#include <iostream>
#include <string>
using namespace std;
const int Sports = 3;

// First base class
class student
{
private:
    string Name;
    string Address;
    char Grade;
    string NameofSchool;
public:
    student(string TempName, string TempAddress, char TempGrade,
    string TempNameofSchool)
    {
        Name = TempName;
        Address = TempAddress;
        Grade = TempGrade;
        NameofSchool = TempNameofSchool;
    }
};

// Second base class
class SportsPerson
{
private:
    string Sport;
    string DetailsOfEvents;
    string Experience;
    int Age;
public:
    SportsPerson(string TempSport, string TempDetailsOfEvents, string TempExperience, int
    TempAge)
    {
        Sport = TempSport;
        DetailsOfEvents = TempDetailsOfEvents;
        Experience = TempExperience;
        Age = TempAge;
    }
};

// Derived class
class SportsStudent : public SportsPerson, public student
{
private:
    string SportsSubjects[Sports];
    int SportsPoints;
public:
    SportsStudent(string TempName, string TempAddress, char TempGrade, string TempNameofSchool,
    string TempSport,
    string TempDetailsOfEvents, string TempExperience, int TempAge,
    int TempSportsSubjects[], int TempSportsPoints) :
    student(TempName, TempAddress, TempGrade, TempNameofSchool),
    SportsPerson(TempSport, TempDetailsOfEvents, TempExperience, TempAge)
```

```
    {
        for(int i = 0; i < Sports; ++i)
        SportsSubjects[i] = TempSportsSubjects[i];
        SportsPoints = TempSportsPoints;
    }
};

void main()
{
    int SportsMarks[] = {59,78,67};
    SportsStudent Carl("Carl Lewis", "US", 'A', "The American school", "Sprint", "Won gold
    in Olympics", "10 years", 40, SportsMarks, 70);
}
```

How the Program Works

This example shows how multiple inheritance can be defined and used in a program. The class `SportsStudent` has been inherited from two classes, namely, `student` and the `SportsPerson` classes. See how the constructors are defined and accessed in the derived class.

The syntax for multiple inheritance is simple. The class name is to be followed by the access specifier. For example,

```
<access specifier> class1 name,
<access specifier> class2 name, ...
```

In this program, it is written as

```
class SportsStudent : public SportsPerson, public student
```

9.10.1 Problems in Multiple Inheritance

Multiple inheritance is touted as a bad feature by some other languages, particularly Java, which discourages a programmer from using it. It is a very important tool, but has to be used with care.

It is important to note that multiple inheritance also has problems. If it is used without proper understanding, or used when a natural solution without multiple inheritance is possible, one has to pay the penalty in terms of efficiency and simplicity of code. Let us analyse the problems of using multiple inheritance in our program.

The idea here is not to restrict the readers from using multiple inheritance but to make them aware of the problems so that they can be avoided while programming.

From the Compiler's Angle

At the time of derivation, the base class is embedded in the derived class. When it is derived further, the inheritance follows a 'natural' chain. The base subobjects are stacked in the order of inheritance in the derived class. In case of multiple inheritance, the path is not simple. The subobject stacking is done using subobjects from multiple classes inserted for multiple inheritance.

Consider Fig. 9.6. If there is a derived class and a further derived class from this derived class, the embedding is straightforward. If ever a compiler needs to convert from a derived class object to a base class object, the lower part is to be neglected. The calculation is simple. On the other hand, if the class contains multiple inheritance, then the selection is not that simple. In such cases, the compiler may need to isolate some part of data (the class `derived1` data) in between, which obviously requires more computation and logic.

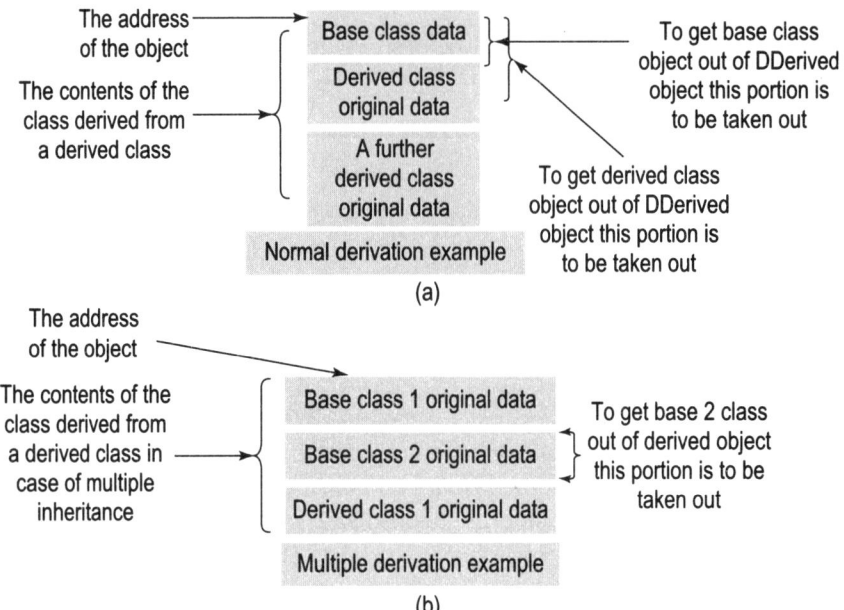

Fig. 9.6 Derivation examples (a) Normal derivation (b) Multiple derivation

Suppose the program contains the following statements:

```
Base BaseObject;
Derived DerivedObject;
DDerived DDerivedObject;
```

If a programmer writes

```
Base *BaseObjPtr = &DerivedObject
```

then the compiler need not do anything in the first case. Similarly, if one writes

```
Base *OtherBasePtr = &DerivedObject
```

then again the compiler need not do anything. The address naturally points to the class needed (base class in the first and derived class in the second). However, this is not observed in the case of multiple inheritance.

Let us assume the class `Derived` is derived from both `Base1` and `Base2`. If one writes the following

```
Derived DerivedObject;
Base2 *BasePtr2 = &DerivedObject;
```

then it is not easy for the compiler to get the right address. If one writes

```
Base1 *BasePtr1 = &DerivedObject
```

the compiler need not intervene.

Notes

1. The compiler has to intervene and properly set the address and provide means of getting correct content for any class that is not the first member of the inheritance list.
2. The compiler has to do more work when there is a long chain or when there is a need to provide virtual base class facility.

From the Designer's Angle

Designers need to take care when they encounter a problem related to a common situation known as *tangled hierarchy*. They need to find the value of an attribute for an object that has inherited multiple number of times. If the attribute cannot be found with the same object, one needs to traverse the hierarchy up to find the value. In the case of multiple inheritance, there is more than one path up. Hence, it is possible to get multiple values for the same attribute, which can at times be conflicting.

Suppose there is a class MyBirds, which is inherited from two classes PetBirds and Ostriches. If one travels up the hierarchy, PetBirds has a base class called Birds. Suppose somebody enquires to know whether MyBirds can fly and travels the hierarchy through Ostriches, then he/she may be misled to believe that MyBirds cannot fly.

On the other hand, if the person chooses the other path (through PetBirds to Birds), he/she would conclude that MyBirds can fly. This is a serious design problem and can be avoided if the classes are designed carefully.

Obviously, avoiding multiple inheritance seems to be the simplest solution. Moreover, multiple inheritance has another drawback. The object becomes more cluttered with the features derived from more than one class and is, therefore, less readable and debuggable than a normal object or singly inherited object.

9.11 DERIVING A CLASS FROM AN ALREADY DERIVED CLASS

We have so far seen the cases of deriving from a base class. It is also possible to derive further. The C++ object model implementation is such that the further derived class will contain all ancestors within its body. Let us look at an example of such a class. We have seen a class student, and further inheritance of it into arts, commerce, and science students. It is possible to have one more derivation from science students, namely the Gujarat University science students. The Gujarat University science students may have some special rules to follow compared to a normal science student, and so, this student object needs to add attributes such as science project details, name of the guide for the science project, and list of subjects offered out of optional subjects. The following program shows how this can be programmed.

```cpp
//FurtherInheritance.cpp
#include <iostream>
#include <string>
using namespace std;

const int Science = 3;
const int OptionalSubjects = 2;

// Base class
class student
{
private:
    string Name;
    string Address;
    char Grade;
    string NameofSchool;
public:
```

```
        student(string TempName, string TempAddress, char TempGrade, string TempNameofSchool)
        {
          Name = TempName;
          Address = TempAddress;
          Grade = TempGrade;
          NameofSchool = TempNameofSchool;
        }
    };
    // Derived class
    class ScienceStudent : public student
    {
      int marks[Science];
      string ScienceName;
      string PractSchedule;
    public:
      ScienceStudent(string TempName, string TempAddress, char TempGrade, string
      TempNameofSchool, int TempMarks[], string TempScienceName, string TempPractSchedule):
      student(TempName, TempAddress, TempGrade, TempNameofSchool)
        {
          for(int i = 0; i < Science; i++)
          marks[i] = TempMarks[i]; ScienceName = TempScienceName; PractSchedule =
          TempPractSchedule;
        }
    };
    // Further derivation from the derived class
    class GUScienceStudent : public ScienceStudent
    {
      string ScienceProjectDetails;
      string GuideName;
      string SubjectsOpted[2];
    public:
      GUScienceStudent(string TempName, string TempAddress, char TempGrade, string
      TempNameofSchool, int TempMarks[], string TempScienceName, string TempPractSchedule,
      string TempScienceProjectDetails, string TempGuideName, string TempSubjectsOpted[])
      : ScienceStudent(TempName, TempAddress, TempGrade, TempNameofSchool, TempMarks,
      TempScienceName, TempPractSchedule)
        {
          ScienceProjectDetails = TempScienceProjectDetails;
          GuideName = TempGuideName;
          for(int i = 0; i < OptionalSubjects; i++)
          SubjectsOpted[i] = TempSubjectsOpted[i];
        }
    };
    void main()
    {
```

```
    int ScienceMarks[] = {89,78,97};
    string BeckhamSubjects[2] = {"Corner","Free kick"};
    GUScienceStudent Beckham("David Beckham", "UK", 'A', "Real Madrid", ScienceMarks,
    "Physics", "12to2daily", "World cup in Germany", "Dribbling", BeckhamSubjects);
}
```

Deriving classes in this way increases the number of arguments to be passed to the constructor. It makes the program less readable. Even with a simple example that has been provided here, a constructor with 10 items needs to be called. A practical solution to this problem is to have a structure containing the items needed and pass it to the constructor. For example,

```
Student(StudSturct)
```

can be written instead of

```
Student(TempName, TempAddress, TempGrade, TempNameofSchool)
```

if a `struct` has been defined as follows:

```
struct Stud
{
    int Name;
    int Address;
    int Grade;
    int NameofSchool;
}
```

9.12 VIRTUAL BASE CLASS

So far, further inheritance is simple to understand. There is a problem with a specific type of further inheritance that has been overlooked. Suppose there is a class `Base` from which two different classes, say, `Derived1` and `Derived2`, are derived. In addition, if a new class `DDerived` is inherited from `Derived1` and `Derived2` (multiple inheritance), then there are two copies of `Base` now copied in `DDerived`, one from `Derived1` and another from `Derived2`. This is diagrammatically shown in Fig. 9.7.

Thus, there are two different copies of all the members of the base class elements. This has two distinct problems. The first one is the bloating of the code size, which is very obvious. The second problem is how to access a member class object from a further derived class. The scope resolution operator is obviously needed to say either 'I need a base class object derived from `Derived1`' or 'I need a base class object derived from `Derived2`'.

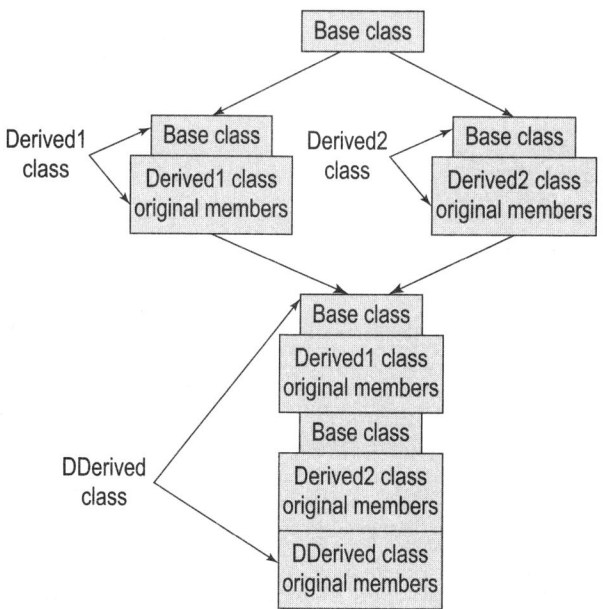

Fig. 9.7   Virtual base class

Consider the following program to understand how to invoke the base class object. It is needless to say that if the object members are not qualified this way, the compiler will get confused (whether to use a base class member from Derived1 or Derived2) and will not compile the program.

```cpp
#include <iostream>
#include <string>
using namespace std;
// Base class
class Base
{
public:
    int BaseInt;
};
// First derived class
class Derived1 : public Base
{
public:
    int Derived1Int;
};
// Second derived class
class Derived2 : public Base
{
public:
    int Derived2Int;
};
// Multiple inheritance
class DDerived : public Derived1, public Derived2
{
public:
    int DDerivedInt2;
};
void main()
{
    DDerived DD;
    // DD.BaseInt = 0;
    // Error: ambiguous access of 'BaseInt' in 'DDerived'
    DD.Derived1::BaseInt = 0; // Now it is not ambiguous
    DD.Derived2::BaseInt = 10;
    /* Yes. This is different from previous BaseInt */
    cout << DD.Derived1::BaseInt << "\n";
    cout << DD.Derived2::BaseInt << "\n";
}
Output
0
10
```

In this example, it is not possible to access the base class member as it is. It needs to be qualified with the derived class name.

Having two different copies and the need to qualify with the base class name is a serious problem in some cases. To solve this problem, it is necessary to precede the first derivation by the keyword virtual. Look at the modified code shown in the following program.

```cpp
//VirtualInheritance.cpp
#include <iostream>
#include <string>
using namespace std;
class Base
{
public:
    int BaseInt;
};
class Derived1 : virtual public Base
// See the keyword virtual preceding public
{
public:
    int Derived1Int;
};
class Derived2 : virtual public Base
{
public:
    int Derived2Int;
};
class DDerived : public Derived1, public Derived2
{
public:
    int DDerivedInt2;
};
void main()
{
    DDerived DD;
    DD.BaseInt = 0;
    // No more ambiguity as there is only one copy of BaseInt present
    DD.Derived1::BaseInt = 0; // This is the same as previous
    DD.Derived2::BaseInt = 10; // We are modifying the same member
    cout << DD.BaseInt << "\n";
    cout << DD.Derived1 :: BaseInt << "\n";
    cout << DD.Derived2 :: BaseInt << "\n";
}
Output
0
0
10
```

The keyword virtual should precede the derivation to provide a virtual base class, that is, a class with only one instance inherited when inherited from multiple paths. One can actually write *virtual public* or *public virtual;* there is no difference between them. The compiler would consider both the definitions the same way. Now, BaseInt is a single copy and there is no ambiguity. Whenever the compiler finds the keyword `virtual` with derivation, it would ensure that two instances of the same base class are not inherited into the class derived from the derived class of `Base`.

The resultant situation is described in Fig. 9.8. We have a single instance of `Base` class in `DDerived` class. This is the advantage of virtual base classes.

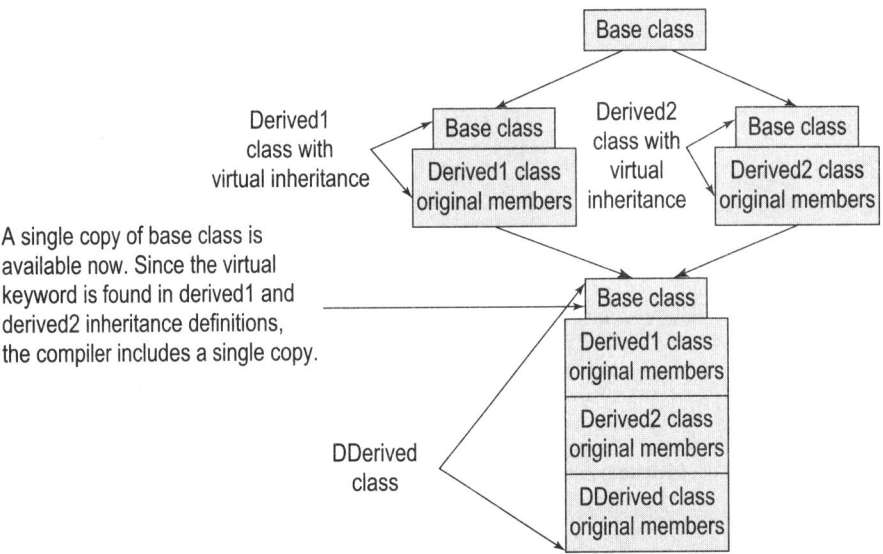

Fig. 9.8 Effect of virtual base class on derived class design

It is actually a challenge for the compiler to provide a single instance of a class from two instances available and still provide compatibility when one type of object is assigned to another, especially while using pointers. It is a complex problem and compilers use complicated mechanisms to solve it.

Note In the case of virtual base classes, the compiler keeps track of those base classes when inherited. If the compiler finds multiple copies of the same class inherited, it will keep only one copy. Such a rework needs a lot of complex mechanisms to be built into the compiler. Moreover, it needs to check the inheritance chain to determine whether the base class is inherited again, which slows down the process.

A general strategy is to divide the members into two regions. One region contains non-virtual base classes that are at a fixed offset from the beginning and can be handled easily. The other region is a shared region where the offset is not fixed and the compiler needs to provide special mechanisms to dynamically access the virtual members.

In a nutshell, using virtual base class is not an efficient way. One should try to avoid it unless one is ready to sacrifice performance and speed. When virtual base classes are combined with multiple inheritance, the situation becomes much more complex for the compiler and must be avoided unless the application demands it. Exhibit 9.1 explains abstract classes.

Exhibit 9.1 Abstract classes

The classes without any objects are known as abstract classes. These classes are usually the outcome of a generalization process that finds the common elements of the classes of interest and stores them in a base class.

In the example for the single inheritance of a single base class into multiple base classes, the `student` class is known as an abstract class. Abstract classes are very important from the designer's point of view. Whenever a designer has to model an abstract concept that cannot have objects, then abstract classes come handy.

9.13 APPLICATIONS OF CONSTRUCTORS AND DESTRUCTORS

We have already seen the applications of constructors when a class is derived from another class. There are a few important things to be noted in such cases, which are as follows:

> When the programmer provides a constructor, the C++ compiler will not provide one.

1. If there is a base class constructor available, the derived class must define one constructor for itself. Why? A base class instance is a part of the derived class; then, how can it be constructed if the derived class does not provide a constructor itself, which calls the constructor of the base class? It should be remembered that when the programmer provides a constructor, C++ will not provide one. This is why the base class subobject needs that base class constructor to be defined by the user. In the case of a default constructor, though, the situation is different. If default constructor is not defined in the derived class and there is one defined in the base, the compiler will define one default constructor for us for the derived class.

2. When `class1 : public class2, public class3, public class4, ..., classN` is defined, then the constructor for `class2` is called first, then the constructor for `class3` is called, and so on until `classN`, and then the *body* of the constructor of `class1` is executed. The call to base class constructors is to be defined outside the body of the constructor, in the MIL. Here, the list that appears after : is sometimes referred to as inheritance list. Hence, the base class constructors are to be called (initialized) using MIL and cannot be called in the body of the derived class.

3. There is an exception to the case mentioned in the point 2. If one of the classes in the list is virtual, then its constructor is called before others. If there are more such virtual base classes, then their constructors are executed in the order of their appearance in the inheritance list.

4. When first `class2 : public class1` and then `class3 : public class2`, that is, `class1->class2->class3` (`->` indicates inherit into) are defined, then the `class1` constructor is called first, then `class2` constructor is called, and then the body of the `class3` constructor is executed when the object of `class3` is defined. When a class is derived from a base class and may be derived further, the inheritance chain is a list that starts with the base class and follows the order of inheritance to the last class. Here, `class1->class2->class3` is the inheritance chain, and it can be seen that the constructor execution order has followed the chain.

5. The destructors of the base classes are called exactly in the reverse order of their initialization when the derived object is destroyed.

6. The argument to the derived constructor will have all the arguments needed for all base classes plus a few for itself. This has already been seen in earlier examples.

9.14 EXCEPTION HANDLING IN CASE OF DERIVATION

It is important to note that C++, while providing very strict type checking, is at times very lenient. If an object of a derived class has been thrown, it can be caught by a handler provided by the base class. If one wants to provide the handler for the derived class objects as a different handler, then it must appear before the handler for the base class; otherwise, that `catch` block will never be executed. Consider the following program to understand the concept.

```cpp
//ExceptionHandling.cpp
#include <iostream>
#include <string>
using namespace std;
const int Languages = 2;
const int Science = 3;
const int Commerce = 2;
class student
{
protected:
   string Name;
   string Address;
   char Grade;
   string NameofSchool;
public:
   student(string TempName, string TempAddress, char TempGrade,
   string TempNameofSchool)
   {
      Name = TempName;
      Address = TempAddress;
      Grade = TempGrade;
      NameofSchool = TempNameofSchool;
   }
};
class ArtsStudent : public student
{
   int marks[Languages];
   string LanguageName;
public:
   ArtsStudent(string TempName, string TempAddress, char TempGrade, string
   TempNameofSchool, int TempMarks[], string TempLanguageName) : student(TempName,
   TempAddress, TempGrade, TempNameofSchool)
   {
      for(int i = 0; i < Languages; ++1)
      {
            marks[i] = TempMarks[i];
      }
      LanguageName = TempLanguageName;
   }
};
class ScienceStudent : public student
{
   int marks[Science];
   string ScienceName;
   string PractSchedule;
public:
   ScienceStudent(string TempName, string TempAddress, char TempGrade,
```

```
      string TempNameofSchool, int TempMarks[], string TempScienceName, string
      TempPractSchedule): student(TempName, TempAddress, TempGrade, TempNameofSchool)
      {
         for(int i = 0; i < Science; i++)
         marks[i] = TempMarks[i];
         ScienceName = TempScienceName;
         PractSchedule = TempPractSchedule;
      }
};
void DelStudent(int Who)
{
   int ArtsMarks[] = {55,75};
   int ScienceMarks[] = {89,78,97};
   ScienceStudent Beckham("David Beckham", "England", 'A', "Germany", ScienceMarks,
   "Physics", "12to2daily");
   ArtsStudent Steffi("Steffi", "C/o Agassi's address", 'A', "Germany", ArtsMarks,
"Silence");
   try
   {
      switch(Who)
      {
              case 0: throw Beckham;
              case 1: throw Steffi;
              default: return;
      }
   }
   catch (ScienceStudent)
   {
      cout << "Caught a science student\n";
   }
   catch (student)
   {
      cout << "Caught a student\n";
   }
   catch (ArtsStudent)
   {
      cout << "Will never catch an arts student\n";
   }
};
void main()
{
   DelStudent(0); // Message to throw Beckham;
   DelStudent(1); // Message to throw Steffi;
}
Output
Caught a science student
Caught a student
```

Unfortunately, the arts student is not caught because the student object handler is written before it. A good compiler might flag a warning while compiling such cases.

The need for such a strategy is to make a base class and derive a lot of classes from it. A single base class catch is still needed to catch the entire group of derived class objects.

> **Note** When an exception is thrown for a derived class, it can always be caught by a base class. If one needs to catch base class as well as derived class exceptions separately, the catch block for the derived class must appear before the catch block for a base class, unless the catch block of the base class captures all exceptions related to the base as well as derived classes and a derived class catch segment will never be executed.

9.15 COMPOSITE OBJECTS (CONTAINER OBJECTS)

Sometimes, the object itself contains some other objects as members. Such objects are known as *composite objects*. This is the *part of* relationship unlike the *is-a* relationship discussed in Section 9.3. It is important to note that there may be no need to call the constructor of the component classes whenever one needs to call the constructor of the container class every time like the derived class. In Program 9.8, the compiler calls the constructor for Employee while initializing the employee collection (CollectionEmp) object. Here, CollectionEmp is a composite object.

A composite object is one that has other objects as members.

PROGRAM 9.8 Composite object

```cpp
//CompositeObject.cpp
#include <iostream>
#include <string>
using namespace std;
class CollectionEmp; // Forward Definition
class employee
{
    int EmpNo;
    string Name;
    string DeptName;
    string Designation;
public:
    employee()
    {
        EmpNo = 0;
    }

    employee(int TempNo, string TempName, string TempDept, string TempDesi)
    {
        EmpNo = TempNo;
        Name = TempName;
        DeptName = TempDept;
        Designation = TempDesi;
    }

    void DisplayDetails()
    {
        cout << "Details of employee number" << EmpNo << "\n";
        cout << "Name is" << Name << "\n";
        cout << "Department is" << DeptName << "\n";
        cout << "Designation is" << Designation << "\n";
    }
```

```
        friend CollectionEmp;
};
class CollectionEmp
{
private:
    employee ColEmp[10];
    int Index;
public:
    bool AddToCol(employee Emp)
    {
        if(Index < 9)
        {
            ColEmp[Index] = Emp;
            Index++;
            return true;
        }
        else
        return false;
    }
void ListDeptWise()
{
    string TempDeptName;
    cout << "Enter the department of the university:";
    cin >> TempDeptName;
    cout << "\n";

    for(int i = 0; i < 10; ++i)
        {
            if(ColEmp[i].DeptName == TempDeptName)
            {
                ColEmp[i].DisplayDetails();
            }
        }
    }

    CollectionEmp()
    {
        Index = 0;
    }

    CollectionEmp(employee TempEmp[], int Size = 10)
    {
        Index = 0;
        for(int i = 0; i < Size; ++i)
        {
            AddToCol(TempEmp[i]);
        }
    }
};

void main()
{
employee UniEmployee[10] =
{
    employee(1, "Lara", "Exam", "Professor"),
    employee(2, "Ponting", Marksheet", "Clerk"),
    employee(3, "Laxman", "Accounts", "Head Clerk"),
    employee(4, "Flintoff", "Exam", "Clerk"),
```

```
      employee(5, "Murlidharan", "Accounts", "CAO"),
      employee(6, "Sarfaraz", "Exam", "Informer"),
      employee(7, "Dean Jones", "Exam", "Invigilator"),
      employee(8, "Madugalle", "Exam", "Examiner"),
      employee(9, "Ganguly", "Marksheet", "Repeater"),
      employee(10, "Nafees", "Accounts", "Clerk")
};
CollectionEmp UniEmpCol(UniEmployee);
UniEmpCol.ListDeptWise();
}
```

How the Program Works

Look at both the constructors of the `CollectionEmp` class. The constructors of `Employee` objects (which are contained by the `CollectionEmp` class) are not called.

```
CollectionEmp()
{
    Index = 0;
}

CollectionEmp(employee TempEmp[], int Size = 10)
{
    Index = 0;
    for(int i = 0; i < Size; ++i)
    {
        AddToCol(TempEmp[i]);
    }
}
```

Let us understand what this program tries to achieve. As this program has already been analysed earlier, let us look at only the additional part. The composite object constructor does not require calling the constructors of the objects it contain.

Earlier we have seen such an example of `item` object as a part of customer object while discussing copy constructors in Chapter 5. Even then, we have not specified any constructor call in the definition of the customer object. Unlike the constructor of a derived class where the base class constructor must be called, *there is no need to call that constructor in this case.* However, there may be a need to call the constructors of contained objects in the constructor of the container class. Program 9.9 is an example that represents the case where such constructor calls are needed.

Calling constructors of contained objects in the composite object   Suppose there is a graphical figure (say, that of a face) that has a triangle, a square, and a pair of circles (to represent the nose, mouth, and pair of eyes). Every instance of the graphical figure determines the position of each of its components, that is, if the first instance of the face is located at (2, 2) on the screen, the components, that is, the pair of circles, the triangle, and the square, will be drawn with respect to (2, 2).

If the next face is drawn at (20, 20), the circles, square, and the triangle will be drawn with respect to position (20, 20). When the face is constructed, all component figures need to be constructed with respect to the position of the face. The constructor of the graphical figure `Face` should be called with the required arguments, one of which must be `Position`, which in turn is used to call the constructors of the embedded (component) objects to find their respective positions. It is a simplified face, which can be positioned where one wants it in two-dimensional space. Depending on the position of the face, the elements (two circles for eyes, one triangle for nose, and one square for mouth) are to be drawn. The issues of orientation of the face (the direction the face is facing) and scaling (making the face bigger and smaller) are ignored here for simplicity.

Program 9.9 is for drawing a face, without really drawing a face on the screen, but printing a message alone. If the face is drawn in the program, then the code becomes compiler dependent (as C++ does not have standard graphics library) and more complicated. Therefore, it is not shown here. It is written just for the purpose of representing the concept of composite objects. The only important part to learn is the call to the constructors while initializing user-defined objects that are a part of the composite object, that is, calling the constructors of circle, triangle, and square while calling the constructor for the face. The positions of the component objects depend on the position of the composite object. The constructors of the component objects should be called using MIL as shown in the program. The values given in the program for X and Y coordinates of all the points is intuitively chosen. Drawing the figure might not draw an exact face but might be something similar to it. One may need to play with X and Y values of all the components to get the face look like an actual face.

PROGRAM 9.9   Composite object where calling constructors of contained objects is necessary

```cpp
//CompositeObj2.cpp
class Point
{
    int X;
    int Y;
public:
    Point(int TempX = 0, int TempY = 0)
    {
        X = TempX;
        Y = TempY;
    }

    int GetX() const
    {
        return X;
    }
    int GetY() const
    {
        return Y;
    }
};

class Square
{
    Point LeftBottom;
    int Length;
public:
    Square(Point TempLeftBottom, int TempLength)
    {
        LeftBottom = TempLeftBottom;
        Length = TempLength;
    }
};
```

```cpp
class Triangle
{
    Point Avertex, Bvertex, Cvertex;
public:
    Triangle(Point TempAvertex, Point TempBvertex, Point TempCvertex)
    {
        Avertex = TempAvertex;
        Bvertex = TempBvertex;
        Cvertex = TempCvertex;
    }
};

class Circle
{
    Point Centre;
    int Radius;
public:
    Circle(Point TempCentre, int TempRadius)
    {
        Centre = TempCentre;
        Radius = TempRadius;
    }
};

class Face
{
    Circle LeftEye;
    Circle RightEye;
    Triangle Nose;
    Square Mouth;
    Point Position;
public:
    Face(Point TempPosition),
    LeftEye(Point((TempPosition.GetX() + 20),
    TempPosition.GetY() + 10), 4),
    RightEye(Point((TempPosition.GetX() + 50),
    TempPosition.GetY() + 10), 4),
    Nose(Point((TempPosition.GetX() + 35),
    TempPosition.GetY() + 20),
    (Point((TempPosition.GetX() + 30),
    TempPosition.GetY() + 25)),
    (Point((TempPosition.GetX() + 40),
    TempPosition.GetY() + 25))),
    Mouth((Point(TempPosition.GetX() + 25),
    TempPosition.GetY() + 30), 20)
    {
        Position = TempPosition;
    }
};

void main()
{
    Face DummyFace(Point(20, 30));
    Face OtherFace(Point(50, 70));
}
```

How the Program Works

Five classes have been defined in this program. The Point class is designed as a platform for deriving all other figures from it. The Point objects are passed to the constructors of Square, Circle, and Triangle. The Point object passed to Square determines the left bottom vertex of the square. The length is also passed as a second argument. Given these two values, a square can easily be drawn. In the case of the triangle, all three vertices are passed. In the case of the circle, a point representing the centre and the radius is passed. The component figures that are under discussion, that is, Square, Circle, and Triangle, are thus composite objects themselves, containing the Point objects within them. There is no need to call the constructor of Point while calling the constructor of any of these objects. Why do we need to call the constructors of Square, Circle, and Triangle in the constructor of their composite object Face? This is because their construction cannot take place in an absolute way. Their construction has one important parameter, the Position, which depends on the construction of the composite object (the position at which the composite object is constructed). So, the constructor of component objects should be called within the body of the composite object.

The program has two objects of type Face. Both are drawn at different places in the two-dimensional space. Since both contain different coordinates, all the objects that are a part of Face need to be drawn at different places. This is achieved by calling the constructor functions in the MIL of the constructor of Face.

Inherited Members vs Contained Members

At times, a beginner in C++ is confused between the inherited members and the contained members. Though they look the same, they are very different. The following are the differences:

1. From the design point of view, inherited members have a relationship that is similar to a subset relationship. If Scooter is inherited from Vehicle, then Scooter objects also belong to Vehicle class (scooters are vehicles; hence, they are a subset of vehicles). All instances of Scooter are instances of Vehicle. In Program 9.9, Face contains the object Circle, but it does not have the subset relationship. It is rather a part of relationship. Nose (a triangle) is a part of the face. Left and right eyes (circles) are again parts of the face. However, all instances of Triangle and Circle are not instances of Face as well.
2. Inherited members must execute their constructors outside the constructor body of the derived class using MIL. If the base class has a constructor, the derived class must also have one itself. Both these restrictions do not apply to contained members. We have seen two different cases, one of the employee collection object in Program 9.8 and the other of the component objects square, circle, and triangle in Program 9.9, where the constructors of the embedded objects are not called.
3. One needs to be careful while assigning values to the constructors of contained objects based on the values passed to the constructor of the container class. Here, one needs to execute the constructors of the contained objects in the constructor of the container class using MIL. (Program 9.9 is an example of such a need. Circles, triangle, and square representing the eyes, nose, and mouth, respectively, need to be drawn depending on the position of the face.)
4. Both types of members (inherited and contained) are treated by C++ in a similar way (embedded in the target class); so, they seem similar while programming.
5. Understanding the difference between the part of and subset relationship helps in one more way. It is called choosing the right link (or inheritance chain) when one is in need of some specific attribute. Suppose an object representing the arm of a sofa is being considered at

the moment. If its colour needs to be found, it is better to travel through the part of the link to know the colour of the sofa. It would be a waste of time if one traverses using subset link to look at the properties of furniture (a class from which the arm of the sofa is inherited).

A similar case is that of a control pasted on a frame in graphical user interface (GUI) programming. The look and feel of the control depends on the parent frame. Consider a button placed on a form. The colour and the font of the button should match with that of the frame in which it is loaded. A programmer may need to know what type of font is to be chosen when pasting it on a specific frame. One needs to traverse the *part of* rather than the *subset of* link. The Button class is having a subset relationship with the Window class while a part of relationship with the Frame or Form.

▓ RECAPITULATION ▓

- Object-oriented programming is based on the concept of inheritance.
- Inheritance is a process to extend an already defined class into a new class with all the properties of the old class plus some additional ones.
- The advantage of inheritance is that there is no need to create objects from scratch.
- Sometimes, the real world has a model that can most intuitively be programmed using inheritance.
- It is also important to understand that one must use inheritance to implement only the subset model. A class having a logical subset of objects of some other class should only be inherited from that class.
- It is possible to derive a class from one or more base classes. When a class is derived from more than one base class, the process is known as multiple inheritance.
- Multiple inheritance is problematic to implement for applications as well as compilers.
- It is also possible to derive from an already derived class.

- If we want only a single copy of the grandparent class, we need to define the parents to inherit the grandparent virtually.
- The compiler needs to keep track of the virtual base classes to ensure that multiple copies of the grandparent do not exist when these classes are inherited further.
- The classes that do not have any objects are known as abstract classes.
- The constructors of the derived class should call the constructors of the base class.
- The order of calling the base class construction follows the order of inheritance list present in the derived class header.
- These constructors can be called only using MIL.
- Exception handling mechanism can catch the base class object when a derived object is thrown.
- Composite objects are different from derived objects. They contain the objects of other classes as data members.

▓ KEYWORDS ▓

Abstract class A class without any object is known as an abstract class.

Access declaration Making a special member (or members) to have a different type of inheritance than specified in the inheritance class is known as access declaration. A different type cannot override the original access specifier used in the base class.

Access specifier and access modifier Public, private, and protected are the ways by which one can define data members. These are known as access specifiers. All three can be specified while a class is being derived from another class. At that point of time, they are known as access modifiers.

Base class The class being extended in the process of inheritance is known as the base class.

Base class subobject When the base class is inherited in the derived class, the base class object is embedded in the derived class object, and this object is known as the base class subobject.

Composite or container object Object that includes other objects as data members is known as composite or container object.

Derived class The extended class itself is known as the derived class.

Inheritance This is a mechanism to extend an existing class into a new class. The new class will have all the attributes of the old class plus some of its own. The new class is said to be inherited or derived from the old class.

Multiple inheritance The inheritance where the derived class is derived from more than one base class is known as multiple inheritance.

Private derivation or private inheritance This refers to inheriting a class in a way that the public and protected members of the base class become the private members of the derived class.

Protected access modifier for data members The protected access modifier works in the same way as the private specifier for the data members of the class,

except that the private members of the base class are not available to the derived class whereas its protected members are available to the derived class.

Protected derivation or protected inheritance This refers to inheriting a class in a way that the public and protected members of the base class become the protected members of the derived class.

Public derivation or public inheritance This refers to inheriting a class in a way that the public and protected members of the base class retain their status in the derived class.

Virtual base class A class that is defined as virtual at the time of inheriting it is known as the virtual base class. The compiler takes a note of it and when it is inherited further using multiple inheritance, the compiler ensures that only one copy of the subobject of the virtual inherited class exists in the derived class.

■ EXERCISES ■

Multiple Choice Questions

1. For handling exceptions in inheritance, what should be sequence of the handlers?
   (a) The base class handler must precede the derived class handler.
   (b) The derived class handler must precede the base class handler.
   (c) No such specific sequence is required.
   (d) The base class handler can never be specified in the presence of the derived class handler.

2. An object becomes more cluttered in case of _____.
   (a) single inheritance
   (b) multi-level inheritance
   (c) multiple inheritance
   (d) hierarchical inheritance

3. The main advantage of protected members is that _____.
   (a) they are available to the derived class functions
   (b) they are available to the derived class objects
   (c) Both
   (d) None

4. What does the following syntax describe?
   `class Derived : public Base1, public Base2;`
   (a) Single inheritance
   (b) Multi-level inheritance
   (c) Multiple inheritance
   (d) Hierarchical inheritance

5. When multiple copies of attributes occur in a derived class, the problem is termed as _____.
   (a) multiple copy problem
   (b) multiple attribute problem
   (c) ambiguity
   (d) ambiguous derived class problem

6. Which of the following is the correct syntax to define a virtual base class?
   (a) `class Derived1 : virtual public Base {};`
   (b) `class Derived1 : public virtual Base {};`
   (c) Both
   (d) None

7. A class with only one instance inherited when inherited from multiple paths is called _____.
   (a) virtual base class
   (b) virtual class
   (c) single inherited class
   (d) single inheritance restricted class

8. The redundancy reduction reduces _____.
   (a) code size
   (b) chances of errors
   (c) Both
   (d) None

9. When a member is protected, it is not different from _____ unless the class is inherited.
   (a) public
   (b) private

(c) Both

(d) None

10. Inheritance is a must for implementing _____ programming.

   (a) object-based programming

   (b) object-oriented programming

   (c) object programming

   (d) All of the above

Conceptual Exercises

1. Differentiate between object-based and object-oriented programming.

2. What are the advantages of using inheritance?

3. What is the difference between public and private inheritance?

4. What is the difference between protected inheritance and other types of inheritance?

5. Explain the statement "The private members of the base class are indirectly available to the derived class".

6. Explain how different types of data members are treated under different types of inheritance.

7. How is protected access specifier different from other access specifiers while further inheriting a class?

8. Why does the C++ object model implement the base class subjects in the derived class object?

9. What are the disadvantages of multiple inheritance?

10. What are the issues one must consider when dealing with multiple inheritance?

11. What is the advantage of access declaration?

12. List few cases where we need to derive multiple classes from a single class.

13. List few cases where we need to derive an already inherited class further.

14. List few cases where we need to have multiple inheritance. (Hint: When we have a classification of the same item in two or more different ways, we need multiple inheritance. For example, fruits can be classified as summer fruits and winter fruits. They can also be classified as sour fruits and sweet fruits. Now, we can have a class summer-sour fruits, which is multiple inherited from summer fruits and also sour fruits).

15. What is the need of virtual base classes? Give an example of your choice to illustrate the need for virtual base class.

16. What are abstract classes? Give some examples of abstract classes.

17. How are constructors of the derived classes executed? What are the issues one must consider while writing derived class constructor?

18. How is exception handling different when the thrown object's class is inherited?

19. How is the behaviour of embedded objects different from that of the inherited objects?

Practical Exercises

1. Define a `Point` class and an `Arc` class. Define a `Graph` class that represents graph as a collection of `Point` objects and of `Arc` objects. Find the following:

   (a) The shortest distance between any two points (use Dijkstra's algorithm). You may also design your own algorithm.

   (b) Find the minimum cost spanning tree using this graph and produce one more graph representing the same minimum cost spanning tree. (Minimum cost spanning tree is the tree derived from a graph after removing the heaviest arcs).

2. Write a program to create classes `Person`, `Examiner`, `Subject`, `Stream`, `Arts`, `Commerce`, `Science`, `Engineering`, and `Student`. A student object will have multiple inheritance from `Person` and either `Arts`, `Commerce`, `Science`, or `Engineering` class. In turn, these classes get inherited from the `Stream` class. Provide routines for enrolling, examination result processing, and granting degree to the students.

3. Write a program to represent part as an object. A part can contain other parts as members. Provide operations to list all the required ingredient parts for any given part looking at the deepest of the hierarchy. Provide routines for inserting and removing parts or the information related to parts.

4. Define a class `Figure` and use inheritance to define the classes `Triangle`, `Square`, `Circle`, and `Rectangle`. Provide a container class `Frame` to contain any number of figures, possibly overlapped in position. Provide operations for drawing frames on the screen and for inserting, modifying, and deleting frames and the contents of frames. (Actual drawing is not required).

5. Define a class `Student`. Inherit this class into `MCAStudent` and `NonMCAStudent`. Also inherit it into `Local` and `NonLocal` students. Multiple inherit `LocalMCAStudent` from `Local` and `MCAStudent`. Define five instances of `LocalMCAStudent` with a constructor, assuming that all classes have a constructor.

Run-time Polymorphism by Virtual Functions

10.1 INTRODUCTION

Polymorphism is the property of the *same object* to *behave differently* in *different contexts* given the *same message*. We have seen that overloaded functions and operators exhibit this property. Suppose there is a class of complex number and the '+' operator has been overloaded for adding two complex numbers as well as a complex number with a normal number. Now, suppose the function Sum() is also defined to perform the same operations.

Look at the following statements:

```
Complex C1, C2, C3;
int i;
C3 = C1.Sum(i);
C3 = C1.Sum(C2);
C3 = C1 + i;
C3 = C1 + C2;
```

In all these cases, the object C3 behaves differently (i.e., calls different functions) when given the same message, that is, either Sum or +, depending on the context (the argument passed). Note that this type of polymorphism is decided at compile time, that is, C++ decides what to do at compile time. This is an important property of an object-oriented (OO) language, and it needs to be extended at run-time.

Suppose there is an abstract base class Vehicle that stores the data and functions common to three other derived classes, namely Car, Bus, and Scooter. Examples of such information are the registration number of the vehicle, date of manufacturing, dealer identity, date of sale, etc. Such information is stored in the Vehicle class because otherwise it needs to be stored in every class derived from the base class. The same issue also arises for the functions. There are two choices, namely, defining it in the base class alone or defining it in every class derived from the base class. Unlike

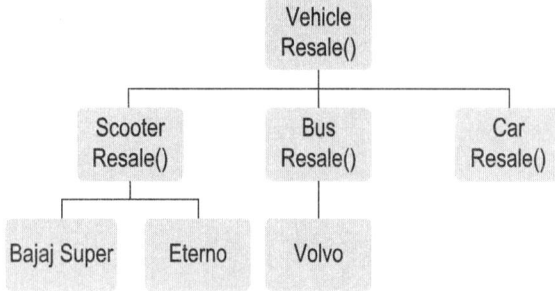

Fig. 10.1   The vehicle hierarchy with a function `Resale()`

the data members, it seems at first sight that there is no sense in making it a member of the base class. For example, if a `Resale()` function has been defined in `Vehicle`, then it is useless in the same class, because an object of the base class cannot be invoked. Another option is to ignore the concept of abstract class and define `Resale()` in all the classes separately. The only problem is that the function call using base class pointer is not possible as there is no such function in the base class.

This example can be compared with another one discussed in Chapter 9, namely, a `Shape` class and its descendents, `Circle`, `Square`, and `Rectangle`. The `Shape` class stores all otherwise redundant information about the objects of the three descendent classes such as the position on the screen, colour, rotation, and angle with origin. The function `draw()`, which is required by all classes, has no significance for the `Shape` class.

If there is a base class, then one can define a pointer to the base class and then that pointer can be made to point to any of the descendent classes. Suppose in the given example, there is a function `Resale()` defined in the `Car`, `Bus`, and `Scooter` classes, as shown in Fig. 10.1. In this case, if the pointer is made to point to the `Vehicle` class, then it can be made to point to any of the descendent classes. Now, when one has a pointer that points to an object of some descendent class, one has to execute the function belonging to that object. This decision cannot be made at compile time because a pointer can be made to point to an object only at *run-time*. At run-time, one has to find which object is the pointer pointing to and execute the function of that class. Here, one has to define a pointer to the `Vehicle` class, and then, if one needs to resale a scooter, one has to make it point to the `Scooter` object and then execute the `Resale()` function of that object. This seems simple, but in reality, it is not. We will learn in the following sections why this is so.

10.2 COMPILE TIME AND RUN-TIME POLYMORPHISM

Compile time polymorphism includes operator and function overloading, while run-time polymorphism includes the decision of using a specific version of a function at run-time. C++ uses virtual functions to deploy run-time polymorphism.

We have seen examples of polymorphism such as function and operator overloading in earlier chapters. A single function name can be used for various purposes (with different arguments) and a single operator can be used to achieve multiple operations (with different types of operands), and the usage of either the function or the operator depends on the context in such cases. The compiler, while compiling the program, resolves the function call or the operator call. This is known as *compile time* or *static polymorphism*. As we have already studied about functions and operator overloading in Chapters 4 and 6 respectively, in this chapter, we will concentrate on achieving polymorphism at run-time. We need to understand some prerequisites before discussion on run-time polymorphism. They are explained in the following sections.

10.3 POINTER TO OBJECT

Pointer to object is a variable containing an address of an object. It is similar to a pointer to any other variable. The normal `address-of` operator has to be used to get the address of an object. One can define a pointer to an object and can assign it the address of the object. Look at the following statements:

```
class Demo
{
// Body of the class
}
Demo DemoObj;
Demo *PtrDemoObj;
PtrDemoObj = &DemoObj;
```

It is similar to other pointers and has no difference.

> **Note** Pointer to object is not different from other pointers. It holds the address of the object instead of some other variable. The same `address-of` operator can be used here as well.

10.4 this POINTER

The `this` pointer is a pointer to an object invoked by the member function. Suppose one writes `DemoObj.DispDemo()`, then a function call to `this` pointer will return the address of `DemoObj`. In other words, `this` pointer is a pointer to `DemoObj`. This is explained in Exhibit 10.1.

> **Exhibit 10.1** Returning `this` pointer
>
> If the code has the following statement
>
> ```
> Object.Function() or *ObjectPointer->Function()
> ```
>
> then whenever `this` is referred to in the `Function()` body, it means a pointer to an object (first case) or an object pointer (second case).
> Similarly, `*this` is the same as `Object` in the first case whereas it is `*ObjectPointer` in the second case. An important statement in such functions is
>
> ```
> return *this
> ```
>
> which means that the function returns the invoking object itself.

The following program explains the usage of `this` pointer to return the invoking object. It has a function where the elder of the two brothers is returned. In case the invoking object represents the elder brother, the function returns `*this`, that is, the object that has invoked the function.

```
//thispointer.cpp
#include <iostream>
#include <string>
using namespace std;
class person
{
    string Name;
    int Age;
```

```
public:
  person(string TempName, int TempAge)
  {
    Name = TempName;
    Age = TempAge;
  }
  person Elder(person OtherPerson)
  {
    if(Age > OtherPerson.Age)
        return *this;
        /* Returning the invoking object, that is the object
        representing Steve in this case */
    else
        return OtherPerson;
  }
  friend ostream & operator <<(ostream& TempOut, person & TempPerson);
  /* The << operator can be overloaded only as a friend */
};
ostream & operator <<(ostream & TempOut, person& TempPerson)
/* The overloaded operator must be passed as a reference
and must return a reference */
{
  TempOut << "The person " << TempPerson.Name << "is ";
  TempOut << TempPerson.Age << " years old \n";
  return TempOut;
}
void main()
{
  person Steve("Steve Waugh", 25);
  person Mark("Mark Waugh", 20);
  person BigBrother = Steve.Elder(Mark);
  cout << BigBrother;
}
Output
The person Steve Waugh is 25 years old
```

10.5 COMPATIBILITY OF DERIVED AND BASE CLASS POINTERS

We have also seen earlier that the base class pointers can point to a derived class object. One does not need any casting for the same. Suppose the code has the following definitions:

```
BaseClass BC;
DerivedClass DC : public BaseClass;
BaseClass *PtrBC;
DerivedClass PtrDC;
```

Now, it is possible to write

```
PtrBC = &BC; // Obvious, pointer and content are of similar types
PtrDC = &DC; // Here too
PtrBC = &DC; // This is done without any casting

// The following is not allowed
PtrDC = &BC
```

> **Note** A base class pointer can point to a derived class object but a derived class pointer cannot point to a base class object.

Though the derived class and base class pointers seem compatible, there are some points to be noted as follows:

1. The base class pointer can be made to point to a derived class object, but it cannot access the original members of the derived class. It can only access the base class members of the derived class object. In fact, it can see only the base class subobject embedded in the derived class object and not the additional part of the derived class. Thus, a base class pointer cannot access a normal function of a derived class. However, if any of the functions defined in the derived class is defined as virtual in the base class, the case is different and is the focus of this chapter.

2. In no case can the derived class object pointer be made to point to the base class (reverse of point 1). It can only be done by casting. One can write `PtrDC = (DC *) &BC`. However, it is an error if one writes `PtrDC = &BC`.

> **Note** Casting a base class pointer to a derived class pointer is called *downcasting*. When we downcast, it results in a successful operation but produces garbage, as the pointer points to the derived class object but contains only the base class subobject. Thus, the address elements after the base class subobject result in garbage. Such behaviour is dangerous and requires some mechanism to check whether the object pointer is really pointing to what it should. Later on, we will see how the dynamic_ cast operator solves the problem in Chapter 11.

3. The increment and decrement operators with base pointer types do not behave as expected. A base class pointer is always incremented as per the base class size and a derived class pointer is always incremented as per the derived class size. Hence, if a base class pointer is pointing to a derived class object, after increment, it might not point to the next derived object. This is explained using Fig. 10.2. If the pointer to `BaseClass1` is incremented by one, then it will now point to somewhere in either `BaseClass2` or `DerivedClass` original contents.

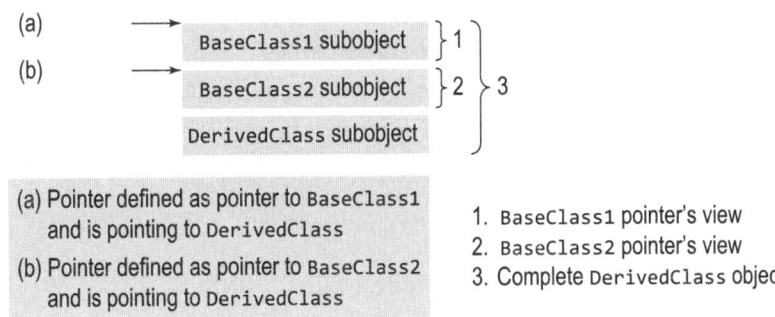

Fig. 10.2 Base class pointer increment

A derived class object always contains a base class subobject within the body of the object. If there are multiple base classes, a derived class contains a base class subject embedded within its body, one for each base class.

10.5.1 Subobject Concept

Whenever a base class is inherited, the derived class contains the base class subobject. We have seen examples of this earlier. In case of multiple inheritance, the derived class contains multiple subobjects. In case of inheritance with more than one level, there are *n* subobjects in the class derived at *n* + 1 level. The subobjects are usually stored before the actual data members of the respective class. We have seen such an example while discussing multiple inheritance in Section 9.10 in Chapter 9. The compiler automatically manages the pointer to point to the respective subobject in case two or more classes inherit into a single derived class.

Suppose a program has the following statements:

```
BaseClass1 BC1;
BaseClass2 BC2;
DerivedClass DC : public BaseClass1, BaseClass2;
BaseClass1 *PtrBC1;
BaseClass2 *PtrBC2;
DerivedClass PtrDC;
```

Now, consider the following statements:

```
PtrBC1 = &DC;
PtrBC2 = &DC;
```

In both the cases, the pointer is made to point to the respective base class subobject of the derived class object. It is important to note that the `BaseClass1` pointer does not need any manipulation at compile time. The address of DC (&DC value) is the same as the address of the subobject of `BaseClass1`. The compiler, however, needs to change the address in the case of the second base class.

It is important to understand that though the base class pointers are allowed to point to the derived class, their access is limited to the original size of the base class. They cannot address beyond their limit. In other words, a base class pointer can be made to point to a derived class object, but it can only access base class members (embedded within a derived class object) and cannot access any of the derived class members. This is also true for multiple inheritance case as shown in the example, that is, it cannot access *other* base class members (as well as derived class members) in the case of multiple inheritance. The concept of object slicing is explained in Exhibit 10.2.

Exhibit 10.2   Object slicing
While inheriting a base class, the base class subobject is embedded within the derived class object. Moreover, a base class pointer pointing to a derived class can access only the base class subobject.   When a base class pointer points to a derived class object, it is said to slice the base class object from derived class object. This process is known as object slicing.

10.6 BASE CLASS AND DERIVED CLASS MEMBER FUNCTIONS

It is possible for two different member functions, one defined in the base class and another defined in the derived class, to have the same name. The function in the derived class is

<table>
<tr><td>When a function with the same name as in the base class is defined in the derived class, it is said to override the original function. The new function is called the overridden function in this case.</td></tr>
</table>

known as an *overridden function* in this case. The process is known as overriding the said function. It is analogous to having a global and a local variable with the same name. Whenever one refers to the variable in the local context, the local variable is in effect. Similarly, if one refers to a function in the derived class, the derived class function is executed. If one refers to the same function in the base class, the base class function is executed.

It is interesting to check the case where the pointer to the base class is made to point to the derived class and the overloaded function is called using that pointer. Let us find which function will be executed using Program 10.1 and then analyse it.

PROGRAM 10.1   Non-virtual function

```
#include <iostream>
using namespace std;

class Shape
{
    int LineStyle;
    int FillColour;
public:

    // Non-virtual function
    void draw()
    {
        cout << "Shape is drawn \n";
    }
};
class Circle : public Shape
{
    int Radius;
    int CentrePointX;
    int CentrePointY;
public:
    void draw()
    {
        cout << "Circle is drawn \n";
    }
};
int main()
{
    Shape SomeShape, *PtrShape;
    Circle Ring;
    SomeShape.draw();
    Ring.draw();

    PtrShape = &Ring;
    PtrShape->draw();
    /* This calls the draw function of the base class and not the
    derived class where the pointer is pointing. */
}
```
Output
```
Shape is drawn
Circle is drawn
Shape is drawn
```

<table>
<tr><td>

A base class pointer will always call a base class function irrespective of where it is pointing to, if the function is a normal (non-virtual) function.

</td><td>

How the Program Works

The sentence `PtrShape->draw();` produces something strange. When a base class pointer pointing to the derived class is used, the function called is from the base class and not from the derived class. Though the pointer is pointing to a derived class object, it still executes the `draw()` function of the base class. If the `draw()` function is called as a normal public function using the objects of the respective class, the `draw()` belonging to the respective class is executed, that is, `Ring.draw()` calls the `draw()` of `Circle` class and `SomeShape.draw()` calls the `draw()` of `Shape` class.

</td></tr>
</table>

When a programmer needs to execute a function of the object pointed to by the pointer at run-time, the function must be defined as virtual.

Here, the function is accessed using an object of the class in the second case (calling `Ring.draw()`). The proper function belonging to the same object is called in this case. When an object is accessed using a pointer, the function of that object is not called. The function of the object where the pointer is *defined to point to* is called. In other words, the pointer type (pointer to base class) matters when the function is called and not where the pointer is pointing to (pointing to an object of type circle). Why is this so?

> **Note** A non-virtual function will always be resolved at compile time, and thus, which function to call is decided by the type and not where it is pointing at run-time. This option is chosen as it is more efficient.

This is simply for the sake of efficiency. When two possible solutions exist (one at the compile time and the other at run-time), C++ tries to favour the solution that can be obtained at compile time. In the given example, there are two possible solutions as follows:

1. Execute a base class function (irrespective of the content of the pointer variable, that is, where the pointer is pointing to, using implicit `this` pointer available at the compile time. (The `this` pointer is pointing to the base class subobject because the pointer variable is defined to point to the base class type). The information about the *type* of the pointer is available at compile time and no run-time overhead is needed to use it.
2. Execute a function of the object it is pointing to (irrespective of the type of the pointer). This solution requires the compiler to find the exact type of the object pointed to by the pointer. This can only be done at run-time in most of the cases.

By default, the first solution is executed by the compiler because the pointer type is always available at compile time whereas where the pointer is pointing to may not be available. The second solution is not preferred because finding out where the pointer is pointing to at run-time, and then loading and executing that function, is not efficient.

> **Note** C++ defaults to *decision-making at compile time* to improve efficiency. The decision to execute base class functions even when a pointer may point to some other inherited object's class is one of the examples of this feature.

10.7 VIRTUAL FUNCTIONS

What should one do if one wants to execute the derived class function using the pointer to base class that is pointing to a derived class object? In such instances, one has to use a virtual function instead of the normal function. Program 10.2 is a modified code of Program 10.1.

PROGRAM 10.2   Virtual function

```
#include <iostream>
using namespace std;

class Shape
{
    int LineStyle;
    int FillColour;
public:
    // Virtual function
    virtual void draw()
    {
        cout << "Shape is drawn \n";
    }
};
class Circle : public Shape
{
    int Radius;
    int CentrePointX;
    int CentrePointY;
public:
    void draw()
    /* This is also a virtual function even though we have not used the keyword. We have
    inherited the virtual property here */
    {
        cout << "Circle is drawn \n";
    }
};
class Rectangle : public Shape
{
    int LeftTopX;
    int LeftTopY;
    int RightBottomX;
    int RightBottomY;
public:
    SomeOtherFunction()
    // No draw defined here
    {
        // Some statements
        /* Whenever there is no function defined for a derived class,
           the virtual function defined in the base class is called. */
    }
};

int main()
{
    Shape SomeShape, *PtrShape;
    Circle Ring;
    SomeShape.draw();
    Ring.draw();
    PtrShape = &Ring;
    PtrShape->draw();            // This draws a circle
    Rectangle Square;
    PtrShape = &Square;
    PtrShape->draw();
    // This would still call draw() of Shape
}
```

Output
```
Shape is drawn
Circle is drawn
Circle is drawn
Shape is drawn
```

How the Program Works

Note the change. Now, `PtrShape->draw()` calls the `draw()` of `Circle` and not of `Shape`. In `Shape` class (base class), the function is defined as `virtual void draw()`. The addition of the keyword `virtual` makes the whole difference. When the statement `PtrShape->draw()` is executed, it looks at the content of the `PtrShape` at run-time and then executes the `draw()` function that is appropriate. This is the difference when virtual functions are used instead of normal functions.

Though the keyword `virtual` is not used in the inherited class, it is still a virtual function, as the virtual property is inherited. One can still use the keyword `virtual` before the function name without changing its working.

Suppose one needs to find the object that is being dealt with at run-time and take an appropriate action depending on the type of object, how can it be done?

For example, one is dealing with customers and provides them some information about the products they are interested in. There is a mix of customers and they are categorized as foreign and Indian customers, service-oriented and cost-sensitive customers, and so on. Suppose there is a new customer who is Indian and cost-sensitive, how would the program decide to provide him/her different options? Suppose there is a function called `DisplayOptions()`, how will the function display the appropriate options? Assume the following code snippet:

```
CustomerDetails(Customer & CurrentCustomer)
{
    ...
    case 3:
        CurrentCustomer = new IndianCostsensitiveCustomer();
        CurrentCustomer->DisplayOptions();
}
```

Look at the function header. The base class reference passed to the function has been used in this program. In case 3, it has been made to point to a derived class object that was just created. It is interesting to see that the base class reference is passed to this function and not to that of the derived class object. The reason is simple. At the time of writing the program, one does not know who is going to query the program and in which order. The first customer may be foreign and cost sensitive, whereas the second customer may be Indian and service oriented, and so on. Hence, the function has to act dynamically at run-time and display appropriate options for a given customer. The program has a case-based logic for that purpose. Now, the problem is to have an object depending on the type of the customer one is dealing with. If a base class reference is available, then one can take advantage of the fact that it can point to any derived class object. So, a base class reference (`Customer &`) has been used here.

The second line is more important for our discussion. When the function `DisplayOptions()` is called, one expects the function to display only those options that the `CurrentCustomer` is pointing to. It is necessary to define `DisplayOptions()` as virtual for this purpose.

A virtual function can be defined in a simple way by just preceding the definition by the keyword `virtual`. The following code snippet shows how virtual function `DisplayOptions()` can be defined.

```
class Customer
{
    ...
    virtual DisplayOptions()
    {
        ...
    }
}
```

For the `Vehicle` class, definitions such as the following are needed:

```
class Vehicle
{
    ...
    virtual Resale()
    {
        ...
    }
}
```

So, the code snippet can be written as follows:

```
ResaleVehicle(Vehicle & SomeVehicle)
{
    ...
    case 3:
        SomeVehicle->Resale();
}
```

One can call the `ResaleVehicle()` function in the following cases:

```
Scooter GJ012345;
Bus GJ024587;
Car GJ274589;

cin >> VehicleForSale

ResaleVehicle(VehicleForSale);
// VehicleForSale = GJ012345
// SomeVehicle points to Scooter object

ResaleVehicle(VehicleForSale);
// VehicleForSale = GJ024587
// SomeVehicle points to Bus object

ResaleVehicle(VehicleForSale);
```

> The virtual table contains pointers to all virtual functions for a given class. The vptr is a pointer to the virtual table. All objects of the class contain the vptr.

> The virtual table also contains RTTI for polymorphic objects when RTTI is enabled.

```
// VehicleForSale = GJ274589
// SomeVehicle points to Car object
```

It can be seen that these three function calls initialize the SomeVehicle reference (which is a reference to Vehicle, a base class) to a Scooter, Bus, and Car object, respectively, *depending on the customer's input at run-time*. The function Resale() must be virtual to provide the effect that is needed here.

It can be seen that the coding is simplified as it has the same statement for all the three descendent classes. In fact, the code does not change even if there are 1,000 descendent classes (or even more). This is the strength of a virtual function.

Virtual functions are special. They are treated differently by the compiler. The class has an additional storage requirement when at least one virtual function is defined inside. A table is created additionally to store the pointers to all virtual functions available to all the objects of the class. This table is known as the virtual table. A single pointer to the virtual table is inserted in all class objects when the class contains at least one virtual function. This pointer is traditionally known as *vptr*. Whenever an object of such class wants to execute a virtual function, the table is referred to and the appropriate function is called. This, as explained earlier, is done at run-time.

The virtual table may also be created when run-time type information (RTTI) is used, even if one does not have any virtual function. This is because the compiler inserts the data type information in the same virtual table that was discussed earlier. This table can be referred at run-time for finding the data type of an object. It is also true with a virtual base class. The compiler either has a special virtual base class table where the pointer to all virtual base classes is kept or may use the same virtual table for the virtual functions to store the information about the virtual base classes (with respective pointer to virtual base classes). The second option is more efficient because a single table is used to address to both virtual functions and virtual base classes; so, it is preferred by most of the compilers.

There are a few syntactical constraints on the use of virtual functions, which are enumerated as follows:

1. The function name must be preceded by the keyword virtual in the base class.
2. The function in the derived class must have the same name and the same prototype as that of the virtual function defined in the base class, such as the draw() function in Program 10.2. If the prototype is different, the function is as good as an overloaded function and is not treated as a virtual function.
3. The function in the derived class need not be preceded by the keyword virtual. Even if it is preceded by the keyword, it makes no difference.
4. If a function with the same name is not defined in the derived class, the original base class function is invoked. For example, if one more class Rectangle is inherited from Shape with no draw() function defined and then if draw() is invoked by a Shape pointer pointing to Rectangle, the draw() of Shape class is called. The given example contains a Rectangle class where the draw() function is not defined; so, the call invokes the base class function.
5. The virtual function must be defined in the base class; it may have an empty body though.
6. For any real problem-solving case using virtual functions, the class hierarchy should be present. The virtual functions are members of the classes of the hierarchy. They are called

It is not possible to have virtual constructors, whereas virtual destructors are possible.

using either pointer to the base class or a reference to the base class. This implies that the functions must be members of the base as well as the derived classes.

7. Polymorphism is achieved only by using pointers (or references) to the base class. It is not possible using objects. `Ring.draw()` would always call `draw()` of `Ring` and not of `Shape` and vice versa. This is known as *static invocation* of virtual function.

8. Virtual constructors are not possible. Constructing a derived class object needs specific construction of the base class subobject within. Obviously, their constructors cannot be virtual. (Rather, the constructor of a derived class calls the constructors of the base class as well) When an object is deleted, one may have a virtual destructor for destroying it; so, the `delete <pointer>` operation works for the object pointed to, irrespective of the pointer type. Here, it is allowed to provide deletion of the entire derived class object while pointed to by a base class pointer (otherwise it would only delete the base class subobject of the derived class). Anyway, it is a good idea to have virtual destructors to avoid memory leaks.

10.7.1 Static vs Dynamic Binding

The virtual function invocation mechanism is sometimes referred to as dynamic binding. Linking is a process of 'attaching' called functions from the `main()` after compilation to create an executable file. Linker is the entity that performs the linking. At the time of linking, the linker does not know which function to call when a virtual function using a pointer to base class is invoked. It is decided at run-time looking at the content of the pointer. Thus, virtual function calls are not resolved until they are called. This implies that such functions are linked at run-time. This also implies that the program using virtual functions would run a bit slower because it involves two steps, namely, linking and executing.

Static binding happens at compile time, whereas dynamic binding happens at run-time.

If virtual functions had not been used, the functions would be linked at linking time (after compilation, before creating executable) and their calls resolved then. There is no run-time overhead as dynamic binding here. This type of binding is known as static binding.

The following program is a simple example to show the difference between static and dynamic binding.

```
#include <iostream>
using namespace std;
class BaseClass
{
public:
    // When called, the function tells which class it is part of
    void testWhichClass()
    {
        cout << "BaseClass" << endl;
    };
    class DerivedClass : public BaseClass
    {
```

```
        public:
        // The same function is also defined in the derived class
        void testWhichClass()
        {
           cout << "DerivedClass" << endl;
        };
        void findClass(BaseClass & SomeClass)
        {
           /* Whenever some class reference is passed to this function,
           it is accepted as a base */
        class reference
        SomeClass.testWhichClass();
        /* This checks which class is the SomeClass passed to this function */
        }
      int main()
      {
        DerivedClass D;
        findClass(D);
        getchar();
      }
```

Output

```
BaseClass
```

A derived class object has been passed, but the output displays BaseClass. If the function testWhichClass() is changed to virtual, the output will be DerivedClass.

> **Note** With a non-virtual function, whenever a base class reference refers to a derived class object, it still calls the base class function. When the function is defined virtual, the same reference referring to the derived class invokes the derived class function.

10.7.2 Default Arguments to Virtual Functions

Default arguments to virtual functions do not behave the way they are expected to behave. Consider Program 10.3:

PROGRAM 10.3   Default arguments do not behave normally with virtual functions

```cpp
//DefArgs.cpp
#include <iostream>
using namespace std;
class Shape
{
    int LineStyle;
    int FillColour;
public:
    virtual int draw(int size = 100)
    /* It will not work as expected. The default argument value will always depend on the
    pointer type and not the content. */

    {
        cout << "Shape is drawn \n";
```

```
            return size;
        }
};

class Circle : public Shape
{
    int Radius;
    int CentrePointX;
    int CentrePointY;
public:
    int draw(int size = 200)
    {
    cout << "Circle is drawn \n";
    return size;
    }
};

int main()
{
    Shape SomeShape, *PtrShape;
    Circle Ring;
    SomeShape.draw();
    Ring.draw();
    PtrShape = &Ring;
    /* Base class pointer pointing to derived class object */

    int DrawSize = PtrShape->draw();
    // This draws a circle

    cout << "Draw size using base class pointer: " << DrawSize << "\n";
    /* This displays 100 instead of 200, as the pointer type is Base */

    Circle *PtrCircle = &Ring;

    DrawSize = PtrCircle->draw();
    /* Now, we are using a derived class pointer to
    point to a derived class object */

    cout << "Draw size using derived class pointer: " << DrawSize << "\n";
    /* This will display 200, as the pointer type is Derived */
}
```

Output
```
Shape is drawn
Circle is drawn
Circle is drawn
Draw size using base class pointer: 100
Circle is drawn
Draw size using derived class pointer: 200
```

How the Program Works

When the following statements are executed

```
int DrawSize = PtrShape->draw();
cout << "Draw size using base class pointer: " << DrawSize << "\n";
```

it displays 100 instead of 200. When the following statements are executed

```
Circle *PtrCircle = &Ring
DrawSize = PtrCircle->draw();
```

```
cout << "Draw size using derived class pointer: " << DrawSize << "\n";
```

it displays 200 correctly.

> **Note** When we use a base class pointer to point to a derived class object, the *default value of the base class function* will be taken. Here, the function that is executed is correct, but with the default value of the base class. On the other hand, when we use a derived class pointer, the default value of the derived class function is taken.

Dummy Default Arguments to the Rescue

Program 10.3 showed that default parameters cannot be used like a normal function. The solution here is to provide a local variable initialized in both such classes and then to use the default argument. If default arguments are needed, they can be assigned values of such local variables, as shown in Program 10.4.

One only needs to see whether the user has supplied a value, and if not, take information from the local variables rather than the default arguments. One can easily check whether the user has supplied a value by keeping a dummy default argument. If the argument equals the dummy value, the user has not supplied the argument, and one can take the value from the local variable. Program 10.4 illustrates how to do it.

PROGRAM 10.4 Using dummy default argument as a solution

```cpp
//SolutionDefArgs.cpp
#include <iostream>
using namespace std;
class Shape
{
    int LineStyle;
    int FillColour;

public:
    virtual int draw(int size = 1)
    /* The size parameter is dummy; it is there to check whether the default argument is
    provided */
    {
        cout << "Shape is drawn \n";
        int ShapeSize = 100;
        /* This is to check whether the default argument is provided with the given
        value 100 */

        if(size == 1)
            size = ShapeSize;
        return size;
    }
};
class Circle : public Shape
{
    int Radius;
    int CentrePointX;
    int CentrePointY;
public:
    int draw(int size = 1)
    {
        cout << "Circle is drawn \n";
        int CircleSize = 200;
```

```
        if(size == 1)
            size = CircleSize;
        return size;
        }
};
int main()
{
    Shape SomeShape, *PtrShape;
    Circle Ring;
    SomeShape.draw();
    Ring.draw();
    PtrShape = &Ring;
    /* Base class pointer pointing to derived class object */

    int DrawSize = PtrShape->draw();
    // This draws a circle

    cout << "Draw size using base class pointer: " << DrawSize << "\n";
    /* This will print the correct value */

    Circle *PtrCircle = &Ring;
    /* Now, we are using a derived class
    pointer to point to a derived class object */

    DrawSize = PtrCircle->draw();
    cout << "Draw size using derived class pointer: " << DrawSize << "\n";
}
```

Output
```
Shape is drawn
Circle is drawn
Circle is drawn
Draw size using base class pointer: 200
Circle is drawn
Draw size using derived class pointer: 200
```

How the Program Works

This trivial patch solves the problem. The code might seem to be strange. When one checks for size == 1, one means to check whether the user has supplied a value. If so, the value 100 is assigned to size in the first function and 200 in the second function. Thus, the value of size is now dependent on the function that is executed. In both these cases, the function of the derived class is executed, and so, the correct answer is obtained.

10.7.3 Advantages of using Virtual Functions

Suppose a video is prepared from a cartoon movie. The video consists of individual frames. An individual frame is what one sees on the screen one after another. Motion is created by generating the frames fast enough such that it appears continuous to our mind (and not the eyes).

Each individual frame contains figures made up of a few basic shapes such as triangle, rectangle, and circle. Individual frames are not stored in the form of photographs or bitmap files as they consume a lot of memory. How can they be stored instead?

Assume that the following figure is to be drawn on the frame.

The information can be stored as follows:

```
Circle(20, 30) radius = 10;    // The face
Rectangle(15, 35, 30, 45)      // The neck
...
```

A frame is described in terms of circles, rectangles, triangles, and lines, which are random in number. How can one write a function that draws a frame? The function algorithm looks as follows:

```
void DrawFrame()
{
    Shape *Element;
    Open the file;
    Do while not end of file
       <Read from file some shape information>
       <Assign element pointer to the address of that shape>
       Element->draw();
    Loop over
}
```

This programming methodology where a base pointer is used to access a bunch of objects from various classes of a single hierarchy is known as OO programming. It is very flexible in the sense that one need not know the exact type of the object in order to manipulate it. The data may come at run-time, either from a file, a communication line, or from user input, and one is able to deal with it.

A program that does a similar job is given in Section 10.8. For simplicity, the program assumes that the input is random. The data coming either from a file, a communication channel, or a user can safely be assumed to be random for testing the program and the concept.

There are plenty of real-life cases that require such flexibility. Take an automated news flash system that takes the latest news as an input and flashes it on the screen based on its priority and importance. The news can be related to politics or sports; political news can be state level or central; sports news can be related to either cricket or gymnastics; and so on. If a specific processing for a specific category is needed when the news is coming without any pre-decided order, a virtual function such as `Processing()` could be very useful. The system need not decide what to do depending on the type of the news object. It would only call the function `Processing()` and the appropriate function for that object would be automatically called.

> Virtual functions make it possible to deal with a mix of objects inherited from a single parent, with a single pointer to the same parent.

This is an example of a general case where a big hierarchy of classes is derived from a root class. It is possible to process any object of the hierarchy at random with this approach. This is the power of true OO programming. However, the power does not come without a cost. Adding and processing virtual functions is a big performance overhead. Languages such as Java have a single root class from which all the classes are derived from (known as the Object class). It enables the Java programmers to enjoy lots of flexibility, but at the cost of speed. In C++, there is a choice. Only if needed, one may go for OO programming; otherwise, object-based programming can be used. Standard Template Library (STL) is an example of object-based programming methodology. We will discuss about it in Chapter 16.

10.7.4 Virtual Destructors

When a destructor is defined virtual, it destroys the proper object pointed to be the pointer and not the subobject of the base class where the pointer is defined to point to.

Virtual destructors are needed for proper deletion of objects of derived class, when pointed to by a base class pointer. If virtual destructors are not defined, only the base class subobject is deleted, and the remaining portion of the derived class object is not deleted. It should be understood that the name of the destructor cannot be the same in the base and the derived classes (because their names must derive from the names of the class). This restriction is relaxed here. It is known that a class can have only one destructor. A derived class destructor is the function called when `delete` is invoked with a base class pointer with the content as the derived class object. Program 10.5 is an example that shows how virtual destructors can be defined and used.

PROGRAM 10.5   Non-virtual destructor destroying incorrect object at run-time

```cpp
//VirtualDestructor.cpp
#include <iostream>
using namespace std;

class BaseClass
{
public:
    BaseClass()
    {
        cout << "BaseClass constructor ..." << endl;
    }

    /* The following destructor is not virtual. This will call for static invocation of the
    function that will call the base class destructor even when the pointer points to a
    derived class object. The result of such a call is undefined */

    ~BaseClass()
    {
        cout << "BaseClass destructor ..." << endl;
    }
};
class DerivedClass : public BaseClass
{
public:
    DerivedClass()
    {
        cout << "DerivedClass constructor ..." << endl;
    }
     ~DerivedClass()
    {
        cout << "DerivedClass destructor ..." << endl;
    }
};
```

```
void main()
{
    BaseClass* ptrBase;
    ptrBase = new DerivedClass();
    delete ptrBase;

    /* This should ideally call for DerivedClass destructor, but will
    call only BaseClass destructor, because the destructor is not virtual.*/

    getchar();
}
```
Output
```
BaseClass constructor ...
DerivedClass constructor ...
```
BaseClass destructor ...

How the Program Works

It can be seen that when the delete operator is executed, it only calls the destructor for the base class and not the derived class. Thus, only the base class subobject of the DerivedClass object pointed to by the ptrBase is destructed and the rest is not. The standard says that the behaviour is undefined, which means the response to such coding depends on the implementation and it is likely to vary.

Instead, if the base class destructor is defined as virtual (which makes all the destructors of all the classes in the hierarchy virtual), it is possible to control that behaviour. The run-time system deletes the object pointed to by the pointer, thus calling a DerivedClass destructor in this case. It is also interesting to note that the DerivedClass contains the base class object and the DerivedClass destructor in turn calls the base class constructor.

```
virtual ~BaseClass()
{
    cout << "BaseClass class destructor ..." << endl;
}
```
```
BaseClass constructor ...
```
```
DerivedClass constructor ...
```
DerivedClass destructor ...
```
BaseClass destructor ...
```

> **Note** Unlike other destructors, virtual destructors are called looking at the context and not by name. A ~<class name> may not destroy the object of <class name> but some other object derived from <class name> depending on where the pointer is pointing to.

10.8 USE OF VIRTUAL FUNCTIONS

Let us now look at the use of virtual functions. Suppose there is a class figure containing 25 small figures. A small figure can be either a Circle, a Square, or a Triangle. Every object of figure class contains some specific combination of squares, circles, and triangles. The following options are available:

1. Fix the total number of squares, triangles, and circles, so they can be defined as, say,
   Circle CircleOfFigure[10], Square SquareOfFigure[10], Triangle TriangleOfFigure[5];

however, this is too rigid and not acceptable for any arbitrary drawing. One needs to have each figure with a fixed number of objects for different types. This is not acceptable in real-life scenario.

2. Use array of pointer to `Shape` class, which is made to point to different objects of `Circle`, `Square`, and `Triangle` type at run-time. Virtual functions are to be used for drawing small figures because normal functions cannot be used, as they would try to execute the `draw()` of the base class. Suppose there is a figure of two triangles, three squares, and one circle. Then, for the two triangles, the `draw()` function of the `Triangle` and not of the `Shape` class should be called. Similarly, for the three squares, the `draw()` function of the `Square` and not of the `Shape` class should be called.

> **Note** A virtual function is designed on the same lines of a void pointer. When a pointer to base class is defined, it acts like a void pointer and can be assigned to any derived class object. When one defines an array of such pointers, the array can be used to define a mix of objects of descendent classes. C programmers use void pointer arrays for similar purpose.

The second approach is more flexible and useful. Let us have a look at Program 10.6, which uses it.

PROGRAM 10.6 Using virtual function

```cpp
//UsingVirtualFunction.cpp
#include <iostream>
#include <ctime>
using namespace std;

class figure;
/* This is forward declaration. This is needed here as the point class contains a friend
statement. The compiler must know that there
exists a class called figure, so that being a friend to it is acceptable. */

class Point
{
    int X;
    int Y;
public:
    Point(int TempX = 0, int TempY = 0)
    {
        X = TempX;
        Y = TempY;
    }

    int GetX() const
    {
        return X;
    }

    int GetY() const
    {
        return Y;
    }

    friend ostream & operator <<(ostream & TempOut, Point & TempPoint);
};

ostream & operator <<(ostream & TempOut, Point & TempPoint)
{
```

```
        TempOut << "(" << TempPoint.GetX() << ", " << TempPoint.GetY() << ")";
        return TempOut;
}

class Shape
{
        Point Position;
        int Colour;
        virtual void draw()
        {
            cout << "Shape is drawn";
        }
        friend figure;
        /* Derived class will use the private members of the Point class, such as X and Y for
        drawing shapes, and hence it must be a friend to the Point class. */
};

// Derived class Square
class Square : public Shape
{
        Point LeftBottom;
        int Length;
public:
        Square(Point TempLeftBottom, int TempLength)
        {
            LeftBottom = TempLeftBottom;
            Length = TempLength;
        }

        void draw()
        {
            cout << "Square is drawn at " << LeftBottom << " and with length as " << Length << "\n";
        }
};

// Derived class Triangle
class Triangle : public Shape
{
        Point Avertex, Bvertex, Cvertex;
public:
        Triangle(Point TempAvertex, Point TempBvertex, Point TempCvertex)
        {
            Avertex = TempAvertex;
            Bvertex = TempBvertex;
            Cvertex = TempCvertex;
        }

        void draw()
        {
            cout << "Triangle is drawn at " << Avertex << " "
            << Bvertex << " " << Cvertex << "\n";
        }
};

// Base class Figure
class figure
{
        Shape * Images[25];
public:
        figure() // Constructor of class figure
```

```
    {
    // Logic to generate random numbers
    srand((unsigned)time(NULL));
    for(int i = 0; i < 25; ++i)
    {
        int RandomValues [6];
        for(int j = 0; j < 6; ++j)
        {
            RandomValues[j] = rand() % 50;
        }

        /* The following statements use random values; however, in real-world cases, the
        values may be coming from some source such as graphics server, a camera, or a file
        generated by an artist, and so on.*/

        Point Position1(RandomValues[0], RandomValues[1]);
        Point Position2(RandomValues[2], RandomValues[3]);
        Point Position3(RandomValues[4], RandomValues[5]);

        switch(int choice = rand() % 3)
        {
            case 0:
            {
                int Length = rand() % 20;
                Images[i] = new Square(Position1, Length);
                break;
            }
            case 1:
                Images[i] = new Triangle(Position1, Position2, Position3);
                break;

            default:
                cout << choice << " is a wrong choice";
        } // End of switch case
    } // End of for loop
} // End of constructor function

    void draw()
    {
        for(int i = 0; i < 15; ++i)
        {
            Images[i]->draw();
        }
    }
}; // End of class figure

void main()
{
    figure MyFigure;
    MyFigure.draw();
}
```

Output
```
Square is drawn at (0, 14) and with length as 18
Triangle is drawn at (14, 41) (14, 24) (28, 17)
Triangle is drawn at (16, 33) (25, 37) (20, 35)
Square is drawn at (0, 22) and with length as 1
Triangle is drawn at (44, 23) (15, 37) (23, 18)
Square is drawn at (10, 1) and with length as 15
Square is drawn at (26, 6) and with length as 19
```

```
Square is drawn at (11, 20) and with length as 1
Triangle is drawn at (1, 38) (47, 48) (14, 27)
Square is drawn at (49, 24) and with length as 17
Triangle is drawn at (43, 48) (41, 26) (20, 11)
Square is drawn at (7, 25) and with length as 3
Square is drawn at (27, 15) and with length as 7
Square is drawn at (3, 0) and with length as 10
Square is drawn at (0, 41) and with length as 0
```

How the Program Works

This program calls for a few explanations.

1. This is an extended version of Program 10.3. This program uses the function rand() available in the library. It also uses a function called srand() for providing the seed value to the rand() function. Current time is used as the seed value; thus, different random numbers are obtained each time. In real-world scenario, the inputs would be coming from a file (when one is reading a file describing the image in digital format of points), a communication channel (while viewing a cartoon drawn using such points), or a temporary buffer (in case of streaming, i.e., when data to draw the image is first stored in the temporary buffer and then allowed to be fed at a constant rate), but the effect would be similar to the draw() function that is used here.

2. This program has a class figure, which contains an array of pointers to Shape class object. Why pointers to Shape class alone? This is because one is not sure about what will be the contents of the figure. The only way to access is to provide a pointer to the base class and access the contents (the small figures) using a pointer to the Shape class. For simplicity, this program uses a fixed array of size 25. This figure class actually represents an image. The Shape and its descendents are the building blocks of the figure.

3. A virtual function draw() is needed. This is because when the draw() function is called, the respective small figure should be drawn.

4. The figure class should be made a friend of Shape, because it uses the private members (the positions of all the derived classes of Shape) to draw the figure. Access methods would be a better solution here, but this program uses a simple solution that serves the purpose.

5. As already studied, as figure is defined after Shape, it is necessary to provide forward definition of figure as a class.

> **Note** Virtual functions are needed when we need to deal with different types of objects with unknown proportion. We may also need to deal with objects belonging to the same generic class but having specific distinct attributes.

An array of base class pointers and dynamic memory allocation is all that are needed to have storage of multiple objects belonging to the same hierarchy.

Think of a program that finds what the customers are interested in by looking at their behaviour. Customers can be of different types, with and without credit cards, regular buyers and casual buyers, those who buy in bulk but once in a while and those who buy at regular intervals, those who belong to teenage and have specific demands and those who are housewives and are interested in specific items, and so on. It is, in this case, required to have them represented by different classes. One may have customer as a base class and then provide all these classes as inherited from customer. Now, this problem involves dealing with customers with unknown proportion at a place (maybe a supermarket). One can only have an array of customer pointer, and only when dealing with a specific type of customer, one has to *new* that customer and then assign the base class pointer to it.

10.9 PURE VIRTUAL FUNCTIONS

When a class does not have any object, there is no need to have functions for it, as there are no objects to utilize those functions. Consider the case of class Shape that was discussed in Program 10.6.

```
class Shape
{
   Point Position;
   int Colour;
   virtual void draw()
   {
      cout << "Shape is drawn";
   }
   friend figure;
};
```

There will never be an object of class Shape in an actual working environment. If draw() is defined in the class, one will never be able to execute it.

It is important to understand that because draw() is a virtual function, it is not possible to have polymorphism without draw() defined inside Shape. In other words, the definition of Shape is needed in the base class but not its body. This can be rewritten as follows:

```
virtual void draw()
{
// Empty
}
```

In this case, the draw() function is defined with an empty body. This can also be achieved by writing

```
virtual void draw() = 0;
```

The body of the function is not needed here, though one can define it outside the class boundary as Shape::draw().

> **Note** Pure virtual functions do not have the body where they are defined, but they can still have it outside the class.

When "= 0" is written in place of the function body after the function header, the function is said to be *pure virtual*. In such a case, the function need not have a body. It offers a great advantage. The function forces the native class to be abstract, that is, it inhibits the object definitions of the class. This means that if a class contains a pure virtual function, it becomes an abstract class, and C++ will not allow defining an object belonging to that class. In a way, when a programmer wants the user not to define

> An abstract class is the one with no objects.

objects of a specific class, he/she can define a pure virtual function (may be a dummy) inside the class.

Pure virtual functions can be invoked statically like normal virtual functions, that is, it is possible to invoke

```
ptrShape->Shape::draw()          // Using only a pointer
```

In this case, the function must be defined outside the class as

```
shape::draw()
{
    // The body
};
```

> **Note** When a single pure virtual function is defined inside a class, it automatically becomes abstract. The program cannot instantiate the abstract class and, thus, cannot have an object of that class.

The concepts of pure virtual function, virtual destructors, and static invocation of virtual functions are illustrated in Program 10.7.

PROGRAM 10.7 Pure virtual function

```cpp
//PureVirtual.cpp
#include <iostream>
using namespace std;
class Shape
{
    int LineStyle;
    int FillColour;

public:
    /* This is a pure virtual function. Though it does not have a
    body in the class, it can have it outside the class itself */

    virtual void draw() = 0;

    virtual ~Shape()// Virtual destructor
    {
        cout << "Shape destroyed\n";
    }
};
void Shape::draw()
{
    cout << "Shape is drawn\n";
}
class Circle : public Shape
{
    int Radius;
    int CentrePointX;
    int CentrePointY;
public:
    ~Circle()
    {
        cout << "Circle destroyed\n";
    };

    void draw()
```

```
    {
        cout << "Circle is drawn\n";
    }
};
int main()
{
    // Shape SomeShape;

    Shape *PtrShape;
    Circle Ring;

    // SomeShape.draw();
    /* We cannot call the draw() function of the Shape class, as we cannot have an object of
    the abstract class. */

    PtrShape->Shape::draw(); //Static call to Shape draw()
    PtrShape = &Ring;
    PtrShape->draw();    // Draws a circle
    cout << "Messages from destructor start now\n";
    PtrShape = new Circle;

    delete PtrShape;
    /* If ~Shape is not virtual, this will not work as expected.
    It will only delete the base class subobject (shape subobject of circle) and not the
    entire derived class object (circle). */
    cout << "Above messages are from delete\n";
    cout << "Following are normal messages exiting the program\n";
}
```

```
Output
Shape is drawn
Circle is drawn
Messages from destructor start now
Circle destroyed
Shape destroyed
Above messages are from delete
Following are normal messages exiting the program
Circle destroyed
Shape destroyed
```

How the Program Works

Defining pure virtual function   The statement

```
virtual void draw() = 0;
```

is important here. It shows the pure virtual function being defined, which makes the class Shape an abstract class. It should also be noted how the body is also defined outside the class.

```
void Shape::draw()
{
    cout << "Shape is drawn\n";
}
```

So, this is how one can define a body for a pure virtual function. It should be remembered that every class that inherits from Shape *must* implement this function (otherwise, it becomes abstract). What a designer wants to convey when he/she defines a pure virtual function is to say that all classes that has objects must be able to handle this message. In the given example, it states that all descendents of Shape must be able to receive the message draw and respond accordingly.

Static invocation of pure virtual function The following statements are commented as it is not possible to define objects of Shape class, which is an abstract class, as the pure virtual function draw() is defined inside. Thus, it is not possible to call the member function using the object dot notation.

```
// Shape SomeShape
// SomeShape.draw();
```

The solution is to use a pointer instead of an object to call that function, with the scope resolution operator. One can call that function using the following syntax, which executes Shape::draw() function using a pointer PtrShape.

```
PtrShape->Shape::draw();      // Static call to Shape draw
```

This is a static call because irrespective of wherever PtrShape may be pointing to, it will always execute the draw() function of the Shape class.

Polymorphic call to pure virtual function If one wants to execute a function belonging to the class object being pointed to, a normal syntax can be used as follows. The draw() function of Ring object will be drawn when the following statements are executed. A statement such as the following means that one takes a pointer pointing to a derived class object (PtrShape in this example), extracts a base class subobject (as PtrShape is defined as a pointer to the base class Shape and not Ring class), and calls a function that is a part of it.

```
PtrShape = &Ring;
PtrShape->draw();
```

Calling virtual destructor The destructor is also an important part of the program. Look at the code

```
PtrShape = new Circle;
delete PtrShape;
```

This **delete** statement invokes the destructor for Circle object and not Shape as the destructor is defined virtual.

```
virtual ~Shape()      // Virtual destructor
{
   cout << "Shape destroyed\n";
};

~Circle()
{
   cout << "Circle destroyed\n";
};
```

If Shape is not defined with a virtual destructor, one will not be able to destroy an object of type Circle while pointed to by pointer of type Shape. See that the destructor for the Circle is called first and then that for the Shape subobject is called.

Notes

1. A virtual destructor to a derived class also invokes the destructor of the base class as the base class subobject buried within the derived class needs it.
2. If a base class contains a pure virtual function, all the other classes in the hierarchy must implement it. If a class does not implement it, it automatically becomes an abstract class, in which case it is not possible to have objects of that class.
3. Pure virtual functions are doing what interfaces do in Java, that is, forcing descendents to implement the function exactly specified in the base class.

10.9.1 Static Invocation of Virtual Function

Virtual functions can also be invoked statically. When a `class name::ptr->virtual function` mechanism is used, they are called statically. Consider the base class `Shape`, virtual function `draw()`, and the derived class `Circle`. Suppose one writes the statements

```
Shape *PtrShape = new Circle;
PtrShape->Shape::draw()
```

In this case, the second statement calls the `draw()` of `Shape` class and not of `Circle` class.

Exhibit 10.3 explains the static evaluation of virtual function content.

Exhibit 10.3 Static evaluation of a virtual function content

When we call a function by the syntax

```
PointerToBaseClass->BaseClassSubObject::FunctionName
```

it is known as the static invocation of the `FunctionName`.
For example,

```
PtrShape->Shape::draw()
```

is the static invocation of `draw()`. Irrespective of the function being virtual and of where `ptrShape` is pointing to, the function that belongs to the base class subobject will be called.

Let us now analyse the topic further with the help of an example. It is related to a problem where the classes are arranged using the type of error. Following is the class hierarchy that is to be modelled in the program.

Define a class `Error`. It should contain error code, description, and possible solutions for the error. Define two derived classes, `SyntaxError` and `LogicalError`, inheriting from the base class `Error`. Define `CompilerError` and `LinkerError` classes inheriting from `SyntaxError` class and `LoopingError` and `InitializationError` inheriting from `LogicalError` class. `PossibleSolutions` is a function that displays what to do if an error has occurred and is defined in all these classes. Define this function such that given any error, it should display all relevant actions to be performed. That is, if an error is an initialization error, it displays possible solutions for initialization errors as well as possible solutions for logical errors and also for generic errors. Figure 10.3 shows the hierarchy that is observed among the classes. Program 10.8 shows how the solution can be coded.

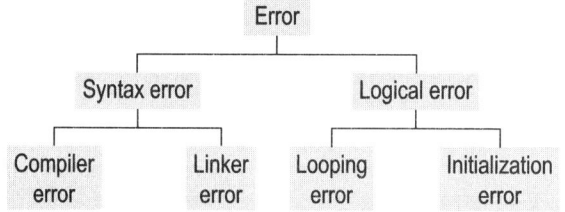

Fig. 10.3 Hierarchy of classes defining different types of errors

PROGRAM 10.8 Invoking the pure virtual function statically

```cpp
//StaticInvocation.cpp
#include <iostream>
using namespace std;

class Error
{
private:
    int ErrorCode;
    string Description;
public:
    virtual void PossibleSolutions() const = 0;
};

// Body of the virtual function defined outside the class
void Error::PossibleSolutions() const
{
    cout << "Generic error\n";
}

// Derived class SyntaxError
class SyntaxError : public Error
{
public:
    void PossibleSolutions()const
    {
        Error::PossibleSolutions();
        cout << "Check the syntax\n";
    }
};

// Derived class LogicalError
class LogicalError : public Error
{
public:
    void PossibleSolutions()const
    {
        Error::PossibleSolutions();
        cout << "Logic is erroneous\n";
    }
};

// Class CompilerError is derived from SyntaxError
class CompilerError : public SyntaxError
{
public:
    void PossibleSolutions()const
    {
```

```
            SyntaxError::PossibleSolutions();
            cout << "Compiler error\n";
        }
};

// Class LinkerError is derived from SyntaxError
class LinkerError : public SyntaxError
{
public:
    void PossibleSolutions()const
    {
        SyntaxError::PossibleSolutions();
        cout << "Linker error\n";
    }
};

// Class LoopingError is derived from LogicalError
class LoopingError : public LogicalError
{
public:
    void PossibleSolutions()const
    {
        LogicalError::PossibleSolutions();
        cout << "Looping error\n";
    }
};

// Class InitializationError is derived from LogicalError
class InitializationError : public LogicalError
{
public:
    void PossibleSolutions()const
    {
        // Static invocation
        LogicalError::PossibleSolutions();
        cout << "Initialization error\n";
    }
};

void main()
{
    Error *pError = new InitializationError;
    pError->PossibleSolutions();
    Error *qError = new LinkerError;
    qError->PossibleSolutions();
}
```
Output
```
Generic error
Logic is erroneous
Initialization error
Generic error
Check the syntax
Linker error
```

How the Program Works

Defining hierarchy of classes and pure virtual functions with body This example illustrates how one can represent the Error class hierarchy as publicly derived C++ classes. It also shows how one can define `PossibleSolutions()` as a pure virtual function as all classes inherited from it must define it. The `Error` class (the base class) must also have generic solutions using `PossibleSolutions()` and, so, must have a body. As explained earlier, the body is defined outside the `Error` class.

Calling a pure virtual function If the `PossibleSolutions()` function of any class is called, it will call the `PossibleSolutions()` function for only that case. For example, consider the following statements:

```
Error *pError = new InitializationError;
pError->PossibleSolutions();
Error *qError = new LinkerError;
qError->PossibleSolutions();
```

This code will only display the possible solutions for initialization errors and linker errors. The need here is that it should also display errors related to their base classes. In case of initialization errors, it should also display the possible solutions for logical errors as well as general errors. In case of linker error, it should display possible solutions for linker errors, syntax errors, and general errors.

Need for static invocation This can be achieved by statically invoking `PossibleSolutions()` function for all the base classes, such as the `PossibleSolutions()` function of `LinkerError` in turn calls syntax as well as generic errors.

It can be seen that the function contains a call to the `PossibleSolutions()` function of the `SyntaxError` class, which in turn calls the `Error::PossibleSolutions()`; thus, one can get all possible solutions related to the error.

`SyntaxError::PossibleSolutions()` and `Error::PossibleSolutions()` are calls to virtual functions. They are different though. They are known as statically invoked calls to virtual functions.

Why is the static invocation needed? A linker error is also a syntax error, which in turn is an error. We need to print the description given by every class. Why a pure virtual function? We want programmers to implement `PossibleSolutions()` for every error that is a part of the hierarchy.

■ RECAPITULATION ■

- Run-time polymorphism is an important feature of OO programming.
- C++ achieves run-time polymorphism using virtual functions.
- Run-time polymorphism adds overhead to the run-time system. Thus, it is not made a default. We have run-time polymorphism only when a function is defined as virtual.
- Run-time polymorphism is different from compile time polymorphism.
- In the case of a normal function being overloaded by the derived class, a base class pointer will always execute the function defined in the base class irrespective of where it is pointing to.
- The pointer, if pointing to a derived class object, executes a derived class function; otherwise, it executes the base class function.
- When a base class pointer is made to point to a derived class object, it can access only the base class subobject buried within the derived class object.
- Whenever a function is defined as virtual, a special pointer is embedded in every object. This pointer points to a table consisting of pointers to virtual functions that the object is capable of invoking.

- Virtual functions are normally linked at run-time.
- Compiler statically binds the virtual function when it can decide the call at compile time.
- Default arguments to virtual functions refer to the pointer type and not the actual function called. Virtual

functions are very useful in flexible OO programming.
- Pure virtual function are virtual functions with "= 0" in the place of the body in the class definition.
- A class with a pure virtual function becomes the abstract class.

■ KEYWORDS ■

Access method   This refers to a function written to return the value of a private variable of a class. When we need to provide read-level access of private variables to objects, access methods are used.

Base class subobject   In C++ object model, when a class is derived into another, the base class object is embedded within the derived class. This embedded base class object is known as the base class subobject in the derived object.

Compile time polymorphism   Polymorphism achieved using operator overloading and function overloading is known as compile time polymorphism.

Dynamic binding   Linking the function at run-time is known as dynamic binding. Virtual functions are dynamically bound. However, it is possible for the compiler to statically bind the static invocations of virtual functions and also in the case where it is possible to decide at compile time. In such cases, the virtual functions are also statically bound.

Polymorphism   The ability of an object to behave differently in different contexts given the same message is known as polymorphism.

Pure virtual function   A virtual function with "= 0" in place of the body in the class. It may not have the body. It is

also possible to have the body of a pure virtual function defined outside the class.

RTTI   Run-time type information is a mechanism to decide the type of the object at run-time.

Run-time polymorphism   Polymorphism achieved using virtual functions is known as run-time polymorphism.

Static binding   Linking a function during linking phase is known as static binding. Normal functions are statically bound.

Static invocation of virtual function   Only when a virtual function is invoked using pointer directly, the virtual function is dynamically invoked. It is possible to call virtual function using an object of the class or using a scope resolution operator. In such case, the virtual function is statically linked. This is known as static invocation of the virtual function.

Virtual function   A function defined with the keyword virtual in the base class is known as virtual function. The compiler will decide the exact class pointed to by the base class pointer and call the respective function of that class if the function is defined as virtual.

Virtual table   This is a table consisting of pointers to all virtual functions of the class. Every class with at least one virtual function will have one copy of the virtual table.

■ EXERCISES ■

Multiple Choice Questions

1. What does the following syntax show?
   ```
   virtual void show() = 0;
   ```
   (a) Member function
   (b) Friend function
   (c) Virtual function
   (d) Pure virtual function

2. The two different types of polymorphism are _____.
   (a) compile time and run-time

   (b) compile time and link time
   (c) compile time and load time
   (d) load time and link time

3. When a programmer does not want a class to be instantiated, it can be achieved by _____.
   (a) defining a member function inside that class
   (b) defining a friend function inside that class
   (c) defining a virtual function inside that class
   (d) defining a pure virtual function inside that class

4. When we write a pure virtual function in any class, _____.
   (a) the class becomes an abstract class
   (b) the class cannot be inherited
   (c) the class becomes a virtual class
   (d) the class becomes a pure virtual base class
5. Pure virtual functions can be invoked statically like normal virtual functions only if the function is defined _____.
   (a) outside the class with empty body
   (b) inside the class with empty body
   (c) outside the class with some body
   (d) inside the class with some body
6. Every class with at least one virtual function _____.
   (a) has multiple copies of virtual functions
   (b) has single copy of the virtual table
   (c) has multiple copies of virtual table
   (d) None of the above
7. The _____ is used to get the address of an object.
   (a) address operator
   (b) address function
   (c) address-of operator
   (d) address-of function
8. What should be used to execute a derived class function using a pointer to base class pointing to a derived class object?
   (a) `this` pointer should be used
   (b) Virtual function should be used
   (c) Virtual pointer should be used
   (d) None of the above
9. _____ cannot help in achieving run-time polymorphism.
   (a) Normal objects
   (b) Pointers to objects
   (c) Virtual functions
   (d) All of the above
10. The _____ manages the pointer to point to the respective subobject in case two or more classes inherit into a single derived class.
    (a) compiler
    (b) linker
    (c) loader
    (d) programmer

Conceptual Exercises

1. What is polymorphism? What is the difference between compile time and run-time polymorphism?

2. What is the importance of `this` pointer in the call to the function using base class pointer?
3. Consider base class B and derived class D. Assume pB is a pointer to base class and pD is a pointer to derived class. Differentiate between these two pointers in terms of accessing the derived class object.
4. What is a subject concept? What is its importance in the case of a base class pointer accessing a derived class pointer?
5. Why is a non-virtual member function of a base class always called even when the base class pointer is pointing to the derived class object?
6. What is the difference between a normal member function and a virtual function?
7. Explain static binding. How do virtual functions enable dynamic binding?
8. What is the problem of default arguments of the virtual function? How can that be solved?
9. What is the requirement of virtual functions in OO programming?
10. Why virtual constructors are not possible but virtual destructor is a good idea?
11. Differentiate between virtual functions and pure virtual functions.
12. What is the need for statically invoking pure virtual or virtual functions?

Practical Exercises

1. Define the `Time` class described in Chapter 9. Inherit Indian Standard Time (IST) and Greenwich Meridian Time (GMT) from it. Write routines that convert from one type of time to another (IST and GMT).
2. Define a class `Stack`. Inherit it into `VariableStack`. Now, inherit this class into `SystemVariableStack` and `UserVariableStack`. Provide constructors and destructors for all the classes.
3. Define a class `Student`. Inherit it into engineering, arts, commerce, and science students. Inherit engineering student into computer science, electronics and communication, and information technology student. Provide constructors for all the classes.
4. For the `Student` class given in Exercise 3, write a program to use a pointer to the `Student` class to access a record of the computer science student. It can be seen that the part defined in computer science is not accessible. Then, define a pointer to computer science student. Now, it can be seen that the part is accessible. Cast the original pointer-to-

student to pointer-to-computer science student and see that now it can access the computer science part.

5. Using the same class given in Exercise 3, now define a virtual function `Display()` for displaying the details for all classes in their respective classes using the same base class pointer (a pointer to student). Now, use the virtual function to access the computer science object. It can be seen that without any pointer casting, the base class pointer can access the derived class object using virtual function.

6. In the class of Exercise 3, provide a virtual function `Registration()`, which registers the respective student for an examination. At the end, display how many students are registered for which examination.

7. In the class of Exercise 2, provide a virtual function `Push()`, which pushes the object into the respective stacks.

8. In Exercise 1, provide a virtual function `Display()`, which displays the time for a given representation.

9. Define a class `Faculty`. It contains the following attributes:
   (a) Name of the faculty
   (b) Qualification of the faculty
   (c) Subjects the faculty can teach

10. Inherit the `Faculty` class in Exercise 9 into a regular faculty, who
    (a) is available full time (no consulting time is specified)

(b) teaches at least three subjects
(c) is part of the institute alone

11. Inherit the `Faculty` class in Exercise 9 into visiting faculty, who
    (a) is available only on two to three days (consulting time is also to be specified)
    (b) teaches a single subject
    (c) is part of some other institute

12. Provide virtual functions for reading and writing class objects of the classes given in Exercises 10 and 11.

13. Define a class `Vehicle`. Inherit this class into two wheelers and four wheelers. Inherit two wheelers into bicycles and scooters and four wheelers into diesel vehicles and petrol vehicles. Provide a virtual function that calculates the mileage of the vehicle (distance travelled in km/ fuel consumed).

14. For Exercise 1, provide virtual destructor for all the classes.

15. Define a class `Employee`. Also define classes of `MaleEmp` and `FemaleEmp` inheriting from the `Employee` class. Define classes `Officers`, `Clerks`, and `Peons` again inheriting from the `Employee` class. Define an array that contains 10 different types of employees. Define a function `ReadDetails()` in all the classes. All array elements should be accessible in the same routine, irrespective of their type.

Chapter 11

Run-time Type Information and Casting Operators

typeid and dynamic_cast are new operators used in RTTI.

Most of the compilers provide RTTI but disable it by default because of performance issues.

Polymorphic objects can be manipulated using virtual functions.

11.1 INTRODUCTION

Run-time type information (RTTI) is a very powerful tool in C++ and is used for finding the type of an object at run-time. Due to run-time functioning, RTTI also impacts the performance of the system to a notable extent. Therefore, most of the compilers provide RTTI but disable it by default. If RTTI is to be used, one needs to enable the option (and accept the performance degradation as well). Though performance is an important issue, it is not most important for some applications. The flexibility and power provided by RTTI scores over the performance problem in such cases.

The ANSI C++ standardization committee has added two keywords to work with RTTI, namely, `typeid` and `dynamic_cast`. `typeid` is an operator that returns the type of objects in a specific form (the `typeinfo` object). `dynamic_cast` is a new type of operator that enables us to cast polymorphic objects in a safe way. It casts the source type to destination type only if valid conversion is possible. Similar operators are `const_cast`, `reinterpret_cast`, and `static_cast`. These operators will be discussed in this chapter. There is a built-in class `typeinfo` introduced here. The `typeinfo` objects hold the information about the type of argument passed to the `typeid` operator.

> **Note** `dynamic_cast`, `const_cast`, `reinterpret_cast`, and `static_cast` are new operators defined in C++ to provide better facility for casting compared to the plain vanilla casting provided in C.

11.1.1 Polymorphic Objects

Using virtual functions, one can point to any object of a derived class with the help of a base pointer. Such objects that can be manipulated using virtual functions are known as *polymorphic objects*. An object with a virtual function and all the objects derived from that object, or any successors in the hierarchy, are all known as polymorphic objects. They can be pointed to by a base class pointer and can be manipulated at run-time.

Consider the case of an `Employee` class, which is inherited into `ProductionEmployee`, `SalesEmployee`, and `OtherEmployee`. Moreover, consider an `Employee` class function `ListLeaves()` that displays the leaves an employee has used so far. Thus, the structure will be as follows:

```
class Employee
{
  ...
public:
   virtual void ListLeaves()
   {...}
}
class ProductionEmployee : public Employee
{
   void ListLeaves()
   {...}
}
class SalesEmployee : public Employee
{
   void ListLeaves()
   {...}
}
class OtherEmployee : public Employee
{
   void ListLeaves()
   {...}
}
main()
{
   Employee *ptrEmp;
   switch(int EmpType)
   {
     ...
     case 1: // Production employee
     ptrEmp = new ProductionEmployee; // Polymorphic object
     ...
   }
   ...
   ptrEmp->ListLeaves()
   ...
}
```

If objects can change their form at run-time, that is, when a pointer changes to point to objects at run-time and the *pointer expression yields different objects depending on where the pointer is pointing to, such objects are known as polymorphic objects.

The object created in this example is a polymorphic object as it takes the form of any of the descendent employee types during run-time.

11.1.2 Need for RTTI

RTTI slows down the process at run-time and thus is used only when needed. Compilers keep it off by default. Alternate solutions using virtual functions are usually better.

RTTI is a powerful tool and it should be avoided if the problem can be solved using virtual functions. However, at times, it is essential to use RTTI. Let us consider a simple example shown in Program 11.1 to understand this better.

Suppose an application has online incoming news. The news can be of different types. For simplicity, let us consider only two types, namely, plain text news and news with images. The application requires having all the news being splashed on the screen with just the headlines. A user can click on any news to view it. It is also possible to right-click on the news to enable some additional operations on it. The right-click option may include the following:

1. Send this news as e-mail.
2. Copy this news in a specific folder.
3. Print this news using a printer.

Suppose that the user does not want the news with images to be printed, as they consume a lot of printer toner. To manage this issue, a **News** class may be defined as the base class. **PlainTextNews** and **NewsWithImages** are two classes derived from it. The News class will be an abstract class, as all the news available are either plain text or with images. No other news types are being considered for the sake of simplicity.

Three functions, SendNews(), StoreNews(), and PrintNews(), are defined in the News class. This design will make NewsWithImages inherit these three functions. However, we do not want NewsWithImages to inherit PrintNews(), which should now be removed from the News class. Where else can it be placed? The next obvious choice is the PlainTextNews class.

The functions SendNews() and StoreNews() are needed for both types of news, and hence, they need to be defined in the News class as virtual. This is shown in Program 11.1:

PROGRAM 11.1   A solution using virtual functions

```cpp
//NewsHierarchy.cpp
#include <iostream>
#include <typeinfo>
#include <string>
using namespace std;

#define SENDNEWS 1
#define STORENEWS 2
#define PRINTNEWS 3

// Base class
class News
{
public:
    virtual void SendNews(string Address){};
    virtual void StoreNews(){};
    virtual ~News() = 0;
};

News::~News()
{
    // Empty body
}
```

```
/* A virtual destructor for making News polymorphic */

// Class for plain text derived from News class
class PlainTextNews : public News
{
public:
    void SendNews(string Address)
    {
        // mailto(Address, this->content)
    }

    void StoreNews()
    {
        // Storing the news in a default folder
    }

    void PrintNews()
    {
        cout << "Printing the news now\n";
    }
};

// Class for news with images
class NewsWithImages : public News
{
public:
    void SendNews(string Address)
    {
        // mailto(Address, &this)
    }
    // Other details
    // Print function is missing here
};

    void StoreNews()
    {
        // Storing the news in a default folder
    }

    /* Right-click function. It takes the reference of the file the
    mouse is pointing to at the moment as an input */

    void MyApp OnRightClick(News & NewsItem, int Choice)
    {
        string Address;
        switch(Choice)
        // Choice represents what is chosen after right-click
        {
            case SENDNEWS:
            cout << "Enter address";
            cin >> Address;
            NewsItem.SendNews(Address);
            break;
            case STORENEWS:
            NewsItem.StoreNews();
            break;

            // The following is not acceptable
            /* case PRINTNEWS:
        NewsItem.PrintNews();  // No print function with News
```

```
        break; */
    }
}
```

> **Note** One needs at least one virtual function to make an object polymorphic. When other functions cannot be made virtual, we may need to define a dummy function virtual. Sometimes, defining a virtual destructor is a good solution.

How the Program Works

This code does not solve the problem completely. Note that sending the news (using e-mail) and storing the news are operations available for both the derived class objects. Thus, it is possible to provide virtual functions in the base class for both these operations, but the print function is not defined for NewsWithImages file. Thus, one cannot define the print function in the News class, and so, it cannot be used.

One needs to write a code that checks for the file type. If the file type is PlainTextNews, it allows printing; if it is NewsWithImages, it does not allow the user to print the news item. The type of news that the mouse is pointing to needs to be known to find whether to provide an option for printing or not. The virtual functions defined in the base class do not support this functionality. RTTI provides a support for checking the type dynamically and, hence, shall prove useful in this situation. A base class pointer is available here. If one can additionally test where it is pointing to, the problem can be solved. For example, if it is known that it is pointing to an object of type PrintTextNews, one can enable the print option, and not otherwise.

It is also important to note that RTTI, similar to virtual functions, requires polymorphic objects to operate, which means that the base class must have at least one virtual function

> RTTI is useful to get the type of an object at run-time and to take decisions based on that information.

defined for RTTI to be operational. Though it is possible to use typeinfo object to work with default types, it is of little use. Section 11.1.4 shows an example of this case. To solve this problem, it is essential to know how RTTI can be used for polymorphic objects.

Before we proceed further, it is imperative that readers have an introduction of the built-in object *typeinfo*.

11.1.3 typeinfo Object and typeid Operator

The <typeinfo> library contains the definition of typeinfo object. This object is automatically created and associated with every data type used in the program when RTTI is enabled. For non-polymorphic data types, it is available even when RTTI is not enabled. The typeinfo

> typeid operator returns the typeinfo object associated with the argument passed to the operator. The argument can be a built-in type or a user-defined object.

object generated depends on the type and not the number of objects. One may have more than one variable of the same type but the typeinfo object generated would be just one. If two integers are defined, one char and the other an user-defined object in the class, then three typeinfo objects are generated, the first one for integer, the second for char, and the third for the user-defined object.

It is possible to get the typeinfo object associated with any object by writing typeid(object). Here, typeid is an operator returning the typeinfo object associated with the object. It can also have a user-defined class argument. In that case, it returns the typeinfo object of that class.

The typeinfo object has three attributes, which are of interest to us. They are described as follows:

Name( ) function   This function returns the type name in a string format.

Operator ==   This operator compares the types of two different typeinfo objects.

Operator !=   This operator compares two typeid objects and returns true if they are of different types.

11.1.4 Using typeid for Non-polymorphic Objects

The following program illustrates the use of RTTI for non-polymorphic objects. RTTI helps the programmer to get the typeinfo object pointed to by the base class pointer and, thus, to check the type of that object at run-time to make decisions. If it is possible to make such decisions, problems such as the news item described in Program 11.1 can be handled easily.

```cpp
//typeinfo.cpp
#include <iostream>
#include <typeinfo>
#include <string>
using namespace std;
class TestClass
{
    int Test;
public:
    TestClass(int TempVal)
    {
        Test = TempVal;
    }
};
int main()
{
    int FirstInt, SecondInt;
    char FirstChar = 'a';
    TestClass TC(5);
    cout << "FirstInt type is ";
    cout << typeid(FirstInt).name(); // Using name()
    cout << "\n";
    // Using ==
    if(typeid(FirstInt) == typeid(SecondInt))
    {
        cout << "FirstInt and SecondInt are of same type\n";
    }
    // Using !=
    if(typeid(FirstInt) != typeid(FirstChar))
    {
        cout << "FirstInt and FirstChar are of different types\n";
    }
```

```
    cout << "Object TC is of type ";
    cout << typeid(TC).name()<< "\n";
}
```

Output

```
FirstInt type is int
FirstInt and SecondInt are of same type
FirstInt and FirstChar are of different types
Object TC is of type class TestClass
```

However, typeid is more useful with polymorphic objects as discussed in Section 11.1.5.

11.1.5 Using typeid for Polymorphic Objects

RTTI has to be enabled for working with polymorphic objects.

Program 11.2 shows how typeid is applied to polymorphic objects. Similar to virtual functions, one needs either a pointer or a reference to the class to enable typeid to provide the correct type contained by a given pointer.

PROGRAM 11.2   typeid for polymorphic objects

```cpp
//PolymorphicTypeid.cpp
#include <iostream>
using namespace std;

class Shape
{
    int LineStyle;
    int FillColour;
public:
    virtual void draw()
    /* A virtual function is a must for us to use RTTI with polymorphic class*/
    {
        cout << "Shape is drawn \n";
    }
};

    class Circle : public Shape
    {
        int Radius;
        int CentrePointX;
        int CentrePointY;
    public:
        void draw()
        {
            cout << "Circle is drawn \n";
        }
    };

class Dot : public Circle
{
    int DotDencity;
public:
    void SomeOtherFunction()
    { // Empty body }
    };

    class Rectangle : public Shape
```

```
    {
        int LeftTopX;
    int LeftTopY;
    int RightBottomX;
    int RightBottomY;
public:
    SomeOtherFunction()  // No draw defined here
    {
        // Some statements
    }
};

int main()
{
    Shape SomeShape, *PtrShape;
    Circle Ring;
    SomeShape.draw();
    Ring.draw();
    PtrShape = &Ring;

    cout << "PtrShape is pointing to " << typeid(*PtrShape).name() << "\n";

    Rectangle Square;
    PtrShape = &Square;
    cout << "PtrShape is pointing to " << typeid(*PtrShape).name() << "\n";
    PtrShape = new Dot;
    cout << "PtrShape is pointing to " << typeid(*PtrShape).name() << "\n";
}
```

Output
```
Shape is drawn
Circle is drawn
PtrShape is pointing to class Circle
PtrShape is pointing to class Rectangle
PtrShape is pointing to class Dot
```

How the Program Works

Program 10.2 in Chapter 10 is modified here to show the use of RTTI for polymorphic objects. It uses `typeid` to display the type of object `PtrShape` is pointing to. `typeid` has (`*PtrShape`) as an argument. It is important because one needs to use a pointer to enable the `typeid` applied to and return an appropriate `typeinfo` object associated with the object pointed to by the pointer. Here, it returns the `typeinfo` object associated with the *content* of `PtrShape`.

`typeid` has been used for displaying the type of the object in statements such as

```
cout << "PtrShape is pointing to" << typeid(*PtrShape).name() << "\n";
```

The `typeid(*PtrShape)` operator returns the `typeinfo` object associated with *PtrShape and the name function gives the name of the object.

11.1.6 Using `typeid` for Solution

Consider Program 11.1 that we have seen earlier in this chapter for dealing with different types of news. It was seen that the problem of adding a printing option when one right-clicks the object could not be solved using virtual functions. Program 11.3 shows how the problem can be solved using `typeid`.

 **PROGRAM 11.3** Solution to printing problem using typeid

```cpp
//NewsHierarchy.cpp
#include <iostream>
#include <typeinfo>
#include <string>
using namespace std;
#define SENDNEWS 1
#define STORENEWS 2
#define PRINTNEWS 3

class News
{
public:
    virtual void SendNews(string Address){};
    virtual void StoreNews(){};
    virtual ~News() = 0;
};

News::~News()
{
    // Empty body
}

class PlainTextNews : public News
{
public:
    void SendNews(string Address)
    {
        // mailto(Address, &this)
    }

    void StoreNews()
    {
        // Storing the news at default position
    }

    virtual void PrintNews()
    {
        cout << "Printing the news now\n";
    }
};

class NewsWithImages : public News
{
public:
    void SendNews(string Address)
    {
        // mailto(Address, &this)
    }
    // Other details
    // Printing is missing out here
};

/* Right-click function */
void MyApp OnRightClick(News & NewsItem, int Choice)
{
    string Address;
    switch(Choice)
```

```
/* Choice represents what is chosen after right-click */
{
    case SENDNEWS:
    cout << "Enter address";
    cin >> Address;
    NewsItem.SendNews(Address);
    break;

    case STORENEWS:
    NewsItem.StoreNews();
    break;
    // The following is not acceptable

    /* case PRINTNEWS:
    NewsItem.PrintNews();  // No print function with News
    break; */
}

    if(typeid(NewsItem) == typeid(PlainTextNews))
    {
        // Provide option for print
        cout << "Printing is enabled\n";
        PlainTextNews & PrintableNewsItem = (PlainTextNews &)NewsItem;
        // Printing is done only for printable items
        PrintableNewsItem.PrintNews();
    }
}
int main()
{
    PlainTextNews TextNews;
    MyApp_OnRightClick(TextNews, 0);
}
```

Output
```
Printing is enabled
Printing the news now
```

> **Note** One can compare the type of objects at run-time using `typeid`.

How the Program Works

This example omits the details about the program itself and only concentrates on the required aspects of RTTI. The important part is the use of `typeid` with the polymorphic object reference `NewsItem`.

```
if(typeid(NewsItem) == typeid(PlainTextNews))
{
    cout << "Printing is enabled \n";
    PlainTextNews & PrintableNewsItem = (PlainTextNews &)NewsItem;
    // Printing is done only for printable items
    PrintableNewsItem.PrintNews();
}
```

`NewsItem`, if referring to `PlainTextNews`, is casted to refer to `PlainTextNews`. Now, one can call the `PrintNews()` function. This is safe as it is already known that `NewsItem` is of printable type.

11.1.7 Applying `typeid` to Class Names and Objects

Program 11.3 has a statement

```
typeid(News) == typeid(PlainTextNews)
```

`typeid` operator can be applied to both a class and an object of the class. In both cases, it returns the `typeinfo` object associated with the class.

Let us analyse this statement to understand the use of the `typeid` operator in a better way. When `typeid(NewsItem)` is applied, the `typeid` operator is being applied to an object of `News` class. In this case, the `typeid` operator returns the `typeinfo` object associated with the class of that object, that is, `News` class. When `typeid` is applied to a class, for example, `typeid(PlainTextNews)`, the `typeinfo` object associated with `PlainTextNews` class will be available. The `typeinfo` object has the `==` operator overloaded, and so, it is possible to compare two `typeinfo` objects.

11.1.8 Cases Where RTTI is Useful

At times, a solution is possible in two different ways, that is, using virtual functions and also using RTTI. We have already seen an example of generating screen objects using virtual functions in Chapter 10 (Program 10.6). RTTI can also be used for this purpose. If virtual functions are used, the complexity lies with the designer of class hierarchy. Prior knowledge of usage of all the classes in the hierarchy such as `draw()`, `getArea()`, and `getCircumference()` would be useful because the designer can then provide them at the beginning. This may not be possible in some cases, and one may need to use RTTI instead. The following are a few such cases:

1. When classes are designed, their ultimate users are not involved in the design; so, all their requirements are not known. When the users start working with the hierarchy, they have to check the specific type and provide the operations they need. For example, a user might be interested in providing a function `Shrink()` to the `Rectangle` class and its derived classes.
2. Users normally require other operations in addition to those provided by the original designer. For example, one may like to add a functionality `FillColour()` to the `Shape` class. More importantly, the user does not have the source code of the original class hierarchy, which is in some form of object code available from the library.
3. The class designer cannot predict all the possible applications of a class while designing its hierarchy. The class hierarchy is designed for a general purpose. The user of the graphics library may be an automobile designer or a movie film designer who requires tweening operations on images. Tweening operation involves generating intermediate images automatically. Suppose the designer wants Mickey Mouse to move from left end to right end. This requires drawing continuous images of Mickey Mouse from the beginning to the end from left to right. It is possible to show Mickey Mouse on the left side of the screen at the beginning and on the right side at the end. The designer may draw these two images and the software should draw all the intermediate images itself. Thus, it may be decided by the user what he/she wants to do with the shape that is being dealt with at the time of working with it. A movie designer can use the same shape hierarchy to add tweening operation on it using RTTI.

Virtual functions are decided when the class is designed and are influenced by the designer's choice. RTTI, on the contrary, is useful when the class is being manipulated by the user and is under the user's control.

The following are a few other cases where RTTI is useful:

> RTTI is to virtual functions what dynamic binding is to static binding.

1. While using templates, one may need to know the actual data type and provide validations. The type is not known while dealing with type variables such as ElementType in the stack. RTTI can be used to find the type of the element in the body of a template function or class. We will study about this in Section 11.6.

> RTTI is useful while using templates, providing special attention to specific class hierarchy when the system is being used, and providing specific task for specific class hierarchy.

2. RTTI enables the user to decide about the type of the object at run-time. Take the case of a network packet observation. It has a virtual function Check(), which checks the network packet for normal cases. In the case of a specific type of attack happening on the network, one may write an ad hoc function to check the type of the packet and take an appropriate action. This can be done without modifying the original design and operation by using RTTI. It is possible to use RTTI to check for the type and apply AdditionalCheck() function in place of Check() only for those packets for which further inspection is needed.

3. One may need to add specific tasks for a specific subset of class hierarchy. For example, for all the shapes derived from the Rectangle class, one may need to provide IncreaseWidth() as a function. While dealing with an object, it is not known whether it is derived from a rectangle or from some other object. Hence, the operation is safe only when the operator IncreaseWidth() is applied to the object of a class derived from the Rectangle class. This requires the facility called *downcasting* to work safely. Downcasting in this case makes the base pointer point to the Rectangle class only if the shape is a Rectangle class or any class derived from it. This is provided by dynamic casting. We will study about dynamic casting in Section 11.2.

11.1.9 Problems with `typeid`

The solution provided in Program 11.3 is better than the one given in Chapter 10. It is possible to determine the type of the file at run-time and make a decision on whether to provide printing option or not. It is still not sufficient in some cases.

Suppose there are two different types of plain text news, namely, HtmlNews (which is still text) and RichTextNews (which is a little better than text). Both of them are inherited from PlainTextNews. Program 11.3 will not work properly for HtmlNews and RichTextNews. Why? If one compares typeid(NewsItem) (which returns the typeinfo object associated with News and neither HtmlNews nor RichTextNews) with typeid(PlainTextNews), then it would be false and the printing option is not provided. One solution here is to change the program code in the following manner:

```
if(typeid(NewsItem) == typeid(PlainTextNews)
|| typeid(NewsItem) == typeid(HtmlNews)
|| typeid(NewsItem) == typeid(RichTextNews))
{
    cout << "Printing is enabled\n";
    PlainTextNews & PrintableNewsItem = (PlainTextNews &) NewsItem;
    // Printing is done only for printable items
    PrintableNewsItem.PrintNews();
}
```

A typeid can help assess whether the object is of a specific single class. However, for assessing whether an object is a member of a hierarchy of class objects, we need dynamic_cast.

This would solve the problem for the time being. However, if later on HtmlNews inherits into TaggedHtmlNews and UntaggedHtmlNews, one needs to add two more lines at that place. Every time a class is added to the hierarchy, a line needs to be added here. This approach is both error-prone and laborious.

Where is the problem? The problem is that the typeid operator checks for the current news type alone. If it checks all news derived from the current news type, the problem is solved.

Thus, if it is possible to assure that the news item one is looking for belongs to some class derived from PlainTextNews, then it is safe to provide printing. To check this, a check is needed for every possible type of class that is derived from the PlainTextNews class. One needs to check for every such class and add that information to modify the code. A solution is needed where it is possible to write a general statement that can work for any descendent of PlainTextNews class, which typeid cannot do. If typeid cannot solve this problem, then how can it be solved? This is explained in the following sections.

11.2 DYNAMIC CASTING USING dynamic_cast

In ANSI C++, there are four additional casting operators available, namely, dynamic_cast, static_cast, const_cast, and reinterpret_cast. The first operator, dynamic_cast, provides a solution to the problem mentioned in Section 11.1.9. Let us learn about dynamic_cast. Though it is a casting operator, it is very special. The following are its salient features:

1. This casting operator is used only for polymorphic object casting. In other words, it can cast only from one polymorphic object to another polymorphic object.
2. It is also known as *safe cast*. It succeeds only when it is properly casted, which means that dynamic_cast succeeds only when the pointer (or reference) being cast is an object of the target type or its derived type.
3. The syntax of dynamic_cast is different from normal C-type casting. It is written as

   dynamic_cast<ToObjectPtrOrRef> (FromObjectPtrOrRef)

   It casts from FromObject to ToObject pointer or reference. Instead of a FromObject pointer or reference, it is also possible to write an expression that yields a FromObject pointer or reference. From this rule, it is clear that for dynamic_cast to succeed, the FromObject must be of the same type as the ToObject, or derived from it. One needs to be very careful with the syntax. The first set of braces are angled, that is, <> and the second set of braces are normal round, that is, ( ).
4. If a Base class and a Derived class are available, then casting from the Derived to the Base pointer always succeeds. However, the casting from the Base to the Derived pointer can succeed only if the Base pointer is actually pointing to an object of the Derived type. This is known as downcasting and we will learn more about it in Section 11.9.
5. Conversion (casting) takes place only with the help of pointers or references. It cannot be done with objects.
6. While working with pointers, if the dynamic_cast fails, it would return null. So, it is important to check for the return value of dynamic_cast similar to a function to see whether the cast is successful. In case of references, the reference cannot be null; so, dynamic_cast will throw bad_cast when it fails.

11.2.1 Using `dynamic_cast`

Polymorphic objects such as `Circle` and `Shape` that we have seen earlier in Program 11.2 can be dynamically casted using `dynamic_cast` to `Shape` pointer. Let us look at Program 11.4 to understand this better.

PROGRAM 11.4   Dynamic casting on polymorphic objects

```cpp
//PolymorphicDynamic_cast.cpp
#include <iostream>
using namespace std;

class Shape
{
    int LineStyle;
    int FillColour;
public:
    virtual void draw()
    {
        cout << "Shape is drawn \n";
    }
};

class Circle : public Shape
{
    int Radius;
    int CentrePointX;
    int CentrePointY;
public:
    void draw()
    {
        cout << "Circle is drawn \n";
    }
};

int main()
{
    Shape SomeShape, *PtrShape;
    Circle Ring, *PtrCircle;

    // Part I
    // Testing four possible cases of conversion
    // A base pointer pointing to base is casted to base

    PtrShape = dynamic_cast<Shape *> (&SomeShape);
    if(PtrShape)
        cout << "Shape pointer to Shape pointer casted\n";
    else
        cout << "Shape pointer to Shape pointer not casted\n";

    /* A derived pointer pointing to derived is casted to derived */
    PtrCircle = dynamic_cast<Circle *> (&Ring);
    if(PtrCircle)
        cout << "Circle pointer to Circle pointer casted\n";
    else
        cout << "Circle pointer to Circle pointer not casted\n";

    /* A base pointer pointing to base is casted to derived */
    PtrCircle = dynamic_cast<Circle *> (&SomeShape);
    if(PtrCircle)
```

```
        cout << "Shape pointer to Circle pointer casted\n";
    else
        cout << "Shape pointer to Circle pointer not casted\n";

    /* A derived pointer pointing to derived is casted to base */
    PtrShape = dynamic_cast<Shape *> (&Ring);
    if(PtrShape)
        cout << "Circle pointer to Shape pointer casted\n";
    else
        cout << "Circle pointer to Shape pointer not casted\n";

    /* Part II
    Casting from base class pointer to derived */
    /* A base pointer pointing to a derived class object
    is casted to a derived class object successfully */

    cout << "Trying to cast a base class pointer\n";
    cout << "pointing to a derived class object\n";
    cout << "to a derived class pointer\n";
    PtrShape = &Ring;

    PtrCircle = dynamic_cast<Circle *> (PtrShape);
    if(PtrCircle)
        cout << "Successful\n";
    else
        cout << "Unsuccessful\n";

    /* A base pointer pointing to a base class object
    failed to cast to a derived class object */

    cout << "Trying to cast a base class pointer\n";
    cout << "pointing to a base class object\n";
    cout << "to a pointer to a derived class object\n";
    PtrShape = &SomeShape;

    PtrCircle = dynamic_cast<Circle *> (PtrShape);
    if(PtrCircle)
        cout << "Successful\n";
    else
        cout << "Unsuccessful\n";

    /* A derived pointer pointing to a derived object
    is casted to a base class pointer successfully */

    cout << "Trying to cast a derived class pointer\n" ;
    cout << "pointing to a derived class object\n";
    cout << "to a base class pointer\n";
    PtrCircle = & Ring;

    PtrShape = dynamic_cast<Shape *> (PtrCircle);
    if(PtrShape)
        cout << "Successful\n";
    else
        cout << "Unsuccessful\n";

    /* The only option left is a derived class pointer
    pointing to a base class object, which is not possible */
}
```

Output
```
Shape pointer to Shape pointer casted
Circle pointer to Circle pointer casted
```

```
Shape pointer to Circle pointer not casted
Circle pointer to Shape pointer casted
Trying to cast a base class pointer
pointing to a derived class object
to a derived class pointer
Successful
Trying to cast a base class pointer
pointing to a base class object
to a pointer to a derived class object
Unsuccessful
Trying to cast a derived class pointer
pointing to a derived class object
to a base class pointer
Successful
```

How the Program Works

Note that the derived class to derived class and the base class to base class conversions are obviously acceptable. Look at the following casting operations. Both of them are successful.

```
PtrShape = dynamic_cast<Shape *> (&SomeShape);
PtrCircle = dynamic_cast<Circle *> (&Ring);
```

It can also be seen that the derived class pointer to base class pointer conversion is also acceptable.

```
PtrShape = dynamic_cast<Shape *> (&Ring);
```

Base class pointer to derived class pointer is possible *only* if base class pointer is actually pointing to a derived class object. So, the following conversion is not successful. Conversion from a Shape pointer to a Circle pointer will fail when the pointer is pointing to a base class object.

```
PtrCircle = dynamic_cast<Circle *> (&SomeShape);
```

However, we will succeed in the following attempt, as the pointer that we are trying to convert is indeed pointing to a derived class.

```
PtrShape = &Ring;
PtrCircle = dynamic_cast<Circle *> (PtrShape);
```

The following is another example where a derived class pointer is casted into a base class pointer successfully. The derived class pointer that is pointing to a derived class object is casted to a base class pointer. This pointer can now access only the base class subobject embedded within the derived class object.

```
PtrCircle = & Ring;
PtrShape = dynamic_cast<Shape *> (PtrCircle);
```

11.2.2 Using dynamic_cast to Replace typeid

In some cases, the code using dynamic_cast can be replaced by one using typeid. It is better and is advisable to do so in such cases. The code using typeid checks for the first slot in the virtual table (where the RTTI information is kept). It has the same performance overhead as

When we encounter multiple checks using typeid where all the classes that we check form some hierarchy, we can replace those multiple typeid statements with a single dynamic_ cast statement.

a virtual function. In contrast, the case with dynamic_cast is different. It traverses the base class objects down in the hierarchy and the result is dependent on the length of the inheritance chain.

It is very simple to convert from dynamic_cast to typeid. When dynamic casting is used to convert a pointer to one polymorphic object into another, it fails if the types do not match. If one is checking for straightforward types as done in Program 11.4, one can write a code with typeid. It involves two steps. The first one is to check the types of two arguments using typeid and the operator '=='. Then, if the answer is yes, plain vanilla C-type casting is used to cast. Consider Program 11.5.

PROGRAM 11.5   Converting from a code using dynamic_cast to one using typeid

```cpp
//dynamic_castToTtypeid.cpp
#include <iostream>
using namespace std;

class Shape
{
    int LineStyle;
    int FillColour;
public:
    virtual void draw()
    {
        cout << "Shape is drawn \n";
    }
};

class Circle : public Shape
{
    int Radius;
    int CentrePointX;
    int CentrePointY;
public:
    void draw()
    {
        cout << "Circle is drawn \n";
    }
};

int main()
{
    Shape SomeShape, *PtrShape;
    Circle Ring, *PtrCircle;

    /* The following is a code using dynamic_cast; later, we will
    show how the same effect can be achieved using typeid */

    PtrShape = &Ring;
    PtrCircle = dynamic_cast<Circle *> (PtrShape);
    if(PtrCircle)
        cout << "Cast is successful\n";
    else
        cout << "Test is not successful\n";

    PtrShape = &SomeShape;
    PtrCircle = dynamic_cast<Circle *> (PtrShape);
```

```
    if(PtrCircle)
        cout << "Cast is successful";
    else
        cout << "Test is not successful\n";

    // The following is an equivalent code using typeid
    PtrShape = &Ring;
    if(typeid(Circle) == typeid(*PtrShape))
    {
        PtrCircle = (Circle *) PtrShape;
        /* C-style casting is now safe because it casts
        only if the types are same */

        cout << "Cast is successful\n";
    }
    else
    {
        PtrCircle = '\0';
        cout << "Cast is not successful\n";
    }

    PtrShape = &SomeShape;
    if(typeid(Circle) == typeid(*PtrShape))
    {
        PtrCircle = (Circle *) PtrShape;
        cout << "Cast is successful\n";
    }
    else
    {
        PtrCircle = '\0';
        cout << "Cast is not successful\n";
    }
}
```

Output
```
Cast is successful
Test is not successful
Cast is successful
Cast is not successful
```

How the Program Works

This program has two different portions. One uses `dynamic_cast` as shown in the following statement:

```
PtrShape = &Ring;
PtrCircle = dynamic_cast<Circle *> (PtrShape);
```

The statement uses `dynamic_cast` and uses a check to null return value for failure. The same job is done using `typeid` in the second portion of the program as in the following statements.

```
if(typeid(Circle) == typeid(*PtrShape))
{
    PtrCircle = (Circle *) PtrShape;

    ...

}
```

The `dynamic_cast` checks for the correct type and then casts only if the types are correct and not otherwise. The `typeid` can only check for identical types; so, a C-type casting is needed to cast once the types are found to be correct.

11.2.3 Using `dynamic_cast` to Solve Problems with `typeid`

If the types are straightforward, it is possible to replace `dynamic_cast` with `typeid`. Consider the problem discussed in Section 11.1.9. In this case, the types being compared are not straightforward. They can be derived types as well. It is easier in that case to replace the code with `typeid` into one with `dynamic_cast`. Look at the following line:

```
PlainTextNews &RefPlainTextNews = dynamic_cast<PlainTextNews&> (NewsItem)
RefPlainTextNews.FPrint();
```

The dynamic_cast operator returns null when unsuccessful when the argument is a pointer. If the reference is passed instead, it throws the exception bad_cast.

The printing takes place only if the `News` is available as a reference to the `PlainTextNews` or a descendent of it; otherwise, `bad_cast` exception is thrown. Now, one need not worry about `HtmlNews` or `RichTextNews`, or `TaggedHtmlNews` or `UntaggedHtmlNews`. For all of them, the `dynamic_cast` would be successful and the job is done.

The only difference is that when one uses `dynamic_cast` using reference, it does not return null reference (because a reference cannot be null). If the cast is not successful, it throws a `bad_cast` exception; so, the part for other files will be written in the `catch` block. Program 11.6 shows how this works.

 **PROGRAM 11.6** More flexible solution to printing problem using dynamic_cast

```cpp
//DynamicPrinting.cpp
#include <iostream>
#include <typeinfo>
#include <string>
using namespace std;

#define SENDNEWS 1
#define STORENEWS 2
#define PRINTNEWS 3

class News
{
public:
    virtual void SendNews(string Address){};
    virtual void StoreNews(){};
    virtual ~News() = 0;
};

News::~News()
{
    // Empty body
}

class PlainTextNews : public News
{
public:
    void SendNews(string Address)
    {
        // mailto(Address, &this)
    }
```

```
    void StoreNews()
    {
        // Storing the news at default position
    }

    void PrintNews()
    {
        cout << "Printing the news now\n";
    }
};

/* The following three classes are added just to show the class
hierarchy. It does not make any difference whether
they have a body or not */

class HtmlNews : public PlainTextNews
{ // Class contents };

class RichTextNews : public PlainTextNews
{ // Class contents };

class TaggedHtmlNews : public HtmlNews
{ // Class contents };

class NewsWithImages : public News
{
public:
    void SendNews(string Address)
    {
        // mailto(Address, &this)
    }
    // Other details
    // Printing is missing out here
};

// Right-click function
void MyApp OnRightClick(News & NewsItem, int Choice)
{
    string Address;
    switch(Choice)
    {
        case SENDNEWS:
        cout << "Enter address";
        cin >> Address;
        NewsItem.SendNews(Address);
        break;

        case STORENEWS:
        NewsItem.StoreNews();
        break;

        case PRINTNEWS:

        try
        {
            PlainTextNews & RefPlainTextNews = dynamic_cast <PlainTextNews&> (NewsItem);

            /* Casting to check if the object belongs to any derived class of PlainTextNews
            class */

            cout << "Printing is enabled \n";
```

```
            RefPlainTextNews.PrintNews();
        }
        catch (bad_cast)
        {
            cout << "Casting not successful \n";
            cout << "Printing is not enabled \n";
            // Executable file has skipped the printing option
        }
    } // End of switch
} // End of function

int main()
{
    TaggedHtmlNews TextNews;
    MyApp_OnRightClick(TextNews, PRINTNEWS);
    NewsWithImages NonTextNews;
    MyApp_OnRightClick(NonTextNews, PRINTNEWS);
}
```

Output
```
Printing is enabled
Printing the news now
Casting not successful
Printing is not enabled
```

> **Note** When we use `dynamic_cast` with reference, we must include it under the `try` block and have a
> `catch` block with `bad_cast` to write code for taking action when the conversion fails.

How the Program Works

An important point to note here is the call to `dynamic_cast` with casting to `PlainTextNews`.
Though the file is actually of type `TaggedHtmlNews`, the cast is still successful; this is because
`TaggedHtmlNews` is a class inherited from `PlainTextNews`. It can also be verified that for
`NewsWithImages` file, printing is not enabled, because the casting is unsuccessful.

The central idea of the program is mentioned in the following statement.

```
PlainTextNews & RefPlainTextNews = dynamic_cast <PlainTextNews&> (NewsItem);
```

The `dynamic_cast` here replaces the three statements using `typeid` in the example mentioned
in Section 11.1.9. It can also be seen that even when many other classes are added to the
hierarchy, there is no need to modify this program, as `dynamic_cast` can handle the situation.
Whenever a `NewsItem` is an object of `PlainTextNews` class or any of its descendents, `dynamic_cast` is successful and, thus, casts the `NewsItem` to `PlainTextNews` reference.

Moreover, consider how failure has been handled using a `catch` block. The `dynamic_cast`
statement is wrapped inside a `try` block and a corresponding `catch` block is written as follows
to take care of a case where the news item is not printable.

```
catch(bad_cast)
{
    cout << "Casting not successful \n";
    cout << "Printing is not enabled \n";
    // Executable file has skipped the printing option
}
```

11.3 CASTING USING `const_cast`

The `const_cast` operator is used to cast a const variable to a non-constant (normal) variable. It is special; no other cast, that is, `dynamic_cast`, `static_cast`, or `reinterpret_cast`, can do this. The cast from const to non-const can be done for reference as well. Consider Program 11.7.

> **PROGRAM 11.7** Const casting

```
//const_cast.cpp
#include <iostream>
#include <string>
using namespace std;

void DangerousFunction(const int *NotActuallyConst)
{
    int *ConvertedNormal = const_cast<int *> (NotActuallyConst); (*ConvertedNormal)++;
}

int main()
{
    int TestForConst = 10;
    cout << "Value of Test: " << TestForConst << "\n";
    DangerousFunction(&TestForConst);
    cout << "After calling dangerous function: " << TestForConst << "\n";
}
```

Output
```
Value of Test: 10
After calling dangerous function: 11
```

How the Program Works

It is important to note that there are two different types of const data; one is the real const, which is defined as

> The `const_cast` removes the const-ness of a contextual const value.

```
const int RealConstInt;
```

and the other is the *contextual const*, which has been used in the program. The variable assumes constness upon entry to the function.

> **Note** Only contextual consts can be converted to non-const. Real const variables such as `RealConstInt` defined in the example cannot be converted to non-const.

11.4 CASTING USING `static_cast`

`static_cast` is a normal non-polymorphic cast. Converting `int` to `double`, `int` to float, etc., should be done using this cast. If applied to a polymorphic object, `static_cast` results in compile-time error. If conversion from a data type is not relevant, it again results in compile-time error. `static_cast` is performed at compile time. It is an ideal replacement for old C-style casting in normal situations.

> A `static_cast` converts a regular data type to some other regular data type.

Program 11.8 is a simple example to understand the use of `static_cast`.

PROGRAM 11.8   Static casting

```
//static_cast.cpp
#include <iostream>
using namespace std;

int main()
{
    int NormalInt = 10;
    float ConvertedFromInt = static_cast<float> (NormalInt);

    /* The following line cannot be compiled
    int *test = static_cast<int *>(NormalInt);
    error: 'static_cast' cannot convert from 'int' to 'int *' */
    return 0;
}
```

Output
There is no output here as we are just casting the normal integer into a float value.

How the Program Works

The program casts a normal integer into a float using the `static_cast` operation.

```
float ConvertedFromInt = static_cast<float>(NormalInt);
```

This is a complicated way of saying the following using C-type casting.

```
float ConvertedFromInt = (float*)NormalInt;
```

The advantage is that the C-type casting casts without looking at the data type. It is fine in the given example but the same C-type cast may also be used to convert an `int` into an `int` pointer. If a similar operation is done using `static_cast`, it results in an error. The following statement, for example, will not be compiled.

```
int *test = static_cast<int *>(NormalInt);
```

If a C-type casting is used as follows, it will, unfortunately, be compiled and also run with surprising results.

> A `static_cast` converts a value only if it is normal conversion; it fails otherwise.

```
int *test = (int*)(NormalInt);
```

This is the advantage of using `static_cast`, It might look complex, but it can check for such errors, which cannot be done by a normal C-type casting.

11.5 CASTING USING `reinterpret_cast`

If a programmer purposefully wants to convert to an irrelevant type, for example, convert an integer value to a pointer, then `reinterpret_cast` provides a way to do it. Program 11.9 shows how this is done.

PROGRAM 11.9   Reinterpret cast

```
//reinterpret_cast.cpp
#include <iostream>
using namespace std;
int main()
```

```
{
    int NormalInt = 10;

    /* The following line will not be compiled */
    // float ConvertedFloatFromInt = reinterpret_cast<float> (NormalInt);

    /* The following line will be compiled */
    int *ConvertedPtrFromInt = reinterpret_cast<int *> (NormalInt);
    cout<< "Int is converted to pointer";
    return 0;
}
```

Output
```
Int is converted to pointer
```

How the Program Works

reinterpret_cast is used to convert a type into an irrelevant type such as an integer to a pointer. It fails when the conversion involves regular data types.

This program demonstrates the exact opposite behaviour of Program 11.8. It compiles the line that converts an integer to a pointer but does not compile the line that converts an integer to a float. Thus, the following line is compiled and it converts an int to an int pointer.

```
int *ConvertedPtrFromInt = reinterpret_cast<int *> (NormalInt);
```

On the contrary, the following line, which converts the int to a float value, is not compiled.

```
float ConvertedFloatFromInt = reinterpret_cast<float> (NormalInt);
```

Note reinterpret_cast is a mechanism by which programmers are saved from typing errors while casting. Only when a programmer is interested in converting to irrelevant types, he/she would use reinterpret_cast.

11.6 RTTI AND TEMPLATES

In Chapter 7, we have learnt how to write generic functions that can work for any type. The type is determined at compile time and a specific function is instantiated that works for the given type. One may need to provide some checks in those generic functions related to the specific types. It is especially useful for validations. Both typeid and dynamic_cast can be used for this purpose. Let us discuss them in the following sections.

11.6.1 Using typeid

In the template function code, if one wants to test the type of the actual variable and try to provide validations according to the type, RTTI can be used. For example, if a programmer is writing a search routine that can operate on any array, a generic search routine has to be written. However, this has a problem.

When templates are needed to check the types of the argument, RTTI is useful, as it checks the type at run-time when the type information is known.

Suppose the integer data contains employee numbers, which cannot be negative. The char * data contains employee names, which are valid names available in the database. The problem is how such validations can be provided once a single routine is written for both these cases (and maybe for many more such cases). It is possible to use typeid here to check the type of the item and then execute specific validation routines for that particular data type. Consider Program 11.10.

PROGRAM 11.10   Template type checking

```cpp
//TemplateTypeChecking.cpp
#include <iostream>
#include <string>
using namespace std;

template <typename Type>

Type Search(Type Array[])
{
Type UserInput;
    cout << "Please input the value";
    cin >> UserInput;
    cout << "\n";
    // Provide integer validation
    if(typeid(Type) == typeid(int))
    {
        cout << "int validation done \n";
    }

    // Provide char validation
    if(typeid(Type) == typeid(char))
    {
        cout << "char validation done \n";
    }

    // Provide string validation
    if(typeid(Type) == typeid(char *))
    {
        cout << "char * validation done \n";
    }

    /* Check for other data types, which can even be user-defined data types */
    /* Search routine is omitted at the moment */

    return 0;
}
int main()
{
    char Array[]= "This is testing";
    int result = Search(Array);
}
```

Output
```
Please input the value 65
char validation done
```

How the Program Works

Readers may be surprised with the output. char validation is called because the array is of type char; 65 in this array is actually A.

What has been discussed so far is also true for generic classes. Program 11.11 is an example where the problem given in Program 11.10 is represented by a class rather than a generic function.

PROGRAM 11.11   Template typeid

```cpp
//TemplateTypeid.cpp
#include <iostream>
#include <string>
using namespace std;

template <typename Type, typename UserInputType = int>
class JustForSearch
{
public:
    Type Search(Type Array[])
    {
        UserInputType UserInput;
        cout << "Please input the value ";
        cin >> UserInput;
        cout << "\n";

        if(typeid(UserInputType) != typeid(Type))
        {
            cout << "Please enter data of type" << typeid(Type).name() << "\n";
        }

        return 0;
    }
};

int main()
{
    char Array[]= "This is testing";
    JustForSearch<char> JS;
    int result = JS.Search(Array);
}
```

Output
```
Please input the value 65
Please enter data of type char
```

How the Program Works

The program is again giving an erroneous output. Now, it is not accepting 65 and wants the user to enter a character.

Surprised again? Look at the default value of type `UserInputType`. It is `int`. Moreover, look at the type arguments passed to `JS`.

```cpp
template <typename Type, typename UserInputType = int>
JustForSearch<char> JS;
```

The second argument has not been passed. Hence, it was taken as `int`, the default type. This does not match with the required type, `char`, and, therefore, generates an error.

One more question arises here. We have discussed about default type arguments to class templates (`int` for `UserInputType` in the given example). Can we have such default type arguments in functions? The answer is no, as already seen in Chapter 7. This is because the default type arguments to template functions were proposed too late for the current standard to accept it. It may be a part of the next C++ standard.

11.6.2 Compatibility and Efficiency Issues

The following are a few other RTTI-related issues:

Backward compatibility with C-style casting It is important to note that compatibility with C is a major concern to C++ designers. C-style casting is still being used in a number of programs. It is not recommended to use it in newer C++ programs though.

Efficiency Using RTTI is not efficient. Even if one does not use `typeid` or `dynamic_cast`, the program runs slowly when RTTI is enabled. It is because the information about type using `typeinfo` object is added to every polymorphic type. The `typeinfo` objects are to be constructed and destroyed similar to other objects, which ultimately slows down the execution.

Using virtual functions in place of RTTI If possible, one must use virtual functions in place of RTTI because they are more efficient. However, it is not possible to use virtual functions in place of RTTI in some cases.

> **Note** C-type cast is still heavily used; however, a good design should use better casting operators mentioned in this chapter.

11.7 CROSS CASTING

Cross casting refers to casting from the derived to the proper base class when there are multiple base classes in case of multiple inheritance.

Consider Program 11.12, which has the following statements:

```
class Derived : public Base1, public Base2;
Base1 *Base1Ptr = new Derived;
Base2 *Base2Ptr;
```

Let us see what happens when one writes

```
Base2Ptr = Base1Ptr;
```

First of all, one needs to make sure that it is allowed. Fortunately, in this case, the compiler allows and automatically adjusts the pointer to point to the base class subobject of the derived class. The value of `Base1Ptr` pointer is incremented to make it point to `Base2` subobject of the derived class and then assigned to the `Base2Ptr` pointer. Thus, in this case, the behaviour of the assignment statement seems valid.

There are two classes, `Base1` and `Base2`, and `Derived` is derived from both `Base1` and `Base2` (multiple inheritance). Now, casting the `Base1` pointer, pointing to a derived class object, to `Base2` is valid when the object is of type `Derived`. (Since `Base1` and `Base2` are both base classes of `Derived`, their pointers can point to the derived class object.) The problem is that the `Base2Ptr` pointer should only be able to address the `Base2` subobject of the derived class. This is why the compiler intervenes and does what has been discussed here.

Unfortunately, when a pointer is casted using C-style casting, this does not happen. Have a look at the following statement:

```
Base2Ptr = (Base2 *) Base1Ptr;
```

Thus, if casting is used instead, what one gets is not what one wants. The address value in the pointer is not incremented to make it point to the `Base2` subobject of the derived class.

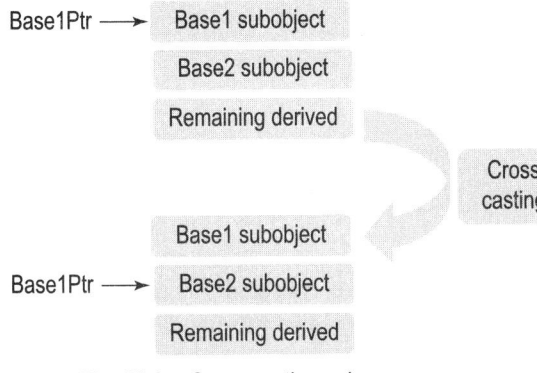

Fig. 11.1 Cross casting using `dynamic_cast`

The first version, unfortunately, does not work for all cases. Assume `Base1Ptr` pointing to a `Base1` class by statement:

```
Base1Ptr = new Base1;
```

Even though `Base1Ptr` is not pointing to a derived class object, the assignment still takes place.

```
Base2Ptr = Base1Ptr;
```

It should not be allowed here. Thus, either of the form is vulnerable to wrong assignment. What is the solution? `dynamic_cast` can be used to solve this problem. If `Base1Ptr` had been pointing to an object of `Base1` class, run-time error would be generated. Refer to Fig. 11.1. The conversion from Base1 pointer to `Base2` pointer actually involves setting it to the address of `Base2` subobject. It is done only when `dynamic_cast` is applied. C-style casting incorrectly keeps the `Base2Ptr` to point to `Base1` subobject. Thus, the solution is to use

```
Base2 *Base2Ptr = dynamic_cast<Base2 *> (Base1Ptr);
```

Notes

1. When a pointer to one base class is to be converted to a pointer to another base class in case of multiple inheritance, it is known as cross casting.
2. For cross casting, `dynamic_cast` is to be used. Neither plain assignment nor C-type casting serves the purpose.

Consider the following program.

```cpp
//CrossCasting.cpp
class Base1
{
    int IntTest;
public:
    virtual ~Base1(){};
    // For making Base1 polymorphic
};
class Base2
{
    float FloatTest;
};
class Derived : public Base1, public Base2
{
    int Test2;
};
int main()
{
    Base1 *Base1Ptr = new Derived;
    Base2 *Base2Ptr = dynamic_cast<Base2 *> (Base1Ptr);
}
```

11.8 DOWNCASTING

The following is a line of code from Program 11.5:

```
PtrShape = &Ring;
PtrCircle = dynamic_cast<Circle *> (PtrShape);
```

When a base class pointer is converted to a derived class pointer, it is known as downcasting. It is safe only when the base class pointer actually points to the derived class object and not otherwise.

The cast from a base class pointer to a derived class pointer is successful because the base class pointer actually points to the derived class object. This type of casting is known as *downcasting*.

Downcasting was considered unsafe and incorrect before RTTI was introduced because C-style casting had to be used, which just converts one type of pointer to another without checking anything. If the base class pointer is pointing to a base class object and not a derived class object, it will create a serious problem. When casted to a derived class pointer, it can now access the derived class portion as well. While referring to the derived class portion using the resultant derived class pointer (which does not exist logically), one may get unexpected results.

■ RECAPITULATION ■

- Run-time type information or RTTI adds overhead at run-time.
- RTTI can work with built-in or user-defined data types.
- When working with polymorphic objects, we need to enable RTTI, which is disabled by default.
- When we define virtual functions in the base class, they can only solve problems of the entire class hierarchy. It is better to use typeid with RTTI in this case.
- `dynamic_cast` helps us to check whether any class is a derived class from some other class.
- `const_cast` converts from a contextual const variable

- pointer to non-const variable pointer.
- `static_cast` coverts from a normal data type into another data type if the conversion is not changing the type drastically.
- When we are in need to covert from one type to another drastically different data type, we need `reinterpret_cast`.
- All these casts, if not used as per specification, generate errors.
- Downcasting and cross casting, which were considered unsafe earlier, are now considered safe with RTTI and `dynamic_cast`.

■ KEYWORDS ■

const_cast This C++ operator casts a contextual const pointer to a non-const variable pointer.

Contextual const This is a const variable that is originally not defined as const but assumes constness due to the `const` operation on it.

Cross casting When a derived class object, originated by multiple inheritance, is pointed to by one of its base class pointers, casting from one base class pointer into another base class pointer is known as cross casting.

Downcasting Casting from a base class pointer to a

derived class pointer is known as downcasting.

dynamic_cast This is a new casting operator provided in C++, which casts a polymorphic object into another if it is correct to do it. Casting from a derived class pointer to a base class is designed to be correct. It is also correct if a base class pointer is converted to a derived class pointer when the base class pointer is actually pointing to a derived class object.

Polymorphic objects If we have a class containing a virtual function, it is possible to point to a derived class object using the base class pointer and manipulate the object. Such objects that can be manipulated are known as polymorphic objects.

reinterpret_cast This is a casting operator for abnormal casting cases such as an integer to a pointer and a pointer to an integer.

RTTI Run-time type information or RTTI is a mechanism by which we can find the type of an object at run-time.

static_cast This is a casting operator for normal casting cases such as `int` to `float` and `char` to `int`.

typeid operator This operator can be applied to any object, class or built-in data type. It returns the `typeinfo` object associated with the object under consideration.

typeinfo object This is an object associated with every built-in and user-defined data type, and also with polymorphic type. This object describes the type of the object. It is available for polymorphic type only when RTTI is enabled.

■ EXERCISES ■

Multiple Choice Questions

1. Casting of _____ to _____ always works in case of `dynamic_cast`.
   (a) base pointer, derived pointer
   (b) derived pointer, base pointer
   (c) derived pointer, abstract pointer
   (d) abstract pointer, derived pointer

2. Even when RTTI is not enabled, the `typeinfo` objects are available for _____.
   (a) built-in data types
   (b) user-defined data types
   (c) polymorphic data types
   (d) non-polymorphic data types

3. While using _____ sometimes, we need to know about the actual data types and provide validations.
   (a) virtual functions
   (b) virtual base classes
   (c) templates
   (d) polymorphic objects

4. If `Base` is base class, `Derived1` and `Derived2` are derived classes, `BasePtr`, `Derived1Ptr` and `Derived2Ptr` are their respective pointers, and `DDerived` is multiple inherited from `Derived1` and `Derived2`, which of the flowing will cast properly when `BasePtr` is pointing to `DDerived`?
   (a) `Base * NewPtr = BasePtr`
   (b) `Derived1 * NewPtr = BasePtr`
   (c) `Derived2 * NewPtr = BasePtr`
   (d) None of the above

5. The cast from const to non-const can be done also for _____ apart from pointers.
   (a) classes
   (b) objects
   (c) variables
   (d) references

6. In case of references, when `dynamic_cast` fails, _____.
   (a) it returns a null
   (b) it gives a compilation error
   (c) it throws an exception
   (d) it throws a `bad_cast` exception

7. Which of the following is the correct syntax for getting the name of a type?
   (a) `name(<type>);`
   (b) `typeid(<type>);`
   (c) `typeid(<type>).name();`
   (d) `name(type_id(<type>));`

8. What does `typeid` return?
   (a) It returns nothing.
   (b) It returns the type of the object in general form.
   (c) It returns the type of the object in a specific form.
   (d) It returns the type and size of the object.

9. _____ are more preferable than RTTI.
   (a) Virtual functions
   (b) Friend functions
   (c) Virtual base classes
   (d) Abstract classes

10. Which built-in class has been introduced with RTTI?
   (a) `type` class
   (b) `typeid` class
   (c) `typeinfo` class
   (d) `RTTI_type` class

Conceptual Exercises

1. Why do we need RTTI? Suggest some cases where we need to use RTTI.
2. What are polymorphic objects?

3. We have seen one case in the text where virtual functions cannot directly solve our problem. We have provided a RTTI-based solution there. Can you suggest some other cases similar to this?

4. What is the need for `typeinfo` object? What is the role of the `typeid` operator in RTTI?

5. Give an example of conversion of a program using `dynamic_cast` to `typeid` other than the one provided in the book.

6. Is it possible to convert a problem solved using `dynamic_cast` to one using `typeid`? Give your views on such conversion.

7. Write down the differences between solutions provided using `typeid` and using `dynamic_cast`.

8. What are the problems with the use of `typeid` mechanism for solving problems?

9. Design a few class hierarchies yourself. Identify cases where we can use virtual functions, `typeid`, and `dynamic_cast`.

10. Draw a comparison between different casting operators.

11. When working with templates, do we need to use RTTI?

12. Suggest a few cases where downcasting or cross casting is useful.

Practical Exercises

1. Read an integer and a float. Try to compare them using `typeid`. Print their type names using a function `name()`. Now, cast the integer into float. Repeat the same thing. Try comparing the types of both the items using the `==` operator.

2. Recall Problem 9 of Chapter 10 related to visiting faculty and regular faculty. Visiting faculty is now divided into visiting faculty from another educational institute and visiting faculty from non-educational institute. All visiting faculty now need facility for transport. Details of such need are stored with their objects and can be retrieved using a function `TransportNeed()`. This function cannot be a part of the faculty base class. Use `typeid` to find whether the faculty is a regular faculty or not, and then read the need for transport.

3. Replace `typeid` with `dynamic_cast` to provide a single statement instead of two different `typeid` statements in Problem 4.

4. Recall Problem 1 of Chapter 10 and define objects of all three (time) classes. Use `dynamic_cast` to provide proper casting. Display error messages when proper casting cannot be done.

5. Replace `dynamic_cast` with `typeid` in Problem 4 and rewrite the program.

6. Write a program that takes the names of two different classes and gives the response 'Yes' when one class is inherited from the other; otherwise, the response is 'No'.

7. Define a class `Variables`. It should contain the variable name, its type, the index in the symbol table, and constructors and destructors. Inherit that into `SystemVariable` and `UserVariable`. `SystemVariable` indicates the system process that has generated that variable. `UserVariable` indicates the user id that initiated that variable. Define `CompilerVariable` as multiple inherited from `SystemVariable` and `UserVariable`. Define a pointer to `Variable` class and use `dynamic_cast` to downcast it to a variable of type `SystemVariable`. Provide error messages if `dynamic_cast` fails. (It fails when the pointer is not actually pointing to `SystemVariable` class.)

8. Provide cross casting for Problem 7. (*Hint*: define a pointer pointing to `SystemVariable`. Now, make it
   point to an object of `CompilerVariable`. Dynamic cast that `SystemVariable` pointer to `UserVariable` pointer.)

9. Rewrite the `DangerousFunction` given in Program 11.7 in the chapter and use the same function to manipulate the string variable. (*Hint*: Use the same `const_cast` with argument `char *`).

10. Recall Problem 3 of Chapter 10. Now, provide `typeid` to check for the type of student that a student pointer is pointing to and then cast it. Provide `dynamic_cast` to do the same.

11. Design a class hierarchy with `student` class as base and `Computer`, `IT`, and `Mechanical` as classes derived from `student` class. Add required attributes to all these classes and provide downcasting from a pointer to student pointing to `IT` student to a `Computer` student.

12. Write a program to read the following hierarchy. `Employee` is derived into `PermanentEmploy-ees` and `DailyEmployees`. `PermanentEmployees` are derived into `DepartmentalEmployees` and `CompanyEmployees`. `CompanyEmployees` are derived into `RegionalManagers` and `AreaManagers`. `DepartmentalEmployees` are derived into `Sales`,

Production, and HumanResource employees. Define a single array for storing all employee objects. Define a function Salary, which displays the salary (do not calculate salary; just display any value) of permanent employees alone. Use dynamic_cast to solve the problem.

(*Hint*: we cannot use virtual functions defined in the Employee class here as DailyEmployees do not have salary functions defined. We have to define salary as a virtual function in the class PermanentEmployees. We have to use Employee pointer to access the objects. Whenever it is valid to cast from Employee to PermanentEmployees, the object belongs to any of the descendants of PermanentEmployees class. dynamic_cast helps us to find this.)

13. Define a Student class. Inherit that into MCAStudents and NonMCAStudents classes. MCAStudents inherits into GLSStudents and NonGLSStudents. A function ShowPracticalHours() can only be applied to MCAStudents. We have a base class Student pointer to point to a GLSStudents object. Use dynamic_cast to check that NonMCAStudents do not call ShowPracticalHours().

Chapter 12

Streams and Formatted Input/ Output

Learning Objectives

- Concept of input/output (I/O) and streams
- Predefined streams in C++
- Formatted and unformatted I/O
- Formatting using I/O members
- fmtflags and displaying the flag information
- Manipulators and their use in formatting
- User-defined manipulators

12.1 INTRODUCTION

Provision for input/output (I/O) is one of the major tasks of a programming language. Streams are (conceptually) pipe-like constructs used for providing I/O. When a programmer needs to handle *input from* or *output to* external entities such as a keyboard, file, or printer, then streams are used.

Different devices have different I/O specifications. For example, printers can be used for output but not for input, keyboard can be used only for input and not for output, and the hard disk is used for both. Conventional monitors of our desktop machines are output devices, but swanky touch screen monitors avoid keyboards by also acting as an input device.

Writing to a disk is a different operation from writing to a printer. In disks, the sector to write is determined, the head is placed on top of it, and the proper representation for input (what magnetic value to write for one and zero) is to be provided. If the sector is full, another empty sector is found to continue writing. It is also to be mentioned somewhere that the new empty sector that has been found is in continuation with the earlier sector. As a result, the content looks contiguous while reading a file. When writing to a disk, it is possible to have multiple disk writes from different users executed (disk being a shared resource).

Writing to a printer is an entirely different case. Here, writing means placing the printer head at the required position (in case of dot matrix) or selecting one from various heads for a given position (in case of line printer); inkjet and laser printers use a totally different technology. Writing to a terminal of a multi-user system involves yet another complexity. Some sort of address manipulation (finding out where the destination machine is) and a communication protocol are to be used.

To conclude, the operation remains same, that is, writing. One can write to both the printer and the hard disk. However, the *execution is different* because the *devices* involved are *different.*

To make things even more complex, vendors keep upgrading their devices with new features and services. An upgraded product may perform

> Though output and input operations look the same, actual devices need different types of attention to complete them.

> Due to competition, vendors keep on adding features to devices. This requires more operations to be managed by the programmers.

the same tasks in a different way. For example, a new laser printer may have the ability to print more number of colours than its predecessor. Given all these complexities, how does a programmer communicate with different I/O devices?

The problem is solved partly by the vendors by providing device drivers and partly by the operating system (OS) by providing an interface of the device drivers to the program. The OS can provide a consistent interface for all such devices in a way that when one asks for write operation, the OS would look at the particular device and execute the write operation that suits the device. For example, if one writes to a printer, the OS sends the *printer driver* a message for writing, and the printer driver sends the commands suited for that brand of printer and gets the job done. Instead, if one writes to a disk, the OS does the same operation, but now communicating to the *disk driver.* Since the OS provides a consistent interface for writing, there is no need to know *where* one is writing. For example, when a printf() statement is written in C, by default, it writes to the screen. However, if the executable were redirected to some file, the same printf() statement would write to that file. If the file were redirected to a printer, it would print on the printer. Thus, the OS provides abstraction by taking all the pressure on its shoulders.

> The OS provides input and output streams, which programmers use for reading and writing to devices.

> The OS provides an interface with which external programs can interact, regardless of the type of the I/O devices and their complexity. All programming languages extend this interface to the programmers so that they can write to or read from the stream. C++, not being an exception, supports stream-based I/O.

The OS soaks in all the complexity and makes the programmer's life easy by providing a consistent interface. This interface, in other words, is known as a *stream*. Streams provide independence from having different operations for different I/O devices. When printf() or cout is used, one is writing to a stream and not to the device directly. Conceptually, it is easier to consider the stream as a pipe-like structure. When one writes to a stream, one is writing to one end of the pipe. The other end is by default attached to the screen. When the OS provides redirection (using > operator with executable files such as test.exe> OutputFile), the other end of the pipe is then attached to the redirected device. This does not make any difference to the user's end; he/she can continue writing in the same way.

12.2 I/O STREAMS OF C VS C++

C++ provides two different stream-based I/O systems. Due to the backward compatibility needed with C, C++ provides C stream I/O *as it is.* One can still include <stdio.h> and use printf() and scanf() in the programs (though it is not recommended). It also provides a new I/O (the one with cout, cin, and << and >> operators overloaded). The new I/O is also stream-based.

Though C I/O is still available and is robust and proven, there are a few distinct advantages of using C++ I/O, which are as follows:

1. C++ I/O is object-oriented. Objects represent streams in C++. cout is an object of the output stream class, whereas cin is an object of the input stream class. << and >> are overloaded operators in those streams. Using objects from istream or ostream class enables the users to overload operators provided by that stream to use it for user-defined types. We have earlier seen examples to overload << and >>

> C++ provides C-type I/O as well as a new object-oriented I/O.

operators for user-defined objects for providing I/O operations. On the contrary, objects are not available in C I/O stream and it has no mechanism to provide such natural I/O to user-defined objects.

2. C++ I/O stream contains richer formatting options than C. It is possible to have the programmer's own format operators known as user-defined manipulators in C++. We will be learning about manipulators in Section 12.11.

3. Though not apparent at first glance, C++ I/O is much easier to use. We have seen the use of `cin` without the '&' operator unlike `scanf()`. We have also used overloaded `<<` and `>>` operators for I/O. For file manipulation, C++ provides constructor functions, which makes it very easy to use files. Writing to and reading from text files can be performed using `>>` and `<<` operators. We will be looking at those operations in Chapter 13.

> **Note** C++ I/O streams are object-oriented, contains richer formatting options, and are more user-friendly than C-type I/O.

12.3 OLD C++ I/O VS ANSI C++ I/O

ANSI C++ I/O has the following two important differences as compared to the original C++ I/O.

Richer set of operations   ANSI C++ I/O has more number of operations than the old I/O. The old I/O was supported by `iostream.h` file, whereas the new I/O is supported by `<iostream>` file. There are some new data types and new features in the newer version of the I/O library. The **ios** class contains the fundamental operations that are possible to be performed on the stream. These operations are provided as member functions. The **ios** class also contains a number of variables that can be manipulated to achieve the desired effect on the stream that is being dealt with. I/O has been enhanced to a large extent in the newer version.

> There are two important differences between old and new C++ IOs; it is richer in operations and uses a separate namespace.

Separate namespace and no global sharing   The old library used to work in the global namespace, but the new library works in the `std` namespace. The difference will be clearer when we study namespaces in Chapter 16. At the moment, consider namespaces as a type of wrapper. If C++ standard library contains one function, one cannot create another function with the same name *in the same namespace.*

> Two functions with the same name can be differentiated if they are a part of two different namespaces.

Suppose there are two `abs()` functions, one for absolute values (provided by the standard library) and another for displaying the absent students in an educational organization, *with the same set of arguments.* In such cases, the compiler is bound to get confused and hence the program will not be compiled. When the standard library is wrapped in `std`, it is possible to define the functions as per the programmer's wish, because the library functions are not available in the global namespace. If the function `abs()` is now defined for absent percentage, one can differentiate between both the functions, `abs()` (programmer's function) and `std::abs()` (the standard library function). Note that here it is assumed that one has not written `using namespace std` as usual.

> Third-party library developers can name functions in their own way without worrying about colliding with names used by standard library or some other library developer.

This facility makes life easier for the programmers of the third-party libraries while naming their global variables and functions. They can name them as they like. If there is a need to develop a library for a client, it is possible to define functions without having to bother about possible conflicts. Without namespaces, there would have been a need to ensure that the programmer does not name the functions the same as those in the C++ standard library itself (or some other third-party library, which is already installed in the target machine). The identifier names of the programmer now have no chance of collision with the standard library identifier names.

12.4 PREDEFINED AND WIDE CHARACTER STREAMS

C++ has a few predefined streams. Whenever a C++ program starts execution, these streams automatically open on their own. Table 12.1 lists the predefined streams.

Table 12.1 Predefined streams

Stream	Meaning	Default source/destination
cin	Standard input stream	Keyboard
cout	Standard output stream	Screen
cerr	Standard error stream with no buffer	Screen
clog	Standard error stream with buffer	Screen

To receive an international standardization from the International Organization for Standardization (ISO), the designers of C++ have added some specific features to enable to work globally. One such feature is the support for *wide character streams*. Some of the languages (e.g., Chinese) cannot accommodate themselves in the small 8-bit footprint of ANSI. They require bigger 16-bit Unicode to represent their character set. These streams are win, wout, werr, and wlog.

12.5 C++ STREAM CLASSES HIERARCHY

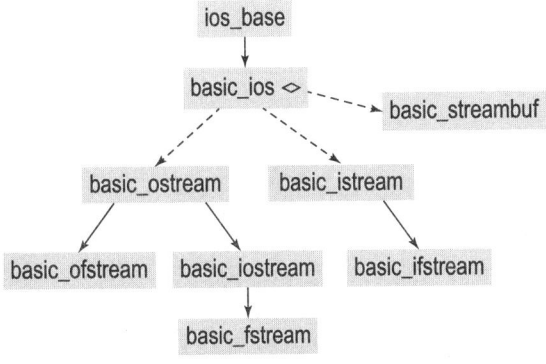

Fig. 12.1 I/O hierarchy

The I/O hierarchy shown in Fig. 12.1 is usually mentioned without the prefix basic_, that is, basic_ios is usually referred to as ios. The ios_base class contains the details not needed for templatization. basic_ios and its descendants are all templatized. basic_streambuf provides the mechanism to access the stream using lower-level functions. It also provides services to other classes. There are a few more items in the hierarchy that are not mentioned here. One can refer to Stroustrup's classic *The C++ Programming Language* for further details.

12.6 FORMATTED AND UNFORMATTED I/O

We have already studied about unformatted I/O using cout. The operator << is usually used with cout object to support unformatted output. Though not used much, there are other ways of formatting I/O. Later on, we will see how rich formatting is possible using operator <<. Besides the default << operator, there are other ways to provide unformatted I/O.

12.6.1 put() and get() Functions for cout

The functions `cout.get()` and `cout.put()` are used for reading and writing to the stream. These functions are similar to `getc()` and `putc()` functions available in C. `cout.get()` has two different versions. The first has the prototype `void get(char)` and the other has the prototype `char get(void)`. The following program looks at both the versions and also shows how `put()` function is used for display. Both functions operate on `char` and are very simple to understand. `get()` reads a `char` at a time from the input stream and `put()` writes a `char` at a time to the output stream.

```cpp
//GetAndPut.cpp
#include <iostream>
using namespace std;
int main()
{
   char ch;
   char Data1Read[100];
   char Data2Read[100];
   for(int i = 0; ; i++)
   {
      cin.get(ch);
      if(ch == '\n')
      {
              Data1Read[i] = '\0';
              break;
      }
      Data1Read[i] = ch;
   }
   for(i = 0; ch = Data1Read[i]; i++)
   {
      cout.put(ch);
   }
   cout.put('\n');
   for(int i = 0; ; i++)
   {
      ch = cin.get();
      // Other version of get()
      if(ch == '\n')
      {
              Data2Read[i] = '\0';
              break;
      }
      Data2Read[i] = ch;
   }
   for(i = 0; ch = Data2Read[i]; i++)
   {
      cout.put(ch);
   }
   cout.put('\n');
}
```

Output
```
This is testing of first get and put
This is testing of first get and put
This is testing of second get and put
This is testing of second get and put
```

Note the two versions of get(). The first is `cin.get(ch)`. Here, the character read from the stream is bound to the argument (ch). In the other case `ch = cin.get()`, the value returned from the get() function is assigned to ch. There are no arguments to the get() function at the moment.

12.6.2 getline(), read(), and write() Functions

C has gets() and puts() functions for reading and writing strings. They are better than using scanf() because scanf() with %s option has a problem of terminating when a white space is encountered. gets() does not have this problem. These functions also provide easy management than scanf() and printf(). A similar functionality is provided in C++ using getline(), read(), and write() functions. In addition to the string parameter for reading and writing by gets() and puts(), these three functions have one additional parameter indicating the size of the string. The prototypes for these three functions are as follows:

> scanf() terminates when a white space is encountered, whereas gets() does not suffer from this problem.

```
cin.getline(string variable, maximum size of string that can be input)
cin.read(string variable, maximum size of string that can be input)
cout.write(string variable, maximum size of string that can be output)
```

These functions are used with old C-style strings. The C++ strings are discussed in Chapter 15. The difference between getline() and read() is that getline() terminates when a new line is entered, whereas read() does not stop when a new line is encountered. It stops only when end of file (ctrl-Z or ^Z for DOS and Windows files, and ctrl-d or ^d for Linux or UNIX files) is encountered. getline() also stops reading from the input if end of file is specified.

> getline() terminates when a new line is entered, whereas read() is not affected by a new line.

Let us look at Program 12.1 to understand this. The maximum number of characters has been specified as 100 while reading, but only 50 while printing; so, some portion of the string is not printed when we write cout.write.

 **PROGRAM 12.1** getline() and write()

```cpp
//GetlineAndWrite.cpp
#include <iostream>
using namespace std;

int main()
{
    char Message[100];
    cin.getline(Message, 100);
    cout.write(Message, 50);
    cout << endl;
    cin.read(Message, 100);
    cout.write(Message, 50);
    cout.write("\n", 1) ;
}
```

Output
```
This is testing of getline and then we have read test
```

```
This is testing of getline and then we have read t
Now the read is being tested
It requires ctrl-Z to end
^Z
Now the read is being tested
It requires ctrl-Z to
```

How the Program Works

The program has demonstrated the use of the three different functions, namely, `cin.getline()`, `cin.read()`, and `cin.write()`. When the user types characters, `getline()` or `read()` accepts only the maximum number of characters specified in the argument. The number of characters printed is taken from the characters read. This is why there is a mismatch between the characters input and the characters displayed as output.

12.7 FORMATTING I/O

Formatting can be done using two different ways. The first method is to use built-in `ios` functions. Table 12.2 lists the various `ios` member functions.

Table 12.2   Use of `ios` functions

ios member function	Use
width()	This specifies the width for display. The output will take up the width specified. It is used in aligning vertical columns of numeric items.
precision()	This specifies the precision of the floating-point number. The default precision is six digits after decimal point.
fill()	This specifies the character for filling up the unused portion of field. It is usually used with width member function. The remaining part of the field will be filled up with the char specified. Default char is space.
setf()	This specifies the format flags that control output display such as left or right justification, padding after sign symbol, scientific notation display, and displaying base of the number (such as hexadecimal, decimal, and octal).
unsetf()	This provides undo operation for the operations with setf().

12.7.1 Member Functions of ios

The prototype for all the following functions is:

> All ios functions return old values of the stream while they are called to set them to new values.

```
<old value of stream> function_name(<specified new value>)
```

The functions set the new value to the stream and return the old value. The `width()` function sets the new width to the argument specified and returns the old width. The `precision()` function sets new precision and returns the old precision. Similarly, `fill()` returns old fill char and sets new fill char.

width()

It specifies the minimum field width for display. The output following this statement will use the width specified. It resets itself after the first output after this statement. The output of the statements

```
cout.width(10);
cout << "C++";
cout << "Language"
```

will be SSSSSSSC++Language. (S is used to indicate a space in the output.)

It can be seen that the output for cout << "C++" was provided in the width of 10, but the output for cout << "Language" is not. If one wants to provide the same width setting to the second cout statement as well, one more width specification should be added to it using one more cout.width in the following way:

```
cout.width(10);
cout << "C++";
cout.width(10);
cout << "Language";
```

Then, the output will be

SSSSSSSC++SSLanguage

Thus, cout.width() must precede any output for which width is to be set as it changes back to original value immediately after executing a single output.

Notes

1. If the actual output exceeds the specified width, the complete output is provided and the value specified in width() is ignored.
2. The formatting function width() operates on a single cout statement. The original width is restored after that.

precision()

It specifies precision, that is, the number of digits to be displayed after the decimal point. As mentioned earlier, the default value is six. The precision function is important while displaying numbers in scientific notation, printing amount data where precision is two, or aligning floating point numbers for vertical alignment.

fill()

The function fill(char) fills the subsequent empty portions of fields by the fill character specified. It is useful to print the '*'s preceding the amount information in cheques.

Consider Program 12.2 to understand the usefulness of the three ios member functions.

PROGRAM 12.2 width(), precision(), and fill()

```cpp
//Width.cpp
#include <iostream>
using namespace std;

int main()
{
    cout << "Roll number"; cout << "Name"; cout << "Marks" << endl;
    cout << 1 << "Lara" << 355.50 << endl;
    cout << 2 << "Beckham" << 275 << endl;
    cout << 3 << "Steffi" << 290.75 << endl;
    cout << 4 << "Jaspal" << 295 << endl;
    cout << 5 << "Ranatunga" << 200.60 << endl;
```

```
    cout.width(15); cout << "Roll number"; cout.width(15);
    cout << "Name"; cout.width(10); cout.precision(2);
    cout << "Marks" << endl;

    cout.fill(' '); cout.width(15); cout << 1; cout.width(15);
    cout << "Lara"; cout.width(10); cout.fill('0');
    cout.precision(2); cout << 355.50 << endl;

    cout.fill(' '); cout.width(15); cout << 2; cout.width(15);
    cout << "Beckham"; cout.width(10); cout.fill('0');
    cout.precision(2); cout << 275 << endl;

    cout.fill(' '); cout.width(15); cout << 3; cout.width(15);
    cout << "Steffi"; cout.width(10); cout.fill('0');
    cout.precision(2); cout << 290.75 << endl;

    cout.fill(' '); cout.width(15); cout << 4; cout.width(15);
    cout << "Jaspal"; cout.width(10); cout.fill('0');
    cout.precision(2); cout << 295 << endl;

    cout.fill(' '); cout.width(15); cout << 5; cout.width(15);
    cout << "Ranatunga"; cout.width(10); cout.fill('0');
    cout.precision(2); cout << 200.60 << endl;
}
```

Output

```
Roll number  Name        Marks
1            Lara        355.5
2            Beckham     275
3            Steffi      290.75
4            Jaspal      295
5            Ranatunga   200.6

Roll number  Name        Marks
1            Lara        003.6e+002
2            Beckham     0000000275
3            Steffi      002.9e+002
4            Jaspal      0000000295
5            Ranatunga   00002e+002
```

How the Program Works

Take a look at the unformatted as well as the formatted outputs. The formatted output looks better than the unformatted output (except names being right justified and marks are not displayed in proper non-scientific notation; we will learn to set it right soon in Program 12.4). Now, look at the code. It seems there are more formatting statements than the actual output statements. These statements are a must in circumstances that involve displaying reports or printing them.

Such statements can be eliminated by using a simple function that does the formatting. The function then should be called using the required values. This is left as an exercise to the reader.

Now, let us see how roll numbers and names can be left aligned, while marks are aligned to their precision. The setf() function needs to be used to set these flags. Note the use of endl in the statements; it is used to provide the same effect as '\n', that is, providing a new line on the output. It is one of the manipulators that will be discussed later in this chapter in Section 12.11.

12.8 SETTING AND CLEARING FORMAT FLAGS

The format flags are attached with every stream that is used. The `ios_base` class defines a bitmask enumeration where 18 flags are defined. Table 12.3 lists the format flags and their roles.

Table 12.3 Format flags

Flag name	Description
skipws	Skip initial white space while reading from a stream.
left	Output is left justified.
right	Output is right justified.
internal	Numeric value is padded with space between sign or base (0x, 0, etc.) character.
oct	Output is displayed in octal format.
hex	Output is displayed in hexadecimal format.
dec	Output is displayed in decimal format.
showbase	Numeric values will be displayed with base character such as displaying Hex 1E as 0x1E (Hex also needs to be specified before this, because decimal is the default).
uppercase	The x in showbase and the e in scientific notation are displayed in lower case. If uppercase is set, they would be displayed as X and E, that is, in upper case.
showpos	A leading + sign is displayed before positive values. This is not displayed by default.
showpoint	Decimal point will be displayed even if it is not present. Trailing zeros will also be displayed for all floating point values (this is needed for the example given earlier).
scientific	Output displays floating point values in scientific notation.
fixed	Output is displayed in fixed (non-scientific) notation.
unibuf	Buffers are flushed after every insertion. It is similar to flushing a stream after reading, so that no more extra chars are left out and subsequent read statements have no problem.
boolalpha	Enable the Boolean values or the input to be displayed as true or false rather than 1 and 0.
basefield	Collection of oct, dec, and hex. Needs to be specified as the second argument if any one of the three is the first argument to `setf()`
adjustfield	Collection of left, right, and internal field. Needs to be specified as the second argument if any one of the three is the first argument to `setf()`
floatfield	Collection of scientific and fixed. Needs to be specified as the second argument if any one of the two is specified as the first argument

All these fields can be set and unset using `setf()` and `unsetf()` functions available with the `cout` object. The following program demonstrates the effect of setting some of the flags on output. After every set and respective display, there is a call to `unsetf()` function to revoke the effect of applying that flag.

Notes

1. If we do not unset the flags, they will remain in effect until the program is over.
2. Operations for setting and unsetting flags are setting bits in a variable of type `fmtflags` defined in `ios_base`. One can use bitwise OR to set or unset multiple bits together.

```cpp
//SetFlags.cpp
#include <iostream>
#include <string>
using namespace std;
int main()
{
    cout << "See that the effect of ios::showpos is to show leading plus sign\n";
    cout.setf(ios::showpos);
    cout << 100.0 << endl; cout.unsetf(ios::showpos); cout << endl;
    cout << "See that the effect of ios::showpoint is to show decimal point\n";
    cout.setf(ios::showpoint);
    cout << 100.0 << endl;
    cout.unsetf(ios::showpoint);
    cout << endl;
    cout << "See the effect of both the above together\n";
    cout.setf(ios::showpoint | ios::showpos);
    cout << 100.0 << endl;
    cout.unsetf(ios::showpoint | ios::showpos);
    cout << endl;
    cout << "See the effect of both upper case and scientific together\n";
    cout.setf(ios::uppercase | ios::scientific);
    cout << 100.123 << endl;
    cout.unsetf(ios::uppercase | ios::scientific);
    cout << endl;
    cout << "See how 100.123 is printed with default right alignment\n";
    cout << "and then see how it changes after left alignment\n";
    cout.width(20);
    cout << 100.123 << endl;
    cout.setf(ios::left);
    cout.width(20);
    cout << 100.123 << endl;
    cout.unsetf(ios::left);
    cout << endl;
    cout << "See the effect of using internal, which displays the sign in the left and
    right justifies the output, thus filling the spaces in between\n";
    cout.setf(ios::internal | ios::showpos);
    cout.width(20);
    cout << 100.123 << endl;
    cout << endl;
    cout << "Now, see the effect of fill char with internal\n";
    cout.width(20);
```

```
        cout.fill('*');
        cout << 100.123 << endl;
        cout.unsetf(ios::internal | ios::showpos);
        cout.fill(' ');
        cout << endl;
        cout << "See how truthfulness is printed as 1 by default and is changed to true when
            boolalpha is set with cout\n";
        bool Test = true;
        cout << Test << endl; // Displays 1
        cout.setf(ios::boolalpha);
        cout << Test << endl; // Displays true
        cout << endl;
        cout << "See how truthfulness is read as 0 or 1 by default. It now accepts false or
        true when boolalpha is set with cin \n";
        cout << "Please enter true or false\n";
        cin.setf(ios::boolalpha);
        cin >> Test;
        cout << Test << endl;
}
```

Output

```
See that the effect of ios::showpos is to show leading plus sign + 100
See that the effect of ios::showpoint is to show decimal point 100.000
See the effect of both the above together +100.000
See the effect of both upper case and scientific together 1.001230E+002
See how 100.123 is printed with default right alignment and then see how it changes
after left alignment 100.123
100.123
See the effect of using internal, which displays the sign in the left and right
justifies the output, thus filling the spaces in between + 100.123
Now, see the effect of fill char with internal +************100.123
See how truthfulness is printed as 1 by default and is changed to true when boolalpha
is set with cout
1
true
See how truthfulness is read as 0 or 1 by default. It now accepts false or true when
boolalpha is set with cin
Please enter true or false
false
false
```

12.9 USING setf() FUNCTION WITH TWO ARGUMENTS

The setf() function can have two arguments instead of one. It is required by most of the implementations to clear other related flags to set a new flag. Suppose one wants to set the internal flag. It may require clearing the left and right flags. All the three flags, that is, left, right, and internal, belong to the same group, and any two of them cannot remain active together at the same point of time.

In case of `unsetf()` and two-argument `setf()`, the feature specified in the second argument is set first. The execution moves from right to left.

Earlier when `cout.setf(ios::left)` was used, the VC++ 7.0 version does the `unsetf(ios::right)` by itself. This is needed because it is not possible to have both the left and right justified flags set at the same point of time. In case the implementation does not take care of the unsetting, the programmer needs to do it. One can use the `unsetf()` function that has been used in the previous program, but it is easier to write `setf()` with two arguments (as a single `setf()` instead of two `unsetf()` and one `setf()`).

The syntax of the two-argument `setf()` is an extension of the simple `setf()` with one argument. When there is a `setf()` with two arguments, both the arguments are of type fmtflags. The following statement can be written

```
cout.setf(ios::showpos, ios::showpos)
```

This statement means set `showpos` if `showpos` is available as the second argument. It clears `showpos` before setting it. The clearing of `showpos` is done because it is mentioned in the second argument.

If the statement is as follows:

```
cout.setf(ios::showpos | ios::left, ios::showpos)
```

then `ios::left` is not applied because it is not specified in the second argument. This strange behaviour of `setf()` is useful in setting values where other values are mutually exclusive to it.

For example, if one writes

```
cout.setf(ios::left, ios::right | ios::left | ios::internal)
```

Writing `cout.setf(ios::left)` and `cout.setf(ios::left, ios::adjustfield)` produces the same result in most of the systems, but the latter is better because it will also work with those systems that require explicit unsetting.

then ios `left` is set, but before that `right`, `left`, and `internal` are all unset. Some implementations may not favour the previous form of `setf()`, and one needs to explicitly `unsetf()` other exclusive items. It is easier to write

```
ios::right | ios::left | ios::internal
```

because it is the same as `ios::adjustfield`, which is provided by C++. So, the code is now reduced to

```
cout.setf(ios::left, ios::adjustfield)
```

Similarly, `ios::basefield` is the same as `ios::oct | ios::dec | ios::hex`. So, for setting display in hexadecimal, one needs to write

```
cout.setf(ios::hex, ios::basefield)
```

Consider Program 12.3, which explains the use of `setf()` with two arguments.

PROGRAM 12.3 setf() with two arguments

```cpp
//Set2ArgFlags.cpp
#include <iostream>
#include <string>
using namespace std;

int main()
{
    cout << "See that the effect of ios::showpos is to show leading plus sign\n";
    cout.setf(ios::showpos, ios::showpos);
    cout << 100.0 << endl;
    cout.unsetf(ios::showpos);
    cout << endl;
```

```
        cout << "See that the effect of ios::showpoint is to show decimal point\n";
        cout.setf(ios::showpoint, ios::showpoint);
        cout << 100.0 << endl;
        cout.unsetf(ios::showpoint);
        cout << endl;
        cout << "See the effect of both the above together\n";
        cout.setf(ios::showpoint | ios::showpos, ios::showpoint | ios::showpos);
        cout << 100.0 << endl;
        cout.unsetf(ios::showpoint | ios::showpos);
        cout << endl;
        cout << "See the effect of scientific \n";
        cout.setf(ios::scientific, ios::floatfield);
        cout << 100.123 << endl;
        cout.unsetf(ios::uppercase | ios::scientific);
        cout << endl;
        cout << "See how 100.123 is printed with default right alignment\n";
        cout << "and then see how it changes after left alignment\n";
        cout.width(20);
        cout << 100.123 << endl;
        cout.setf(ios::left, ios::adjustfield);
        cout.width(20);
        cout << 100.123 << endl;
        cout.unsetf(ios::left);
        cout << 100.123 << endl;
        cout.setf(ios::hex, ios::basefield);
        cout << 100 << endl;        // Prints 64
        cout.setf(ios::oct, ios::basefield);
        cout << 100 << endl;        // Prints 144
        cout.setf(ios::dec, ios::basefield);
        cout << 100 << endl;        // Prints 100
        cout.setf(ios::showbase);     // Prints the base
        cout.setf(ios::hex, ios::basefield);
        cout << 100 << endl;            // Prints 0x64
        cout.setf(ios::oct, ios::basefield);
        cout << 100 << endl;            // Prints 0144
        cout.setf(ios::dec, ios::basefield);
        cout << 100 << endl;            // Prints 100
}
```

Output
```
See that the effect of ios::showpos is to show leading plus sign
+ 100
See that the effect of ios::showpoint is to show decimal point
100.000
See the effect of both the above together
+100.000
See the effect of scientific
1.001230e+002
See how 100.123 is printed with default right alignment and then see how it changes after
left alignment
100.123
100.123 100.123
64
144
100
0x64
0144
100
```

How the Program Works

Note that most of the `setf()` statements are those that have successfully worked in the single argument version. The `setf()` for setting base may not work in some installations. In that case, one needs to provide the two-argument `setf()` to print it right. The conclusion is that if one wants the program to be portable across various platforms, it is safer to use the two-argument `setf()`, even if it may be a little tedious.

Program 12.2 is rewritten as Program 12.4 to display the names left justified and marks in scientific notation.

PROGRAM 12.4   Printing mark sheet

```
//MarksheetPrinting.cpp
#include <iostream>
using namespace std;

int main()
{
    cout.width(15);
    cout.setf(ios::left);cout.setf(ios::fixed);cout.precision(2);cout.setf(ios::showpoint);

    /* The same code that we had in Program 12.2 comes here */
}
```

Output

```
Roll number  Name       Marks
1            Lara       355.50
2            Beckham    275.00
3            Steffi     290.75
4            Jaspal     295.00
5            Ranatunga  200.60
```

How the Program Works

The important line here is

```
cout.setf(ios::left); cout.setf(ios::fixed); cout.precision(2);
cout.setf(ios::showpoint);
```

> Setting and unsetting multiple flags are done by combining them using the pipe character (bitwise OR)

The output is left justified, and non-scientific format is used for displaying the floating point numbers. Precision of two is applied for displaying marks with two digits after the decimal and showing a decimal point even when there is no need. This is done to have the marks aligned properly.

12.10 EXAMINING AND CLEARING FLAGS

It is possible to find which flags are set and also possible to clear them using the `setf()` function. The argument to `setf()` is of type `fmtflags`. It is defined as an *enumeration of bitmask* in `ios`.

> The argument to `setf()` function is of type `fmtflags`, which is an enumeration of bitmask.

Every `ios` function described in this chapter returns the previous status of the stream in the form of `fmtflags`. There are also function *flags* as a member function of `cout`, which return flags settings. Let us look at Program 12.5 to understand how to use it.

PROGRAM 12.5   Examining and resetting flags

```cpp
//ExamineAndResetFlags.cpp
#include <iostream>
using namespace std;
void DispFlags()
{
    ios::fmtflags FlagStatus;
    long Flag1by1;

    FlagStatus = (long) cout.flags();
    cout << endl;
    for(Flag1by1 = 0x4000; Flag1by1; Flag1by1 >>= 1)
    if(Flag1by1 & FlagStatus)
        cout << 1;
    else
        cout << 0;
}
void SetAndDispFlag(long FlagVal)
{
    cout.flags(FlagVal);
    DispFlags();
}
int main()
{
    cout << "Current set of flags";
    DispFlags();
    long NoFlagsOn = 0;
    cout.flags(NoFlagsOn);

    DispFlags();
    SetAndDispFlag(ios::boolalpha); cout << "boolalpha";
    SetAndDispFlag(ios::fixed); cout << "Fixed";
    SetAndDispFlag(ios::scientific); cout << "Scientific";

    SetAndDispFlag(ios::hex); cout << "Hex"; SetAndDispFlag(ios::oct); cout << "Oct";
    SetAndDispFlag(ios::dec); cout << "Dec";

    SetAndDispFlag(ios::internal); cout << "Internal";
    SetAndDispFlag(ios::right); cout << "Right";
    SetAndDispFlag(ios::left); cout << "Left";

    // SetAndDispFlag(ios::showpos);
    SetAndDispFlag(ios::showpoint); cout << "Showpoint";
    SetAndDispFlag(ios::uppercase); cout << "Upper case";
    SetAndDispFlag(ios::skipws); cout << "Skip white space";

    SetAndDispFlag(ios::floatfield); cout << "Float field";
    SetAndDispFlag(ios::adjustfield); cout << "Adjust field";
    SetAndDispFlag(ios::basefield); cout << "Base field \n";
}
```

Output
```
Current set of flags 000001000000001
000000000000000 // All the flags are cleared here
100000000000000 boolalpha
010000000000000 Fixed
001000000000000 Scientific
000100000000000 Hex
000010000000000 Oct
000001000000000 Dec
```

```
000000100000000 Internal
000000010000000 Right
000000001000000 Left
00000000001000  Showpoint
000000000000100 Upper case
000000000000001 Skip white space
011000000000000 Float field
000000111000000 Adjust field
000111000000000 Base field
```

How the Program Works

We have to look at the last 14 bits of the value returned from the flags function. It is a long variable. We start with 4,000 hex given to a variable `Flag1By1`. That is, the 14th bit from the left-hand side is one and all other bits are zero. We bitwise-AND the same value (4,000 hex) with the status we have received from the flags function. If it is one, then the 14th bit is set in the status. It indicates the `boolalpha` flag being on. We then right-shift `Flag1By1` to get the 13th bit and repeat the process until the last bit is checked. We continue until the value of `Flag1By1` becomes zero, that is, every bit of the status is examined.

But why is the line displaying status for `showpos` commented? Observe the output after uncommenting this line. Is there a problem? The solution to this problem is left as an exercise to the reader.

12.11 MANIPULATORS

Manipulators are special functions for formatting. They can do all the formatting that is done by the `ios` member functions. So why do we need both manipulators and `ios` functions? Manipulators are better in some circumstances and provide an alternative way to solve the same problem. The choice between manipulators and `ios` functions to solve formatting problems sometimes depends on the preference of the user. Besides, there are a few other differences as well. We will discuss that after checking how manipulators can replace the `ios` functions.

12.11.1 Using Manipulators instead of `ios` Functions

Table 12.4 lists a few manipulators and their equivalent `ios` functions.

Table 12.4   Manipulators and their equivalent `ios` functions

Manipulators	Equivalent `ios` function
`setw()`	`width()`
`setprecision()`	`precision()`
`setfill()`	`fill()`
`setiosflags()`	`setf()`
`resetiosflags()`	`unsetf()`

Let us now look at the following program, which is a sample code that shows how to use manipulators in place of `ios` functions. Program 12.4 has been modified as follows:

```
//Manipulator1.cpp
#include <iostream>
#include <iomanip>
using namespace std;
int main()
{
    cout << setw(15) << setiosflags(ios::left)
    << setiosflags(ios::fixed) << setprecision(2)
    << setiosflags(ios::showpoint);
    cout << "Roll number" << setw(15) << "Name" << setw(10) << setprecision(2)
    << "Marks" << endl;
    cout << setw(15) << 1 << setw(15) << "Lara" << setw(10) << setprecision(2) << 355.50
    << endl;
    /* setw and setprecision are required in each cout as their setting stays for only
    one cout statement */
    cout << setw(15) << 2 << setw(15) << "Beckham" << setw(10)
    << setprecision(2) << 27 5.00 << endl;
    cout << setw(15) << 3 << setw(15) << "Steffi" << setw(10)
    << setprecision(2) << 2 90.75 << endl;
    cout << setw(15) << 4 << setw(15) << "Jaspal" << setw(10)
    << setprecision(2) << 295.0 << endl;
    cout << setw(15) << 5 << setw(15) << "Ranatunga" << setw(10)
    << setprecision(2)<< 200.60 << endl;
}
```

The output of this program is the same as that of Program 12.4 written using ios functions.

This program uses manipulators whereas Program 12.4 used ios functions. There are a few differences between manipulators and ios functions. The differences between manipulators and ios functions are listed in Section 12.11.2.

12.11.2 Differences between Manipulators and ios Functions

The differences between manipulators and ios functions are as follows:

1. Unlike ios functions, manipulators do not return the previous status. Suppose one wants to change the current width to 15 and then revert to the previous width, or change the precision to 2 and then switch back to the previous precision, it is possible using ios functions. Take a look at the following code.

```
int PrevWidth = width(15);
int PrevPrecision = precision(2);
/* Call a third-party function that might change the settings */
width(PrevWidth);
precision(PrevPrecision);
```

Such a code segment is better when it is a part of a function and one does not want the user to apply his/her own setting while calling the function.

> **Note** Format changes made on the stream are global. Formatting cin or cout at any place anywhere affects the program as a whole. To write a foolproof function, we must set the required setting and then unset everything upon exit to a previous setting. Thus, ios can prove useful in cases where the previous value of a flag must be preserved.

2. Manipulators have a distinct advantage. It is possible to write our own manipulator and use it in the program. Thus, the program using manipulators can define its own manipulator and use it for printing the mark sheet. It makes the program much more readable and short. We will learn how to do it in Section 12.11. It is possible and more readable to overload the '<<' operator for an object to display in a formatted way using functions (or manipulators).

3. `ios` functions are single. They cannot be combined to have multiple effects together. One has to write

```
cout.precision(2);
cout.width(15);
```

as two separate sentences. On the contrary, it is possible to combine manipulators as follows:

```
cout << setprecision(2) << setw(15)
```

When a large set of formatting options is needed, manipulators are easy to write and produce more readable codes.

4. `ios` functions require only the `<iostream>` file, whereas manipulators need the `<iomanip>` file to be included additionally.

5. For some manipulators, there are no equivalent `ios` functions. One such example is `endl` that outputs a newline character. As an additional job, it flushes the stream as well. Another example is `boolalpha`. It is used to turn on or off displaying Boolean values as true or false rather than one or zero. We have a `setf()` equivalent for doing this in `ios` functions

```
cout.setf(ios::boolalpha)
```

and also using `setiosflags` as follows:

```
cout << setiosflags(ios::boolalpha)
```

However, it is possible to write `cout << boolalpha` to have the same effect using a simple representation. Similar manipulators are available for almost all the flags, which we can set using `setiosflags`. Thus, there is almost no need to use `setiosflags` while working with manipulators, whereas one needs to use `setf()` for such work with `ios` functions. Such manipulators are known as shorthand manipulators.

6. When a manipulator does not take an argument, it is passed without parentheses, that is, (). For example, we do not use `endl()`. Instead, only `endl` is used. Similarly, only `hex` is used instead of `hex()`. On the contrary, the `ios` functions cannot be called without parentheses.

7. Some of the manipulators are needed in pairs to provide the toggle effect, for example, `showbase` and `noshowbase`, `boolalpha` and `noboolalpha`, `showpoint` and `noshowpoint`, etc. There are no such `ios` functions. The `setf()` and `unsetf()` functions with respective arguments need to be used to have the same effect.

8. `ios` functions are member functions (static functions, which can be called `ios::<function>`), whereas manipulators are non-member functions.

12.12 USING MANIPULATORS

In this section, we will discuss some more ways of using manipulators. We can left or right align, display in upper or lower case, fill the range with a specific character, display bool values as true or false, etc., using manipulators.

12.12.1 Setting and Testing Flags using Manipulators

The following program shows how to set and reset flags using manipulators. We have already seen a similar example for ios functions in Section 12.8.

```cpp
//SetFlagManip.cpp
#include <iostream>
#include <string>
#include <iomanip>
using namespace std;
int main()
{
    cout << "See that the effect of ios::showpos is to show leading plus sign\n";
    cout << setiosflags(ios::showpos) << 100.0 << endl
    << resetiosflags(ios::showpos) << endl;
    cout << "See that the effect of ios::showpoint is to show decimal point\n";
    cout << setiosflags(ios::showpoint) << 100.0 << endl
    << resetiosflags(ios::showpoint) << endl;
    cout << "See the effect of both the above together\n";
    cout << setiosflags(ios::showpoint | ios::showpos) << 100.0 << endl <<
    resetiosflags(ios::showpoint | ios::showpos) << endl;
    cout << "See the effect of both upper case and scientific together\n";
    cout << setiosflags(ios::uppercase | ios::scientific) << 100.123 << endl <<
    resetiosflags(ios::uppercase | ios::scientific) << endl;
    cout << "See how 100.123 is printed with default right alignment\n";
    cout << "and then see how it changes after left alignment\n";
    cout << setw(20) << 100.123 << endl << setiosflags(ios::left) << setw(20) << 100.123
    << endl << resetiosflags(ios::left) << endl;
    cout << "See the effect of using internal, which displays the sign in the left and
    right justifies the output, thus filling the spaces in between\n";
    cout << setiosflags(ios::internal | ios::showpos) << setw(20) << 100.123 << endl;
    cout << "Now see the effect of fill char with internal\n";
    cout << setw(20) << setfill('*') << 100.123 << endl
    << resetiosflags(ios::internal | ios::showpos) << setfill(' ')
    << endl;
    cout << "See how truthfulness is printed as 1 by default and is changed to true when
    boolalpha is set with cout\n";
    bool Test = true;
    cout << Test << endl;// This will display 1
    cout << setiosflags(ios::boolalpha);
    cout << Test << endl;// This will display true
    cout << "See how truthfulness is read as 0 or 1 by default. It now accepts false or
    true when boolalpha is set with cin\n";
    cout << "Please enter true or false\n";
    cin >> setiosflags(ios::boolalpha);
    cin >> Test;
    cout << Test << endl;
}
```

Both manipulators and ios functions can be used to produce identical results by setting and resetting format flags of streams.

The output of the program is the same as that of the program in Section 12.8. This is done to show that both the ways of formatting produce exactly the same results.

This contains many calls to `setiosflags`, which can be eliminated in most of the cases. Instead of writing

```
cin >> setiosflags(ios::boolalpha)
```

one can write

```
cin >> boolalpha
```

and it will have the same effect. The `boolalpha` here is a *shorthand manipulator* for the job. The following two programs show the use of such manipulators.

12.12.2 Manipulators for Toggle Effect

The following program shows how to toggle from `boolalpha` to `noboolalpha`, `showpoint` to `noshowpoint`, etc.

```cpp
//ToggleValues.cpp
#include <iostream>
using namespace std;
#include <iomanip>
int main()
{
    bool Test = false;
    cout << boolalpha << Test << endl;
    cout << noboolalpha << Test << endl;
    cout << showpoint << 100.00 << endl;
    cout << noshowpoint << 100.00 << endl;
    cout << showpos << 100.00 << endl;
    cout << noshowpos << 100.00 << endl;
    cout << showpoint << uppercase << scientific << 100.20 << endl;
    cout << nouppercase << 100.20 << endl;
}
```
Output
```
false
0
100.000
100
+ 100
100
1.002000E+002
1.002000e+002
```

12.12.3 Shorthand Manipulators

The long versions of manipulators can be cumbersome to use. Therefore, shorthand manipulators are available. `Setiosflags` and its arguments can be replaced by shorthand versions of manipulators. For example,

```
setiosflags(ios::internal | ios::showpos)
```

can be replaced by just `showpos`. Program 12.6 shows how to use such shorthand manipulators.

PROGRAM 12.6   Shorthand manipulators

```
//SetFlagDirectManip.cpp
#include <iostream>
#include <string>
#include <iomanip>
using namespace std;

int main()
{
    cout << "See that the effect of showpos is to show leading plus sign\n";
    cout << showpos << 100.0 << endl << noshowpos << endl;
    cout << "See that the effect of showpoint is to show decimal point\n";
    cout << showpoint << 100.0 << endl << noshowpoint << endl;
    cout << "See the effect of both the above together\n";
    cout << showpoint << showpos << 100.0 << endl << noshowpoint << showpos << endl;

    cout << "See the effect of both upper case and scientific together\n";
    cout << uppercase << scientific << 100.123 << endl << nouppercase << fixed << endl;

    cout << "See how 100.123 is printed with default right alignment\n";
    cout << "and then see how it changes after left alignment\n";
    cout << setw(20) << 100.123 << endl << left << setw(20) << 100.123 << endl << right <<
    endl;

    cout << "See the effect of using internal, which displays the sign in the left and right
    justifies the output, thus filling the spaces in between\n";
    cout << internal << showpos << setw(20) << 100.123 << noshowpos << endl;

    cout << "Now see the effect of fill char with internal\n";
    cout << setw(20) << setfill('*') << 100.123 << endl << internal << showpos << setfill(' ')
    << endl;
}
```

How the Program Works

This program is similar to the one in Section 12.12.1 with `setiosflags`. The output is similar. It is important to see that shorthand manipulators are shorter and easier to work with. For example, look at the following statements from the program in Section 12.12.1.

```
cout << setiosflags(ios::showpos) << 100.0 << endl
  << resetiosflags(ios::showpos) << endl;
```

Now, they are converted to a single statement as follows in Program 12.6.

```
cout << showpos << 100.0 << endl << noshowpos << endl;
```

The program contains similar examples for all such manipulators.

12.13 USER-DEFINED MANIPULATORS

Manipulators can also be defined to suit particular requirements. Program 12.7 shows how one can write and use one's own manipulators. The example prints the mark sheet, now in a much better form as compared to the output of Program 12.4 discussed earlier.

PROGRAM 12.7 User-defined manipulators

```cpp
//ManipMarksheetPrint.cpp
#include <iostream>
#include <iomanip>
using namespace std;

// First manipulator
ostream & PrintHeading(ostream & TempOut)
{
    TempOut << setw(80) << setiosflags(ios::left);
    TempOut << "GLS Higher Secondary School" << endl
    << setw(80) << "Standard XII" << endl;
    return TempOut;
}

// Second manipulator
ostream & PrintMarksheetHeading(ostream & TempOut)
{
    TempOut << setw(15) << setiosflags(ios::left) << setiosflags(ios::fixed) << setprecision(2)
    << setiosflags(ios::showpoint);
    TempOut << "Roll number" << setw(15) << "Name" << setw(10)
    << setprecision(2) << "Marks" << endl;
    return TempOut;
}

// Third manipulator
ostream & PrintLine(ostream & TempOut)
{
    TempOut << "-------";
    TempOut << endl;
    return TempOut;
}

int main()
{
    cout << PrintLine;
    cout << PrintHeading << PrintLine << PrintMarksheetHeading;
    cout << PrintLine;
    cout << setw(15) << 1 << setw(15) << "Lara" << setw(10) << setprecision(2) << 355.50 << endl;
    cout << setw(15) << 2 << setw(15) << "Beckham" << setw(10)
    << setprecision(2) << 27 5.00 << endl;
    cout << setw(15) << 3 << setw(15) << "Steffi" << setw(10)
    << setprecision(2) << 290.75 << endl;

    cout << PrintLine;
}
```

Output
```
---------------------------------------------
GLS Higher Secondary School Standard XII
---------------------------------------------

 Roll number  Name       Marks

  1           Lara       355.50

  2           Beckham    275.00

  3           Steffi     290.75
---------------------------------------------
```

How the Program Works

Simpler manipulators are sometimes more useful. For example, the `PrintLine` manipulator used for drawing lines is more useful. One may ask what happens if the call to these manipulators are jumbled? For example, what happens if `PrintHeading` is called at the end? In that case, the output displays the heading at the end. The output depends on the sequence in which the manipulators are called in the `main()` function. To understand the definition of the manipulators, let us have a look at the manipulator for printing the heading for the mark sheet. The manipulator function looks similar to the functions we have seen earlier for overloading `<<` and `>>`. In fact, they are bound to be similar because they are doing almost the same action.

Note the header. The headers of manipulators have the following structure:

```
ostream <manipulator name> (ostream & <stream reference variable>)
{
    // Manipulators and ios functions to do all formatting
    return <stream reference variable>
}
```

The corresponding code in the given program is

```
ostream & PrintHeading(ostream & TempOut)
{
    TempOut << setw(80) << setiosflags(ios::left);
    TempOut << "GLS Higher Secondary School" << endl
        << setw(80) << "Standard XII" << endl;
    return TempOut;
}
```

There are three user-defined manipulators in this program. The name of the first manipulator is `PrintHeading` and the stream reference variable is `TempOut`. Note that `TempOut` is also returned from the manipulator. All manipulators will have the same format.

Note how the manipulator is called from the main function.

```
cout << PrintHeading << PrintLine << PrintMarksheetHeading;
```

This is similar to calling the overloaded `<<` function. In a true sense, the overloaded `<<` does the same action. It takes the ostream reference as argument and returns the same.

12.13.1 Passing and Returning Streams as Reference

A close look at the manipulator definition given reveals that the stream is passed and returned as a reference. The same `cout` that has been received is being returned. It is important to do so. If one does not return the output stream as reference, it is not possible to use

```
cout << PrintHeading << PrintLine << PrintMarksheetHeading;
```

in a chaining way. If `PrintHeading` does not return the same `cout` passed to it, the output of `cout << PrintHeading` does not yield `cout`, and `<< PrintLine` does not have `cout` as a left-hand side operator. So, it cannot be executed.

> Returning a reference helps chaining multiple user-defined manipulators in a single cout statement.

The importance of passing reference is also to be noted. If one does not pass `ostream &`, then when `ostream TempOut` (instead of `ostream & TempOut`) is encountered, a temporary stream object is created and copied from `TempOut` (a reference to `cout`, i.e., `cout`) and *that* is returned back. Being a local object, it would be destroyed upon exit, and hence, the output is garbage. These arguments are similar to the arguments we had quoted in favour of passing and returning references when we were using overloaded << and >>.

12.13.2 Using a Function for Formatting

A function can also be used instead of repeating identical formatting codes. The following program shows how this can be done. In the example, the function `FormatPrint()` prints the data passed to it in the format required.

Manipulators are handy for using argument-less formatting and functions can be used for formatting with arguments. It is also possible to format using manipulators having arguments, but it is cumbersome. Combining both, it is possible to produce professional quality report preparation tools for our project.

```cpp
//FinalMarksheet.cpp
#include <iostream>
#include <string>
#include <iomanip>
using namespace std;
/* Here we have three manipulators defined earlier in Program 12.7 */
void FormatPrint(int TempRollNo, string TempName, float TempMarks);
int main()
{
    cout << PrintLine;
    cout << PrintHeading << PrintLine << PrintMarksheetHeading;
    cout << PrintLine;
    FormatPrint(1, "RamChandra", 275.0);
    FormatPrint(2, "Beckham", 275.0);
    FormatPrint(3, "Steffi", 290.75);
    FormatPrint(4, "Jaspal", 295.0);
    FormatPrint(5, "Ranatunga", 200.60);
}
void FormatPrint(int TempRollNo, string TempName, float TempMarks)
{
    cout << setw(15) << TempRollNo << setw(15) << TempName << setw(10) <<
    setprecision(2) << TempMarks << endl;
}
```
Output
The output of the program is the same as in the version without the function.

▣ RECAPITULATION ▣

- Streams connect the I/O devices with the I/O operations of our programs.
- The I/O operations of computer programs are written with reference to the streams and not with reference to the devices.

- The streams with which the I/O operations of computer programs are connected are attached to the I/O device at the other end.
- There are two different ways to handle streams. The unformatted way of handling does not require any

formatting statements to be specified before output or input. Most of the cases, however, need formatting.

- There are two different ways of formatting in C++, namely, using `ios` member functions and using manipulators.
- The `ios` functions return the original format, whereas manipulators are more flexible and are easy to use.
- The function `width()` is similar to `setw()` manipulator, `fill()` is similar to `setfill()` manipulator, and so on.

- The `ios` functions include the `setf()` function. This function can be used for a variety of purposes. It has two versions, one with a single argument and the other with two arguments.
- There is a member function `flags()`, which returns flag settings.
- It is also possible to construct our own manipulators and use them wherever needed in the program.

■ KEYWORDS ■

Device drivers These are routines written by the device manufacturer to make it work when plugged with the computer.

Format functions from ios These functions are defined in the `ios_base` class and are useful in formatting. Being member functions, they are called by following a dot (.) after the `cout` object.

Manipulators These are functions that are non-members but provide similar formatting mechanism as ios functions.

Namespace This is a kind of enclosure for functions, classes, and variables to separate them from other entities.

Shorthand manipulators There are some manipulators that work as a shorthand to the longer versions, for example, using `boolalpha` for `setiosflags(ios::boolalpha)`. These are called shorthand manipulators.

Stream A stream is a conceptual pipe-like structure, which can have one end attached to the program and the other end attached by default to a keyboard, screen, or file. It is possible to change where one end is pointing to, while keeping the other end as it is.

■ EXERCISES ■

Multiple Choice Questions

1. C++ I/O is _____ to use compared to C I/O.
   - (a) easier
   - (b) harder
   - (c) moderate
   - (d) never easy

2. Which of the following functions is used to specify the precision of the floating number?
   - (a) `width()`
   - (b) `precision()`
   - (c) `setf()`
   - (d) `unsetf()`

3. Which of the following functions undo the operations done by `setf()`?
   - (a) `width()`
   - (b) `precision()`
   - (c) `setf()`
   - (d) `unsetf()`

4. After every set and respective display, we have a call to the _____ function to revoke the effect of applying the format flag.
   - (a) `setf()`
   - (b) `unsetf()`

   - (c) `clear()`
   - (d) Any of the above

5. _____ are conceptually pipe-like constructs for providing I/O.
   - (a) Files
   - (b) Devices
   - (c) Both
   - (d) None

6. What will be the output from the following statements? (S indicates space)
   ```
   cout.width(5);
   cout << "C++";
   cout.width(5);
   cout << "C++";
   ```
   - (a) SSSSSSSC++C++
   - (b) SSC++SSC++
   - (c) SSSSSC++C++
   - (d) SSSSSC++SSSSSC++

7. We can write _____ and use it in the program.
   - (a) our own manipulator
   - (b) our own ios function

(c) our own format flag

(d) our own format specifier

8. We can use _____ to set or unset multiple flags together.

(a) bitwise AND

(b) bitwise OR

(c) bitwise XOR

(d) bitwise NOT

9. Which default destination is used by the following cout, cerr, and clog predefined streams?

(a) Keyboard

(b) Mouse

(c) Screen

(d) Printer

10. The setf() function can have maximum _____ arguments.

(a) one

(b) two

(c) three

(d) multiple

Conceptual Exercises

1. What are streams? Why they are useful?

2. What is the difference between I/O provided by C and C++?

3. What is new in I/O provided by the ANSI C++ compared to the older I/O of C++?

4. What is the importance of ios member flags in formatting I/O?

5. What is the difference between I/O using put() and get() and that using getline() and write()?

6. What is the advantage of giving two arguments to setf()? Why does it require two arguments?

7. Discuss how various member functions of ios can be used for formatting I/O.

8. How can we clear all the flags for formatting at the same time?

9. What are the differences between manipulators and ios functions?

10. What is the requirement for passing and returning reference from a manipulator function?

Practical Exercises

1. Write a program to read the marks of a student and print his mark sheet. Define at least two user-defined manipulators for reading and printing. Use either ios functions or manipulators for formatting.

2. Design your own manipulator that displays a line and then displays your name, address, and phone number in proper format and then displays a line again.

3. Design a manipulator for printing your institute letterhead's header and footer. Now, write a function to display a congratulating note to you for getting first class in MCA from your institute head.

4. Define a cricket scoreboard class. It should have the innings details for both the teams, bowling analysis of bowlers, and list of wickets fallen. Design a presentation style such that any information can be seen easily. Use ios functions or manipulators to achieve the effect.

Using Files for Input/Output

13.1 SPECIALTY OF INPUT/OUTPUT

So far we have seen many operations that are performed by C++, such as constructing objects from classes, taking care of objects coming into existence and going out of context, and making virtual base class effect visible when the classes are being inherited. However, input/output (I/O) operations are special because they are to be performed with the help of the operating system (OS) and the device drivers. Exhibits 13.1 and 13.2 describe an OS and a device driver.

Exhibit 13.1 Operating system

An operating system is the primary interface between the user and the computer. DOS, Windows, Unix, and Linux are all examples of operating systems. Excluding I/O, no other operation requires active participation from the OS. The compiler and the C++ object model take care of them in the form that suits them. However, I/O operations do not come under the direct purview of the C++ compiler or the run-time system. The C++ system has to work in sync with other entities to get the job done.

Exhibit 13.2 Device driver

A device driver is a small program that comes with every device that we attach to a computer, be it a hard disk, a scanner, a mouse, a web camera, or any other additional device. This small program acts as an interpreter between the OS and the device. When the OS issues a command, the driver makes the device understand it.

Let us consider an example to see the roles of the other entities in the I/O. Suppose one writes type `<filename>` in the command prompt, double clicks on a file, or writes cat `<filename>` in the Linux console, the operating system makes a request to the device driver to open the required file. The device driver, in turn, passes the message to the disk and when the disk responds to the message, the device driver passes it on to the OS. Then, the OS passes it to the screen. It is usually not possible to access the device directly. It is to be done using specific calls to the OS. Thus, a C++ program is not capable of performing I/O operations on its own. One may wonder where streams have gone. Streams are the interface and not the entity

> A C++ program cannot perform I/O operations on its own. It has to depend on the OS and the device drivers to access a device.

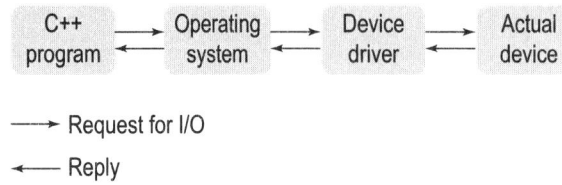

———▶ Request for I/O

◀——— Reply

Fig. 13.1   Request for I/O and its reply

involved in the operation, and thus, they are not discussed. Since we have already learnt about streams, there is no need for further exploration of that topic.

Figure 13.1 illustrates how a request from a C++ program for I/O travels via the OS and the device driver to the actual device and how reply comes back traversing the reverse path.

There is one more player in the whole process, which is not shown in Fig. 13.1. A C++ program generally does not request directly to the OS. It invokes an I/O function from a standard library. The standard library comes with the C++ compiler and is made available when C++ is installed. This I/O function, in turn, invokes the request to the OS and passes on the request back to the program when the reply comes back.

The standard library and the I/O functions make the programmer's job easy. One has to call fopen() to open the file (or .open in C++, which we will study in Section 13.2). The function fopen() is from the standard library, which manages all the complexities. The programmer need not worry about using any OS interface, which is usually far more complex than using standard library functions such as fopen() and fclose(). There is one more reason for this indirection. It makes the program more portable. The function fopen() is found wherever C is installed and .open is available when C++ is installed.

If the OS changes, the implementation of fopen() (the way fopen() is programmed; it may be in assembly language) may be different, but the way it is called remains the same, that is, the program need not change when it runs under a different OS.

> **Note**   As a programmer, we cannot have direct control over an I/O device for reading and writing. This is for our own benefit. How? It is because devices and their drivers keep changing, and it is up to the driver designer to ensure compatibility with existing programs. As a result, we do not have to alter an existing program to suit the current requirements of an upgraded driver.

13.2 PROCESS OF INPUT/OUTPUT

The devices perform I/O operations under the control of device drivers, which accept commands from the OS. If a programmer wants to perform I/O operations using a device, it is imperative that he/she requests the OS for the same. See Fig. 13.2.

Since different OSs employ different mechanisms to provide I/O, it is very hard to provide a unique I/O standard for all C++ compilers. This standardization is achieved by providing standard I/O libraries. The C++ programmer views the interface provided by the I/O library and not its implementation. A programmer will look at the functions such as fwrite(), fread(), fopen(), and fclose() and not how these functions actually communicate with the OS.

> **Note**   Functions such as cin.getline() and cin.read() are very easy to use. The design of a library tries to hide the OS-dependent details deep into implementation. For example, when cin.getline() is used, the programmer is not aware of how cin.getline() function is written. The getline() function in VC++ is coded in a different way than in GNU C++ (Linux). A simple rule of thumb is the more the efforts towards standardizing the library function calls, the easier it is for the programmer. The same C++ program should work with all the compilers. The C++ standard I/O library is a step in that direction.

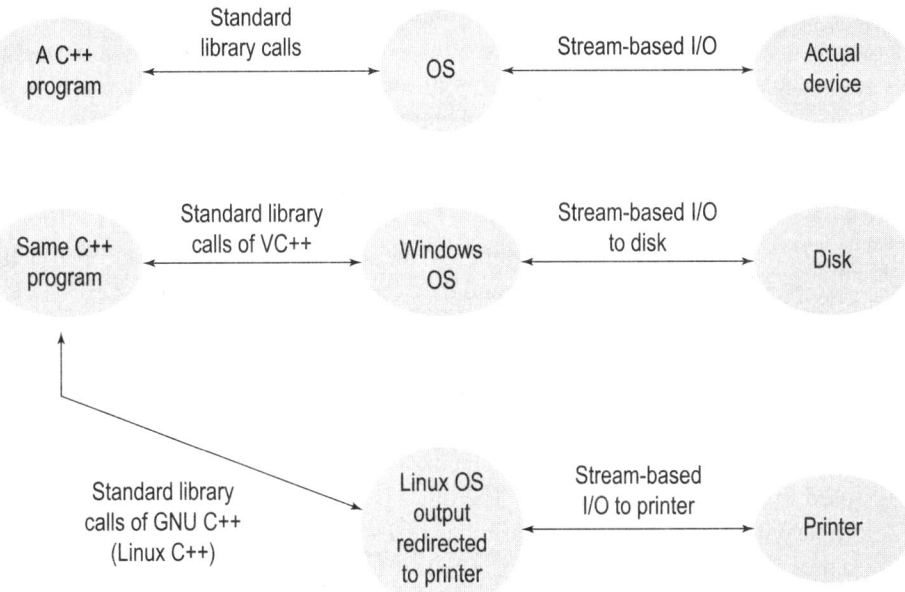

Fig. 13.2 Common interface for programmer for different OSs by standard I/O

When a program uses a built-in library function call, it is likely to be available on other suitably configured platforms. Thus, using the standard library makes the programs portable.

The C++ I/O, or even the C I/O for that matter, is stream based. When a C or C++ program performs I/O, it is being done with the streams rather than any device. The standard library helps them in the process. It makes the I/O standard the same for most of the devices. The following sections deal mostly with the disk I/O, but most of the points described here can easily be applied to other devices as well. Figure 13.2 illustrates the point.

A diligent reader may ask where the stream connection to the C++ program is when the OS and a device indulge in stream-based I/O. The point is that a standard library function such as `fopen()` opens a file irrespective of the physical device it is attached to. The call to `fopen()` may be for opening a disk file, a console, or a printer; the programmer only provides a call to `fopen()` and related arguments. Thus, the standard library and the OS make the programmers feel that they are dealing with a file without really knowing the actual device it is attached to. Streams facilitate such a mechanism.

Note The standard library functions are designed with streams in mind. Thus, using them with different devices will work in the same manner. For example, `fwrite()` can be used to write to a disk file, the terminal, or some other device without really changing the code.

13.3 FILE I/O PROGRAMMING

File I/O programming in C++ is far easier than in C. It is because we have properly written constructors and overloaded << and >>, although programming without using constructors is also possible. Any I/O involves the following steps:

1. Ask for hard disk space to store file. The OS will respond positively in most of the cases and provide hard disk space. It is also important to note that the OS knows the file by some other name than the name given by the programmer. Usually the name given by the programmer is known as the *logical file name* and the OS-given name is known as the *physical file name*.

Text files can be read using text editors, whereas binary files can be opened only using a program.

2. The second step is to ask for the association of the physical file with the logical file. If we are dealing with an existing file, this is the first step. It is a kind of linking the file that we treat in our program as, say, "InputFile" to "Input.dat" file known to OS. This step also involves specifying the type of linking, that is, if we are interested in just reading from the physical file, just writing to it, doing both read and write together, etc. This specification is known as *file mode*. It is possible to open the same physical file in different modes at different times, may be by the same program. We can open a file in write mode, close the file, and then reopen the file in read mode.

File handles are unique identifiers assigned by the OS to identify different files.

3. When we describe different modes of the file we are opening, we are usually specifying the stream that we are going to work with. Specifying the stream is the third step. There are two types of streams associated with C++ files. The default stream is *text*. The files created using text stream are known as text files and are readable without using the program. Any standard text editor such as notepad, vi, or edit can be used to open and read that file. The other type of stream is known as the *binary stream*. Binary stream files are known as binary files. They can be opened and read only by using a program. Even though there are such restrictions with binary files, they are usually more suitable for commercial programs. Section 13.4 elaborates the difference between text and binary streams.

Note To provide I/O operations, first, allocate disk space for file and allocate buffers, second, relate the physical file name with a logical file name, and third, specify the way you are going to access the file (text or binary).

4. When we finish these three operations, the file is opened and can now be used. The OS gives our file some buffer to store intermediate data. It also provides us a unique identifier, usually known as *file handle*, to describe that file. This point onwards, all our requests to manipulate the file will bear this identifier. The handle is represented by the logical file name in our context. We would never be using the actual handle in our programs. Rather, we would use the logical file name to access the file.

Note All I/O functions where a logical file name is specified map it to a file handle. The OS will operate on a specified file using a specified handle.

The buffers allocated by the OS may be *read buffers* or write *buffers*. Read buffers are needed when the file content is read from the disk and write buffers are needed when the program intends to write to the disk. Buffers enable read and write operation done in bulk.

Note If we were doing lower level I/O using C, we would use the file handle directly in our programs. For example, a call to low-level read function may look like fd = read(...), where fd is the file handle. A handle is an index to the array where file-related information is stored. Though we are using the logical file name to address the file (similar to Student in fprintf(Student, "This is testing");), the OS inherently transforms the file name into an ID. For an analogy, assume that we are a customer of some company. The company has allocated us a customer ID. We are requested to quote the customer ID in all our conversation with the company. This customer ID is equivalent to a file handle.

Exhibit 13.3 describes a file pointer and a file handle.

Exhibit 13.3 File pointer and file handle

File pointer has two different meanings in two different contexts. When we are dealing with file handles to access files, a file handle is sometimes referred to as a file pointer. In C conventionally, the file handle is called the file pointer and usually written as

```
FILE *fp;
```

where fp is actually a handle but is called a pointer. Another meaning of file pointer is a place in the file where the next read or write is to take place.

> There are three file modes, namely, read, write, and read–write.

5. Next are the read and write operations to the file. The acceptance of read-write operations from OS depends on the mode in which the file is opened for both types of streams. For example, if the file is opened in read or read-write mode, we can read from it. If the file is opened in write mode; we cannot read from it. At times, before reading a file, we would like to reach to a specific location in the file. It is possible with both types of streams, though it is useful only in binary files in most of the cases.

> It is important to close files after operating on them. It helps flush the allocated buffers.

6. The last operation involved with files is closing a file. When a file is no longer in use, the OS decides to close it. The OS deallocates the buffers and frees the handle associated with it. If there are write buffers to be deallocated, then they are written completely to the file before deallocation starts. This is known as *flush operation*. Users can themselves initiate a flush operation if it is required without closing the file.

Note By including the header `<fstream>`, we have an access to classes `ifstream` (input file stream), `ofstream` (output file stream), and `fstream` (file stream), which are needed for input mode files, output mode files, and I/O mode files, respectively. Thus, `<fstream>` is an important header to have when we are manipulating files.

13.4 TEXT AND BINARY STREAMS

There are two different types of streams, namely, text streams and binary streams.

The text stream accepts data in ASCII form. If 0 is typed, the ASCII value of 0, that is, 48, would be inserted. If the <Enter> key is pressed, two characters, that is, CR and LF (carriage return and line feed) are inserted in the Windows environment. This is known as *conversion*. When one reads back, conversion is again needed to convert from CR–LF to the visual interpretation of the <Enter> key.

Binary streams are pure binary streams; when 0 is typed, binary zeroes are inserted in the stream. When one writes to binary streams, no conversion takes place. For example, if the user enters 15 in a binary file, the binary value equivalent to 15 (00000111) is entered in the stream. On the contrary, the text file converts it to the ASCII values of 1 and 5 and then sends it through the stream. Similarly, if the user presses the <Enter> key, only the value 13 is sent, unlike two values in the case of a text file. The meaning of this is that when one reads, no conversion is needed in binary.

The files created using text streams are more general in the sense that they can be manipulated using a text editor without having to depend on the source program. On the contrary, files created using binary streams are restricted to the application that creates the file. One may create a binary file containing customer data such as customer_id, name, address, and items. Now, this file can only be opened by a particular C++ program that knows the exact structure of that file. No other application can open that file. The differences between text stream files and binary stream files are summarized as follows:

1. Text files are made up of ASCII characters, that is, the information stored is in the form of binary values representing their ASCII equivalent. If A is to be stored, it is stored as 65. If 0 is to be stored, it is stored as 48. In the case of binary files, the numbers are stored as numbers, that is, 0 is stored as binary zeroes, though characters are still stored as their ASCII equivalents.
2. Text files storage and retrieval may require character conversions. That is, the number of characters read from the screen may differ when written to a file or read from it. This is not the case with binary files.
3. Text file records are separated by CR–LF sequence (in Windows) and by CR in Linux and Unix. Each visible line forms a record in the text file. Unless special care is taken to have the same number of characters in all lines, each record (line) will have a different size. While using binary files, a record is usually of the same size. It is also, then, possible to provide the user a random access. That is, reaching the first record, tenth record, or nth record is possible. In text files, it is not possible to reach a specific record without knowing the exact location of that record.
4. Text files are more general. They can be opened by other editors, and can also be opened by OS commands such as *type* of DOS and *cat* of Unix. It is also possible to open text files created by a C++ program by programs written in other languages such as COBOL.
5. Binary files on the contrary are not that flexible. They are stored as bytes by C++. The original record format is not saved in the file. For example, if in our customer file, the items are customer id (`int`), then customer name of 30 `char`, and then address of 60 `char`, then only those programs that are aware of this design can open and manipulate this file. Any other program, which is not aware of this design, may be able to open that file, but it will get only bytes, because these programs do not know how to interpret these bytes. This means that such programs will not be able to effectively manipulate these files. No text editor can manipulate that file. OS commands will also not be able to show the contents of such files. Even if they are shown, the contents are not decipherable (because OS commands assume ASCII input). Try to type a '.exe' file on the screen and see the output. Table 13.1 illustrates all the differences in a nutshell.

Table 13.1 Differences between text and binary stream files

Criterion	Text	Binary
Char representation	ASCII	ASCII
Digit representation	ASCII	binary
Char conversion	Done	Not done
Separated by	CR or CR–LF	Size
Size of every record	May or may not be equal	Equal
Who can open	Any editor or program	Only programs
Portability across various platforms	Yes	No

13.5 OPENING AND CLOSING FILES

Before using a file, it must be initialized for usage. One must initiate a request to the OS to open a file and get a file handle. As mentioned earlier, a file handle is usually an index to the array where the information about the file being used is kept. It stores or points to the information about the owner of the file, the file rights, the current location of the file pointer, etc. One will be able to manipulate the content of that file with such a file handle, which in our case, we will not be directly operating with. The call to I/O functions is going to perform that operation. Opening a file does one more action. The OS, upon accepting the request to open a file, allocates some read and/or write buffers to that file depending on the mode. For example, if the file is opened in read mode, only read buffers are allocated.

> When we call an I/O function, the function maps the logical name that we provide to a file handle and accesses the OS services using that file handle.

> **Note** An OS, depending on its processing speed, can only handle a few files at a time. The OS can only allocate a finite number of file handles. Unless we close the file or terminate the program, the file handle allocated is not returned to the OS. If one tries to open more files than what the OS can handle, the program would not respond. So, it is imperative that we close the files properly.

For text files, a special byte indicating the end of file is written at the end when the file is closed. This byte is known as EOF (end of file) mark for OS; it is ^Z (ctrl-Z) for Windows and ^D (ctrl-D) for Unix or Linux. Any program such as a text editor, when displaying that file, understands that the file has come to an end when it reads the EOF mark. If the file is not closed, write buffers are not flushed. If the program terminates properly, the files opened by the program would be automatically closed by the OS. If program terminates abnormally, the file that is opened but not closed is likely to be damaged.

13.6 TEXT FILES

We start with text files because they are easier to deal with. We start with a program where a file accepts a few lines as input and then displays those lines one by one. We start with the simplest of functions to be used for this operation.

13.6.1 Defining Files

Files can be defined in three possible types.

1. `ifstream <filename>`   (input file stream)
2. `ofstream <filename>`   (output file stream)
3. `fstream <filename>`   (I/O file stream)

The `ifstream` file is a read-only file, and one can only read from the file defined as `ifstream`. The `ofstream` file is an output-only file, and one can only write to the file defined as `ofstream`. The `fstream` file is used for both input and output.

> `ifstream` opens a file in read mode and `ofstream` opens it in write mode, whereas `fstream` opens it in read–write mode.

13.6.2 Opening Files

Files can be opened using constructors and open functions. Using constructors, one can open a file with a statement such as

```
ofstream EntryFile("FewLines.dat")
```

The file modes have not been specified. It is assumed to be `ios::out` (output mode) when the object of `ofstream` class (the `EntryFile`) is defined. Now, take a look at the following statement:

```
ifstream DisplayFile("FewLines.dat");
```

Again, the file mode has not been specified. It is assumed to be `ios::in` (input mode) for the objects of `ifstream` class (the `DisplayFile`) in this case.

Note that the physical file name (`FewLines.dat`) remains the same in both the statements. It is needed because only then is it possible to read the same physical file that has been created and in which the records have been inserted. The single statement given defines logical as well as physical file names and also provides the links between these names.

After defining `FewLines.dat` to be a physical name for `EntryFile` logical name, the data written to the `EntryFile` will be written to `FewLines.dat`. The logical name (`EntryFile`) will vanish when the program is over, but the physical file name will be there until somebody renames or deletes the file.

Buffer allocation will be done accordingly. In the first case (`ofstream`), a few output buffers are allocated, and in the second case (`ifstream`), a few input buffers are allocated. Note that only constructors have been used in Programs 13.1 and 13.2; however, one could equally use open methods.

13.6.3 Reading from and Writing to Files

It is very simple to read from and write to a file. Overloaded << and >> operators need to be used as they were used with `cout` and `cin`.

13.6.4 Closing Files

The function `close()` is used without any arguments to close a file. The allocated file handle is deallocated and the buffers are flushed when a file is closed.

13.6.5 Using Text Files

Program 13.1 is a simple program to read a few lines and then display each word in a different line.

 **PROGRAM 13.1** Working on a text file

```
//WriteReadText.cpp
#include <iostream>
#include <string>
#include <fstream>
using namespace std;

int main()
{
    string InputLine, OutputLine;
    ofstream EntryFile("FewLines.dat")
    cout << "Input :" << endl;
    while(true)
    {
        cin >> InputLine;
        if(InputLine == "End") break;
        EntryFile << InputLine << endl;  // Writing to EntryFile
    }
}
```

```
        EntryFile.close();
        cout << "Output: " << endl;
        ifstream DisplayFile("FewLines.dat");
        while(IDisplayFile.eof())
        {
            DisplayFile >> OutputLine;
            cout << OutputLine << "\n";
        }
        DisplayFile.close();
        return 0;
}
```

Input
It was a fight
for pride and ego
for one
It was a fight for
duty and self-respect
for another
who won it at the End

Output
It
was
a
fight
...
who
won
it
at
the

How the Program Works

Why does not the program display the original lines *as they are* in the output? Why are the lines broken into words? It is because the bare ifstream object (such as cin) is not capable of doing it. The problem of using an ifstream object in its bare form (i.e., using >>) is that it cannot work with strings containing *spaces*.

> Using either << or >> will be a problem when a string contains spaces, as it considers each item separated by a space as an individual item.

If a string contains spaces, each word is counted as a separate record. One needs to use either get() and put() (for reading char by char) or use getline() function for reading lines with spaces. Program 13.2 shows how to use get() and put().

13.6.6 Using get() and put()

Program 13.2 reads lines until $ and displays the lines as they are back on the screen. It uses two functions for reading and writing characters, that is, get() and put(). Their syntax is as follows:

> get() and put() functions are useful for reading from and writing to files character by character.

cin.get(ch) (reads a character from cin and stores what is read in ch)
cout.put(ch) (reads a character ch and writes to cout)
get() has few other varieties; kindly look at the help of your compiler to find more details.

PROGRAM 13.2   get() and put() functions

```cpp
//GetPut.cpp
#include <iostream>
#include <string>
#include <fstream>
using namespace std;
#include <iomanip>

int main()
{
    char ch;
    ofstream EntryFile("FewLines.dat");
    while(true)
    {
        cin.get(ch);
        if(ch == '$') break;
        EntryFile << ch;
    }
    EntryFile.close();

    ifstream DisplayFile("FewLines.dat");
    while(!DisplayFile.eof())
    {
        // Do not skip white space
        DisplayFile.unsetf(ios::skipws);
        DisplayFile >> ch;
        cout << ch;
    }

    DisplayFile.close();
    return 0;
}
```

Input
The battle
between One and Another
is
between light and darkness
between truthfulness and falsehood
between duty and ego
$

Output
The battle
between One and Another
is
between light and darkness
between truthfulness and falsehood
between duty and ego

How the Program Works

The program begins with opening a file in the write mode, so that a few lines can be written into it.

```cpp
ofstream EntryFile("FewLines.dat");
```

The `put()` function is called to write characters into this file. One can read a character, stop if $ is encountered or continue otherwise, and write that character in the `EntryFile` using three statements as follows. Look at how << is used to enter data in a file.

```
cin.get(ch);
if(ch == '$') break;
EntryFile << ch;
```

After this, the same file is opened in the read mode so that one can read from it. The following statements perform exactly the reverse process of what has been done now.

```
DisplayFile >> ch;
cout << ch;
```

The statement before these two lines, which uses `unsetf()`, needs mention. While reading, `get()` skips the white spaces before any character. Thus, if `get()` is reading `"...this is testing"`, it will skip the first three spaces and then read and return `'t'` (the first character of the string). This is correct for normal cases, but here the need is not to skip the whitespaces. Therefore, `unsetf(ios::skipws)` needs to be provided for unsetting the usual setting of skipping the whitespaces.

13.6.7 Using getline( )

`getline()` is useful for reading entire lines.

One can even use `cout` and `cin` with `getline()` to provide the same result. Look at Program 13.3. The same `getline()` available with `cin` is also available to all `istream` objects. It is also available to the `DisplayFile()`.

PROGRAM 13.3 getline() function

```cpp
//Getline.cpp
#include <iostream>
#include <cstring>
#include <fstream>
using namespace std;

int main()
{
    char InputLine[80], OutputLine[80];
    ofstream EntryFile("FewLines.dat");
    while(true)
    {
        cin.getline(InputLine, 80);
        if(!strcmp(InputLine, "End")) break;
        EntryFile << InputLine << endl;
    }
    EntryFile.close();

    ifstream DisplayFile("FewLines.dat");
    while(!DisplayFile.eof())
    {
        DisplayFile.getline(OutputLine, 80);
        cout << OutputLine << endl;
    }
    DisplayFile.close();
    return 0;
}
```

Input
```
Imagination is
more important
```

```
than knowledge
End
```

Output
```
Imagination is more important than knowledge
```

How the Program Works

The only important part of this program involves using `getline()` function. When the following statements are executed, the line (maximum 80 characters as specified in the argument or until the carriage return is encountered) is read into the input (if `cin is used to` invoke `getline()`) or read from the file (if file name is used to invoke `getline()`).

```
cin.getline(InputLine, 80);

DisplayFile.getline(OutputLine, 80);
```

One can try commenting the file generation code from this program, construct a file using an editor, and see how the program outputs. The program will work like a DOS-type command and display the contents of the file.

> **Note** When we read a string in a file, the file does not take <CR> as input. Thus, pressing the <Enter> key terminates the string entry, but the file will not contain that <Enter>. When the file is read back, we will not be able to see different outputs in different lines.

13.7 BINARY FILES

In this section, we will focus our concentration on binary files. These files are more useful for storing structures of information.

13.7.1 Opening a Binary File

A binary file can be opened using a constructor. The constructors for `ofstream` and `ifstream` that we have seen so far are acceptable for text files. For binary files, another constructor with two arguments is needed. The first argument is the name of the file and the second one is the file mode. Look at the following statements, which are examples for both the methods.

```
// Using open methods
ofstream MCA_StudFile_Out;

MCA_StudFile_Out.open("MCA.dat", ios::out | ios::binary | ios::trunc);
// Using constructor
ifstream MCA_StudFile_In("MCA.dat", ios::in | ios::binary);
```

The first example is using the open method and the second one is using a constructor. There is no significant difference between the two ways of opening a file. The first method uses two statements instead of one and needs a little more typing than the second to achieve the same result. Programmers, therefore, usually use the second method of using constructors.

An open function can also be used with a file to open a file. If ever we need to open the same file using different modes, open() is useful.

The same effect can be achieved by writing either of the following:

```
ofstream MCA_StudFile_Out("MCA.dat", ios::out | ios::binary | ios::trunc);

ifstream MCA_StudFile_In;

MCA_StudFile_In.open("MCA.dat", ios::in | ios::binary);
```

> **File read and write operations are done with objects, and not the elements of the objects.**

Constructor calls and open functions produce similar effects. Only in the case when the file is already open and there is a need to reopen the file with new modes, one may type `close()` and then use `.open` method to open the same file in different modes. Note that pipes (|) are used in the second argument to add multiple nodes.

13.7.2 Reading from and Writing to Binary Files

Two member functions for ifstream and ofstream objects are useful in reading and writing. Both of them have similar syntax. They are

```
OfstreamFileObject.write((char *) &<the object>, sizeof(<the same object>))
```

for writing in the file and

```
IfStreamFileObject.read((char *) &<the object>, sizeof(<the same object>))
```

for reading from the file.

It is important to understand that the file read and write is performed *objectwise* and not *elementwise*. One reads the complete object from the file or writes the complete object to the file using a single read or write. The object here can even be a `struct` variable such as `struct student` of Program 13.4.

> **Reading an object from the keyboard and writing it to the screen is done element by element.**

Respective statements are needed to read from the keyboard and construct the object for providing input to the file, that is, one has to first read the student object and then write to a file. Similarly, one needs to write the object on the screen after reading it from the file. Here, both *reading the object from the keyboard and writing it to the screen are done elementwise*. Only when one is reading from a file or writing to it, one reads and writes objectwise.

13.7.3 Closing Binary Files

Closing of binary files is similar to closing text files. A `close()` function is needed to close the binary file.

Look at the statement taken from Program 13.4.

```
MCA_StudFile_Out.close();
```

The syntax for closing a file is

```
FileObject.close()
```

It also deallocates the file handle and flushes the allocated buffers as in the case of text files.

13.7.4 Using Binary Files

Let us consider an example of a structure student. It contains the following entities: roll number, name, address, and an array of five subjects the student has opted for. There are two simple programs; Program 13.4 allows the user to add the details of a few students to the student file and Program 13.5 displays the data. Both open methods and

> **For commercial programming, binary file is the usual choice.**

constructors have been used to open the files. Thus, it is again a proof that both methods yield the same result. The `fail()` and `eof()` functions used in the program are explained in Section 13.8.

PROGRAM 13.4   Writing to a binary file

```cpp
//WriteFile.cpp
#include <iostream>
#include <fstream>
using namespace std;

struct student
{
    int RollNo;
    char Name[30];
    char Address[40];
};

void ReadStudent(student & TempStud)
{
    cout << "\n Enter roll no.: ";
    cin >> TempStud.RollNo;

    cout << "\n Enter name: ";
    cin >> TempStud.Name;

    cout << "\n Enter address: ";
    cin >> TempStud.Address;
    cout << "\n";
}

int main()
{
    struct student MCA_Student_Out;
    ofstream MCA_StudFile_Out;
    MCA_StudFile_Out.open("MCA.dat", ios::out | ios::binary | ios::trunc);

    if(!MCA_StudFile_Out.is_open())
    cout << "File cannot be opened \n";
    char Continue = 'y';
    do
    {
        ReadStudent(MCA_Student_Out);

        MCA_StudFile_Out.write((char*) &MCA_Student_Out, sizeof(struct student));
        if(MCA_StudFile_Out.fail())
        cout << "File write failed";
        cout << "Do you want to continue? (y/n): ";
        cin >> Continue;
    } while(Continue != 'n');

    MCA_StudFile_Out.close();
    return 0;
}
```

Input
```
Enter roll no.: 1
Enter name: Lara
Enter address: West Indies
Do you want to continue? (y/n): y

Enter roll no.: 2
Enter name: Ranatunga
Enter address: Sri Lanka
Do you want to continue? (y/n): y
Enter roll no.: 3
```

```
Enter name: Steffi
Enter address: Germany
Do you want to continue? (y/n): n
```

PROGRAM 13.5   Reading from a binary file

```cpp
//ReadFile.cpp
#include <iostream>
#include <fstream>
#include <string>
using namespace std;

struct student
{
    int RollNo;
    char Name[30];
    char Address[40];
};

void WriteStudent(student TempStud)
{
    cout << "\n The roll no.: ";
    cout << TempStud.RollNo;
    cout << "\n The name: ";
    cout << TempStud.Name;
    cout << "\n The address: ";
    cout << TempStud.Address;
    cout << "\n";
}

int main()
{
    struct student MCA Student In;
    ifstream MCA_StudFile_In("MCA.dat", ios::in | ios::binary);
    while(!MCA_StudFile_In.eof())
    {
        MCA_StudFile_In.read((char*) &MCA_Student_In, sizeof(struct student));

        if(MCA_StudFile_In.fail())
        break;

        WriteStudent(MCA_Student_In);
    }

    MCA_StudFile_In.close();
    return 0;
}
```

Output
```
The roll no.: 1
The name: Lara
The address: West Indies

The roll no.: 2
The name: Ranatunga
The address Sri Lanka

The roll no.: 3
The name: Steffi
The address Germany
```

How the Program Works

Both these programs describe a few important points about files and their use. They are listed as follows:

> write() is used to write into and read() is used to read from a binary file.

1. File is a communication mechanism between two distinct programs. In this example, Program 13.4 writes the file and Program 13.5 reads it.
2. The binary file, unlike text, is program dependent; this is proved by the fact that the structures defined in both these programs are identical (the definition of struct student). If the structures are different, the programs will not work as expected.

> fail() is used to check if the preceding file operation is successful or failed.

```
struct student
{
    int RollNo;
    char Name[30];
    char Address[40];
};
```

> The function eof() can be used to check the end of a file. It works for both text and binary files.

3. We have used read() for reading data and write() for writing data in file. In both the cases, the data is the student structure.

```
MCA_StudFile_Out.write((char*) &MCA_Student_Out, sizeof(struct student));
MCA_StudFile_In.read((char*) &MCA_Student_In, sizeof(struct student));
```

4. Note how it has been tested whether the operation has failed, as in the following case:

```
if(MCA_StudFile_In.fail())
    break;
```

13.8 END OF FILE

The eof() function is an important function for checking the end of file. It returns one when the file pointer reaches the end of a file and reads the end of file mark. This function can be used for both text and binary files. One needs to check if reading has failed in the program. When one reads the last record, eof() is not true. When one tries to read after that, the reading operation fails and eof() becomes true.

There are two ways to implement this. One way is to check after each read; if read has failed, it has to terminate. This has been done in Program 13.5. The other solution is to use the return value from the read() function and not use eof() at all. In that case, the while loop would be written as follows:

```
while(MCA_StudFile_In.read((char*) &MCA_Student_In, sizeof(struct student))
{
    WriteStudent(MCA_Student_In);
}
```

13.9 RANDOM ACCESS USING seek()

Unlike C, C++ keeps two different file pointers for random access. In C, the seek() function moves the file pointer to the desired place for both read and write. C++ is more elaborate. For any given file opened in read-write mode, **seekg()** is a pointer for reading (or getting) and

seekp() is a pointer for writing (or putting). If the file is opened in the read mode, it would only have **seekg()**, and if the file is opened in the write mode, it would only have **seekp()**.

Random access allows us to reach any record of any file skipping other records in between. **Seekg()** and **seekp()** help programmers to move to any byte and not record of the file. If the address from where (i.e., from which byte) a record starts is known, one can reach that record using the two given functions. For example, assume there is a file containing customer records. Here, suppose it is known that the record of Steffi starts at byte number 100; then, one can reach 100 using **seekg()** or **seekp()** and perform read or write operations, respectively.

How can the address from where a record starts be obtained? It is an important question. If it is known that Steffi's record is 11th in sequence, then there are 10 records before Steffi's. If a customer record size is 10 bytes each, it is simple to calculate 101 as the first byte of Steffi's record. One can *seek* the 100th byte and then start reading Steffi's record. In Program 13.6, Steffi's record is being read at the third position. One has to skip two records to reach the third record. One would actually skip 2 * sizeof(customer) bytes to reach the beginning of the third record. Before we look at the program, a brief introduction to **seekg()** and **seekp()** follows.

13.9.1 seekg() and seekp()

seekg() is a function to move the get or read pointer of the file concerned. The function takes the following two arguments:

1. Number of bytes to skip
2. From where to skip

seekp() is a function to move the put or write pointer and takes the same set of arguments. Let us understand a few important points related to the arguments of these two functions.

1. The first argument is obvious. The second is also obvious if one remembers the bits of C's I/O. One can count or skip the number of bytes from the

   (a) beginning of the file
   (b) end of the file
   (c) current position of the file pointer

2. The first argument can be positive as well as negative. A negative value of first argument moves file pointer backwards. It is obvious that if the second argument is the beginning of the file, the first argument cannot be negative. Similarly, if the second argument is the end of the file, the first argument cannot be positive.

3. For the first argument, the data type is integer. For the second argument, it is an enumeration containing the following values:

   (a) ios::beg   Beginning of the file
   (b) ios::end   End of file
   (c) ios::cur   Current position of the file

seekg() and seekp() are functions but they also are referred to as file pointers, in the sense that they show where the current file pointer is, that is, from where the next read or write will take place.

We can apply multiple I/O modes together using pipe (|) character.

Let us look at a simple example given in Program 13.6, which swaps two records of a file using both these pointers. When we use read, it reads from the place where seekg() is pointing. When we use write, it writes to a place where seekp() is pointing.

PROGRAM 13.6   Swap two records of a file

```
//SwapRecords.cpp
#include <iostream>
#include <fstream>
#include <string>
#include <iomanip>
using namespace std;

class customer
{
    int CustId;
    string Name;
public:
    customer()
    {
        CustId = 0;
        Name = "Dummy";
    }

    customer(int TempCustId, string TempName)
    {
        CustId = TempCustId;
        Name = TempName;
    }

    friend operator <<(ostream TempOut, customer TempCustomer)
    {
        TempOut << TempCustomer.CustId << " " << TempCustomer.Name << endl;
    }
};

int main()
{
    fstream CustomerFile("Cust.dat", ios::in | ios::out | ios::trunc | ios::binary);
    /* Opening customer file in binary mode; trunc ensures deletion of file if exists */

    customer Lara(1, "Brian Charles Lara");
    customer Beckham(2, "David Beckham");
    customer Steffi(3, "Steffi Graf");
    // Three customer objects are defined

    customer Answer1, Answer2;

    CustomerFile.write((char *) &Lara, sizeof(Lara));
    CustomerFile.write((char *) &Beckham, sizeof(Beckham));
    CustomerFile.write((char *) &Steffi, sizeof(customer));

    /* sizeof operator can be applied to both a class and an object; so, sizeof(customer)
    and sizeof(Beckham) yield the same value */

    cout << "Record no. 1 is as follows: \n";

    CustomerFile.seekg(0, ios::beg);
    // Reaching the beginning of the file
    if(!CustomerFile.read((char *) &Answer1, sizeof(customer)))
    cout << "Error in reading file";
    // Reading the customer record from file
    cout << Answer1;
    // Writing the record on the screen
    cout << "Record no. 3 is as follows: \n";
```

```
        CustomerFile.seekg(2 * sizeof(customer), ios::beg);

        CustomerFile.read((char *) &Answer2, sizeof(customer));
        cout << Answer2;
        cout << "Swap record no. 1 with record no. 3 \n";
        CustomerFile.seekp(0, ios::beg);
        CustomerFile.write((char *) &Answer2, sizeof(customer));
        // Writing record 3 at the beginning of the file
        CustomerFile.seekp(2 * sizeof(customer), ios::beg);
        CustomerFile.write((char *) &Answer1, sizeof(customer));
        // Writing record no. 1 at the third position in the file

        cout << "Swapped record no. 1 is as follows \n";
        CustomerFile.seekg(0, ios::beg);
        CustomerFile.read((char *) &Answer1, sizeof(customer));
        cout << Answer1;

        cout << "Swapped record no. 3 is as follows \n";
        CustomerFile.seekg(2 * sizeof(customer), ios::beg);
        CustomerFile.read((char *) &Answer2, sizeof(customer));
        cout << Answer2;
        CustomerFile.close();
        return 0;
}
```

Output
```
Record no. 1 is as follows
1 Brian Charles Lara

Record no. 3 is as follows
3 Steffi Graf

Swap record no. 1 with record no. 3

Swapped record no. 1 is as follows
3 Steffi Graf

Swapped record no. 3 is as follows
1 Brian Charles Lara
```

How the Program Works

We have studied about the other details of this program earlier; so, we will only concentrate on the new things specified here. First, we will look at the call to seekg(). For example, look at the following statement:

```
CustomerFile.seekg(0, ios::beg);
```

The call takes the first argument as zero, that is, there will be zero byte displacement. The second argument indicates from the beginning of the file. Thus, this call indicates that the file pointer will move to the beginning of file with zero displacements, that is, the beginning of the file. Now consider another example.

```
CustomerFile.seekg(2 * sizeof(customer), ios::beg);
```

The displacement is for two customer records; thus, the file pointer now moves to the end of the second record, that is, the beginning of the third record. Hence, when one reads next, the third record will be read.

13.9.2 `tellg()` and `tellp()`

`tellg()` and `tellp()` are functions to find where the read and write pointers of a file are pointing to in terms of bytes from the beginning (i.e., the offset from the beginning). `tellg()` shows where the get pointer is pointing to and `tellp()` shows where the put pointer is pointing to.

Program 13.7 shows how `tellp()` can be used (in conjunction with `seekp()`). It plays with a file and changes its content using `tellp()`, `seekp()`, and `write()` functions.

PROGRAM **13.7**   tellp() function

```
//Tellp.cpp
#include <fstream>
using namespace std;

int main()
{
    long FilePosition;
    ofstream OutputFile;
    OutputFile.open("FewLines.txt");
    OutputFile.write("Oxford University Press", 23);
    FilePosition = OutputFile.tellp();
    OutputFile.seekp(FilePosition-5);
    OutputFile.write("India", 5);

    OutputFile.close();

    return 0;
}
```

How the Program Works

The file `FewLines.txt` is generated and entered with a string `Oxford University Press` by the following statement:

```
OutputFile.write("Oxford University Press", 23);
```

The file position (the current pointer must be at the end of the file after writing) can be learnt using `tellp()`, which returns the file position at the end of file, now in a long variable `FilePosition`, by the following statement:

```
FilePosition = OutputFile.tellp();
```

Now, this position is reduced by five to reach the position where character `P` resides (at the beginning of statement, i.e., `Press`); `seekp()` is used to move to that place.

```
OutputFile.seekp(FilePosition-5);
```

Then, `India` is written there. The resultant content of the file is as follows:

```
Oxford University India
```

Let us look at one more program to see how `tellg()` works. Program 13.8 loads the entire file in memory. The file `FewLines.txt` is already created and available.

PROGRAM **13.8**   tellg() function

```
//SeekgTellg.cpp
#include <iostream>
#include <fstream>
```

```
using namespace std;
int main()
{
    int Length;
    Char * DataBuffer;

    ifstream InputFile;
    InputFile.open("FewLines.txt", ios::binary);

    // Length of the file is calculated
    InputFile.seekg(0, ios::end);
    Length = InputFile.tellg();
    Cout << "Length of the file is" << Length << endl;
    InputFile.seekg(0, ios::beg);

    // Buffer memory allocated
    DataBuffer = new char[Length];

    // Read data into buffer
    InputFile.read(DataBuffer, Length);

    InputFile.close();

    cout.write(DataBuffer, Length);

    delete[] DataBuffer;
    return 0;
}
```

Output
```
Length of the file is 75
This is testing
and testing should continue
until the result is successful
```

How the Program Works

The following two statements are of interest to us. The first statement places the file pointer at the end of file and `tellg()` informs the file position in terms of bytes, that is, the length of file in bytes. One can see the usefulness of `seekg()` and `tellg()` here.

```
InputFile.seekg(0, ios::end);
Length = InputFile.tellg();
```

Additionally, a dynamically allocated `DataBuffer` has been used to read everything the file has and then dump it on the screen, as it is.

Now that we know how both the pointers are used, let us modify Program 13.6 in such a way that it displays where `get` and `put` pointers are pointing to every time. This is shown in Program 13.9.

PROGRAM 13.9   tellg( ) and tellp( ) functions

```
//ShowPointers.cpp
#include <iostream>
#include <fstream>
#include <string>
#include <iomanip>
using namespace std;
```

```
class customer
{
    int CustId;
    string Name;
public:
    customer()
    {
        CustId = 0;
        Name = "Dummy";
    }

    customer(int TempCustId, string TempName)
    {
        CustId = TempCustId;
        Name = TempName;
    }

    friend ostream & operator <<(ostream & TempOut, customer TempCustomer);
};

ostream & operator <<(ostream & TempOut, customer TempCustomer)
{
    TempOut << TempCustomer.CustId << " " << TempCustomer.Name << endl;
    return TempOut;
}

int main()
{
    fstream CustomerFile("Customers.dat", ios::in | ios::out | ios::trunc| ios::binary);

    customer Lara(1, "Brian Charles Lara");
    customer Beckham(2, "David Beckham");
    customer Steffi(3, "Steffi Graf");
    customer Answer1, Answer2;
    CustomerFile.write((char *) &Lara, sizeof(Lara));
    CustomerFile.write((char *) &Beckham, sizeof(Beckham));
    CustomerFile.write((char *) &Steffi, sizeof(customer));

    cout << "Initial stage \n";
    cout << "The get pointer is at byte no. " << CustomerFile.tellg() << endl;
    cout << "The put pointer is at byte no. " << CustomerFile.tellp() << endl;

    CustomerFile.seekg(0, ios::beg);
    cout << "After seekg() is moved to the beginning of the file \n";

    cout << "The get pointer is at byte no. " << CustomerFile.tellg() << endl;
    cout << "The put pointer is at byte no. " << CustomerFile.tellp() << endl;
    cout << "Record no. 1 is as follows \n";

    if(!CustomerFile.read((char *) &Answer1, sizeof(customer)))
    cout << "Error in reading file";
    cout << Answer1;

    cout << "Record no. 3 is as follows \n";
    CustomerFile.seekg(2 * sizeof(customer), ios::beg);

    cout << "After seekg() is moved to the end of the second record \n";

    cout << "The get pointer is at byte no. " << CustomerFile.tellg() << endl;
    cout << "The put pointer is at byte no. " << CustomerFile.tellp() << endl;
    CustomerFile.read((char *) &Answer2, sizeof(customer));
    cout << Answer2;
```

```
        cout << "Now let us swap record no. 1 with record no. 3 \n";
        CustomerFile.seekp(0, ios::beg);
        CustomerFile.write((char *) &Answer2, sizeof(customer));

        CustomerFile.seekp(2 * sizeof(customer), ios::beg);
        CustomerFile.write((char *) &Answer1, sizeof(customer));
        cout << "After seekp() is moved to the end of the second record \n";

        cout << "The get pointer is at byte no. " << CustomerFile.tellg() << endl;
        cout << "The put pointer is at byte no. " << CustomerFile.tellp() << endl;
        cout << "Swapped record no. 1 is as follows \n";
        CustomerFile.seekg(0, ios::beg);
        CustomerFile.read((char *) &Answer1, sizeof(customer));
        cout << Answer1;

        cout << "Swapped record no. 3 is as follows \n";
        CustomerFile.seekg(2 * sizeof(customer), ios::beg);
        CustomerFile.read((char *) &Answer2, sizeof(customer));
        cout << Answer2;

        CustomerFile.close();
        return 0;
}
```

Output
```
Initial stage
The get pointer is at byte no. 96
The put pointer is at byte no. 96

After seekg() is moved to the beginning of the file
The get pointer is at byte no. 0
The put pointer is at byte no. 0

Record no. 1 is as follows
1 Brian Charles Lara

Record no. 3 is as follows
3 Steffi Graf

After seekg() is moved to the end of the second record
The get pointer is at byte no. 96
The put pointer is at byte no. 96
3 Steffi Graf

Now let us swap record no. 1 with record no. 3

After seekp() is moved to the end of the second record
The get pointer is at byte no. -1
The put pointer is at byte no. -1

Swapped record no. 1 is as follows
1 Brian Charles Lara

Swapped record no. 3 is as follows
3 Steffi Graf
```

Notes

1. Changing the put pointer changes the value of the get pointer and vice versa. Although mentioned as two different pointers, get for read and put for write, they refer to a single pointer, as in C.

2. Regardless of what pointer we use (seekg() or seekp()), the other pointer moves with it. At any given point of time, both read and write pointers point to a single location of the file.

How the Program Works

This program is the same as Program 13.6, except that statements such as the following have been added to display file position after every operation.

```
cout << "The get pointer is at byte no. " << CustomerFile.tellg() << endl;
cout << "The put pointer is at byte no. " << CustomerFile.tellp() << endl;
```

An important observation can be made about both the pointers; they contain an identical value every time. This means that changing a read pointer changes the write pointer and vice versa.

13.10 I/O MODES

Most of the I/O modes used in the given programs are quite easy to understand. `ios::in` for input and `ios::out` for output are the simplest ones. However, there are a few points to be noted about the other I/O modes.

1. `ios::ate` puts the file pointer at the end of the file, though one can move anywhere in the file to read and write. On the contrary, ios::app opens the file in the append mode and puts the file pointer at the end and one can only write at the end of the file. Both would work only with existing files.

2. With constructors, some of the modes are usually provided as default arguments. If the `ifstream` constructor is used, `ios::in` is the default, and if the `ofstream` constructor is used, `ios::out` is the default. For example, writing

> One can determine the options associated with the process of opening a file by specifying the different I/O modes.

```
ifstream InputFile("MyFile.dat")
```

is similar to writing

```
ifstream InputFile("MyFile.dat", ios::in)
```

Table 13.2 gives a summary of the I/O modes available to the programmer.

Table 13.2 I/O modes

IO mode	Effect
ios::in	File opens in input mode.
ios::out	File opens in output mode.
ios::app	File opens in append mode; we can add records at the end of an existing file.
ios::ate	When file is opened the file pointers move at the end of file. We can read and write anywhere in the file depending on other modes provided with this mode. The file must exist when this mode is applied. ios::trunc cannot be provided with this mode.
ios::trunc	When the file is opened, the contents are erased.
ios::noreplace	Checks if the file exists; if file does not exist, the call to open fails.
ios::nocreate	Checks if the file exists; if file exists, the call to open fails.
ios::binary	The file is opened in binary rather then default text mode.

13.11 OBJECT PERSISTENCE AND SERIALIZING

Serializing is a process of storing and retrieving of objects on and from auxiliary devices. The objects that can be stored and retrieved later are known as *persistent objects*. Serializing is not available to C++ programmers directly. The objects have to be written in a binary file as was done using the customer file in earlier cases. Writing to and reading from binary files do not make objects serialized. The object states and their dependencies are also to be preserved. Binary files are just the beginning.

> C++ cannot provide persistent objects; so, programmers must adopt solutions with object identification and a few other tricks in order to get this feature.

It is important to note that when objects are written to a file, it is similar to writing a `struct` variable to the file. The functions that are provided with the class are stored neither with the objects stored in the main memory (normal objects with which we have dealt so far) nor with the objects stored in a file. Any virtual base class information (such as the information whether a specific function is virtual or not, or which objects are embedded in a class with similar values) cannot be stored. Using the built-in features of C++, it is impossible to store an object with its status values and extract it later after restarting the program.

> The process of serialization relates to storing and retrieving objects and retaining their status during storage and retrieval. Such objects are known as persistent objects. C++ does not provide any facility for serialization.

The problem of object persistence becomes more complicated while dealing with polymorphic objects, because objects do not bear any 'type' tag. For example, if a few letters and a few memos are stored as document object (a parent object from which letters and memos are derived), there is no way to differentiate between them once stored. The simplest possible solution is to store documents and memos in the file. Unfortunately, `vptr` is not stored in the file and that information is lost. The entire inheritance chain information is just lost. Even when there are embedded objects, the trace of `vptr` of those objects and the related values are lost. When one wants this process by the base class pointer, it becomes more difficult as one needs to store different `vptr` entries for each inherited class. How can a C++ programmer provide serialization of professional degree is difficult to explain here, but one can visualize the difficulty of the task. Some of the other object-oriented programming languages, most notably Java, provide serialization.

Why would one like to store objects in the auxiliary devices? It is because one would like to preserve the status of the object. For example, if there is a `TeachingStaff` object derived from an `employee` object where the designation is changed from `Professor` to `Director` and one would like to have that information available the next time onwards. Assume the program is printing salary slips of employees; it can use this information to print the proper salary slips. If an `employee` pointer is being used to access the different types of employees, the change in the object of a specific person must be noted, which is not possible in C++ directly. There is no method in C++ to identify objects uniquely. All standard extensions provide some form of wrapping, which adds an identifier and a few other important information that one can use to provide serialization.

13.12 I/O ERRORS

The OS has to be requested for file handles and disk space for the files. In most of the cases, the OS complies with the requests; however, it might not comply in some specific cases. It is actually the programmer's responsibility to check whether the operation is successfully completed or not. Let us enumerate a few such cases here.

One must test for errors after different file operations. C++ has no default mechanism to check and correct errors.

Error handling is possible by calling functions such as `fail()` or `is_open()` or by testing the return value of most of the I/O functions.

1. When one is providing paths in phrases such as `Customer.dat`, the OS looks at the current directory to find that file. The current directory is different when the program is running elsewhere. If the path is not provided to retrieve the file in different situations, the same program running fine at one place will not be able to work at another place.

2. While working with multi-user OS such as Linux or Windows 2000, it is also important to know that files can be created or read only where there is a permission to write or read, respectively. The same program running perfectly on one machine or one account might just not work on another.

3. A program copied from one user account to another might not work as expected in the other user account on the same machine because of permission restrictions for different files and folders to different users.

The errors can be checked in the following ways:

1. While opening a file:

   (a) A function `is_open()` is available to all file objects. It is possible to write

   ```
   if(filename.is_open())
   ```

   to check whether a file has opened or not after an `open()` call.

   (b) One can open the file using `ios::nocreate` option when one does not want the file to be accidentally overwritten, if it already exists. This option ensures that a file is created only when there is no such file.

   (c) One can open the file using `ios::noreplace` option when one does not want to generate a new file if an old file with the same name exists.

2. While reading or writing a file:

   (a) Both `read()` and `write()`, when successful, return the stream, and return zero otherwise. Adding `read()` and `write()` inside the `if` statement's condition part is also a common practice. It is done as follows:

   ```
   if(MCA_StudFile_In.read((char*) &MCA_Student_In, sizeof(struct student)))
   {
     // Actions to be taken
   }
   else
   {
     // Actions to be taken when error occurs
   }
   ```

   This construct automatically checks for errors and there is no need to write specific code for finding whether an error has occurred or not.

   (b) After executing a `read()` or `write()` statement, one can check whether it has failed by calling the function `fail()`. It is done as follows:

   ```
   MCA_StudFile_In.read((char*) &MCA_Student_In, sizeof(struct student));
   if(MCA_StudFile_In.fail())
   break;
   ```

The `fail()` function is quite generic. One can call `fail()` after any file-related operation to check whether the operation was successful or not.

▪ RECAPITULATION ▪

- I/O is a special operation as the program needs to take the help of the OS and other devices to perform.
- For providing I/O, an I/O library is used in C++. The I/O library helps in the portability of the program.
- A file on the auxiliary device has minimum four operations possible; they are open(), read(), write(), and close().
- The files mechanism is provided in C++ by the <fstream> header. It has two different mechanisms to open files, one using constructors and the other using the open() function.
- Text and binary are the two different streams provided.

- Text is more portable than binary, but binary is preferable for commercial programs.
- It is also possible to use get() and put() functions on text stream for reading and writing single characters.
- It is possible to use getline() for reading a single line.
- Binary files require read() and write() functions for reading from and writing in a file.
- seekg() and seekp() are functions for seek in the read and the write modes, respectively.
- tellp() and tellg() are functions for tell in the write and read modes, respectively.
- C++ does not provide object serialization.

▪ KEYWORDS ▪

Binary files   Files containing integers in binary and other data in ASCII format are known as binary files.

eof()   This denotes the end of a file. In text file, it is indicated by a special character. In binary files, this is determined implicitly using the length of the file.

File pointer   This term has two different meanings in two different contexts. When we are dealing with file handles to access files, a file handle is sometimes referred to as the file pointer. In C, conventionally, the file handle is called the file pointer and is usually written as FILE *fp; where fp is actually a handle but called a pointer. Another meaning of file pointer is a place in the file where the next read or write is to take place.

I/O modes   These are the different modes such as read only, write only, read-write, and append in which we can open files.

Logical file name   This is the name of the file that we refer in our program.

Physical file name   This is the name of the file that is referred by the OS.

seekg() and seekp()   These are similar to the seek pointer in C. 'g' indicates get() or read() and 'p' indicates put() or write(). Thus, seekg() is for seeking while reading, whereas seekp() is for seeking while writing

Seek   This is an operation to move the file pointer (second definition above) to the place we want.

Serialization   This is the process of placing the objects in auxiliary memory for later retrieval and later getting them back as it is.

Text files   Files containing integers and other data in ASCII format are known as text files.

tellg() and tellp()   These are similar to the tell pointer in C. 'g' indicates get() or read() and 'p' indicates put() or write(). Thus tellg() is for indicating the file position while reading, whereas tellp() is for indicating it while writing.

▪ EXERCISES ▪

Multiple Choice Questions

1. The logical and the physical file needs to be _____ to enable a programmer to work on that file.
   - (a) created
   - (b) executed
   - (c) associated
   - (d) de-referenced

2. _____ helps read and write operations to be carried out in bulk.
   - (a) File handle
   - (b) File pointer
   - (c) File buffers
   - (d) Any of the above

3. The objects that can be stored and retrieved later are known as _____.
   (a) serial objects
   (b) serialized objects
   (c) persistent objects
   (d) persisted objects

4. When we write to binary streams, _____ does not take place.
   (a) insertion
   (b) conversion
   (c) Both
   (d) None

5. The name by which we refer to a file in our program is known as _____.
   (a) logical file name
   (b) physical file name
   (c) file handle
   (d) program file name

6. Text file storage and retrieval may require _____.
   (a) character conversions
   (b) numeric conversions
   (c) Both
   (d) None

7. The more the _____ of library functions, the easier it is for the programmer.
   (a) dependency
   (b) independency
   (c) standardization
   (d) modularization

8. The operation to move the file pointer to the place we want is known as _____.
   (a) jump operation
   (b) seek operation
   (c) Both
   (d) None

9. The device driver accepts commands from _____.
   (a) the user
   (b) the operating system
   (c) the programmer
   (d) the device

10. The end of file mark in Unix is _____.
   (a) ^Z (ctrl Z)
   (b) ^D (ctrl D)
   (c) Any of the above depending on the programmer
   (d) Any of the above depending on the compiler

Conceptual Exercises

1. What is the need for I/O libraries?
2. Discuss the role of a programmer, C++ I/O library, and OS in I/O.
3. Explain the process of open, read, write, and close for files.
4. Explain the difference between text and binary streams.
5. How can we open a text file and read from it?
6. How can we open a binary file and write to it?
7. Explain the method of read-write using `get()` and `put()` functions and using `getline()`.
8. Explain the method of read-write using `read()` and `write()` functions in binary streams.
9. Explain the roles of `seekg()`, `seekp()`, `tellg()`, and `tellp()` functions in the process of random access in a binary file.
10. How can we determine errors while dealing with files?

Practical Exercises

1. Write a program to read text file and count the number of characters in it.
2. Write a program to read a text file and copy it to another text file.
3. Write a program to read a text file and convert a specific word to another in the entire file.
4. Pick up any employee class defined in earlier chapters. Store the information about employees in sorted order of their employee numbers in the file. Read an employee number from the keyboard and display the corresponding employee details.
5. Write a similar program for customer class. Pick up any customer class defined earlier.

Namespaces

14.1 NAME CONFLICT PROBLEM

When the initial version of C++ was introduced, vendors started shipping third-party libraries to be used by programmers. These libraries help programmers to get routine job functions off the shelf. For example, statisticians require additional functions for finding the regression, mode, etc. Similarly, graphic designers require functions to draw basic shapes such as lines and squares and, at times, more advanced functions such as three-dimensional images, shadows, and projection. Libraries reduce the burden on the programmers by providing the basic building blocks so that they can concentrate on the core design.

When a programmer uses one such library, he/she does not face any problem. The problem starts when one uses multiple libraries that define a function *with the same name*. Let us consider an example. We have a `math` library with a function `abs()`, which returns the absolute value of the number passed to it. We may also be using a library where `abs()` returns the number of students absent in a class. When we use `abs()` in a program, the compiler cannot identify which `abs()` is required. This problem can be easily avoided if we could name both the functions differently. Unfortunately, it is not in our hands to pick names that do not conflict, as they are decided by the developer who develops that library. Whenever we use any third-party library, we might run into one or the other name clash with previously installed libraries. This problem cannot be solved locally. Neither can a third-party library designer solve this problem because he/she does not know anything about the other libraries installed in our computer. This is called the *name conflict problem*.

> **Note** The name conflict problem is analogous to putting all the students of a school in one big room. If you call out to one student just by name, say 'Arun', there is a likelihood of more than one student replying.

To resolve the name conflict problem, we need to have enclosures for functions. Each enclosure should have a unique name and contain unique functions. However, the same name may exist in different enclosures. Each such enclosure is known as a *namespace*.

> When we use two third-party libraries with the same name given to at least one of the elements of both the libraries, we have a name conflict problem.

> The name conflict problem can be avoided by placing the elements of different libraries in different namespaces.

14.1.1 Global Namespace

The global namespace is the enclosure where the program runs. It is the environment accessible to the program while being executed. Any function, variable, or class must be brought to the global namespace to be accessible.

Every program can use the global namespace elements without qualification.

The problem arose because all the libraries installed insert their functions into a global namespace. In simpler terms, all functions are assembled together in a single space in an indiscriminate manner. One does not have any discrimination between library element names once the library is installed. Hence, the global namespace cannot identify a library element uniquely in case of a name conflict.

Namespaces identify logical groups.

14.1.2 Logical Grouping

The solution to the global namespace problem lies in logical grouping. It is analogous to placing the students of a specific standard in a separate room. Now, one can easily identify the Arun of third standard uniquely. One can also find that the 'Arun' of third standard is different from the Arun of sixth standard.

namespace:: element is a fully qualified name, for example, `std::cout` and `math::abs()` are fully qualified names of the elements of `std` and `math` namespaces, respectively. `math` is a user-defined namespace here.

Namespaces are introduced to provide this logical grouping of names. Once the logical grouping is in place, one just has to worry about uniquely identifying a name in a single group. Again, this is analogous to making sure there are no more than one Arun in a single standard. While programming, one can actually disallow similar names for objects in a single namespace or can rename them. This is not a big problem, as a single library is designed by a single team of developers; so, a leader can always decide better naming conventions with no conflict.

Thus, namespaces identify the logical group of elements. These elements could be variables, classes, and their objects, and non-member functions as well.

There are many ways to use namespaces: using directive, using declaration, and fully qualified names are examples.

14.1.3 Fully Qualified Names

Once the elements are logically grouped using namespaces, any name can be qualified using the syntax `namespace::element`. Suppose there are two `abs()` functions, one in `math` namespace and the other in `Academic` namespace. Here, it is possible to use `math::abs()` and `Academic::abs()` to identify both `abs()` functions in an unambiguous way.

The name `math::abs()` is said to be a fully qualified name. When the `abs()` function is used by some other function of the same library, that is, `math` library, it is situated in the same namespace where `abs()` is situated. It does not need to use `math::abs()`; it can simply use `abs()`. If some other function defined outside the `math` namespace uses `abs()`, then it should use the fully qualified name, that is, `math::abs()`.

We will learn how to define and use namespaces in the following sections. First, let us discuss how the `std` namespace can be used in different ways than `'using namespace std'`, which we have been doing so far.

14.2 WAYS OF USING NAMESPACES

Namespaces can be used in various ways. It is possible to move every element of a namespace into the global namespace or only a part of it. It is also possible to use fully qualified names instead. Let us see how it is done.

14.2.1 using Syntax

using is a keyword that is used when one does not want to use fully qualified names repeatedly. There are two ways in which it can be used.

using Declaration

The syntax that uses using namespace ::element is called the using declaration.

The using declaration follows the `namespace::element` syntax for making only the element of a given namespace available. Look at the following code:

```
//usingDeclaration.cpp
#include <iostream>
// NO "using namespace std"

int main()
{
    using std::cout;
    using std::operator <<;
    cout << "Hi";
    return 0;
}
```

The usual **using namespace std;** has not been specified in this code; yet, we are able to use `cout` as a normal `ostream` object. This is because the **using** declaration has been provided for both `cout` object and the operator << overloaded in `cout`.

The following statements are considered to be `using` declarations.

```
using std::cout;
using std::operator <<;
```

using Directive

The usual **using namespace std;** statement is known as the `using` directive. Note that the word `namespace` is included inside the definition. This makes all the names defined in the `std` namespace to be available to the global namespace. This is the simplest of mechanisms to use namespaces. We will see how to define user-defined namespaces in Section 14.3.1. Assume that a namespace called `mynamespace` has been defined. The `using` directive examples are as follows:

```
using namespace std;
using mynamespace;
```

Look at the difference between a directive and a declaration. Directives introduce the entire namespace to a global namespace, whereas declarations only introduce the objects that the programmer wants to use.

The syntax using namespace namspacename is an example of using directive.

Code without using Directive or Declaration

Look at the following program:

When we use fully qualified names such as std::cin, we do not require the using directive or decla-ration.

```
//WithoutUsing.cpp
#include <iostream>
// NO "using namespace std"
int main()
{
    using std::operator <<;
    std::cout << "Hi";
    return 0;
}
```

The statement `using std::cout;` is now missing in the code. Instead, `cout` has been used with its fully qualified name, that is, `std::cout`. There is no need for the `using` directive with fully qualified names. As we are using all the names of the `std` namespace quite frequently in our programs so far, we are using the `using` directive. We can instead use either `using` declarations or fully qualified names.

14.3 DEFINING A NAMESPACE

Namespaces can be defined to accommodate variables, functions, and classes. A namespace can be defined inside another namespace. It is also possible to define a namespace as an alias of another namespace. It can also be defined in parts. Let us see some examples to understand this better.

14.3.1 Defining Variables Inside a Namespace

One can define user-defined namespaces and use the variables defined therein. The following program defines a namespace `MyNamespace` containing a few variables. The code uses fully qualified names.

```
//MyNamespace.cpp
#include <iostream>
#include <string>
using namespace std;
// User-defined namespace with two variables
namespace MyNamespace
{
   int MyNumber;
   string MyString;
}
int main()
{
   cin >> MyNamespace::MyNumber;
   cin >> MyNamespace::MyString;
   cout << MyNamespace::MyNumber << endl;
   cout << MyNamespace::MyString << endl;
}
```

Observe how the namespace and two variables have been defined within that namespace. Moreover, note the way these variables are used. This seems to be a laborious approach. One can use the `using` declaration or directive as shown in the following programs.

```
//UsingDeclarationMyNameSpace.cpp
#include <iostream>
#include <string>
using namespace std;

namespace MyNamespace
{
   int MyNumber;
```

```
        string MyString;
}

int main()
{
    using MyNamespace::MyNumber;
    using MyNamespace::MyString;
    cin >> MyNumber;
    cin >> MyString;
    cout << MyNumber << endl;
    cout << MyString << endl;
}

//UsingDirectiveMyNameSpace.cpp
#include <iostream>
#include <string>
using namespace std;

namespace MyNamespace
{
    int MyNumber;
    string MyString;
}

int main()
{
    using namespace MyNamespace;
    cin >> MyNumber;
    cin >> MyString;
    cout << MyNumber << endl;
    cout << MyString << endl;
}
```

14.3.2 Defining Functions Inside a Namespace

> Similar to std namespace, the using directives and declarations are also available to user-defined namespaces.

Besides variables, a namespace can hold functions as well. One can define functions inside a namespace and access them using the same technique. The following program illustrates how this can be done.

```
//DefiningFunctions.cpp
#include <iostream>
#include <string>
using namespace std;

namespace MyNamespace
{
    int MyNumber;
    string MyString;
    void InputAndDisplay()
    {
```

```
            cin >> MyNumber;
            cin >> MyString;
            cout << MyNumber << endl;
            cout << MyString << endl;
        }
    }

    int main()
    {
        MyNamespace::InputAndDisplay();
    }
```

One can define a function inside a namespace and call it using a fully qualified name.

Note how the function is called. It is fully qualified similar to the variables, using the namespace and the function names. One can use the `using` directive or declaration to access the functions defined inside a namespace.

14.3.3 Defining Classes Inside a Namespace

One can even define classes inside a namespace. Look at Program 14.1.

PROGRAM 14.1   Defining classes inside a namespace

```cpp
//DefineClassOutsideNS.cpp
#include <iostream>
#include <string>
using namespace std;

namespace MyNamespace
{
    class brother
    {
        string Name;
    public:
        brother(string BrotherName)
        {
            Name = BrotherName;
        }
        friend ostream & operator <<(ostream & TempOut, brother TempBrother);
    };

    ostream & operator <<(ostream & TempOut, brother TempBrother)
    {
        TempOut << TempBrother.Name;
        return TempOut;
    }
}

int main()
{
    MyNamespace::brother Lara("Brian Charles Lara");
    cout << Lara;
}
```

Note   When one defines a class inside a namespace, `namespace::classname` can be used to access the class outside that namespace.

How the Program Works

The class `brother` is now defined inside `MyNamespace` and accessed like any other variable. Defining the objects of the `brother` class is done using the following statement:

```
MyNamespace::brother Lara("Brian Charles Lara");
```

that is, fully qualifying the class name and using it. One can also use the `using` declaration or directive as used in the earlier programs.

```
// using directive
int main()
{
   using namespace MyNamespace;
   brother Lara("Brian Charles Lara");
   cout << Lara;
}
```

```
// using declaration
int main()
{
   using MyNamespace::brother;
   brother Lara("Brian Charles Lara");
   cout << Lara;
}
```

In both the cases, the operator `<<` is being used without qualifying it, that is, the code does not contain the statement **using MyNamespace::operator <<**. How does it work then? This is explained in Section 14.8 where we discuss Koenig lookup.

14.3.4 Declaring Inside and Defining Outside the Namespace

Similar to a class definition, one can *declare* an element inside a namespace and *define* it outside. In the following program, the function `InputAndDisplay()` is defined outside the namespace.

```
//DefineOutsideNS.cpp
#include <iostream>
#include <string>
using namespace std;

namespace MyNamespace
{
   int MyNumber;
   string MyString;
   void InputAndDisplay();  // Declaration
}
/* Qualifying the function name and defining it outside */
void MyNamespace::InputAndDisplay()
{
   cin >> MyNumber;
   cin >> MyString;
   cout << MyNumber << endl;
```

```
        cout << MyString << endl;
    }
    int main()
    {
        using namespace MyNamespace;
        InputAndDisplay();
    }
```

> When a function is defined outside the namespace, it requires qualification.

It is important to note that the definition of the function lies outside the namespace, and so, it needs a qualification. Earlier, when it was defined inside the namespace, this was not required.

Program 14.2 shows how to define the class member functions outside the namespace. However, similar to a non-member function, its declaration has to be done inside the namespace.

PROGRAM 14.2   Define a member function outside the namespace

```
//DefineClassOutsideNS2.cpp
#include <iostream>
#include <string>
using namespace std;

namespace MyNamespace
{
    class brother
    {
        string Name;
    public:
        brother(string BrotherName);    // Compulsory declaration
        friend ostream & operator <<(ostream & TempOut, brother TempBrother);
    };
}
MyNamespace::brother::brother(string BrotherName)
{
    MyNamespace::brother::Name = BrotherName;
}
std::ostream & MyNamespace::operator <<(ostream & TempOut, MyNamespace::brother TempBrother)
{
    TempOut << TempBrother.Name;
    return TempOut;
}
int main()
{
    MyNamespace::brother Lara("Brian Charles Lara");
    cout << Lara;
}
```

How the Program Works

The constructor function is now defined as follows:

```
MyNamespace::brother::brother(string BrotherName)
```

Moreover, the variable assignments are as follows:

```
MyNamespace::brother::Name = BrotherName;
```

One can extend a namespace by defining additional components inside the namespace with the same name.

Both the constructs seem very long. One way to reduce their length is to use the using declaration or directive. There is one more way to solve this problem. It is known as *namespace aliasing*. We will learn about that in Section 14.6.

14.3.5 Extending a Namespace

It is possible to extend a previously defined namespace. Take a look at Program 14.3. Where would one need this feature? A big project usually involves more than one developer. All of them can develop their own portion of namespace, which add up when inserted in the program code if they use the same namespace name for defining their own part of the namespace.

PROGRAM 14.3 Extending a namespace

```cpp
//ExtendingNamespace.cpp
#include <iostream>
#include <string>
using namespace std;

namespace MyNamespace
{
    class brother
    {
        string Name;
    public:
        brother(string BrotherName)
        {
            Name = BrotherName;
        }
        friend ostream & operator <<(ostream & TempOut, brother TempBrother);
    };

    ostream & operator <<(ostream & TempOut, brother TempBrother)
    {
        TempOut << TempBrother.Name;
        return TempOut;
    }
}

/* This definition extends the previous definition; does not overwrite it */
namespace MyNamespace
{
    int Test = 20;
}

int main()
{
    MyNamespace::brother Lara("Brian Charles Lara");
    cout << Lara;
    cout << endl << MyNamespace::Test;
}
```

How the Program Works

As shown in the program, the second definition *extends* the previous definition. This is very useful in some cases. It is possible to have a code as follows:

```cpp
#include <FirstHeaderFile>
```

```
#include <SecondHeaderFile>
// Rest of the program
```

Here, it is possible to have a namespace `TheNameSpace` defined in the `FirstHeaderFile` as well as the `SecondHeaderFile`. The contents of `TheNameSpace` in both the header files will be added to the rest of the program.

This implies that one can define a namespace *in parts*. In the example, the first part of `TheNameSpace` has been defined in the first header file and the second part in the second header file.

One can easily consider two different programmers developing these two parts. It becomes easy for them to continue working and evolving their own parts without being merged into a single set of code and retain the same effect.

14.3.6 Using Namespaces in .h Files

The following are two different versions of Program 14.2. Both now have a namespace embedded in the .h file. Look at the examples.

The first is the .h file.

```
//NamedNamespace.h
#include <string>
namespace MyNamespace
{
   class brother
   {
      string Name;
   public:
      brother(string BrotherName)
      {
         Name = BrotherName;
      }
   friend ostream & operator <<(ostream & TempOut, brother TempBrother);
   };
   ostream & operator <<(ostream & TempOut, brother TempBrother)
   {
      TempOut << TempBrother.Name;
      return TempOut;
   }
}
```

The second is the .cpp file.

```
//NamedNamespace.cpp
#include <iostream>
#include <string>
using namespace std;
#include "NamedNamespace.h"

int main()
{
```

```
    MyNamespace::brother Lara("Brian Charles Lara");
    cout << Lara;
}
```

The program separates the namespace definition from the .cpp file, which contains the C++ code that uses the namespace. This is a usual programming practice, as the core coding part is done by expert coders and is stored in the namespace. Other programmers use that namespace for their own programs using that .h file. It works the same as other versions of the same program written earlier.

14.4 UNNAMED NAMESPACES

The name of the namespace plays an important role in namespace declarations. One writes

`<namespace name> <element name>`

> An unnamed namespace can contain anything a named namespace may contain. The only difference is that we do not need a qualification for accessing any of its elements.

to qualify and uniquely identify an element. The namespaces that we have used so far are known as *named namespaces*. Here, the name of the namespace is useful for conflict resolution. If there are two namespaces Academic and Maths, then Maths::abs() is certainly different from Academic::abs().

Surprisingly, it is also possible to have a namespace without a name. Such namespaces are called *unnamed namespaces*. The variables of the unnamed namespaces are used like normal variables without qualifying with the namespace name, because there is no name for the namespace. What is the difference between a normal global variable and a variable defined in an unnamed namespace? Let us consider Program 14.4 to understand it.

PROGRAM 14.4   Unnamed namespace

```cpp
//UnnamedNS.cpp
#include <iostream>
#include <string>
using namespace std;

namespace // Unnamed namespace
{
    int MyNumber;
    string MyName;
}

int main()
{
    cout << "Enter the number: ";
    cin >> MyNumber;
    cout << endl;
    cout << "Enter the name: ";
    cin >> MyName;
    cout << "\n The name and number are " << MyName << " and " << MyNumber << endl;
    return 0;
}
```

How the Program Works

It can be seen how MyName and MyNumber are used in the main program. Both the variables are used as both have been defined globally. Though apparently similar, this mechanism has an important difference. Although variables are available globally in this physical file, they are not available to any other file linked with this file. This means that the variables `MyName` and `MyNumber` are available anywhere inside `UnNamedNamespace.cpp`, but they will not be available in any other file.

Let us try to understand this point further. The file `UnnamedNamespace.cpp` is as follows:

```
namespace
{
    // Definition of variables MyName and MyNumber
}

int main()
{
    // Using the variables
}
```

Suppose some other file `xyz.cpp` contains statements such as the following:

```
{
    extern MyName
    // Using MyName
}
```

It will not work because `MyName` is not available to other files. Suppose our file is as follows:

```
/* Definition of variables globally without being wrapped into unnamed namespace */
int main()
{
    // Using the variables
}
```

Then, the second file not only compiles properly but works properly too.

Note An unnamed namespace element behaves similar to a static global variable. Something defined as static globally is available only in the file in which it is defined.

Let us consider the following program. Now, `UnNamedNameSpace.cpp` alone contains the definition of the unnamed namespace. There is one more file `CheckUNNS.cpp` that uses the unnamed namespace. The program compiles properly but does not link. It will not be able to resolve both the variables at linking time. The program does not work as expected.

```
//UnnamedNamespace.cpp
#include <iostream>
#include <string>
using namespace std;

namespace
{
    int MyNumber;
    string MyName;
}
```

```
//CheckUNNS.cpp
#include <iostream>
#include <string>
using namespace std;
extern string MyName;
extern int MyNumber;

int main()
{
    cout << "Enter the number: ";
    cin >> MyNumber;    // Generates compile-time error
    cout << endl;
    cout << "Enter the name: ";
    cin >> MyName;    // This too will generate compile-time error
    cout << "\n The name and number are " << MyName << " and " << MyNumber << endl;
    return 0;
}
```

> An unnamed name-space is not available to the components of the program defined in other physical files.

An unnamed namespace can produce the same effect as static global definition. However, it is advisable to use unnamed namespaces because the static global definition is now deprecated and future versions of the compilers may not accept it.

14.5 NESTED NAMESPACES

One can define a namespace within another namespace. The following program has two namespaces; the inner namespace `InnerNamespace` is contained in the outer namespace `OuterNamespace`. The `brother` class now is deep inside the inner namespace. How can we access an element of such a nested namespace? We need to provide qualification using the following syntax:

> A nested namespace is defined inside another namespace.

`outer namespace::inner namespace::element name`

This can be understood better using the following program.

```
//NestedNamespaces.cpp
#include <iostream>
#include <string>
using namespace std;

namespace OuterNamespace
    {
    namespace InnerNamespace
    {
        class brother
        {
        private:
            string Name;

        public:
            brother(string BrotherName)
            {
```

```
                            Name = BrotherName;
                    }
                    friend std::ostream & operator <<(ostream & TempOut,  OuterNamespace::Inn
                    erNamespace::brother TempBrother);
            };
        }
    }
    std::ostream & OuterNamespace::InnerNamespace::operator <<(ostream & TempOut,
    OuterNamespace:: InnerNamespace::brother TempBrother)
    {
        TempOut << TempBrother.Name;
        return TempOut;
    }
    int main()
    {
        OuterNamespace::InnerNamespace::brother Lara("Brian Charles Lara");
        cout << Lara;
    }
```

A nested namespace is required in cases involving more than two levels of hierarchy. A::B::C is a case where we are addressing the third level of hierarchy.

The fully qualified names are even longer now. The solution to reduce the length of the names is given in Section 14.6.

Note A namespace is similar to a Java package. For example, `java.Applet.applet` represents the third level of hierarchy.

14.6 NAMESPACE ALIASES

A namespace name can act as an alias of another namespace. It can help reduce the length of long fully qualified names. Let us look at Program 14.5 to see how namespace aliases can be defined and used.

PROGRAM 14.5 Namespace alias

```
//NamespaceAliases.cpp
#include <iostream>
#include <string>
using namespace std;

namespace OuterNamespace
{
    namespace InnerNamespace
    {
        class brother
        {
        private:
            string Name;
        public:
            brother(string BrotherName)
            {
                Name = BrotherName;
            }
            friend std::ostream & operator <<(ostream & TempOut, OuterNamespace::InnerName
            space::brother TempBrother);
```

```
        };
    }
}
std::ostream & OuterNamespace::InnerNamespace::operator <<(ostream & TempOut, OuterNamespace::
InnerNamespace::brother TempBrother)
{
    TempOut << TempBrother.Name;
    return TempOut;
}

int main()
{
    // Namespace alias
    namespace NS = OuterNamespace::InnerNamespace;

    NS::brother Lara("Brian Charles Lara");
    NS::brother Beckham("David Beckham");
    NS::brother Steffi("Steffi Graf");

    cout << Lara << endl;
    cout << Beckham << endl;
    cout << Steffi << endl;
}
```

How the Program Works

> A namespace alias is a new name given to an existing namespace. This is useful for reducing the length of long and nested namespace names.

Observe the following statements:

```
namespace NS = OuterNamespace::InnerNamespace;
NS::brother Lara("Brian Charles Lara");
```

Here, NS acts as a replacement for OuterNamespace::InnerNamespace, and thereby shortens the long fully qualified names.

Exhibit 14.1 describes namespaces and dynamism.

Exhibit 14.1 Namespaces and dynamism

Namespace aliases can be used for providing dynamism such as #define symbols in C. Let us try to understand their usefulness with the help of an example.

Suppose we are developing a software product called Product. We may then have a new version of Product, still called Product. How can we differentiate the new Product from the old one? What will happen if one of our old customers, still having the old Product, uses the new version of software? How can he/she get similar functionality? Let us try to find a solution using namespace aliasing.

```
namespace OldProduct
{
    class Product
    {
        void registration()
        {...}
    }...
}
namespace NewProduct
{
```

```
        class Product
        {
            void registration()
            {...}
        }
    }

    int main()
    {
        namespace Product = NewProduct;
        /* The most important line */

        Product::Product MyProduct;
        /* The first is the name of namespace and the second is the class in
        Product::Product */
        MyProduct.registration();
    }
```

Look at the most important line

```
namespace Product = NewProduct
```

Changing that single line to

```
namespace Product = OldProduct
```

changes it to the old Product for the rest of the program.

The beauty of this design is that we keep everything related to both versions of the product separate in two different namespaces. Still, we can use the same code including the functions that appear in both the namespaces such as `register()` to work differently. Such a design helps programmers to use the same name repeatedly for a function with additional features for a new product.

For example, let us suppose the new `registration()` function for a new product requires the customer's address in a different format. The old registration function may still be there in the `OldProduct` namespace and the new and updated registration function will be a part of the `NewProduct` namespace. The code used to register the customer, thus, still remains the same as follows:

```
MyProduct.registration();
```

If `MyProduct` aliases `NewProduct`, the new registration function is called; on the other hand, if `MyProduct` aliases `OldProduct`, the old registration function is called.

14.7 `std` NAMESPACE

`std` is a namespace where the standard library routines are defined. One can use objects such as `cout` or `cin` without any qualification if one writes `using namespace std` at the beginning of a program. The inclusion of `std` namespace makes all the standard library routines wrapped in the `std` namespace available in the global namespace.

If `using namespace std` is not written at the beginning, then the elements of `std` can be called using the qualifier `std::`.

The new headers that are used such as `<iostream>` and `<cstdlib>` instead of `<iostream.h>` and `<stdio.h>` are using the `std` namespace. The older design directly inserts the content of

'.h' headers in the global namespace and does not use std namespace; hence, it cannot solve problems of name conflict. On the contrary, a programmer can easily avoid adding the entire std namespace to the global namespace by avoiding using directive. One may use either using declaration or fully qualified names to avoid conflict. This was not possible with the older design. In the newer version, the library elements can be separated by the using declaration. Thus, if programmers define class abs themselves and do not write using <cmath>, they can call cmath::abs() to call the absolute function of the library and OurLib::abs() to access abs() of their library.

We have also seen that namespaces can be extended. However, the std namespace is an exception. It is not possible to add new definitions to the std namespace.

14.8 KOENIG LOOKUP

If **using std::cout** is written initially and then **cout** is used with <<, the program works. We have seen this earlier in the chapter. The operator << is a part of the std namespace. How does the compiler find and qualify the operator even when the namespace in which it is defined is not specified? It is because of an algorithm by Andrew Koenig, which is now implemented in most of the compilers. It is mandatory for all ANSI C++-compliant compilers. The formal name of the algorithm is *augment-dependent lookup*. The Koenig lookup is automatically applied by any ANSI/ISO standard-compliant compiler; hence, there is no need to enable or disable anything.

Koenig lookup enables the compiler to search namespaces to locate an element even if one does not use the using directive or even a fully qualified name. Consider the following program.

```
//KoenigLookup.cpp
#include <iostream>
// using namespace std is missing here

int main()
{
    using std::cout;
    // The following line is now commented // using std::operator <<;
    cout << "Hi";
    return 0;
}
```

The program still works as before. The operator << will be found from the std namespace by the Koenig lookup algorithm.

14.9 OVERHEAD WITH NAMESPACES

Namespaces are resolved at compile time. All using directives, using declarations, fully qualified names, etc. are handled statically by the compiler. There is nothing to be done at run-time. In short, there is no run-time overhead with namespaces.

Thus, it is advised to use namespaces when necessary without worrying about performance overhead at run-time. However, it is important to note that if one builds unnecessary namespaces, it may affect the readability of the program.

■ RECAPITULATION ■

- Use of third-party libraries introduces name conflict problem.
- If the functions are grouped and every group is given a specific name, then we can qualify the function as a part of a group.
- Namespace is a logical grouping mechanism for grouping objects and qualifying objects by that group to avoid name conflict issues.
- Namespace enables the programmer to unambiguously specify the objects of different libraries.
- A using declaration can make a single element of the library available to us and a using directive can make the entire library available.
- It is possible to use an object of the namespace without the using directive or declaration. In such cases, we can use fully qualified names.
- We can define variables, functions, and classes inside namespaces.
- It is possible to extend the namespace (except the std namespace) with additional objects.

- Unnamed namespace, that is, namespaces without any name is also possible.
- Variables defined in unnamed namespaces are available to the program in the same file similar to global static variables.
- It is possible to define one namespace inside another one. Such a namespace is known as nested namespace.
- A long namespace name can be shortened by using namespace alias.
- When the user does not specify the namespace name for any object, it is possible for a compiler to apply argument-dependent lookup algorithm to find that namespace name from the context. This algorithm is popularly known as the Koenig lookup algorithm.
- Namespaces incur no overhead at run-time as all processing related to the namespaces is resolved at compile time.

■ KEYWORDS ■

Fully qualified name This is the name of any object, variable, or function with the names of the namespace and the scope resolution operator (::).

Global namespace This is the namespace where every function or class is copied in older C++ by default.

Koenig lookup The ability of the compiler to find the exact namespace of the object in use even when not specified by the programmer is known as Keonig lookup.

Namespace This is an enclosure of logical nature, which helps libraries to have separate existence and solves the name conflict problem.

Namespace aliases A shorter name given to a long fully qualified name using namespace aliasing syntax

is known as a namespace alias for the long fully qualified name. This process is known as namespace aliasing.

Nested namespaces Namespaces defined inside another are known as nested namespaces.

Unnamed namespace This is a namespace without any name specified for it. It is now recommended to use unnamed namespaces in place of global static variables.

using declaration This is a mechanism for making a single element of a library available to the program.

using directive This is a mechanism for making all elements of a library available to the program at a single stretch.

■ EXERCISES ■

Multiple Choice Questions

1. When a namespace with the same name as previous namespace is defined, _____.
   - (a) the new namespace overwrites the previous namespace
   - (b) the new namespace overrides the previous namespace
   - (c) the new namespace extends the previous namespace
   - (d) the compiler generates an error

2. Which of the following is the correct syntax of defining namespace with only variables as members?
   - (a) `namespace MyNamespace { int myNumber; string myString; }`
   - (b) `MyNamespace { int myNumber; string myString; }`
   - (c) `namespace MyNamespace { myNumber; myString; }`
   - (d) `MyNamespace namespace { int myNumber; string myString; }`

3. The _____ enables the compiler to find the namespace of an element even if it is not mentioned either using a directive or a fully qualified name.
   - (a) lookup
   - (b) global lookup
   - (c) dependent lookup
   - (d) Koenig lookup

4. There is no _____ overhead with namespaces.
   - (a) compile time
   - (b) link time
   - (c) load time
   - (d) run-time

5. Namespaces can be defined _____.
   - (a) in compiled libraries
   - (b) in external programs
   - (c) in parts
   - (d) as whole namespaces only

6. When logically grouped using namespaces, any name can be qualified using the syntax _____.
   - (a) `namespace::element`
   - (b) `element::namespace`
   - (c) `namespace::<data type> element`
   - (d) `<data type> element::namespace`

7. Namespace `ABC{...};` is an example of _____.
   - (a) unnamed namespace
   - (b) namespace alias
   - (c) a regular namespace
   - (d) None of the above

8. How can an object of a class named `MyClass` defined inside a namespace called `MyNamespace` be created with the use of `using` directive?
   - (a) `using namespace MyNamespace; MyClass <object name>;`
   - (b) `using MyNamespace; MyClass <object name>;`
   - (c) Both
   - (d) None of the above

9. Which of the following syntax shows the use of any element of a given namespace?
   - (a) `namespace::element`
   - (b) `element::namespace`
   - (c) `using namespace::element`
   - (d) `using element::namespace`

10. The name conflict problem can be solved by _____.
    - (a) having the same enclosure for all conflicting names
    - (b) having different enclosures for the conflicting names
    - (c) having unique names; else, it is not possible to resolve
    - (d) it cannot be resolved

Conceptual Exercises

1. What is the name conflict problem? How can it be solved using namespaces?

2. How is logical grouping provided by the namespaces? How can objects with the same name be handled?

3. What is a fully qualified name? When do we need to use a fully qualified name?

4. What is the difference between `using` declaration and `using` directive?

5. How can we define an object without using either `using` directive or `using` declaration?

6. How can we define our own namespace? How can we define our functions inside the namespace and use them outside?

7. How can we define a function or a class in a namespace and use it outside?

8. How can we extend a namespace already defined? What is its advantage?

9. What is unnamed namespace? What is the use of unnamed namespace?

10. How can we define one namespace inside another? How can we use the objects defined in the inner namespace outside the outer namespace?

11. What are namespace aliases? What is their use?

12. What is std namespace? How is it different from other namespaces?

13. What is Koenig lookup? When is it applied?

Practical Exercises

1. Write a program to define a namespace and define an employee class inside that. (Use any definition of employee class encountered so far). Define at least two member functions outside the namespace. Write a main() program and use the employee class objects there.

2. Get the definition of a student class from any of the previous chapters. Define the class in a namespace Student. Define a function abs() in the class to indicate absence. Also use the function in the main program with abs() from the math library.

3. Get the definition of Time class from Chapter 6. Define a function DifferenceTime() as its member. Define the Time class inside the namespace. Define DifferenceTime() outside the namespace and use namespace alias to access that function in main().

4. Get the definition of a student class from any of the earlier chapters. Define a NewStudent class with a new data member MobileNumber indicating the mobile phone number of the student. Use namespace alias such that the main() function can use either of the student class.

5. Get the definition of any student class from earlier chapters. Overload << operator. Define the student class in a namespace and use it in the main program. Use using declaration for the student class alone. Use << operator to display the student object in the main() and to see that it is available without specifying.

Chapter 15

String Objects

Learning Objectives

- Introduction to string objects
- Methods of using constructors for the string class
- Application of substring operations to a string object
- Handling multiple strings
- Attributes of the string object

15.1 INTRODUCTION

Strings are implemented in C as character arrays. However, character arrays have a few limitations when treated as strings. They are as follows:

1. They cannot be compared like other variables. One cannot write `String1 == String2` to compare two strings.
2. They cannot be assigned like normal variables. One cannot write `String1 = String2` to assign `String1` the same value as `String2`.
3. Direct initialization with another string is not possible. One cannot write

   `string String1(String2)` or `string String1 = String2`

   One can write

   `char * String2 = String1`

   However, here one is actually initializing a character pointer and not the string itself. It means the contents are shared but not copied; that is, if one string changes, the other changes too.
4. There are functions provided for strings in the library, the prototypes of which are accessible using the `string.h` file (or `cstring` file). These functions are not string functions in the true sense. They operate on character pointers. They can malfunction in some cases. Suppose one has copied character by character into a character array, the null character will not be present at the end of the character array. Now, if one uses the `strlen()` function, which calculates the length of the string by counting until the null character, it would return a wrong value.

Therefore, it is desirable that strings are treated as separate objects and not as character arrays. C++ overcomes these limitations by providing string objects.

15.2 OPERATIONS ON STRING OBJECTS

The string class is designed in such a way that the objects work like natural strings. It provides all the required operations a user expects from an object. Thus, the string class has become one of the most useful classes for C++ programmers.

The operations possible on string objects are explained in the following sections.

15.2.1 Creating Strings

A string object can be created in three ways:

Normal way One can write string StringName; to define a string object in the normal way. This has been done in the previous chapters to define strings. This is illustrated in the program that follows.

Through initialization One can write string AStringObject(AnotherStringObject); or string AStringObject = AnotherStringObject; to define and initialize AStringObject using AnotherStringObject. This is also illustrated in the following program.

By a constructor One can write string AStringObject(Value) or string AStringObject = Value to use a single-argument constructor to define AStringObject and initialize it with a value.

The following program shows how string objects can be created.

```
//DefineStrings.cpp
#include <iostream>
#include <string>
using namespace std;

int main()
{
    string FirstString;   // Normal definition
    string SecondString("Hi");   // Using one-argument constructor
    string ThirdString(SecondString); // Using initialization
    FirstString = "How Are You?";
    string FourthString = FirstString;   // Defining and initializing
}
```

> **Note** The use of a conversion function for conversion from normal string to string object is as follows:
>
>   FirstString = "How Are You?";
>
> This conversion function is an outcome of a non-explicit one-argument constructor.

15.2.2 Substring Operations

There are a few substring operations as well. Most of the functions defined here have more than one overloaded versions. The most useful versions have been chosen to show as examples.

Locate substring or character There is a function find(), which finds a specific substring or a character in a given string. It returns the position of the specific character or substring in a given string. As in C strings, the first position is numbered as zero. The second is numbered as one, and so on. This is why FirstString.find("You") returns eight in Program 15.1. The same function can also be used with a character argument. Thus, FirstString.find('Y'); is also allowed and it returns eight. Surprisingly enough, the function returns the largest possible unsigned integer value when the character or the substring is not found in the string.

> **Note** Such behaviour is common among all standard template library (STL) objects, and not only strings. They return a value given by the function end(), which returns the end position + 1 of that STL object.

Find character at given location in given string There is a function `at()` that displays the character located at a given position in a string. If one defines

```
string FirstString("This is testing");
FirstString.at(1);
```

It returns `'h'` because this is the character at the first position. Program 15.1 shows how `at()` command can be used to display each character of the string.

Insert substring at specific place One can insert a specific substring at a given place by using the function `insert()`. Its syntax is as follows:

```
insert(PositionAtWhichInsertionToBeMade, StringToBeInserted)
```

It takes two arguments as shown here. Program 15.1 will show how a substring `'busy'` is inserted at position number 4 in the string `'How Are You?'` to make it `'How busy Are You?'`.

Replace specific characters One can replace a specific sequence of characters (a substring) by another sequence of characters (i.e., another substring). Program 15.1 shows how `'busy'` is replaced by `'lazy'`. Here, the same number of characters has been used in the replacement string; however, it is not necessary. One can even replace `'busy'` with `'busy and tired'`.

Append substring to string The `append()` function is available to add a substring at the end of a given string. It is called with just one argument, that is, the substring to append. Program 15.1 has one such use of `append()`. It appends `'friend'` to the `SecondString` variable to make it `'Hi friend!'`.

Erase part of string The `erase()` function is used for erasing a part of the string. It takes three arguments, the string itself, the beginning character position, and the total number of characters. Program 15.1 illustrates the operations described here.

> `at()` command is helpful in finding the character that is present at a given position.

> `find()` finds a given substring or a character in a given string; `insert()` inserts a given substring in a given string at a specified position; `replace()` replaces a substring by another; `append()` appends a string to another; `erase()` erases a substring from a given string.

PROGRAM 15.1 Substring operations

```cpp
//SubstringOperations.cpp
#include <iostream>
#include <string>
using namespace std;

int main()
{
    string FirstString = "How Are You?";
    string SecondString ("Hi");

    // Using find()
    cout << FirstString.find('A') << endl;
    /* Returns where A appears in the string*/
    /* Example of char argument */

    cout << FirstString.find("You") << endl;
    /* Returns where You appears in the string*/
    /* Example of string argument */

    cout << FirstString.find("Nowhere") << endl;
    /* Substring not present in the string*/

    cout << FirstString.find('B') << endl;
    /* char not present in the string*/
```

```
// Using at()
for (unsigned int i = 0; i < FirstString.length(); i++)
cout << FirstString.at(i);
cout << endl;

// Using insert()
FirstString.insert(4, "busy");
cout << FirstString << endl;

// Using append()
SecondString.append("friend!");
cout << SecondString << endl;

// Using replace()
FirstString.replace(4, 4, "lazy");   // Replace busy with lazy
cout << FirstString << endl;

// Using erase()
FirstString.erase(4,5);   // Now removing lazy
cout << FirstString << endl;
}
```

Output
```
4
8
4294967295
4294967295
How Are You?
How busy Are You?
Hi friend!
How lazy Are You?
How Are You?
```

How the Program Works

In the output, it is important to note that the value 4294967295 returned is one more than the maximum capacity of the string object. When a character or a substring is not found, this is what is returned.

There is a function called `max_size`, which returns the maximum capacity of a string object. We will discuss how to get the characteristics of a string later in Section 15.2.4. Strings, being STL objects, return the end as one past the last value.

15.2.3 Operations Involving Multiple Strings

There are quite a few operators that deal with multiple strings. They are described in the following sections. Their use is illustrated in Program 15.2.

+, =, ==, and compare() functions The following are the ways to concatenate and compare two strings:

1. We have already used '=' to assign one string object to another.
2. We can use '+' to concatenate two strings into one. Suppose String2 is 'abc' and String3 is 'def'. If we write String1 = String2 + String3, then String1 becomes 'abcdef'.
3. We can use the '==' operator to compare two string objects.
4. We can also use the `compare()` function to compare two string objects. This function is analogous to the `strcmp()` function. Apart from just comparing, it can also determine whether either string is smaller than the other.

5. There is also an overloaded version of `swap()`, which compares a part of a given string to a part of another string. This, however, has not been shown in Program 15.2.

Swapping two strings The function `swap()` helps in swapping two different string object values. If `st1` and `st2` are two string objects, then `st1.swap(st2)` copies the value of `st1` to `st2` and vice versa. By using the `swap()` function, one avoids the use of a temporary variable and the three assignment statements generally used for swapping.

> Relational operators such as ==, !=, <, >, ≤, and ≥, and other operators such as <<, >>, and [] are available for string objects with obvious meanings.

Operators available with string objects We have already discussed the use of operators such as '+' and '=' for strings. We have used them for concatenating and assigning strings. Besides these, there are a few other operators available for string operations. Let us have a look at them.

1. Operator '!=' is used for checking whether two strings are equal.
2. Operators < , >, ≤, and ≥ are used to check whether one string is lexicographically (in the alphabetical order) greater than the other, etc.
3. We have already seen the use of << and >> operators for reading and writing string objects.
4. The [] operator is also available to access an element (a character) from the string object. `StringName[ElementIndex]` will return the character at `ElementIndex` from the `StringName`. In Program 15.2, we have accessed each element of the string, starting from the zeroth element to the first element and so on until the end of the string. Here, `FirstString.length()` is similar to `strlen()`, which returns the length of the string in the elements.

15.2.4 String Characteristics

There are built-in functions available to check the characteristics of a given string. These functions are listed as follows:

1. The `empty()` function is a simple but useful function; it checks whether a string object contains any data. One can write `st1.empty()` to check if `st1` is an empty string object. The function returns a Boolean value, that is, the empty function returns one (1) if the function is empty and returns zero (0) otherwise. Program 15.2 illustrates its use.
2. The `size()` function returns the size of a string. The syntax is `st1.size()` for string object `st1`. There is one more function, `length()`, which provides the same value. This has been used while writing the `for` loop using the [] operator to access a character from the string in Program 15.2. The `size()` function can be used here instead.
3. The maximum permissible size of a string in a given system can be found using the `max_size()` function. The syntax is `st1.max_size()` for string object `st1`.
4. There is another function `resize()`, which resizes the string by the number supplied as an argument.

Program 15.2 illustrates the use of all the operators discussed here.

PROGRAM 15.2 String characteristics

```
//OtherOp.cpp
#include <iostream>
#include <string>
using namespace std;
```

```cpp
void DisplayDetails(string TempString);
void ResizeString(string, int);

int main()
{
    cout << boolalpha;
    // String details display
    string FirstString;
    string SecondString;

    DisplayDetails(FirstString);
    SecondString = "This is testing";
    DisplayDetails(SecondString);
    FirstString = "Testing is difficult";
    DisplayDetails(FirstString);

    // Relational operators
    cout << endl << "****Illustrating relational operators";
    cout << "****"  << endl;

    if(FirstString > SecondString)
    {
        cout << "\"" << FirstString << "\"";
        cout << " is lexicographically greater than ";
        cout << "\""<< SecondString<< "\"" << endl;
    }
    else
    {
        cout << "\"" << SecondString << "\"";
        cout << "is lexicographically greater than ";
        cout << "\""<< FirstString<< "\"" << endl;
    }

    // Equality checking
    if(FirstString != SecondString)
    {
        cout << "\"" << FirstString << "\"";
        cout << " and "<< "\"" << SecondString ;
        cout << "\""<<" are not equal\n";
    }

    string ThirdString(SecondString);
    if(SecondString == ThirdString)
    {
        cout << "\"" <<  SecondString<< "\"";
        cout << " and "<< "\"" << ThirdString;
        cout << "\""<<" are equal\n";
    }

    // Using the [] operator
    cout << endl << "****Illustrating the use of [] operator";
    cout << "****"  << endl;;
    cout << "using [] operator\n";
    for(unsigned int i = 0; i < FirstString.length(); i++)
    cout << FirstString[i];
    cout << endl;

    // Using compare()
    cout << endl << "****Illustrating compare() function";
    cout << "****" << endl;
```

```
        switch(FirstString.compare(SecondString))
        {
            case 0:
                cout << "Both the strings are equal\n";
                break;
            case 1:
                cout << "\"" << SecondString << "\"";
                cout << " is lexicographically greater than ";
                cout << "\""<< FirstString<< "\"" << endl;
                break;
            case 2:
                cout << "\"" << FirstString << "\"";
                cout << " is lexicographically greater than ";
                cout << "\""<< SecondString<< "\"" << endl;
                break;
        }

        cout << endl << endl;

        // Swapping strings
        cout << "****Illustrating swap" << "****"  << endl;
        cout << "Strings before swapping \n";
        cout <<"First string is " << "\"" << FirstString;
        cout << "\"" << endl;
        cout <<"Second string is " << "\"" << SecondString;
        cout << "\"" << endl;
        FirstString.swap(SecondString);

        // SecondString.swap(FirstString) will have the same effect

        cout << "****Strings after swapping****\n";
        cout <<"First string is " << "\"" << FirstString;
        cout << "\"" << endl;
        cout <<"Second string is " << "\"" << SecondString;
        cout << "\"" << endl;
        cout << endl << endl;

        // Resizing the strings
        cout << endl << "****Illustrating resizing****" << endl;
        ResizeString(FirstString, 100);
        ResizeString(SecondString, 10);
        return 0;
}
void DisplayDetails(string TempString)
{
    cout << endl << "****Displaying the details of string\"";
    cout << TempString << "\"" << "****" ;
    cout << "\n The size of the string is " << TempString.size();
    cout << "\n Is the string empty? " << TempString.empty();
    cout << "\n The maximum size of string in this system is " ;
    cout << TempString.max_size();
    cout << endl ;
}

void ResizeString(string TempString, int NewSize)
{
    cout << "****Now resizing\"" << TempString;
    cout << "\" to size ";
    cout << NewSize << "****" <<endl;
```

```
    cout << "Original string is: \"" << TempString;
    cout << "\"" << endl;
    cout << "Original size is: " << TempString.size() << endl;
    TempString.resize(NewSize);
    cout << "String size after resize: ";
    cout << TempString.size()<< endl;
    cout << "The resized string is: \"";
    cout << TempString << "\" "<<endl;
    cout << endl;
}
```

Output
```
****Displaying the details of string****
The size of the string is 0
Is the string empty? true
The maximum size of string in this system is 4294967294

****Displaying the details of string "This is testing"****
The size of the string is 15
Is the string empty?  false
The maximum size of string in this system is 4294967294

****Displaying the details of string "Testing is difficult"****
The size of the string is 20
Is the string empty?  false
The maximum size of string in this system is 4294967294

****Illustrating relational operators****
"This is testing" is lexicographically greater than "Testing is difficult"
"Testing is difficult" and "This is testing" are not equal
"This is testing" and "This is Testing" are equal

****Illustrating the use of [] operator****
using [] operator
Testing is difficult

****Illustrating compare() function****
"This is testing" is lexicographically greater than "Testing is difficult"

****Illustrating swap****
Strings before swapping
First string is "Testing is difficult"
Second string is "This is testing"
****Strings after swapping****
First string is "This is testing"
Second string is "Testing is difficult"

****Illustrating resizing ****
*****Now resizing "This is testing" to size 100****
Original string is: "This is testing"
Original size is: 15
string size after resize: 100
The resized string is: "This is testing"

*****Now resizing "Testing is difficult" to size 10****
Original string is: "Testing is difficult"
Original size is: 20
string size after resize: 10
The resized string is: "Testing is"
```

How the Program Works

The output provides reinforcement to what we have studied earlier.

1. When the string `'This is testing'` is resized to 100, blanks are padded at the end to make it 100 characters long. Thus, there is a blank second line after it.
2. When the `SecondString` is resized to a smaller value (from original 20 to 10), then the remaining part of the string (the word `'difficult'`) is lost.
3. Note the use of `boolalpha` manipulator to print `true` or `false` instead of `1` or `0` for Boolean values.

The difference between C++ strings and C strings is explained in Exhibit 15.1.

Exhibit 15.1 C++ strings vs C strings

The string objects of C++ are closer to the actual strings. This is because C++ works with string data type, unlike the array of characters in C. It also improves the ease of use and applicability. Moreover, C++ strings are as efficient as C strings, if not more. By virtue of string objects being a part of the STLs, there are plenty of generic algorithms and built-in functions such as find(), replace(), merge(), and sort() that can be used with strings.

▪ RECAPITULATION ▪

- The string is an important class of C++.
- The string class contains many useful member functions.
- The C-type strings have problems of various kinds such as assignment using '=' is not possible, comparison of two strings using '==' is not possible, and initializing a string with another is not possible. All these problems are solved in C++ by using string objects.
- String, being a class, can have overloaded =, ==, and != operators.
- String class also has a few important constructors that help in initializing one string object with another, initializing a string object with C-type string, or having a normal definition without initialization.
- It is also possible to have few substring operations on the strings such as finding the position of a substring or a character within a string, inserting a specific substring at a specific place, replacing a specific substring by another, and appending a string to another.
- It is also possible to use + to concatenate two different strings and use a function compare() to match two strings (similar to strcmp() in C).
- Swap function is also available as a member function for swapping two strings.
- The functions empty() to check whether the string is empty or not, size() to check the size of the string, resize() to resize the string to a new size, and max_size() to find the maximum size of the string possible are available as member functions.
- Generic algorithms such as find(), replace(), and sort() are also available for operations on string objects in C++.

▪ KEYWORDS ▪

C-type strings Character arrays are used as strings in C. They are also called C-type strings.

Size of string This is the number of characters in a string.

String objects These are objects of type string.

■ EXERCISES ■

Multiple Choice Questions

1. When the specified character or substring is not found, the find() function returns _____.
   - (a) zero
   - (b) a null value
   - (c) the smallest possible unsigned integer
   - (d) the largest possible unsigned integer

2. Which of the following is the correct syntax of using the find() function?
   - (a) `myString.find("You");`
   - (b) `myString.find(&loqus; Y&roqus;);`
   - (c) Both
   - (d) None

3. C++ string objects are _____.
   - (a) easy to use
   - (b) easily applicable
   - (c) Both
   - (d) None

4. When the string is resized to reduce than the original capacity, _____.
   - (a) the resize does not take place
   - (b) the data is truncated to the new size
   - (c) the compiler will generate an error
   - (d) an exception will be raised

5. Which of the following function provides the size of a given string?
   - (a) `size()`
   - (b) `length()`
   - (c) Both
   - (d) None

6. We can insert a specific substring in a given place in the string using the function _____.
   - (a) `insert(PositionAtWhichInsertionIsToBeMade, StringToBeInserted);`
   - (b) `insertAt(PositionAtWhichInsertionIsToBeMade, StringToBeInserted);`
   - (c) `insert(StringToBeInserted, PositionAtWhichInsertionIsToBeMade);`
   - (d) `insertAt(StringToBeInserted, PositionAtWhichInsertionIsToBeMade);`

7. Which of the following is the correct syntax of defining a string object?
   - (a) `string myString(intNumber);`
   - (b) `string myString("Hi");`
   - (c) `string myString(&loqus; H&roqus;);`
   - (d) All of the above

8. Which of the following is not the correct way of using the find() function?
   - (a) `myString.find("You");`
   - (b) `myString.find(&loqus; Y&roqus;);`
   - (c) `myString("Y");`
   - (d) `myString(7.5);`

9. When a string is empty, the empty() function _____.
   - (a) returns a zero
   - (b) returns false
   - (c) returns null
   - (d) raises an exception

10. Which of the following operators are used to check that a given string is lexicographically same as or different than the other string?
    - (a) < and > operators
    - (b) ≤ and ≥ operators
    - (c) Both
    - (d) None

Conceptual Exercises

1. What are the problems with C-type strings?
2. List different constructors for string objects.
3. What are the facilities available for substring operations on the string object?
4. Write functions that can help us in finding the different characteristics of the string object.
5. Compare C strings with C++ strings.

Practical Exercises

1. Write a program to read and count the elements in a string.
2. Write a program to compare two strings and display whether one string is lexicographically smaller than the other.
3. Write a program that searches for a specific word inside the text.
4. Write a program that reads from a file and converts each character of that file to another using some algorithm.
5. Write a program that accepts two strings from the user in a text file. Read the first string from the user in the text file. Replace that string with the second string in that file. For example, if the user enters 'Test' and 'Pure', then we have to find Test in the file and replace it with Pure.

Chapter 16

Standard Template Library

Learning Objectives

- Generic programming, generic software components or containers, generic algorithms, and iterators
- Sequence containers such as vector, list, and deque
- Sorted associative containers such as map, multimap, set, and multiset
- Sample algorithms of STL find(), copy(), and sort()
- Function objects, predicate objects, and allocators

STL contains containers and generic algorithms connected by iterators.

Generic algorithm is the strength of STL. It allows fewer and optimized algorithms in the system.

16.1 INTRODUCTION

Standard Template Library (STL) is a collection of generic software components (generic containers) and generic algorithms, glued by objects called *iterators*.

STL is different from normal libraries. All other libraries defined need entities as classes. The operations required in that class are written as member functions of the class. This is not needed for STL. It has a large number of non-member functions designed to work on multiple classes of container types. This approach has a significant advantage.

Assume that an efficient algorithm to find an element from some sequence is written. When it is implemented as a non-member function, any sequence can be used as an input to it. Thus, there is a single function for multiple sequences. For X such sequences and Y such operations, the earlier case needs $X * Y$ member functions (Y operations on each of the X classes), whereas non-member functions are just Y in the second case. Thus, the number of implementations required for a class becomes very less. There is going to be a single function for most of the classes, if not all. Hence, it becomes feasible to implement all operations in an efficient manner, as they are required to be implemented only once.

For example, consider a function called find() for finding an element from a sequence of elements. Being a non-member, find() can be used with any sequence of the programmer's choice. On the other hand, if find() is a member function of a specific class, it will have to be used only with that class object and one needs to redefine similar functions for all classes where this generic functionality is needed.

STL has one more advantage. It is also possible to have a new sequence designed. All such operations designed for a generic case are readily available for the new sequence. These non-member functions are known as *generic algorithms*. STL contains so many useful algorithms such as find(), replace(), merge(), and sort(). Being generic, these algorithms are non-member functions and can be used with all the containers.

Apart from generic algorithms, STL has generic software components (containers). These containers are classes that can, in turn, contain other objects. We will be looking at a few of the components of this library in due course:

1. Vector (implementation is like an array), list (implementation of doubly linked list), and deque (implementation of deque) are called *sequence containers.*
2. Set, multiset, map, and multimap are known as *associative sorted containers.* Unlike sequence containers, these containers keep the contents in a sorted form.
3. There are adapted containers such as queue and stack that are not true containers but are implemented using sequence containers.

Iterators　One can think of iterators as generic pointers. The designers of C used void pointers in many cases where they would like a pointer to be assigned to any other type later. malloc() is an excellent example; it returns the void pointer that a programmer can assign to the type he/she deems fit. In true sense, iterators are far more capable than void pointers.

If there is an array, one will traverse the array using an index. On the contrary, if there is a linked list, one can traverse it using a pointer designed to point to the node of that linked list. If some other structure is used, then some other mechanism is needed to traverse the container. The array index used to traverse an array sequentially or randomly and the pointer used in a linked list to traverse the list sequentially are basically doing the same job, which is, traversing a sequence of elements. In the case of STL, a generalized concept called iterator is used to traverse a sequence of container elements.

An important problem in generalizing such a concept is to ensure that it is not bound to a type. For example, consider designing a pointer that can be used to point to any linked list node; it is just impossible. Say, if there is a linked list of integers, the pointer to be used is int*, and if there is a linked list of node of type NodeType, the pointer to be used is NodeType*. In such a situation, templates are used to avoid type-related issues. For example, if there is a pointer defined as Type *ptr, the ptr is a generic pointer. Iterator is a kind of generic index that helps one to iterate through some specific sequence. The following code segment helps us understand the same.

```
vector <int>::iterator IntIndex;

for(IntIndex = vi.begin(); IntIndex < vi.end(); IntIndex++)
{
    cout << *IntIndex << endl;
}
```

The IntIndex variable is of type iterator (of vector int type), which will help one iterate through a vector (a container type quite similar to an array) vi. We will soon see other details about how to program with containers, generic algorithms, and containers.

Iterators, thus, help a user to iterate through a sequence of elements of a container; hence, the name.

The beauty of matching generic algorithms with generic containers lies in the use of templates and objects known as iterators. They are pointer-like objects, but unlike pointers, they are categorized into five different categories, namely, input, random access, bidirectional, forward, and output.

Generic algorithms are written to work on iterator objects rather than any data structure. The find() algorithm works on a category of iterators called *input iterators.*

Containers are also designed in terms of iterators rather than normal pointers. Thus, iterators are able to join algorithms with containers. It is also important to note that not all algorithms are efficient with all data structures. For example, `sort()`, which is usually implemented as `quicksort()`, requires random access to the data. For linked list, this algorithm is painfully slow. Here, `sort()` is defined to require *random access iterators*.

> Software components (containers) and algorithms are connected to each other by iterators.

The list (the doubly linked list) container is defined to have *bidirectional iterators*. Thus, `sort()` cannot be used with a list. There will be compilation errors if a generic `sort()` algorithm is used with a list. Vector and deque containers are defined to have *random access iterators* and, therefore, the `sort()` algorithm can work with them. Hence, it is clear that the choice of iterators also impacts the efficiency.

Exhibit 16.1 provides a brief history of STL.

Exhibit 16.1   A brief history of STL

STL is a broad topic and is beyond the scope of this text, which only provides an introduction to it. The following is a brief history of STL.

STL is the brainchild of Alexander Stepanov. When Stepanov was working with the General Electric Research and Development Centre in 1979, he started working on generic programming concepts. Surprisingly, the idea of generic programming has nothing to do with C++. It was first implemented in the Ada language. Stepanov later joined AT&T and then Hewlett-Packard where he worked on C++.

Due to the efforts of Andrew Koenig, a member of the Standardization Committee, Stepanov was invited to present his ideas about generic programming and STL to the C++ Standardization Committee in 1993. The Committee accepted his ideas unanimously, and in 1994, STL was added to the ANSI standard. A number of C++ experts have quoted STL to be the biggest addition to the standard.

16.2 GENERIC PROGRAMMING

STL is not a normal library. It is designed on the basis of a few very important principles independent of C++ itself.

> STL is a templatized, generic library that provides standard storage of elements in a type-independent form.

Generic programming has nothing to do with C++. It is a mechanism of designing generic software components such as vector, list, and deque. The next element of STL is generic algorithms. Unlike normal programming practice, these algorithms are not designed having any software component in mind. The algorithms are designed to suit the minimum level of requirements. Thus, these algorithms can work with many variants of different software components (containers) without any change.

> The model using inheritance is known as the object-oriented model and the model presented by STL is called the object-based model.

It is important to understand that this model of programming is different from the sharing model of inheritance and virtual functions, where the base class, the common attributes storage in base class, base class pointers, and virtual functions provide a very flexible model of programming with great runtime control. In contrast, the model presented by STL offers similar advantages but with a more efficient architecture. Generality is achieved by using templates, iterators, and a good design rather than having class hierarchy.

16.3 GENERIC SOFTWARE COMPONENTS

STL aims to provide 'reusable' components such as vector, list, and deque. Earlier, programmers used to write their own routines for using arrays, lists, and queues. STL provides tested and debugged components readily available. They are reusable in the sense that one can use them as a building block for other software development projects. These generic software components are also called *containers*, as they are basically a collection of the other objects. Thus, containers are objects themselves, which in turn contain other objects. These readymade components offer the following advantages:

Small in number The software components are few in number (nearly 12) and so are easy to master. Though small in number, they are extremely useful in solving a myriad of problems.

Generic They are generic in nature. It is possible to use them at various places without much trouble.

Efficient, tested, debugged, and standardized These software components are designed for speed. Every component has been designed with a specific time requirement as an efficiency measure and it is seen that it matches that efficiency requirement. STL components are already running in a large number of user programs, and hence, they are thoroughly tested and debugged. They have already become a standard. Thus, programs written using STL components are easier to program and to read.

Portability and reusability STL is already a standard. If a program uses STL, it becomes more portable because the stacks, queues, and vectors are all available on the destination machine in the same form. STL uses templates to a large extent to make it as independent of type as possible.

16.4 GENERIC ALGORITHMS

As STL is designed for speed, the algorithms that operate on the software components are designed in such a way that they depend very little on the data structure of the component (e.g., an algorithm called find() does not vary much in speed if it is finding in the vector, stack, or queue). Programmers can write their own algorithms in place of generic algorithms. This is, however, not preferred, as there are some distinct advantages of using generic algorithms:

1. Programmers are free from writing routines such as sort(), merge(), binary-search(), and find() with different variations in each case. They are available readymade in the STL.
2. The algorithms use the best mechanisms to be as efficient as possible, designing which may not be generally possible for most of the programmers. All the algorithms are designed taking the best of the breed components, and most of the efficiency concerns are addressed. For example, the sort() algorithm applies quick sort but it might switch over to merge sort if the input data is more suited (almost sorted elements).
3. Generic algorithms are standardized and, hence, have more acceptability than proprietary algorithms. Some software organizations adopt STL only because of it being a standard. Some of the US clients expect designers to code using STL and consider it as one of the fundamental requirements of their contract.

4. Similar semantics are designed for all these algorithms. For example, checking an end of list is similar to checking an end of a vector. Learning how to learn one algorithm improves the learning curve for the other algorithms.

16.5 ITERATORS

The software components being dealt with are collections of other objects. Efficient methods are needed to traverse these containers. Iterators provide a way to do it. Iterators can be safely assumed to be generic pointers for the time being.

There are two different models of managing multiple objects, one using the *address mechanism* and the other using the *function mechanism*. C or C++ arrays can be accessed using the [] operator as well as pointers. Files are accessed using get() and put() methods. One cannot directly point to a file element like a pointer does and directly increment it to get the next element. Such increment is possible while using pointers for arrays.

The functional model of managing multiple objects is described in Exhibit 16.2.

Exhibit 16.2   Functional model

The pointers to array elements represent a *model of address mechanism,* whereas the file access using get() and put() uses a *functional model.* Some languages, noticeably Java, assume that the pointers are too dangerous to be given to programmers, and are better hidden. Such languages try to provide functional interface to the programmers like a file interface.

The functional approach is simpler but has one big disadvantage. The address mechanism enables the programmer to have complete control on the process by having the pointer. It is then possible for the programmer to tailor the solution to the most efficient one. This flexibility is not possible with the functional approach. The functional approach loses finer control in order to provide better readability and avoidance of complex problems.

STL is based on the address model, which is a little more complex but more flexible than the functional model.

STL designers provided iterators to allow finer control. They are not only provided but are also open to the programmer. Programmers not only can define and use iterators like pointers to the component objects, but they can also dereference them, assign them, and manipulate them, just like pointers.

In the following example, IntIndex is assigned a value returned by the function vi.begin(). It is compared against vi.end and incremented exactly like an array index. Its value is displayed exactly like using a dereferenced pointer syntax.

```
vector <int>::iterator IntIndex;
for(IntIndex = vi.begin(); IntIndex < vi.end(); IntIndex++)
{
    cout << *IntIndex << endl;
}
```

One may ask why pointers are not made available directly. Why not just define something as follows:

```
vector <int> * IntIndex;
```

and use it? Instead of iterators, which are internally implemented using pointers, why not use the pointers directly? Why is the additional layer of iterators provided? This is so because

> Iterator is a more general term than pointer. It helps manage the traversal better and can be designed to suit the particular needs of a system.

of two reasons. First, iterators are more general than pointers and are classified according to different code requirements. One can choose an appropriate iterator for a specific operation. Second, although iterators are implemented as pointers in most of the cases, one can choose a more fitting implementation for a special case. If programmers design one more software component themselves and would like to use the same set of generic algorithms, they can design their own iterators to traverse their containers. For example, consider a special case, which is basically a linked list of huge images. Here, one may not use memory addresses as iterators (pointers are memory addresses); it requires a specialized iterator to suit the storage of such images.

Table 16.1 lists the five categories of iterators and their roles.

Table 16.1   Types of iterators and their meanings

Type	Meaning
Input	Used for reading in
Output	Used for writing out
Forward	Used for travelling in the forward direction from start to end; it is possible to save a forward iterator and use it later. It is also an input and output iterator.
Bidirectional	Used for travelling in both directions, that is, start to end and vice versa; it is otherwise similar to a forward iterator, and thus, is also a forward iterator.
Random access	Used for both reading and writing randomly; it is otherwise similar to a bidirectional iterator, and thus, is also a bidirectional iterator.

The efficiency of the STL iterators depends heavily on two principles:

1. Open design having iterators open for programmers to manipulate. One can assign values, compare them with other iterators, increment them, etc.
2. Address manipulation by which it is possible to do the job in minimum steps. One can just deference an iterator to get the object they are pointing to.

Iterators are categorized unlike pointers. One can have additional checks before applying an algorithm. For example, one can check whether the sort() algorithm is provided with random access iterators or not. Thus, one can prevent the user from calling sort() with the list container.

It is an important design principle to have loose coupling between the components involved. STL container objects that interact with generic algorithms can identify only iterators. For example, if a vector v has been defined and a function v.find(...) is invoked, it returns the iterator that points to the element being searched in that container. Similarly, if there is a list 1, then 1.find(...) returns an integrator pointing to the element of the list that is being searched. The algorithm only returns the iterator that the programmer manipulates later on. Iterators being generic, the find() function need not worry about the container calling it, and neither should the container worry about the design of find().

Exhibit 16.3 states the advantages of STL containers.

16.6 CONTAINERS AND THEIR TYPES

Containers are objects that contain other objects. They are of two different types, namely, *sequence containers* and *sorted associative containers*.

An STL container can be either a sequence container or a sorted associative container.

1. A sequence container stores the elements in a sequence of some sort. Examples include vectors, deques, and lists.

2. Unlike sequence containers, an *associative sorted container* keeps the contents in a sorted form. Examples include sets, multisets, maps, and multimaps.

16.6.1 Vectors

Let us consider Program 16.1, which shows how a vector can be defined and used in a simple way.

PROGRAM 16.1 Vectors

```cpp
#include <vector>
#include <iostream>
#include <string>
using namespace std;

class Student
{
    int RollNumber;
    string Name;
public:
    Student(int TempRollNumber, string TempName)
    {
        RollNumber = TempRollNumber;
        Name = TempName;
    }

    bool operator < (Student AnotherStudent)
    {
        return(RollNumber < AnotherStudent.RollNumber);
    }

    friend ostream & operator <<(ostream & TempOut, Student TempStud)
    {
        TempOut << "Roll number is: " << TempStud.RollNumber << endl;
        TempOut << "Name is: " << TempStud.Name << endl;
    }
};
```

```
int main()
{
    vector <Student> vs;
    vector <int> vi;

    vi.push_back(12); // Inserting at the end of vector
    vi.push_back(20); vi.push_back(16);
    vi.push_back(29); vi.push_back(24);
    Student Lara(1, "Brian Charles Lara");
    Student Beckham(2, "David Beckham");
    Student Steffi(3, "Steffi Graf");
    Student Maradona(4, "Diego Maradona");
    Student Tiger(5, "Tiger Woods");
    Student Carl(6, "Carl Lewis");

    vs.push_back(Lara); vs.push_back(Beckham);
    vs.push_back(Steffi); vs.push_back(Maradona);
    vs.push_back(Tiger); vs.push_back(Carl);

    vector <int>::iterator IntIndex;
    vector <Student>::iterator StudentIndex;
    cout << "Integer vector listing" << endl;

    for(IntIndex = vi.begin(); IntIndex < vi.end(); IntIndex++)
    {
        cout << *IntIndex << endl;
    }
    cout << "Student vector listing" << endl;
    for(StudentIndex = vs.begin(); StudentIndex < vs.end(); StudentIndex++)
    {
        cout << *StudentIndex;
    }
}
```

Output
```
Integer vector listing
12
20
16
29
24

Student vector listing
Roll number is: 1
Name is: Brian Charles Lara
Roll number is: 2
Name is: David Beckham
Roll number is: 3
Name is: Steffi Graf
Roll number is: 4
Name is: Diego Maradona
Roll number is: 5
Name is: Tiger Woods
Roll number is: 6
Name is: Carl Lewis
```

How the Program Works

Look at the **include** statements. <vector> needs to be included to use the vector container.
Next, the Student class is defined. The important part is the < operator and the << operator

being overloaded. We will discuss their usefulness soon. Two vectors are defined in `main()`.

```
vector <Student> vs;
vector <int> vi;
```

vs is a vector of **Student** type and **vi** is of **int** type. Note that vector is a class template and the data type needs to be passed to it as an argument enclosed within <> brackets.

Next, data is inserted in the `int` vector. An important function for vectors is `push_back()`, which inserts the element at the end of the vector. If the vector is full, unlike an array, it extends itself and then accommodates that value.

A few `Student` objects are then defined and inserted in the same manner in the `Student` vector. It can be seen that the vector `push_back()` function is used in a similar fashion here.

The vector container provides other constructors to define vectors in a different way. It is also possible to access various elements of the vector using the [ ] operator, similar to an array. Next in the example are the iterator definitions.

```
vector <int>::iterator IntIndex;
vector <Student>::iterator
StudentIndex;
```

Here, two different iterators for `int` vector and `Student` vector are defined. They have been used like pointers in the rest of the program.

Vectors provide two useful functions (all containers provide both these functions). The first one is known as `begin()`. It returns the iterator pointing to the first element of the vector. The second one is the `end()` function. This function *does not* return the iterator pointing to the last element. It returns the iterator pointing to the one after the last element. Remember our discussion regarding string objects in Chapter 15 and the return of value that is one more than the size; it is due to this property of the `end()` function. The iterator range ID is denoted as [first, last) in mathematics as open interval.

In this program, both have been used in the `for` loop defined next.

```
for(IntIndex = vi.begin(); IntIndex < vi.end(); IntIndex++)
{
    cout << *IntIndex << endl;
}
```

The statement `IntIndex = vi.begin()` does the initialization. It makes the `IntIndex` iterator pointing to the first element of the `int` vector. Please note that vi, being an `int` vector, returns the iterator of type vector <int>, which is matching with the right-hand side (RHS) (IntIndex = vi.begin()). Similarly, the condition for termination is also checked using the '<' operator (IntIndex < vi.end).

> A vector is a container similar to an array. However, unlike an array, it can grow and shrink and, thus, is not confined to a fixed size.

The vector iterator is a random access iterator. It has < operator overloaded and, hence, can be used here. The increment `IntIndex++` is similar to incrementing the pointer to make it point to the next element in the sequence. This operator is also overloaded for all containers. One can refer to vector elements by dereferencing the iterator. Thus, `*IntIndex` returns an integer, which is printed on the screen.

Similar explanation can be provided for the other `for` loop for `Student` vector. The only difference is the use of `StudentIndex` as an `iterator` of type vector <Student>::iterator rather than vector <int>::iterator in the earlier case.

Note the importance of overloading << for the Student object. cout << *StudentIndex can be written as the << operator is overloaded.

Let us consider one more example to see how a generic algorithm can be used with vector. Program 16.2 shows how Student objects can be sorted on the total mark obtained to print a merit list.

PROGRAM 16.2   Vector with a generic algorithm

```cpp
//MeritList.cpp
#include <iostream>
#include <vector>
#include <algorithm>
using namespace std;
class Student
{
private:
    int RollNumber;
    float TotalMarks;

public:
    Student(){};
    Student(int TempRollNumber, float TempTotalMarks)
    {
        RollNumber = TempRollNumber;
        TotalMarks = TempTotalMarks;
    }

    void operator = (Student TempStud)
    {
        RollNumber = TempStud.RollNumber;
        TotalMarks = TempStud.TotalMarks;
    }

    bool operator < (Student TempStud)
    {
        return(TotalMarks < TempStud.TotalMarks);
    }

    friend ostream & operator <<(ostream & TempOut, Student & TempStud);
};

ostream & operator <<(ostream & TempOut, Student & TempStud)
{
    TempOut << "The mark of roll number " << TempStud.RollNumber << " is " << TempStud.
    TotalMarks;
    return TempOut;
}

void main()
{
    vector <Student> StudMarks;
    float TempMarks;
    int i = 0;

    for(;;)
    {
        cout << "Enter the mark for roll number " << i + 1 << " Enter -1 to stop: ";
        cin >> TempMarks;
        if(TempMarks == -1) break;
        StudMarks.push_back(Student(i + 1, TempMarks));
```

```
        ++i;
    }
    cout << "The size of StudMarks is " << StudMarks.size()<< endl;

    vector <Student>::iterator index;
    sort(StudMarks.begin(), StudMarks.end());

    for(index = StudMarks.begin(); index < StudMarks.end(); ++index)
    cout << *index << endl;
}
```

How the Program Works

We can have a vector with built-in as well as user-defined types as its element. This is true for all containers.

Let us try to understand the program. The Student class is used in this program as well. It is important to note that the operators, = and < have been defined along with the << operator in the class. The Sort() algorithm needs < operator to be overloaded.

The following statement defines a vector StudMarks, which contains the Student objects.

```
vector <Student> StudMarks;
```

Then, there is a for loop, which reads the mark of each student and then uses push_back to insert it in the vector.

A member function size() has been used to find the size of the vector, which is the number of elements in the vector. Thus, the following statement displays number of elements in the vector.

```
cout << "The size of StudMarks is " << StudMarks.size() << endl;
```

The next statement defines an iterator index for vector <Student>. The generic algorithm sort() is called here.

```
sort(StudMarks.begin(), StudMarks.end());
```

The algorithm requires only two arguments; both are of type random access iterators. This sort algorithm is *in-place sort algorithm*. It sorts the very vector that is passed to it. The vector range is provided again as [first, last), which includes all the elements between the first and the last, including the first but not the last.

The printing of the Student data is done next using a similar for loop as seen earlier.

It has been stated earlier that vectors can grow dynamically. Program 16.3 illustrates this property. The function capacity() returns the number of elements a vector can accommodate without *growing*.

PROGRAM 16.3   Growing vector

```
//GrowingVector.cpp
#include <vector>
#include <iostream>
#include <string>
using namespace std;

class Student
{
int RollNumber;
```

```
        string Name;
public:
        Student(int TempRollNumber, string TempName)
        {
            RollNumber = TempRollNumber;
            Name = TempName;
        }
};

int main()
{
        vector <Student> vs;
        vector <int> vi;
        cout << "The capacity of the Student vector is " << vs.capacity() << endl;
        cout << "The capacity of the integer vector is " << vi.capacity() << endl;
        int TempSizeInt = vi.capacity();
        int TempSizeStudent = vs.capacity();
        for(int i = 0; i < 200; i++)
        {
            vi.push_back(i);
            if(vi.capacity() != TempSizeInt)
            {
                cout << "The capacity of the vector changes to " << vi.capacity() << endl;
                TempSizeInt = vi.capacity();
            }
        }

        Student Lara(1, "Brian Charles Lara");
        for(int i = 0; i < 200; i++)
        {
            vs.push_back(Lara);
            if(vs.capacity() != TempSizeStudent)
            {
                cout << "The capacity of the vector changes to " << vs.capacity() << endl;
                TempSizeStudent = vs.capacity();
            }
        }
}
```

Output (in VC++ 7.0)
```
The capacity of the Student vector is 0
The capacity of the integer vector is 0
The capacity of the vector changes to 1
The capacity of the vector changes to 2
The capacity of the vector changes to 3
The capacity of the vector changes to 4
The capacity of the vector changes to 6
The capacity of the vector changes to 9
The capacity of the vector changes to 13
The capacity of the vector changes to 19
The capacity of the vector changes to 28
The capacity of the vector changes to 42
The capacity of the vector changes to 63
The capacity of the vector changes to 94
The capacity of the vector changes to 141
```
The capacity of the vector changes to 211
```
// Student vector output
The capacity of the vector changes to 1
```

```
The capacity of the vector changes to 2
The capacity of the vector changes to 3
The capacity of the vector changes to 4
The capacity of the vector changes to 6
The capacity of the vector changes to 9
The capacity of the vector changes to 13
The capacity of the vector changes to 19
The capacity of the vector changes to 28
The capacity of the vector changes to 42
The capacity of the vector changes to 63
The capacity of the vector changes to 94
The capacity of the vector changes to 141
The capacity of the vector changes to 211

The output from Linux is as follows:
The capacity of the Student vector is 0
The capacity of the integer vector is 0
The capacity of the vector changes to 1
The capacity of the vector changes to 2
The capacity of the vector changes to 4
The capacity of the vector changes to 8
The capacity of the vector changes to 16
The capacity of the vector changes to 32
The capacity of the vector changes to 64
The capacity of the vector changes to 128
The capacity of the vector changes to 256

// Student vector output
The capacity of the vector changes to 1
The capacity of the vector changes to 2
The capacity of the vector changes to 4
The capacity of the vector changes to 8
The capacity of the vector changes to 16
The capacity of the vector changes to 32
The capacity of the vector changes to 64
The capacity of the vector changes to 128
The capacity of the vector changes to 256
```

How the Program Works

Let us try to understand this program and its outputs. It has a Student vector and an int vector similar to Program 16.1. vi.capacity() and vs.capacity() have been used to find the capacity of both the vectors and an integer TempSizeInt is used to calculate their capacity. The program uses vi.push_back(i) to insert an int object in the int vector vi and vs.push_back(Lara) to insert a Student object in the Student vector vs. If the capacity of the vector now is different from the earlier capacity, the new capacity is displayed. Then, it continues to add 200 elements in the vector in both cases.

A vector's capacity increases when it is full and insertion is attempted. It automatically manages the growth. The way a vector grows depends on the specific compiler.

Now, look at the output produced by two different compilers that the program was tested on. The first compiler is VC++ 7.0. The vector here grows arbitrarily. The output from Linux compiler is far more straightforward. Every time a vector is full, its size is doubled. Note that for a built-in type or a user-defined class, the growth is similar. It may be different for large class objects.

16.6.2 List

List is the next container type, which is a templatized implementation of doubly linked list. It is easy to learn another container after the first, as the way one can manipulate containers is quite similar. Let us look at an example where the vector has been replaced by a list, except at one place. Program 16.4 prints the merit list, now using a list rather than a vector.

PROGRAM 16.4   STL list object

```cpp
//MeritList.cpp
#include <iostream>
#include <list>
#include <algorithm>
using namespace std;

class Student
{
private:
    int RollNumber;
    float TotalMarks;
public:
    Student(){};
    Student(int TempRollNumber, float TempTotalMarks)
    {
        RollNumber = TempRollNumber;
        TotalMarks = TempTotalMarks;
    }

    void operator = (Student TempStud)
    {
        RollNumber = TempStud.RollNumber;
        TotalMarks = TempStud.TotalMarks;
    }

    bool operator < (Student TempStud)
    {
        return(TotalMarks < TempStud.TotalMarks);
    }
    friend ostream & operator <<(ostream & TempOut, Student & TempStud);
};

ostream & operator <<(ostream & TempOut, Student & TempStud)
{
    TempOut << "The mark of roll number " << TempStud.RollNumber << " is " << TempStud.
    TotalMarks;
    return TempOut;
}

void main()
{
    list <Student> StudMarks;
    float TempMarks;
    int i = 0;
    for(;;)
    {
    cout << "Enter mark for roll number " << i + 1 << " Enter -1 to stop: ";
    cin >> TempMarks;
    if(TempMarks == -1) break;
    StudMarks.push_back(Student(i + 1, TempMarks)); ++1
    }
```

```
        cout << "The size of StudMarks is " << StudMarks.size() << endl;
        list <Student>::iterator index;
        for(index = StudMarks.begin(); index != StudMarks.end(); ++index)
        cout << *index << endl;
}
```

Output
```
Enter mark for roll number 1 Enter -1 to stop: 13
Enter mark for roll number 2 Enter -1 to stop: 23
Enter mark for roll number 3 Enter -1 to stop: 34
Enter mark for roll number 4 Enter -1 to stop: 45
Enter mark for roll number 5 Enter -1 to stop: 32
Enter mark for roll number 6 Enter -1 to stop: 23
Enter mark for roll number 7 Enter -1 to stop: 24
Enter mark for roll number 8 Enter -1 to stop: 1
Enter mark for roll number 9 Enter -1 to stop: -1
The size of StudMarks is 8
The mark of roll number 1 is 13
The mark of roll number 2 is 23
The mark of roll number 3 is 34
The mark of roll number 4 is 45
The mark of roll number 5 is 32
The mark of roll number 6 is 23
The mark of roll number 7 is 24
The mark of roll number 8 is 1
```

How the Program Works

The program does the same job as Program 16.4 with only one change in it; `'vector'` is replaced by `'list'` everywhere. The output of the program using the vector has not been given. It is the same as the output given for this program. This shows how easy it is to learn more containers once we learn one .

List vs Vector

Lists seem to work similar to vectors. Why are they provided then? The emphasis is on three operations, namely, insertion, deletion, and access. The list is implemented using a doubly linked list; hence, insertion and deletion at random require reshuffling the pointers alone, and it is very fast. Unfortunately, accessing a random member requires moving to that place from either the beginning or the end, which is not efficient. A list is better when insertion and deletion at random places are to be performed, and access to elements is not done in random but in sequence. This is similar to the advantage of linked list over arrays.

> **Note** Vectors can grow automatically, but it comes with a cost. Extending a vector is similar to having a new large vector and copying the old vector elements in it. This is a *linear time operation*, that is, the time of insertion depends on the number of elements in the vector. On the other hand, growth in a list is a *constant time operation*, that is, the time of insertion remains constant irrespective of the number of elements to be inserted.

Table 16.2 lists the differences between a vector and a list.

There is a difference between Programs 16.4 and 16.2. The `for` loop does not contain test such as `index < StudMarks.end()` because operator `'<'` is not overloaded for bidirectional iterators provided by the list. It is only available for random access iterators. Fortunately, there is the inequality operator `'!='` overloaded for bidirectional operators. Thus, the `'!='`

Table 16.2 Differences between vector and list

Criterion	Vector	List
Insertion time	Depends on the number of elements	Constant
Access time	Constant	Depends on traversal time
Extension	Liner time operation	Constant time
Library	<vector>	<list>
Size	Increase when full	No such issue
Best when	Random access	Random insertion or deletion
Storage	Contiguous locations	Non-contiguous; based on insertion and deletion patterns
Implementation	Array type	Doubly linked list with two pointers for each node
Management of insertion and deletion	Rearranging elements	Rearranging pointers

Technically, the '!=' operator is available to input iterators, which is the lowest level of iterators, and thus, it is available to all the other containers too.

operator has been used here instead of '<'. This is not actually a big difference. The '!=' operator could have been used in Program 16.2. It was done here to show the difference between iterators, algorithms, and the containers using them.

Program 16.5 uses list because insertion at random place is most efficient in this case as it will have to manipulate only two pointers instead of shifting all the remaining elements downwards as in the vector.

PROGRAM 16.5 Inserting at a specific location in a list

```cpp
//ListInsert.cpp
#include <list>
#include <iostream>
#include <string>
#include <algorithm>

// For find()
using namespace std;

class Student
{
    int RollNumber;
    string Name;
public:
    Student(int TempRollNumber, string TempName)
    {
        RollNumber = TempRollNumber;
        Name = TempName;
    }

    bool operator < (Student AnotherStudent)
    {
```

```
            return(RollNumber < AnotherStudent.RollNumber);
        }
        friend ostream & operator <<(ostream & TempOut, Student TempStud)
        {
            TempOut << "Roll number is: " << TempStud.RollNumber << endl;
            TempOut << "Name is: " << TempStud.Name << endl;
        }
        // Essential for find() to work
        bool operator == (Student AnotherStudent)
        {
            return(RollNumber == AnotherStudent.RollNumber);
        }
};
int main()
{
    list <Student> ls;
    list <int> li;
    li.push_back(12);
    li.push_back(20);
    li.push_back(16);
    li.push_back(29);
    li.push_back(24);

    Student Lara(1, "Brian Charles Lara");
    Student Beckham(2, "David Beckham");
    Student Steffi(3, "Steffi Graf");
    Student Maradona(4, "Diego Maradona");
    Student Tiger(5, "Tiger Woods");
    Student Carl(6, "Carl Lewis");
    ls.push_back(Lara);
    ls.push_back(Beckham);
    ls.push_back(Steffi); ls.push_back(Maradona);
    ls.push_back(Tiger); ls.push_back(Carl);

    list <int>::iterator IntIndex;
    list <Student>::iterator StudentIndex;
    for(IntIndex = li.begin(); IntIndex != li.end(); IntIndex++)
    {
        cout << *IntIndex << endl;
    }

    /* The following is the most efficient operation in the list container: adding at
    arbitrary place */
    Student Jaspal(7, "Jaspal Rana");
    StudentIndex = find(ls.begin(), ls.end(), Maradona);
    ls.insert(StudentIndex, Jaspal);

    for(StudentIndex = ls.begin(); StudentIndex != ls.end(); StudentIndex++)
    {
        cout << *StudentIndex;
    }
}
```

How the Program Works

In this program, the following three statements are important to us at the moment.

```
Student Jaspal(7, "Jaspal Rana");
```

A list can insert or delete an element just by rearranging the pointers, which is a constant time operation.

```
StudentIndex = find(ls.begin(), ls.end(), Maradona);
ls.insert(StudentIndex, Jaspal);
```

A new student Jaspal has been defined. The find() algorithm is used to get the iterator that points to Maradona. Next, Jaspal is inserted there using a member function insert() for list (ls.insert()). Here, the iterator is used like a file pointer for having seek-like operation. The insert() member function is available with all the containers.

> **Note** List is the only container where insertion is a constant time operation irrespective of the location. A vector has constant time operation for insertion in the end and deque at the beginning and the end, but not at any location.

16.6.3 Deque

Deque, pronounced 'deck', is a useful container adapted into two other containers, namely, the stack and the queue. We are not going to discuss stacks and queues in this text, but they are as easy to work with as deques. Let us understand how a deque works with the help of Program 16.6.

PROGRAM 16.6 Deques

```cpp
//DeQueue.cpp
#include <deque>
#include <iostream>
#include <string>
using namespace std;
class Student
{
    int RollNumber;
    string Name;
public:
    Student(int TempRollNumber, string TempName)
    {
        RollNumber = TempRollNumber;
        Name = TempName;
    }

    bool operator < (Student AnotherStudent)
    {
        return(RollNumber < AnotherStudent.RollNumber);
    }

    friend ostream & operator <<(ostream & TempOut, Student & TempStud)
    {
        TempOut << "Roll number is: " << TempStud.RollNumber << endl;
        TempOut << "Name is: " << TempStud.Name << endl;
        return TempOut;
    }
};

int main()
{
    deque <Student> ds;
    Student Lara(1, "Brian Charles Lara");
    Student Beckham(2, "David Beckham");
    Student Steffi(3, "Steffi Graf");
    Student Maradona(4, "Diego Maradona");
```

```
        Student Tiger(5, "Tiger Woods");
        Student Carl(6, "Carl Lewis");
        ds.push_front(Lara);
        ds.push_front(Beckham);
        ds.push_front(Steffi);
        ds.push_front(Maradona);
        ds.push_front(Tiger);
        ds.push_front(Carl);
        deque <Student>::iterator StudentIndex;

        for(StudentIndex = ds.begin(); StudentIndex < ds.end(); StudentIndex++)
        {
            cout << *StudentIndex;
        }
}
```

Output
```
Roll number is: 6
Name is: Carl Lewis
Roll number is: 5
Name is: Tiger Woods
Roll number is: 4
Name is: Diego Maradona
Roll number is: 3
Name is: Steffi Graf
Roll number is: 2
Name is: David Beckham
Roll number is: 1
Name is: Brian Charles Lara
```

How the Program Works

> Deque is a structure that allows insertion at the end as well as at the beginning in constant time.

> push_front() with a constant time function is a unique feature of deque.

This program is similar to Program 16.2 where the names of different students have been entered and have been printed at the end. However, there is an important difference. The push_front() function has been used instead of the push_back() function in vectors. Deque is a structure where insertion at the end as well as at the beginning is possible to be done in constant time. List is the other container where insertions at the beginning take constant time. Both these containers (deque and list) provide push_front() function.

The push_front() function adds at the beginning; hence, the data entered is printed in the reverse order. A statement such as the following is possible for deque and list; for other containers, it results in a compile-time error.

```
ds.push_front(Lara);
```

There is a need for a container that always remains sorted. All database indexes are of this type. Any form of indexing mechanism needs a solution by which the index always remains sorted, irrespective of the insertions and deletions made. Sorted associative containers help us to achieve this.

16.6.4 Sorted Associative Containers

Sorted associative containers are containers where the content is always sorted, irrespective of the order of insertions and deletions. Every element, when inserted, is inserted at the exact place where it is to be inserted in the sorted order.

An important requirement for insertion in sorted associative container is that the object that is inserted must obey some form of ordering. This ordering can be achieved by overloading `operator < () const` for each of the objects that is to be inserted in these sorted associative containers.

The operator function must be defined as `const`. It is also important to note that these containers are also associative, and an element of the record can be used to access the entire record.

A *sequence container* element is accessed by the index or position of the element (similar to an array), whereas a *sorted associative container* element is accessed by a key value, which is a part of the element, similar to indexed sequential files. However, sorted associative container also allows sequential operation.

> **Note** Associative containers are named so because they help accessing elements in an associative manner rather than indexed manner. Associative search is quite usual in human processing system. It is common for us to hear a few bars of music associated with a specific song and recall that song rather than being provided with information such as the name of the movie and singer and then recalling it.

16.6.5 Maps

We are going to look at map first, which is a container that can have two items, namely, a key and a value stored in itself. It is automatically sorted on the key item at the time of insertion. As mentioned earlier, the key item must have some form of ordering. For user-defined objects, it is important to overload `operator <` as `const` to have the ordering.

Let us look at Program 16.7 first. There are two items; the first is a `Student` object, used as a key, and the second (the value) is an integer. As mentioned earlier, the `Student` object must observe some order. The order here is maintained on the basis of the total mark the student possesses. Thus, it is possible to have the merit list. The perception of ordering depends on the context. If one wants a roll-call to be programmed, maybe the roll number is the key in ordering, or if students list is to be printed namewise, the name of the student may form the key for ordering.

> Map is a container with a pair of items, namely, a key and a value stored in a sorted order of key.

PROGRAM 16.7 Map

```cpp
//Map.cpp
#include <map>
#include <string>
#include <iostream>
#include <algorithm>
using namespace std;
class Student
{
private:
    int RollNumber;
    float TotalMarks;

public:
    Student(){};
    Student(int TempRollNumber, float TempTotalMarks)
    {
        RollNumber = TempRollNumber;
        TotalMarks = TempTotalMarks;
    }

    bool operator < (Student TempStud) const
```

```
        // Without const, it will not work with map
        {
            return(TotalMarks < TempStud.TotalMarks);
        }
        friend ostream & operator <<(ostream & TempOut, Student & TempStud);
};

int main()
{
    map <string, float> StudentData;
    StudentData["Lara"] = 12000;
    StudentData["Sachin"] = 11000;
    StudentData["Sunil"] = 10500;

    Student Lara(1, 65);
    Student Sachin(2, 55);
    Student Sunil(3, 60);

    map <Student, float> StudClassData;
    StudClassData[Lara] = 12000;
    StudClassData[Sachin] = 11000;
    StudClassData[Sunil] = 10500;
}
```

> **Note** A map allows a programmer to use other types of indexes, besides the integer index.

How the Program Works

It should be noted that `<map>` needs to be included for both map and multimap. The difference between map and multimap is that map can only have one record with a single key whereas multimap can have multiple records with a single key. Map and multimap are designed to have a pair of values, namely, a key and a value. Insertion in the map is done using array-like notation. The following is a statement for defining map with the string object.

```
map <string, float> StudentData;
```

`StudentData` is now a map with two items; `string` is the key and `float` is the value. The following is the definition for the `StudClassData` map.

```
map <Student, float> StudClassData;
```

`StudClassData` is a map with two items; `Student` object is the key and `float` is the value. The [] operator can be used for insertion in both the maps, as shown in the following examples.

```
StudentData["Lara"] = 12000; // String is the key
StudClassData[Lara] = 12000; // Student class object is the key
```

It is also possible to use insert member function instead of []. Program 16.8 shows the form of insert function for multimap. Map and multimap both have the same syntax for insertion. Multimap retains the key and the old value pair when a key and a new value pair is inserted.

Unlike maps, a multimap does not provide the simpler notation of []. One must use a pair < > to insert a function.

16.6.6 Multimap

Multimap is a container that can have entry with multiple values for a single key. Program 16.8 demonstrates the use of multimap. The insert method is being used for inserting an element. This method is also possible with map as discussed in Section 16.6.5. It is important to note that the [] operator is not available for multimap, and hence, the insert method must be used to insert an element.

 **PROGRAM 16.8** Multimap

```cpp
//MultiMap.cpp
#include <map>
#include <string>
#include <iostream>
#include <algorithm>
using namespace std;

class Student
{
private:
    int RollNumber;
    float TotalMarks;

public:
    Student(){};
    Student(int TempRollNumber, float TempTotalMarks)
    {
        RollNumber = TempRollNumber;
        TotalMarks = TempTotalMarks;
    }

    /* Without const, it will not work with multimap */
    bool operator < (Student TempStud) const
    {
        return(TotalMarks < TempStud.TotalMarks);
    }

    // For cout Student objects
    friend ostream & operator <<(ostream & TempOut, const Student & TempStud)
    {
        TempOut << "Roll number is:" << TempStud.RollNumber << endl;
        TempOut << "Total mark is:" << TempStud.TotalMarks << endl;
        return TempOut;
    }
};

int main()
{
    Student Lara(1, 65);
    Student Sachin(2, 55);
    Student Sunil(3, 60);

    multimap <Student, float> StudClassData;

    StudClassData.insert(pair<Student, float>(Lara, 12000));
    StudClassData.insert(pair<Student, float>(Sachin, 11000));
    StudClassData.insert(pair<Student, float>(Sunil, 10500));
    StudClassData.insert(pair<Student, float>(Lara, 12001));
    StudClassData.insert(pair<Student, float>(Sachin, 11001));
    StudClassData.insert(pair<Student, float>(Sunil, 10501));

    multimap <Student, float>::iterator Position;

    for(Position = StudClassData.begin(); Position != StudClassData.end(); Position++)
    {
        cout << Position->first;
        cout << "Runs scored are:";
        cout << Position->second;
        cout << endl;
```

```
        }
}
```

Output
```
Roll number is: 2
Total mark is: 55
Runs scored are: 11000
Roll number is: 2
Total mark is: 55
Runs scored are: 11001
Roll number is: 3
Total mark is: 60
Runs scored are: 10500
Roll number is: 3
Total mark is: 60
Runs scored are: 10501
Roll number is: 1
Total mark is: 65
Runs scored are: 12000
Roll number is: 1
Total mark is: 65
Runs scored are: 12001
```

How the Program Works

In this program, #include <map> has been used. This is necessary for both maps and multimaps.

The Student class definition has nothing new. Note the need for operator < () const as for map. Moreover, << has also been overloaded for simplifying the display of Student object. The following is the definition of multimap:

```
multimap <Student, float> StudClassData;
```

This definition is similar to map definition that was seen in Program 16.7. A pair of elements has been inserted in the multimap using the statement

```
StudClassData.insert(pair<Student, float>(Lara, 12000));
```

The insert member function expects a pair object to be inserted. Pair is a template class provided by STL. It needs explicit argument specification such as <Student, float> in StudClassData.insert(pair<Student, float>(Lara, 12000));

The first element in the pair class is known as first and second element is known as second. The StudClassData elements are all pairs with the first item as Student and the second item as float value. Next, an iterator for the map is defined by using the following statement:

```
multimap <Student, float>::iterator Position;
```

It is important to note that the iterator is pointing to multimap elements, and each element is a pair. Thus, Position->first is the first element of the Student object and Position->second is the second element (the float value). Now, there is a simple for loop from the beginning to the end of the multimap to print both the elements of the pair.

```
for(Position = StudClassData.begin(); Position != StudClassData.end(); Position++)
{
    cout << Position->first;
```

```
        cout << "Runs scored are:";
        cout << Position->second;
        cout << endl;
    }
```

The << operator has been overloaded for the Student object. Hence, the statement

```
cout << Position->first;
```

works without any problem, as Position->first returns a Student object.

Now, look at the output. As each data has been entered twice, there are two entries for each data. If a map had been used instead, there would have been only one copy for each of them.

16.6.7 Sets

A set is a collection of keys in a sorted order.

The set is a collection of keys in a sorted form. When one is interested only in verifying whether a key is valid, one can use sets. All keys can be inserted and when the key is referenced, it can be seen whether the key belongs to an inserted data or not. Program 16.9 explains this concept.

PROGRAM 16.9   Sets

```
//Set.cpp
#include <set>
#include <vector>
#include <iostream>
#include <string>
using namespace std;

class Student
{
    int RollNumber;
    string Name;

public:
    Student(int TempRollNumber, string TempName)
    {
        RollNumber = TempRollNumber;
        Name = TempName;
    }

    friend ostream & operator <<(ostream & TempOut, Student & TempStud)
    // For cout Student objects
    {
        TempOut << "Roll number is: " << TempStud.RollNumber << endl;
        TempOut << "Name is: " << TempStud.Name << endl;
        return TempOut;
    }

    // This const is must for set
    bool operator < (Student AnotherStudent) const
    {
        return(RollNumber < AnotherStudent.RollNumber);
    }
};
int main()
{
```

```
        vector <Student> vs;

        Student Lara(1, "Brian Charles Lara");
        Student Beckham(2, "David Beckham");
        Student Steffi(3, "Steffi Graf");
        Student Maradona(4, "Diego Maradona");
        Student Tiger(5, "Tiger Woods");
        Student Carl(6, "Carl Lewis");

        vs.push_back(Lara);
        vs.push_back(Beckham);
        vs.push_back(Steffi);
        vs.push_back(Maradona);
        vs.push_back(Tiger);
        vs.push_back(Carl);
        // Inserting the same data second time
        vs.push_back(Lara);
        vs.push_back(Beckham);
        vs.push_back(Steffi);
        vs.push_back(Maradona);
        vs.push_back(Tiger);
        vs.push_back(Carl);

        set <Student> SetStudent;

        vector <Student>::iterator StudentIndex;

        for(StudentIndex = vs.begin(); StudentIndex < vs.end(); StudentIndex++)
        {
            SetStudent.insert(*StudentIndex);
        }

        set <Student>::iterator SetStudentIndex;
        for(SetStudentIndex   =   SetStudent.begin();   SetStudentIndex   !=   SetStudent.end();
        SetStudentIndex++)
        {
            cout << *SetStudentIndex ;
        }
}
```

Output
```
Roll number is: 1
Name is: Brian Charles Lara
Roll number is: 2
Name is: David Beckham
Roll number is: 3
Name is: Steffi Graf
Roll number is: 4
Name is: Diego Maradona
Roll number is: 5
Name is: Tiger Woods
Roll number is: 6
Name is: Carl Lewis
```

How the Program Works

Let us try to understand this program. It should be noted that `<set>` has to be included for using sets. The following statement defines a set of `Student`.

```
set <Student> SetStudent;
```

In the program, first, there is a vector with some students data entered using the push_back() function that we've seen earlier. The following loop is executed using the vector iterator.

> A set uses insert function to insert a key in the set.

```
for(StudentIndex = vs.begin(); StudentIndex < vs.end(); StudentIndex++)
{
    SetStudent.insert(*StudentIndex);
}
```

> A set accepts only one copy of the key. If the key is inserted twice, the set will retain only one copy.

The insert member function of the set is called for SetStudent object. The item inserted is obtained by dereferencing the vector iterator StudentIndex. It is known that this vector is of Student objects. Thus, *StudentIndex is a Student object itself and is possible to be inserted in SetStudent. Now, the set is traversed using the set iterator and all the elements (the Student objects stored in SetStudent) are printed. The following two statements define an iterator and traverse the set to do so.

```
set <Student>::iterator SetStudentIndex;
for(SetStudentIndex = SetStudent.begin(); SetStudentIndex != SetStudent.end();
SetStudentIndex++)
{
    cout << *SetStudentIndex ;
}
```

The coding of a set is similar to the printing of vector or list elements using vector or list iterators. An important part to be observed is the output. The data of about six students has been inserted *twice*. The output shows only a single copy of them. This is because the set stores only a single copy. If multiple copies of a single item are needed, multiset, which is discussed in Section 16.6.8, should be used.

> Multisets are similar to sets except the case that multiple key entries result in multiple keys inserted. Thus, multiset is a set with multiple key values possible.

16.6.8 Multiset

A set can only have a single copy of a key. If more than one key is required, one needs to use a multiset. Program 16.10 uses a multiset instead of a set. The program has just one change from Program 16.9. The output is very different though. Have a look at the program.

PROGRAM 16.10   Multiset

```
//MultiSet.cpp
#include <set>
#include <vector>
#include <iostream>
#include <string>
using namespace std;

class Student
{
    int RollNumber;
    string Name;
public:
    Student(int TempRollNumber, string TempName)
    {
        RollNumber = TempRollNumber;
        Name = TempName;
```

```
        }

        // For cout Student objects
        friend ostream & operator <<(ostream & TempOut, Student & TempStud)
        {
            TempOut << "Roll number is: " << TempStud.RollNumber << endl;
            TempOut << "Name is: " << TempStud.Name << endl;
            return TempOut;
        }

        // This const is must for set
        bool operator < (Student AnotherStudent) const
        {
            return(RollNumber < AnotherStudent.RollNumber);
        }
};

int main()
{
    vector <Student> vs;

    Student Lara(1, "Brian Charles Lara");
    Student Beckham(2, "David Beckham");
    Student Steffi(3, "Steffi Graf");
    Student Maradona(4, "Diego Maradona");
    Student Tiger(5, "Tiger Woods");
    Student Carl(6, "Carl Lewis");

    vs.push_back(Lara); vs.push_back(Beckham);
    vs.push_back(Steffi); vs.push_back(Maradona);
    vs.push_back(Tiger); vs.push_back(Carl);

    // Inserting the same data the second time
    vs.push_back(Lara); vs.push_back(Beckham);
    vs.push_back(Steffi); vs.push_back(Maradona);
    vs.push_back(Tiger); vs.push_back(Carl);
    multiset <Student> SetStudent;
    vector <Student>::iterator StudentIndex;

    for(StudentIndex = vs.begin(); StudentIndex < vs.end(); StudentIndex++)
    {
        SetStudent.insert(*StudentIndex);
    }
    multiset <Student>::iterator SetStudentIndex;

    for(SetStudentIndex  =  SetStudent.begin();  SetStudentIndex  !=  SetStudent.end();
    SetStudentIndex++)
    {
        cout << *SetStudentIndex ;
    }
}

Output
Roll number is: 1
Name is: Brian Charles Lara
Roll number is: 1
Name is: Brian Charles Lara
Roll number is: 2
Name is: David Beckham
Roll number is: 2
Name is: David Beckham
```

```
Roll number is: 3
Name is: Steffi Graf
Roll number is: 3
Name is: Steffi Graf
Roll number is: 4
Name is: Diego Maradona
Roll number is: 4
Name is: Diego Maradona
Roll number is: 5
Name is: Tiger Woods
Roll number is: 5
Name is: Tiger Woods
Roll number is: 6
Name is: Carl Lewis
Roll number is: 6
Name is: Carl Lewis
```

How the Program Works

This program differs from Program 16.9 in the following statement.

```
multiset <Student> SetStudent;
```

Other statements remain the same. Now, look at the output. When all keys have been inserted twice, there are two copies of each. As can be seen, output is sorted, and hence, duplicate keys are displayed together.

16.6.9 Adapted Containers

Stack and queue are adapted containers. A stack can be defined using stack <int> or stack <Student> and can have push() and pop() operations. Similarly, one can have queue <int> or queue <Student> and also have push() and pop() operations on it.

These containers are implemented using deque. They can also be implemented using other sequence containers.

16.7 GENERIC ALGORITHMS

In this section, we will look at a sample of algorithms from STL. An explanation for each of the algorithms provided by STL is out of scope of this introductory text.

16.7.1 find() Algorithm

find() is a generic algorithm to find an element in the container by traversing the container in *sequence*. Consider Program 16.11.

 **PROGRAM 16.11** find() algorithm

```
//Find.cpp
#include <vector>
#include <list>
#include <deque>
#include <algorithm>
#include <iostream>
#include <string>
using namespace std;
```

```
class Student
{
    int RollNumber;
    string Name;
public:
    Student(int TempRollNumber, string TempName)
    {
        RollNumber = TempRollNumber;
        Name = TempName;
    }

    bool operator == (Student AnotherStudent) const
    {
        return(RollNumber == AnotherStudent.RollNumber);
    }

    friend ostream & operator <<(ostream & TempOut, Student TempStud)
    {
        TempOut << "Roll number is: " << TempStud.RollNumber << endl;
        TempOut << "Name is: " << TempStud.Name << endl;
    }
};

int main()
{
    vector <Student> vs;
    int IntArray[6];

    for(int i = 0; i < 6; i++)
    {
        IntArray[i] = i;
    }

    Student Lara(1, "Brian Charles Lara");
    Student Beckham(2, "David Beckham");
    Student Steffi(3, "Steffi Graf");
    Student Maradona(4, "Diego Maradona");
    Student Tiger(5, "Tiger Woods");
    Student Carl(6, "Carl Lewis");
    vs.push_back(Lara); vs.push_back(Beckham);
    vs.push_back(Steffi); vs.push_back(Maradona);
    vs.push_back(Tiger); vs.push_back(Carl);

    // Using find for vector
    vector <Student>::iterator StudentIndex;
    StudentIndex = find(vs.begin(), vs.end(), Maradona);
    cout << *StudentIndex;
    // Using find for integer array
    int *pos = find(IntArray, IntArray + 6, 3);
    cout << *pos << endl;

    // Using find for a list
    list <Student> ls(vs.begin(), vs.end());

    // Creating list from a vector data
    list <Student>::iterator ListIndex;
    ListIndex = find(ls.begin(), ls.end(), Tiger);
    cout << *ListIndex;

    // Using find for a deque
    deque <Student> ds(vs.begin(), vs.end());
```

```
    // Creating deque from a vector data
    deque <Student>::iterator DeqIndex;
    DeqIndex = find(ds.begin(), ds.end(), Steffi);
    cout << *DeqIndex;
}
```

How the Program Works

Let us try to understand the program, which includes vector, list, and deque. It can be seen that the same find() algorithm works for each of them. To enable to access find(), the program also includes <algorithm>. For find() to work on a Student object, the == operator needs to be overloaded, which has been done in the Student class. The function needs to compare each element of the container with the passed argument. This comparison is not possible for user-defined objects unless == is overloaded.

> find(), similar to other generic algorithms, can be called in a similar manner irrespective of the container involved. Only iterators differ according to the container involved.

Since the other statements of the programs have been encountered by us earlier, we will look only at the calls to the find() algorithm:

```
int *pos = find(IntArray, IntArray + 6, 3);
StudentIndex = find(vs.begin(), vs.end(), Maradona);
ListIndex = find(ls.begin(), ls.end(), Tiger);
DeqIndex = find(ds.begin(), ds.end(), Steffi);
```

> A very convenient type of constructors available for all types of container is to provide begin() and end() values of some other type of container, already existing with data.

All the statements look similar. find() takes three arguments; the first two are iterators pointing to some places in the container and the third one is the element to find in that range. find() returns the *same* type of iterator that is passed as the first and second arguments. With integer arrays, it expects integer pointers and returns an integer pointer; in vector case, it expects two vector iterators and returns a vector iterator; and so on. find() can work with all types of containers because the iterators expected are of the category called input iterators, which are supported by all containers.

One more very interesting issue is the use of constructors for containers using the other container, thus producing one container from another. The following statements in turn generate list and deque from a vector range.

```
list <Student> ls(vs.begin(), vs.end());
deque <Student> ds(vs.begin(), vs.end());
```

16.7.2 copy() Algorithm

The following is an example of one more algorithm that is capable of copying data from one container to another. Consider Program 16.12. This algorithm does not require us to overload any operator for user-defined objects.

PROGRAM 16.12   copy() algorithm

```
//Copy.cpp
#include <vector>
#include <list>
#include <deque>
#include <algorithm>
#include <iostream>
```

```cpp
#include <string>
using namespace std;

class Student
{
    int RollNumber;
    string Name;
public:
    Student()
    {
        RollNumber = 0;
    }

    Student(int TempRollNumber, string TempName)
    {
        RollNumber = TempRollNumber;
        Name = TempName;
    }

    friend ostream & operator <<(ostream & TempOut, Student TempStud)
    {
        TempOut << "Roll number is: " << TempStud.RollNumber << endl;
        TempOut << "Name is: " << TempStud.Name << endl;
    }
};

int main()
{
    vector <Student> vs;
    Student Lara(1, "Brian Charles Lara");
    Student Beckham(2, "David Beckham");
    Student Steffi(3, "Steffi Graf");
    Student Maradona(4, "Diego Maradona");
    Student Tiger(5, "Tiger Woods");
    Student Carl(6, "Carl Lewis");

    vs.push_back(Lara); vs.push_back(Beckham);
    vs.push_back(Steffi); vs.push_back(Maradona);
    vs.push_back(Tiger); vs.push_back(Carl);

    // Copy from one vector to another
    vector <Student> AnotherVector(vs.size());
    // This requires default constructor of Student

    // Copy from vector to vector
    copy(vs.begin(), vs.end(), AnotherVector.begin());

    // Copy from vector to list
    list <Student> ls(vs.size());
    copy(vs.begin(), vs.end(), ls.begin());

    // Copy from vector to deque
    deque <Student> ds(vs.size());
    copy(vs.begin(), vs.end(), ds.begin());

    deque <Student>::iterator DeqIndex;
    list <Student>::iterator ListIndex;
    vector <Student>::iterator StudentIndex;

    for(StudentIndex  =  AnotherVector.begin();  StudentIndex  <  AnotherVector.end();
    StudentIndex++)
    {
```

```
        cout << *StudentIndex;
    }
    for(ListIndex = ls.begin(); ListIndex != ls.end(); ListIndex++)
    {
        cout << *ListIndex;
    }
    for(DeqIndex = ds.begin(); DeqIndex != ds.end(); DeqIndex++)
    {
        cout << *DeqIndex;
    }
}
```

How the Program Works

Let us analyse the program, Consider the following statements in the program:

```
// Copy from vector to vector
copy(vs.begin(), vs.end(), AnotherVector.begin());

// Copy from vector to list
list <Student> ls(vs.size());
copy(vs.begin(), vs.end(), ls.begin());

// Copy from vector to deque
deque <Student> ds(vs.size());
copy(vs.begin(), vs.end(), ds.begin());
```

Copy algorithm has three arguments. The first two arguments are the same type of iterators indicating a range of values. The third argument is the place where the range is to be copied. The third iterator can be of a different type than the first two iterators. Let us consider the statement

```
copy(vs.begin(), vs.end(), ls.begin());
```

It contains `vs.begin()` and `vs.end()`, both of which return an iterator of type

```
vector <Student>::iterator
```

> Copy algorithm copies from one container into another; it has three arguments— beginning and end of the first container and beginning of the second container.

The third iterator is of type

```
list <Student>::iterator.
```

`copy()`, similar to `find()`, works the same for all the examples using various containers.

One interesting part of the program is the need for default constructor for the `Student` object. It is required because of the following statement:

```
vector <Student> AnotherVector(vs.size());
```

> `copy()` is a simpler method for copying the contents of one container into another, irrespective of their types.

This statement creates a vector (the `AnotherVector`) of size `vs.size` and requires the values to be default `Student` objects for each element in `AnotherVector`. This demands the default constructor calling for `Student` class. It is important to note that since a parameterized constructor has already been defined, it is the programmer's job to provide the default constructor as well.

16.7.3 `sort()` Algorithm

`sort()` is an important algorithm that sorts the container data using overloaded `'<'` similar to the sorted associative containers for user-defined objects. One may or may not have it `const`. Consider Program 16.13.

PROGRAM 16.13 sort( ) algorithm

```cpp
//Sort.cpp
#include <vector>
#include <deque>
#include <algorithm>
#include <iostream>
#include <string>
using namespace std;

class Student
{
    int RollNumber;
    string Name;
public:
    Student(int TempRollNumber, string TempName)
    {
        RollNumber = TempRollNumber;
        Name = TempName;
    }

    bool operator < (Student AnotherStudent) const
    {
        return(Name < AnotherStudent.Name);
    }

    friend ostream & operator <<(ostream & TempOut, Student TempStud)
    {
        TempOut << "Roll number is: " << TempStud.RollNumber << endl;
        TempOut << "Name is: " << TempStud.Name << endl;
    }
};

int main()
{
    vector <Student> vs;

    Student Lara(1, "Brian Charles Lara");
    Student Beckham(2, "David Beckham");
    Student Steffi(3, "Steffi Graf");
    Student Maradona(4, "Diego Maradona");
    Student Tiger(5, "Tiger Woods");
    Student Carl(6, "Carl Lewis");

    vs.push_back(Lara); vs.push_back(Beckham);
    vs.push_back(Steffi); vs.push_back(Maradona);
    vs.push_back(Tiger); vs.push_back(Carl);

    // Using sort for deque
    deque <Student> ds(vs.begin(), vs.end());
    // Creating deque from a vector data

    cout << "Unsorted deque \n";
    deque <Student>::iterator DeqIndex;
    for(DeqIndex = ds.begin(); DeqIndex != ds.end(); DeqIndex++)
```

```
    {
        cout << *DeqIndex;
    }
    sort(ds.begin(), ds.end());
    cout << "Sorted deque \n";
    for(DeqIndex = ds.begin(); DeqIndex != ds.end(); DeqIndex++)
    {
        cout << *DeqIndex;
    }

    // The following also prints the same
    // Using sort for vector
    vector <Student>::iterator StudentIndex;
    sort(vs.begin(), vs.end());
    for(StudentIndex = vs.begin(); StudentIndex < vs.end(); StudentIndex++)
    {
        cout << *StudentIndex;
    }
}
```

Output
```
Unsorted deque
Roll number is: 1
Name is: Brian Charles Lara
Roll number is: 2
Name is: David Beckham
Roll number is: 3
Name is: Steffi Graf
Roll number is: 4
Name is: Diego Maradona
Roll number is: 5
Name is: Tiger Woods
Roll number is: 6
Name is: Carl Lewis

Sorted deque
Roll number is: 1
Name is: Brian Charles Lara
Roll number is: 2
Name is: David Beckham
Roll number is: 4
Name is: Diego Maradona
Roll number is: 6
Name is: Carl Lewis
Roll number is: 3
Name is: Steffi Graf
Roll number is: 5
Name is: Tiger Woods
```

How the Program Works

The output shows that the data is sorted by name in lexicographical order (the order observed in a book library). The vector output is not shown as it is identical to the deque output. This program has the following statements using the algorithm sort() for sorting deque and a vector.

```
sort(ds.begin(), ds.end());
sort(vs.begin(), vs.end());
```

The output confirms that `sort()` delivers what is asked from it. It takes two arguments and both are iterators of the same type. In this program, both are deque iterators in the first case and vector iterators in the second case. It is important to note that `sort()` requires a different type of iterators than `find()` and `copy()`. It requires random access iterators, which are provided by both vector and deque. A list provides only bidirectional iterators and not random access iterators; hence, it cannot work with `sort()`. A statement such as the following where `ls` is a list produces runtime error.

> A list provides only bidirectional iterators and not random access iterators; hence, it cannot work with `sort()`.

```
sort(ls.begin(), ls.end()) // Erroneous statement
```

Notes

1. If ever it is required to sort the list elements, one can use a member function of list; for example, it is possible for `ls.sort()` to call sort `ls`.
2. By default, `sort()` provides the result in an ascending order. It is possible to change the default behaviour by providing a third argument, which is a function object; it is an object of the class with the `()` operator overloaded. A function object with the return value `bool` is known as a *predicate object*.

Exhibit 16.4 describes allocators.

Exhibit 16.4 Allocators

Containers can grow and shrink as and when required. For automating this dynamic growth, STL has predefined default memory allocation and deallocation mechanism for all the containers and the types of elements. In most of the cases, the default mechanism is good enough.

Allocators are memory management mechanisms. By default, a default allocator is used with the containers. The call to `vector <int>` is actually

```
vector <int, allocator <int>)
```

where the second argument `allocator <int>` determines the memory allocation mechanism for `int` vectors as default. Some other allocators can be passed if the programmers want to manage the memory themselves.

▪ RECAPITULATION ▪

- The Standard Template Library (STL) is different from other libraries.
- STL contains containers, which in turn contain other objects within, and algorithms, which operate containers to do some job.
- Iterators are pointer-like devices that help us in connecting the containers and the algorithms.
- STL-based design follows the concept of object-based programming rather than object-oriented programming.
- Generic programming is a mechanism for designing generic software components and algorithms such that maximum amount of reusability is achieved with maximum efficiency.
- The generic software components used in STL are called containers as they are able to contain other objects within themselves.
- Containers are of two types. The first type, known as sequence containers, is able to hold elements in an unordered form as inserted. The second type of containers is known as sorted associative containers. They keep themselves sorted irrespective of the insertions and deletions taking place on them.

- Sorted associative containers are also of two types. The first type stores only the keys and the second type stores an element as well with the key.
- Containers that only store keys are of two types—set and map. Both these accept only one instance of key in the data.
- If we want multiple entries, we need to use multi-key versions, namely, multiset and multimap.
- Generic algorithms free the programmer to code the core part without worrying about the routines such as sort() and merge() that are to be programmed.
- Iterators provide open design such that we are able to access the elements pointed to by them directly using pointer notations.
- Vector, list, and deque can all have arbitrary length and can expand or shrink when needed.
- New algorithms and containers can be added without being really bothered about other containers or algorithms.
- Algorithms such as find() work the same for all containers, whereas sort() requires random access iterators, which cannot be provided by lists.
- There are containers such as stack and queue, which are implemented in terms of other sequence containers. They are known as adapted containers.

▪ KEYWORDS ▪

Address manipulation approach   This is a pointer-like approach to access elements one by one.

Container   This refers to a software component that can contain other objects.

Functional approach   This refers to file operations such as put() and get() in instances where directly reaching the next element is not possible; a specific function is to be called for that purpose.

Generic algorithms   Non-member functions that are capable of working with many objects of container type are known as generic algorithms.

Generic programming   Programming in a way that the algorithms and the containers are separated in an orthogonal way and adding an algorithm or container is possible with least interoperability problems is known as generic programming.

Iterator   This is a pointer-type object capable of pointing to objects of a specific container.

Sequence containers   These are containers where the values are stored as inserted and not sorted upon insertion.

Sorted associative container   These are containers where the element is sorted upon insertion.

Vector capacity   This refers to the capability of the vector class to accommodate elements without growing.

▪ EXERCISES ▪

Multiple Choice Questions

1. The generic non-member algorithms can be used _____.
   - (a) only with classes
   - (b) only inside member functions
   - (c) with all containers
   - (d) only with generic containers

2. A map can have _____ record(s) with a single key.
   - (a) single
   - (b) two
   - (c) three
   - (d) multiple

3. The function mechanism provides _____.
   - (a) better readability
   - (b) avoidance of complex problems
   - (c) Both (a) and (b)

   - (d) None of the above

4. The pointer-like approach to access elements one by one is called _____.
   - (a) address mechanism approach
   - (b) pointer access approach
   - (c) reference access approach
   - (d) All of the above

5. The storage requirements for STL components is _____.
   - (a) static
   - (b) fixed
   - (c) dynamic
   - (d) None of the above

6. STL uses templates to a large extent to make it as _____ as possible.
   - (a) independent of type

(b) dependent of type

(c) specific

(d) All of the above

7. In map container, the elements are automatically sorted on the _____ at the time of the insertion.

(a) key item

(b) value item

(c) Both (a) and (b)

(d) None of the above

8. _____ is the only container where insertion is a constant time operation irrespective of the location.

(a) List

(b) Vector

(c) Queue

(d) Deque

9. The generic containers and generic algorithms in STL are connected together by _____.

(a) templates

(b) classes

(c) objects

(d) iterators

10. Function object is _____.

(a) an object with a function

(b) a function declaring a local object

(c) a function using a global object

(d) an object of a class with ( ) operator overloaded

Conceptual Exercises

1. What is the difference between STL and other libraries?

2. What is the advantage of using generic algorithms?

3. What is the need for iterators? What is their role in STL?

4. List the different types of containers.

5. What is the need for sorted associative containers? What is the difference between sorted associative containers and sequence containers?

6. What is the advantage of having readymade components?

7. Explain how sequence iterators work.

8. Explain how sorted associative containers work.

9. List the differences between list and vector containers.

10. List the differences between set and map containers.

11. List a few algorithms other than the ones described in this chapter.

Practical Exercises

1. Write a program to use an employee class and then provide the following:

(a) Listing of the employee class in the order of their employee ID

(b) Listing of employees by their name

(c) Sorting employees by their employee ID

(d) Finding an employee based on the residence address

2. Write a program to read details about some players and provide the following:

(a) Data inserted about the player should be sorted by the sport he/she plays and the name of the player at the time of insertion.

(b) It is possible that a player plays more than one game. This is also to be incorporated in the program.

3. Write a program for students to enrol in college-wide contests. A student registered in one contest cannot be registered in another. The data about the students must be sorted by the contest name and student name.

4. Write a program to register employees for a daily function of some sort. Any employee can register at any time. The listing can be in any order. An employee can prefer to register after any other employee of his/her choice.

5. Write a program to read and generate a sequence of projects that are to be completed. Assume the project to be a string. Whenever a new project is inserted, it must be either at the beginning or at the end.

Appendix

Case Study

LEARNING OBJECTIVE

The single objective of this appendix is to apply the concepts studied so far in a real-world application.

A.1 INTRODUCTION

C++ is an important player in designing compilers, operating systems, graphics applications, and networking and communication programs. If we choose a case study from any one of these domains, it would be difficult to understand. Hence, we will work on an example in a domain with which both teachers and students are familiar. The case study that is discussed here by no means gives a complete solution to the problem. A real commercial solution will contain many more features and, more importantly, a graphical user interface (GUI) component for the users to interact with.

One may wonder why C++ does not provide GUI as a built-in component, whereas VB and JAVA provide it. In this book, we have hardly used GUI features in any of the programs. Here are a few reasons:

1. C++ is traditionally considered good for generating dynamic link libraries (DLLs), network level programming (coding TCP/IP-like protocols), and building compilers, operating systems (Windows and Linux have significant parts written in C++), and other application development tools (VB is built using C++). GUI is not a necessary component for building these applications as there is no interaction with the user.
2. Unlike Java, which does not run directly on top of the operating system, or VB, which is confined to a single OS, C++ needs to work with many operating systems. For example, a TCP/IP protocol needs to run on top of multiple operating systems and must be designed in a way that the same program runs on top of any given operating system. GUI requirement hinders that possibility.
3. VC++ is the only exception that is designed to provide GUI, which is only in Windows environment. This design is not a part of the standard and, thus, is not useful elsewhere. The windows GUI model is fairly complex and is not easy for a normal user to work with.
4. Linux environment has a few solutions that provide GUI with C++. They too are complex and are not at all compatible with other solutions.
5. Some lightweight solutions such as `conio` in TC++ and `curses` in Linux are used to confine the output to a specific part of the text. Both `conio` and `curses` are text-based graphics and, therefore, have their own limitations. For example, they cannot have buttons and cannot provide event-driven programming. Even with these limitations, they are quite useful for generating different windows on the screen, and they make the program interface look better. Unfortunately, there are no standards for even these solutions, and hence, they are not recommended.

A.2 MARKS ENTRY PROBLEM

Let us first have a briefing of the problem. Here, a teacher assigns his/her students two sessional examinations, two practical examinations, and a presentation in a given subject. The following points need to be noted:

1. In a given subject, five different types of marks are to be entered. Each type is known as a *head*. Thus, marks are to be entered under five different heads.
2. The teacher should be able to enter marks at any time. Sessional1 marks may be entered when Sessional1 theory answer sheets are checked. Similarly, Sessional2 marks are entered when Sessional2 answer sheets are checked. Practical1 and Practical2 marks are entered immediately after conducting the practical examination.
3. The teacher usually teaches more than one subject. He/she must be able to enter marks according to the subjects and also be able to enter the list of subjects once. He/ she should be able to choose from the subjects for marks entry every time the program is executed.
4. When the program is executed for the first time, it should read the subject and the year of entry. Next, it should read the marks for (usually) Sessional1 marks. Then, the entry is made for some other head; either Sessional2 or Practical1, etc.
5. It is important to get the Sessional1 marks entered earlier to be displayed with new marks. It is also important to tell the user that Sessional1 marks are already entered. Similarly, when the marks of the third head are being entered, the user should be informed that marks of two of the other heads are already entered.
6. The marks should be displayed in a formatted manner when needed.

This problem may look simple, but it is not. Some of the requirements are very challenging to meet.

1. Marks once entered should be available next time and every time. It demands that the marks are to be stored in some form of file.
2. The file that stores the information should be named such that it can be used without the user's intervention.
3. Two different types of files are required for entry of marks. The first file would store all the marks of different students. The second file would store information about the marks themselves (metadata). It stores information such as the subject and the year for which the marks are meant and under which of the five heads are they entered.
4. One more file is needed for storing information about the subjects. This file should be used to display the names of subjects available to select from, when the user starts entering marks.
5. None of these files exist initially, but they would later. When we program, we must understand the difference while dealing with files.
6. For all the marks heads, we can have a single class to store all the information for a single student and then have a vector large enough to hold the data about all the students.
7. Here again, we have to deal with two different types of information; one is related to the roll numbers and marks of each student and the other is related to the subject, year, associated file name, whether marks are entered for each head, and what is being entered currently. All these data are present as a single copy for all bunch of marks objects. We need to define them as static.

8. We need to use menus for the user to select from. Take the case of marks entry. We need to provide choices for the subject for which data is to be entered and also for the head. Both the requirements are different. The subjects are not known a priori. The list of subjects depends on the entry made by the user. We need to have some form of a dynamic menu. This menu is to be generated from the data entered by the user about subjects. The second menu is static and can be generated by simple cout statements.

9. The marks need to be entered for unknown number of students. Without the Standard Template Library (STL), we need either a large array or some form of dynamic memory manipulation. Fortunately, vectors are handy.

Essential Components of the Project

Files and streams Why do we need files? Is our storage in a vector not enough? Unfortunately, it is not possible to use vectors in our case. We need to keep the status of the marks entered between multiple runs of our program. When we are entering Sessional2 marks, Sessional1 marks should be available and so on. The heads that are entered so far and those that are not entered should also be known. When the program is not executing, the values stored in the vector are just lost. It is important to reload the values in the vector when the program is rerun.

Menu-driven program The need for menus is not all that stringent. We can have a program without menus. Menus are used to improve the user interface so that users can easily choose from the given options. A GUI interface might have other types of user interfaces, but text-based interface is almost impossible without menus.

STL vector and student array We could have a normal array in the program instead of vectors. However, the problem is that we have no idea, while writing the program, about the number of students for which marks are to be entered. In such a case, we need to have a very large array or some form of dynamic memory mechanism. Fortunately, we do not need that if we use vectors because they can grow dynamically.

Classes and important functions We have two classes, Marks and Subject, and functions for data entry of marks of a subject and choosing a subject. Displaying the mark sheet is also done by a function. An important non-member function ChooseSubject() is provided for the user to choose subjects and related details.

A.3 PROGRAM CONSTRUCT

Let us now analyse the following code. It is followed by one possible output, which consists of a total of 13 output screenshots.

```cpp
//CaseStudy.cpp
#include <iostream>
#include <fstream>
#include <string>
#include <vector>
#include <list>
#include <algorithm>
#include <cstdlib>
#include <iomanip>
```

```
using namespace std;
// The following is an itoa function for Linux users
// from the website www.jb.man.ac.uk/~slowe/cpp/itoa.html._
// The author is Robert Jan Schaper
char* itoa(int val, int base)
{
   static char buf[32] = {0};
   int i = 30;
   for(; val && i; --i, val /= base)
   buf[i] = "0123456789abcdef"[val % base];
   return &buf[i + 1];
}
enum
ReadingStatus {ReadingSessional1, ReadingSessional2, ReadingPractical1,
ReadingPractical2, ReadingPresentation};
class Marks
{
   // Metadata about Marks
public:
   static ReadingStatus Status;
   static char Sessional1Entered;
   static char Sessional2Entered;
   static char Practical1Entered;
   static char Practical2Entered;
   static char PresentationEntered;
   static string FileName;
   static string Subject;
   static int Year;
   static void GetMetaData();
   // Normal Data
private:
   int RollNo;
   int Sessional1;
   int Sessional2;
   int Practical1;
   int Practical2;
   int Presentation;
   static int CurrentRollNo;
public:
   Marks() : RollNo(0)
   { };
   friend istream & operator >>(istream & TempIn, Marks & TempMarks)
   {
      cout << "\n Enter marks for roll number" << TempMarks.RollNo << " ";
      if(Status == ReadingSessional1)
              TempIn >> TempMarks.Sessional1;
```

```
        if(Status == ReadingSessional2)
                TempIn >> TempMarks.Sessional2;
        if(Status == ReadingPractical1)
                TempIn >> TempMarks.Practical1;
        if(Status == ReadingPractical2)
                TempIn >> TempMarks.Practical2;
        if(Status == ReadingPresentation)
                TempIn >> TempMarks.Presentation;
        return TempIn;
    }
    friend ostream & operator <<(ostream & TempOut, Marks & TempMarks)
    {
        TempOut << setw(12);
        TempOut << TempMarks.RollNo;
        TempOut << setw(12);
        TempOut << TempMarks.Sessional1;
        TempOut << setw(12);
        TempOut << TempMarks.Sessional2;
        TempOut << setw(12);
        TempOut << TempMarks.Practical1;
        TempOut << setw(12);
        TempOut << TempMarks.Practical2;
        TempOut << setw(12);
        TempOut << TempMarks.Presentation;
        TempOut << "\n";
        return TempOut;
    }
    void AssignNextRollNo()
    {
        RollNo = ++CurrentRollNo;
    }
}; // End of class Marks
// Mandatory definitions of static variables
int Marks::CurrentRollNo = 0;
ReadingStatus Marks::Status = ReadingSessional1;
char Marks::Sessional1Entered;
char Marks::Sessional2Entered;
char Marks::Practical1Entered;
char Marks::Practical2Entered;
char Marks::PresentationEntered;
string Marks::Subject = "OOCP";
int Marks::Year = 2007;
char *StringYear = itoa(Marks::Year, 10);
string Marks::FileName = "Marks" + Marks::Subject + StringYear;
void Marks::GetMetaData()
{
```

```cpp
        string ChooseSubject();
        Marks::Subject = ChooseSubject();
        cout << "Please enter the year \n";
        cin >> Marks::Year;
        char *StringYear = itoa(Marks::Year, 10);
        Marks::FileName = "Marks" + Marks::Subject + StringYear;
    }
    class Subject
    {
        int SubjectNo;
        string Name;
    public:
        Subject()
        {
            SubjectNo = 0;
        }
        Subject(int TempSubjectNo, string TempName)
        {
            SubjectNo = TempSubjectNo;
            Name = TempName;
        }
        string getName()
        {
            return Name;
        }
        int getNo()
        {
            return SubjectNo;
        }
        friend istream & operator >>(istream & TempIn, Subject & TempSubject)
        {
            cout << "\n Enter subject no.: ";
            TempIn >> TempSubject.SubjectNo;
            cout <<   "\n Enter name: ";
            TempIn >> TempSubject.Name;
            cout << "\n";
            return TempIn;
        }
        friend ostream & operator <<(ostream & TempOut, Subject & TempSubject)
        {
            TempOut << "Subject no.: ";
            TempOut << TempSubject.SubjectNo;
            TempOut << "\t Name: ";
            TempOut << TempSubject.Name;
            return TempOut;
```

```
      }
}; // End of class Subject
string ChooseSubject()
{
   string SubjectFileName = "Subject";
   ifstream SubjectFile(SubjectFileName, c_str());
   if(!SubjectFile.is_open())
   perror("Subject file open error: ");
   int NoOfSubjects = 0;
   int Choice = 0;
   vector <Subject> Subjects;
   vector <Subject>::iterator SubjectIndex = Subjects.begin();
   while(!SubjectFile.eof())
   {
      int TempNo;
      string TempName;
      SubjectFile >> TempNo;
      SubjectFile >> TempName;
      NoOfSubjects++;
      Subject MCA_Subject_In(TempNo, TempName);
      Subjects.push_back(MCA_Subject_In);
   }
   SubjectFile.close();
   cout << "Total subjects are " << NoOfSubjects << endl;
   while(Choice < 1 || Choice > NoOfSubjects)
   {
      int i;
      for(SubjectIndex = Subjects.begin(), i = 1; SubjectIndex < Subjects.end();
      SubjectIndex++, i++)
      {
            cout << endl << i << "." << SubjectIndex->getName();
      }
      cout << "\n\n Please enter your choice";
      cin >> Choice;
      cout << endl;
   } // End of while
   return Subjects[Choice - 1].getName();
} // End of function ChooseSubject()
// Please add the role of this function
void SubjectEntry()
{
   string SubjectFileName = "Subject";
   ofstream SubjectFile(SubjectFileName, c_str());
   int NoOfSubjects = 0;
   Subject MCA_Subject_Out;
```

```
    cout << "How many subjects? ";
    cin >> NoOfSubjects;
    int i;
    for(i = 0; i < NoOfSubjects; i++)
    {
        cin >> MCA_Subject_Out;
        SubjectFile << MCA_Subject_Out.getNo();
        SubjectFile << " ";
        SubjectFile << MCA_Subject_Out.getName();
        /* Except the last record, add a space to separate the records */
        if(i + 1 < NoOfSubjects)
                SubjectFile << " ";
    }
    SubjectFile.close();
} // End of function SubjectEntry()
int main()
{
    void SubjectEntry();
    void MarksEntry();
    void DisplayMarks();
    int Choice = 0;
    while(Choice != 4)
    {
        cout << "1. Enter subjects "<< endl;
        cout << "2. Enter marks " << endl;
        cout << "3. Display marks for a given subject for a specific year " << endl;
        cout << "4. Exit" << endl;
        cin >> Choice;
        switch(Choice)
        {
                case 1: SubjectEntry(); break;
                case 2: MarksEntry(); break;
                case 3: DisplayMarks(); break;
                case 4: exit(0);
                default: continue;
        }
    }
    return 0;
} // End of main
// Marks entry for a given subject and exam
void MarksEntry()
{
    vector <Marks> StudMarks;
    char Answer;
    cout << "Do you want to enter marks for subject";
```

```
cout << "other than OOCP for the year 2007? ";
cin >> Answer;
if(Answer =='y')
{
    Marks::GetMetaData(); cout << Marks::FileName;
}
bool NewFile = false;
int NoOfRecords = 0;
Marks DummyMarks;
fstream MarkStatus;
ofstream NewMarkStatus;
fstream MarksFile;
ofstream NewMarksFile;
MarksFile.open(Marks::FileName.c_str(), ios::in | ios::out | ios::binary);
if(!MarksFile.is open())
{
    NewFile = true;
    NewMarksFile.open(Marks::FileName.c_str(), ios::out | ios::binary);
    if(!NewMarksFile.is_open())
            perror("New marks file cannot be opened:);
    NewMarkStatus.open((Marks::FileName + "Status").c_str());
    if(!NewMarkStatus.is_open())
            perror("New file for mark status cannot be opened");
}
cout << "\n Welcome to Mark Sheet Entry System!";
if(NewFile)
{
    cout << "How many records?";
    cin >> NoOfRecords;
    StudMarks.reserve(NoOfRecords);
    Marks::Sessional1Entered ='n';
    Marks::Sessional2Entered = 'n';
    Marks::Practical1Entered = 'n';
    Marks::Practical2Entered = 'n';
    Marks::PresentationEntered = 'n';
}
else
{
    while(MarksFile.read((char *) &DummyMarks, sizeof(Marks)))
    {
            StudMarks.push_back(DummyMarks);
            NoOfRecords++;
    }
    MarkStatus.open((Marks::FileName + "Status").c_str(), ios::in | ios::out);
    if(!MarkStatus.is_open())
```

```
                perror("Mark Status file: ");
        cout << endl
        Marks::Sessional1Entered = MarkStatus.get();
        Marks::Sessional2Entered = MarkStatus.get();
        MarkStatus >> Marks::Practical1Entered;
        MarkStatus >> Marks::Practical2Entered;
        MarkStatus >> Marks::PresentationEntered;
        MarkStatus >> Marks::Year;
        MarkStatus >> Marks::Subject;
        cout << "Status read from file is  \n";
        cout << "Subject is  "<< Marks::Subject << endl;
        cout << "Year is  " << Marks::Year << endl;
        if(Marks::Sessional1Entered ==  'y')
                cout << "Sessional 1 marks are available \n";
        else
                cout << "Sessional 1 marks are yet to be entered\n";
        if(Marks::Sessional2Entered ==  'y')
                cout << "Sessional 2 marks are available\n";
        else
                cout << "Sessional 2 marks are yet to be entered\n";
        if(Marks::Practical1Entered ==  'y')
                cout << "Practical 1 marks are available\n";
        else
                cout << "Practical 1 marks are yet to be entered\n";
        if(Marks::Practical2Entered ==  'y')
                cout <<  "Practical 2 marks are available\n";
        else
                cout << "Practical 2 marks are yet to be entered\n";
        if(Marks::PresentationEntered ==  'y')
                cout <<  "Presentation marks are available\n";
        else
                cout << "Presentation marks are yet to be entered\n";
        // cout << "Status is" << Marks::Status;
    }
    cout << "Please enter marks one by one \n";
    int Choice = 0;
    while(Choice < 1 || Choice > 5)
    {
        cout << "1. First sessional marks \n";
        cout << "2. Second sessional marks \n";
        cout << "3. First practical marks \n";
        cout << "4. Second practical marks \n";
        cout << "5. Presentation marks \n";
        cin >> Choice;
    }
```

```
switch(Choice)
{
   case 1:
          Marks::Status = ReadingSessional1;
          Marks::Sessional1Entered = 'y';
          break;
   case 2:
          Marks::Status = ReadingSessional2;
          Marks::Sessional2Entered = 'y';
          break;
   case 3:
          Marks::Status = ReadingPractical1;
          Marks::Practical1Entered = 'y';
          break;
   case 4:
          Marks::Status = ReadingPractical2;
          Marks::Practical2Entered = 'y';
          break;
   case 5:
          Marks::Status = ReadingPresentation;
          Marks::PresentationEntered = 'y';
}
int i;
for(i = 0; i < NoOfRecords; ++i)
{
   if(NewFile)
          StudMarks[i].AssignNextRollNo();
   cin >> StudMarks[i];
}
if(!NewFile)
{
   MarksFile.clear();
   MarksFile.seekg(0, ios::beg);
   MarkStatus.close();
   NewMarkStatus.open((Marks::FileName+"Status").c_str());
   if(!NewMarkStatus.is open())
          perror("Error re-opening mark status file: ");
   for(i = 0; i < NoOfRecords; ++i)
   {
          cout << StudMarks[i];
          MarksFile.write((char *) &StudMarks[i], sizeof(Marks));
          if(!MarksFile)
                 perror("Error writing the old marks file: ");
          cout << endl;
   }
```

```
            }
            else
            {
               for(i = 0; i < NoOfRecords; ++i)
               {
                       cout << StudMarks[i];
                       NewMarksFile.write((char *) &StudMarks[i], sizeof(Marks));
                       if(!NewMarksFile)
                               perror("Error writing the new marks file: ");
                       cout << endl;
               }
            }
            NewMarkStatus << Marks::Sessional1Entered;
            if(!NewMarkStatus)
               perror("Error writing the status file: ");
            cout << endl;
            NewMarkStatus << Marks::Sessional2Entered;
            if(!NewMarkStatus)
               perror("Error writing the status file: ");
            cout << endl;
            NewMarkStatus << Marks::Practical1Entered;
            if(!NewMarkStatus)
               perror("Error writing the status file: ");
            cout << endl;
            NewMarkStatus << Marks::Practical2Entered;
            if(!NewMarkStatus)
               perror("Error writing the status file: ");
            cout << endl;
            NewMarkStatus << Marks::PresentationEntered;
            if(!NewMarkStatus)
               perror("Error writing the status file: ");
            cout << endl;
            NewMarkStatus << Marks::Subject;
            NewMarkStatus << Marks::Year;
            cout << "\n The mark status is \n";
            cout << Marks::Subject;
            cout << Marks::Year;
            cout << Marks::Sessional1Entered;
            cout << Marks::Sessional2Entered;
            cout << Marks::Practical1Entered;
            cout << Marks::Practical2Entered;
            cout << Marks::PresentationEntered;
            cout << endl;
        }
        ostream & PrintHeading(ostream & TempOut)
```

```
{
   TempOut << setw(30) << setiosflags(ios::right);
   TempOut << "Marks for subject" << setw(20) << Marks::Subject << endl;
   TempOut << setw(30) << setiosflags(ios::right) << "for the year" << setw(20) <<
   setiosflags(ios::right) << Marks::Year << endl;
   return TempOut;
}
ostream & PrintMarkSheetHeading(ostream & TempOut)
{
   TempOut << setw(12) << setiosflags(ios::left) << setiosflags(ios::fixed) <<
   setprecision(2) << setiosflags(ios::showpoint);
   TempOut << "Roll number" << setw(12) << "Sessional1";
   TempOut << setw(12) << "Sessional2";
   TempOut << setw(12) << "Practical1";
   TempOut << setw(12) << "Practical2";
   TempOut << setw(12) << "Presentation";
   return TempOut;
}
ostream & PrintLine(ostream & TempOut)
{
   TempOut << endl << "          ";
   TempOut << endl;
   return TempOut;
}
void DisplayMarks()
{
   cout << "Please specify the subject \n"; cin >> Marks::Subject;
   cout << "Please specify the year \n";
   cin >> Marks::Year;
   char *StringYear = itoa(Marks::Year, 10);
   Marks::FileName = "Marks" + Marks::Subject + StringYear;
   fstream MarksFile(Marks::FileName.c_str(), ios::in | ios::out | ios::binary);
   fstream MarkStatus((Marks::FileName + "Status").c_str());
   if(!MarksFile.is_open())
   {
      cout << "Marks file for the year that you have specified does not exist.";
      cout << "\n Make sure the file exists\n";
      exit(0);
   }
   vector <Marks> StudMarks;
   Marks DummyMarks;
   int NoOfRecords = 0;
   while(MarksFile.read((char *) &DummyMarks, sizeof(Marks)))
   {
      StudMarks.push_back(DummyMarks);
```

```
            NoOfRecords++;
        }
        MarkStatus.open((Marks::FileName+"Status").c_str(), ios::in | ios::out);
        if(!MarkStatus.is_open())
        {
            perror("Mark status file: ");
            exit(0);
        }
        cout << endl;
        Marks::Sessional1Entered = MarkStatus.get();
        Marks::Sessional2Entered = MarkStatus.get();
        MarkStatus >> Marks::Practical1Entered;
        MarkStatus >> Marks::Practical2Entered;
        MarkStatus >> Marks::PresentationEntered;
        // Now printing it
        cout << PrintHeading << PrintMarkSheetHeading << PrintLine << PrintLine;
        int i;
        for(i = 0; i < NoOfRecords; i++)
        {
            cout << StudMarks[i];
        }
    };
```

Output

The following screenshots depict one specific run of the program.

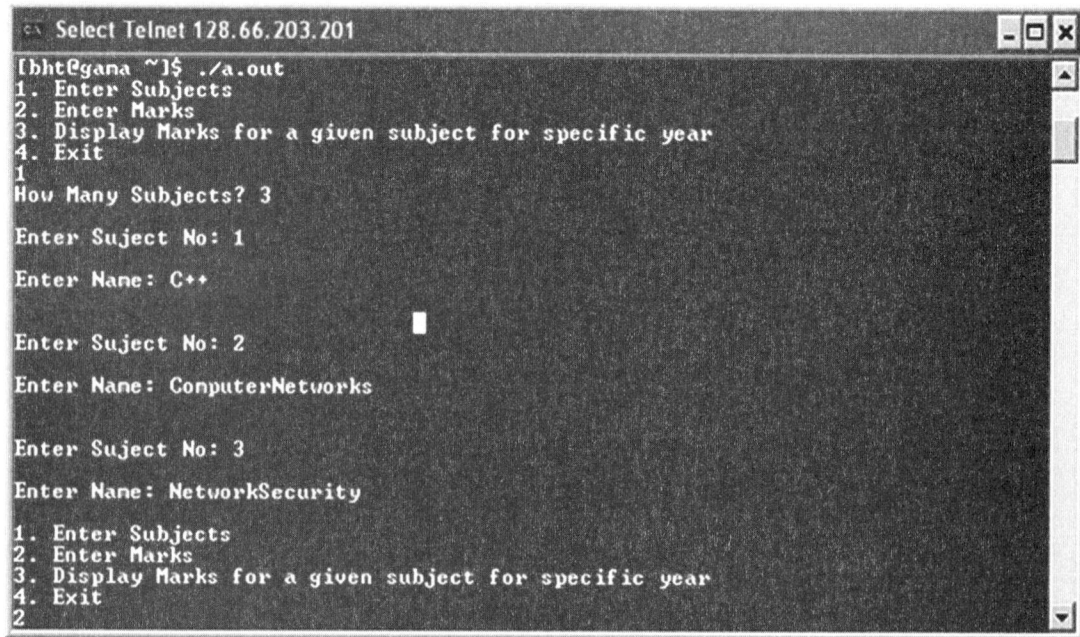

Fig. A.1   Screen 1 of output

Screen 1 This shows the subject detail entry and ends with a selection for entering marks for a subject.

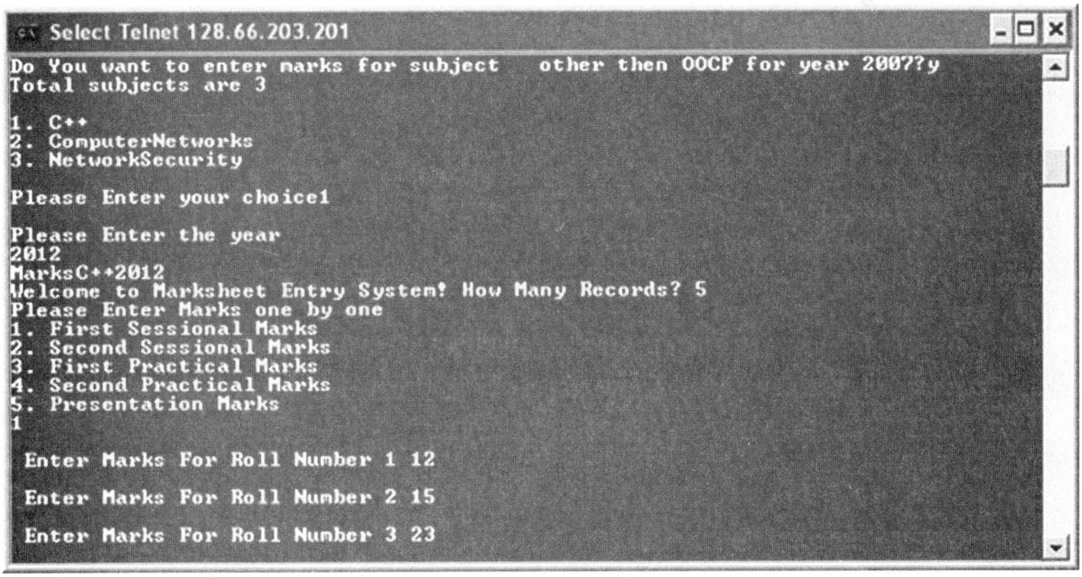

```
Select Telnet 128.66.203.201                                    _ □ ×
Do You want to enter marks for subject    other then OOCP for year 2007?y
Total subjects are 3

1. C++
2. ComputerNetworks
3. NetworkSecurity

Please Enter your choice1

Please Enter the year
2012
MarksC++2012
Welcome to Marksheet Entry System! How Many Records? 5
Please Enter Marks one by one
1. First Sessional Marks
2. Second Sessional Marks
3. First Practical Marks
4. Second Practical Marks
5. Presentation Marks
1

 Enter Marks For Roll Number 1 12

 Enter Marks For Roll Number 2 15

 Enter Marks For Roll Number 3 23
```

Fig. A.2   Screen 2 of output

Screen 2 This screen begins with the query for the subject name and year. The default is OOCP and 2007. It asks for the number of subjects and a subject and starts marks entry.

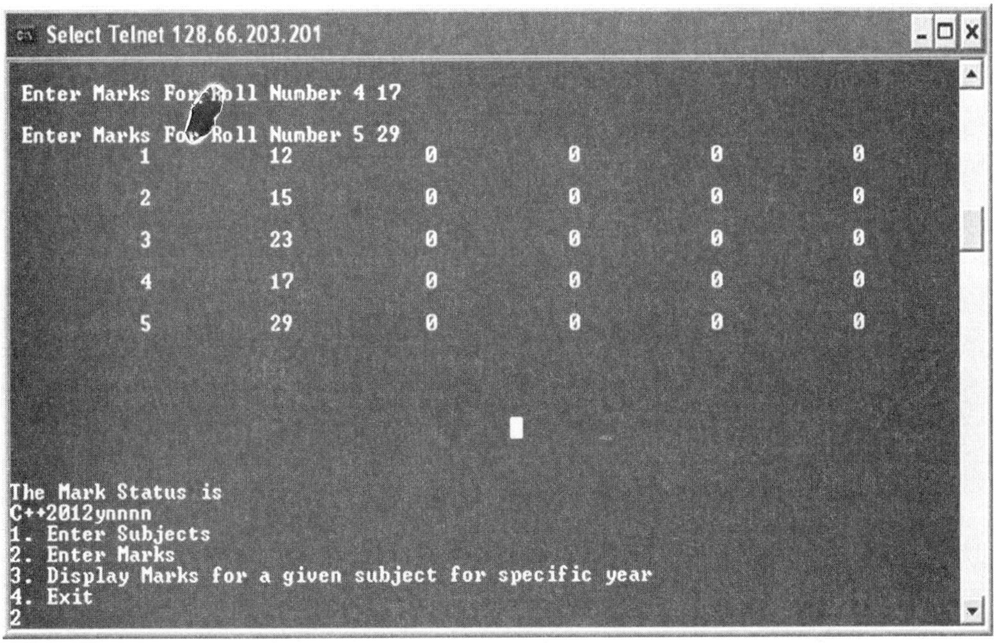

```
Select Telnet 128.66.203.201                                    _ □ ×

 Enter Marks For Roll Number 4 1?

 Enter Marks For Roll Number 5 29
         1          12          0          0          0          0

         2          15          0          0          0          0

         3          23          0          0          0          0

         4          1?          0          0          0          0

         5          29          0          0          0          0




                              █


The Mark Status is
C++2012ynnnn
1. Enter Subjects
2. Enter Marks
3. Display Marks for a given subject for specific year
4. Exit
2
```

Fig. A.3   Screen 3 of output

Screen 3 This shows the marks of each student in a matrix form, displays mark status, and loops back to the menu where the user chooses to enter the marks once again.

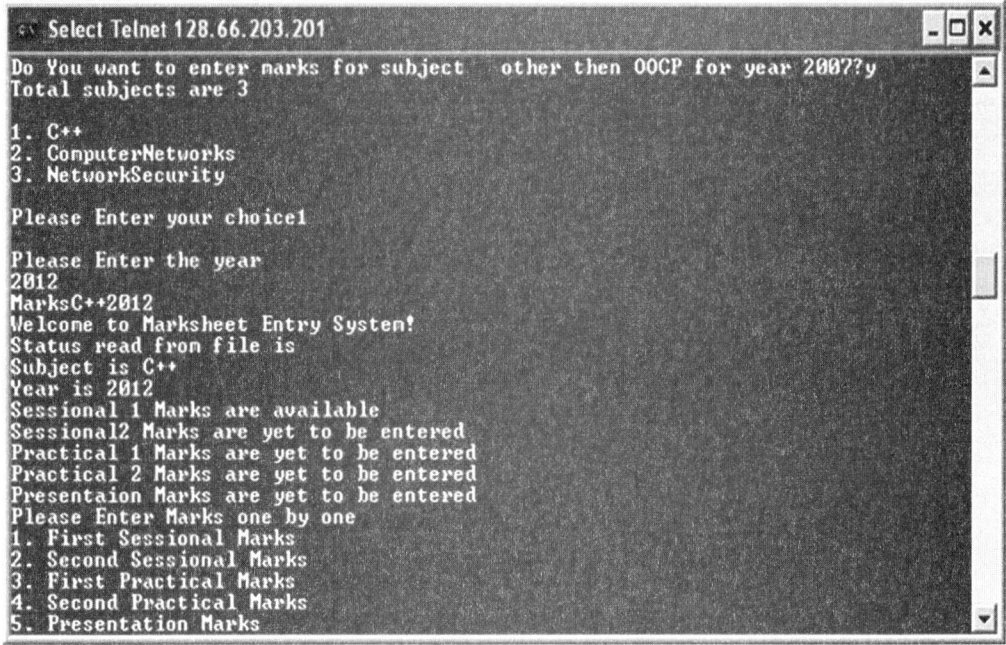

Fig. A.4 Screen 4 of output

Screen 4 The user is prompted again for the subject and marks; the program displays the marks that are entered and are not.

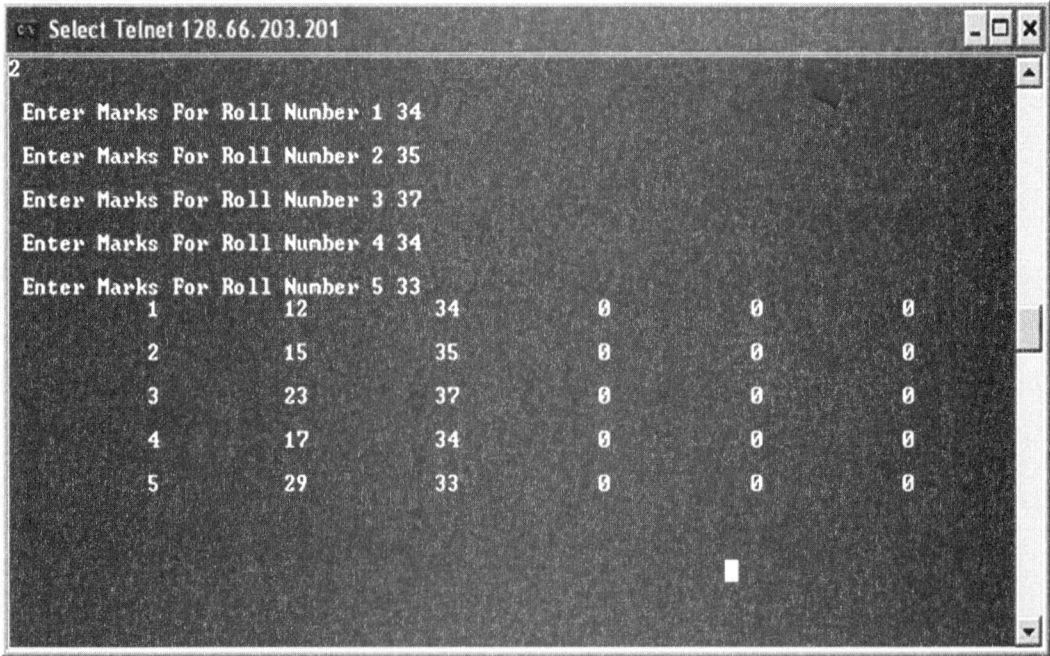

Fig. A.5 Screen 5 of output

Screen 5 Marks are displayed in the matrix form after the entry.

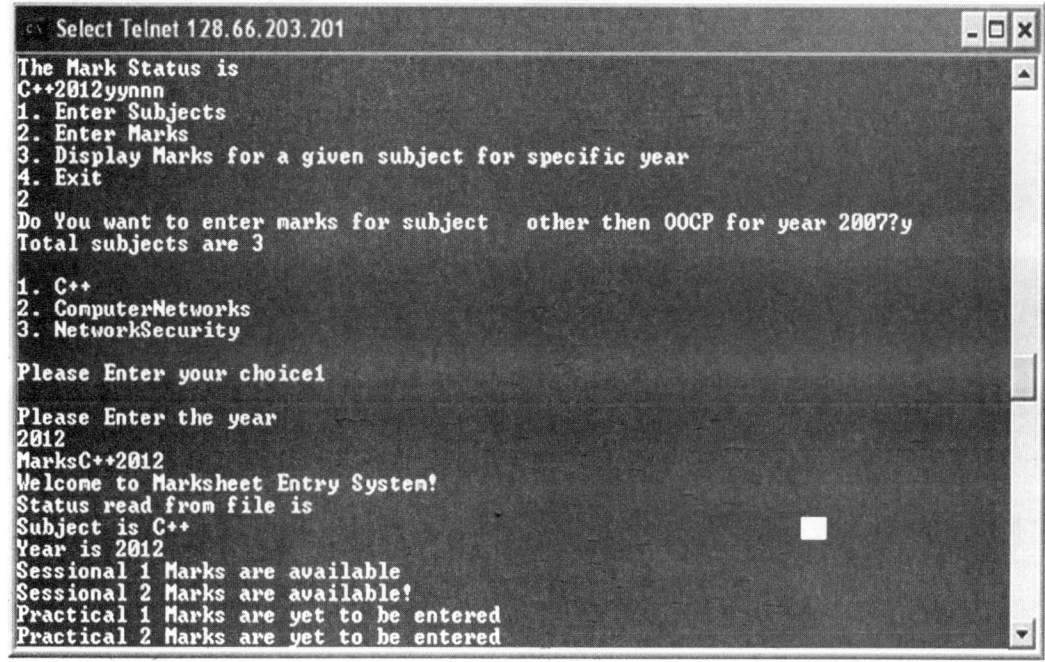

Fig. A.6 Screen 6 of output

Screen 6 The loop comes back to ask for entry and shows the status of the specific subject with specific year.

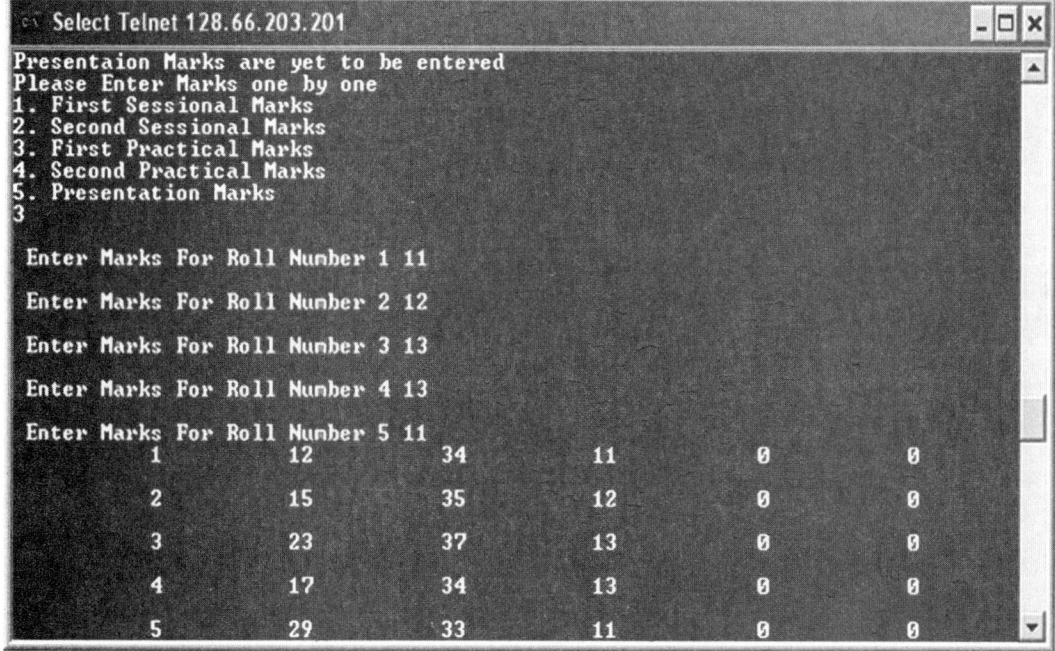

Fig. A.7 Screen 7 of output

Screen 7 The practical marks are entered and information is displayed.

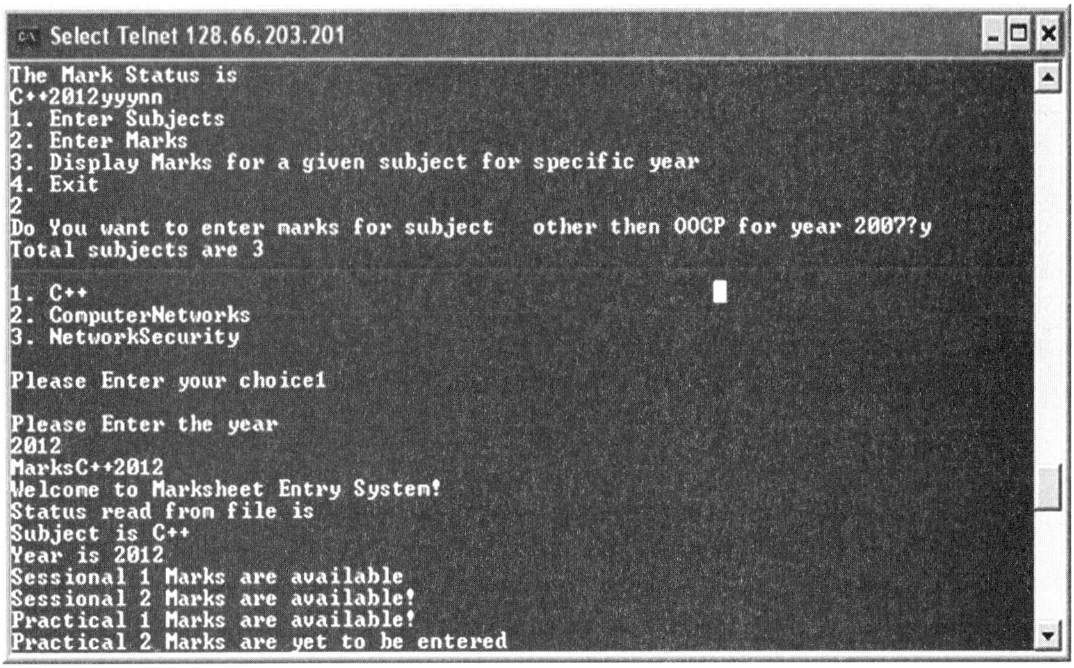

Fig. A.8   Screen 8 of output

Screen 8   The marks are entered and looped back.

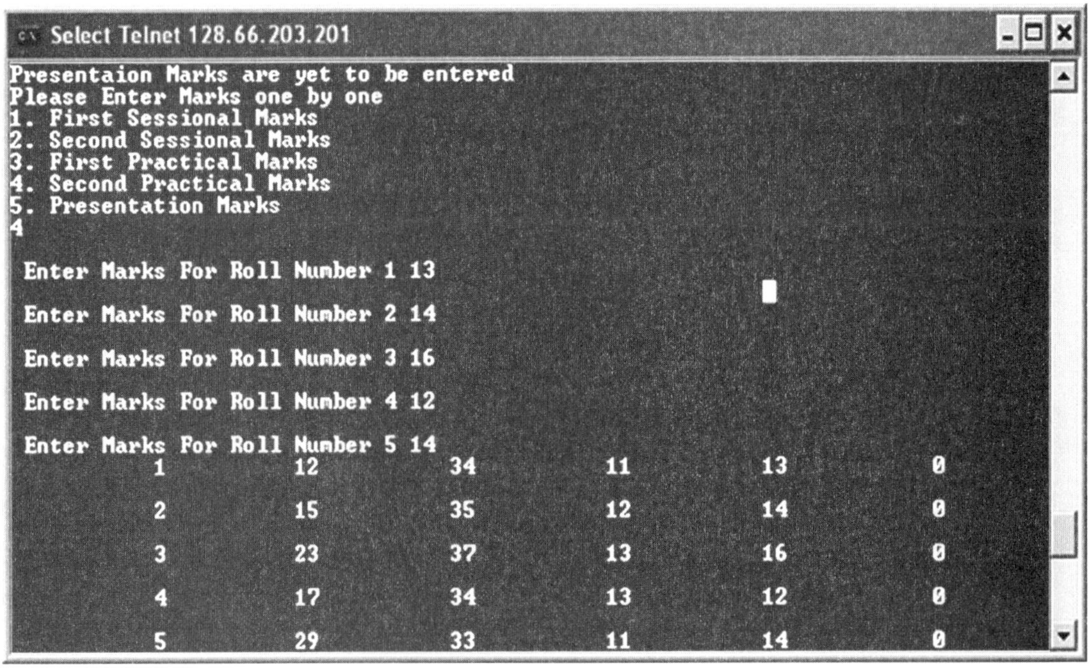

Fig. A.9   Screen 9 of output

Screen 9   Practical second test marks are entered as shown.

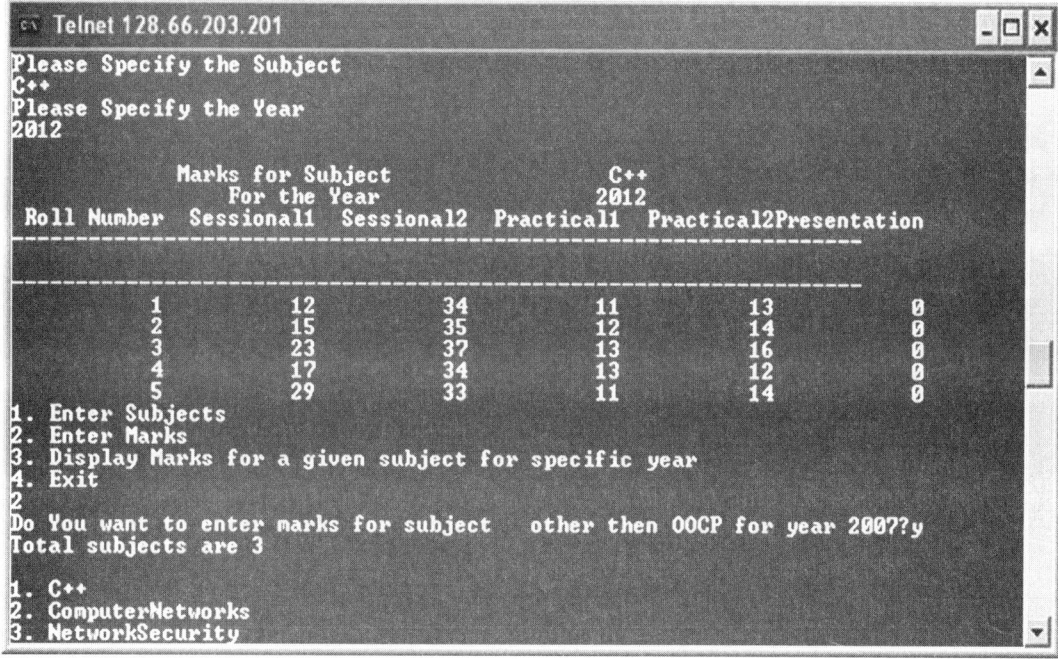

Fig. A.10   Screen 10 of output

Screen 10   The intermediate mark sheet is displayed.

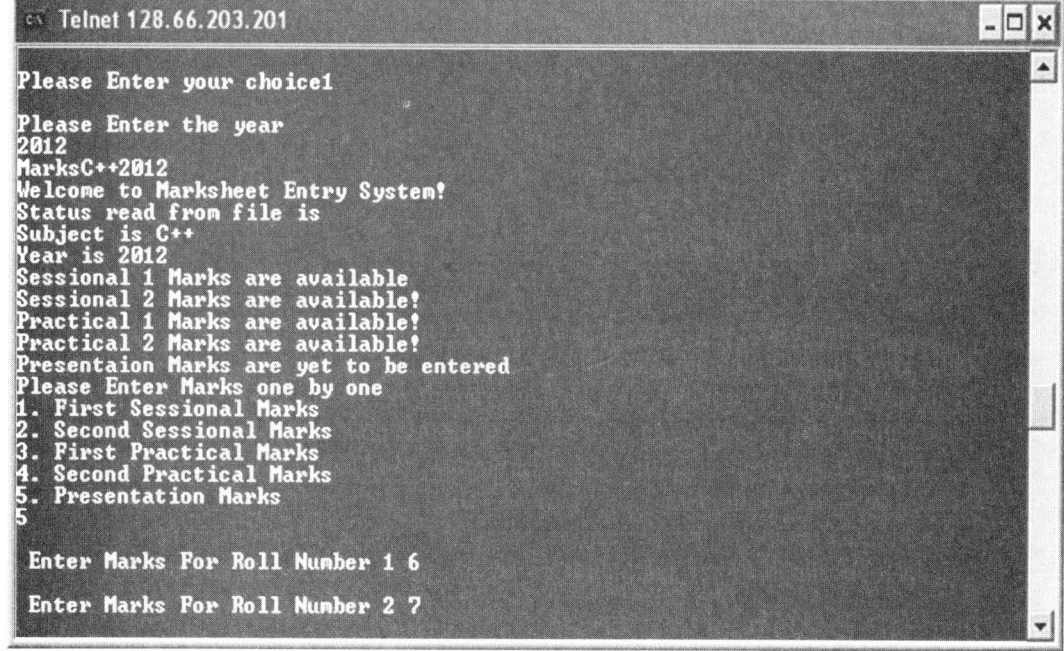

Fig. A.11   Screen 11 of output

Screen 11   The presentation marks are being entered.

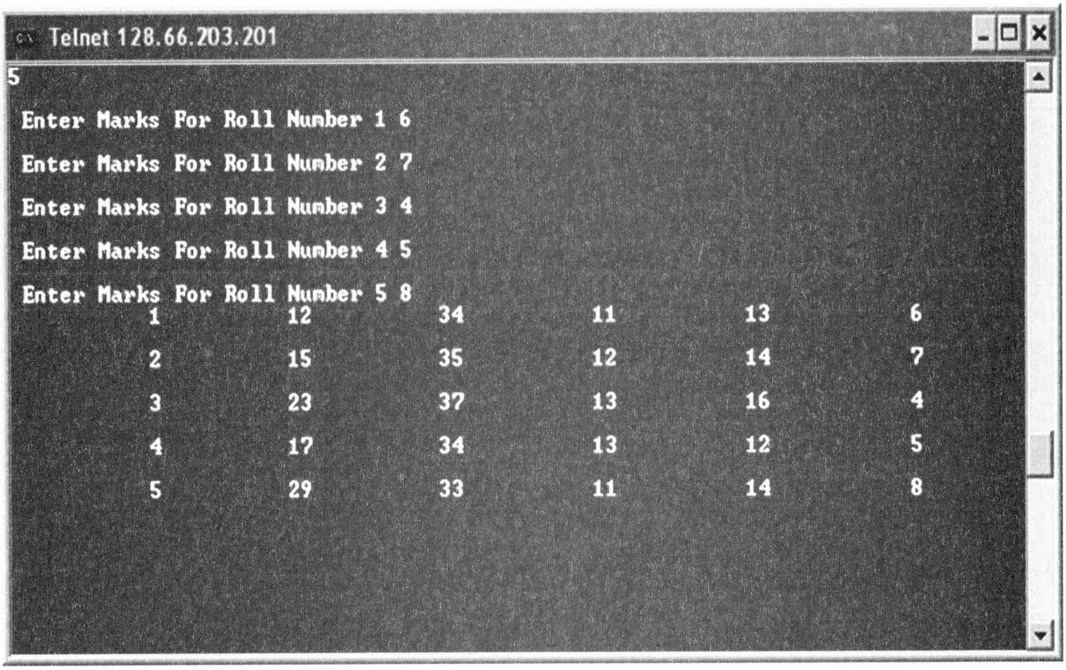

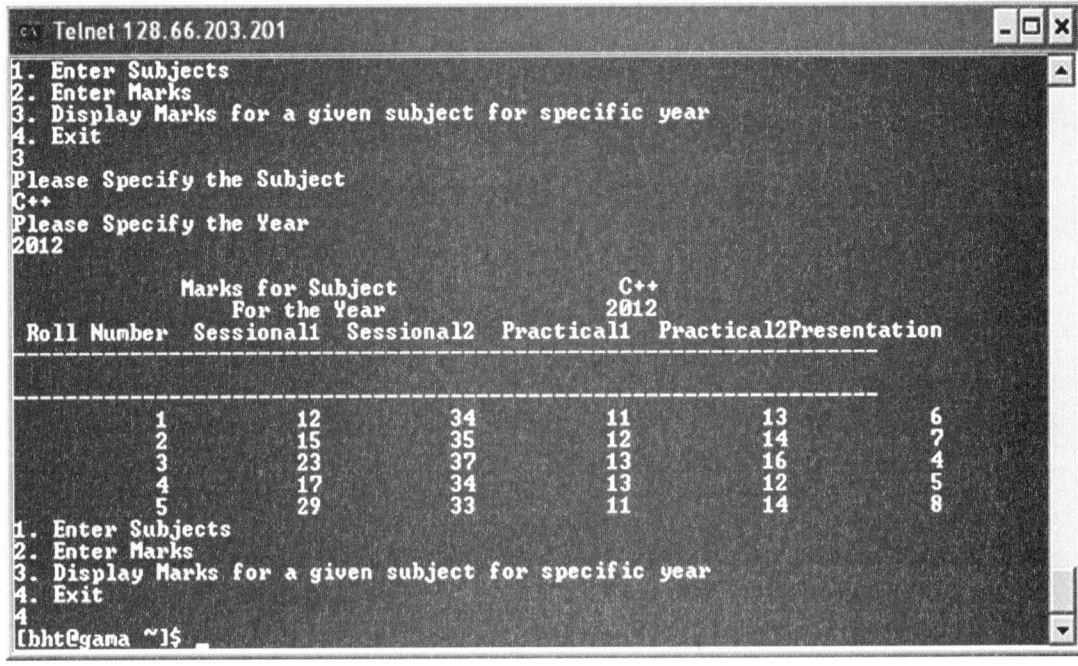

Fig. A.12 Screen 12 of output

Screen 12 Complete marks are entered.

Fig. A.13 Screen 13 of output

Screen 13 The final mark sheet is printed.

A.4 EXPLANATION

The program begins with two important definitions. One is a function for getting a string from an **int** value. There is a function **itoa** available in Windows or TC++, but it is not available in Linux. We need such a function to run the program under Linux.[1]

The other definition is an **enum**, which describes the reading status. We have already seen that the program may be reading marks about any head at any given point of time. It is **enum** that tells us what we are reading.

Then, we have the most important class of our program, namely, **Marks**. The members of the class are divided into two parts. Static members represent the metadata about the class, whereas other members are integers representing the different heads of marks of a student. We have our static members defined and given default values outside the body of the class. It is important to note that the name of the file is a concatenation of three strings. The first string is always 'Marks', the second is the subject for which the data entry is made, and the third is the string representation of the year value. Thus, this makes the name of the file unique for each subject for each year. For example, the file name could be **MarksOOCP2007**, **MarksAI2008**, etc.

These files cannot store their metadata. We need an additional file to store the same. We name that file as the original filename plus the word 'Status'. Thus, status files for the given two cases will be **MarksOOCP2007Status** and **MarksAI2008Status**. These are long but unambiguous names.

It is interesting to see that the argument requires a C-type string; hence, we need to call **c_str()** function with the file name to get the C-type string from a string object.

Next is the **Subject** class. This class stores only two bits of information, the subject name and number. Ideally, it should also store the name of the file for each subject where syllabus is stored for that subject.

It is needless to state the importance of the overloaded **<<** and **>>** operators for both the classes and that we have proper constructors for them as well.

Next is the function **ChooseSubject()**. This is an important function, which reads from the **SubjectFile** and lets us choose the subject. The following statements are worth having a look.

```
while(!SubjectFile.eof())
{
    int TempNo;
    string TempName;
    SubjectFile >> TempNo;
    SubjectFile >> TempName;
    NoOfSubjects++;
    Subject MCA_Subject_In(TempNo, TempName);
```

[1] This function has been taken from the web. The website and the author's name have been specified in the program itself. As programmers need to invest time and energy to program and debug various cases, it is always a viable option to look for readymade solutions on the web and incorporate them in a program. The advantage of such solutions is that they are usually tested and designed for generic cases. Incorporating such codes makes the program more robust and generic. One must carefully look at the copyright warnings in such cases though.

```
    Subjects.push_back(MCA_Subject_In);
}
```

This code reads the `SubjectFile` and populates the `Subject` vector for us. Look at the `push_back()` function for the vector to accommodate arbitrary number of elements. The following code is for the dynamic menu:

```
for(SubjectIndex = Subjects.begin(), i = 1; SubjectIndex < Subjects.end();
SubjectIndex++, i++)
{
    cout << endl << i << "." << SubjectIndex->getName();
}
```

Our loop runs from the beginning to the end of `Subject` vector and prints each subject with a proper choice value. Look at the use of the iterator `SubjectIndex` and the usefulness of `getName()` access method.

Marks are stored in the binary file. For storing mark status and subject information, we have chosen text files. The function `SubjectEntry()` shows how subjects are read and a file is created. The interesting part here is to have additional spaces between fields for separating them at the time of reading. Note that the string records are separated by white spaces.

It is also important not to add a space at the end of the file, as it adds a dummy record to our file.

```
for(i = 0; i < NoOfSubjects; i++)
{
    cin >> MCA_Subject_Out;
    SubjectFile << MCA_Subject_Out.getNo();
    SubjectFile << "  ";
    SubjectFile << MCA_Subject_Out.getName();
    /* Except the last record, add a space to separate the records */
    if(i + 1 < NoOfSubjects)
        SubjectFile << " ";
}
```

Next is the `main()` containing only a static menu.

The function `MarksEntry()`, which follows next, has the default of marks of subject OOCP for the year 2007. We have two versions of input from file for the status file. One is using `get()` and the other is using the overloaded `>>`.

Next, we encounter the code that checks and opens two files related to marks entry. The same file has two different names. The version with `New` prefix is opened using `ofstream` and is initialized with proper initial values when the file is created for the first time. Otherwise, the files are read, and the vector and the metadata are populated with the values stored in the file.

We have the menu presented next, which displays the choices about marks entry heads. If a specific head, for example, `Sessional1` is chosen, the `Status` variable is set accordingly. We also mark that head as read. The `for` loop reads the records into the vector. If the new file is generated, it generates the roll number and adds to the record.

Next, we check if we have an old file with marks with us. We create a new status file, as the status of the file is changed after reading records. The original marks file records are rewritten in the file from the vector. In the end, we encounter a function for printing the marks in a lightly formatted way.

A.5 IMPROVING THE PROGRAM

Real-world application-oriented programs include a number of features to facilitate easy debugging and frequent updates. They are robust and are executed without exerting much load on the system. In the given project, we have opted to have a limited set of features in order to keep the program simple and restrict its length. However, the program can be modified to suit additional requirements, for which it requires additional discipline. We have not considered all the features to reduce the complexity. Nevertheless, you, as a reader, should try and incorporate new features in the existing program to make it better. Here is a list of features you can add:

1. A professional program should be as dynamic as possible. We could have dynamic menus in the program. The menu for selecting heads can be made dynamic similar to the menu for selecting subjects; it is not made here.
2. It is possible that multiple faculties teach the subject in a shared fashion and they give their marks separately. We must be able to accumulate them into a single mark sheet. This is not provided in our program, as it would increase the level of complexity. We have assumed that all teachers use the same set of heads. It may not be true for some subjects where practicals are not involved and where we need other heads such as group discussion or quiz. Providing such dynamism is neither important nor feasible in our case.
3. Professional programs use different components and readymade programmed modules, which we can use in our program. VC++ provides components such as text box and list box for data entry. Menus are also available. Calendar control is available for validating dates. We have obviously used none. There is another feature called 'report writer' available with all professional systems, which helps us format our reports in a detailed way. We have used only basic formatting features of C++ in our program.
4. The printing does not take care of multi-page, multi-column display, which demands additional logic.
5. Similarly, all professional programs use some form of database and the code contains calls to create and manipulate databases. We will not be using such approach.
6. One more important issue is of validations. Ideally, all data entered in the system should be allowed only after proper sanitation. It is not uncommon to see half the program being dedicated to validation code. We will use minimal validations in the program. It is not that validations are not all that important; they are very important, but they need difficult logic and more redundancy in the code.
7. A small but important issue is to use more general mechanism of programming. For example, we could have decided to have menu() function, which takes inputs from the respective file and populate the menu for us. It has not been done for simplicity and length-of-code issues.

The program has two menus; one is dynamic and the other is static. Usually, menus are provided for cases such as add, delete, modify, and display single item. You can add such features by choosing sorted associative containers in place of vectors.

Possible extensions The program can be extended, with a little effort, to include the following features:

1. The format can become a little more portable. It is possible to provide a DLL, which reads from a file and sends the mark sheet out. There would be no input/output (IO) in the program, but only processing. In that case, the interface would be function-based. Functions could be called at runtime and mark sheets and marks of the students can be produced and updated as and when required. The calling program manages the IO.
2. More generality can be provided for reading validated input by using wrapper classes.
3. A student module such as subject can be provided to accept the roll numbers and names of the students so that we can print the names of students in place of roll numbers.
4. The program can hold a mobile application programming interface, which will make it accessible as a mobile application.

Index

Related Titles

SOFTWARE ENGINEERING: CONCEPTS AND APPLICATIONS

Subhajit Dutta, *Senior Specialist, Accenture Technology Labs, Bangalore*
9780195696561 | Paperback

Software Engineering: Concepts and Applications bridges the critical gap between software engineering as taught in the classroom and as practised in the real world. Primarily designed as a book for students of software engineering, it offers key insights for succeeding as professional software engineers.

Key Features
- Discusses the theory of software engineering in the context of its practice
- Covers topics best suited to readers with limited or no prior exposure to software engineering

COMPUTER NETWORKS

Bhushan Trivedi, *GLS Institute of Computer Technology, Ahmedabad*
9780198066774 | Paperback

Computer Networks is designed to serve as a textbook for undergraduate students of computer science engineering as well as those pursuing MCA and IT. Following the tried-and-tested layered approach, it gives equal weight to all the network layers and their protocols.

Key Features
- Incorporates the layered approach with emphasis on TCP/IP model, Internet, and Ethernet technologies
- Explains several new topics such as bluetooth, IPv6, QoS provided by WiMax, and the use of scalable OFDM in 802.16

WEB TECHNOLOGIES

Uttam K. Roy, *Jadavpur University, Kolkata*
9780198066224 | Paperback

Web Technologies is a textbook specially designed for undergraduate and postgraduate students of Computer Science, Information Technology, and Computer Applications (BE/B Tech/BCA/MCA).

Key Features
- Provides a thorough understanding of the working of each technology through extensive examples, along with program codes and screenshots
- Provides relevant software installation and configuration information, wherever necessary

PROGRAMMING IN JAVA

Sachin Malhotra, *Chairperson, PGDM-IT, IMS Ghaziabad*
Saurabh Choudhary, *Dean, Academics, IMS Ghaziabad*
9780198063582 | Paperback

Programming in Java provides a comprehensive discussion of the latest features of Java such as enumerations, generics, logging API, console class, StringBuilder class, NetworkInterface class, and assertions. The book gives an insight into some advanced concepts such as servlets, RMI, and JDBC.

Key Features
- Provides line-by-line explanations along with comments in the programs for in-depth understanding
- Introduces advance topics such as Java beans, servlets, and swings

Other Related Titles

- 9780195681529 Sahay: *Object-oriented Programming with C++*
- 9780198066231 Patil: *Data Structures using C++*
- 9780198061847 Chauhan: *Software Testing: Principles and Practices*
- 9780198068914 Raj Kamal: *Mobile Computing* (2e)
- 9780198071068 Nagpal: *Formal Languages and Automata Theory*
- 9780198061861 Mahajan and Shah: *Distributed Computing*
- 9780198070887 Pal: *Systems Programming*
- 9780198070788 Sridhar: *Digital Image Processing*